*The Voices of Prose*

*The Voices of*

**WILLIAM STAFFORD**

Lewis and Clark College


**FREDERICK CANDELARIA**

Simon Fraser University

McGraw-Hill Book Company

New York    St. Louis
San Francisco    Toronto

# THE VOICES OF PROSE

Library of Congress Catalog Card Number   65-20108

60632

1234567890   MP   7210698765

**Roger Ascham,** from "The Schoolmaster," reprinted from *Renaissance England,* selected and edited by Roy Lamson and Hallett Smith, © 1942, 1956. By permission of W. W. Norton & Company, Inc.

**Francis Bacon,** "Idols of the Mind," from "Novum Organum," reprinted from *English Prose of the XVII Century,* selected and edited by Roberta F. Brinkley. By permission of W. W. Norton & Company, Inc., 1951.

**Sheridan Baker,** "Scholarly Style, or the Lack Thereof," from *AAUP Bulletin,* 42, Autumn, 1956, pp. 464-470. By permission of the American Association of University Professors.

**Henry Adams,** "The Virgin and the Dynamo," from *The Education of Henry Adams.* Copyright 1918 by the Massachusetts Historical Society and 1946 by Charles F. Adams. Reprinted by permission of the publisher, Houghton Mifflin Company.

**Jacques Barzun,** "The Ivory Lab," from *Teacher in America* by Jacques Barzun. Copyright 1944, 1945 by Jacques Barzun. By permission of Little, Brown and Company–Atlantic Monthly Press.

**James Baldwin,** "My Dungeon Shook: Letter to My Nephew on the One Hundredth Anniversary of the Emancipation." Reprinted from *The Fire Next Time* by James Baldwin. Copyright © 1963, 1962 by James Baldwin. Used by permission of the publisher, The Dial Press, Inc.

**William Barrett,** "Existentialism as a Symptom of Man's Contemporary Crisis," from *Spiritual Problems in Contemporary Literature,* S. R. Hopper (ed.). Copyright 1952 by The Institute for Social and Religious Studies. Used by permission of Harper & Row, Publishers, Incorporated.

**Joyce Cary,** "Idea and Form" from *Art and Reality* by Joyce Cary. Copyright © 1958 by Arthur Lucius Michael Cary and David Alexander Ogilvie, Executors of Joyce Cary Estate. Reprinted by permission of Harper & Row, Publishers, Incorporated, and Curtis Brown, Ltd.

**Robert Gorham Davis,** "Logical Fallacies," from *Handbook for English A.* Copyright 1941 by the President and Fellows of Harvard College. Published by Harvard University Press. Reprinted by permission of Robert Gorham Davis.

**Albert Einstein,** "Science and Religion," from *Out of My Later Years.* New York: Philosophical Library, 1950. By permission of the Estate of Albert Einstein. "Science and Ethics," from Foreword to *Relativity—A Richer Truth* by Philipp Frank, 1950. By permission of Beacon Press and the Estate of Albert Einstein.

**Loren Eiseley,** "The Fire Apes," from *Harper's Magazine,* September, 1949. By permission of Loren Eiseley.

**William Faulkner,** "Appendix. Compson: 1699–1945," pages 3-22 from *The Sound and The Fury and As I Lay Dying* by William Faulkner (ML-187). Copyright 1946 by Random House, Inc. Reprinted from *The Sound and The Fury,* by William Faulkner. By permission of Random House, Inc.

*Preface*
To the Teacher

**The Voices of Prose** claims for college writers a domain far wider than the reading and practicing of the plain or encyclopedia style. The book offers a range of distinctive prose pieces, composition in all its variety and imaginative vitality, even some extremes of acrobatic performance. Principal emphasis is on the essay, varied and dynamic; extremes of possibility, however, extend into the realm of fiction and experimental writing.

Every selection has to meet a simple criterion: It must serve as a helpful model of good prose; it must bear up and continue to be rewarding under close and continued analysis. No other limit is set. The pieces range from classic to contemporary, from private letters to public addresses. Quality, the welding of content and manner, the continuous sustaining of purpose in the natural flow of the writer's native tongue—these essentials have required pieces which ring true, which arrived at their form under complete control, as original English.

Headnotes and introductions to sections of the book are brief and are intended as guides rather than as imposed interpretations, but the exercises which follow the selections are extensive and rigorous, meant as inducements to individual analysis. After every selection students are led through discussion ques-

tions to analyze the strategies employed and then to apply that analysis to original composition. To aid the teacher in seeking out appropriate selections for any sequence of study, the appendixes arrange selections according to rhetorical categories and forms and functions.

For assistance in the preparation of this book, we give special thanks to Marliss Strange for her work on the Topics for Discussion and Composition, to Marion Candelaria for her many labors on different portions of the text, and to Marilyn Triplett for her invaluable secretarial help.

**William Stafford**

**Frederick Candelaria**

# *Introduction*

## To the Student

Writers are persons who write. It is almost as easy as talking, which everyone does. Talk, though, evaporates, whereas writing lasts; you can look at it and find it hard to forgive—or good to cherish. A student must learn to forgive, both himself and others, and to make steady judgments. A good student learns to treasure his good impulses in writing, to modify them with conscious craft, and to string them together. This process is composition.

A book of readings to aid composition should invite reactions, and some of them quick reactions. Further, the reading should display ideas, maneuvers, patterns of action used by many kinds of writers. But there are dangers in any set of readings: some are excellent but paralyzing; others are exciting but dangerous and habit-forming.

In this book are pieces by varied, distinctive writers; in their voices are any number of tones, including the ironic, the satiric, the earnest, and the impassioned. The purpose is to induce immediate responses which can become writings in turn. As in a good class, where talk flows with ready rejoinders, there must be easy reaction, confident participation. We may be impressed, but we must not be immobilized and simply admiring. The job of the student writer is to encounter good prose and to

respond accordingly. Some analytical vocal engagement with these pieces, and then considered written reaction—that is the plan.

As in conversation, the initial exchange between you and the reading should be spontaneous. Only writers who deserve your respect are here, but they do not demand abject allegiance. They invite participation. Do not linger till you become great before you respond— great writers did not. Write it today, improve it tomorrow. Imagine meeting a person who confesses that he does not talk because he does not feel adequate, that he is waiting to learn how to exchange words with you!

For perspective and variety, some selections come from as far back as the Renaissance, the beginning of modern English. To ensure the kind of control present when language, thought, and a writer all find each other at once, only works originally in English are included. The topics range far for the interests of alert students, but a good piece should appeal early and also on reflection: there are no superficial selections.

The Table of Contents will show at a glance that we claim for college students far more than the reading and practicing of the plain or encyclopedia style. Composition in all its variety and imaginative vitality is the province of this book.

# Contents

## 2  *Issues: Styles in Persuasion*

### EDUCATION

### FREEDOM

### SCIENCE

### BELIEF

# 3    *Forms and Occasions*

# 4   *Selections for Further Analysis*

## APPENDIX

PART *1*

*Resources*

When you write even the simplest prose you make a chain of decisions; you wield resources in the language and the habits and the funded accomplishments of your culture. No one can lead you to make "right" choices; no one can outline the resources which surround you. And no reading plan could ever be complex enough—or flexible enough—to match the essential liveliness of your own mind. All that a reading plan can do is to supply some worthy examples of writing, to order and classify these pieces for suggested uses, and to hint at some possible connections and emphases.

This section of the book offers you groups of notable articles on the writer's resources. These groups focus your attention on language itself, on resources in art and form, on logic, and on some extreme and exemplary accomplishments —accomplishments which are striking enough to demonstrate possibilities for student writers. None of these pieces can do more than launch into the suggested topics. But for an interval, with successive authors, you can glimpse beginnings of endless opportunities. Resources are beginnings; they suggest further action and fuller use. The task of the student, the writer, is to see and then to adjust, to compose, and to be ready to go on.

1

**GILBERT HIGHET (1906–     )** combines scholarly excellence and
public acceptance. Professor of Greek and Latin at Columbia University, he has
by turns been reviewer for Harper's Magazine, editor for The Book-of-the
Month Club, conductor of a weekly radio program on literature, and a prolific
writer of books and articles. Starting with an M.A. from the University at
Glasgow, he went on for a double first at Oxford. Coming to the United States
in 1938, with an interlude as British liaison officer during World War II, he quickly
achieved academic and general recognition. *The Art of Teaching* represents
him at his best, as he delivers the results of scholarship in a direct and
interesting way. The following article manifests that same skill.

## *The First Few Words*

If you have ever tried to write a book, you will know that it is an exciting
experience. It is full of passionate moments. The greatest, no doubt, is the
wonderful instant when you open the parcel from the publishers, and, for
the first time, see your own offspring: your own long-nourished thoughts,
and your own carefully arranged words, at last objectively real, independent,
alive. But there is another moment, almost as exciting: the moment when,
after thinking about your book for many months or years, you take up a
pad of paper and write down the first words.

The first words of a book—they are intensely important. They will
kindle the reader's interest; or they will puzzle him; they may repel him or
challenge him. Both for him, the reader, and for you, the author, they are
the opening of a new experience.

Whether he is conscious of it or not, the first words of a book are likely
to remain in the reader's mind. And, if the book proves to be a good one,
whenever he thinks of it later or picks it up to reread, he will find that

his enthusiasm is rekindled simply by those first sentences. To put it another way, it seems to be a reliable rule that great books very rarely open badly, and very often open with a few impressive sentences. The first words need not be dramatic; they need not even be clear; but they must grip the mind of the reader and begin to mold his mood.

Here is the most famous beginning in American literature, three words only:

> Call me Ishmael.

This is the opening of *Moby Dick*. In those three words, Melville has shown us the character of his hero, or his narrator; an exile, a wanderer, with a taste for the Bible, and a rough, lonely, combative character. In its abrupt power, its violence, and its sense of doom, that is the right beginning for a book which is to end with a lonely ship sinking deep in the desert sea.

But here is another opening, far less clear, and very undramatic:

> It was the best of times, it was the worst of times, it was the age of wisdom, it was the age of foolishness, it was the epoch of belief, it was the epoch of incredulity, it was the season of Light, it was the season of Darkness, it was the spring of hope, it was the winter of despair, we had everything before us, we had nothing before us, we were all going direct to Heaven, we were all going direct the other way—in short, the period was so far like the present period, that some of its noisiest authorities insisted on its being received, for good or for evil, in the superlative degree of comparison only.

That is the overture to Dickens's *Tale of Two Cities*. It describes the years just before the French Revolution, in the same satirical tones as Dickens used about his own period; it warns us that that was a period of confusion, it makes us feel much of its unrest, it prepares for the extremes of the French Revolution, and at the same time it shows, without announcing the fact directly, that Dickens will take no sides: he will neither oppose the French Revolution as a frightful crime, nor praise it as though it were heaven on earth. He was a skilful writer.

Now take a contemporary. Here are the first words of one of his best novels:

> Through the fence, between the curling flower spaces, I could see them hitting. They were coming toward where the flag was and I went along the fence. Luster was hunting in the grass by the flower tree. They took the flag out, and they were hitting. Then they put the flag back and they went to the table, and he hit and the other hit.

Is this unintelligible? No. It makes sense. It describes something we have all seen; but it describes it as seen by a special mind. It is simply an account of two golfers approaching the green, holing out, and moving on to the next tee. But the description is given in the words of a man who is mentally defective: he can recognize people and simple events, but he cannot follow

the structure of anything so complicated as a game of golf, he can merely describe it as a disconnected series of actions. These sentences are the opening of William Faulkner's *The Sound and the Fury*—a tale told partly by an idiot. They take you at once inside the mind of poor imbecile Benjy; they hint at one of his obsessions (golf balls); and they prepare you for the effort of understanding his story, not in the terms he uses, but in our own more rational and complete context. And also, in a pathetic simple way, they are beautiful. "Through the fence, between the curling flower spaces, I could see them hitting."

The chief mistake made by many authors in their opening sentences is to try to put in too much. Turn to the best known of all modern American books, and read the first sentence:

> Scarlett O'Hara was not beautiful, but men seldom realized it when caught by her charm as the Tarleton twins were.

It is a good novel, *Gone with the Wind,* full of spanking incident and vigorous character drawing, but it is not sensitively written. It is clear, but it is clumsy. This opening shows that Margaret Mitchell was an amateurish stylist. She wanted to describe her heroine on the very first page, to show that she was unusual, not the regular classical Southern beauty. That she did, and did quite well; her description of Scarlett goes on for two paragraphs. But she also wanted to get the story going, and so she dragged in the Tarleton twins, who do not even speak for two or three pages, and the result is a sentence with a stumble. She ought to have been more courageous, and written:

> Scarlett O'Hara was not beautiful, but men seldom realized it when caught by her charm.

Or even, if I might venture to suggest it:

> Scarlett O'Hara was not beautiful, but men seldom realized it.

The same mistake appears in the opening sentence of a world-famous novel, Dostoevski's *The Brothers Karamazov.* It begins with a long and absorbing character sketch of the man whose murder is the central theme of the book, old Karamazov: he occupies the reader's attention for the first ten or twelve pages; therefore he should have been introduced first. But Dostoevski also had in his mind the son, Alexey, who was to become the most important and most positive character in the novel: so, foolishly, he dragged him into the first sentence and then dropped him, thus:

> Alexey Fyodorovitch Karamazov was the third son of Fyodor Pavlovitch Karamazov, a land owner well known in our district in his own day, and still remembered among us owing to his gloomy and tragic death, which happened 13 years ago, and which I shall describe in its proper place.

No, it is better to be simple. One of the most remarkable of all modern novels begins with a sentence which is brief, undramatic, almost naïve:

> For a long time I went to bed early.

Silly, isn't it? And yet it is the opening of Marcel Proust's *Remembrance of Things Past,* one of the *least* naïve books of our epoch, and composed in a most exquisite style. Gently, imperceptibly, after that sentence, the reader is drawn into a meditation on sleep and dreams so subtle that—although sleep and dreaming is a universal experience—almost every thought in it seems quite new to him. Proust goes on:

> Sometimes, almost before my candle was out, my eyes closed, so quickly that I had no time to say to myself "I am falling asleep." And, half an hour afterwards, the thought that it was time to try to sleep would awake me: I attempted to put down the book which I thought I was still holding, and to blow out the light; as I slept, I had gone on thinking about what I had just read, but my reflections had taken an unusual turn: it seemed to me that I myself was the subject of the work: a church, a quartet, the rivalry of Francis I and Charles V. . . .

And this prepares the reader for the long voyage through the world described by Proust—a world which, even while the author describes it, changes as curiously and irrationally as the phenomena of a dream, and from which, at the end, as though life were itself a long slumber, we awake to find ourselves facing one of the few permanent realities: Death.

Equally clear, but less apparently naïve, is this introduction:

> It is a truth universally acknowledged, that a single man in possession of a good fortune must be in want of a wife.

In that epigram there is a dry and almost bitter tone; we know from it that we are to read a comedy; we are prepared for irony; there is something both of amusement and of derision in the author's trick of elevating the vulgar wish to catch a rich husband into a general principle, half way between economics and psychology. That is the exquisitely appropriate overture, almost Mozartian in its simplicity, to Jane Austen's *Pride and Prejudice.*

Many of the bad novels in the world are bad because, throughout, their author has no clear conception of the emotional tone he wants to create. This also often appears in the opening paragraph. I have a particular blind spot for Henry James; I can never read his books with any interest—apart from *The Turn of the Screw* and *The Aspern Papers.* The first sentence of *Daisy Miller* will explain why:

> At the little town of Vevey, in Switzerland, there is a particularly comfortable hotel. There are, indeed, many hotels; for the entertainment of tourists is the business of the place, which, as many travellers well remember, is

seated upon the edge of a remarkably blue lake—a lake that it behooves every tourist to visit.

Well, are you interested? Do you find that perceptive, or amusing? Does the description make you long to read on and on? Is there not something a little snobbish about "as many travellers will remember," something a little patronizing about the crack at the touristy charm of the Lake of Geneva, something bored, something boring about the whole sentence?

But consider this opening, somber, romantic, and mystical:

It was late in the evening when K. arrived. The village was deep in snow. The Castle hill was hidden, veiled in mist and darkness, nor was there even a glimmer of light to show that a castle was there. On the wooden bridge leading from the main road to the village K. stood for a long time gazing into the illusory emptiness above him.

That comes from Franz Kafka's weird unfinished book, *The Castle,* in which the hero K. constantly tries, in vain, to get into communication with a mysterious castle which dominates his life, yet which he can never visit, and sometimes not even see.

A mystical aphorism and a mystical question stand together at the entrance to a novel which may or may not be a masterpiece: the reconstruction of the story of Joseph by Thomas Mann. Its Prelude begins:

Very deep is the well of the past. Should we not call it bottomless?

So says Mann, because his entire book is devoted to taking us back, far back, into the remote past, where figures almost mythical become real individuals; and to showing us that they thought of themselves as modern, and felt behind them a long, long reach of tradition and history: so that, when we read of their acts and lives, we feel ourselves not creatures of a single generation, but inheritors of the ages.

While Mann was working on his Joseph stories, another author even more deeply fascinated by the process of history was exploring the past. His novel, issued in 1939, is not much read; yet it haunts those who know something of it. This was James Joyce's *Finnegans Wake.* While Mann saw history as a movement in one main direction, Joyce thought of it as following a pattern of constant recurrence, the rains to the river, the river to the sea, the sea to the rain clouds, and so forever on and on. Therefore *Finnegans Wake* begins in the middle of a sentence and ends in the middle of a sentence, the two joining to give the effect of a continuous cycle. Here is the opening, without even a capital letter to break its continuity:

riverrun, past Eve and Adam's, from swerve of shore to bend of bay, brings us by a commodius vicus of recirculation back to Howth Castle and Environs.

That half-sentence contains the theory on which the book is based, the

initials of its hero, the name of the philosopher Vico who helped to inspire it, its setting, Dublin and the River Liffey, and half a dozen other themes of great interest and charm. Joyce expected his readers to devote their entire lives to reading his works; he is not a great enough man to justify that demand, but as a hobby, to be taken up from time to time, he is fascinating.

The first words of a book are not simply those which happen to stand at the top of the first page. They are the beginning of a new experience for both the author and the reader, and they point toward the end of that experience. Once we have read the blunt ominous opening of Melville's *Moby Dick,* we can never forget it. That short hammering sentence prepares for the terrible last scene, in which the doomed whale crashes into the whale-ship, and the ship sinks, carrying down all its men, a sea hawk enfolded in its flag.

> Now small fowls flew screaming over the yet yawning gulf; a sullen white surf beat against its steep sides; then all collapsed, and the great shroud of the sea rolled on as it rolled five thousand years ago.

## TOPICS FOR DISCUSSION

1 What does a good beginning in fiction do?

2 How does each example here perform its part? What is gained by the examples which fail? Do you agree with Highet about the failures?

3 In what ways does nonfiction resemble fiction in the use of the first few words? How does a newspaper story differ from a by-line editorial or from a long magazine article?

4 Is anything gained by addressing the article to a "you"? Is Highet consistent in his pronoun usage? Why is consistency important to the coherence of a work?

5 In what way does the *Moby Dick* illustration give unity to the essay?

## ...AND COMPOSITION

6 Find five or ten first sentences of fiction or nonfiction that kindle your interest and explain why.

7 Write several introductory paragraphs which both pose problems and hint at probable developments. Briefly *outline* the course of subsequent developments.

8 Write an introductory paragraph creating suspense. Do not use the word "suspense."

**GEORGE ORWELL [ERIC BLAIR] (1903–1950)**   achieved great popularity
through his novels *1984* and *Animal Farm,* both disquieting projections of
modern political life. In revulsion against dishonesties, Orwell made of
truth-telling a moral passion; in his writings there is a yearning for directness
and clarity and a nausea brought on by what he identified as evasions and
cruelties in modern man. Some of his concerns and obsessive allegiances
animate the following selection.

# Politics and the English Language

Most people who bother with the matter at all would admit that the
English language is in a bad way, but it is generally assumed that we
cannot by conscious action do anything about it. Our civilization is decadent
and our language—so the argument runs—must inevitably share in the
general collapse. It follows that any struggle against the abuse of language
is a sentimental archaism, like preferring candles to electric light or hansom
cabs to aeroplanes. Underneath this lies the half-conscious belief that
language is a natural growth and not an instrument which we shape for
our own purposes.

Now, it is clear that the decline of a language must ultimately have
political and economic causes: it is not due simply to the bad influence of
this or that individual writer. But an effect can become a cause, reinforcing
the original cause and producing the same effect in an intensified form, and
so on indefinitely. A man may take to drink because he feels himself to
be a failure, and then fail all the more completely because he drinks. It is
rather the same thing that is happening to the English language. It becomes
ugly and inaccurate because our thoughts are foolish, but the slovenliness
of our language makes it easier for us to have foolish thoughts. The point
is that the process is reversible. Modern English, especially written English,
is full of bad habits which spread by imitation and which can be avoided if
one is willing to take the necessary trouble. If one gets rid of those habits
one can think more clearly, and to think clearly is a necessary first step
toward political regeneration: so that the fight against bad English is not
frivolous and is not the exclusive concern of professional writers. I will
come back to this presently, and I hope that by that time the meaning of
what I have said here will have become clearer. Meanwhile, here are five
specimens of the English language as it is now habitually written.

These five passages have not been picked out because they are especially
bad—I could have quoted far worse if I had chosen—but because they
illustrate various of the mental vices from which we now suffer. They are
a little below the average, but are fairly representative samples. I number
them so that I can refer back to them when necessary:

[1]    I am not, indeed, sure whether it is not true to say that the Milton
who once seemed not unlike a seventeenth-century Shelley had not
become, out of an experience ever more bitter in each year, more alien
[*sic*] to the founder of that Jesuit sect which nothing could induce him
to tolerate.
PROFESSOR HAROLD LASKI
*Essay in "Freedom of Expression"*

[2]    Above all, we cannot play ducks and drakes with a native battery of
idioms which prescribes such egregious collocations of vocables as
the Basic *put up with* for *tolerate* or *put at a loss* for *bewilder*.
PROFESSOR LANCELOT HOGBEN
*"Interglossa"*

[3]    On the one side we have the free personality: by definition it is not
neurotic, for it has neither conflict nor dream. Its desires, such as they
are, are transparent, for they are just what institutional approval keeps
in the forefront of consciousness; another institutional pattern would
alter their number and intensity; there is little in them that is natural,
irreducible, or culturally dangerous. But *on the other side,* the social
bond itself is nothing but the mutual reflection of these self-secure
integrities. Recall the definition of love. Is not this the very picture of
a small academic? Where is there a place in this hall of mirrors for
either personality or fraternity?
*Essay on psychology in "Politics" (New York)*

[4]    All the "best people" from the gentlemen's clubs, and all the frantic
fascist captains, united in common hatred of Socialism and bestial
horror of the rising tide of the mass revolutionary movement, have
turned to acts of provocation, to foul incendiarism, to medieval
legends of poisoned wells, to legalize their own destruction of proletarian organizations, and rouse the agitated petty-bourgeoisie to
chauvinistic fervour on behalf of the fight against the revolutionary
way out of the crises.
*Communist pamphlet*

[5]    If a new spirit *is* to be infused into this old country, there is one thorny
and contentious reform which must be tackled, and that is the human-
ization and galvanization of the B.B.C. Timidity here will bespeak
cancer and atrophy of the soul. The heart of Britain may be sound
and of strong beat, for instance, but the British lion's roar at present
is like that of Bottom in Shakespeare's *Midsummer Night's Dream*—as
gentle as any sucking dove. A virile new Britain cannot continue
indefinitely to be traduced in the eyes, or rather ears, of the world
by the effete languors of Langham Place, brazenly masquerading as
"standard English." When the Voice of Britain is heard at nine

o'clock, better far and infinitely less ludicrous to hear aitches honestly dropped than the present priggish, inflated, inhibited, school-ma'amish arch braying of blameless bashful mewing maidens!
*Letter in "Tribune"*

Each of these passages has faults of its own, but quite apart from avoidable ugliness, two qualities are common to all of them. The first is staleness of imagery: the other is lack of precision. The writer either has a meaning and cannot express it, or he inadvertently says something else, or he is almost indifferent as to whether his words mean anything or not. This mixture of vagueness and sheer incompetence is the most marked characteristic of modern English prose, and especially of any kind of political writing. As soon as certain topics are raised, the concrete melts into the abstract and no one seems able to think of turns of speech that are not hackneyed: prose consists less and less of *words* chosen for the sake of their meaning, and more and more of *phrases* tacked together like the sections of a prefabricated hen-house. I list, below, with notes and examples, various of the tricks by means of which the work of prose-construction is habitually dodged:

### DYING METAPHORS

A newly invented metaphor assists thought by evoking a visual image, while on the other hand a metaphor which is technically "dead" (e.g., *iron resolution*) has in effect reverted to being an ordinary word and can generally be used without loss of vividness. But in between these two classes there is a huge dump of worn-out metaphors which have lost all evocative power and are merely used because they save people the trouble of inventing phrases for themselves. Examples are: *Ring the changes on, take up the cudgels for, toe the line, ride roughshod over, stand shoulder to shoulder with, play into the hands of, no axe to grind, grist to the mill, fishing in troubled waters, on the order of the day, Achilles' heel, swan song, hotbed.* Many of these are used without knowledge of their meaning (what is a "rift," for instance), and incompatible metaphors are frequently mixed, a sure sign that the writer is not interested in what he is saying. Some metaphors now current have been twisted out of their original meaning without those who use them even being aware of the fact. For example, *toe the line* is sometimes written *tow the line*. Another example is *the hammer and the anvil*, now always used with the implication that the anvil gets the worst of it. In real life it is always the anvil that breaks the hammer, never the other way about: a writer who stopped to think what he was saying would be aware of this, and would avoid perverting the original phrase.

### OPERATORS OR VERBAL FALSE LIMBS

These save the trouble of picking out appropriate verbs and nouns, and at the same time pad each sentence with extra syllables which give it an

appearance of symmetry. Characteristic phrases are: *render inoperative, militate against, make contact with, be subjected to, give rise to, give grounds for, have the effect of, play a leading part (role) in, make itself felt, take effect, exhibit a tendency to, serve the purpose of, etc., etc.* The keynote is the elimination of simple verbs. Instead of being a single word, such as *break, stop, spoil, mend, kill,* a verb becomes a *phrase,* made up of a noun or adjective tacked on to some general-purpose verb such as *prove, serve, form, play, render.* In addition, the passive voice is wherever possible used in preference to the active, and noun constructions are used instead of gerunds (*by examination of* instead of *by examining*). The range of verbs is further cut down by means of the *-ize* and *de-* formation, and the banal statements are given an appearance of profundity by means of the *not un-* formation. Simple conjunctions and prepositions are replaced by such phrases as *with respect to, having regard to, the fact that, by dint of, in view of, in the interests of, on the hypothesis that,* and the ends of sentences are saved from anticlimax by such resounding commonplaces as *greatly to be desired, cannot be left out of account, a development to be expected in the near future, deserving of serious consideration, brought to a satisfactory conclusion,* and so on and so forth.

### PRETENTIOUS DICTION

Words like *phenomenon, element, individual* (as noun), *objective, categorical, effective, virtual, basic, primary, promote, constitute, exhibit, exploit, utilize, eliminate, liquidate,* are used to dress up simple statements and give an air of scientific impartiality to biased judgments. Adjectives like *epoch-making, epic, historic, unforgettable, triumphant, age-old, inevitable, inexorable, veritable,* are used to dignify the sordid processes of international politics, while writing that aims at glorifying war usually takes on an archaic colour, its characteristic words being: *realm, throne, chariot, mailed fist, trident, sword, shield, buckler, banner, jackboot, clarion.* Foreign words and expressions such as *cul de sac, ancien régime, deus ex machina, mutatis mutandis, status quo, gleichschaltung, weltanschauung,* are used to give an air of culture and elegance. Except for the usual abbreviations *i.e., e.g.,* and *etc.,* there is no real need for any of the hundreds of foreign phrases now current in English. Bad writers, and especially scientific, political and sociological writers, are nearly always haunted by the notion that Latin or Greek words are grander than Saxon ones, and unnecessary words like *expedite, ameliorate, predict, extraneous, deracinated, clandestine, subaqueous* and hundreds of others constantly gain ground from their Anglo-Saxon opposite numbers. The jargon peculiar to Marxist writing (*hyena, hangman, cannibal, petty bourgeois, these gentry, lacquey, flunkey, mad dog, White Guard,* etc.) consists largely of words and phrases translated from Russian, German or French; but the normal way of coining a new word is to use a Latin or Greek root with the appropriate affix and,

where necessary, the *-ize* formation. It is often easier to make up words of this kind (*deregionalize, impermissible, extramarital, non-fragmentary* and so forth) than to think up the English words that will cover one's meaning. The result, in general, is an increase in slovenliness and vagueness.

### MEANINGLESS WORDS

In certain kinds of writing, particularly in art criticism and literary criticism, it is normal to come across long passages which are almost completely lacking in meaning. Words like *romantic, plastic, values, human, dead, sentimental, natural, vitality,* as used in art criticism, are strictly meaningless in the sense that they not only do not point to any discoverable object, but are hardly ever expected to do so by the reader. When one critic writes, "The outstanding feature of Mr. X's work is its living quality," while another writes, "The immediately striking thing about Mr. X's work is its peculiar deadness," the reader accepts this as a simple difference of opinion. If words like *black* and *white* were involved, instead of the jargon words *dead* and *living,* he would see at once that language was being used in an improper way. Many political words are similarly abused. The word *Fascism* has now no meaning except in so far as it signifies "something not desirable." The words *democracy, socialism, freedom, patriotic, realistic, justice,* have each of them several different meanings which cannot be reconciled with one another. In the case of a word like *democracy,* not only is there no agreed definition, but the attempt to make one is resisted from all sides. It is almost universally felt that when we call a country democratic we are praising it: consequently the defenders of every kind of régime claim that it is a democracy, and fear that they might have to stop using the word if it were tied down to any one meaning. Words of this kind are often used in a consciously dishonest way. That is, the person who uses them has his own private definition, but allows his hearer to think he means something quite different. Statements like *Marshal Pétain was a true patriot, The Soviet Press is the freest in the world, The Catholic Church is opposed to persecution,* are almost always made with intent to deceive. Other words used in variable meanings, in most cases more or less dishonestly, are: *class, totalitarian, science, progressive, reactionary, bourgeois, equality.*

Now that I have made this catalogue of swindles and perversions, let me give another example of the kind of writing that they lead to. This time it must of its nature be an imaginary one. I am going to translate a passage of good English into modern English of the worst sort. Here is a well-known verse from *Ecclesiastes:*

> I returned and saw under the sun, that the race is not to the swift, nor the battle to the strong, neither yet bread to the wise, nor yet riches to men of understanding, nor yet favour to men of skill; but time and chance happeneth to them all.

Here it is in modern English:

Objective consideration of contemporary phenomena compels the conclusion that success or failure in competitive activities exhibits no tendency
to be commensurate with innate capacity, but that a considerable element
of the unpredictable must invariably be taken into account.

This is a parody, but not a very gross one. Exhibit (3), above, for instance, contains several patches of the same kind of English. It will be
seen that I have not made a full translation. The beginning and ending of
the sentence follow the original meaning fairly closely, but in the middle
the concrete illustrations—race, battle, bread—dissolve into the vague
phrase "success or failure in competitive activities." This had to be so,
because no modern writer of the kind I am discussing—no one capable of
using phrases like "objective consideration of contemporary phenomena"—
would ever tabulate his thoughts in that precise and detailed way. The
whole tendency of modern prose is away from concreteness. Now analyze
these two sentences a little more closely. The first contains forty-nine words
but only sixty syllables, and all its words are those of everyday life. The
second contains thirty-eight words of ninety syllables: eighteen of its words
are from Latin roots, and one from Greek. The first sentence contains six
vivid images, and only one phrase ("time and chance") that could be called
vague. The second contains not a single fresh, arresting phrase, and in spite
of its ninety syllables it gives only a shortened version of the meaning contained in the first. Yet without a doubt it is the second kind of sentence that
is gaining ground in modern English. I do not want to exaggerate. This
kind of writing is not yet universal, and outcrops of simplicity will occur
here and there in the worst-written page. Still, if you or I were told to
write a few lines on the uncertainty of human fortunes, we should probably
come much nearer to my imaginary sentence than to the one from *Ecclesiastes*.

As I have tried to show, modern writing at its worst does not consist
in picking out words for the sake of their meaning and inventing images
in order to make the meaning clearer. It consists in gumming together long
strips of words which have already been set in order by someone else, and
making the results presentable by sheer humbug. The attraction of this
way of writing is that it is easy. It is easier—even quicker, once you have
the habit—to say *In my opinion it is a not unjustifiable assumption that*
than to say *I think*. If you use ready-made phrases, you not only don't have
to hunt about for words; you also don't have to bother with the rhythms
of your sentences, since these phrases are generally so arranged as to be
more or less euphonious. When you are composing in a hurry—when you
are dictating to a stenographer, for instance, or making a public speech—
it is natural to fall into a pretentious, Latinized style. Tags like *a consideration which we should do well to bear in mind* or *a conclusion to which all
of us would readily assent* will save many a sentence from coming down

with a bump. By using stale metaphors, similes and idioms, you save much mental effort, at the cost of leaving your meaning vague, not only for your reader but for yourself. This is the significance of mixed metaphors. The sole aim of a metaphor is to call up a visual image. When these images clash—as in *The Fascist octopus has sung its swan song, the jackboot is thrown into the melting pot*—it can be taken as certain that the writer is not seeing a mental image of the objects he is naming; in other words he is not really thinking. Look again at the examples I gave at the beginning of this essay. Professor Laski (1) uses five negatives in fifty-three words. One of these is superfluous, making nonsense of the whole passage, and in addition there is the slip *alien* for akin, making further nonsense, and several avoidable pieces of clumsiness which increase the general vagueness. Professor Hogben (2) plays ducks and drakes with a battery which is able to write prescriptions, and, while disapproving of the everyday phrase *put up with,* is unwilling to look *egregious* up in the dictionary and see what it means. (3), if one takes an uncharitable attitude towards it, is simply meaningless: probably one could work out its intended meaning by reading the whole of the article in which it occurs. In (4), the writer knows more or less what he wants to say, but an accumulation of stale phrases chokes him like tea leaves blocking a sink. In (5), words and meaning have almost parted company. People who write in this manner usually have a general emotional meaning—they dislike one thing and want to express solidarity with another—but they are not interested in the detail of what they are saying. A scrupulous writer, in every sentence that he writes, will ask himself at least four questions, thus: What am I trying to say? What words will express it? What image or idiom will make it clear? Is this image fresh enough to have an effect? And he will probably ask himself two more: Could I put it more shortly? Have I said anything that is avoidably ugly? But you are not obliged to go to all this trouble. You can shirk it by simply throwing your mind open and letting the ready-made phrases come crowding in. They will construct your sentences for you—even think your thoughts for you, to a certain extent—and at need they will perform the important service of partially concealing your meaning even from yourself. It is at this point that the special connection between politics and the debasement of language becomes clear.

In our time it is broadly true that political writing is bad writing. Where it is not true, it will generally be found that the writer is some kind of rebel, expressing his private opinions and not a "party line." Orthodoxy, of whatever colour, seems to demand a lifeless, imitative style. The political dialects to be found in pamphlets, leading articles, manifestos, White Papers and the speeches of under-secretaries do, of course, vary from party to party, but they are all alike in that one almost never finds in them a fresh, vivid, home-made turn of speech. When one watches some tired hack on the platform mechanically repeating the familiar phrases—*bestial atrocities,*

*iron heel, bloodstained tyranny, free peoples of the world, stand shoulder to shoulder*—one often has a curious feeling that one is not watching a live human being but some kind of dummy: a feeling which suddenly becomes stronger at moments when the light catches the speaker's spectacles and turns them into blank discs which seem to have no eyes behind them. And this is not altogether fanciful. A speaker who uses that kind of phraseology has gone some distance towards turning himself into a machine. The appropriate noises are coming out of his larynx, but his brain is not involved as it would be if he were choosing his words for himself. If the speech he is making is one that he is accustomed to make over and over again, he may be almost unconscious of what he is saying, as one is when one utters the responses in church. And this reduced state of consciousness, if not indispensable, is at any rate favourable to political conformity.

In our time, political speech and writing are largely the defense of the indefensible. Things like the continuance of British rule in India, the Russian purges and deportations, the dropping of the atom bombs on Japan, can indeed be defended, but only by arguments which are too brutal for most people to face, and which do not square with the professed aims of political parties. Thus political language has to consist largely of euphemism, question-begging and sheer cloudy vagueness. Defenceless villages are bombarded from the air, the inhabitants driven out into the countryside, the cattle machine-gunned, the huts set on fire with incendiary bullets: this is called *pacification*. Millions of peasants are robbed of their farms and sent trudging along the roads with no more than they can carry: this is called *transfer of population* or *rectification of frontiers*. People are imprisoned for years without trial, or shot in the back of the neck or sent to die of scurvy in Arctic lumber camps: this is called *elimination of unreliable elements*. Such phraseology is needed if one wants to name things without calling up mental pictures of them. Consider for instance some comfortable English professor defending Russian totalitarianism. He cannot say outright, "I believe in killing off your opponents when you can get good results by doing so." Probably, therefore, he will say something like this:

> While freely conceding that the Soviet régime exhibits certain features which the humanitarian may be inclined to deplore, we must, I think, agree that a certain curtailment of the right to political opposition is an unavoidable concomitant of transitional periods, and that the rigours which the Russian people have been called upon to undergo have been amply justified in the sphere of concrete achievement.

The inflated style is itself a kind of euphemism. A mass of Latin words falls upon the facts like soft snow, blurring the outlines and covering up all the details. The great enemy of clear language is insincerity. When there is a gap between one's real and one's declared aims, one turns as it were

instinctively to long words and exhausted idioms, like a cuttlefish squirting out ink. In our age there is no such thing as "keeping out of politics." All issues are political issues, and politics itself is a mass of lies, evasions, folly, hatred and schizophrenia. When the general atmosphere is bad, language must suffer. I should expect to find—this is a guess which I have not sufficient knowledge to verify—that the German, Russian and Italian languages have all deteriorated in the last ten or fifteen years, as a result of dictatorship.

But if thought corrupts language, language can also corrupt thought. A bad usage can spread by tradition and imitation, even among people who should and do know better. The debased language that I have been discussing is in some ways very convenient. Phrases like *a not unjustifiable assumption, leaves much to be desired, would serve no good purpose, a consideration which we should do well to bear in mind,* are a continuous temptation, a packet of aspirins always at one's elbow. Look back through this essay, and for certain you will find that I have again and again committed the very faults I am protesting against. By this morning's post I have received a pamphlet dealing with conditions in Germany. The author tells me that he "felt impelled" to write it. I open it at random, and here is almost the first sentence that I see: "[The Allies] have an opportunity not only of achieving a radical transformation of Germany's social and political structure in such a way as to avoid a nationalistic reaction in Germany itself, but at the same time of laying the foundations of a co-operative and unified Europe." You see, he "feels impelled" to write— feels, presumably, that he has something new to say—and yet his words, like cavalry horses answering the bugle, group themselves automatically into the familiar dreary pattern. This invasion of one's mind by ready-made phrases (*lay the foundations, achieve a radical transformation*) can only be prevented if one is constantly on guard against them, and every such phrase anaesthetizes a portion of one's brain.

I said earlier that the decadence of our language is probably curable. Those who deny this would argue, if they produced an argument at all, that language merely reflects existing social conditions, and that we cannot influence its development by any direct tinkering with words and constructions. So far as the general tone or spirit of a language goes, this may be true, but it is not true in detail. Silly words and expressions have often disappeared, not through any evolutionary process but owing to the conscious action of a minority. Two recent examples were *explore every avenue* and *leave no stone unturned,* which were killed by the jeers of a few journalists. There is a long list of flyblown metaphors which could similarly be got rid of if enough people would interest themselves in the job; and it should also be possible to laugh the *not un-* formation out of existence, to reduce the amount of Latin and Greek in the average sentence, to drive out foreign phrases and strayed scientific words, and, in general, to make

pretentiousness unfashionable. But all these are minor points. The defence of the English language implies more than this, and perhaps it is best to start by saying what it does *not* imply.

To begin with it has nothing to do with archaism, with the salvaging of obsolete words and turns of speech, or with the setting up of a "standard English" which must never be departed from. On the contrary, it is especially concerned with the scrapping of every word or idiom which has outworn its usefulness. It has nothing to do with correct grammar and syntax, which are of no importance so long as one makes one's meaning clear, or with the avoidance of Americanisms, or with having what is called a "good prose style." On the other hand it is not concerned with fake simplicity and the attempt to make written English colloquial. Nor does it even imply in every case preferring the Saxon word to the Latin one, though it does imply using the fewest and shortest words that will cover one's meaning. What is above all needed is to let the meaning choose the word, and not the other way about. In prose, the worst thing one can do with words is to surrender to them. When you think of a concrete object, you think wordlessly, and then, if you want to describe the thing you have been visualizing you probably hunt about till you find the exact words that seem to fit. When you think of something abstract you are more inclined to use words from the start, and unless you make a conscious effort to prevent it, the existing dialect will come rushing in and do the job for you, at the expense of blurring or even changing your meaning. Probably it is better to put off using words as long as possible and get one's meaning as clear as one can through pictures or sensations. Afterwards one can choose —not simply *accept*—the phrases that will best cover the meaning, and then switch round and decide what impressions one's words are likely to make on another person. This last effort of the mind cuts out all stale or mixed images, all prefabricated phrases, needless repetitions, and humbug and vagueness generally. But one can often be in doubt about the effect of a word or a phrase, and one needs rules that one can rely on when instinct fails. I think the following rules will cover most cases:

(i)   Never use a metaphor, simile or other figure of speech which you are used to seeing in print.
(ii)  Never use a long word where a short one will do.
(iii) If it is possible to cut a word out, always cut it out.
(iv)  Never use the passive where you can use the active.
(v)   Never use a foreign phrase, a scientific word or a jargon word if you can think of an everyday English equivalent.
(vi)  Break any of these rules sooner than say anything outright barbarous.

These rules sound elementary, and so they are, but they demand a deep change of attitude in anyone who has grown used to writing in the style now fashionable. One could keep all of them and still write bad English,

but one could not write the kind of stuff that I quoted in those five specimens at the beginning of this article.

I have not here been considering the literary use of language, but merely language as an instrument for expressing and not for concealing or preventing thought. Stuart Chase and others have come near to claiming that all abstract words are meaningless, and have used this as a pretext for advocating a kind of political quietism. Since you don't know what Fascism is, how can you struggle against Fascism? One need not swallow such absurdities as this, but one ought to recognize that the present political chaos is connected with the decay of language, and that one can probably bring about some improvement by starting at the verbal end. If you simplify your English, you are freed from the worst follies of orthodoxy. You cannot speak any of the necessary dialects, and when you make a stupid remark its stupidity will be obvious, even to yourself. Political language—and with variations this is true of all political parties, from Conservatives to Anarchists—is designed to make lies sound truthful and murder respectable, and to give an appearance of solidity to pure wind. One cannot change all this in a moment, but one can change one's own habits, and from time to time one can even, if one jeers loudly enough, send some worn-out and useless phrase—some *jackboot, Achilles' heel, hotbed, melting pot, acid test, veritable inferno* or other lump of verbal refuse—into the dustbin where it belongs.

## TOPICS FOR DISCUSSION

1    How does Orwell explain the circular cause-and-effect relationship between the decline of language and the decline of a civilization? Is the analogy of the man who takes the first drink appropriate here? Although figurative language can be vivid and concrete, can it run counter to concreteness?

2    What are the two modern "mental vices" apparent in the five passages quoted, and how do they manifest themselves?

3    Is the section on meaningless words convincing, or are there times when one can use with meaning some of those words Orwell finds too vague? Give an example.

4    What is the "special connection between politics and the debasement of language"? Is the argument convincing?

5    Is Orwell guilty of using the word "orthodoxy" in a meaningless way? Does his use of the word give you any hint as to his political views?

6    When does language corrupt thought? Does the process end here?

7    How can language be cured of its decadence? Is the cure of the language likely to affect society as a whole? Why? Is this another indication of Orwell's politics?

8    Does his main objective seem literary or political?

## ...AND COMPOSITION

9    Do you agree that "politics itself is a mass of lies, evasions, folly, hatred and schizophrenia"? Avoid meaningless words.

10   Orwell's political beliefs are easy to recognize even though they appear in fragments in this essay. Write a short paper illustrating how his basic assumptions assist his argument. Could one of different political persuasions share his opinions of the ultimate relationship of language and politics?

11   Using Orwell's six rules for writing, analyze two newspaper editorials written on the same subject.

12   Analyze the public speeches of a major political officeholder using Orwell's six rules. Do you believe insincerity or lax thinking prompted whatever offenses you found?

**SHERIDAN BAKER (1918–    )** professor of English at the
University of Michigan, has devoted himself to teaching—and to exemplifying—
effective composition. Two of his books, *The Essayist* and *The Practical Stylist,*
provide good examples and careful guidance. In the preface to *The Essayist,*
Mr. Baker quotes Samuel Johnson: "You can never be wise unless you love reading."
And in witnessing about his own guides he goes on to say of Thoreau: "I
think I have learned more about writing from him than from anyone." In the
following essay, Mr. Baker passes along some of his accumulated wisdom
about writing.

# Scholarly Style, or the Lack Thereof

Teachers and scholars are constantly picking at faulty writing. Indeed, instructors in English do little else. But the writing of the college professor himself, I think, could stand one more attack, though I repeat much said before. Recently, as I was getting together a volume from different scientific and scholarly fields, several things from freshman handbooks and articles on composition came home.[1] Regardless of person or field, I saw, writing always fails in the same way. Words should count, they should make sense, and the great enemy of counting sensibly is wordiness. I saw also that behind the professor's wordiness lay a failure of attitude, a mistaken stance encouraged by both our scientific and our pedantic selves.

We mistake, I think, how scholarship should look and sound in public. Picture a young man in a rusty cutaway and striped pants, a celluloid collar and flowing tie, face serious, eyes glazed, gesticulating with his gloves, mumbling long words while no one at the party pays him the slightest attention. Or perhaps he is dapper, nose-in-the-air, full of jargon and wind. Picture either one and you will have some idea of the way a great many scholars attempt to address their readers. Both have the wrong attitude. Our scientific temper has made our syntax ponderous, and our dignity strings out long words like so much bunting.

Now, both scholar and scientist owe first allegiance to the scientific method. Whether he works with books or social behavior or metallic salts, the researcher collects his facts, weighs them, and shapes from probability an hypothesis about the truth. But the scientific attitude has nevertheless, I think, done much to load our sentences with nouns, and to teach us the passive voice.

Because the scientist, social or natural, prefers *things* to *qualities,* he prefers nouns to adjectives. Indeed, whenever he can, he makes qualities

[1] I am especially indebted to George Orwell, "Politics and the English Language," in *Shooting an Elephant* (New York: Harcourt, Brace and Co., 1950), pp. 77–92, and to Robert C. Waddell, *Grammar and Style* (New York: Dryden Press, 1951).

into things by building nouns around them. He will write *Spanish-type* instead of *Spanish*. He will write *in size* instead of *long*. He will always say *of a peculiar order* when he means *peculiar*, and *of an indefinite nature* when he means *indefinite*, and *of great importance* when he means *important*. He will encumber prepositions with nouns, apparently because this makes the preposition more substantial, less like a disembodied process. He will say *in order to* rather than *to*, and *by means of* rather than *by*. Where *and* or *with* would serve, he writes *in relation to*. When he wants to add a phrase, he will select the relative pronoun—usually *which*—rather than the adjective or participle: "a subject *which was* popular a decade ago" rather than "a subject popular a decade ago."

The trouble with this is its density—more words, less light, and almost no movement. The *ofs* and the *whiches* have thrown our prose into a hundred-years' sleep. Here is a piece typically respectable and drowsy:

> Many biological journals, especially those *which* regularly publish new scientific names, now state in each issue the exact date *of* publication *of* the preceding issue. In dealing with journals *which* do not follow this practice, or with volumes *which* are issued individually, the biologist often needs *to* resort *to* indexes . . . *in order to* determine the actual date *of* publication *of* a particular name.

By eliminating *ofs* and the nouns they bring, by changing *which*-phrases into participles, and nouns into verbs, we can cut this passage almost to half without touching the sense:

> Many biological journals, especially those regularly *publishing* new scientific names, now give the date of each preceding issue. With journals not *following* this practice, and with some books, the biologist must turn to indexes . . . *to date* a particular name.

Our heavy preference for nouns, moreover, leads to a habit worse than any indulgence in *whiches* and *ofs:* we modify nouns by nouns instead of by adjectives. The social sciences here sin more than most. Working with intangibles, the scientist seems urged to stiffen his nouns with nouns, and the reader can separate main thought from modifier only after initiation. "Child sex education" stands for "the sexual education of children," I think, unless it stands for "educating someone about the sex of children." Is sex educational, or is education sexual? The noun-habit often carries us completely away from what words mean, and keeps us there by elevated sound alone. And even if by habit we learn to read these constructions, they remain lumpy and unattractive: *body consciousness, human body function, significance level, sign situation, population theory, art ability, teacher grades, nature-nurture evidence.* If we can't drop one of the nouns or find its related adjective, the only cure is homeopathic—a cautious shot of *ofs*.

II

Our scientific taste prefers not only the solid noun but the impersonal passive voice—an opiate which cancels responsibility, hides identity, and numbs the reader. And our adherence to officialdom and groups strengthens the preference.

We have almost forgotten that the simple English sentence, the basis of good writing, moves. It moves from *subject* through *verb* to *object:* "Smith laid the cornerstone on April 1." But because we must sound important, because the institution must be bigger than Smith, we write "the cornerstone was laid on April 1," and the human being vanishes from the earth. The doer and the writer both—all traces of individuality—disappear behind elongated verbs. Men don't do things, things merely are done; stones move into place, whole campuses emerge from the ground, regulations crystallize overhead. Committees always write this way—and the ecological effect on scholarly writing is deadly. "It was moved that a conference would be held," the secretary writes, to avoid pinning the rap on anybody.

Unfortunately, we like this. We use the passive voice at every opportunity, even with nothing to hide and no one to protect. The passive voice seems dignified and authoritative, and, for all this, it makes our writing dreary with extra *ises, beens* and *bys.* It overruns every scholarly field:

> Public concern *has also been given* a tremendous impetus *by* the findings of the Hoover Commission in the federal government, and "little Hoover" commissions to survey the organizational structure and functions of many state governments *have been established.* [In the federal government, the findings of the Hoover Commission have also greatly stimulated public concern, and many states have established "little Hoover" commissions to survey their governments.]

> The algal mats *are made up of* the interwoven filaments of several genera. [The interwoven filaments of several genera make up these algal mats.]

> Many of the remedies *would probably be shown to be* "faith cures." [Many of the remedies are probably "faith cures."]

> In this way less developed countries *can be enabled* to participate in the higher production system of the Western World. [These programs can help backward countries to Western productivity.]

> Anxiety and emotional conflict *are lessened* when latency sets in. The total personality *is oriented* in a repressive, inhibitory fashion so as to maintain the barriers, and what Freud has called "psychic dams," against psychological impulses. [When latency sets in, anxiety and emotional conflict subside. The personality inhibits itself, maintaining its barriers—Freud's "psychic dams"—against psychosexual impulses.]

The passive voice, simply in its wordiness, is unclear; but, eliminating the real subject of the verb, as it does, it is intrinsically unclear also. An essay,

getting started, will state, "it was demonstrated," and one can only guess as to whether the writer or his rivals had done the demonstrating.

The passive voice is the natural voice of science. Not only officialdom but scientific objectivity tempts us to it. It sounds dispassionate and impersonal; it stops time and holds life still so we can catalogue it. (Flowers never grow in this dry land; they "are found.") Perhaps scientific German has had something to do with it. At any rate, since the scientist describes what *is,* since our dignity demands *is laid* instead of *laid, is* becomes almost our only verb. All of us, following first the natural and then the social scientist, define, partition, arrange categories, and cement our writing into blocks with an equals-sign our only predication.

*Is* so besets us—we are so willing to sit back on our *ises*—that we not only replace active with passive voice, but active verbs with sedentary ones. We can almost see the roadblocks—separated by a narrow *was,* inverted to look passive—in this opening sentence:

> Typical of the rationalism of the eighteenth century was a view of prose fiction which developed during the middle decades.

After a little blasting, we might get on into the essay, leaving something like this behind:

> A new view of prose fiction, typically rational, developed in the middle decades of the eighteenth century.

To make matters worse, we spread our *is*ms by handing out *exists* and *existences* at every opportunity. We write "this association is not known to exist," not "this association is unknown." And we like to carry phrases around in a stretcher that looks like this: "There is ———— which." *It* may substitute for *there. That* or *who* may substitute for *which.* But they are all equally wordy: "Moreover, *there is* one class of worker *which* never seeks regular employment." If we drop the italicized words, nothing diminishes but clumsiness.

### III

If we straighten out our syntax, however, we are still left with the ornate vocabulary we think proper to scholarship. Vocabulary is a matter of tone. Tone is a matter of attitude. All our *ofs,* our *whiches* our passives, our clumps of substantives—all rise from the same source as our vocabulary: the pompous and circumstantial attitude so common to our scholarly, scientific pages. Official anonymity is in our ears. We wish to be modest and objective. We want to impress other zoologists, psychologists, economists, and literary men by writing like them. And the result is an inky, back-bay fog. We should work like scholars and scientists, but we should write like writers. We should take our subjects seriously but ourselves with grains of salt, with the knowledge that we are all sinners, all wordy, and all—whether courtly or pontifical—too fond of big Latin words.

Two scientific fishermen have compared numbers of bass in the pond to numbers in the basket, and have watched imported bass survive in mixed company. Their article begins:

Of the many things which influence angling success, the size of population of the species sought must be a prime factor. In order to gain information on the relationship between population and yield to fishermen in a fishery based mainly on large mouth bass, *Micropterus salmoides* (Lacépède), we have experimented. . . .

The trouble with this is not *Micropterus salmoides*. Technical Latin words are precise and useful. The trouble lies in *influence, success, population, factor, information, relationship, population,* and the ambiguous *yield to*—all slushing along together through the weedy connectives. Does your subject seem mundane or trivial? Then give it a Latin diploma and it will graduate into elegant dullness. Actually, this article soon begins to read quite well. After a Latin period or two the writers get down to ponds and fish; they leave the academic procession and get out their waders. If we traded our Latin words for Anglo-Saxon ones wherever we could make a bargain, and long words for short ones; if we wrote *find* for *determine, see* for *inquire, watch* for *observe, book* for *volume;* if we banished all words containing *tion,* and then let not more than three sneak back into any one paragraph, our writing would be clearer. Subjects needing Latin technicalities should insist the more stoutly on short English words for the writing in between.

But the social sciences—especially sociology and psychology—unblessed with Latin genera, are in a bad way. They must make their own terms as they go, and few men have Freud's command of words. Some words, like *schizophrenia* and *psychosomatic,* describe what they represent; *ego* and *id* are clear enough. But, for the most part, poor writers have endowed psychology with a technical vocabulary that would put even Solomon on the couch. We hear of *reaction fixation,* of *reaction to action. Factors, aspects,* and *situations* are *functions* of every sentence, and a word like *motivation* takes on private meanings which force the writer to new definitions. *Affect* changes into a noun and affects the sanity of everyone trying to write effectively.

Language is public property that must not be rough-hewn to private ends. A real knowledge of Latin might save us from this—a real understanding of what a word means at the root. But we are not Latinists; we are merely Latinate. Always looking for an exact scientific language, we never write with an alert and delighted sense that words have more than one meaning, that our sentences can strike harmonics and still be precise. Beware of the writer who must define his terms, I say. He may be unable to use language, as it runs, to express his meaning, and—whatever his motivation—the result is pomposity. He is Humpty Dumpty, the original

egghead, making words say what he wants them to mean instead of meaning what he wants to say. He is either evading the toil of finding the right word, or defining the obvious:

> Let us agree to use the word *signal* as an abbreviation for the phrase "the simplest kind of sign." (This agrees fairly well with the customary meaning of the word "signal.")

A definer of words is usually a bad writer. The man, above, who had to get his signals straight, a semanticist, by the way, grinds out about three parts sawdust to every one of meat. In the following excerpt, the italics are his; the brackets, mine. Read the sentence first as it was written; then read it again, omitting the bracketed words:

> The moral of such examples is that *all intelligent criticism [of any instance] of language [in use] must begin with understanding [of] the motives [and purposes] of the speaker [in that situation].*

Here, each of the bracketed phrases is already implied in the others. Attempting to be precise, our writer has only clouded his meaning. We have reached our last infirmity of scientific mind. Naturally the speaker would be "in that situation"; naturally a sampling of language would be "an instance" of language "in use." And even if *motives* are not *purposes,* the difference is too small to dawdle over. His next sentence deserves some kind of immortality. He means "muddy language causes trouble":

> Unfortunately, the type of case that causes trouble in practice is that in which the kind of use made of language is not transparently clear. . . .

IV

Clearly, it is hard to be transparent. Writing is hard. Even divinity has found it necessary to write in the middle of the night with great commotion. Writing is probably more than half of the researcher's job, as anyone will testify who has found himself hunting up one more fact, and running one more test, postponing the awful hour when he must face the mystery of the word, to gather his thoughts and to communicate. It is a matter of finding first the right attitude, and then the right words—and no more. If we have little to say, we will be pompous, we will write in the passive voice, we will throw phrases in the air like dust.

But if you have something to say and still sound tumid, we can work out our salvation. Here are some suggestions:

1   Economize. Think of explaining what you have to say clearly, simply and pleasantly to a small mixed group of intelligent people.
2   Never use a long word when you can find a short one, or a Latin word when you can find a good Old English one.
3   Suspect yourself of wordiness whenever you see an *of,* a *which* or a *that.* Inspect all areas surrounding any form of *to be.* Never use *exist.*

4   Resolve not to use the passive voice. Simply fly in the face of convention and begin your sentence with "I" or "we" or "the writer."
5   Take pains to avoid modifying a noun with a noun.
6   Make sure that each word really makes sense. No one who had inspected the meaning of his words could have written: "Every seat in the auditorium was filled to capacity."
7   Beware of the metaphor. It is the spirit of good prose. It gives the reader a picture, a glimpse of what the subject really looks like to the writer. But it is dangerous, can easily get tangled and insistent, the more so when it almost works: don't have a violent explosion pave the way for a new growth.

The important thing is, I think, to pick up each sentence in turn, asking ourselves if we can possibly make it shorter. This done, clarity will come of itself, and with it the peculiar pleasure of having wrestled—the struggle itself will be agony—with the written word, and written well. We may even live in a style in which we never dreamed we could become accustomed.

## TOPICS FOR DISCUSSION

1   Do you think Orwell and Baker are working over the same points? How do they differ? Which of their arguments do you consider more direct and valid? On what do you base your judgment?

2   What do the four divisions of the essay contribute to the general thesis? What simple transitional device is found at the beginning of sections 2, 3, and 4?

3   How has the scientific method been responsible, rightly or wrongly, for ponderous syntax and excessively long words? What is the particular offense of nouns?

4   Why is the passive voice the "natural voice of science"? Are there ever times when the process rather than the individual should be emphasized? How does the passive voice make a subject unclear?

5   What does Baker mean when he says: "A definer of words is usually a bad writer"? Can you think of any situation in which definitions are necessary?

6   How can Latin both assist and hinder exact communication? Should we regard as fixed the meaning of Latin roots?

7   How does Baker's suggestion 7 agree with C. S. Lewis's remarks on effective writing? Do they disagree, or are they merely emphasizing different aspects of metaphoric writing?

## ...AND COMPOSITION

**8**  Analyze two or three examples of failure in scholarly writing or of ineffectiveness in political writing, using the suggestions of Baker and Orwell.

**9**  Using the examples you analyze above, rewrite the sections into clear prose, following Baker's suggestions.

**10**  Find ten examples of poor use of the passive construction and ten examples of necessary use; comment on the reasons for the passive constructions.

**C. S. LEWIS (1898–1963)** eminent in Renaissance and medieval
literature at Cambridge, wrote fantasy and science fiction, Christian polemics, and
literary criticism. He ranged through courtly love and Heaven and Hell—
all of which turned out to bear on current issues. In his lively book *The Screwtape
Letters*, he even undertook to realize the complexity of Satan's plans,
ironically assuming Satan's point of view. Here C. S. Lewis has applied
himself to the complex topic of language.

# At the Fringe of Language

Language exists to communicate whatever it can communicate. Some things it communicates so badly that we never attempt to communicate them by words if any other medium is available. Those who think they are testing a boy's "elementary" command of English by asking him to describe in words how one ties one's tie or what a pair of scissors is like, are far astray. For precisely what language can hardly do at all, and never does well, is to inform us about complex physical shapes and movements. Hence descriptions of such things in the ancient writers are nearly always unintelligible. Hence we never in real life voluntarily use language for this purpose; we draw a diagram or go through pantomimic gestures. The exercises which such examiners set are no more a test of "elementary" linguistic competence than the most difficult bit of trick-riding from the circus ring is a test of elementary horsemanship.

Another grave limitation of language is that it cannot, like music or gesture, do more than one thing at once. However the words in a great poet's phrase interinanimate one other and strike the mind as a quasi-instantaneous chord, yet strictly speaking, each word must be read or heard before the next. That way, language is as unilinear as time. Hence, in narrative, the great difficulty of presenting a very complicated change which happens suddenly. If we do justice to the complexity, the time the reader must take over the passage will destroy the feeling of suddenness. If we get in the suddenness we shall not be able to get in the complexity. I am not saying that genius will not find its own ways of palliating this defect in the instrument; only that the instrument is in this way defective.

One of the most important and effective uses of language is the emotional. It is also, of course, wholly legitimate. We do not talk only in order to reason or to inform. We have to make love and quarrel, to propitiate and pardon, to rebuke, console, intercede, and arouse. "He that complains," said Johnson, "acts like a man, like a social being." The real objection lies not against the language of emotion as such, but against language which, being in reality emotional, masquerades—whether by plain hypocrisy or subtler self-deceit—as being something else.

All my generation are much indebted to Dr. I. A. Richards for having fully called our attention to the emotional functions of language. But I am hardly less indebted to Professor Empson for having pointed out that the conception of emotional language can be very easily extended too far. It was time to call a halt.

We must obviously not call any utterance "emotional" language because it in fact arouses, even because it must arouse, emotion. "It is not cancer after all," "The Germans have surrendered," "I love you"—may all be true statements about matter of fact. And of course it is the facts, not the language, that arouse the emotion. In the last, the fact communicated is itself the existence of an emotion but that makes no difference. Statements about crime are not criminal language; nor are statements about emotions necessarily emotional language. Nor, in my opinion, are value-judgments ("this is good," "this is bad") emotional language. Approval and disapproval do not seem to me to be emotions. If we felt at all times about the things we judge good the emotion which is appropriate, our lives would be easier. It would also be an error to treat "I am washed in the blood of the Lamb" as emotional language. It is of course metaphorical language. But by his metaphor the speaker is trying to communicate what be believes to be a fact. You may of course think the belief false in his particular case. You may think the real universe is such that no fact which corresponded to such a statement could possibly occur. You may say that the real cause which prompts a man to say things like that is a state of emotion. But if so an emotion has produced erroneous belief about an impossible fact and it is the fact erroneously believed in which the man is stating. A man's hasty belief that the Germans had surrendered (before they did) might well be caused by his emotions. That would not make "The Germans have surrendered" a specimen of emotional language. If you could find a man nowadays capable of believing, and saying, "The Russians have all been annihilated by magic," even this would not be emotional language, though his belief in magic might be a belief engendered by emotion.

All this is fairly plain sailing. We reach something harder in the things said by poets. For there the purpose of the utterance would be frustrated if no emotion were aroused. They do not merely, like the sentences cited above, arouse emotion in fact; it is their purpose—at any rate, part of their purpose—to do so. But we must be very careful here. Having observed that a poetical utterance in fact arouses emotion, and is intended to arouse emotion, and that if taken as a statement about reality—or even about the make-believe "realities" of a fictitious narrative—it would be nonsensical or at least false, can we conclude that it communicates nothing but emotion? I think not.

Nothing will convince me that "My soul is an enchanted boat" is simply a better way—however much better—of doing what might be done by some exclamation like "Gee! Asia has risen from the dark cave of Demogorgon.

She is floating upwards. She is saluted as Life of Life!" The reversed temporal process in [lines] 97—103 ("We have passed Age's icy caves" etc.),[1]
borrowed from Plato's *Politicus* (269ᶜ *sq*.), marks the fact that at this
moment the whole cycle is reversed and cosmos begins anew. She is undergoing apotheosis. What did it feel like? The poet says to us in effect "Think
of going in a boat. But quite effortless" ("Like a sleeping swan" gliding with
the current, he adds in the next line), "Like a boat without sail or oar; the
motive power undiscoverable. Like a magic boat—you must have read or
dreamed of such things—a boat drawn on, drawn swiftly on, irresistibly,
smoothly, by enchantment." Exactly. I know now how it felt for Asia. The
phrase has communicated emotion. But notice how. By addressing in the
first instance my imagination. He makes me imagine a boat rushing over
waves, which are also identified with sounds. After that he need do no more;
my emotion will follow of itself. Poetry most often communicates emotions,
not directly, but by creating imaginatively the grounds for those emotions.
It therefore communicates something more than emotion; only by means of
that something more does it communicate the emotion at all.

Burns compares his mistress to "a red, red rose"; Wordsworth his to
"a violet by a mossy stone Half hidden from the eye." These expressions
do communicate to me the emotion each poet felt. But it seems to me that
they do so solely by forcing me to imagine two (very different) women. I see
the rose-like, overpowering, midsummer sweetness of the one; the reticent,
elusive freshness, the beauty easily overlooked in the other. After that my
emotions may be left to themselves. The poets have done their part.

This, which is eminently true of poetry, is true of all imaginative writing.
One of the first things we have to say to a beginner who has brought us
his MS. is, "Avoid all epithets which are merely emotional. It is no use
*telling* us that something was 'mysterious' or 'loathsome' or 'awe-inspiring'
or 'voluptuous.' " Do you think your readers will believe you just because
you say so? You must go quite a different way to work. By direct description, by metaphor and simile, by secretly evoking powerful associations,
by offering the right stimuli to our nerves (in the right degree and the right
order), and by the very beat and vowel-melody and length and brevity of
your sentences, you must bring it about that we, we readers, not you,
exclaim 'how mysterious!' or 'loathsome' or whatever it is. Let me taste
for myself, and you'll have no need to *tell* me how I should react to the
flavour."

In Donne's couplet

Your gown going off, such beautious state reveals
As when from flowry meads th'hills shadow steales[2]

*beautious* is the only word of the whole seventeen which is doing no work.

---

[1] *Prometheus Unbound* ii, v, 72.
[2] *Elegy* xix, 13.

There are exceptions to this principle. By very successful placing, a great author may sometimes raise such words to poetic life. Wordsworth's lines are a specimen:

Which, to the boundaries of space and time,
Of melancholy space and doleful time,
Superior—[3]

Here we have almost the reverse of the process I have been describing. The object (space and time) is in one way so familiar to our imaginations and in another so unimaginable—we have read so many tedious attempts to exalt or over-awe us with mere superlatives or even with simple arithmetic —that nothing can be made of it. This time, therefore, the poet withdraws the object (the ground for emotion) altogether and appeals directly to our emotions; and not to the quite obvious ones. Another exception is naturally to be found in drama or very dramatic lyric, where the poet—with discretion and a proper use of illusion—imitates the speech of people in some highly emotional situation—even, at need, their inarticulate cries. This in its purity, which purity a good poet never sustains for long, belongs to poetry not in so far as poetry is a special use of language but in so far as poetry is *mimesis*. In themselves the "Ah! Ah!" or "Otototoi" or "Iou! Iou!" of characters in a Greek tragedy are not specimens of poetry any more than the "Bé, bé" of the lamb or the "Au! Au!" of the dog in Aristophanes.

In general, however, the poet's route to our emotions lies through our imaginations.

We must also exclude from the category "emotional language" words such as I have taken *supernatural* to be. The class of things which they refer to may be bound together chiefly by a common emotion; but the purpose of using the words is to assign something to that class, not merely to communicate the emotion which led to the classification.

Having thus narrowed the field, we can now make a new start. It will be noticed that I have throughout used the word *emotional* rather than *emotive*. This is because I think the latter word applicable to only one aspect of emotional language. For an "emotive word" ought to mean one whose function is to arouse emotion. But surely we ought to distinguish utterances which arouse, from those which express, emotion? The first is directed towards producing some effect on a (real or imagined) hearer; the second discharges our own emotion, cleanses our stuffed bosom of some perilous stuff.

The distinction will seem straw-splitting if we have in mind the language of love. For, as Samson says, "love seeks to have love," and it would be hard to say whether endearments serve more as expressions of love in the speaker or incitements to it in the beloved. But that tells us more about the

[3] *Prelude* vi, 134.

nature of love than about the nature of language. One of my old head-masters once wisely said it was a pity that *amare* was the first Latin verb we all learn. He thought this led to an imperfect grasp of the difference between the active and the passive voice. It might be better to begin with *flagellare*. The difference between flogging and being flogged would come home to the business and bosoms of schoolboys far more effectively than that of loving and being loved. On the same principle, we can best see the distinction between the stimulant and the expressive functions of emotional language in a quarrel; and best of all where the same word performs both. The man who calls me a low hound both expresses and (actually or intentionally) stimulates emotion. But not the same emotion. He expresses contempt; he stimulates, or hopes to stimulate, the almost opposite emotion of humiliation.

Again, in the language of complaint we often find the expressive without the stimulant. When two people who have missed the last train stand on the silent platform saying "Damn" or "Bloody" or "Sickening," they neither intend nor need to stimulate each other's disappointment. They are just "getting it off their chests."

The vocabulary of endearment, complaint, and abuse, provides, I think, almost the only specimens of words that are purely emotional, words from which all imaginative or conceptual content has vanished, so that they have no function at all but to express or stimulate emotion, or both. And an examination of them soon convinces us that in them we see language at its least linguistic. We have come to the frontier between language and inarticulate vocal sounds. And at that frontier we find a two-way traffic going on.

On the one hand we find inarticulate sounds becoming words with a fixed spelling and a niche in the dictionary. Thus English *heigh-ho* and Latin *eheu* are clearly formalised imitations of the sigh; *ah,* of the gasp; *tut-tut,* of the tongue clicked against the hard palate. These are general. In particular situations the "verbification" of the inarticulate may occur *ad hoc.* A voluntary scream may become a cry for mercy. A voluntary groan, from a wounded man, uttered to attract the attention of the stretcher-bearers, may be the equivalent of a sentence ("There is a wounded man in this ditch").

But we also see the frontier being crossed in the opposite direction. In the vocabulary of abuse and complaint we see things that once were words passing out of the realm of language (properly so called) and becoming the equivalents of inarticulate sounds or even of actions; of sighs, moans, whimperings, growls, or blows.

The "swear-words"—*damn* for complaint and *damn you* for abuse—are a good example. Historically the whole Christian eschatology lies behind them. If no one had ever consigned his enemy to the eternal fires and believed that there were eternal fires to receive him, these ejaculations would never have existed. But inflation, the spontaneous hyperboles of

ill temper, and the decay of religion, have long since emptied them of that lurid content. Those who have no belief in damnation—and some who have —now damn inanimate objects which would on any view be ineligible for it. The word is no longer an imprecation. It is hardly, in the full sense, a word at all when so used. Its popularity probably owes as much to its resounding phonetic virtues as to any, even fanciful, association with hell. It has ceased to be profane. It has also become very much less forceful. You may say the same of *sickening* in its popular, ejaculatory, use. There are alarms and disappointments which can actually produce nausea, or, at least, emotions which we feel to be somehow similar to it. But the man who says *sickening!* when he has missed the train is not thinking about that. The word is simply an alternative to *damn* or *bloody*. And of course far weaker than it would be if it still carried any suggestion of vomiting.

So with abusive terms. No one would now call his schoolfellow or next door neighbour a *swine* unless someone had once used this word to make a real comparison between his enemy and a pig. It is now a mere alternative to *beast* or *brute* or various popular unprintable words. They are all interchangeable. *Villain,* as we know, once really compared your enemy to a *villein*. Once, to call a man *cad* or *knave* assigned to him the status of a servant. And it did so because, earlier still, these words meant "boy" or "junior" (you address a slave as "boy" in Greek and a waiter as *garçon* in French).

Thus all these words have come down in the world. None of them started by being *merely* abusive, few of them by being abusive at all. They once stimulated emotion by suggesting an image. They made the enemy odious or contemptible by asserting he was like somebody or something we already disliked or looked down on. Their use was a sort of passionate parody of the syllogism: pigs (or servants or my juniors) are contemptible—John is like a pig (or servant or adolescent)—therefore John is contemptible. That was why they really hurt; because hurting was not the whole of what they did. They stimulated emotion because they also stimulated something else; imagination. They stimulated emotion in the particular case because they exploited emotions which already existed towards whole classes of things or persons. Now that they are nothing whatever but emotional stimulants, they are weak emotional stimulants. They make no particular accusation. They tell us nothing except that the speaker has lost his temper.

And even this they do not tell us linguistically, but symptomatically; as a red face, a loud voice, or a clenched fist, might do equally well. The fact of the other person's anger may hurt or frighten us; hurt us if we love him, or frighten us if he is larger and younger than ourselves and threatens violence. But his language as such has very little power to do the only thing it is intended to do. It would have been far more wounding to be called *swine* when the word still carried some whiff of the sty and some echo of a grunt; far more wounding to be called a *villain* when this still conjured up an image of the unwashed, malodorous, ineducable, gross,

belching, close-fisted, and surly boor. Now, who cares? Language meant solely to hurt hurts strangely little.

This can be seen clearly when we catch a word "just on the turn." *Bitch* is one. Till recently—and still in the proper contexts—this accused a woman of one particular fault and appealed, with some success, to our contempt by calling up an image of the she-dog's comical and indecorous behaviour when she is in heat. But it is now increasingly used of any woman whom the speaker, for whatever reason, is annoyed with—the female driver who is in front of him, or a female magistrate whom he thinks unjust. Clearly, the word is far more wounding in its narrower usage. If that usage is ever totally lost—as I think it will be—the word will sink to the level of *damn her*. Notice, too, how *cat* (of a woman) is still strong and useful because the image is still alive in it.

An important principle thus emerges. In general, emotional words, to be effective, must not be solely emotional. What expresses or stimulates emotion directly, without the intervention of an image or concept, expresses or stimulates it feebly. And in particular, when words of abuse have hurting the enemy as their direct and only object, they do not hurt him much. In the field of language, however it may be in that of action, hatred cuts its own throat, and those who are too "willing to wound" become thereby impotent to strike. And all this is only another way of saying that as words become exclusively emotional they cease to be words and therefore of course cease to perform any strictly linguistic function. They operate as growls or barks or tears. "Exclusively" is an important adverb here. They die as words not because there is too much emotion in them but because there is too little—and finally nothing at all—of anything else.

In this there is not much to be lamented. If a mother with a baby, or lovers in each other's arms, use language so emotional that it is really not language at all, I see no ground for shame or offence; and if men in an orgy of resentment, though (in the physical sense) they articulate, are really no more speaking—are saying no more—than a snarling animal, this is perhaps all for the best. The real corruption comes when men whose purpose in speaking is in fact purely emotional conceal this from others, and perhaps from themselves, by words that seem to be, but are not, charged with a conceptual content.

We have all heard *bolshevist, fascist, Jew,* and *capitalist,* used not to describe but merely to insult. Rose Macaulay noticed a tendency to prefix "so called" to almost any adjective when it was used of those the speaker hated; the final absurdity being reached when people referred to the Germans as "these so-called Germans." *Bourgeois* and *middle class* often suffer the same fate.

A literary man of my acquaintance, on reading an unfavourable reference to his own works, called it *vulgar.* The charge brought against him was one that only highly educated people ever bring; the tone of the passage not otherwise offensive than by being unfavourable; the phrasing perfectly good

English. If he had called it false, unintelligent, or malicious, I could have understood, though I might have disagreed. But why *vulgar?* Clearly, this word was selected solely because the speaker thought it was the one that the enemy, if he could hear it, would most dislike. It was the equivalent of an oath or a growl. But that was concealed from the speaker because "This is vulgar" sounds like a judgement.

When we write criticism we have to be continually on our guard against this sort of thing. If we honestly believe a work to be very bad we cannot help hating it. The function of criticism, however, is "to get ourselves out of the way and let humanity decide," not to discharge our hatred but to expose the grounds for it; not to vilify faults but to diagnose and exhibit them. Unfortunately, to express our hatred and to revenge ourselves is easier and more agreeable. Hence there is a tendency to select our pejorative epithets with a view not to their accuracy but to their power of hurting. If writing which was intended to be comic has set our teeth on edge, how easily the adjectives *arch* or *facetious* trickle out of the pen! But if we do not know exactly what we mean by them, if we are not prepared to say how comic work which errs by *archness* and *facetiousness* differs from comic work which errs in any other way, it is to be feared that we are really using them not to inform the reader but to annoy the author—*arch* or *facetious* being among the most effective "smear-words" of our period. In the same way work which obviously aspires and claims to be mature, if the critic dislikes it, will be called *adolescent*; not because the critic has really seen that its faults are those of adolescence but because he has seen that adolescence is the last thing the author wishes or expects to be accused of.

The best protection against this is to remind ourselves again and again what the proper function of pejorative words is. The ultimate, simplest and most abstract, is *bad* itself. The only good purpose for ever departing from that monosyllable when we condemn anything is to be more specific, to answer the question "Bad in what way?" Pejorative words are rightly used only when they do this. *Swine,* as a term of abuse is now a bad pejorative word, because it brings no one accusation rather than another against the person it vilifies; *coward* and *liar* are good ones because they charge a man with a particular fault—of which he might be proved guilty or innocent. As applied to literate, *dull, hackneyed, incoherent, monotonous, pornographic, cacophonous,* are good pejoratives; they tell people in what particular way we think a book faulty. *Adolescent* or *provincial* are not so good. For even when they are honestly used, to define, not merely to hurt, they really suggest a cause for the book's badness instead of describing the badness itself. We are saying in effect "He was led into his faults by being immature" or "by living in Lancashire." But would it not be more interesting to indicate the faults themselves and leave out our historical theory about their causes? If we find words like these—and *vulgar,* and others—indispensable to our criticism, if we find ourselves

applying them to more and more different kinds of things, there is grave reason to suspect that—whether we know it or not—we are really using them not to diagnose but to hurt. If so, we are assisting in verbicide. For this is the downward path which leads to the graveyard of murdered words. First they are purely descriptive; *adolescent* tells us a man's age, *villain,* his status. Then they are specifically pejorative; *adolescent* tells us that a man's work displays "mawkishness and all the thousand bitters" confessed by Keats, and *villain* tells that a man has a churl's mind and manners. Then they become *mere* pejoratives, useless synonyms for *bad,* as *villain* did and as *adolescent* may do if we aren't careful. Finally they become terms of abuse and cease to be language in the full sense at all.

## TOPICS FOR DISCUSSION

1   What is the author's main point? What preliminary points does he make before beginning his final statement in paragraph 3, page 34?

2   Much of this essay is definition and analysis; why is it useful in such an essay to begin by establishing what a subject is not?

3   Paragraph 3, page 28, introduces the major subject. How do the next few paragraphs clarify or add to the subject?

4   Why do poets present a more complicated problem than writers of prose? What is the similarity between poetry and all imaginative writing? How are the examples and the exceptions used to make this function of language clear?

5   What does Lewis mean by the "two-way traffic" at the frontier of language and inarticulate sound?

6   What is the "proper function of pejorative words"?

7   Find explicit and implicit transitional devices between sections of Lewis's argument.

8   What pattern, if any, does Lewis follow in his paragraphing with regard to the grouping of examples? Why do some examples take a whole and others fall into groups in one paragraph?

## ...AND COMPOSITION

9   Define your career plans only by negation, and yet give a clear indication of your hopes.

10   Try to evoke the emotions of "mysterious," "loathsome," or some other such epithet without using the word itself.

11   Find a recent editorial or essay that employs pejorative words; comment on the effectiveness of these words.

**JOYCE CARY (1888–1957)** seems conservative compared with acrobatic writers like Joyce and Stein. He wrote the steady view, the coherent judgment; but he makes us aware of how relevant parts of the truth surround the consciousness, demanding consideration, offering the ambitious writer limitless possibilities. The following pieces, bit by bit, with apt allusions, reveal both the value of focus in writing and the writer's knowledge that no work of art is ever enough.

# *Idea and Form*

I

The question of truth in art is an old one. It was always obvious that most writers were biased. And one school of novelists, the French school of the Goncourts, Flaubert, and finally Zola, set themselves deliberately to write novels that should be true to fact. They said, "We shall have nothing to do with romance, with drama, we shall study life as it is, and write from life." The consequence, for all four, was that they were accused of a libel on human nature and their countrymen. Flaubert was taken to court for *Madame Bovary*. He pleaded that he was interested only in art, he had no wish to attack anybody. This was, of course, untrue. Flaubert was intent on giving what he believed to be the truth about people, and especially the bourgeois, whom he detested. His prejudice was so violent that his last work, *Bouvard et Pécuchet,* a satire on two retired clerks, is unreadable. It is as boring as a tune on two notes. On the other hand, the attack on him was equally beside the point unless you believe in censorship. And Zola was even more violently abused for what was called his vicious distortion of the truth.

In *L'Assommoir* Zola sets his story in the Paris of the Second Empire. The plot turns on the drink traffic. His heroine Gervaise, a good, virtuous, decent working girl, marries Coupeau, a worker in zinc. They have a daughter, Nana. Gervaise starts a small laundry and does well. Then Coupeau has a fall, damages himself and takes to drink, and gradually ruins both himself and Gervaise. She is too gentle, too decent, or too weak to leave him or fight him. She ends on the streets and dies of exposure— Coupeau of delirium tremens at a hospital.

The book is a masterpiece, full of magnificent descriptions of working-class life in Paris at that time. And Zola studied every detail from life; the drink trade, the pubs, laundry work, the public laundries, a dozen crafts and the obscure courts where they were carried on. But the French accused him of giving a completely false picture of the Paris working class.

It is true that Zola probably exaggerated drunkenness among working men because he was writing about drink—a consequence of the book was the abolition by law of the kind of absinthe which destroyed Coupeau. From that time absinthe has been quite a different stuff. Drink was Zola's theme, and his plot is built upon it. Concentration upon drink as an evil among the working class was essential to him as a writer not only because he felt strongly about drink, but because he had to have a centre for his plot.

As Henry James writes to Hugh Walpole about his novel, *Mr Perrin and Mr Traill,*

> I don't quite recognise here the *centre of your subject,* that absolutely and indispensably fixed and constituted point from which one's ground must be surveyed and one's material wrought. If you can say it's (that centre) in Mr P.'s exasperated consciousness I can only reply that if it might be it yet isn't treated as such.

Without some unifying idea, it is impossible for a book to have a form. As Flaubert in *Madame Bovary* built his whole complex structure around Emma Bovary's romantic dream, so Zola built on the tragedy of Coupeau's drunkenness. Flaubert chose his characters, his background, to illuminate the dreams of a frustrated woman; he gives her a dull husband, and buries her in the boredom of a small country village, he ruins her through the moneylender who plays upon her love of finery. He brings in the country Don Juan to make love to her at the agricultural prize-giving, and draws a provincial clerk whom she pursues in her turn at Rouen. We have, that is, the whole picture of a rural society, of its leading characters from the apothecary and the doctor to the farmers, tradespeople, the small squire, even a glimpse, in the famous ball, of its lords, constructed round Emma Bovary, to illustrate Flaubert's theme of the futility and vulgarity of middle-class existence. But without Emma Bovary's character and the story of her tragedy, it would have no form at all as a novel, it would not, so to speak, add up to a whole of meaning, an experience of Flaubert's world. *Madame*

*Bovary* makes an unforgettable impact upon the reader. It is a permanent possession of his imagination. But it owes that memorable power even more to the formal unity of its plot than to the excellence of the writing, which is of course, seen as completed and achieved form, an aspect of that unity. The mood of the style is in the mood of the whole book. It affects even the choice of what should be in narrative, what in dialogue. But that unity is obtained by selection of facts, of characters, by special interpretation of events, which is partial and so far untrue. Country life is not necessarily a bore, country doctors are not necessarily fools, and their wives are often sensible, cheerful and even faithful. So Zola, in *L'Assommoir,* in order to achieve his form, was obliged to give a false impression of Paris working-class life as a whole. This is true of all novels. They must have an angle in order to have form and meaning, and this angle is usually even narrower, sweeps a narrower range of truth, than the writer's own angle, on account of the limitations of the craft itself. Zola's *Nana,* which succeeded *L'Assommoir,* giving us the life of the daughter as an actress and a demi-mondaine, deals throughout with that half-world of prostitution and the comedy theatre. Drink takes no place in it. It would simply complicate the plot, the form, without adding any significance to it. The truth of *Nana,* so strongly felt by the respectable bourgeois Zola, is a quite different truth from that of *L'Assommoir,* equally important in Zola's feeling. But as an artist, as novelist, he knew too much of his craft to attempt to combine them in one work.

He existed, like all of us, in his own particular world of fact and feeling, created in his imagination from childhood, and he could not write about any other. This picture gave him the valuation by which he selected from the confusion of the active scene what was significant to him. From what was significant, again, he selected that part which could be made significant in a novel, given the limitations of that art. He left out anything that could confuse the plot and therefore the reader.

For a reader must never be left in doubt about the meaning of a story. I mean, of course, the ideal reader; in the first place, the writer himself.

II

So we have the position, a novel has to be a partial view of things. First, because all views are partial and personal, and secondly, because of the limitations of the form of the novel, of which the first and most important is this: that the more comprehensive a novel in scope, in width of scene, the more it loses in power and significance. *Anna Karenina* has much more power than *War and Peace,* and *The Kreutzer Sonata* has more than *Anna Karenina.* The truth given by a novel is in close relation with the power of its expression. It is truth for feeling, it is truth about values. It is a personal truth. For Zola, drink was a fearful truth because it was a fearful evil, and to make light of it, to make it subordinate to any other issue in *L'Assommoir* would have been falsifying the truth of his feeling.

It is not valid to charge a writer with falsification because he emphasises one truth rather than another. As for saying that he does not give the whole, that is absurd because the whole truth cannot be known. It would have to include not only events which are happening all the time and changing the phenomenal world while I speak, but the valuation of events. The most important part of truth is what humanity is suffering, is feeling and thinking at any moment, and this cannot be known, as a totality, to any person. It is not known completely to the individuals themselves. For immediately life takes place in the subconscious, before it is known to reflection; and its sources, the active nature of being itself, are completely beyond the human imagination.

A novelist, therefore, can give only very partial truth in any one book, and that truth with an angle.

It is often said that the only truth a writer can give is a point of view, that the truth of a work of art is simply its coherence, its meaning as a work of art. The "meaning" here is frequently given a pragmatic sense, as effect. A whole school of criticism, in the twenties, took this view. A work of art was to be judged by what it does to the reader, the observer. Its truth was merely in relation to that reader and could be a lie in any other relation. That is to say, it could be founded in the Nazi philosophy or in Marx, and if on that account it gave a Nazi or a Stalinite more satisfaction, say, than a masterpiece by a Tolstoy or a Hardy, it would be a greater and truer work.

This theory was in accord with the general fashion of thirty years ago; it was in reaction against the religiosity of the Victorians before and any belief in real values. It went with atheism, dadaism, Marxism, Freudianism and the rest. It is now old-fashioned and generally on the defensive. But it could find a lot of support still in the experience of writers and readers. For the first duty of a writer is to compose a form of meaning which shall be coherent to the reader, even if that reader be himself. And the meaning is addressed finally to the emotions, the sensibility. The writer must seize upon the sympathy of the reader for his characters, and as every professional knows, a major problem for the novelist is to maintain the emotional continuity of the work. To do this, even so masterly a technician as Jane Austen will break a rule. In the third chapter of *Pride and Prejudice* she writes about Mr Bingley that Mrs Bennet, being unable to draw from her husband any satisfactory description of the gentleman, was obliged to accept the second-hand intelligence of her neighbour, Lady Lucas. At the bottom of the page we read that Mrs Bennet said to her husband, "If I can but see one of my daughters happily settled at Netherfield, I shall have nothing to wish for."

This is something we know very well. Mrs Bennet, on the second page of the book has said already that she is thinking of marrying one of her daughters to Mr Bingley or his friend; that is to say, Jane Austen has

repeated herself, a thing no novelist does if he can avoid it. A repetition at once brings before the reader's mind an anxious author trying to make a point, and authors ought not to be present in readers' minds.

Obviously Jane Austen repeats herself in order to show us that Mrs Bennet, having consulted Sir William and Lady Lucas about Mr Bingley, has now returned home. She cannot say so because the mere statement would break the emotional continuity, the mood of the book, consistently satiric from the beginning. Probably, too, as a technician she reflected or discovered that a remark by Mrs Bennet introducing any new matter would surprise and check the reader. The satiric vein has to continue unbroken in Mrs Bennet's words, but without attracting too much attention from the reader to their real purpose, that is, to get her home.

The transition, the handling of space in this case is so deft that probably only a professional would notice the technical device. Yet it is one in which Jane Austen has sacrificed a certain integrity in order to hold the reader in his mood, and that integrity of form is one of the things for which we chiefly value her, and, I imagine, she valued herself.

The reader thus carefully handled, is regarded, even in Jane Austen's day, a hundred years before any behaviourist theory of human conduct, as a mere reaction mass, a kind of emotional piano, on which the artist plays his little tune. This view seems true to our practice. How often are we told that to read we must put away all prejudice, relax, make ourselves completely receptive, await reactions.

This attitude of the writer towards his readers is founded not on any *a priori* theory but on experience. Every writer as reader and critic of his own work is aware of emotional continuity as a prime technical demand of his craft. And this gives at once a very strong support to the behaviourist theory of art—that art has nothing to do with truth or the representation of any objective real. It is intended to produce certain psychological reactions in a passive mind.

All the same, I think it completely false. In the first place, we do, as readers, notice a difference between truth of art and truth of revelation. We can enjoy a masterpiece of form without in the least accepting it as true. Our meaning when we say, "That's good," is quite different from the sense of revelation with which we say, "That's true." We accept *The Kreutzer Sonata* as a masterpiece of form, but we don't accept its meaning as a general truth. And this sense of revelation certainly appears to be the same as that with which we intuit the real.

## TOPICS FOR DISCUSSION

1   Although devoted to writing realistic novels, Flaubert and Zola distorted the facts. What was the nature of these distortions? What

produced them? Does Cary think this a necessary procedure in fictional works? Do you think the selection and emphasis of details can distort the world of facts in expository writing as well?

2  Why is the limited view more powerful and significant than the comprehensive view? Do you agree with Cary, basing your opinion on specific works you have read? Does it follow that the epic, with its comprehensive view, is necessarily a lesser form than the lyric?

3  How are plot unity and emotional continuity both necessary to attain conviction about a book's central effect?

4  What is the difference between the truth of art and the truth of revelation? Yet, are they similar?

5  Why are the specific examples of the novelists especially helpful in a work treating abstractions? Can you supply from your reading other novels which would illustrate Cary's thesis?

## ...AND COMPOSITION

6  Pick a large subject, such as education, and write an essay on an extremely limited aspect of it. You might pick a particularly inspiring teacher, a moment of great enlightenment, a remarkable failure, or a brilliant success. Remember to keep the larger subject in the background and let the limited view carry the weight of the paper.

7  Try to explain your notion of beauty or some other abstraction equally difficult of explanation, relying heavily on the use of examples.

8  Find an editorial which purports to use facts; analyze it in light of other facts you know to have been omitted and show how the omissions distort the whole effect.

**HERBERT READ (1893–    )** operates as a lively and independent critic of
the arts, which he sees as crucial in our lives. The disquisition following—
just one little distinction amid many which have to be made—cannot
reveal his range and relevance for a serious student. He stands for openness and
receptivity, and his place is with the Romantics: human feeling validates
judgments. His *English Prose Style* is a handy book for a student of writing.

# Art and Beauty

I

The simple word "art" is most usually associated with those arts which
we distinguish as "plastic" or "visual," but properly speaking it should
include the arts of literature and music. There are certain characteristics
common to all the arts, and though in these notes we are concerned only
with the plastic arts, a definition of what is common to all the arts is the
best starting-point of our enquiry.

It was Schopenhauer who first said that all arts aspire to the condition
of music; that remark has often been repeated, and has been the cause of
a good deal of misunderstanding, but it does express an important truth.
Schopenhauer was thinking of the abstract qualities of music; in music,
and almost in music alone, it is possible for the artist to appeal to his
audience directly, without the intervention of a medium of communication
in common use for other purposes. The architect must express himself in
buildings which have some utilitarian purpose. The poet must use words
which are bandied about in the daily give-and-take of conversation. The
painter usually expresses himself by the representation of the visible world.
Only the composer of music is perfectly free to create a work of art of his
own consciousness, and with no other aim than to please. But all artists
have this same intention, the desire to please; and art is most simply and
most usually defined as an attempt to create pleasing forms. Such forms
satisfy our sense of beauty and the sense of beauty is satisfied when we
are able to appreciate a unity or harmony of formal relations among our
sense-perceptions.

2

Any general theory of art must *begin* with this supposition: that man
responds to the shape and surface and mass of things present to his senses,
and that certain arrangements in the proportion of the shape and surface
and mass of things result in a pleasurable sensation, whilst the lack of such
arrangement leads to indifference or even to positive discomfort and
revulsion. The sense of pleasurable relations is the sense of beauty; the

opposite sense is the sense of ugliness. It is possible, of course, that some people are quite unaware of proportions in the physical aspect of things. Just as some people are colour-blind, so others may be blind to shape and surface and mass. But just as people who are colour-blind are comparatively rare, so there is every reason to believe that people wholly unaware of the other visible properties of objects are equally rare. They are more likely to be undeveloped.

### 3

There are at least a dozen current definitions of beauty, but the merely physical one I have already given (beauty is a unity of formal relations among our sense-perceptions) is the only essential one, and from this basis we can build up a theory of art which is as inclusive as any theory of art need be. But it is perhaps important to emphasize at the outset the extreme relativity of this term beauty. The only alternative is to say that art has no necessary connection with beauty—a perfectly logical position to hold if we confine the term to that concept of beauty established by the Greeks and continued by the classical tradition in Europe. My own preference is to regard the sense of beauty as a very fluctuating phenomenon, with manifestations in the course of history that are very uncertain and often very baffling. Art should include all such manifestations, and the test of a serious student of art is that, whatever his own sense of beauty, he is willing to admit into the realm of art the genuine manifestations of that sense in other people at other periods. For him, Primitive, Classical and Gothic are of equal interest, and he is not so much concerned to assess the relative merits of such periodical manifestations of the sense of beauty as to distinguish between the genuine and false of all periods.

### 4

Most of our misconceptions of art arise from a lack of consistency in the use of the words art and beauty. It might be said that we are only consistent in our misuse of them. We always assume that all that is beautiful is art, or that all art is beautiful, that what is not beautiful is not art, and that ugliness is the negation of art. This identification of art and beauty is at the bottom of all our difficulties in the appreciation of art, and even in people who are acutely sensitive to aesthetic impressions in general, this assumption acts like an unconscious censor in particular cases when art is not beauty. For art is not necessarily beauty: that cannot be said too often or too blatantly. Whether we look at the problem historically (considering what art has been in past ages) or sociologically (considering what art actually is in its present-day manifestations all over the world) we find that art often has been or often is a thing of no beauty.

## TOPICS FOR DISCUSSION

1   What does each of the four sections contribute to the definition of art? How does each section reflect the previous material?
2   How do the words of the poet, "bandied about in the daily give-and-take of conversation," keep his works from having the abstract qualities of music?
3   What is Read's definition of beauty? Do you agree with his idea of the relativity of this term?
4   What is the alternative to his definition? Why is this a crucial distinction?
5   When is art not beauty?

## ...AND COMPOSITION

6   Define in an increasingly limiting way any abstraction as if your definition were preliminary to a thorough study of that abstraction.
7   Sheridan Baker ("Scholarly Style, or the Lack Thereof") said we should be wary of the definer. Comment on Baker's remarks as well as on Read's use of the defining technique, trying to justify both men.
8   Comment on the relativity of your reactions to an art form which strikes you as ugly but which was obviously highly respected by a foreign culture.

SUSANNE K. LANGER (1895–    )  a leading authority on aesthetics, is best known for *Philosophy in a New Key*, which attempts to make the transforming processes of the mind a recognized part of our way of thinking about philosophical questions. In the following, she analyzes how an organism works and then leads into her central concern: how do the conditions of the self relate to those of man's creations which grow out of and satisfy that self? Answers could help to account for that reverberation between self and object—the experience of art.

# Living Form

One of the most widely used metaphors in the literature of art is the metaphor of the living creature applied to the artistic product. Every artist finds "life," "vitality," or "livingness" in a good work of art. He refers to the "spirit" of a picture, not meaning the spirit in which it was painted, but its own quality; and his first task is to "animate" his canvas. An unsuccessful work is "dead." Even a fairly good one may have "dead spots." What do people mean when they speak as though a picture or a building or a sonata were a living and breathing creature?

Another metaphor of the studio, borrowed from the biological realm, is the familiar statement that every art work must be organic. Most artists will not even agree with a literal-minded critic that this is a metaphor. "Organic" simply and directly refers, in their vocabulary, to something characteristic of good pictures and statues, poems and plays, ballets and buildings and pieces of music. It does not refer to biological functions like digestion and circulation. But—breathing? Heartbeat? Well, maybe. Mobility? Yes, perhaps. Feeling? Oh yes, certainly.

For a work to "contain feeling," as that phrase is commonly used, is precisely to be alive, to have artistic vitality, to exhibit "living form." We discussed yesterday why a form that expresses feeling appears not merely to connote it, as a meaning, but to contain it, as a quality. Since, however, we know that for a work to contain feeling is really to be an expressive form which articulates feeling, we may well ask, at this point, why such articulation requires a symbol having the appearance of vital organization and autonomous life; and furthermore, how this appearance is achieved. For, certainly, works of art are not really organisms with biological functions. Pictures do not really pulse and breathe; sonatas do not eat and sleep and repair themselves like living creatures, nor do novels perpetuate their kind when they are left unread in a library. Yet the metaphors of "life" and "organic form" in art are so strong that I have known a serious, reflective artist to be actually shocked at such philistine statements as I have just made, calling those terms metaphors.

Let us consider, first, what feeling and emotion have to do with organic life; secondly, what are the characteristics of actual organisms; thirdly, what are the most general features of artistic creation by virtue of which the semblance of life is produced, and finally, how this semblance empowers the artist to imagine and articulate so much of human mentality, emotion, and individual experience as men of genius do in fact put before us.

Sentience—the most elementary sort of consciousness—is probably an aspect of organic process. Perhaps the first feeling is of the free flow or interruption of vital rhythms in the creature itself, as the whole organism interacts with the surrounding world. With higher phases of functional development, more specialized sentience develops, too—sensations, distinct emotions rather than total, undifferentiated excitements, desires in place of bodily discomfort, directed drives and complex instincts, and with every complication of activity a richer subjective immediacy.

It is a misconception, I believe, to think of sentience as something *caused* by vital activities. It is not an effect, but an aspect of them; as the red of an apple is not caused by the apple, but is an aspect of the apple itself in its mature phase. Sentience arises *in* vital functioning rather than *from* it; life as such is sentient. Naturally, then, life as it is felt always resembles life as it is observed; and when we become aware of feeling and emotion as ingredients in a non-physical nexus, the mind, they still seem to lie close to the somatic and instinctive level of our being. They are, indeed, like high-lights on the crests of the turbulent life-stream. Naturally, then, their basic forms are vital forms; their coming and going is in the pattern of growth and decline, not of mechanical occurrences; their mutual involvements reflect the mold of biological existence. If, therefore, a created sensuous symbol—a work of art—is to be in their image, it must present itself somehow as a version, or projection, of living process; it must be of a logical form that is commensurable with the essential forms of life.

What are the distinctive features of life? What properties divide living from non-living things?

All living matter that we have identified as such is organic; living creatures are organisms. They are characterized by what we call organic process—the constant burning-up and equally constant renewal of their substance. Every cell, and indeed every part of every cell (and the functionally distinct parts are infinitesimal), is perpetually breaking down, and perpetually being replaced. The cell, the tissue composed of diverse cells, the organ to which the tissue belongs, the organism that subsumes the organ—that whole vast system is in unceasing flux. It actually has no sameness of material substance from second to second. It is always changing; and if the exchanges of matter stop for even a few seconds, the effect is cataclysmic; the system is destroyed. Life is gone.

An organism, which seems to be the most distinct and individual sort of thing in the world, is really not a *thing* at all. Its individual, separate,

thing-like existence is a pattern of changes; its unity is a purely functional unity. But the integration of that functional whole is so indescribably complex and intimate and profound that the self-identity of the higher organisms (that is, the most elaborately integrated ones) is more convincing than the self-identity of the most permanent material concretion, such as a lump of lead or a stone. If you reflect on this strange fact, you realize why human identity is always felt to lie not so much in bodily permanence as in personality. It is a functional identity, a pattern of physical and mental process, a continuum of activity.

Let us hark back, for a moment, to a concept that was discussed in the first lecture—the concept of *dynamic form*. You may remember that the example we considered there was a waterfall. You can photograph a waterfall with an ordinary little camera, if you stand back enough, just as you can photograph a house or a mountain. The waterfall has a shape, moving somewhat, its long streamers seeming to shift like ribbons in a wind, but its mobile shape is a permanent datum in the landscape, among rocks and trees and other things. Yet the water does not really ever stand before us. Scarcely a drop stays there for the length of one glance. The material composition of the waterfall changes all the time; only the form is permanent; and what gives any shape at all to the water is the motion. The waterfall exhibits a *form of motion,* or a *dynamic form.*

If you put a dot of color on the rim of a wheel and spin it, you see a colored circle instead of a dot. This again is the form of the dot's motion— a purely dynamic form—made visible.

Vital form is always dynamic. An organism, like a waterfall, exists only while it keeps going. Its permanence is not endurance of a material, but of a functional pattern. The most elementary feeling, therefore—one might say, the sheer sense of life—is a sense of that dialectic of permanence and change that governs the existence of every cell, every fibre in a living creature. That is the foundation of what Henry James called "felt life."

But dynamic form is not enough. A waterfall is not an organism. The waterfall has no biography. It cuts its groove into the resisting rock; its own shape changes somewhat with that process, and very much more with any changes in the water supply, with hot and cold weather, etc.—but under steady conditions the waterfall does not grow, age, decline, and cease forever, as an organism does. If the water source fails, the fall stops, but with renewed supply it begins again.

An organism has an entirely different relation to the outside world from that of a simple dynamism like the waterfall. It is also a dynamism, but not a stream; it contains a myriad of distinct activities represented by permanent structures, and coinciding with each other in ways that seem a miracle of timing and complementation. All its processes form a single system. In the higher organisms, certain very elaborate processes acquire control over the simpler and perhaps phylogenetically older ones; in man,

for instance, the nervous system is so involved with all the other organic functions that any extensive injury done to it is likely to disturb or even abrogate the whole functional system. The organism is, to a great extent, inviolable if it is to exist at all. It can undergo many changes, survive many accidents, but only as long as the basic process of life goes on.

This basic process is the constant breaking down and reconstitution of every living part. For an organism is always taking in material that is not of its own system, splitting it up, and transforming some of it into living matter. Concomitantly, some living matter is always breaking down and resigning from the total activity. The one process is growth, and the other decay. Every organism is always both growing and decaying. When growth exceeds decay, the system increases (the process we commonly mean by "growth"); when they are evenly balanced, it maintains itself; when decay has the ascendancy, it ages. Finally, growth stops all at once; the life is done, and decay quickly dissolves the whole structure.

The character of inviolability and fragility marks all living things. Even the most persistent—redwood trees, and very long-lived creatures like crocodiles—are always maintaining themselves precariously against ravaging influences, from temperature-changes and bacterial blights to the brute hand of man. The nature of life is transient; even without accident, it is a passage from youth to age, no matter what its span.

The reason why so complex a network of events as the life of an individual can possibly go on and on in a continuous dynamic pattern is, that this pattern of events is rhythmic. We all know that many of our actions, like walking, rowing, even wood-chopping and rug-beating, are more easily done when they are rhythmic. People usually think of rhythm as a succession of similar events at fairly short, even intervals of time; that is, they think of rhythm as *periodic succession*. But what about a tennis player whose motions impress one as rhythmic? He probably does not repeat a single action; even his step is less metrical than that of a drunkard walking. What, then, is rhythm?

It is, I think, something related to *function* rather than to time. What we call an *event* is not simply anything that goes on in an arbitrary segment of time. An event is a change in the world having a beginning and a completion. The fall of an apple is the sort of thing we mean, ordinarily, by an event; it begins with the breaking of the stem from the twig that bears it, and ends with the apple's coming to rest somewhere. Its falling may include its rolling on the ground, or we may call that another event, and say that after the apple fell it rolled. At any rate, what we identify as an event in nature (except for certain highly specialized, scientific purposes) is not something instantaneous, but a change that is begun and completed.

A rhythmic pattern arises whenever the completion of one distinct event appears as the beginning of another. The classic example is the swinging of a pendulum. The momentum of its drop drives the weight

upward in the opposite direction, and builds up the potential energy that will bring it down again; so the first swing prepares the second; the second swing was actually begun in the first one, and similarly, after that, each swing is prepared by the one before. The result is a rhythmical series. Or, consider the breaking of waves in a steady surf on a beach: the momentum of the water drives it up the beach, until that momentum is spent, and the slant of the shore causes the water to run seaward again; but the piling of the second, incoming wave is also sucking back the spent water, and making its return a downward rush, that stops the bottom part of the new wave and causes it to break over itself. Here, again, is a rhythmic pattern. The completion of each breaker's history is already the beginning of the next one's.

In a living organism, practically all activities are rhythmically conditioned, sometimes interconnected not only by one chain of events but by many, functioning in many different rhythmic relationships at once. The most obvious rhythmic processes are, of course, heartbeat and breath. In the heart, every systole starts a diastole, and vice versa. In breathing, the process starts all the time throughout the whole body; as the oxygen of a breath is used up, it builds up the imperative need of oxygen that is really the beginning of the new breath. This sort of mutual conditioning is the law of organic function; the more closely you look into the entire physiological process that constitutes the dynamic form we call "life," the more minutely, diversely, and elaborately rhythmic it proves to be. In every cell, the very process of its oxidation—its burning away, breaking down—is the condition that has already started the chemical change which builds up its characteristic substance again. The rhythmic interaction is incredible.

Many fundamental rhythms in the world are periodic; in fact, so many that periodicity is often taken to be the essence of rhythm. But the view we have just taken of rhythm as a functional involvement of successive events makes periodic rhythms a special sort, despite their immense importance, and lets us see why a tennis player, a wheeling bird, and a modern dancer who does not necessarily repeat any motion may exhibit rhythm, too.

Living form, then, is in the first place dynamic form, that is, a form whose permanence is really a pattern of changes. Secondly, it is organically constructed; its elements are not independent parts, but interrelated, interdependent centers of activity—that is, organs. Thirdly, the whole system is held together by rhythmic processes; that is the characteristic unity of life. If its major rhythms are greatly disturbed, or suspended for more than a few moments, the organism collapses, life stops. Therefore living form is inviolable form. And finally, the law of living form is the dialectic of growth and decay, with its characteristic biographical phases.

In the higher organisms, secondary rhythms develop, specialized responses to the surrounding world, tensions and their resolutions within the

system: emotions, desires, attentive perception and action. Finally, at the human level, instinct is largely replaced by intuition, direct responses by symbolic responses—imagination, memory, reason—and simple emotional excitement is superseded by the continuous, personal life of feeling. But all these typically human functions have evolved from the deeper vital complex, and still exhibit its fundamental traits—its dynamism, inviolable unity, organization, rhythmic continuity, and growth. These are the principles of living form.

If art is, as I believe it is, the expression of human consciousness in a single metaphorical image, that image must somehow achieve the semblance of living form. All the principles we have just considered must have their analogues in those of artistic creation. This is indeed the case. But it must be remembered that analogous principles are not identical. The semblance of life need not be constructed on the same plan as life itself; a device that serves to create a sense of change need not involve any actual change, nor the most forcible presentation of growth any actual accumulation. Artistic form is a projection, not a copy. Consequently there is no direct correlation between the constituents of an organism and the elements in a work of art. Art has its own laws, which are laws of expressiveness. Its own elements are all created forms, not material ingredients; such elements cannot be compared to physical factors, nor their functions to physical functions. Only their product—the expressive form, the work of art— has characteristics symbolically related to those of life itself.

There are countless devices in the arts for the creation or enhancement of "living form." In the brief hour of a lecture we cannot do more than mention and illustrate a few of the major resources that artists draw upon for this purpose.

As I said earlier today, our sense of change in permanence, the balance of becoming and passing, is one of the profoundest aspects of human consciousness. If we look at even the most elementary forms of visual art— say, a purely decorative design, a wavy line adorning the rim of a pot, a repeated pattern on a cloth—the line, which is stationary, is said to "run" around the rim, and the over-all design, if it is good, seems to spread out over the cloth from any point where we happen to start. Let us talk about the line.

In talking about dynamic form we considered the effect of a dot of color on a rotating wheel: the little dot is seen as a circle, an even, closed line. This line expresses the form not of the dot, but of its motion. It projects this dynamic form as an apparently fixed visual datum, a circular line.

The relationship between lines and motions of objects rests upon the natural laws of our perception. Swift motions are actually seen as motionless lines. Objects that deposit a trail, like a crayon, leave an actual, permanent line; this line, too, expresses the motion of the object, though it is not

physically a dynamic form like the circle made by the spinning dot. But such a line does not naturally connote the thing that made it; what it connotes is only the directedness of its motion. It is a path; and in our seeing, every continuous line is a path, though it need not be the path of any imagined thing.

Lines, however, have another function, too: they are divisions of space, contours that define volumes. Volumes are the stabilizing elements in our world. In virtual space, lines express both motion and rest; and as virtual space is a pure creation, the lines that articulate it create both motion and rest, and, moreover, create both at the same time. A contour—as the word itself tells—is a turn, or path, that carves out a space. The way a line is handled makes it predominantly a dynamic or a static element, as the case may be. A space created by lines is *ipso facto* a temporal space, that is, a spatio-temporal form, which may readily be molded to express the dialectic of permanence and change which is characteristic of life.

Let us take another basic principle of art, that artists and critics are forever talking about: organic structure. Obviously, a picture or a poem does not really have organs and vital functions. But something about artistic structure exemplifies the principle of organization, too, though not in the same way that natural organisms do.

Every element in a work of art is so involved with other elements in the making of the virtual object, the work, that when it is altered (as it may be—artists make many alterations after the composition is well under way) one almost always has to follow up the alteration in several directions, or simply sacrifice some desired effects. A key word in a poetic verse, for instance, has literal sense, perhaps obvious metaphorical sense, emotional overtones, grammatical cognates, familiar and unfamiliar uses. Each of these different functions may relate it in a different way from any other. Let us take William Blake's very perfect little poem, "Love's Secret," and examine the functions of a few words in it:

> Never seek to tell thy love,
> Love that never told can be;
> For the gentle wind doth move
> Silently, invisibly.
>
> I told my love, I told my love,
> I told her all my heart,
> Trembling, cold, in ghastly fears.
> Ah! she did depart!
>
> Soon after she was gone from me,
> A traveller came by,
> Silently, invisibly:
> He took her with a sigh.

The first two lines exhibit three repetitions, but all of different degrees. "Never" is exactly repeated, but stands in different relations to the respective lines; "tell" is repeated in different grammatical form, at corresponding points in both lines; "love"—the key word—occurs in diametrically opposed positions, i.e., at the end of the one line and the beginning of the next; and in the two clauses which it dominates it has both different meaning and different syntactical value. The first "love" is the indirect object of "tell" and designates a person; the second "love" is the direct object of the same verb, and designates an emotion. And the two uses of love are in juxtaposition, but differently emphasized by the metrical structure of the lines. They are different elements, intimately related, at once, by their apparent identity; then by the shift of sense from one to the other which makes them homonyms instead; by the fact that their meanings, though distinct, are cognate; by the fact that they both complete the sense of the same verb, "tell," but in different ways. Finally, they serve in conjunction to link the two lines in a special way, making them seem like counterparts, a symmetrical pair. Symmetry is a strong form; this purely formal strength of the first two lines makes possible the erratic shift of thought in the following verses, which is logically, of course, a complete *non sequitur* introduced by the word "for." In the third line, another function of the word "love" (in its first occurrence) comes to light: it has also prepared the rhyme; and to save the poem from too much symmetry, it is a near-rhyme.

The use of "for" to link the first and second thoughts is a bold construction; it creates the feeling of a rational connection where literally there is none; but it refers the wind's movements—"silently, invisibly"—directly to love, and transforms them at a stroke into metaphors for its ineffable nature.

This many-sided involvement of every element with the total fabric of the poem is what gives it a semblance of organic structure; like living substance, a work of art is inviolable; break its elements apart, and they no longer are what they were—the whole image is gone.

I wish we could analyze all the leading principles; but I have already made great demands on your attention, and the two remaining subjects, rhythm and the illusion of development, or growth, are difficult. So I can only say, in conclusion, that the more you study artistic composition, the more lucidly you see its likeness to the composition of life itself, from the elementary biological patterns to the great structures of human feeling and personality that are the import of our crowning works of art; and it is by virtue of this likeness that a picture, a song, a poem is more than a thing—that it seems to be a living form, created, not mechanically contrived, for the expression of a meaning that seems inherent in the work itself: our own sentient being, Reality.

## TOPICS FOR DISCUSSION

   **1**  Using the four points given in paragraph 4, outline the argument.

   **2**  Distinguish between sentience as caused by an activity and sentience as an aspect of it.

   **3**  What is an organism? Why is this definition critical to the entire argument?

   **4**  What is the difference between dynamic and organic form?

   **5**  What is a rhythmic pattern? Why is repetition not a necessary ingredient of such patterns?

   **6**  How is a work of art able to produce a semblance of life?

   **7**  What do "philistine," "nexus," "somatic," "dialectic," and "abrogate" mean?

## ...AND COMPOSITION

   **8**  Just as Langer did, develop a four-step argument, indicating early in the essay your anticipated procedure for the entire work.

   **9**  Comment on those details of style that indicate this essay was designed originally as a lecture. What special problems does a lecturer have which an essayist does not?

   **10**  Analyze C. Day Lewis's poem "The Gate" (in "The Making of a Poem"), using the method Langer used on the William Blake poem.

**ROBERT GORHAM DAVIS (1908–    )** now at Columbia University, has
taught in many universities including Harvard, where he was educated
and where he published this now classic essay on traps that threaten the unwary
writer and reader. Among Professor Davis's special interests is the study of
contemporary literature and the history of prose fiction. He has lectured
abroad, both in Europe and in South America, and has twice participated
in the Salzburg Seminar in American Studies.

# *Logical Fallacies*

## UNDEFINED TERMS

The first requirement for logical discourse is knowing what the words
you use actually mean. Words are not like paper money or counters in a
game. Except for technical terms in some of the sciences, they do not have
a fixed face value. Their meanings are fluid and changing, influenced by
many considerations of context and reference, circumstance and association. This is just as true of common words such as *fast* as it is of literary
terms such as *romantic*. Moreover, if there is to be communication, words
must have approximately the same meaning for the reader that they have
for the writer. A speech in an unknown language means nothing to the
hearer. When an adult speaks to a small child or an expert to a layman,
communication may be seriously limited by lack of a mature vocabulary
or ignorance of technical terms. Many arguments are meaningless because
the speakers are using important words in quite different senses.

Because we learn most words—or guess at them—from the contexts in
which we first encounter them, our sense of them is often incomplete or
wrong. Readers sometimes visualize the Assyrian who comes down like
the wolf on the fold as an enormous man dressed in cohorts (some kind

of fancy armor, possibly) gleaming in purple and gold. "A rift in the lute" suggests vaguely a cracked mandolin. Failure to ascertain the literal meaning of figurative language is a frequent reason for mixed metaphors. We are surprised to find that the "devil" in "the devil to pay" and "the devil and the deep blue sea" is not Old N:ck, but part of a ship. Unless terms mean the same thing to both writer and reader, proper understanding is impossible.

### ABSTRACTIONS

The most serious logical difficulties occur with abstract terms. An abstraction is a word which stands for a quality found in a number of different objects or events from which it has been "abstracted" or taken away. We may, for instance, talk of the "whiteness" of paper or cotton or snow without considering qualities of cold or inflammability or usefulness which these materials happen also to possess. Usually, however, our minds carry over other qualities by association. See, for instance, the chapter called "The Whiteness of the Whale" in *Moby Dick*.

In much theoretic discussion the process of abstraction is carried so far that although vague associations and connotations persist, the original objects or events from which the qualities have been abstracted are lost sight of completely. Instead of thinking of words like *sincerity* and *Americanism* as symbols standing for qualities that have to be abstracted with great care from examples and test cases, we come to think of them as real things in themselves. We assume that Americanism is Americanism just as a bicycle is a bicycle, and that everyone knows what it means. We forget that before the question, "Is Arthur Godfrey sincere?" can mean anything, we have to agree on the criteria of sincerity.

When we try to define such words and find examples, we discover that almost no one agrees on their meaning. The word *church* may refer to anything from a building on the corner of Spring Street to the whole tradition of institutionalized Christianity. *Germany* may mean a geographical section of Europe, a people, a governing group, a cultural tradition, or a military power. Abstractions such as *freedom, courage, race, beauty, truth, justice, nature, honor, humanism, democracy,* should never be used in a theme unless their meaning is defined or indicated clearly by the context. Freedom for whom? To do what? Under what circumstances? Abstract terms have merely emotional value unless they are strictly defined by asking questions of this kind. The study of a word such as *nature* in a good unabridged dictionary will show that even the dictionary, indispensable though it is, cannot determine for us the sense in which a word is being used in any given instance. Once the student understands the importance of definition, he will no longer be betrayed into fruitless arguments over such questions as whether free verse is "poetry" or whether you can change "human nature."

## NAME-CALLING

It is a common unfairness in controversy to place what the writer dislikes or opposes in a generally odious category. The humanist dismisses what he dislikes by calling it *romantic;* the liberal, by calling it *fascist;* the conservative, by calling it *communistic.* These terms tell the reader nothing. What is *piety* to some will be *bigotry* to others. *Non-Catholics* would rather be called *Protestants* than *heretics.* What is *right-thinking* except a designation for those who agree with the writer? Social security measures become *creeping socialism;* industrial organizations, *forces of reaction;* investigation into Communism, *witch hunts;* prison reform, *coddling;* progressive education, *fads and frills.* Such terms are intended to block thought by an appeal to prejudice and associative habits. Three steps are necessary before such epithets have real meaning. First, they must be defined; second, it must be shown that the object to which they are applied actually possesses these qualities; third, it must be shown that the possession of such qualities in this particular situation is necessarily undesirable. Unless a person is alert and critical both in choosing and in interpreting words, he may be alienated from ideas with which he would be in sympathy if he had not been frightened by a mere name.

## GENERALIZATION

Similar to the abuse of abstract terms and epithets is the habit of presenting personal opinions in the guise of universal laws. The student often seems to feel that the broader the terms in which he states an opinion, the more effective he will be. Ordinarily the reverse is true. An enthusiasm for Thomas Wolfe should lead to a specific critical analysis of Wolfe's novels that will enable the writer to explain his enthusiasm to others; it should not be turned into the argument that Wolfe is "the greatest American novelist," particularly if the writer's knowledge of American novelists is somewhat limited. The same questions of *who* and *when* and *why* and under what *circumstances* which are used to check abstract terms should be applied to generalizations. Consider how contradictory proverbial wisdom is when detached from particular circumstances. "Look before you leap," but "he who hesitates is lost."

Superlatives and the words *right* and *wrong, true* and *untrue, never* and *always* must be used with caution in matters of opinion. When a student says flatly that X is true, he often is really saying that he or his family or the author of a book he has just been reading, persons of certain tastes and background and experience, *think* that X is true. If his statement is based not on logic and examination of evidence, but merely reproduces other people's opinions, it can have little value or relevance unless these people are identified and their reasons for thinking so explained. Because many freshmen are taking survey courses in which they read a single work by an author or see an historical event through the eyes

of a single historian whose bias they may not be able to measure, they must guard against this error.

### SAMPLING

Assertions of a general nature are frequently open to question because they are based on insufficient evidence. Some persons are quite ready, after meeting one Armenian or reading one medieval romance, to generalize about Armenians and medieval romances. One ought, of course, to examine objectively as many examples as possible before making a generalization, but the number is far less important than the representativeness of the examples chosen. The Literary Digest Presidential Poll, sent to hundreds of thousands of people selected from telephone directories, was far less accurate than the Gallup Poll which questioned far fewer voters, but selected them carefully and proportionately from all different social groups. The "typical" college student, as portrayed by moving pictures and cartoons, is very different from the "average" college student as determined statistically. We cannot let uncontrolled experience do our sampling for us; instances and examples which impress themselves upon our minds do so usually because they are exceptional. In propaganda and arguments extreme cases are customarily treated as if they were characteristic.

If one is permitted arbitrarily to select some examples and ignore others, it is possible to find convincing evidence for almost any theory, no matter how fantastic. The fact that the mind tends naturally to remember those instances which confirm its opinions imposes a duty upon the writer, unless he wishes to encourage prejudice and superstition, to look carefully for exceptions to all generalizations which he is tempted to make. We forget the premonitions which are not followed by disaster and the times when our hunches failed to select the winner in a race. Patent medicine advertisements print the letters of those who survived their cure, and not of those who died during it. All Americans did not gamble on the stock exchange in the twenties or become Marxists in the thirties, and all Vermonters are not thin-lipped and shrewd. Of course the search for negative examples can be carried too far. Outside of mathematics or the laboratory, few generalizations can be made airtight, and most are not intended to be. But quibbling is so easy that resort to it is very common, and the knowledge that people can and will quibble over generalizations is another reason for making assertions as limited and explicitly conditional as possible.

### FALSE ANALOGY

Illustration, comparison, analogy are most valuable in making an essay clear and interesting. It must not be supposed, however, that they prove anything or have much argumentative weight. The rule that what is true of one thing in one set of circumstances is not necessarily true of another thing in another set of circumstances seems almost too obvious to need

stating. Yet constantly nations and businesses are discussed as if they were human beings with human habits and feelings; human bodies are discussed as if they were machines; the universe, as if it were a clock. It is assumed that what held true for seventeenth century New England or the thirteen Atlantic colonies also holds true for an industrial nation of 160,000,000 people. Carlyle dismissed the arguments for representative democracy by saying that if a captain had to take a vote among his crew every time he wanted to do something, he would never get around Cape Horn. This analogy calmly ignores the distinction between the lawmaking and the executive branches of constitutional democracies. Moreover, voters may be considered much more like the stockholders of a merchant line than its hired sailors. Such arguments introduce assumptions in a metaphorical guise in which they are not readily detected or easily criticized. In place of analysis they attempt to identify their position with some familiar symbol which will evoke a predictable, emotional response in the reader. The revival during the 1932 presidential campaign of Lincoln's remark, "Don't swap horses in the middle of the stream," was not merely a picturesque way of saying keep Hoover in the White House. It made a number of assumptions about the nature of depressions and the function of government. This propagandist technique can be seen most clearly in political cartoons.

## DEGREE

Often differences in degree are more important than differences in kind. By legal and social standards there is more difference between an habitual drunkard and a man who drinks temperately, than between a temperate drinker and a total abstainer. In fact differences of degree produce what are regarded as differences of kind. At known temperatures ice turns to water and water boils. At an indeterminate point affection becomes love and a man who needs a shave becomes a man with a beard. The fact that no men or systems are perfect makes rejoinders and counter-accusations very easy if differences in degree are ignored. Newspapers in totalitarian states, answering American accusations of brutality and suppression, refer to lynchings and gangsterism here. Before a disinterested judge could evaluate these mutual accusations, he would have to settle the question of the degree to which violent suppression and lynching are respectively prevalent in the countries under consideration. On the other hand, differences in degree may be merely apparent. Lincoln Steffens pointed out that newspapers can create a "crime wave" any time they wish, simply by emphasizing all the minor assaults and thefts commonly ignored or given an inch or two on a back page. The great reported increases in insanity may be due to the fact that in a more urban and institutionalized society cases of insanity more frequently come to the attention of authorities and hence are recorded in statistics.

## CAUSATION

The most common way of deciding that one thing causes another thing is the simple principle: *post hoc, ergo propter hoc,* "After this, therefore because of this." Rome fell after the introduction of Christianity; therefore Christianity was responsible for the fall of Rome. Such reasoning illustrates another kind of faulty generalization. But even if one could find ten cases in which a nation "fell" after the introduction of Christianity, it still would not be at all certain that Christianity caused the fall. Day, it has frequently been pointed out, follows night in every observable instance, and yet night cannot be called the cause of day. Usually a combination of causes produces a result. Sitting in a draught may cause a cold, but only given a certain physical condition in the person sitting there. In such instances one may distinguish between necessary and sufficient conditions. Air is a necessary condition for the maintenance of plant life, but air alone is not sufficient to produce plant life. And often different causes at different times may produce the same result. This relation is known as plurality of causes. If, after sitting in a stuffy theatre on Monday, and then again after eating in a stuffy restaurant on Thursday, a man suffered from headaches, he might say, generalizing, that bad air gave him headaches. But actually the headache on Monday may have been caused by eye-strain and on Thursday by indigestion. To isolate the causative factor it is necessary that all other conditions be precisely the same. Such isolation is possible, except in very simple instances, only in the laboratory or with scientific methods. If a picture falls from the wall every time a truck passes, we can quite certainly say that the truck's passing is the proximate or immediate cause. But with anything as complex and conditional as a nation's economy or human character, the determination of cause is not easy or certain. A psychiatrist often sees a patient for an hour daily for a year or more before he feels that he understands his neurosis.

Ordinarily when we speak of cause we mean the proximate or immediate cause. The plants were killed by frost; we had indigestion from eating lobster salad. But any single cause is one in an unbroken series. When a man is murdered, is his death caused by the loss of blood from the wound, or by the firing of the pistol, or by the malice aforethought of the murderer? Was the World War "caused" by the assassination at Sarajevo? Were the Navigation Acts or the ideas of John Locke more important in "causing" the American Revolution? A complete statement of cause would comprise the sum total of the conditions which preceded an event, conditions stretching back indefinitely into the past. Historical events are so interrelated that the isolation of a causative sequence is dependent chiefly on the particular preoccupations of the historian. An economic determinist can "explain" history entirely in terms of economic developments; an idealist, entirely in terms of the development of ideas.

## SYLLOGISTIC REASONING

The formal syllogism of the type,

All men are mortal
John is a man
Therefore John is mortal,

is not so highly regarded today as in some earlier periods. It merely fixes an individual as a member of a class, and then assumes that the individual has the given characteristics of the class. Once we have decided who John is, and what "man" and "mortal" mean, and have canvassed all men, including John, to make sure that they are mortal, the conclusion naturally follows. It can be seen that the chief difficulties arise in trying to establish acceptable premises. Faults in the premises are known as "material" fallacies, and are usually more serious than the "formal" fallacies, which are logical defects in drawing a conclusion from the premises. But although directly syllogistic reasoning is not much practiced, buried syllogism can be found in all argument, and it is often a useful clarification to outline your own or another writer's essay in syllogistic form. The two most frequent defects in the syllogism itself are the undistributed and the ambiguous middle. The middle term is the one that appears in each of the premises and not in the conclusion. In the syllogism,

All good citizens vote
John votes
Therefore John is a good citizen,

the middle term is not "good citizens," but "votes." Even though it were true that all good citizens vote, nothing prevents bad citizens from voting also, and John may be one of the bad citizens. To distribute the middle term "votes" one might say (but only if that is what one meant),

All voters are good citizens
John is a voter
Therefore John is a good citizen.

The ambiguous middle term is even more common. It represents a problem in definition, while the undistributed middle is a problem in generalization. All acts which benefit others are virtuous, losing money at poker benefits others, therefore losing at poker is a virtuous act. Here the middle term "act which benefits others" is obviously used very loosely and ambiguously.

## NON-SEQUITUR

This phrase, meaning "it does not follow," is used to characterize the kind of humor found in pictures in which the Marx Brothers used to perform. It is an amusing illogicality because it usually expresses, beneath

its apparent incongruity, an imaginative, associative, or personal truth. "My ancestors came over on the Mayflower; therefore I am naturally opposed to labor unions." It is not logically necessary that those whose ancestors came over on the Mayflower should be opposed to unions; but it may happen to be true as a personal fact in a given case. It is usually a strong personal conviction which keeps people from realizing that their arguments are non-sequiturs, that they do not follow the given premises with logical necessity. Contemporary psychologists have effectively shown us that there is often such a wide difference between the true and the purported reasons for an attitude that, in rationalizing our behavior, we are often quite unconscious of the motives that actually influence us. A fanatical antivivisectionist, for instance, may have temperamental impulses toward cruelty which he is suppressing and compensating for by a reasoned opposition to any kind of permitted suffering. We may expect, then, to come upon many conclusions which are psychologically interesting in themselves, but have nothing to do with the given premises.

### IGNORATIO ELENCHI

This means, in idiomatic English, "arguing off the point," or ignoring the question at issue. A man trying to show that monarchy is the best form of government for the British Empire may devote most of his attention to the charm of Elizabeth II and the affection her people felt for her. In ordinary conversational argument it is almost impossible for disputants to keep to the point. Constantly turning up are tempting side-issues through which one can discomfit an opponent or force him to irrelevant admissions that seem to weaken his case.

### BEGGING THE QUESTION; ARGUING IN A CIRCLE

The first of these terms means to assume in the premises what you are pretending to prove in the course of your argument. The function of logic is to demonstrate that because one thing or group of things is true, another must be true as a consequence. But in begging the question you simply say in varying language that what is assumed to be true is assumed to be true. An argument which asserts that we shall enjoy immortality because we have souls which are immaterial and indestructible establishes nothing, because the idea of immortality is already contained in the assumption about the soul. It is the premise which needs to be demonstrated, not the conclusion. Arguing in a circle is another form of this fallacy. It proves the premise by the conclusion and the conclusion by the premise. The conscience forbids an act because it is wrong; the act is wrong because the conscience forbids it.

### ARGUMENTS AD HOMINEM AND AD POPULUM

It is very difficult for men to be persuaded by reason when their interest or prestige is at stake. If one wishes to preach the significance of

physiognomy, it is well to choose a hearer with a high forehead and a determined jaw. The arguments in favor of repealing the protective tariff on corn or wheat in England were more readily entertained by manufacturers than by landowners. The cotton manufacturers in New England who were doing a profitable trade with the South were the last to be moved by descriptions of the evils of slavery. Because interest and desire are so deeply in human nature, arguments are frequently mingled with attempts to appeal to emotion, arouse fear, play upon pride, attack the characters of proponents of an opposite view, show that their practice is inconsistent with their principles; all matters which have, strictly speaking, nothing to do with the truth or falsity, the general desirability or undesirability, of some particular measure. If men are desperate enough they will listen to arguments proper only to an insane asylum but which seem to promise them relief.

After reading these suggestions, which are largely negative, the student may feel that any original assertion he can make will probably contain one or several logical faults. This assumption is not true. Even if it were, we know from reading newspapers and magazines that worldly fame is not dimmed by the constant and, one suspects, conscious practice of illogicality. But generalizations are not made only by charlatans and sophists. Intelligent and scrupulous writers also have a great many fresh and provocative observations and conclusions to express and are expressing them influentially. What is intelligence but the ability to see the connection between things, to discern causes, to relate the particular to the general, to define and discriminate and compare? Any man who thinks and feels and observes closely will not want for something to express.

And in his expression a proponent will find that a due regard for logic does not limit but rather increases the force of his argument. When statements are not trite, they are usually controversial. Men arrive at truth dialectically; error is weeded out in the course of discussion, argument, attack and counterattack. Not only can a writer who understands logic show the weaknesses of arguments he disagrees with, but also, by anticipating the kind of attack likely to be made on his own ideas, he can so arrange them, properly modified with qualifications and exceptions, that the anticipated attack is made much less effective. Thus, fortunately, we do not have to depend on the spirit of fairness and love of truth to lead men to logic; it has the strong support of argumentative necessity and of the universal desire to make ideas prevail.

## TOPICS FOR DISCUSSION

1 All the fallacies described represent errors in conclusion resulting from faulty reasoning. Which specific fallacies might an advertising man intentionally use? Why? How might advertisements be

written to suggest conclusions to prospective clients but not make the conclusions themselves? What specific fallacies are likely to be used by campaigning politicians?

2   What is a "distributed middle"? What is an "ambiguous middle"?

3   Construct a logical syllogism.

4   Analogy is a useful method of supporting or developing arguments but not of proving them. Why not? Reflecting on the readings presented earlier in this text, how many writers relied heavily on analogies? Did these analogies ever seem to prove arguments?

## ... AND COMPOSITION

5   From your own experience or reading, supply two examples of each fallacy.

6   Locate the logical fallacies of a newspaper or magazine editorial and comment on them, paying special attention to them as probable accidents of careless thinking or as intentional deceptions.

7   Construct a logical argument supporting a belief of yours.

**FRANCIS BACON (1561–1626)** glimpsed a whole new era in man's relation
to the world: we know something of nature, but we do not know enough;
we are weak and fallible, but we are not helpless; by careful investigation we can
steadily enlarge our control and use of the world around us. A hazard
to the success of this investigation lies in certain common obstacles to the senses
and the understanding. In his *Novum Organum,* a guide to the new
method, Bacon identifies those obstacles as four kinds of "idols" in the mind. His
analysis of those idols marks a great step toward man's understanding of himself
and hence a great step in that incremental program of discovery, modern science.

# Idols of the Mind

### XXXVIII

The idols and false notions which are now in possession of the human
understanding, and have taken deep root therein, not only so beset men's
minds that truth can hardly find entrance, but even after entrance obtained,
they will again in the very instauration of the sciences meet and trouble us,
unless men being forewarned of the danger fortify themselves as far as may
be against their assaults.

### XXXIX

There are four classes of idols which beset men's minds. To these for
distinction's sake I have assigned names—calling the first class *Idols of the
Tribe;* the second, *Idols of the Cave;* the third, *Idols of the Market-place;*
the fourth, *Idols of the Theater.*

### XL

The formation of ideas and axioms by true induction is no doubt the
proper remedy to be applied for the keeping off and clearing away of
idols. To point them out, however, is of great use; for the doctrine of idols
is to the interpretation of nature what the doctrine of the refutation of
sophisms is to common logic.

### XLI

The *Idols of the Tribe* have their foundation in human nature itself,
and in the tribe or race of men. For it is a false assertion that the sense of
man is the measure of things. On the contrary, all perceptions as well of the
sense as of the mind are according to the measure of the individual and
not according to the measure of the universe. And the human understanding is like a false mirror, which, receiving rays irregularly, distorts and
discolors the nature of things by mingling its own nature with it.

### XLII

The *Idols of the Cave* are the idols of the individual man. For every-one (besides the errors common to human nature in general) has a cave or den of his own, which refracts and discolors the light of nature; owing either to his own proper and peculiar nature; or to his education and conversation with others; or to the reading of books, and the authority of those whom he esteems and admires; or to the differences of impressions, accordingly as they take place in a mind preoccupied and predisposed or in a mind indifferent and settled; or the like. So that the spirit of man (ac-cording as it is meted out to different individuals) is in fact a thing variable and full of perturbation, and governed as it were by chance. Whence it was well observed by Heraclitus that men look for sciences in their own lesser worlds, and not in the greater or common world.

### XLIII

There are also idols formed by the intercourse and association of men with each other, which I call *Idols of the Market-place,* on account of the commerce and consort of men there. For it is by discourse that men asso-ciate; and words are imposed according to the apprehension of the vulgar. And therefore the ill and unfit choice of words wonderfully obstructs the understanding. Nor do the definitions or explanations wherewith in some things learned men are wont to guard and defend themselves, by any means set the matter right. But words plainly force and overrule the understanding, and throw all into confusion and lead men away into numberless empty controversies and idle fancies.

### XLIV

Lastly, there are idols which have immigrated into men's minds from the various dogmas of philosophies, and also from wrong laws of demonstra-tion. These I call *Idols of the Theater;* because in my judgment all the received systems are but so many stage-plays, representing worlds of their own creation after an unreal and scenic fashion. Nor is it only of the systems now in vogue, or only of the ancient sects and philosophies, that I speak; for many more plays of the same kind may yet be composed and in like artificial manner set forth; seeing that errors the most widely different have nevertheless causes for the most part alike. Neither again do I mean this only of entire systems, but also of many principles and axioms in science, which by tradition, credulity, and negligence, have come to be received.

But of these several kinds of idols I must speak more largely and exactly, that the understanding may be duly cautioned.

### XLV

The human understanding is of its own nature prone to suppose the existence of more order and regularity in the world than it finds. And

though there be many things in nature which are singular and unmatched, yet it devises for them parallels and conjugates and relatives which do not exist. Hence the fiction that all celestial bodies move in perfect circles; spirals and dragons being (except in name) utterly rejected. Hence too the element of fire with its orb is brought in, to make up the square with the other three which the sense perceives. Hence also the ratio of density of the so-called elements is arbitrarily fixed at ten to one. And so on of other dreams. And these fancies affect not dogmas only, but simple notions also.

### XLVI

The human understanding when it has once adopted an opinion (either as being the received opinion or as being agreeable to itself) draws all things else to support and agree with it. And though there be a greater number and weight of instances to be found on the other side, yet these it either neglects and despises, or else by some distinction sets aside and rejects; in order that by this great and pernicious predetermination the authority of its former conclusions may remain inviolate. And therefore it was a good answer that was made by one who when they showed him hanging in a temple a picture of those who had paid their vows as having escaped shipwreck, and would have him say whether he did not now acknowledge the power of the gods—"Ay," asked he again, "but where are they painted that were drowned after their vows?" And such is the way of all superstition, whether in astrology, dreams, omens, divine judgments, or the like; wherein men having a delight in such vanities, mark the events where they are fulfilled, but where they fail, though this happen much oftener, neglect and pass them by. But with far more subtlety does this mischief insinuate itself into philosophy and the sciences; in which the first conclusion colors and brings into conformity with itself all that come after, though far sounder and better. Besides, independently of that delight and vanity which I have described, it is the peculiar and perpetual error of the human intellect to be more moved and excited by affirmatives than by negatives; whereas it ought properly to hold itself indifferently disposed towards both alike. Indeed, in the establishment of any true axiom, the negative instance is the more forcible of the two.

### XLVII

The human understanding is moved by those things most which strike and enter the mind simultaneously and suddenly, and so fill the imagination; and then it feigns and supposes all other things to be somehow, though it cannot see how, similar to those few things by which it is surrounded. But for that going to and fro to remote and heterogeneous instances, by which axioms are tried as in the fire, the intellect is altogether slow and unfit, unless it be forced thereto by severe laws and overruling authority.

XLVIII

The human understanding is unquiet; it cannot stop or rest, and still presses onward, but in vain. Therefore it is that we cannot conceive of any end or limit to the world, but always as of necessity it occurs to us that there is something beyond. Neither again can it be conceived how eternity has flowed down to the present day; for that distinction which is commonly received of infinity in time past and in time to come can by no means hold; for it would thence follow that one infinity is greater than another, and that infinity is wasting away and tending to become finite. The like subtlety arises touching the infinite divisibility of lines, from the same inability of thought to stop. But this inability interferes more mischievously in the discovery of causes: for although the most general principles in nature ought to be held merely positive, as they are discovered, and cannot with truth be referred to a cause; nevertheless, the human understanding being unable to rest still seeks something prior in the order of nature. And then it is that in struggling towards that which is further off, it falls back upon that which is more nigh at hand; namely, on final causes: which have relation clearly to the nature of man rather than to the nature of the universe, and from this source have strangely defiled philosophy. But he is no less an unskilled and shallow philosopher who seeks causes of that which is most general, than he who in things subordinate and subaltern omits to do so.

XLIX

The human understanding is no dry light, but receives an infusion from the will and affections; whence proceed sciences which may be called "sciences as one would." For what a man had rather were true he more readily believes. Therefore he rejects difficult things from impatience of research; sober things, because they narrow hope; the deeper things of nature, from superstition; the light of experience, from arrogance and pride, lest his mind should seem to be occupied with things mean and transitory; things not commonly believed, out of deference to the opinion of the vulgar. Numberless in short are the ways, and sometimes imperceptible, in which the affections color and infect the understanding.

L

But by far the greatest hindrance and aberration of the human understanding proceeds from the dullness, incompetency, and deceptions of the senses; in that things which strike the sense outweigh things which do not immediately strike it, though they be more important. Hence it is that speculation commonly ceases where sight ceases; insomuch that of things invisible there is little or no observation. Hence all the working of the spirits enclosed in tangible bodies lies hid and unobserved of men. So also

all the more subtle changes of form in the parts of coarser substances (which they commonly call alteration, though it is in truth local motion through exceedingly small spaces) is in like manner unobserved. And yet unless these two things just mentioned be searched out and brought to light, nothing great can be achieved in nature, as far as the production of works is concerned. So again the essential nature of our common air, and of all bodies less dense than air (which are very many) is almost unknown. For the sense by itself is a thing infirm and erring; neither can instruments for enlarging or sharpening the senses do much; but all the truer kind of interpretation of nature is effected by instances and experiments fit and apposite; wherein the sense decides touching the experiment only, and the experiment touching the point in nature and the thing itself.

LI

The human understanding is of its own nature prone to abstractions and gives a substance and reality to things which are fleeting. But to resolve nature into abstractions is less to our purpose than to dissect her into parts; as did the school of Democritus, which went further into nature than the rest. Matter rather than forms should be the object of our attention, its configurations and changes of configuration, and simple action, and law of action or motion; for forms are figments of the human mind, unless you will call those laws of action forms.

LII

Such then are the idols which I call *Idols of the Tribe;* and which take their rise either from the homogeneity of the substance of the human spirit, or from its preoccupation, or from its narrowness; or from its restless motion, or from an infusion of the affections, or from the incompetency of the senses, or from the mode of impression.

LIII

The *Idols of the Cave* take their rise in the peculiar constitution, mental or bodily, of each individual; and also in education, habit, and accident. Of this kind there is a great number and variety; but I will instance those the pointing out of which contains the most important caution, and which have most effect in disturbing the clearness of the understanding.

LIV

Men become attached to certain particular sciences and speculations, either because they fancy themselves the authors and inventors thereof, or because they have bestowed the greatest pains upon them and become most habituated to them. But men of this kind, if they betake themselves to philosophy and contemplations of a general character, distort and color

them in obedience to their former fancies; a thing especially to be noticed in Aristotle, who made his natural philosophy a mere bondservant to his logic, thereby rendering it contentious and well nigh useless. The race of chemists again out of a few experiments of the furnace have built up a fantastic philosophy, framed with reference to a few things; and Gilbert also, after he had employed himself most laboriously in the study and observation of the loadstone, proceeded at once to construct an entire system in accordance with his favorite subject.

LV

There is one principal and, as it were, radical distinction between different minds, in respect of philosophy and the sciences, which is this: that some minds are stronger and apter to mark the differences of things, others to mark their resemblances. The steady and acute mind can fix its contemplations and dwell and fasten on the subtlest distinctions: the lofty and discursive mind recognizes and puts together the finest and most general resemblances. Both kinds however easily err in excess, by catching the one at gradations, the other at shadows.

LVI

There are found some minds given to an extreme admiration of antiquity, others to an extreme love and appetite for novelty; but few so duly tempered that they can hold the mean, neither carping at what has been well laid down by the ancients, nor despising what is well introduced by the moderns. This however turns to the great injury of the sciences and philosophy; since these affectations of antiquity and novelty are the humors of partisans rather than judgments; and truth is to be sought for not in the felicity of any age, which is an unstable thing, but in the light of nature and experience, which is eternal. These factions therefore must be abjured, and care must be taken that the intellect be not hurried by them into assent.

LVII

Contemplations of nature and of bodies in their simple form break up and distract the understanding, while contemplations of nature and bodies in their composition and configuration overpower and dissolve the understanding: a distinction well seen in the school of Leucippus and Democritus as compared with the other philosophies. For that school is so busied with the particles that it hardly attends to the structure; while the others are so lost in admiration of the structure that they do not penetrate to the simplicity of nature. These kinds of contemplation should therefore be alternated and taken by turns; that so the understanding may be rendered at once penetrating and comprehensive, and the inconveniences above mentioned, with the idols which proceed from them, may be avoided.

LVIII

Let such then be our provision and contemplative prudence for keeping off and dislodging the *Idols of the Cave,* which grow for the most part either out of the predominance of a favorite subject, or out of an excessive tendency to compare or to distinguish, or out of partiality for particular ages, or out of the largeness or minuteness of the objects contemplated. And generally let every student of nature take this as a rule,—that whatever his mind seizes and dwells upon with peculiar satisfaction is to be held in suspicion, and that so much the more care is to be taken in dealing with such questions to keep the understanding even and clear.

LIX

But the *Idols of the Market-place* are the most troublesome of all: idols which have crept into the understanding through the alliances of words and names. For men believe that their reason governs words; but it is also true that words react on the understanding; and this it is that has rendered philosophy and the sciences sophistical and inactive. Now words, being commonly framed and applied according to the capacity of the vulgar, follow those lines of division which are most obvious to the vulgar understanding. And whenever an understanding of greater acuteness or a more diligent observation would alter those lines to suit the true divisions of nature, words stand in the way and resist the change. Whence it comes to pass that the high and formal discussions of learned men end oftentimes in disputes about words and names; with which (according to the use and wisdom of the mathematicians) it would be more prudent to begin, and so by means of definitions reduce them to order. Yet even definitions cannot cure this evil in dealing with natural and material things; since the definitions themselves consist of words, and those words beget others: so that it is necessary to recur to individual instances, and those in due series and order; as I shall say presently when I come to the method and scheme for the formation of notions and axioms.

LX

The idols imposed by words on the understanding are of two kinds. They are either names of things which do not exist (for as there are things left unnamed through lack of observation, so likewise are there names which result from fantastic suppositions and to which nothing in reality responds), or they are names of things which exist, but yet confused and ill-defined, and hastily and irregularly derived from realities. Of the former kind are Fortune, the Prime Mover, Planetary Orbits, Element of Fire, and like fictions which owe their origin to false and idle theories. And this class of idols is more easily expelled, because to get rid of them it is only necessary that all theories should be steadily rejected and dismissed as obsolete.

But the other class, which springs out of a faulty and unskilled abstraction, is intricate and deeply rooted. Let us take for example such a word as *humid;* and see how far the several things which the word is used to signify agree with each other; and we shall find the word *humid* to be nothing else than a mark loosely and confusedly applied to denote a variety of actions which will not bear to be reduced to any constant meaning. For it both signifies that which easily spreads itself round any other body; and that which in itself is indeterminate and cannot solidize; and that which readily yields in every direction; and that which easily divides and scatters itself; and that which easily unites and collects itself; and that which readily flows and is put in motion; and that which readily clings to another body and wets it; and that which is easily reduced to a liquid, or being solid easily melts. Accordingly when you come to apply the word,—if you take it in one sense, flame is humid; if in another, air is not humid; if in another, fine dust is humid; if in another, glass is humid. So that it is easy to see that the notion is taken by abstraction only from water and common and ordinary liquids, without any due verification.

There are however in words certain degrees of distortion and error. One of the least faulty kinds is that of names of substances, especially of lowest species and well-deduced (for the notion of *chalk* and of *mud* is good, of *earth* bad); a more faulty kind is that of actions, as *to generate, to corrupt, to alter;* the most faulty is of qualities (except such as are the immediate objects of the sense), as *heavy, light, rare, dense,* and the like. Yet in all these cases some notions are of necessity a little better than others, in proportion to the greater variety of subjects that fall within the range of the human sense.

### LXI

But the *Idols of the Theater* are not innate, nor do they steal into the understanding secretly, but are plainly impressed and received into the mind from the play-books of philosophical systems and the perverted rules of demonstration. To attempt refutations in this case would be merely inconsistent with what I have already said: for since we agree neither upon principles nor upon demonstrations, there is no place for argument. And this is so far well, inasmuch as it leaves the honor of the ancients untouched. For they are no wise disparaged—the question between them and me being only as to the way. For as the saying is, the lame man who keeps the right road outstrips the runner who takes a wrong one. Nay, it is obvious that when a man runs the wrong way, the more active and swift he is the further he will go astray.

But the course I propose for the discovery of sciences is such as leaves but little to the acuteness and strength of wits, but places all wits and understandings nearly on a level. For as in the drawing of a straight line or perfect circle, much depends on the steadiness and practice of the hand, if it be

done by aim of hand only, but if with the aid of rule or compass, little or nothing; so is it exactly with my plan. But though particular confutations would be of no avail, yet touching the sects and general divisions of such systems I must say something; something also touching the external signs which show that they are unsound; and finally something touching the causes of such great infelicity and of such lasting and general agreement in error; that so the access to truth may be made less difficult, and the human understanding may the more willingly submit to its purgation and dismiss its idols.

### LXII

*Idols of the Theater,* or of systems, are many, and there can be and perhaps will be yet many more. For were it not that now for many ages men's minds have been busied with religion and theology; and were it not that civil governments, especially monarchies, have been averse to such novelties, even in matters speculative; so that men labor therein to the peril and harming of their fortunes,—not only unrewarded, but exposed also to contempt and envy; doubtless there would have arisen many other philosophical sects like to those which in great variety flourished once among the Greeks. For as on the phenomena of the heavens many hypotheses may be constructed, so likewise (and more also) many various dogmas may be set up and established on the phenomena of philosophy. And in the plays of this philosophical theater you may observe the same thing which is found in the theater of the poets, that stories invented for the stage are more compact and elegant, and more as one would wish them to be, than true stories out of history.

In general, however, there is taken for the material of philosophy either a great deal out of a few things, or a very little out of many things; so that on both sides philosophy is based on too narrow a foundation of experiment and natural history, and decides on the authority of too few cases. For the rational school of philosophers snatches from experience a variety of common instances, neither duly ascertained nor diligently examined and weighed, and leaves all the rest to meditation and agitation of wit.

There is also another class of philosophers, who having bestowed much diligent and careful labor on a few experiments, have thence made bold to educe and construct systems; wresting all other facts in a strange fashion to conformity therewith.

And there is yet a third class, consisting of those who out of faith and veneration mix their philosophy with theology and traditions; among whom the vanity of some has gone so far aside as to seek the origin of sciences among spirits and genii. So that this parent stock of errors—this false philosophy—is of three kinds; the sophistical, the empirical, and the superstitious. . . .

LXVIII

So much concerning the several classes of idols, and their equipage: all of which must be renounced and put away with a fixed and solemn determination, and the understanding thoroughly freed and cleansed; the entrance into the kingdom of man, founded on the sciences, being not much other than the entrance into the kingdom of heaven, whereinto none may enter except as a little child.

## TOPICS FOR DISCUSSION

1 What relationship do you see between Bacon's idols and the logical fallacies analyzed by Davis? Are any of the idols logical fallacies?

2 What pattern or patterns of paragraph organization does Bacon use? Are the paragraphs inductive or deductive?

3 What overall organization is there in Bacon's presentation of the idols? Is there a logical progression in Bacon's organization?

4 How would you describe Bacon's sentence patterns and diction?

5 Compare Bacon's style in this selection with his style in the versions of his essay "Of Studies."

## ... AND COMPOSITION

6 If Bacon were writing today, how would he describe the idols of our tribes, or caves, or marketplaces, or theaters? Rewrite the discussion of one of the idols in twentieth-century terms.

7 What twentieth-century idols can you *add* to Bacon's list? Present your idols in paragraphs patterned after Bacon's.

8 Are the idols altogether to be despised ? Write an essay defending them as best you can.

**LEWIS CARROLL [CHARLES LUTWIDGE DODGSON]** (1832–1898)   a solid
citizen, a mathematician, lives in fame as Lewis Carroll, writer of nonsense. *Alice in
Wonderland* and *Through the Looking Glass* have delighted
generations of children, and their parents, with calm
assertions based on playful, indirect flashes of reason.

# The Mad Tea-party

There was a table set out under a tree in front of the house, and the March Hare and the Hatter were having tea at it: a Dormouse was sitting between them, fast asleep, and the other two were using it as a cushion, resting their elbows on it, and talking over its head. "Very uncomfortable for the Dormouse," thought Alice; "only as it's asleep, I suppose it doesn't mind."

The table was a large one, but the three were all crowded together at one corner of it. "No room! No room!" they cried out when they saw Alice coming. "There's *plenty* of room!" said Alice indignantly, and she sat down in a large arm-chair at one end of the table.

"Have some wine," the March Hare said in an encouraging tone.

Alice looked all round the table, but there was nothing on it but tea. "I don't see any wine," she remarked.

"There isn't any," said the March Hare.

"Then it wasn't very civil of you to offer it," said Alice angrily.

"It wasn't very civil of you to sit down without being invited," said the March Hare.

"I didn't know it was *your* table," said Alice: "it's laid for a great many more than three."

"Your hair wants cutting," said the Hatter. He had been looking at Alice for some time with great curiosity, and this was his first speech.

"You should learn not to make personal remarks," Alice said with some severity: "It's very rude."

The Hatter opened his eyes very wide on hearing this; but all he *said* was. "Why is a raven like a writing-desk?"

"Come, we shall have some fun now!" thought Alice. "I'm glad they've begun asking riddles—I believe I can guess that," she added aloud.

"Do you mean that you think you can find out the answer to it?" said the March Hare.

"Exactly so," said Alice.

"Then you should say what you mean," the March Hare went on.

"I do," Alice hastily replied; "at least—at least I mean what I say— that's the same thing, you know."

"Not the same thing a bit!" said the Hatter. "Why, you might just as well say that 'I see what I eat' is the same thing as 'I eat what I see'!"

"You might just as well say," added the March Hare, "that 'I like what I get' is the same thing as 'I get what I like'!"

"You might just as well say," added the Dormouse, which seemed to be talking in its sleep, "that 'I breathe when I sleep' is the same thing as 'I sleep when I breathe'!"

"It *is* the same thing with you," said the Hatter, and here the conversation dropped, and the party sat silent for a minute, while Alice thought over all she could remember about ravens and writing-desks, which wasn't much.

The Hatter was the first to break the silence. "What day of the month is it?" he said, turning to Alice: he had taken his watch out of his pocket, and was looking at it uneasily, shaking it every now and then, and holding it to his ear.

Alice considered a little, and then said "The fourth."

"Two days wrong!" sighed the Hatter. "I told you butter wouldn't suit the works!" he added, looking angrily at the March Hare.

"It was the *best* butter," the March Hare meekly replied.

"Yes, but some crumbs must have got in as well," the Hatter grumbled: "you shouldn't have put it in with the bread-knife."

The March Hare took the watch and looked at it gloomily: then he dipped it into his cup of tea, and looked at it again: but he could think of nothing better to say than his first remark, "It was the *best* butter, you know."

Alice had been looking over his shoulder with some curiosity. "What a funny watch!" she remarked. "It tells the day of the month, and doesn't tell what o'clock it is!"

"Why should it?" muttered the Hatter. "Does *your* watch tell you what year it is?"

"Of course not," Alice replied very readily: "but that's because it stays the same year for such a long time together."

"Which is just the case with *mine*," said the Hatter.

Alice felt dreadfully puzzled. The Hatter's remark seemed to her to have no sort of meaning in it, and yet it was certainly English. "I don't quite understand you," she said, as politely as she could.

"The Dormouse is asleep again," said the Hatter, and he poured a little hot tea upon its nose.

The Dormouse shook its head impatiently, and said, without opening its eyes, "Of course, of course: just what I was going to remark myself."

"Have you guessed the riddle yet?" the Hatter said, turning to Alice again.

"No, I give it up," Alice replied. "What's the answer?"

"I haven't the slightest idea," said the Hatter.

"Nor I," said the March Hare.

Alice sighed wearily. "I think you might do something better with the time," she said, "than wasting it in asking riddles that have no answers."

"If you knew Time as well as I do," said the Hatter, "you wouldn't talk about wasting *it*. It's *him*."

"I don't know what you mean," said Alice.

"Of course you don't!" the Hatter said, tossing his head contemptuously. "I dare say you never even spoke to Time!"

"Perhaps not," Alice cautiously replied; "but I know I have to beat time when I learn music."

"Ah! That accounts for it," said the Hatter. "He won't stand beating. Now, if you only kept on good terms with him, he'd do almost anything you liked with the clock. For instance, suppose it were nine o'clock in the morning, just time to begin lessons: you'd only have to whisper a hint to Time, and round goes the clock in a twinkling! Half-past one, time for dinner!"

("I only wish it was," the March Hare said to itself in a whisper.)

"That would be grand, certainly," said Alice thoughtfully; "but then— I shouldn't be hungry for it, you know."

"Not at first, perhaps," said the Hatter: "but you could keep it to half-past one as long as you liked."

"Is that the way *you* manage?" Alice asked.

The Hatter shook his head mournfully. "Not I!" he replied. "We quarreled last March—just before *he* went mad, you know—" (pointing with his teaspoon at the March Hare,) "—it was at the great concert given by the Queen of Hearts, and I had to sing

*Twinkle, twinkle, little bat!*
*How I wonder what you're at!*

You know the song, perhaps?"

"I've heard something like it," said Alice.

"It goes on, you know," the Hatter continued, "in this way:—

*Up above the world you fly,*
*Like a tea-tray in the sky.*
   *Twinkle, twinkle——"*

Here the Dormouse shook itself, and began singing in its sleep *"Twinkle, twinkle, twinkle, twinkle—"* and went on so long that they had to pinch it to make it stop.

"Well, I'd hardly finished the first verse," said the Hatter, "when the Queen bawled out 'He's murdering the time! Off with his head!'"

"How dreadfully savage!" exclaimed Alice.

"And ever since that," the Hatter went on in a mournful tone, "he wo'n't do a thing I ask! It's always six o'clock now."

A bright idea came into Alice's head. "Is that the reason so many tea-things are put out here?" she asked.

"Yes, that's it," said the Hatter with a sigh: "it's always tea-time, and we've no time to wash the things between whiles."

"Then you keep moving round, I suppose?" said Alice.

"Exactly so," said the Hatter: "as the things get used up."

"But what happens when you come to the beginning again?" Alice ventured to ask.

"Suppose we change the subject," the March Hare interrupted, yawning. "I'm getting tired of this. I vote the young lady tells us a story."

"I'm afraid I don't know one," said Alice, rather alarmed at the proposal.

"Then the Dormouse shall!" they both cried. "Wake up, Dormouse!" And they pinched it on both sides at once.

The Dormouse slowly opened its eyes. "I wasn't asleep," it said in a hoarse, feeble voice, "I heard every word you fellows were saying."

"Tell us a story!" said the March Hare.

"Yes, please do!" pleaded Alice.

"And be quick about it," added the Hatter, "or you'll be asleep again before it's done."

"Once upon a time there were three little sisters," the Dormouse began in a great hurry; "and their names were Elsie, Lacie, and Tillie; and they lived at the bottom of a well—"

"What did they live on?" said Alice, who always took a great interest in questions of eating and drinking.

"They lived on treacle," said the Dormouse, after thinking a minute or two.

"They couldn't have done that, you know," Alice gently remarked. "They'd have been ill."

"So they were," said the Dormouse; "*very* ill."

Alice tried a little to fancy to herself what such an extraordinary way of living would be like, but it puzzled her too much: so she went on: "But why did they live at the bottom of a well?"

"Take some more tea," the March Hare said to Alice, very earnestly.

"I've had nothing yet," Alice replied in an offended tone: "so I ca'n't take more."

"You mean you ca'n't take *less*," said the Hatter: "It's very easy to take *more* than nothing."

"Nobody asked *your* opinion," said Alice.

"Who's making personal remarks now?" the Hatter asked triumphantly.

Alice did not quite know what to say to this: so she helped herself to some tea and bread-and-butter, and then turned to the Dormouse, and repeated her question. "Why did they live at the bottom of a well?"

The Dormouse again took a minute or two to think about it, and then said "It was a treacle-well."

"There's no such thing!" Alice was beginning very angrily, but the Hatter and the March Hare went "Sh! Sh!" and the Dormouse sulkily remarked "If you ca'n't be civil, you'd better finish the story for yourself."

"No, please go on!" Alice said very humbly. "I wo'n't interrupt you again. I dare say there may be *one*."

"One, indeed!" said the Dormouse indignantly. However, he consented to go on. "And so these three little sisters—they were learning to draw, you know—"

"What did they draw?" said Alice, quite forgetting her promise.

"Treacle," said the Dormouse, without considering at all, this time.

"I want a clean cup," interrupted the Hatter: "let's all move one place on."

He moved on as he spoke, and the Dormouse followed him: the March Hare moved into the Dormouse's place, and Alice rather unwillingly took the place of the March Hare. The Hatter was the only one who got any advantage from the change; and Alice was a good deal worse off than before, as the March Hare had just upset the milk-jug into his plate.

Alice did not wish to offend the Dormouse again, so she began very cautiously: "But I don't understand. Where did they draw the treacle from?"

"You can draw water out of a water-well," said the Hatter; "so I should think you could draw treacle out of a treacle-well—eh, stupid?"

"But they were *in* the well," Alice said to the Dormouse, not choosing to notice this last remark.

"Of course they were," said the Dormouse: "well in."

This answer so confused poor Alice, that she let the Dormouse go on for some time without interrupting it.

"They were learning to draw," the Dormouse went on, yawning and rubbing its eyes, for it was getting very sleepy; "and they drew all manner of things—everything that begins with an M—"

"Why with an M?" said Alice.

"Why not?" said the March Hare.

Alice was silent.

The Dormouse had closed its eyes by this time, and was going off into a doze; but, on being pinched by the Hatter, it woke up again with a little shriek, and went on: "—that begins with an M, such as mouse-traps, and the moon, and memory, and muchness—you know you say things are 'much of a muchness'—did you ever see such a thing as a drawing of a muchness!"

"Really, now you ask me," said Alice, very much confused, "I don't think—"

"Then you shouldn't talk," said the Hatter.

This piece of rudeness was more than Alice could bear: she got up in great disgust, and walked off: the Dormouse fell asleep instantly, and neither of the others took the least notice of her going, though she looked back once or twice, half hoping that they would call after her: the last time she saw them, they were trying to put the Dormouse into the teapot.

"At any rate I'll never go *there* again!" said Alice, as she picked her way through the wood. "It's the stupidest tea-party I ever was at in all my life!"

Just as she said this, she noticed that one of the trees had a door leading right into it. "That's very curious!" she thought. "But everything's curious to-day. I think I may as well go in at once." And in she went.

Once more she found herself in the long hall, and close to the little glass table. "Now, I'll manage better this time," she said to herself, and began by taking the little golden key, and unlocking the door that led into the garden. Then she set to work nibbling at the mushroom (she had kept a piece of it in her pocket) till she was about a foot high: then she walked down the little passage: and *then*—she found herself at last in the beautiful garden, among the bright flower-beds and the cool fountains.

## TOPICS FOR DISCUSSION

1 Why is "meaning what you say" not the same as "saying what you mean"?

2 How many "certainly English" words are made meaningless in this multimeaningful text?

3 Can the lapses of logic be identified formally as fallacies of conclusion, or are they rather gaps in coherence?

4 Is there another kind of thought that holds the episode together?

5 How many "times" are there? How is this confusion of times characteristic of Carroll's style?

## ...AND COMPOSITION

6 Try to write a paragraph of Carrollesque prose.

7 How do you account for the appeal this text has for imaginative children?

8 What kind of sense can you make out of the tea-party?

**ROGER ASCHAM (1515–1568)** English scholar and teacher attached to the royal court, as indicated by the essay below believed in training the young by arranging their reading and writing. His ideas were so influential in his day that they prevailed in the management of the promising young lady who became Queen Elizabeth. Some of his most engaging traits show up in the care he demonstrates for the welfare of the young—and in his optimism about education. They *knew* how to be reasonable, then. Of course, it was a long time ago.

# The Schoolmaster

### THE FIRST BOOK FOR THE YOUTH

After the child hath learned perfitly the eight parts of speech, let him then learn the right joining together of substantives with adjectives, the noun with the verb, the relative with the antecedent. And in learning farther his syntaxis, by mine advice, he shall not use the common order in common schools, for making of Latins: whereby the child commonly learneth, first, an evil choice of words (and "right choice of words," saith Caesar, "is the foundation of eloquence"); then, a wrong placing of words; and lastly, an ill framing of the sentence, with a perverse judgment, both of words and sentences. These faults, taking once root in youth, be never or hardly plucked away in age. Moreover, there is no one thing that hath more either dulled the wits or taken away the will of children from learning, than the care they have to satisfy their masters in making of Latins.

For the scholar is commonly beat for the making, when the master were more worthy to be beat for the mending, or rather marring of the same; the master many times being as ignorant as the child, what to say properly and fitly to the matter.

Two schoolmasters have set forth in print, either of them a book of

such kind of Latins, Horman and Whittington. A child shall learn of the better of them that which another day, if he be wise and come to judgment, he must be fain to unlearn again.

There is a way, touched in the first book of *Cicero de Oratore,* which, wisely brought into schools, truly taught, and constantly used, would not only take wholly away this butcherly fear in making of Latins, but would also with ease and pleasure, and in short time, as I know by good experience, work a true choice and placing of words, a right ordering of sentences, an easy understanding of the tongue, a readiness to speak, a facility to write, a true judgment both of his own and other men's doings, what tongue soever he doth use.

The way is this. After the three concordances learned, as I touched before, let the master read unto him the Epistles of Cicero, gathered together and chosen out by Sturmius, for the capacity of children. First let him teach the child cheerfully and plainly the cause and matter of the letter; then let him construe it into English so oft, as the child may easily carry away the understanding of it; lastly, parse it over perfitly. This done thus, let the child, by and by, both construe and parse it over again; so that it may appear that the child doubteth in nothing that his master taught him before. After this, the child must take a paper book, and sitting in some place, where no man shall prompt him, by himself, let him translate into English his former lesson. Then showing it to his master, let the master take from him his Latin book, and pausing an hour at the least, then let the child translate his own English into Latin again in another paper book. When the child bringeth it turned into Latin, the master must compare it with Tully's book, and lay them both together; and where the child doth well, either in choosing or true placing of Tully's words, let the master praise him, and say, "Here ye do well." For I assure you, there is no such whetstone to sharpen a good wit, and encourage a will to learning, as is praise.

But if the child miss, either in forgetting a word, or in changing a good with a worse, or misordering the sentence, I would not have the master either frown or chide with him, if the child have done his diligence, and used no truantship therein. For I know by good experience that a child shall take more profit of two faults gently warned of, than of four things rightly hit; for then the master shall have good occasion to say unto him, "*N.,*[1] Tully would have used such a word, not this; Tully would have placed this word here, not there; would have used this case, this number, this person, this degree, this gender: he would have used this mood, this tense, this simple, rather than this compound; this adverb here, not there: he would have ended the sentence with this verb, not with that noun or participle," etc.

[1] "Nomen." Here the teacher writes the name of the student whom he is instructing. (ED. NOTE)

In these few lines I have wrapped up the most tedious part of grammar; and also the ground of almost all the rules that are so busily taught by the master, and so hardly learned by the scholar, in all common schools; which, after this sort, the master shall teach without all error, and the scholar shall learn without great pain; the master being led by so sure a guide, and the scholar being brought into so plain and easy a way. And therefore we do not contemn rules, but we gladly teach rules; and teach them more plainly, sensibly, and orderly, than they be commonly taught in common schools. For when the master shall compare Tully's book with his scholar's translation, let the master, at the first, lead and teach his scholar to join the rules of his grammar book with the examples of his present lesson, until the scholar by himself be able to fetch out of his grammar every rule for every example; so as the grammar book be ever in the scholar's hand, and also used of him as a dictionary for every present use. This is a lively and perfit way of teaching of rules; where the common way used in common schools, to read the grammar alone by itself, is tedious for the master, hard for the scholar, cold and uncomfortable for them both.

Let your scholar be never afraid to ask you any doubt, but use discreetly the best allurements ye can to encourage him to the same; lest his overmuch fearing of you drive him to seek some misorderly shift; as to seek to be helped by some other book, or to be prompted by some other scholar; and so go about to beguile you much and himself more.

With this way of good understanding the matter, plain construing, diligent parsing, daily translating, cheerful admonishing, and heedful amending of faults, never leaving behind just praise for well doing, I would have the scholar brought up withal, till he had read and translated over the first book of Epistles chosen out by Sturmius, with a good piece of a comedy of Terence also.

All this while, by mine advice, the child shall use to speak no Latin; for as Cicero saith in like matter, with like words, "Loquendo, male loqui discunt";[2] and that excellent learned man G. Budaeus, in his Greek commentaries, sore complaineth that when he began to learn the Latin tongue, use of speaking Latin at the table and elsewhere unadvisedly did bring him to such an evil choice of words, to such a crooked framing of sentences, that no one thing did hurt or hinder him more all the days of his life afterward, both for readiness in speaking and also good judgment in writing.

In very deed, if children were brought up in such a house, or such a school, where the Latin tongue were properly and perfitly spoken, as Tiberius and Caius Gracchi were brought up in their mother Cornelia's house; surely then the daily use of speaking were the best and readiest way to learn the Latin tongue. But now commonly in the best schools in England, for words, right choice is smally regarded, true propriety wholly neglected,

---

[2] "By speaking, they learn to speak badly."

confusion is brought in, barbariousness is bred up so in young wits, as afterward they be not only marred for speaking, but also corrupted in judgment, as with much ado, or never at all, they be brought to the right frame again.

## TOPICS FOR DISCUSSION

1  Outline Ascham's steps for learning Latin. Is the process made perfectly clear to the reader? How? What specific words in the text indicate steps in the procedure?
2  What is the teacher's role?
3  Why is this a "lively and perfit way of teaching of rules"?
4  What assumption about the structure of English made the study of Latin so important?

## ...AND COMPOSITION

5  Describe a process—writing a theme, teaching a little brother or sister about language, learning about college conversations.
6  Defend or repudiate the learning of Latin as a transferable discipline.
7  Study a short passage from a book; then put the book away and try to write the passage from memory. Check your own with the original. How many lines did you remember exactly? Were these passages especially effective? Why? Describe your experience in a short essay, commenting briefly on what you learned about language generally from this exercise.

**FRANCIS BACON (1561–1626)** one of the great organizing intellects of history (as noted earlier on page 65), wielded language—and distrusted it—as public official (up to the office of Lord Chancellor for James I), as literary man (so highly regarded that people still try to prove that he wrote the the the works of Shakespeare), and as scientist (commonly accorded a primary role in the rise of modern science). Such brief mention here—and in the earlier note for "Idols of the Mind"—can scarcely indicate the tribute he deserves; but the three versions of the essay reprinted below will demonstrate his distinction—and his care with language.

# Of Studies

Studies serve for pastimes, for ornaments, and for abilities. Their chief use for pastime is in privateness and retiring; for ornament is in discourse; and for ability is in judgment. For expert men can execute, but learned men are fittest to judge or censure.

¶ To spend too much time in them is sloth; to use them too much for ornament is affectation; to make judgment wholly by their rules is the humour of a scholar. ¶ They perfect Nature, and are perfected by experience. ¶ Crafty men contemn them, simple men admire them, wise men use them: for they teach not their own use, but that is a wisdom without them, and above them, won by observation. ¶ Read not to contradict, nor to believe, but to weigh and consider. ¶ Some books are to be tasted, others to be swallowed, and some few to be chewed and digested: that is, some books are to be read only in parts; others to be read, but cursorily; and some few to be read wholly and with diligence and attention. ¶ Reading maketh a full man, conference a ready man, and writing an exact man. And therefore if a man write little, he had need have a great memory; if he confer little, he had need have a present wit; and if he read little, he had need have much cunning, to seem to know that he doth not. ¶ Histories make men wise, poets witty; the mathematics subtle, natural philosophy deep; moral grave, logic and rhetoric able to contend.

*1597 Version.*

Studies serve for delight, for ornament, and for ability; their chief use for delight, is in privateness and retiring; for ornament, is in discourse; and for ability, is in judgment. For expert men can execute, but learned men are fittest to judge or censure. To spend too much time in them, is sloth; to use them too much for ornament, is affectation; to make judgment wholly by their rules, is the humour of a scholar. They perfect nature, and are perfected by experience. Crafty men contemn them, simple men admire them, and wise men use them. For they teach not their own use, but that is a wisdom without them, and above them, won by observa-

tion. Read not to contradict, nor to believe, but to weigh and consider. Some books are to be tasted, others to be swallowed, and some few to be chewed and digested. That is, some books are to be read only in parts; others to be read, but not curiously; and some few to be read wholly, and with diligence and attention. Reading maketh a full man, conference a ready man, and writing an exact man. And therefore if a man write little, he had need have a great memory; if he confer little, he had need have a present wit; and if he read little, he had need have much cunning, to seem to know that he doth not. Histories make men wise, poets witty, the· mathematics subtle, natural philosophy deep, morall grave, logic and rhetoric able to contend. *Abeunt studia in mores.*[1] Nay, there is no stond or impediment in the wit, but may be wrought out by fit studies: like as diseases of the body may have appropriate exercises. Bowling is good for the stone and reins; shooting for the lungs and breast; gentle walking for the stomach; riding for the head, and the like. So if a man's wit be wandering, let him study the mathematics; if his wit be not apt to distinguish, or find difference, let him study the schoolmen; if it be not apt to beat over matters and to find out resemblances, let him study lawyers' cases. So every defect of the mind may have a special receipt.

*1612 Version.*

Studies serve for delight, for ornament, and for ability. Their chief use for delight, is in privateness and retiring; for ornament, is in discourse; and for ability, is in the judgment and disposition of business. For expert men can execute, and perhaps judge of particulars, one by one; but the general counsels, and the plots and marshalling of affairs, come best from those that are learned. To spend too much time in studies is sloth; to use them too much for ornament is affectation; to make judgment wholly by their rules, is the humour of a scholar. They perfect nature, and are perfected by experience: for natural abilities are like natural plants, that need pruning by study; and studies themselves do give forth directions too much at large, except they be bounded in by experience. Crafty men contemn studies, simple men admire them, and wise men use them; for they teach not their own use; but that is a wisdom without them, and above them, won by observation. Read not to contradict and confute; nor to believe and take for granted; nor to find talk and discourse; but to weigh and consider. Some books are to be tasted, others to be swallowed, and some few to be chewed, and digested; that is, some books are to be read only in parts; others to be read, but not curiously; and some few to be read wholly, and with diligence and attention. Some books also may be read by deputy, and extracts made of them by others; but that would be only in the less important arguments, and the meaner sort of books; else

[1] "Studies lead to manners."

distilled books are like common distilled waters, flashy things. Reading maketh a full man; conference a ready man; and writing an exact man. And therefore, if a man write little, he had need have a great memory; if he confer little, he had need have a present wit; and if he read little, he had need have much cunning, to seem to know that he doth not. Histories make men wise; poets witty; the mathematics subtle; natural philosophy deep; moral grave; logic and rhetoric able to contend. *Abeunt studia in mores.* Nay, there is no stond or impediment in the wit, but may be wrought out by fit studies: like as diseases of the body may have appropriate exercises. Bowling is good for the stone and reins; shooting for the lungs and breast; gentle walking for the stomach; riding for the head, and the like. So if a man's wit be wandering, let him study the mathematics; for in demonstrations, if his wit be called away ever so little, he must begin again. If his wit be not apt to distinguish and find differences, let him study the schoolmen, for they are *cymini sectores.*[2] If he be not apt to beat over matters, and to call up one thing to prove and illustrate another, let him study the lawyers' cases. So every defect of the mind may have a special receipt.

*1625 Version.*

## TOPICS FOR DISCUSSION

1  We have reprinted the three successive versions of this famous essay so that you may examine the care with which Bacon revised his work. What sentences remain unchanged through the revisions? Is there a quality common to most of these sentences? How would you characterize it?

2  Find instances of parallel structure in the 1625 version. Were these passages ever altered from nonparallel form? Are they uniformly more precise, or is there any indication that a desire for grace and balance may have motivated the alteration?

3  Consider the following sentence, in which metaphors are supplemented by explanations: "Some books are to be tasted, others to be swallowed, and some few to be chewed and digested; that is, some books are to be read only in parts; others to be read, but not curiously; and some few to be read wholly, and with diligence and attention." Are the explanations necessary? Which is the more effective, the metaphoric or the explanatory half of the sentence?

4  How is understanding increased by the description of the "school-

2 "Hairsplitters."

men" as hairsplitters in the next to the last sentence of the 1625 version?

5 What, according to Bacon, is the aim of studies? Is this a broad or a narrow view of education? What standards of value evidence themselves in this view?

6 Explain the following sentence: "They perfect nature, and are perfected by experience: for natural abilities are like natural plants, that need pruning by study; and studies themselves do give forth directions too much at large, except they be bounded in by experience." Is this an apt analogy? Can you think of another subject to which this analogy has been applied?

## ...AND COMPOSITION

7 Write a short essay on the aim of your studies.

8 Write a paragraph, using an extended metaphor or an analogy as the method of development.

9 Write a critique from Bacon's point of view of the educational program of the modern trade school, the small liberal arts college, or the large, diversified modern university.

**JOHN DONNE (1573–1631)** sustained by his wit a most dazzling and incoherent set of abilities and impulses and made for himself a career as churchman and poet. He welds poetry and religion, love and science, into literature. The following meditations demonstrate his power to force disparate elements of experience into patterns that hint at occult resemblances between the material and the spiritual. His mind threaded space and time and brought back little trophies of discovery. Figuratively he sailed to the New World; in thought, he discovered Northwest Passages in the originality of his poetry. He demonstrates one extreme among many ways to write.

# Devotions upon Emergent Occasions

## MEDITATION XVI

We have a *Convenient Author,* who writ a *Discourse of Bells,* when hee was prisoner in *Turky.* How would hee have enlarged himselfe if he had beene my *fellow-prisoner* in this *sicke bed,* so neere to that *steeple,* which never ceases, no more than the *harmony of the spheres,* but is more heard. When the *Turkes* took *Constantinople,* they melted the *Bells* into *Ordnance;* I have heard both *Bells* and *Ordnance,* but never been so much affected with those, as with these *Bells.* I have *lien* near a *steeple,* in which there are said to be more than *thirty Bels,* And neere another, where there is one so bigge, as that the *Clapper* is said to weigh more than *six hundred pound,* yet never so affected as here. Here the *Bells* can scarse solemnise the *funerall* of any person, but that I knew him, or knew that he was my *Neighbour:* we dwelt in houses neere to one another before, but now hee is gone into that house, into which I must follow him. There is a way of correcting the *Children* of great persons, that other *Children* are corrected in their *behalfe,* and in their *names,* and this workes upon them, who indeed had more deserved it. And when these *Bells* tell me, that now one, and now another is buried, must not I acknowledge, that they have the *correction* due to me, and paid the *debt* that I owe? There is a story of a *Bell* in a *Monastery* which, when any of the house was sicke to death, rung alwaies *voluntarily,* and they knew the inevitablenesse of the danger by that. It rung once, when no man was sick; but the next day one of the house, fell from the *steeple,* and died, and the *Bell* held the reputation of a *Prophet* still. If these *Bells* that warne to a *Funerall* now, were appropriated to none, may not I, by the houre of the *funerall,* supply? How many men that stand at an *execution,* if they would aske, for what dies that man, should heare their owne faults condemned, and see themselves executed, by *Atturney?* We scarce heare of any man *preferred,* but wee thinke of our

selves, that wee might very well have beene that *Man;* Why might not I have beene that *Man,* that is carried to his *grave* now? Could I fit my selfe, to *stand,* or *sit* in any Mans *place,* and not to lie in any mans *grave?* I may lacke much of the *good parts* of the meanest, but I lacke nothing of the *mortality* of the weakest; They may have acquired better *abilities* than I, but I was borne to as many *infirmities* as they. To be an *incumbent* by lying down in a *grave,* to be a *Doctor* by teaching *Mortification* by *Example,* by *dying,* though I may have *seniors,* others may be *elder* than I, yet I have proceeded apace in a good *University,* and gone a great way in a little time, by the furtherance of a vehement *fever;* and whomsoever these *Bells* bring to the ground to day, if hee and I had beene compared yesterday, perchance I should have been thought likelier to come to this preferment, then, than he. *God* hath kept the power of *death* in his owne hands, lest any Man should *bribe death.* If man knew the *gaine of death,* the *ease of death,* he would solicite, he would provoke death to assist him, by any hand, which he might use. But as when men see many of their owne professions preferd, it ministers a hope that that may light upon them; so when these hourely *Bells* tell me of so many *funerals* of men like me, it presents, if not a *desire* that it may, yet a *comfort* whensoever mine shall come. . . .

> Nunc lento sonitu dicunt,
>   Morieris.

> *Now, this Bell tolling softly for another, saies to me, Thou must die.*


## MEDITATION XVII

Perchance hee for whom this *Bell* tolls, may bee so ill, as that he knowes not it tolls for him; And perchance I may thinke my selfe so much better than I am, as that they who are about mee, and see my state, may have caused it to toll for mee, and I know not that. The *Church* is *Catholike, universall,* so are all her *Actions; All* that she does, belongs to *all.* When she *baptizes a child,* that action concernes mee; for that child is thereby connected to that *Head* which is my *Head* too, and engraffed into that *Body,* whereof I am a *member.* And when she *buries a Man,* that action concernes me: All *mankinde* is of one *Author,* and is one *volume;* when one Man dies, one *Chapter* is not *torne* out of the *booke,* but *translated* into a better *language;* and every *Chapter* must be so translated; *God* emploies several *translators;* some peeces are translated by *Age,* some by *sicknesse,* some by *warre,* some by *justice;* but *Gods* hand is in every *translation;* and his hand shall binde up all our scattered leaves againe, for

that *Librarie* where every *booke* shall lie open to one another: As therefore the *Bell* that rings to a *Sermon,* calls not upon the *Preacher* onely, but upon the *Congregation* to come; so this *Bell* calls us all: but how much more *mee,* who am brought so neere the *doore* by this *sicknesse.* There was a *contention* as farre as a *suite,* (in which both *pietie* and *dignitie, religion,* and *estimation,* were mingled) which of the religious *Orders* should ring to *praiers* first in the *Morning;* and it was *determined,* that *they should ring first that rose earliest.* If we understand aright the *dignitie* of this *Bell,* that tolls for our *evening prayer,* wee would be glad to make it ours, by rising early, in that *application,* that it might bee ours, as wel as his, whose indeed it is. The *Bell* doth toll for him that *thinkes* it doth; and though it *intermit* againe, yet from that *minute,* that that occasion wrought upon him, hee is united to *God.* Who casts not up his *Eye* to the *Sunne* when it rises? but who takes off his *Eie* from a *Comet* when that breakes out? who bends not his *care* to any *bell,* which upon any occasion rings? but who can remove it from that *bell,* which is passing a *peece of himselfe* out of this *world?* No man is an *Iland,* intire of it selfe; every man is a peece of the *continent,* a part of the *maine;* if a *Clod* bee washed away by the *Sea, Europe* is the lesse, as well as if a *Promontorie* were, as well as if a *Mannor* of thy *friends* or of *thine owne* were; Any mans *death* diminishes *me,* because I am involved in *Mankinde;* And therefore never send to know for whom the *bell* tolls; It tolls for *thee.* Neither can we call this a *begging* of *Miserie* or a *borrowing* of *Miserie,* as though we were not miserable enough of our selves, but must fetch in more from the next house, in taking upon us the *Miserie* of our *Neighbours.* Truly it were an excusable *covetousnesse* if wee did; for *affliction* is a *treasure,* and scarce any man hath *enough* of it. No man hath *affliction* enough that is not matured, and ripened by it, and made fit for *God* by that *affliction.* If a man carry *treasure* in *bullion,* or in a *wedge of gold,* and have none coined into *currant Monies,* his *treasure* will not defray him as he travells. *Tribulation* is *Treasure* in the *nature* of it, but it is not *currant money* in the *use* of it, except wee get nearer and nearer our *home, heaven,* by it. Another man may be *sicke* too, and sicke to *death,* and this *affliction* may lie in his *bowels,* as *gold* in a *Mine,* and be of no use to him; but this *bell,* that tels me of his *affliction,* digs out, and applies that *gold* to *mee:* if by this consideration of anothers danger, I take mine owne into Contemplation, and so secure my selfe, by making my recourse to my *God,* who is our onely securitie. . . .

    At inde
Mortuus es, Sonitu celeri,
   pulsuque agitato.

*The Bell rings out, and tells me in*
*him, that I am dead.*

## TOPICS FOR DISCUSSION

1   At what point in the meditations does the author expand his subject from the immediate physical situation to the spiritual level? How is the transition made smooth? Does he continue this method of moving from the literal to the figurative level?

2   How is the story of the bell that rang voluntarily used to advance the argument?

3   What is the effect of a sentence like the following: "I may lacke much of the *good parts* of the meanest, but I lacke nothing of the *mortality* of the weakest"?

4   Why is the personification of death more moving than a mere treatment of death as a cessation of life?

5   What is the unifying idea of meditation 17?

6   What are the steps in the argument beginning with the statement "The *Church* is *Catholike, universall,* so are all her Actions"? Is this a deductive argument? On what does it all depend?

7   How many correspondences are present in the section on the burial of a man as a translation?

8   What does Donne mean by "The *Bell* doth toll for him that *thinkes* it doth"? How has death in a literal sense been converted into communion with God?

## ...AND COMPOSITION

9   Write a short paper on any subject, beginning with a literal object and converting it, by the end of the essay, into a figurative object.

10   Write a paper reversing the process described above.

11   Hemingway used the passage "No man is an island" as an epigraph for *For Whom the Bell Tolls,* his novel of an American's involvement and self-sacrifice for the Loyalist cause in the Spanish Civil War. If you have read the novel, write a paper on Hemingway's use of the passage, answering some of the following questions: Does Hemingway distort the meaning of the passage—or have the intervening centuries justified the new context? In considering the complete passage, can the humanitarian goals of modern man be substituted for the spiritual values of seventeenth-century man?

**THOMAS BROWNE (1605–1682)** was an enormously learned physician in the
quiet little town of Norwich. King Charles II recognized his quality and
made him Sir Thomas in 1671. In his several books, Sir Thomas wrought so
intricately that he put a great strain on prose; no one else ever put more balance
and reverberation into phrasing, and greater intensity of allusion. Though
his style in this selection, Chapter 5 of *Urn Burial* (as finally corrected by Browne),
is far from the current mode, the demands he puts on the reader and the tonality
he elicits from the language can remind us of what resources are available.
His effects are latently present in even the simplest prose, and reading Browne
should aid one's realization: the language is alive with opportunities
and shimmering options. Luxuriate in his work; as a writer he is one of
the richest men who ever lived.

# Urn Burial

Now since these dead bones have already out-lasted the living ones of
*Methuselah,* and in a yard under ground, and thin walls of clay, out-worn
all the strong and specious buildings above it; and quietly rested under the
drums and tramplings of three conquests; what Prince can promise such
diuturnity unto his Reliques, or might not gladly say,

Sic ego componi versus in ossa velim.[1]

Time which antiquates Antiquities, and hath an art to make dust of all
things, hath yet spared these *minor* Monuments. In vain we hope to be
known by open and visible conservatories when to be unknown was the
means of their continuation and obscurity their protection: If they dyed by
violent hands, and were thrust into their Urnes, these bones become considerable, and some old Philosophers would honour them, whose souls
they conceived most pure, which were thus snatched from their bodies;
and to retain a stronger propension unto them: whereas they weariedly left
a languishing corps, and with faint desires of re-union. If they fell by long
and aged decay, yet wrapt up in the bundle of time, they fall into indistinc-
tion, and make but one blot with Infants. If we begin to die when we
live, and long life be but a prolongation of death; our life is a sad composition; We live with death, and die not in a moment. How many pulses made
up the life of *Methuselah,* were work for *Archimedes:* Common Counters
summe up the life of *Moses* his man. Our dayes become considerable like
petty sums by minute accumulations; where numerous fractions make up
but small round numbers; and our dayes of a span long make not one
little finger.

If the nearnesse of our last necessity, brought a nearer conformity
into it, there were a happinesse in hoary hairs, and no calamity in half

[1] "Thus I, when dead, should wish to go to rest."

senses. But the long habit of living indisposeth us for dying; when Avarice makes us the sport of death; When even *David* grew politickly cruell; and *Solomon* could hardly be said to be the wisest of men. But many are too early old, and before the date of age. Adversity stretcheth our dayes, misery makes *Alcmenas* nights, and time hath no wings unto it. But the most tedious being is that which can unwish itself, content to be nothing, or never to have been, which was beyond the *male*-content of *Job,* who cursed not the day of his life, but his Nativity: Content to have so farre been, as to have a Title to future being; Although he had lived here but in an hidden state of life, and as it were an abortion.

What Song the *Syrens* sang, or what name *Achilles* assumed when he hid himself among women, though puzling Questions, are not beyond all conjecture. What time the persons of these Ossuaries entred the famous Nations of the dead, and slept with Princes and Counsellours, might admit a wide solution. But who were the proprietaries of these bones, or what bodies these ashes made up, were a question above Antiquarism. Not to be resolved by man, nor easily perhaps by spirits, except we consult the Provinciall Guardians, or tutellary Observators. Had they made as good provision for their names, as they have done for their Reliques, they had not so grosly erred in the art of perpetuation. But to subsist in bones, and be but Pyramidally extant, is a fallacy in duration. Vain ashes, which in the oblivion of names, persons, times, and sexes, have found unto themselves, a fruitless continuation, and only arise unto late posterity, as Emblemes of mortall vanities; Antidotes against pride, vain-glory, and madding vices. Pagan vain-glories which thought the world might last for ever, had encouragement for ambition, and, finding no *Atropos* unto the immortality of their Names, were never dampt with the necessity of oblivion. Even old ambitions had the advantage of ours, in the attempts of their vain-glories, who acting early, and before the probable Meridian of time, have by this time found great accomplishment of their designes, whereby the ancient *Heroes* have already out-lasted their Monuments, and Mechanicall preservations. But in this latter Scene of time, we cannot expect such mummies unto our memories, when ambition may fear the Prophecy of *Elias,* and *Charles* the fifth can never hope to live within two *Methuselae's of Hector.*

And therefore restlesse inquietude for the diuturnity of our memories unto present considerations, seems a vanity almost out of date, and superannuated peece of folly. We cannot hope to live so long in our names, as some have done in their persons, one face of *Janus* holds no proportion unto the other. 'Tis too late to be ambitious. The great mutations of the world are acted, or time may be too short for our designes. To extend our memories by Monuments, whose death we daily pray for, and whose duration we cannot hope, without injury to our expectations, in the advent of the last day, were a contradiction to our beliefs. We whose generations

are ordained in this setting part of time, are providentially taken off from such imaginations; And being necessitated to eye the remaining particle of futurity, are naturally constituted unto thoughts of the next world, and cannot excusably decline the consideration of that duration, which maketh Pyramids pillars of snow, and all that's past a moment.

Circles and right lines limit and close all bodies and the mortall right-lined circle must conclude and shut up all. There is no antidote against the *Opium* of time, which temporally considereth all things; Our Fathers finde their graves in our short memories, and sadly tell us how we may be buried in our Survivors. Grave-stones tell truth scarce fourty years. Generations passe while some trees stand, and old families last not three oaks. To be read by bare Inscriptions like many in *Gruter,* to hope for Eternity by Ænigmaticall Epithetes or first letters of our names, to be studied by Antiquaries, who we were, and have new Names given us like many of the Mummies, are cold consolations unto the Students of perpetuity, even by everlasting Languages.

To be content that times to come should only know there was such a man, not caring whether they knew more of him, was a frigid ambition in *Cardan:* disparaging his horoscopal inclination and judgment of himself, who cares to subsist like *Hippocrates* Patients, or *Achilles* horses in *Homer,* under naked nominations, without deserts and noble acts, which are the balsame of our memories, the *Entelechia* and soul of our subsistences. To be namelesse in worthy deeds exceeds an infamous history. The *Canaanitish* woman lives more happily without a name, than *Herodias* with one. And who had not rather have been the good theef, then *Pilate?*

But the iniquity of oblivion blindely scattereth her poppy, and deals with the memory of men without distinction to merit of perpetuity. Who can but pity the founder of the Pyramids? *Herostratus* lives that burnt the Temple of *Diana,* he is almost lost that built it; Time hath spared the Epitaph of Adrians horse, confounded that of himself. In vain we compute our felicities by the advantage of our good names, since bad have equall durations, and *Thersites* is like to live as long as *Agamemnon;* Who knows whether the best of men be known? or whether there be not more remarkable persons forgot, then any that stand remembred in the known account of time? Without the favour of the everlasting register, the first man had been as unknown as the last, and *Methuselahs* long life had been his only Chronicle.

Oblivion is not to be hired: The greater part must be content to be as though they had not been, to be found in the Register of God, not in the record of man. Twenty-seven Names make up the first story, and the recorded names ever since contain not one living Century. The number of the dead long exceedeth all that shall live. The night of time far sur-passeth the day, and who knows when was the Æquinox? Every hour adds unto that current Arithmetique which scarce stands one moment. And since

death must be the *Lucina* of life, and even Pagans could doubt, whether thus to live, were to dye. Since our longest Sunne sets at right descensions, and makes but winter arches, and therefore it cannot be long before we lie down in darknesse, and have our light in ashes. Since the brother of death daily haunts us with dying *memento's*, and time that grows old in it self, bids us hope no long duration: Diuturnity is a dream and folly of expectation.

Darknesse and light divide the course of time, and oblivion shares with memory, a great part even of our living beings; we slightly remember our felicities, and the smartest stroaks of affliction leave but short smart upon us. Sense endureth no extremities, and sorrows destroy us or themselves. To weep into stones are fables. Afflictions induce callosities, miseries are slippery, or fall like snow upon us, which notwithstanding is no unhappy stupidity. To be ignorant of evils to come, and forgetfull of evils past, is a mercifull provision in nature, whereby we digest the mixture of our few and evil dayes, and our delivered senses not relapsing into cutting remembrances, our sorrows are not kept raw by the edge of repetitions. A great part of Antiquity contented their hopes of subsistency with a transmigration of their souls. A good way to continue their memories, while having the advantage of plurall successions, they could not but act something remarkable in such variety of beings, and enjoying the fame of their passed selves, make accumulation of glory unto their last durations. Others, rather then be lost in the uncomfortable night of nothing, were content to recede into the common being, and make one particle of the public soul of all things, which was no more then to return into their unknown and divine Originall again. Ægyptian ingenuity was more unsatisfied, contriving their bodies in sweet consistencies, to attend the return of their souls. But all was vanity, feeding the winde, and folly. The Ægyptian Mummies, which *Cambyses* or time hath spared, avarice now consumeth. Mummie is become Merchandise, *Mizraim* cures wounds, and *Pharaoh* is sold for balsoms.

In vain do individuals hope for Immortality, or any patent from oblivion, in preservations below the Moon: Men have been deceived even in their flatteries above the Sun, and studied conceits to perpetuate their names in heaven. The various Cosmography of that part hath already varied the names of contrived constellations; *Nimrod* is lost in *Orion,* and *Osyris* in the Dogge-starre. While we look for incorruption in the heavens, we finde they are but like the Earth; Durable in their main bodies, alterable in their parts: whereof beside Comets and new Stars, perspectives begin to tell tales. And the spots that wander about the Sun, with *Phaetons* favour, would make clear conviction.

There is nothing strictly immortall, but immortality; whatever hath no beginning, may be confident of no end—which is the peculiar of that necessary essence that cannot destroy itself; And the highest strain of omnipotency, to be so powerfully constituted as not to suffer even from

the power of itself: All others have a dependent being, and within the reach of destruction. But the sufficiency of Christian Immortality frustrates all earthly glory, and the quality of either state after death, makes a folly of posthumous memory. God who can only destroy our souls, and hath assured our resurrection, either of our bodies or names hath directly promised no duration. Wherein there is so much of chance, that the boldest Expectants have found unhappy frustration; and to hold long subsistence, seems but a scape in oblivion. But man is a Noble Animal, splendid in ashes, and pompous in the grave, solemnizing Nativities and Deaths with equal lustre, nor omitting Ceremonies of bravery in the infamy of his nature.

Life is a pure flame, and we live by an invisible Sun within us. A small fire sufficeth for life, great flames seemed too little after death, while men vainly affected precious pyres, and to burn like *Sardanapalus,* but the wisedom of funerall Laws found the folly of prodigall blazes, and reduced undoing fires unto the rule of sober obsequies, wherein few could be so mean as not to provide wood, pitch, a mourner, and an Urne.

Five Languages secured not the Epitaph of *Gordianus.* The man of God lives longer without a Tomb then any by one, invisibly interred by Angels, and adjudged to obscurity, though not without some marks directing humane discovery. *Enoch* and *Elias,* without either tomb or buriall, in an anomalous state of being, are the great Examples of perpetuity, in their long and living memory, in strict account being still on this side death, and having a late part yet to act upon this stage of earth. If in the decretory term of the world we shall not all dye but be changed, according to received translation; the last day will make but few graves; at least quick Resurrections will anticipate lasting Sepultures; Some Graves will be opened before they be quite closed, and *Lazarus* be no wonder. When many that feared to dye, shall groane that they can dye but once, the dismall state is the second and living death, when life puts despair on the damned; when men shall wish the coverings of Mountaines, not of Monuments, and annihilations shall be courted.

While some have studied Monuments, others have studiously declined them: and some have been so vainly boisterous, that they durst not acknowledge their Graves; wherein *Alaricus* seems most subtle, who had a River turned to hide his bones at the bottome. Even *Sylla,* that thought himself safe in his Urne, could not prevent revenging tongues, and stones thrown at his Monument. Happy are they whom privacy makes innocent, who deal so with men in this world, that they are not afraid to meet them in the next, who when they dye, make no commotion among the dead, and are not touched with that poetical taunt of *Isaiah.*

*Pyramids, Arches, Obelisks,* were but the irregularities of vain glory, and wilde enormities of ancient magnanimity. But the most magnanimous resolution rests in the Christian Religion, which trampleth upon pride,

and sets on the neck of ambition, humbly pursuing that infallible perpetuity, unto which all others must diminish their diameters, and be poorly seen in Angles of contingency.

Pious spirits who passed their dayes in raptures of futurity, made little more of this world, then the world that was before it, while they lay obscure in the Chaos of pre-ordination, and night of their forebeings. And if any have been so happy as truly to understand Christian annihilation, extasis, exolution, liquefaction, transformation, the kisse of the Spouse, gustation of God, and ingression into the divine shadow, they have already had an handsome anticipation of heaven; the glory of the world is surely over, and the earth in ashes unto them.

To subsist in lasting Monuments, to live in their productions, to exist in their names and prædicament of *chymera's,* was large satisfaction unto old expectations, and made one part of their *Elyziums.* But all this is nothing in the Metaphysicks of true belief. To live indeed is to be again our selves, which being not only an hope but an evidence in noble beleevers; 'Tis all one to lye in St. *Innocents* churchyard, as in the Sands of *Ægypt:* Ready to be anything, in the ecstasie of being ever, and as content with six foot as the Mole of *Adrianus.*

> *Tabesne cadavera solvat*
> *An rogus haud refert.*[2]
> —LUCAN.

## TOPICS FOR DISCUSSION

1 The discovery of an ancient burial urn prompts Browne's meditations and adds some unity to the chapter, but is it the main subject? What is?

2 The classical and biblical allusions add useful illustrations but contribute, in addition, much to the tone of the essay. How? Do you think such allusions could contribute to any other tone?

3 How many simple sentences might be rewritten from the following sentence: "Time which antiquates Antiquities, and hath an art to make dust of all things, hath yet spared these *minor* Monuments"? What is gained in effectiveness with subordination? Find further examples of subordination in the essay.

4 How does "antiquates Antiquities" emphasize the aging power of time? What is unexpected in *"minor* Monuments"?

5 The repetition of structure in paragraph 2, sentences 2, 3, and 4,

[2] "By the swift funeral pyre or slow decay
(No matter which) the bodies pass away."

is significantly altered in sentence 4 and is especially effective in advancing the subject. How?

6  Infinitive phrases appear in a major way in paragraphs 5, 6, and 7, pages 94-95. How do they vary in structure? How does the variation help to develop the subject?

7  How is fire used in the second paragraph on page 97?

## ...AND COMPOSITION

8  Browne's writing is prompted by the associations surrounding the uncovering of an ancient burial urn. Like Donne, he meditates on these associations, allowing his mind to review various matters but always heading toward a goal: the affirmation of Christian immortality. Try the same pattern in developing a subject, aiming always toward a clear goal. The subject need not be as exotic as ancient bones or as grave as death; it can be a souvenir of a past experience, an old book, a memento of an old friend or relative, or any object that has associations.

9  Write a paragraph using as an illustration a reference to a classical or biblical legend. You might begin with "The best man always wins" or "The best man does not always win" or some other such general statement.

10  Imitate the following sentence: "Generations passe while some trees stand, and old families last not three oaks."

**JOSEPH ADDISON (1672–1719)**   is usually linked with Richard Steele and identified as among the earliest journalists (*The Spectator* and *The Tatler*). Addison has come to stand for modern prose. His manner is easy; he turns the language with little adjustments toward any topic, always ready to assert and modify. He assumes a social tone which invites acceptance by readers who share the general assumptions of the writer. The following essay demonstrates these early—and lasting—qualities.

# The Spectator

*Monday, September 3, 1711.*

There is no character more frequently given to a writer than that of being a genius. I have heard many a little sonneteer called a fine genius. There is not a heroic scribbler in the nation that has not his admirers who think him a great genius; and as for your smatterers in tragedy, there is scarce a man among them who is not cried up by one or other for a prodigious genius.

My design in this paper is to consider what is properly a great genius, and to throw some thoughts together on so uncommon a subject.

Among great geniuses those few draw the admiration of all the world upon them, and stand up as the prodigies of mankind, who, by the mere strength of natural parts, and without any assistance of art or learning, have produced works that were the delight of their own times and the wonder of posterity. There appears something nobly wild and extravagant in these great natural geniuses, that is infinitely more beautiful than all the turn and polishing of what the French call a *bel esprit,* by which they would express a genius refined by conversation, reflection, and the reading of the most polite authors. The greatest genius which runs through the arts and sciences takes a kind of tincture from them and falls unavoidably into imitation.

Many of these great natural geniuses, that were never disciplined and broken by rules of art, are to be found among the ancients, and in particular among those of the more eastern parts of the world. Homer has innumerable flights that Virgil was not able to reach, and in the Old Testament we find several passages more elevated and sublime than any in Homer. At the same time that we allow a greater and more daring genius to the ancients, we must own that the greatest of them very much failed in, or, if you will, that they were much above the nicety and correctness of the moderns. In their similitudes and allusions, provided there was a likeness, they did not much trouble themselves about the decency of the comparison: thus

Solomon resembles the nose of his beloved to the tower of Lebanon which looketh toward Damascus, as the coming of a thief in the night is a similitude of the same kind in the New Testament. It would be endless to make collections of this nature. Homer illustrates one of his heroes encompassed with the enemy, by an ass in a field of corn that has his sides belaboured by all the boys of the village without stirring a foot for it; and another of them tossing to and fro in his bed, and burning with resentment, to a piece of flesh broiled on the coals. This particular failure in the ancients opens a large field of raillery to the little wits, who can laugh at an indecency, but not relish the sublime in these sorts of writings. The present Emperor of Persia, conformable to this eastern way of thinking, amidst a great many pompous titles, denominates himself "the sun of glory" and "the nutmeg of delight." In short, to cut off all cavilling against the ancients, and particularly those of the warmer climates, who had most heat and life in their imaginations, we are to consider that the rule of observing what the French call the *bienséance* in an allusion has been found out of latter years, and in the colder regions of the world, where we would make some amends for our want of force and spirit by a scrupulous nicety and exactness in our compositions. Our countryman, Shakespeare, was a remarkable instance of this first kind of great geniuses.

I cannot quit this head without observing that Pindar was a great genius of the first class, who was hurried on by a natural fire and impetuosity to vast conceptions of things and noble sallies of imagination. At the same time can anything be more ridiculous than for men of a sober and moderate fancy to imitate this poet's way of writing in those monstrous compositions which go among us under the name of Pindarics? When I see people copying works which, as Horace has represented them, are singular in their kind, and inimitable; when I see men following irregularities by rule, and by the little tricks of art straining after the most unbounded flights of nature, I cannot but apply to them that passage in Terence:

—Incerta hæc si tu postules
Ratione certa facere, nihilo plus agas,
Quam si des operam, ut cum ratione insanias.[1]

In short, a modern Pindaric writer compared with Pindar is like a sister among the Camisars compared with Virgil's Sibyl; there is the distortion, grimace, and outward figure, but nothing of that divine impulse which raises the mind above itself, and makes the sounds more than human.

There is another kind of great geniuses which I shall place in a second class, not as I think them inferior to the first, but only for distinction's sake, as they are of a different kind. This second class of great geniuses are those that have formed themselves by rules, and submitted the greatness of their

[1] "If you pretend to be mad and sane at the same time, you would not be more rash than if you think of reducing these uncertain things to any certainty by reason."

natural talents to the corrections and restraints of art. Such among the Greeks were Plato and Aristotle; among the Romans, Virgil and Tully; among the English, Milton and Sir Francis Bacon.

The genius in both these classes of authors may be equally great, but shows itself after a different manner. In the first it is like a rich soil in a happy climate, that produces a whole wilderness of noble plants rising in a thousand beautiful landscapes without any certain order or regularity; in the other it is the same rich soil, under the same happy climate, that has been laid out in walks and parterres, and cut into shape and beauty by the skill of the gardener.

The great danger in these latter kind of geniuses is lest they cramp their own abilities too much by imitation, and form themselves altogether upon models, without giving the full play to their own natural parts. An imitation of the best authors is not to compare with a good original; and I believe we may observe that very few writers make an extraordinary figure in the world who have not something in their way of thinking or expressing themselves that is peculiar to them, and entirely their own.

It is odd to consider what great geniuses are sometimes thrown away upon trifles.

"I once saw a shepherd," says a famous Italian author, "who used to divert himself in his solitudes with tossing up eggs and catching them again without breaking them; in which he had arrived to so great a degree of perfection that he would keep up four at a time for several minutes together playing in the air, and falling into his hand by turns. I think," says the author, "I never saw a greater severity than in this man's face, for by his wonderful perseverance and application he had contracted the seriousness and gravity of a privy councillor, and I could not but reflect with myself that the same assiduity and attention, had they been rightly applied, might have made him a greater mathematician than Archimedes."

## TOPICS FOR DISCUSSION

1   The main subject of the essay is the nature of geniuses. Into how many subdivisions or classifications is the subject arranged? Are there still further divisions? What are the characteristics attributed to the major and minor divisions?

2   How do geography and climate affect the nature of genius? Are the notions phrased by Addison still applied popularly today? Do you agree or disagree?

3   What does "sublime" mean? Do you think it could be an eighteenth-century "meaningless word," to use Orwell's term?

4   What is the ever-present danger of figurative language that Addison finds so evident in the nose-tower of Lebanon simile?

5  What rhetorical methods of paragraph development does Addison use in his opening paragraph?

## ... AND COMPOSITION

6  Classify a subject into its divisions. You might start with a broad subject like a major political party and then break it down into types within the larger divisions, further dividing these divisions.
7  Write a paragraph comparing and contrasting the ancients and the moderns, paraphrasing Addison's remarks.

**WILLIAM HAZLITT (1778–1830)** helped to create the freedom and directness of modern prose. Acquainted with the great in his day, he wrote of them and of art and literature. He ranks as one of the most respected critics of his time. One of his characteristics is a readiness for combat. Can you find hints of it in the following essay? Though he announced the principles of modern prose, it is possible that you will not think his practice modern, but he is *approachable;* what he says, he says to you. And there is the assumption that ordinary human beings are addressed, appealed to, and depended on.

# On Familiar Style

It is not easy to write a familiar style. Many people mistake a familiar for a vulgar style, and suppose that to write without affectation is to write at random. On the contrary, there is nothing that requires more precision, and, if I may so say, purity of expression, than the style I am speaking of. It utterly rejects not only all unmeaning pomp, but all low, cant phrases, and loose, unconnected, *slipshod* allusions. It is not to take the first word that offers, but the best word in common use; it is not to throw words together in any combinations we please, but to follow and avail ourselves of the true idiom of the language. To write a genuine familiar or truly English style, is to write as any one would speak in common conversation, who had a thorough command and choice of words, or who could discourse with ease, force, and perspicuity, setting aside all pedantic and oratorical flourishes. Or to give another illustration, to write naturally is the same thing in regard to common conversation, as to read naturally is in regard to common speech. It does not follow that it is an easy thing to give the true accent and inflection to the words you utter, because you do not attempt to rise above the level of ordinary life and colloquial speaking. You

do not assume indeed the solemnity of the pulpit, or the tone of stage-declamation: neither are you at liberty to gabble on at a venture, without emphasis or discretion, or to resort to vulgar dialect or clownish pronunciation. You must steer a middle course. You are tied down to a given and appropriate articulation, which is determined by the habitual associations between sense and sound, and which you can only hit by entering into the author's meaning, as you must find the proper words and style to express yourself by fixing your thoughts on the subject you have to write about. Any one may mouth out a passage with a theatrical cadence, or get upon stilts to tell his thoughts: but to write or speak with propriety and simplicity is a more difficult task. Thus it is easy to affect a pompous style, to use a word twice as big as the thing you want to express: it is not so easy to pitch upon the very word that exactly fits it. Out of eight or ten words equally common, equally intelligible, with nearly equal pretensions, it is a matter of some nicety and discrimination to pick out the very one, the preferableness of which is scarcely perceptible, but decisive. The reason why I object to Dr. Johnson's style is, that there is no discrimination, no variety in it. He uses none but "tall, opaque words," taken from the "first row of the rubric":—words with the greatest number of syllables, or Latin phrases with merely English terminations. If a fine style depended on this sort of arbitrary pretension, it would be fair to judge of an author's elegance by the measurement of his words, and the substitution of foreign circumlocutions (with no precise associations) for the mother-tongue. How simple it is to be dignified without ease, to be pompous without meaning! Surely, it is but a mechanical rule for avoiding what is low to be always pedantic and affected. It is clear you cannot use a vulgar English word, if you never use a common English word at all. A fine tact is shewn in adhering to those which are perfectly common, and yet never falling into any expressions which are debased by disgusting circumstances, or which owe their signification and point to technical or professional allusions. A truly natural or familiar style can never be quaint or vulgar, for this reason, that it is of universal force and applicability, and that quaintness and vulgarity arise out of the immediate connection of certain words with coarse and disagreeable, or with confined ideas. The last form what we understand by *cant* or *slang* phrases.—To give an example of what is not very clear in the general statement. I should say that the phrase *To cut with a knife,* or *To cut a piece of wood,* is perfectly free from vulgarity, because it is perfectly common: but to *cut an acquaintance* is not quite unexceptionable, because it is not perfectly common or intelligible, and has hardly yet escaped out of the limits of slang phraseology. I should hardly therefore use the word in this sense without putting it in italics as a license of expression, to be received *cum grano salis.* All provincial or bye-phrases come under the same mark of reprobation—all such as the writer transfers to the page from his fireside or a particular *coterie,* or that he invents for his own sole

use and convenience. I conceive that words are like money, not the worse for being common, but that it is the stamp of custom alone that gives them circulation or value. I am fastidious in this respect, and would almost as soon coin the currency of the realm as counterfeit the King's English. I never invented or gave a new and unauthorized meaning to any word but one single one (the term *impersonal* applied to feelings) and that was in an abstruse metaphysical discussion to express a very difficult distinction. I have been (I know) loudly accused of revelling in vulgarisms and broken English. I cannot speak to that point: but so far I plead guilty to the determined use of acknowledged idioms and common elliptical expressions. I am not sure that the critics in question know the one from the other, that is, can distinguish any medium between formal pedantry and the most barbarous solecism. As an author, I endeavour to employ plain words and popular modes of construction, as were I a chapman and dealer, I should common weights and measures.

The proper force of words lies not in the words themselves, but in their application. A word may be a fine-sounding word of an unusual length, and very imposing from its learning and novelty, and yet in the connection in which it is introduced, may be quite pointless and irrelevant. It is not pomp or pretension, but the adaptation of the expression to the idea that clenches a writer's meaning:—as it is not the size or glossiness of the materials, but their being fitted each to its place, that gives strength to the arch; or as the pegs and nails are as necessary to the support of the building as the large timbers, and more so than the mere shewy, unsubstantial ornaments. I hate any thing that occupies more space than it is worth. I hate to see a load of band-boxes go along the street, and I hate to see a parcel of big words without any thing in them. A person who does not deliberately dispose of all his thoughts alike in cumbrous draperies and flimsy disguises, may strike out twenty varieties of familiar everyday language, each coming somewhat nearer to the feeling he wants to convey, and at last not hit upon that particular and only one, which may be said to be identical with the exact impression in his mind. This would seem to shew that Mr. Corbett is hardly right in saying that the first word that occurs is always the best. It may be a very good one; and yet a better may present itself on reflection or from time to time. It should be suggested naturally, however, and spontaneously, from a fresh and lively conception of the subject. We seldom succeed by trying at improvement, or by merely substituting one word for another that we are not satisfied with, as we cannot recollect the name of a place or person by merely plaguing ourselves about it. We wander farther from the point by persisting in a wrong scent, but it starts up accidentally in the memory when we least expected it, by touching some link in the chain of previous association.

There are those who hoard up and make a cautious display of nothing but rich and rare phraseology;—ancient medals, obscure coins, and Spanish

pieces of eight. They are very curious to inspect; but I myself would neither offer nor take them in the course of exchange. A sprinkling of archaisms is not amiss; but a tissue of obsolete expressions is more fit *for keep than wear.* I do not say I would not use any phrase that had been brought into fashion before the middle or the end of the last century; but I should be shy of using any that had not been employed by any approved author during the whole of that time. Words, like clothes, get old-fashioned, or mean and ridiculous, when they have been for some time laid aside. Mr. Lamb is the only imitator of old English style I can read with pleasure; and he is so thoroughly imbued with the spirit of his authors, that the idea of imitation is almost done away. There is an inward unction, a marrowy vein both in the thought and feeling, an intuition, deep and lively, of his subject, that carries off any quaintness or awkwardness arising from an antiquated style and dress. The matter is completely his own, though the manner is assumed. Perhaps his ideas are altogether so marked and individual, as to require their point and pungency to be neutralised by the affectation of a singular but traditional form of conveyance. Tricked out in the prevailing costume, they would probably seem more startling and out of the way. The old English authors, Burton, Fuller, Coryate, Sir Thomas Browne, are a kind of mediators between us and the more eccentric and whimsical modern, reconciling us to his peculiarities. I do not, however, know how far this is the case or not, till he condescends to write like one of us. I must confess that what I like best of his papers under the signature of Elia (still I do not presume, amidst such excellence, to decide what is most excellent) is the account of *Mrs. Battle's Opinions on Whist,* which is also the most free from obsolete allusions and turns of expressions—

A well of native English undefiled.

To those acquainted with his admired prototypes, these *Essays* of the ingenious and highly gifted author have the same sort of charm and relish, that Erasmus's *Colloquies* or a fine piece of modern Latin have to the classical scholar. Certainly, I do not know any borrowed pencil that has more power or felicity of execution than the one of which I have here been speaking.

It is as easy to write a gaudy style without ideas, as it is to spread a pallet of shewy colours, or to smear in a flaunting transparency. "What do you read?"—"Words, words, words."—"What is the matter?"—"*Nothing,*" it might be answered. The florid style is the reverse of the familiar. The last is employed as an unvarnished medium to convey ideas; the first is resorted to as a spangled veil to conceal the want of them. When there is nothing to be set down but words, it costs little to have them fine. Look through the dictionary, and cull out a *florilegium,* rival the *tulipomania. Rouge* high enough, and never mind the natural complexion. The vulgar, who are not in the secret, will admire the look of preternatural health and vigour; and

the fashionable, who regard only appearances, will be delighted with the imposition. Keep to your sounding generalities, your tinkling phrases, and all will be well. Swell out an unmeaning truism to a perfect tympany of style. A thought, a distinction is the rock on which all this brittle cargo of verbiage splits at once. Such writers have merely *verbal* imaginations, that retain nothing but words. Or their puny thoughts have dragon-wings, all green and gold. They soar far above the vulgar failing of the *Sermo humi obrepens*[1]—their most ordinary speech is never short of an hyperbole, splendid, imposing, vague, incomprehensible, magniloquent, a cento of sounding common-places. If some of us, whose "ambition is more lowly," pry a little too narrowly into nooks and corners to pick up a number of "unconsidered trifles," they never once direct their eyes or lift their hands to seize on any but the most gorgeous, tarnished, thread-bare patch-work set of phrases, the left-off finery of poetic extravagance, transmitted down through successive generations of barren pretenders. If they criticise actors and actresses, a huddled phantasmagoria of feather, spangles, floods of light, and oceans of sound float before their morbid sense, which they paint in the style of Ancient Pistol. Not a glimpse can you get of the merits or defects of the performers: they are hidden in a profusion of barbarous epithets and wilful rhodomontade. Our hypercritics are not thinking of these little fantoccini beings—

That strut and fret their hour upon the stage—

but of tall phantoms of words, abstractions, *genera* and *species,* sweeping clauses, periods that unite the Poles, forced alliterations, astounding antitheses—

And on their pens *Fustian* sits plumed.

If they describe kings and queens, it is an Eastern pageant. The Coronation at either House is nothing to it. We get at four repeated images—a curtain, a throne, a sceptre, and a foot-stool. These are with them the wardrobe of a lofty imagination; and they turn their servile strains to servile uses. Do we read a description of pictures? It is not a reflection of tones and hues which "nature's own sweet and cunning hand laid on," but piles of precious stones rubies, pearls, emeralds, Golconda's mines, and all the blazonry of art. Such persons are in fact besotted with words, and their brains are turned with the glittering, but empty and sterile phantoms of things. Personifications, capital letters, seas of sunbeams, visions of glory, shining inscriptions, the figures of a transparency, Britannia with her shield, or Hope leaning on an anchor, make up their stock in trade. They may be considered as *hieroglyphical* writers. Images stand out in their minds isolated and important merely in themselves, without any ground-work of

---

[1] "Talk creeping on the grounds."

feeling—there is no context in their imaginations. Words affect them in the same way, by the mere sound, that is, by their possible, not by their actual application to the subject in hand. They are fascinated by first appearances, and have no sense of consequences. Nothing more is meant by them than meets the ear: they understand or feel nothing more than meets their eye. The web and texture of the universe, and of the heart of man, is a mystery to them: they have no faculty that strikes a chord in unison with it. They cannot get beyond the daubings of fancy, the varnish of sentiment. Objects are not linked to feelings, words to things, but images revolve in splendid mockery, words represent themselves in their strange rhapsodies. The categories of such a mind are pride and ignorance—pride in outside show, to which they sacrifice every thing, and ignorance of the true worth and hidden structure both of words and things. With a sovereign contempt for what is familiar and natural, they are the slaves of vulgar affection—of a routine of high-flown phrases. Scorning to imitate realities, they are unable to invent any thing, to strike out one original idea. They are not copyists of nature, it is true; but they are the poorest of all plagiarists, the plagiarists of words. All is far-fetched, dear-bought, artificial, oriental in subject and allusion: all is mechanical, conventional, vapid, formal, pedantic in style and execution. They startle and confound the understanding of the reader, by the remoteness and obscurity of their illustrations: they soothe the ear by the monotony of the same everlasting round of circuitous metaphors. They are the *mock-school* in poetry and prose. They flounder about between fustian in expression, and bathos in sentiment. They tantalise the fancy but never reach the head nor touch the heart. Their Temple of Fame is like a shadowy structure raised by Dulness to Vanity, or like Cowper's description of the Empress of Russia's palace of ice, as "worthless as in shew 'twas glittering"—

It smiled, and it was cold!

## TOPICS FOR DISCUSSION

1 How much of Hazlitt's discussion states what the familiar style is not? Why is the negative approach useful when the subject is difficult to define?

2 Summarizing it both positively and negatively, what is a familiar style?

3 Using modern standards of diction, would you describe Hazlitt's essay as familiar?

4 Distinguish between exactness and pretentiousness.

5 What do "perspicuity," "rubric," "cento," "rhodomontade," and

"fantoccini beings" mean? Can you find exact synonyms? Are they necessarily pretentious words?

6 In what ways can figurative language be either refreshing and familiar or inexact and pretentious? Find instances of figurative language in Hazlitt's essay and judge their effectiveness.

## ... AND COMPOSITION

7 Choose a subject and write a paragraph in the familiar style; then rewrite it in a pretentious style. In a third paragraph comment on ways in which you achieved the pretentiousness.

8 Write a three-paragraph definition of a subject. Then make a list of all your verbs, altering any that might be made more exact; make a list of the adjectives, improving as many as you can without being stilted and unidiomatic.

9 Using Hazlitt's definition of the familiar style, comment on the style of an editorial writer or popular radio or television commentator.

**H. L. MENCKEN (1880–1956)**   lived by the acid ink he displays
below. Attacking the "booboisie" and ridiculing "Bible Belt" types in
America, he entertained and tried to reform his time. Himself not immune to the
nostrums he derided, he nevertheless gained enthusiastic readers, partly because
his methods did have as targets the kind of person addicted to vanity.
His readers willingly enjoyed the exaggeration of Mencken's attacks. His scholarly
book *The American Language* might appear to endanger his separation
from professors or pedants, but his way of writing and his lively stance in the
culture give him grounds for consistently opposing the narrow and the pretentious.

## On Style

With only one or two exceptions, all the books on prose style in English are by writers quite unable to write. The subject, indeed, seems to exercise a special and dreadful fascination over schoolma'ams, bucolic college professors, and other such pseudo-literates. In a thousand texts they set forth their depressing ideas about it, and millions of suffering high-school pupils have to study what they say. Their central aim, of course, is to reduce the whole thing to a series of simple rules—the overmastering passion of their melancholy order, at all times and everywhere. They aspire to teach it as bridge whist, the flag-drill and double-entry bookkeeping are taught. They fail as ignominiously as that Athenian of legend who essayed to train a regiment of grasshoppers in the goose-step.

For the essence of a sound style is that it cannot be reduced to rules—that it is a living and breathing thing, with something of the demoniacal in it—that it fits its proprietor tightly and yet ever so loosely, as his skin fits him. It is, in fact, quite as securely an integral part of him as that skin is. It hardens as his arteries harden. It is gaudy when he is young and gathers decorum when he grows old. On the day after he makes a mash on a new girl it glows and glitters. If he has fed well, it is mellow. If he has gastritis it is bitter. In brief, a style is always the outward and visible symbol of a man, and it cannot be anything else. To attempt to teach it is as silly as to set up courses in making love.

The schoolma'am theory to the contrary is based upon a faulty inference from a sound observation. The sound observation is that the great majority of American high-school pupils, when they attempt to put their thoughts upon paper, produce only a mass of confused and puerile nonsense. The faulty inference is to the effect that what ails them is a defective technical equipment—that they can be trained to write clearly as a dog may be trained to walk on its hind legs. This is all wrong. What ails them is not a defective technical equipment but a defective natural equipment. They write badly simply because they cannot think clearly. They cannot think

clearly because they lack the brains. Trying to teach them is as hopeless as trying to teach a dog with only one hind leg. Any human being who can speak English understandably has all the materials necessary to write English clearly, and even beautifully. There is nothing mysterious about the written language; it is precisely the same, in essence, as the spoken language. If a man can think in English at all, he can find words enough to express his ideas. The fact is proved abundantly by the excellent writing that often comes from so-called ignorant men. Such writing commonly arouses little enthusiasm among pedagogues. Its transparency excites their professional disdain, and they are offended by its use of homely words and phrases. They prefer something more ornate and complex—something, as they would probably put it, demanding more thought. But the thought they yearn for is the kind, alas, that they secrete themselves—the muddled, highfalutin, vapid thought that one finds in their own textbooks.

I do not denounce them because they write so badly; I merely record the fact in a sad, scientific spirit. Even in such twilight regions of the intellect the style remains the man. What is in the head infallibly oozes out of the nub of the pen. If it is sparkling Burgundy the writing is full of life and charm. If it is mush the writing is mush too. The late Dr. Harding, twenty-ninth President of the Federal Union, was a highly self-conscious stylist. He practised prose composition assiduously, and was regarded by the pedagogues of Marion, Ohio, and vicinity as a very talented fellow. But when he sent a message to Congress it was so muddled in style that even the late Henry Cabot Lodge, a professional literary man, could not understand it. Why? Simply because Dr. Harding's thoughts, on the high and grave subjects he discussed, were so muddled that he couldn't understand them himself. But on matters within his range of customary meditation he was clear and even charming, as all of us are. I once heard him deliver a brief address upon the ideals of the Elks. It was a topic close to his heart, and he had thought about it at length and *con amore*. The result was an excellent speech—clear, logical, forceful, and with a touch of wild, romantic beauty. His sentences hung together. He employed simple words, and put them together with skill. But when, at a public meeting in Washington, he essayed to deliver an oration on the subject of Dante Alighieri, he quickly became so obscure and absurd that even the Diplomatic Corps began to snicker.

A pedagogue, confronted by Harding in class, would have set him to the business of what is called improving his vocabulary—that is, to the business of making his writing even worse than it was. In point of fact, he had all the vocabulary that he needed, and a great deal more. Any idea that he could formulate clearly he could convey clearly. Any idea that genuinely moved him he could invest with charm. But style cannot go beyond the ideas which lie at the heart of it. If they are clear, it too will be clear. If they are held passionately, it will be eloquent. Trying to teach

it to persons who cannot think, especially when the business is attempted by persons who also cannot think, is a great waste of time, and an immoral imposition upon the taxpayers of the nation. It would be far more logical to devote all the energy to teaching, not writing, but logic—and probably just as useless. For I doubt that the art of thinking can be taught at all— at any rate, by school-teachers. It is not acquired, but congenital. Some persons are born with it. Their ideas flow in straight channels; they are capable of lucid reasoning; when they say anything it is instantly understandable; when they write anything it is clear and persuasive. They constitute, I should say, about one-eighth of one percent of the human race. The rest of God's children are just as incapable of logical thought as they are incapable of jumping over the moon. Trying to teach them is as vain an enterprise as trying to teach a streptococcus the principle of Americanism. The only thing to do with them is to make Ph.D.'s of them, and set them to writing handbooks on style.

## TOPICS FOR DISCUSSION

1    Can those belonging to Mencken's majority who are congenitally unable to think and write do anything about it, according to Mencken? What do you think about his position?

2    How does Mencken define style? Does his statement approximating a definition help or hinder your acceptance of his argument? Does the argument seem to encourage a logical response?

3    In speaking of "Dr. Harding," Mencken says: "He had all the vocabulary that he needed. . . . Any idea that he could formulate clearly he could convey clearly." Does possession of a new word in your vocabulary improve clarity of thought? Always? Never?

4    What effect on the tone has the simile at the end of paragraph 1? Is it convincing? Colorful?

5    Is Mencken exaggerating his anti-intellectualism? How can you tell?

6    Aside from specific names and topics, what makes the essay seem dated?

## . . . AND COMPOSITION

7    "A style is always the outward and visible symbol of a man, and it cannot be anything else." If Mencken is correct in so saying, what kind of man is symbolized by Mencken's style? Write a short essay touching on such matters as choice of words, sentence structure, and figures of speech.

8  Comment specifically on the appropriateness, fairness, and effectiveness of Mencken's use of similes and metaphors.

9  Discuss the feasibility of a public education system based on belief in congenital intelligence or lack of intelligence; include your judgment on what such a basic belief would imply for democracy.

**F. L. LUCAS 1894–    )** writes novels, poems, plays, and
essays; in the following he demonstrates his deep concern with how different people
write—how their ideas occur to them, how the ideas are induced to join
and to proceed. Contrast the tone of the following with that of the piece by
Mencken, the assertive, strident claimant for your attention.
Lucas here dwells spaciously and lovingly on details. And the end of his
essay asserts a justification for the time and care.

# Methods of Writing

Temperaments are so various that there may be even more than
"nine-and-sixty ways" of writing books. Rousseau, for example, could not
compose with pen in hand: but then Chateaubriand could not compose
without. Wordsworth did it while walking, riding, or in bed; but Southey,
only at his desk. Shakespeare, we are told, never blotted a line; Scott could
toss first drafts unread to the printer; Trollope drilled himself, watch on
desk, to produce two hundred and fifty words every quarter of an hour;
Hilaire Belloc, so Desmond MacCarthy once told me, claimed to have
written twenty thousand of them in a day; and in ten days Balzac could
turn out sixty thousand.[1] On the other hand Ronsard and Montaigne,
FitzGerald and George Moore, went on sedulously repolishing even their
published works. One need not believe too literally in Oscar Wilde's account
of how he spent the morning putting in a comma, and the afternoon in
taking it out again; but Flaubert could really toil for three days to grind out
eight lines—"qu'il faut pourtant raturer encore."

None the less, varieties of method are usually interesting, sometimes
instructive; and though every writer has to work out his own by trial and
error, certain ways of writing seem intrinsically more promising.

Clearly the main problem is, again, one of practical psychology. When
a writer thinks of brilliant ideas or phrases, such that neither he nor others
can think how he thought of them, men used to call it "inspiration." "Hé
bien, Monsieur," King Murat of Naples would cry to Samuel Rogers (of
all people), when he met him out riding, "êtes-vous inspiré aujourd'hui?"[2]
When Dickens was asked where he got Mr. Pickwick, he could only reply
that he had *thought* of Mr. Pickwick. Such sudden illuminations the Hebrew
prophet attributed to the spirit of the Lord; the Greek poet assigned them
to the gracious hands of a Muse (etymologically akin to *mania,* "madness,"

---

[1] Cf. his boast to Mme. Hanska in 1835: "Il fallait dix ans à un auteur, dans le XVIII^me
siècle, pour faire dix volumes. J'en aurai fait quatorze cette année." ("In the 18th century
it took an author ten years to write ten volumes. I shall have written fourteen this year.")
Perhaps the eighteenth-century method, however, had more advantages than Balzac supposed.
[2] "Well, Monsieur, are you inspired to-day?"

and *mantis,* "seer"); but we appear to owe them rather to that amorphous and sinister monster, the Unconscious.[3]

That things go on in our heads without our knowing is, of course, no new idea. From time immemorial men perplexed by some problem have found it wise to sleep on it. Medieval poets repeatedly pretended to fall asleep and dream their poems. The ancient Persians, according to Herodotus, gave scope to their less conscious thinking by deliberating on important matters twice—first drunk, then sober; or first sober; then drunk. Dryden speaks vividly in the dedication of *The Rival Ladies* of "a confused mass of Thoughts, tumbling over one another in the dark," and of the Fancy (what we should call "Imagination") "moving the sleeping images of things towards the light." Similarly Johnson refers to "the lucky moments of animated imagination"; to "those felicities which cannot be produced at will by wit and labour, but must arise unexpectedly in some hour propitious to poetry"; to the influence exerted "by causes wholly out of the performer's power, by hints of which he perceives not the origin, by sudden elevations of mind which he cannot produce in himself, and which sometimes rise when he expects them least." Stevenson had his nocturnal Brownies. Ibsen, again, writes of putting his characters "out to grass," in the hope that they will fatten. And the mathematician Henri Poincaré noted three phases in his own thinking—conscious effort; unconscious fermentation; and a final conscious analysis of the new combination thus formed. But to Freud, whatever else may be questioned in his work, belongs the great discovery, not that unconscious mental processes exist, but that they are much more extensive and important than anyone had dreamed. Men know far less than they think; but they also think far more than they know.[4]

A great part of the writer's problem, then, is how to catch the ideas that creep forth in the stillness, like magic mice, from their holes. Here I suspect that the dog's method is less effective than the cat's. "Wise passiveness" may succeed better than impatient rush and pounce. No doubt the artist or the thinker may carry his day-dreaming to excess, so that it becomes a vice—Balzac called it "smoking enhanted cigars." But it pays, I think, to meditate a good deal, both before beginning to write, and at intervals while writing. The processes of creation may refuse to be bustled. The writer's reverie with a cigarette by the fire may not be as wasteful as

[3] Further details in the chapters on "Wit" and on "Creation and Criticism" in my *Literature and Psychology.*

[4] Cf. Proust: "Il y a plus d'analogie entre la vie instinctive du public et le talent d'un grand écrivain qui n'est qu'un instinct réligieusement écouté, au milieu du silence imposé à tout le reste, un instinct perfectionné et compris, qu'avec le verbiage superficiel et les critères changeants des juges attitrés." "There is more in common between the instinctive life of the public and the talent of a great writer (which is simply an instinct religiously listened to, while silence is imposed on everything else—an instinct perfected and understood) and either shares with the superficial verbiage and changing criteria of the official judges." *Le Temps Retrouvé* (1927), II, p. 46. "Instinct" seems hardly the right word. But it remains true, I think, that many critics live to excess in conscientious consciousness; thinking too much, feeling and dreaming too little, blinded by inability to shut their peering eyes.

Balzac suggests. It may not only turn paper into smoke; it may also turn smoke into paper.

But besides the Unconscious there is a second important master to be served—the conscious, critical Reason. Otherwise one wanders into the bedlam of the Surrealist. And it is important that neither conscious mind nor unconscious should usurp on the domain of the other. "Render unto Caesar. . . ."

On the one hand, the Unconscious may breed happy ideas in incubation. Therefore it needs time to incubate. Therefore it is usually undesirable that a writer should be hurried or worried, hectically overworked or hectically dissipated. But this incubation need not always involve indolence— change of occupation may do better. Thus Scott found that it suited him to have a dozen irons in the fire at once. Metternich told Varnhagen von Ense that he could not concentrate on a problem day after day; he left it to work in him by itself, and got his best ideas in the middle of other occupations—eating, driving, ordinary talk. Others have gained their most illuminating thoughts on a subject while reading about another subject quite irrelevant; or again an inspiration for Chapter Ten may present itself as the writer toils at Chapter Two. It is often as if the Unconscious were a wayward child, playing truant when it is called, then offering help unasked. In other words, Muses are often coquettes.

But the suggestions of the Unconscious should be seized as soon as offered—or, as Samuel Butler phrased it, one must "put salt on their tails." For what the Unconscious thus unaccountably gives, it can as unaccountably take away again—often beyond recall. It will be remembered how Pope could mercilessly drag a poor domestic four times from bed on a freezing night to note inspirations that rose like apparitions from the dark. Similarly the eccentric Duchess of Newcastle kept a servant ready to take down her nocturnal inspirations: "John," she would cry, "I conceive!" The soberer Bentham, again, would write with a green curtain beside him, where he pinned his stray notions on scraps of paper, like butterflies.

But luckily not all good ideas insist on arriving at the wrong moment. They may also, when a writer is in the vein, be called forth by the rush and excitement of composition; just as the excitement of conversation may stimulate a talker to wit or wisdom that he would never have hit on in hours of solitary thought.[5] It follows that the process of composition should, if possible, have some rush of excitement about it—not remain too slow,

---

[5] Cf. Montesquieu's idea that one can give one's thoughts order and logic in one's study; but "dans le monde, au contraire, on apprend à imaginer; on heurte tant de choses dans les conversations que l'on imagine des choses; on y voit les hommes comme agréables et comme gais; on y est pensant par la raison qu'on ne pense pas, c'est à dire que l'on a les idées de hasard, qui sont souvent les bonnes." ("In society, on the contrary, one learns to use one's imagination; one encounters so many different matters in the conversations there, that one imagines things; one sees men there in a light that is agreeable, and gay; one is thinking, just because one is *not* thinking, that is to say one has fortuitous ideas, which are often the really good ones.") Happy age, when such conversation was to be found!

cold, calculated, and self-critical. For this is not only chilling; it may lead the more conscious side of the mind to cramping interference. In tennis, to play with gritted teeth and tense concentration may merely stiffen the muscles: once the necessary reflexes have been formed by practice, it may work far better to use one's head to think where to put the ball, but leave it to one's body how to put it there. And so some have found (again like Scott) that their swiftest compositions were their best; and have gained inspiration from printers' devils rapping at their doors. This may arise partly from the challenge of working against time; partly from the stimulus of feeling that their words would be before the world within a few days, instead of after a year or more; but partly also from the lack of leisure to be hypocritical. For by taking too much thought a man may, not add, but even subtract a cubit from his literary stature.

Such tense self-consciousness was one of the weaknesses of our eighteenth-century poets—even Gray. They tended too much, while they wrote, to let their other, critical selves gaze with freezing eyes over their shoulders. What would Society say? Similarly in her later writing Fanny Burney seemed, paradoxically, to know less of life as an experienced woman, than she had known as a spontaneous girl; while her style degenerated into a false and lumbering Johnsonese.

For the orator, again, self-criticism may prove more crippling still. De Tocqueville attributed his failure in speaking to his habit of listening to himself, instead of being carried away. Other speakers have been known to do best on some occasion when they happened to have lost their carefully composed manuscripts: for *now* they had no time to think too much. In Parliament, above all as a debater, Charles James Fox seems to have been, in the phrase of his opponent Pitt, "a magician"; yet he never prepared a speech; but his *James II,* written "drop by drop," with a purism that carefully restricted itself to the vocabulary of Dryden, remains today only a name. "Tom Birch," said Johnson, "is brisk as a bee in conversation; but no sooner does he take a pen in his hand, than it becomes a torpedo to him, and benumbs all his faculties." And of his own most successful work, *The Lives of the Poets,* Johnson records that he wrote them "in my usual way, dilatorily and hastily, unwilling to work and working with vigour and haste."[6]

Therefore it seems that a writer may often gain by writing at high speed. It is rash to do so for long at a time; but he should perhaps often write in spurts. Flaubert's method was, on the contrary, a slow elaboration, like Gray's. For writers with their temperament no other way may have been possible. None the less Flaubert's letters, which must have been written faster and more freely, often seem to me better, even as style,

---

[6] It seems to me not impossible that the superior ease of the *Lives* owes something to the incessant conversation, often with minds above the average, of Johnson's later years, when he had become a lion.

than some of his more laboured work. (And, more important, I have heard a Frenchman say the same.) Therefore I suspect that in general it may answer better to follow the practice of Virgil who, we are told, would write a number of lines rapidly in the morning, then lick them into shape, as a few perfect verses, in the course of the day.

There are, indeed, limits to this. It may not answer at all well to write a first draft so quickly and carelessly that it needs to be not merely polished, but totally recast. For this not only wastes time; it is sometimes curiously difficult, once a piece of writing has been started on the wrong lines, to obliterate the memory of it, and begin afresh. Once the metal has cooled in the wrong shape, it may prove unexpectedly hard to remelt and remould. Gray, himself a slow writer, warned Mason against this danger of too rapid first drafts.[7]

On the whole, however, I think Johnson was probably wiser in urging that one should learn to write well by writing fast than Quintilian in advertising, on the contrary, that one should learn to write fast by writing well. A Chinese connoisseur of painting put it more tersely still: "Thinkee long. Work chop-chop."

This does not of course mean that one should paint a whole picture, or write a whole book, at express speed. It is usually wiser to leave intervals for meditation and incubation; as a chick emerging from its egg alternately struggles and rests, struggles and rests. It merely means that a given passage is often better written fast and not one word at a time, with pauses to seek inspiration from the ceiling, or sustenance from gnawing one's pen.

Further, where hard thinking is needed it may often be better done *before* a man sits down to his desk. The students in the Bardic Schools of Medieval Ireland (eleventh to fifteenth centuries), who—unlike some more modern poets—underwent six or seven years' hard training in their art, lay all day abed in darkened cubicles to compose; in the evening, lights were brought and then they wrote down their poems. Similarly, in a very different world, James Brindley, the canal-engineer (1716–72), when grappling with some difficult problem, would retire to bed to find ideas. For the mind may meditate best when the body is relaxed and the other world shut off. "Thinkee long. Work chop-chop."

To sum up what I have said so far, a good many of these principles are embodied in the practice of Kant. He let his imagination work on a subject beforehand, but read works on quite different topics, such as stories

---

[7] Cf. Quintilian, X, 3, 17-8: "manet in rebus temere congestis quae fuit levitas. Protinus ergo adhibere curam rectius erit atque ab initio sic opus ducere ut caelandum, non ex integro fabricandum sit. Aliquando tamen adfectus sequemur, in quibus fere plus calor quam diligentia valet." "Things hastily thrown together keep their original flimsiness. Accordingly it will answer better to take more care, and conduct one's work from the start in such a way that it will need merely to be chiselled, not wholly recast. Still, at times we shall be wise to follow the moods of the moment, where warmth of feeling commonly provides more force than any laboured effort."

or travel-books. He set a high value on sudden ideas ("dasjenige, worauf man sich am wenigsten präpariert, ist das naïvste") and carefully noted them down. Then he would read his notes, sketch his scheme in short sentences, and write ahead. If new ideas occurred during this process, he quickly left a space with a note of them, then pressed forward.[8]

But if I suggest the need for giving the less conscious levels of the mind their chance by long incubation and rapid writing, it is not that I wish to minimize the share of the conscious reason. On the contrary, with Jane Austen, I feel that "to be rational in anything is great praise." Our century has produced only too much tipsy literature. I much prefer Rossetti's "fundamental brainwork"—first of all, before incubation begins (for the unconscious mind may fail to work seriously unless the conscious mind has worked seriously first); and again during actual composition. Unless he indulges in free association and automatic writing, or is carried away by "poetic fury," or is drugged like Coleridge over *Kubla Khan,* the writer needs to keep his head as well as use it. For instance, it sometimes proves easier to write freely at night; but the results are apt, like fairy gold, to reveal themselves as withered leaves in the cold light of morning. For though at night the invention is sometimes more fertile, that may be only because the judgment is then drowsier. Just as alcohol does not really stimulate the brain, but merely drugs the part of it that acts as censor.

But it is, above all, in the final stage of revision that the conscious critical reason can play its most dominant part. A work may have been composed with happy ease, or with intoxicated ardour; but now comes the time—for writers that can do it—to view the result with cold detachment.[9] After Sainte-Beuve had drafted each of his *Lundis,* he would hand it to his secretary and say, "Lisez-moi en ennemi."[10]

The vital importance of this last stage, especially for style, is seldom realized by the general public. But it is here that some truth emerges from Buffon's paradox: "Le génie n'est qu'une grande aptitude à la patience."

---

[8] Coleridge's much-discussed distinction between Fancy and Imagination seems not irrelevant here. These terms do not strike me as happy, for in older English Fancy and Imagination are the same thing; and if one wishes to make scientific distinctions of this kind, it may be wiser, as scientsts do, to coin new words, free from muddling associations. And the distinction itself seems to have occasioned a lot of false profundity. In general, what Coleridge would call "imaginative" appears to differ from what he would call "fanciful" merely by being more serious, more deeply felt, more an expression of real emotion than an exhibition of cleverness. But it may also be true that "imaginative" ideas often gain their finer quality from having been brooded in the Unconscious, like the materials of *The Ancient Mariner;* not superficially juggled together by the fully conscious intellect. It would follow (as seems likely anyway) that no sharp line can be drawn between the "fanciful" and the "imaginative"—one fades into the other, like colours in the spectrum.

[9] The neo-Classic age already knew this. Cf. Roscommon—
    And write with fury, but correct with phlegm;
and Walsh's notion that, ideally, one should be in love to write love-poems, and out of love to correct them.

[10] "Read it to me as an enemy would."

No doubt there are writers who revolt at revision—such as Shakespeare, or Dryden (in this, the reverse of Pope), or Byron who, if he missed his first spring, went growling back to his jungle.[11] But those who refuse to revise may pay dearly—though, of course, they may be rich enough to afford it. Even in Shakespeare there is plenty of "sad stuff"; Scott's style is uneven; Trollope's,[12] undistinguished. Indeed, I can think of no constantly perfect stylist who has not laboured like an emmet.

Here I am not thinking so much of the toilsome apprenticeship needed to acquire a style—of Demosthenes five times copying out all Thucydides, or of Stevenson composing careful pastiches of older authors; of Buffon saying at seventy, "J'apprends tous les jours a ecrire,"[13] or of Goethe's, "At length after forty years I have learnt to write German."[14] I am thinking rather of the endless rewriting done, even by established writers, to an extent that the public little guesses—of Plato's variant versions of the first words of *The Republic,* or Ariosto's of the first line of *Orlando.*

In fine, there is much to be said for the principle "Write in haste; and revise at leisure." And revision is usually best when one has had time to forget what has been written, and comes back to it with fresh eyes.

La Bruyère took ten years to write his *Caractères;* and nearly ten more to revise them. La Fontaine, seemingly so simple and so idle, revised indefatigably.

Pascal, it is said, composed his eighteenth *Provinciale* thirteen times;[15] Buffon made eighteen drafts of his *Epoques de la Nature,* and Xavier de Maistre seventeen of his *Lépreux.* Chateaubriand polished and repolished his *Mémoires* over a period of thirty years. Tolstoy's long-suffering countess copied out for him seven times the vast bulk of *War and Peace;* and he would send telegrams to change a word. No wonder his great works left him in a state of collapse. Virginia Woolf wrote parts of *The Waves* twenty times. Anatole France liked eight proofs. Balzac, for all his feverish haste, might go as far as twenty-seven. Indeed, he boasted that, if there were a million lines in his *Comédie Humaine,* they must have cost him two francs apiece in corrections (say £80,000, when the pound itself had a very

---

[11] "I can't correct, I can't and I won't. Nobody ever succeeds in it, great or small." But Byron should have been content to speak for himself. And at times even he would revise, and discuss alternative revisions, with considerable care. (See R. E. Prothero, *Byron's Works* (*Letters and Journals*), II, pp. 145–161.)

[12] I find myself gasping at Trollope's advice, in his admirable *autobiography,* to young writers: "That their work should be read after it has been written is a matter of course— that it should be read twice at least before it goes to the printers, I take to be a matter of course." Twice!

[13] "Every day I am learning to write."

[14] Similarly Rodin at sixty observed that he was beginning to understand his art; Hokusaï (1760–1849) made a like remark at seventy-three.

[15] His sixteenth *Provinciale* had to be produced in haste: "cette lettre est donc plus *longue* qu'il ne souhaitait." ("Accordingly this letter is *longer* than he wished.") As usual, brevity needed time.

different value from today). Obviously this passion for perfection can degenerate into a mania. Rousseau would run from his attic to recapture a note and revise it; Paul-Louis Courier would make seventeen drafts of a letter.[16] But, in general, the lesson is clear—good writing is often far harder work than most people suppose.

Yet I notice that most of my pupils feel it a hardship if I suggest that they should make even one rough draft of their essays. Clearly they cannot, as Horace advises, keep them nine years before bringing them out; but it is optimistic to think one can write well without a tenth of the pains that it has cost even the masters. After all, no less labour is often needed to excel in other arts. Giardini, when asked how long it took to learn the fiddle, replied, "Twelve hours a day for twenty years." Paganini would practise the same passage for ten hours running. Leonardo would walk the length of Milan to change a single tint in his *Last Supper*. Monet painted a haystack eighty-three times. On many subjects an easy style may be one of the very hardest things to produce. "Naturalness," says Anatole France, "is what is added last." Or in the words of Michael Angelo: "What one takes most pains to do, should look as if it had been thrown off quickly, almost without effort—nay, despite the truth, as if it had cost no trouble. Take infinite pains to make something that looks effortless."[17]

[16] A. Albalat, *Le Travail du Style* (1903), p. 105. (A highly instructive book.)
[17] The reader may like to be reminded by some examples of the vast improvements sometimes made by revision.

(1) Since then at an uncertain hour,
    Now ofttimes and now fewer,
    That anguish comes and makes me tell
    My ghastly aventure.

(2) Since then at an uncertain hour
    That agony returns:
    And till my ghastly tale is told,
    My heart within me burns.
    COLERIDGE,
    *Ancient Mariner*

(1) Underneath the bearded barley,
    The reaper, reaping late and early,
    Hears her ever changing cheerly,
        Like an angel, singing clearly,
            O'er the stream of Camelot.
    Piling the sheaves in furrows airy,
    Beneath the moon, the reaper weary
    Listening whispers, " 'tis the fairy
        Lady of Shalott."

(2) Only reapers, reaping early
    In among the bearded barley,
    Hear a song that echoes cheerly
    From the river winding clearly,
        Down to tower'd Camelot:
    And by the moon the reaper weary,
    Piling sheaves in uplands airy,

    Listening, whispers "Tis the fairy
        Lady of Shalott."
    TENNYSON,
    *Lady of Shalott*

Compare the development of Housman's *"coloured* countries" from "sunny," through "pleasant," "checkered," "patterned," "planted" (in a dream), to its final form.

One has also to remember that revision is a means not only of polishing, but also of compressing. For perfect brevity—I need not repeat my praises of it—can seldom be had without long filing and cutting. Quintilian spoke the truth: "A pen may be just as usefully employed in crossing out as in writing." Kipling, who kept some of his short stories from three to five years, shortening them annually, had a special method for this, which he called "the Higher Editing." "Take of well-ground Indian Ink as much as suffices and a camel-hair brush proportionate to the interspaces of your lines. In an auspicious hour, read your final draft and consider faithfully every paragraph, sentence and word, blacking out where requisite. Let it lie by to drain as long as possible. At the end of that time, re-read and you should find it will bear a second shortening. Finally, read it aloud alone and at leisure. Maybe a shade more brushwork will then indicate or impose itself. If not, praise Allah and let it go, and 'when thou hast done, repent not.' "[18]

In principle this seems to me most sound; but in method, too elaborate. Kipling may have felt a natural partiality for *Indian* ink and the hair of camels; but why delete the first version so irrevocably? One may wish, in places, to restore it after all. Therefore I would suggest that it would be more practical, though less poetical, to revise with humble pencil and rubber, and leave all this painting to pictorial artists.

It is only honest, however, to add that all such heroic efforts in the end be worse than wasted. One's second thoughts—or one's twenty-second —are not always best; and too much revision may only sacrifice happy spontaneity for a tired correctness. Isocrates polished his *Panegyric* for ten or fifteen years; but Isocrates remains a minor writer. Cardinal Bembo made his manuscripts migrate through sixteen portfolios in turn, revising them at each migration from one to the next; it sounds a marvellous system; yet, somehow, it seems not to have brought the diligent cardinal much immortality. Again, the final versions of Wordsworth's *Prelude,* for instance, or FitzGerald's *Omar* please many readers less than the earlier versions they replaced.[19] Whether truly or not, it was said of the excellence

---

[18] Quoted in R. Lynd, *Books and Writers* (1952), p. 93.
[19] Examples of second thoughts that do *not* seem better.

> (1) She took me to her elfin grot,
> And there she wept and sigh'd full sore,
> And there I shut her wild wild eyes
> With kisses four.

> (2) She took me to her elfin grot,
> And there she gaz'd and sighed deep,
>
> And there I shut her wild sad eyes—
> So kiss'd to sleep.
> KEATS,
> *La Belle Dame Sans Merci*

of Sainte-Beuve's *Lundis,* "il n'a pas le temps de les gâter." And Pope made a similar comment on Addison, who was a great corrector, except in his *Spectators.*

Therefore it is important, not only to revise, but to know when to stop revising. Personally, I take it as a warning-signal when I find myself deleting what stands in the last revision, and reinstating what stood there in the last but one; then one had better give over.

So far I have been thinking mainly of creative literature and, in that literature, of the element of style. But there is another problem that seems worth briefly considering, since bad management here can have disastrous effects on style as well. I mean documentation. A critic or scholar, for example, even a novelist or poet, may need to master a large body of facts. In practice, I come across this particular problem most in advising research students; but it is of far more general application.

Now the first impulse of the conscientious writer may be to assume that he should pore through everything written on his subject, before he puts pen to paper. Thus Flaubert relates on 25 January 1880, that he has devoured over one thousand five hundred books for his *Bouvard et Pécuchet.* (In the end he was to read some two thousand.) "Cette surabondance de documents m'a permis de n'être pas pédant."[20] I doubt it.

So apparently, sooner or later, did Flaubert himself. Elsewhere he groans that he would gladly give up all the ninety-eight volumes he has so far read, and the half-ream of notes he has compiled, if only for three seconds he could feel really moved by the passions of his characters. And his niece records that he came to feel he had spent too long on such pre-liminary researches, and wanted to give the rest of his life to pure art.

Of course, different minds vary enormously in their power to amass information without growing gorged and surfeited. Nothing in Gibbon's vast history is more astounding than the calm enjoyment with which he

(The "Knight at arms" also declines into a "wretched wight.")

(1) Awake! for Morning in the Bowl of Night
   Has flung the Stone that puts the Stars to Flight:
       And lo! the Hunter of the East has caught
   The Sultán's Turret in a Noose of Light.

(2) Wake! for the Sun, who scatter'd into flight
   The Stars before him from the Field of Night,
       Drives Night along with them from Heav'n, and
       strikes
   The Sultán's Turret with a Shaft of Light.
   FITZGERALD,
   *Omar Khayyam*

(The desert Arabs flung a stone into a cup as signal for striking camp. In the later version this vivid local colour fades away.)
[20] "This super-abundance of documents has enabled me *not* to be pedantic."

seems to have produced it. He talks of it in the tone other men use of their hobbies. "This work," he writes, *"amused* and exercised nearly twenty years." And again: "Some fame, some profit, and the assurance of daily *amusement* encourage me to persist." Whereas his great contemporary Montesquieu, toiling through Visigothic statutes, compared himself wearily to Saturn swallowing stones; and the completion of *L'Esprit des Lois* was reported to have left him too exhausted to read anything profounder than fairy-tales. All the more honour to him that his work yet remains so readable and so alive.

But since for most of us the accumulation of facts does often prove highly exhausting, the vital point is to avoid getting stale. Often, indeed, the ideal of reading everything ever written on a subject seems to me a vain idol. Five centuries ago such an ambition was often feasible;[21] today it is often fantastic; tomorrow it will become still more so. Therefore it is important to develop a quick eye for fools whose books are not worth reading; and a quick power of disembowelling other books less foolish, but still of minor importance.[22] Otherwise, before the author puts pen to his own paper, he may easily have become a stuffed owl, with nothing new to say and with no energy for saying it.

The second point, I think, is not to delay writing till too late. If one is going to read a hundred books on a given subject, it may often be better to start writing as soon as one has read, say, fifty of them. The rest can be taken in the intervals of writing, or after the first draft is written. In this way the writer will feel less like one of those Alpine peasants one sees scaling hillsides with haystacks on their heads. He will have more chance to produce original ideas of his own; and his style will be less likely to lose all life and lightness of touch.

Later on, when the stage of revision arrives, he can complete his reading of what really must be read; then he can add what he has omitted, and rectify what he has forgotten or failed to grasp, with a memory refreshed, and with spirits raised by a sense that the body of his work is already created and it now remains only to make it better and better.

No doubt there is a danger that such additions may overload or distort his original structure; but it proves, as a rule, far easier to lengthen a book than to shorten it. No doubt, too, one can be overtimid about losing inspiration while mastering material. I think Matthew Arnold sometimes was. He would write a poem like *Sohrab and Rustum,* based merely on

[21] Still more, nine centuries ago, when the happy Benedict of Clusa could boast in 1028 (whether or not one believes him): "I have two large houses filled with books. . . . There is not in the whole earth a book that I have not."

[22] "Sir," said Johnson, "do you read books through?" There are many, no doubt, that is a pity not to; but many more where he that runs and skips, reads quite enough.

some stray article in a French journal, without bothering to read further, either then or afterwards.

However, the essential point is that good writing can seldom come from a jaded body or a bloated mind. Indeed, I am constantly astonished that scholars and men of letters should overstrain and overburden their own irreplaceable minds and bodies as no prudent general would ever do with his troops, no prudent rider with his horse, no prudent driver with his car. For a time, indeed, slavery may be made to pay—as with Balzac, writing eighteen hours a day on black coffee. But not only was the end of all that a total collapse; it is hard not to feel that Balzac's output, had it been less in quantity, might have gained in quality and in style.[23] One who would be a stylist, I believe, should be a careful steward of his own vitality.

To recapitulate, the method of writing I have suggested, though there are doubtless many others, falls roughly into these stages.

1 (a) Meditation and documentation.

(b) Incubation.

2 Periods of alternate thought, quick writing, and partial revision, till the first draft is complete.

3 Revision; further documentation, correction, curtailment, and amplification. This can be repeated indefinitely, subject to the danger of the book's growing unwieldy, overloaded, or stale.

There are also various minor questions of method. Gibbon got a paragraph perfect in his head before writing it down; so did Pascal; it is probably far commoner to write, and to revise, sentence by sentence, clause by clause. Gibbon's way may have advantages; but it requires an exceptional memory. Besides, I never know whether a sentence will seem right till I have *seen* it with my eyes in print. As one cannot afford in these times to have Balzac's twenty-seven proofs (and even in that period of sweated compositors these lavish habits of his helped to drown him in debt), one has to be content with typescript. But see it one must. Even then, there are faults that only reveal themselves when one reads it aloud. Lytton Strachey, who followed Gibbon's method, once argued to me that one cannot alter a word here and a word there, because each alteration of a word upsets other words which would have in their turn to be altered—and so *ad infinitum.* My only answer is, "In that case the impossible perpetually happens. Look at a manuscript-page of *Madame Bovary."* To some minds, however, I admit that this method of piecemeal alteration seems repugnant.

---

[23] Cf. Browning's remark to Gosse, according to Mr. Harold Nicolson (quoted by Miss B. Patch, *Thirty Years with G. B. S.,* p. 243). Gosse had congratulated the poet on having nothing to regret. But Browning replied that he regretted not having been a civil servant: "Had I been a civil servant, I should have been at my office all day and only written in the evening. I have written too much, my dear Mr. Gosse; I have over-written; I have written myself out. If I had been a civil servant, I should have written better and much less." Of how many other professional writers might the same be said!

Morris, for example, if dissatisfied with a piece of work, would write the whole thing afresh from the start.

None the less, when I read of authors rewriting whole volumes a dozen times (if they really mean what they say), I cannot help wondering whether it might not have been better to revise more and rewrite less. The mere mechanical labour of a dozen rewritings is enormous; and unless there is careful collation, good things may get scrapped along with the bad; suppose what one wrote at some point in the second draft was, after all, better than what replaced it in the sixth, what labour to unearth it! And what a risk that it may get forgotten! Whereas if one writes the first draft on only a third or a quarter of each page, with plenty of space between lines, the rest of the page can be used for rewritings and additions. Then, all the variants remain under the writer's eye; and he continues free to change his choice, and revert if necessary to his first ideas. Finally, if a whole page grows too congested, it can then be retyped, in its revised version, with minimum waste of time, since any page contains only a few lines. Further, the less matter there is on each page, the easier it is to alter the order of passages, or to insert new. In this way it is possible to do an equal amount of revising with far fewer rewritings of the whole. But I should not dare to suggest anything so obvious if writers did not often seem in practice to do the opposite, and so crowd their manuscripts as to leave themselves no room to turn. Paper may have grown costly; but it remains less precious than time, life, and energy.

There is also a slight problem in the mechanical means employed for writing. I have known authors compose with a pencil in an armchair; but I think *that* process, if carried on for any length of time, can prove curiously demoralizing, and lead to slovenly style. Some can compose on a typewriter; but it needs considerable familiarity for that clicking, mechanical contraption to become second nature, whereas a pen soon grows a mere extension of one's own forefinger. Lastly, there are those who, like Stendhal or the later Henry James, dictate.[24] This does well enough for business documents; but even antiquity saw its dangers for a writer. Habit, I suppose, may triumph even over these; but I feel that a serious writer should create in solitude; and the stylistic results of dictation can easily become abominable—facile, verbose, and sluttish. I have suggested that, in general, prose style should be neither too unlike talk, nor yet too like it; with dictation it may grow too like loose chatter.

However, the main point in methods of composition remains, I think, this—to hold the balance between the more and the less conscious parts of the mind. Otherwise one may become either too coldly correct or too wildly eccentric. But naturally men will always disagree what the right

[24] The blind Milton had to. But then he had presumably composed his verses first, and memorized them before dictating.

balance is, or perhaps whether there should be any balance at all. Blake would deny the importance I have given to the criticizing reason. Flaubert, on the contrary, might claim a higher value for cold detachment. "Il faut écrire froidement. Tout doit se faire à froid, posément. Quand Louvel a voulu tuer le duc de Berri, il a pris une carafe d'orgeat, et n'a pas manqué son coup."[25] He might indeed have quoted Diderot's paradox on the self-possession of great actors. For it seems likely that, whereas the passionate player may be marvellous on Monday, but mediocre on Tuesday, only his calmer colleagues can be trusted to maintain a steady excellence.

However, from the beginning of recorded time some temperaments seem born to prefer Dionysus, others Apollo. Men have never long agreed how drunk they liked art or literature to be. Most critical quarrels are really about nothing else. For myself, I have come passionately to prefer sense to sensibility, and even cynics (if one must have either) to rhapsodists and rapturists. To argue which gives more artistic pleasure is futile (though nothing seems able to stop men arguing about it). I can only suggest that humanity seems throughout its history to have suffered far worse from mental intoxications and fanaticisms than from any rare excess of sober reason. Both the Apolline and the Dionysiac types have produced memorable writers; but the bad writer of the Apolline type can seldom become anything worse than a bore, whereas the bad writer in the Dionysiac style may prove a mere maniac, disseminating mania. In short, though the pleasure-values of literature are outside argument, its influence-values seem to me in favour of balance and restraint. One cannot destroy Dionysus (as Pentheus found to his cost). And Dionysus has his gifts. But there are other powers better to trust than he.

There remains another respect in which I think it is important for a writer not to let himself be tyrannized over by the less conscious portions of his mind. He should not wait passively for "inspiration." Ronsard, Herrick, Gray averred that they could not write except when the mood took them; Shelley denied that any man could will to produce a poem; Macaulay attributed his own success to never writing except when he felt in the humour, and his ideas flowed fast. But about inspiration there is a temptation to talk cant. Inevitably Gray's view irritated Johnson who had lived on fourpence-halfpenny a day, and learned that "a man can always write if he sets himself doggedly to it"; though what he called "fantastick foppery" in Gray was rather lack of resolution, or of compulsion. Poetry, indeed, may be harder to force than prose; but if Shelley's adage were true, how could any long poem ever be written? Crabbe could set himself his steady thirty lines a day. You may not admire Crabbe. But Milton's *Paradise Lost*,

---

[25] "One should write coldly. Everything should be done in cold blood, tranquilly. When Louvel wanted to assassinate the Duc de Berri, he drank a carafe of barley-water, and did not miss."

or the hundred and twenty dramas of Sophocles, could hardly have been composed by waiting on the whimsies of an imaginary Muse.[26] As for Macaulay, who appears to have expressed himself at dinner-tables like a cloudburst, one doubts if there were ever many days when *he* was disinclined to express himself on paper. There seems more sense in honest Trollope's scornful comment that a tallow-chandler might as well await "the divine moment of melting." Certainly Trollope lived up to his principles, and wrote even at sea, in the intervals of running out to be sick. Probably most writers have to drag themselves to their desks. There are minds that, like motor-cars, are hard to start from cold; but if one's self-starter fails, the remedy is not to go for a walk, but to swing the engine. A man can make himself put down what comes, even if it seems nauseating nonsense; tomorrow some of it may not seem wholly nonsense after all. "Not a day without a line"—or, as Swiss guides say, "doucement, mais toujours"—seems to me in general a wiser policy than an alternating diet of lotus and midnight oil. For often, as Gautier put it, "L'inspiration consiste à s'asseoir à son bureau et à prendre la plume"—"Inspiration consists in sitting down at one's desk and taking up one's pen."

It may be said, however, "Granted that good writing turns out to depend less on inspiration, and more on hard grind, than most people suppose, is there any real need for all this rewriting and repolishing?" As Shelley is supposed to have said of Ariosto's traditional fifty-six versions, "is it worth so much trouble?"

I agree that, like most things, the passion for perfection can be overdone. It is part of that good sense which is so valuable to style itself, to remember that fine phrases are not, after all, the summit of human achievement. Few of us will shed tears over the Italian author who, spying a textual error in the volume he was going to present to the Pope, died of heart-failure in the carriage; or even feel much sympathy with Alfred de Musset passing three sleepless nights over a misprinted comma. Even Flaubert's distress at having written a double "de" in "un bouquet *de* fleurs *d*'oranger" may seem a little excessive.[27]

Again, it is a truism that art should not be obtrusive; and ages more interested than ours in the conception of "the gentleman," or "l'honnête homme," have included among his qualities, not without reason, a certain grace of negligence. Some readers are irritated by the too careful polish of Stevenson; the accomplished diction and rhythm of Tennyson's *Idylls* works less well for narrative than the less jewelled style of Chaucer or of Morris. For narrative generally gains by a rapidity like Homer's; whereas

---

[26] Milton preferred to compose between the autumnal and spring equinoxes; but if he was thus limited to six months in the year, he could all the less afford to be capricious while they lasted.

[27] On the other hand Thackeray seems a little too slipshod with his "wife *of* a clergyman *of* the Church *of* England."

verbal felicities may have a delaying effect, as the golden apples on Atalanta.

There is also something irritating to robuster minds in the delicacy like Pater's, who would not read Stevenson or Kipling for fear their stronger style might infect his own. Better, some may feel, if it had; better a muscular Philistine like Macaulay than such finicky valetudinarianism. Similarly with Amiel who sterilized himself by a fastidiousness that could never "brutaliser son sujet."[28]

Literature itself, it may be urged, is only lessened by being made an idol, and only degraded by being exalted from human to divine. "Ce qui fit le bonheur de la littérature sous Louis XIV, c'est qu'alors c'était une peu d'importance"—"Les passions et les arts ne sont qu'une importance ridicule attachée à quelque petite chose"[29]—these cynicisms of Stendhal have yet an element of truth often forgotten in Universities, studios, and salons. It is good to be a great writer: it remains more important to be an honest man.

More important for the man himself—yes. But not always for society. There have been writers whose lives were warped by excessive concentration on literature, yet of whom the world must say, as Hal of Falstaff, "I could have better spar'd a better man." Whether their infinite pains were really worth while for Pope or Flaubert or Tennyson, no one can know; but they were well worth while for us.

In any case there does not seem much practical danger of many authors rewriting their books seventeen times, or even seven. I suspect, on the contrary, that most authors do not revise enough, and that most books would be better for more pains.

In his interesting volume, *Modern Prose Style,* Professor Dobrée has said, "The modern writer must not think of style"; and again, thirteen pages later, "In a sense all good live prose is experimental—as all good poetry is—a desperate attempt to say what has never been said before in spite of having to use the same words to say it in. Any original writer is engaged in a continual struggle with words, to wrest out of them, to hammer into them, meanings they never had before; if he did not want to do this, he would not be an original writer."

I hope he will forgive me if I do not find these two precepts altogether easy to reconcile; nor either of them altogether wise. I should have thought that any serious writer would do well to think quite a lot about style; but I doubt if all these "desperate" efforts to hammer new meanings into words are likely to do much service either to the writer or to the language. In the end it is the reader that may become "desperate." I distrust frantic

[28] "Treat his subject roughly, brutally."
[29] "What made the fortune of literature under Louis XIV was the fact that literature was then a matter of trivial importance."—"The passions and the arts are simply a ridiculous importance attached to some trifle."

resolutions to be "original." I believe that a writer should try, not to be different from others, but to be himself; not to write "originally," but as well as he possibly can. Real originality is spontaneous. Aeschylus or Herodotus, Shakespeare or Milton, even lesser writers like Beddoes or Landor, could hardly have hidden theirs, even had they tried. Caesar (not usually reckoned a timid character) held that a writer should shun an unusual word as a mariner a reef; he would hardly have been more favourable to unusual "meanings." His attitude towards language seems to me *too* conservative: perhaps it was a compensation for an attitude towards politics the reverse of conservative. But it is a tenable attitude; certainly I doubt if one can reasonably dogmatize that "all live prose" must now do the opposite. Again, imagine Swift or Voltaire taking off their coats to hammer new meanings into words!

Those who chase originality (as is far too common today) are more likely to find they have caught instead her ugly sister, eccentricity—like Seneca and Lyly, Meredith and Shaw. Progress may come from aiming, however hopelessly, at perfection; I question if perfection has often come in literature, from aiming at "progress." Indeed, progress in literature has probably been as often downwards as upwards.

My simple conclusion is that any writer with an artistic conscience must share that passion of any honest craftsman which will not let him rest till a piece of work is as good as he can make it: but, even so, he should also remember the eternal wisdom of Greece, "Nothing too much"; or of Israel, "Be not righteous overmuch; why shouldst thou destroy thyself?"

Here are a great many words I have uttered about words—more than I had meant. The subject is indeed important, as I said at the beginning, not only to writers, but to all of us—both as readers and as ordinary human beings, who have to think in words, and to talk them, and to write them, at least in letters. It is important to us, too, as inheritors of our native tongue, which each of us, in his own minute degree, must help to leave better or worse for those that come after us. We may question, indeed, whether style has ever been much improved by books on style. The influence of creative writers, of national history, of social change, surely weighs far more. And no teaching can give talent; yet sometimes, perhaps, it may help to save talent from being wasted. A lot of writing is too confused and obscure; a lot is too wordy; a lot is too peevish or pompous or pretentious; a lot is too lifeless; a lot is too lazy. These are not hopeless faults to cure oneself of, if only one can remember them. If you *can* remember to pursue clarity, brevity, and courtesy to readers; to be, if not gay, at least good-humoured; never to write a line without considering whether it is really true, whether you have not exaggerated your statement, or its evidence; to shun dead images, and cherish living ones; and to revise unremittingly—then, though you may not, even so, write well, you are at least to write less badly. For, obvious as such precepts are, nine-tenths

of the books that are written seem to me to ignore one or more of them.

At least it is well that such things should be discussed. A civilized language cannot develop as the unselfconscious child of circumstance, like the tongue of a primitive people. And perhaps even primitive peoples are less unselfconscious about it than we think. Even Athenian fishwives had strong views on Attic Greek. In any case, once education comes, it inevitably brings with it rules and precepts; some for better, some for worse. And these rules and precepts must constantly be open to thought and questioning. Such has been my object. But those who try to contribute to such questioning would be foolish to hope too much. They must rest in the end, as Pope said he was,

> Content, if hence th' unlearn'd their wants may view,
> The learn'd reflect on what before they knew.

What the world will be like a century hence, was never so impossible to foresee. Like a gigantic snowball, larger and larger, faster and faster, science hurtles with us all into the unknown. Let us at least hope it is not towards a world of swarming ant-heaps populated by highly mechanized barbarians, a new Dark Age, with technocrats in place of theologians. But whatever the future, no part of our traditional inheritance from the past seems less likely to be superseded than human speech—together with the memorable things that men have made with words.

The English of that future, even if its bounds are ever more widely set, will inevitably differ more and more from ours.[30] That is part of the eternal change of things, and can be accepted without too much regret. But what that English of the hereafter is like, depends, as I have said, in its minute degree on what each of us says each day of our lives. One may hope that it will still be a language plain yet rich, simple yet subtle, graceful yet strong. Whether the effort to keep it so succeeds or fails, I trust that even those who disagree most strongly with all I have said, will agree that this effort needs, generation after generation, to be made.

## TOPICS FOR DISCUSSION

1 "Methods" means the variety of aspects related to creative writing, from the way a pen is held to intimacies with one's muse. Make a list of the various aspects and a list of examples used to illustrate

---

[30] Broadcasting, for example, may perhaps tend to make style less pompous by bringing it closer to ordinary talk; there remains the danger that it might bring style *too* close to talk—that it might vulgarize, as well as simplify. One can sometimes see this happening already.

each. Why is the use of examples the most effective way of developing this subject?

2   Because they vary in function, you should examine individual examples *in context*. Do they support a general statement? Do they help to define a term or concept? Do they contribute to an understanding of the reason for, or cause of, such an aspect of method? Do they ever seem to illustrate the opposite of the general statement?

3   What does Lucas mean in the following: "Men know far less than they think; but they also think far more than they know." What has this to do with the incubation period of writing? Is this a problem merely in creative writing, or is it equally vital in expository writing?

4   How can the "less conscious levels of the mind" have "their chance" without ignoring the critical faculties?

5   How can one "develop a quick eye for fools whose books are not worth reading; and a quick power of disembowelling other books less foolish, but still of minor importance"?

## ...AND COMPOSITION

6   In the press find a broad statement supported by an authority (a form of development by example) and comment on how the broad statement advances communication. Is the authority reliable? Is the statement representative of widespread opinion? Is it apt? Does it seem to be quoted in context? Does the quotation influence your acceptance of the statement?

7   Write a short essay on your own method of writing, using Lucas's terminology as a guide.

8   Develop one of the following topics, being careful to use examples to develop the subject: extremism in politics, admirable characteristics in friends, preferred reading materials.

**GERTRUDE STEIN (1874–1946)**   the writer who figured out the simplest
construction for saying a rose really is a rose ("A rose is a rose is a rose."),
provides in the following one of the extremes for any array of writing styles: writing
that not only is like talking, but is talking, and is talking as it might be done
from a rocking chair by a person willfully drifting toward the condition of
brooding or chant: "A long complicated sentence should force itself upon you,
make you know yourself knowing it and the comma, well at the most a
comma is a poor period that it lets you stop and take a breath but if you want to
take a breath you ought to know yourself that you want to take a breath."
Gertrude Stein entertained and influenced other American writers many of
whom visited her during her long residence in France; and she accomplished
spectacularly what many of them tried to do—offending the stodgy.

# Poetry and Grammar

What is poetry and if you know what poetry is what is prose.

There is no use in telling more than you know, no not even if you do not know it.

But do you do you know what prose is and do you know what poetry is.

I have said that the words in plays written in poetry are more lively than the same words written by the same poet in other kinds of poetry. It undoubtedly was true of Shakespeare, is it inevitably true of everybody. That is one thing to think about. I said that the words in a play written in prose are not as lively words as the words written in other prose by the same writer. This is true of Goldsmith and I imagine it is true of almost any writer.

There again there is something to know.

One of the things that is a very interesting thing to know is how you are feeling inside you to the words that are coming out to be outside of you.

Do you always have the same kind of feeling in relation to the sounds as the words come out of you or do you not. All this has so much to do with grammar and with poetry and with prose.

Words have to do everything in poetry and prose and some writers write more in articles and prepositions and some say you should write in nouns, and of course one has to think of everything.

A noun is a name of anything, why after a thing is named write about it. A name is adequate or it is not. If it is adequate then why go on calling it, if it is not then calling it by its name does no good.

People if you like to believe it can be made by their names. Call anybody Paul and they get to be a Paul call anybody Alice and they get to be an Alice perhaps yes perhaps no, there is something in that, but

generally speaking, things once they are named the name does not go on doing anything to them and so why write in nouns. Nouns are the name of anything and just naming names is alright when you want to call a roll but is it any good for anything else. To be sure in many places in Europe as in America they do like to call rolls.

As I say a noun is a name of a thing, and therefore slowly if you feel what is inside that thing you do not call it by the name by which it is known. Everybody knows that by the way they do when they are in love and a writer should always have that intensity of emotion about whatever is the object about which he writes. And therefore and I say it again more and more one does not use nouns.

Now what other things are there beside nouns, there are a lot of other things beside nouns.

When you are at school and learn grammar grammar is very exciting. I really do not know that anything has ever been more exciting than diagraming sentences. I suppose other things may be more exciting to others when they are at school but to me undoubtedly when I was at school the really completely exciting thing was diagraming sentences and that has been to me ever since the one thing that has been completely exciting and completely completing. I like the feeling the everlasting feeling of sentences as they diagram themselves.

In that way one is completely possessing something and incidentally one's self. Now in that diagraming of the sentences of course there are articles and prepositions and as I say there are nouns but nouns as I say even by definition are completely not interesting, the same thing is true of adjectives. Adjectives are not really and truly interesting. In a way anybody can know always has known that, because after all adjectives effect nouns and as nouns are not really interesting the thing that effects a not too interesting thing is of necessity not interesting. In a way as I say anybody knows that because of course the first thing that anybody takes out of anybody's writing are the adjectives. You see of yourself how true it is that which I have just said.

Besides the noun and the adjectives there are verbs and adverbs. Verbs and adverbs are more interesting. In the first place they have one very nice quality and that is that they can be so mistaken. It is wonderful the number of mistakes a verb can make and that is equally true of its adverb. Nouns and adjectives never can make mistakes can never be mistaken but verbs can be so endlessly, both as to what they do and how they agree or disagree with whatever they do. The same is true of adverbs.

In that way any one can see that verbs and adverbs are more interesting than nouns and adjectives.

Besides being able to be mistaken and to make mistakes verbs can change to look like themselves or to look like something else, they are, so to speak on the move and adverbs move with them and each of them

find themselves not at all annoying but very often very much mistaken. That is the reason any one can like what verbs can do. Then comes the thing that can of all things be most mistaken and they are prepositions. Prepositions can live one long life being really being nothing but absolutely nothing but mistaken and that makes them irritating if you feel that way about mistakes but certainly something that you can be continuously using and everlastingly enjoying. I like prepositions the best of all, and pretty soon we will go more completely into that.

Then there are articles. Articles are interesting just as nouns and adjectives are not. And why are they interesting just as nouns and adjectives are not. They are interesting because they do what a noun might do if a noun was not so unfortunately so completely unfortunately the name of something. Articles please, a and an and the please as the name that follows cannot please. They the names that is the nouns cannot please, because after all you know well after all that is what Shakespeare meant when he talked about a rose by any other name.

I hope now no one can have any illusion about a noun or about the adjective that goes with the noun.

But an article an article remains as a delicate and a varied something and any one who wants to write with articles and knows how to use them will always have the pleasure that using something that is varied and alive can give. That is what articles are.

Beside that there are conjunctions, and a conjunction is not varied but it has a force that need not make any one feel that they are dull. Conjunctions have made themselves live by their work. They work and as they work they live and even when they do not work and in these days they do not always live by work still nevertheless they do live.

So you see why I like to write with prepositions and conjunctions and articles and verbs and adverbs but not with nouns and adjectives. If you read my writing you will you do see what I mean.

Of course then there are pronouns. Pronouns are not as bad as nouns because in the first place practically they cannot have adjectives go with them. That already makes them better than nouns.

Then beside not being able to have adjectives go with them, they of course are not really the name of anything. They represent some one but they are not its or his name. In not being his or its or her name they already have a greater possibility of being something than if they were as a noun is the name of anything. Now actual given names of people are more lively than nouns which are the name of anything and I suppose that this is because after all the name is only given to that person when they are born, there is at least the element of choice even the element of change and anybody can be pretty well able to do what they like, they may be born Walter and become Hub, in such a way they are not like a noun. A noun has been the name of something for such a very long time.

That is the reason that slang exists it is to change the nouns which have been names for so long. I say again. Verbs and adverbs and articles and conjunctions and prepositions are lively because they all do something and as long as anything does something it keeps alive.

One might have in one's list added interjections but really interjections have nothing to do with anything not even with themselves. There so much for that. And now to go into the question of punctuation.

There are some punctuations that are interesting and there are some punctuations that are not. Let us begin with the punctuations that are not. Of these the one but the first and the most the completely most uninteresting is the question mark. The question mark is alright when it is all alone when it is used as a brand on cattle or when it could be used in decoration but connected with writing it is completely entirely completely uninteresting. It is evident that if you ask a question you ask a question but anybody who can read at all knows when a question is a question as it is written in writing. Therefore I ask you therefore wherefore should one use it the question mark. Beside it does not in its form go with ordinary printing and so it pleases neither the eye nor the ear and it is therefore like a noun, just an unnecessary name of something. A question is a question, anybody can know that a question is a question and so why add to it the question mark when it is already there when the question is already there in the writing. Therefore I never could bring myself to use a question mark, I always found it positively revolting, and now very few do use it. Exclamation marks have the same difficulty and also quotation marks, they are unnecessary, they are ugly, they spoil the line of the writing or the printing and anyway what is the use, if you do not know that a question is a question what is the use of its being a question. The same thing is true of an exclamation. And the same thing is true of a quotation. When I first began writing I found it simply impossible to use question marks and quotation marks and exclamation points and now anybody sees it that way. Perhaps some day they will see it some other way but now at any rate anybody can and does see it that way.

So there are the uninteresting things in punctuation uninteresting in a way that is perfectly obvious, and so we do not have to go any farther into that. There are besides dashes and dots, and these might be interesting spaces might be interesting. They might if one felt that way about them.

One other little punctuation mark one can have feelings about and that is the apostrophe for possession. Well feel as you like about that, I can see and I do see that for many that for some the possessive case apostrophe has a gentle tender insinuation that makes it very difficult to definitely decide to do without it. One does do without it, I do, I mostly always do, but I cannot deny that from time to time I feel myself having regrets and from time to time I put it in to make the possessive case. I absolutely do not like it all alone when it is outside the word when the

word is a plural, no then positively and definitely no, I do not like it and in leaving it out I feel no regret, there it is unnecessary and not ornamental but inside a word and its s well perhaps, perhaps it does appeal by its weakness to your weakness. At least at any rate from time to time I do find myself letting it alone if it has come in and sometimes it has come in. I cannot positively deny but that I do from time to time let it come in.

So now to come to the real question of punctuation, periods, commas, colons, semi-colons and capitals and small letters.

I have had a long and complicated life with all these.

Let us begin with these I use the least first and these are colons and semi-colons, one might add to these commas.

When I first began writing, I felt that writing should go on, I still do feel that it should go on but when I first began writing I was completely possessed by the necessity that writing should go on and if writing should go on what had colons and semi-colons to do with it, what had commas to do with it, what had periods to do with it what had small letters and capitals to do with it to do with writing going on which was at that time the most profound need I had in connection with writing. What had colons and semi-colons to do with it what had commas to do with it what had periods to do with it.

What had periods to do with it. Inevitably no matter how completely I had to have writing go on, physically one had to again and again stop sometime and if one had to again and again stop some time then periods had to exist. Beside I had always liked the look of periods and I liked what they did. Stopping sometime did not really keep one from going on, it was nothing that interfered, it was only something that happened, and as it happened as a perfectly natural happening, I did believe in periods and I used them. I really never stopped using them.

Beside that periods might later come to have a life of their own to commence breaking up things in arbitrary ways, that has happened lately with me in a poem I have written called Winning His Way, later I will read you a little of it. By the time I had written this poem about three years ago periods had come to have for me completely a life of their own. They could begin to act as they thought best and one might interrupt one's writing with them that is not really interrupt one's writing with them but one could come to stop arbitrarily stop at times in one's writing and so they could be used and you could use them. Periods could come to exist in this way and they could come in this way to have a life of their own. They did not serve you in any servile way as commas and colons and semi-colons do. Yes you do feel what I mean.

Periods have a life of their own a necessity of their own a feeling of their own a time of their own. And that feeling that life that necessity that time can express itself in an infinite variety that is the reason that I have always remained true to periods so much so that as I say recently I have felt that one could need them more than one had ever needed them.

You can see what an entirely different thing a period is from a comma, a colon or a semi-colon.

There are two different ways of thinking about colons and semi-colons you can think of them as commas and as such they are purely servile or you can think of them as periods and then using them can make you feel adventurous. I can see that one might feel about them as periods but I myself never have, I began unfortunately to feel them as a comma and commas are servile they have no life of their own they are dependent upon use and convenience and they are put there just for practical purposes. Semi-colons and colons had for me from the first completely this character the character that a comma has and not the character that a period has and therefore and definitely I have never used them. But now dimly and definitely I do see that they might well possibly they might have in them something of the character of the period and so it might have been an adventure to use them. I really do not think so. I think however lively they are or disguised they are they are definitely more comma than period and so really I cannot regret not having used them. They are more powerful more imposing more pretentious than a comma but they are a comma all the same. They really have within them deeply within them fundamentally within them the comma nature. And now what does a comma do and what has it to do and why do I feel as I do about them.

What does a comma do.

I have refused them so often and left them out so much and did without them so continually that I have come finally to be indifferent to them. I do not now care whether you put them in or not but for a long time I felt very definitely about them and would have nothing to do with them.

As I say commas are servile and they have no life of their own, and their use is not a use, it is a way of replacing one's own interest and I do decidedly like to like my own interest my own interest in what I am doing. A comma by helping you along holding your coat for you and putting on your shoes keeps you from living your life as actively as you should lead it and to me for many years and I still do feel that way about it only now I do not pay as much attention to them, the use of them was positively degrading. Let me tell you what I feel and what I mean and what I felt and what I meant.

When I was writing those long sentences of The Making of Americans, verbs active present verbs with long dependent adverbial clauses became a passion with me. I have told you that I recognize verbs and adverbs aided by prepositions and conjunctions with pronouns as possessing the whole of the active life of writing.

Complications make eventually for simplicity and therefore I have always liked dependent adverbial clauses. I have liked dependent adverbial clauses because of their variety of dependence and independence. You can see how loving the intensity of complication of these things that commas

would be degrading. Why if you want the pleasure of concentrating on the final simplicity of excessive complication would you want any artificial aid to bring about that simplicity. Do you see now why I feel about the comma as I did and as I do.

Think about anything you really like to do and you will see what I mean.

When it gets really difficult you want to disentangle rather than to cut the knot, at least so anybody feels who is working with any thread, so anybody feels who is working with any tool so anybody feels who is writing any sentence or reading it after it has been written. And what does a comma do, a comma does nothing but make easy a thing that if you like it enough is easy enough without the comma. A long complicated sentence should force itself upon you, make you know yourself knowing it and the comma, well at the most a comma is a poor period that it lets you stop and take a breath but if you want to take a breath you ought to know yourself that you want to take a breath. It is not like stopping altogether which is what a period does stopping altogether has something to do with going on, but taking a breath well you are always taking a breath and why emphasize one breath rather than another breath. Anyway that is the way I felt about it and I felt that about it very very strongly. And so I almost never used a comma. The longer, the more complicated the sentence the greater the number of the same kinds of words I had following one after another, the more the very many more I had of them the more I felt the passionate need of their taking care of themselves by themselves and not helping them, and thereby enfeebling them by putting in a comma.

So that is the way I felt punctuation in prose, in poetry it is a little different but more so and later I will go into that. But that is the way I felt about punctuation in prose.

Another part of punctuation is capital letters and small letters. Anybody can really do as they please about that and in English printing one may say that they always have.

If you read older books you will see that they do pretty well what they please with capitals and small letters and I have always felt that one does do pretty well what one pleases with capitals and small letters. Sometimes one feels that Italians should be with a capital and sometimes with a small letter, one can feel like that about almost anything. I myself do not feel like that about proper names, I rather like to look at them with a capital on them but I can perfectly understand that a great many do not feel that way about it. In short in prose capitals and small letters have really nothing to do with the inner life of sentences and paragraphs as the other punctuation marks have as I have just been saying.

We still have capitals and small letters and probably for some time we will go on having them but actually the tendency is always toward

diminishing capitals and quite rightly because the feeling that goes with them is less and less of a feeling and so slowly and inevitably just as with horses capitals will have gone away. They will come back from time to time but perhaps never really come back to stay.

Perhaps yes perhaps not but really and inevitably really it really does not really make any difference.

But and they will be with us as long as human beings continue to exist and have a vocabulary, sentences and paragraphs will be with us and therefore inevitably and really periods will be with us and it is of these things that will be always inevitably with us in prose and in poetry because prose and also poetry will also always always be with us that I will go on telling to you all I know.

Sentences and paragraphs. Sentences are not emotional but paragraphs are. I can say that as often as I like and it always remains as it is, something that is.

I said I found this out first in listening to Basket my dog drinking. And anybody listening to any dog's drinking will see what I mean.

When I wrote The Making of Americans I tried to break down this essential combination by making enormously long sentences that would be as long as the longest paragraph and so to see if there was really and truly this essential difference between paragraphs and sentences, if one went far enough with this thing with making the sentences long enough to be as long as any paragraph and so producing in them the balance of a paragraph not a balance of a sentence, because of course the balance of a paragraph is not the same balance as the balance of a sentence.

It is only necessary to read anything in order to know that. I say if I succeeded in making my sentences so long that they held within themselves the balance of both both sentences and paragraphs, what was the result.

I did in some sentences in The Making of Americans succeed in doing this thing in creating a balance that was neither the balance of a sentence nor the balance of a paragraph and in doing so I felt dimly that I had done something that was not leading to anything because after all you should not lose two things in order to have one thing because in doing so you make writing just that much less varied.

That is one thing about what I did. There is also another thing and that was a very important thing, in doing this in achieving something that had neither the balance of a sentence nor the balance of a paragraph but a balance a new balance that had to do with a sense of movement of time included in a given space which as I have already said is a definitely American thing.

An American can fill up a space in having his movement of time by adding unexpectedly anything and yet getting within the included space everything he had intended getting.

A young french boy he is a red-haired descendant of the niece of

Madame Recamier went to America for two weeks most unexpectedly and I said to him what did you notice most over there. Well he said at first they were not as different from us frenchmen as I expected them to be and then I did see that they were that they were different. And what, said I, well he said, when a train was going by at a terrific pace and we waved a hat the engine driver could make a bell quite carelessly go ting ting ting, the way anybody playing at a thing could do, it was not if you know what I mean professional he said. Perhaps you do see the connection with that and my sentences that had no longer the balance of sentences because they were not the parts of a paragraph nor were they a paragraph but they had made in so far as they had come to be so long and with the balance of their own that they had they had become something that was a whole thing and in so being they had a balance which was the balance of a space completely not filled but created by something moving as moving is not as moving should be. As I said Henry James in his later writing had had a dim feeling that this was what he knew he should do.

And so though as I say there must always be sentences and paragraphs the question can really be asked must there always be sentences and paragraphs is it not possible to achieve in itself and not by sentences and paragraphs the combination that sentences are not emotional and paragraphs are.

## TOPICS FOR DISCUSSION

1    Presenting rules of grammar and punctuation is not the intent of the essay, apparently. What is?

2    Did you learn anything about grammar from the lecture?

3    Locate as many types of deviations from handbook grammar as you can. Were any of the "errors" useful to you in understanding the reason for the rule?

4    What is it in the punctuation that produces the monotone effect? Copy out some of the longer sentences and punctuate them, indicating major and minor elements; does this help?

5    The lecturer addresses herself to most problems of grammar (and punctuation) from her own point of view; that is, she discusses why she does or does not for her own purposes follow a prescription. Is this the best way to approach grammar?

## ...AND COMPOSITION

6    Write a paper on your choice of subject. Revise it, noticing particularly the way emphasis and subordination within sentences

(and in the larger units as well) clarify your subject and make it more precise. Submit both papers with a paragraph commenting on the special improvements in the revision.

7  Compare and contrast the punctuation styles of Lucas and Stein, including in your comments the specific instances of, the possible motives for, and the effects of, the deviations from the normal style.

8  Write a critical review of the Stein lecture.

**EDGAR ALLAN POE (1809–1849)** composed the most extreme and romantic of poems and stories; indeed, he represents in American literature the occult and strange. At the same time, however, he maintained in his prose that composition was for him a conscious and controlled process. Fortunately for us, he applied his analysis carefully to one of his own poems. The poem and the analysis follow. As in all such explanations, we must remember that both pieces are compositions: a writer may claim anything; readers must judge. Poe has been moved to write an emphatic exposition about what he claims to be a mechanically constructed poem. The essay may be more poetic than the poem.

# The Raven

Once upon a midnight dreary, while I pondered, weak and weary,
Over many a quaint and curious volume of forgotten lore,
While I nodded, nearly napping, suddenly there came a tapping,
As of some one gently rapping, rapping at my chamber door.
" 'Tis some visitor," I muttered, "tapping at my chamber door—    5
      Only this and nothing more."

Ah, distinctly I remember it was in the bleak December,
And each separate dying ember wrought its ghost upon the floor.
Eagerly I wished the morrow; vainly I had sought to borrow
From my books surcease of sorrow—sorrow for the lost Lenore,    10
For the rare and radiant maiden whom the angels name Lenore—
      Nameless *here* for evermore.

And the silken, sad, uncertain rustling of each purple curtain
Thrilled me—filled me with fantastic terrors never felt before;
So that now, to still the beating of my heart, I stood repeating,    15
" 'Tis some visitor entreating entrance at my chamber door—
Some late visitor entreating entrance at my chamber door—
      This it is and nothing more."

Presently my soul grew stronger: hesitating then no longer,
"Sir," said I, "or Madam, truly your forgiveness I implore;    20
But the fact is I was napping, and so gently you came rapping,
And so faintly you came tapping, tapping at my chamber door,
That I scarce was sure I heard you"—here I opened wide the door—
      Darkness there and nothing more.

Deep into that darkness peering, long I stood there, wondering, fearing,    25
Doubting, dreaming dreams no mortal ever dared to dream before;
But the silence was unbroken, and the stillness gave no token,
And the only word there spoken was the whispered word "Lenore!"

This I whispered, and an echo murmured back the word "Lenore!"
    Merely this and nothing more.                    30

Back into the chamber turning, all my soul within me burning,
Soon again I heard a tapping, somewhat louder than before.
"Surely," said I, "surely that is something at my window lattice;
Let me see, then, what thereat is, and this mystery explore,—
Let my heart be still a moment and this mystery explore—     35
    'Tis the wind and nothing more."

Open here I flung the shutter, when, with many a flirt and flutter,
In there stepped a stately Raven of the saintly days of yore.
Not the least obeisance made he, not a minute stopped or stayed he,
But with mien of lord or lady perched above my chamber door—  40
Perched upon a bust of Pallas just above my chamber door—
    Perched and sat, and nothing more.

Then, this ebony bird beguiling my sad fancy into smiling
By the grave and stern decorum of the countenance it wore,
"Though thy crest be shorn and shaven, thou," I said, "art sure
    no craven,                                        45
Ghastly grim and ancient Raven, wandering from the nightly
    shore—
Tell me what thy lordly name is on the Night's Plutonian shore!"
    Quoth the Raven, "Nevermore."

Much I marveled this ungainly fowl to hear discourse so plainly,
Though its answer little meaning—little relevancy bore;       50
For we cannot help agreeing that no living human being
Ever yet was blessed with seeing bird above his chamber door—
Bird or beast upon the sculptured bust above his chamber door,
    With such name as "Nevermore."

But the Raven, sitting lonely on the placid bust, spoke only   55
That one word, as if his soul in that one word he did outpour.
Nothing further then he uttered, not a feather then he fluttered;
Till I scarcely more than muttered, "Other friends have flown before:
On the morrow *he* will leave me, as my hopes have flown before."
    Then the bird said, "Nevermore."                  60

Startled at the stillness broken by reply so aptly spoken,
"Doubtless," said I, "what it utters is its only stock and store,
Caught from some unhappy master whom unmerciful Disaster
Followed fast and followed faster till his songs one burden bore,
Till the dirges of his hope that melancholy burden bore        65
    Of 'Never—nevermore.' "

But the Raven still beguiling my sad fancy into smiling,

Straight I wheeled a cushioned seat in front of bird and bust and door;
Then, upon the velvet sinking, I betook myself to linking
Fancy unto fancy, thinking what this ominous bird of yore,                70
What this grim, ungainly, ghastly, gaunt, and ominous bird of yore
    Meant in croaking "Nevermore."

This I sat engaged in guessing, but no syllable expressing
To the fowl, whose fiery eyes now burned into my bosom's core;
This and more I sat divining, with my head at ease reclining            75
On the cushion's velvet lining that the lamplight gloated o'er,
But whose velvet violet lining with the lamplight gloating o'er,
    *She* shall press, ah, nevermore!

Then, methought, the air grew denser, perfumed from an unseen censer
Swung by seraphim whose foot-falls tinkled on the tufted floor.         80
"Wretch," I cried, "thy God hath lent thee—by these angels he
    hath sent thee
Respite—respite and nepenthe from thy memories of Lenore!
Quaff, oh quaff this kind nepenthe, and forget this lost Lenore!"
    Quoth the Raven, "Nevermore."

"Prophet!" said I, "thing of evil! prophet still, if bird or devil!     85
Whether Tempter sent, or whether tempest tossed thee here ashore,
Desolate yet all undaunted, on this desert land enchanted—
On this home by Horror haunted—tell me truly, I implore:
Is there—*is* there balm in Gilead?—tell me—tell me, I implore!"
    Quoth the Raven, "Nevermore."                    90

"Prophet!" said I, "thing of evil! prophet still, if bird or devil!
By that Heaven that bends above us—by that God we both adore,
Tell this soul with sorrow laden if, within the distant Aidenn,
It shall clasp a sainted maiden whom the angels name Lenore—
Clasp a rare and radiant maiden whom the angels name Lenore"            95
    Quoth the Raven, "Nevermore."

"Be that word our sign of parting, bird or fiend!" I shrieked, upstarting:
"Get thee back into the tempest and the Night's Plutonian shore!
Leave no black plume as a token of that lie thy soul hath spoken!
Leave my loneliness unbroken! quit the bust above my door!             100
Take thy beak from out my heart, and take thy form from off my door!"
    Quoth the Raven, "Nevermore."

And the Raven, never flitting, still is sitting, still is sitting
On the pallid bust of Pallas just above my chamber door;
And his eyes have all the seeming of a demon's that is dreaming,       105
And the lamp-light o'er him streaming throws his shadow on the floor;
And my soul from out that shadow that lies floating on the floor
    Shall be lifted—nevermore!

# The Philosophy of Composition

Charles Dickens, in a note now lying before me, alluding to an examination I once made of the mechanism of "Barnaby Rudge," says— "By the way, are you aware that Godwin wrote his 'Caleb Williams' backwards? He first involved his hero in a web of difficulties, forming the second volume, and then, for the first, cast about him for some mode of accounting for what had been done."

I cannot think this the *precise* mode of procedure on the part of Godwin—and indeed what he himself acknowledges, is not altogether in accordance with Mr. Dickens' idea—but the author of "Caleb Williams" was too good an artist not to perceive the advantage derivable from at least a somewhat similiar process. Nothing is more clear than that every plot, worth the name, must be elaborated to its *dénouement* before anything be attempted with the pen. It is only with the *dénouement* constantly in view that we can give a plot its indispensable air of consequence, or causation, by making the incidents, and especially the tone at all points, tend to the development of the intention.

There is a radical error, I think, in the usual mode of constructing a story. Either history affords a thesis—or one is suggested by an incident of the day—or, at best, the author sets himself to work in the combination of striking events to form merely the basis of his narrative—designing, generally, to fill in with description, dialogue, or authorial comment, whatever crevices of fact, or action, may, from page to page, render themselves apparent.

I prefer commencing with the consideration of an *effect*. Keeping originality *always* in view—for he is false to himself who ventures to dispense with so obvious and so easily attainable a source of interest—I say to myself, in the first place, "Of the innumerable effects, or impressions, of which the heart, the intellect, or (more generally) the soul is susceptible, what one shall I, on the present occasion select?" Having chosen a novel, first, and secondly a vivid effect, I consider whether it can be best wrought by incident or tone—whether by ordinary incidents and peculiar tone, or the converse, or by peculiarity both of incident and tone—afterward looking about me (or rather within) for such combinations of event, or tone, as shall best aid me in the construction of the effect.

I have often thought how interesting a magazine paper might be written by any author who would—that is to say who could—detail, step by step, the processes by which any one of his compositions attained its ultimate point of completion. Why such a paper has never been given to the world, I am much at a loss to say—but, perhaps, the authorial vanity has had more to do with the omission than any one other cause. Most

writers—poets in especial—prefer having it understood that they compose by a species of fine frenzy—an ecstatic intuition—and would positively shudder at letting the public take a peep behind the scenes, at the elaborate and vacillating crudities of thought—at the true purposes seized only at the last moment—at the innumerable glimpses of idea that arrived not at the maturity of full view—at the fully matured fancies discarded in despair as unmanageable—at the cautious selections and rejections—at the painful erasures and interpolations—in a word, at the wheels and pinions—the tackle for scene-shifting—the step-ladders and demon-traps—the cock's feathers, the red paint and the black patches, which, in ninety-nine cases out of a hundred, constitute the properties of the literary *histrio*.

I am aware, on the other hand, that the case is by no means common, in which an author is at all in condition to retrace the steps by which his conclusions have been attained. In general, suggestions, having arisen pell-mell, are pursued and forgotten in a similar manner.

For my own part, I have neither sympathy with the repugnance alluded to, nor, at any time the least difficulty in recalling to mind the progressive steps of any of my compositions; and, since the interest of an analysis, or reconstruction, such as I have considered a *desideratum,* is quite independent of any real or fancied interest in the thing analyzed, it will not be regarded as a breach of decorum on my part to show the *modus operandi* by which some one of my own works was put together. I select "The Raven," as most generally known. It is my design to render it manifest that no one point in its composition is referrible either to accident or intuition—that the work proceeded, step by step, to its completion with the precision and rigid consequence of a mathematical problem.

Let us dismiss, as irrelevant to the poem, *per se,* the circumstance—or say the necessity—which, in the first place, gave rise to the intention of composing *a* poem that should suit at once the popular and the critical taste.

We commence, then, with this intention.

The initial consideration was that of extent. If any literary work is too long to be read at one sitting, we must be content to dispense with the immensely important effect derivable from unity of impression—for, if two sittings be required, the affairs of the world interfere, and every thing like totality is at once destroyed. But since, *ceteris paribus,* no poet can afford to dispense with *any thing* that may advance his design, it but remains to be seen whether there is, in extent, any advantage to counterbalance the loss of unity which attends it. Here I say no, at once. What we term a long poem is, in fact, merely a succession of brief ones—that is to say, of brief poetical effects. It is needless to demonstrate that a poem is such, only inasmuch as it intensely excites, by elevating, the soul; and all intense excitements are, through a psychal necessity, brief. For this reason, at least one half of the "Paradise Lost" is essentially prose—a succession of poetical excitements interspersed, *inevitably,* with corresponding depressions—the

whole being deprived, through the extremeness of its length, of the vastly important artistic element, totality, or unity, of effect.

It appears evident, then, that there is a distinct limit, as regards length, to all works of literary art—the limit of a single sitting—and that, although in certain classes of prose composition, such as "Robinson Crusoe," (demanding no unity,) this limit may be advantageously overpassed, it can never properly be overpassed in a poem. Within this limit, the extent of a poem may be made to bear mathematical relation to its merit—in other words, to the excitement or elevation—again in other words, to the degree of the true poetical effect which it is capable of inducing; for it is clear that the brevity must be in direct ratio of the intensity of the intended effect:—this, with one proviso—that a certain degree of duration is absolutely requisite for the production of any effect at all.

Holding in view these considerations, as well as that degree of excitement which I deemed not above the popular, while not below the critical taste, I reached at once what I conceived the proper *length* for my intended poem—a length of about one hundred lines. It is, in fact, a hundred and eight.

My next thought concerned the choice of an impression, or effect, to be conveyed: and here I may as well observe that, throughout the construction, I kept steadily in view the design of rendering the work *universally* appreciable. I should be carried too far out of my immediate topic were I to demonstrate a point upon which I have repeatedly insisted, and which, with the poetical, stands not in the slightest need of demonstration—the point, I mean, that Beauty is the sole legitimate province of the poem. A few words, however, in elucidation of my real meaning, which some of my friends have evinced a disposition to misrepresent. That pleasure which is at once the most intense, the most elevating, and the most pure, is, I believe, found in the contemplation of the beautiful. When, indeed, men speak of Beauty, they mean, precisely, not a quality, as is supposed, but an effect—they refer, in short, just to that intense and pure elevation of *soul—not* of intellect, or of heart—upon which I have commented, and which is experienced in consequence of contemplating "the beautiful." Now I designate Beauty as the province of the poem, merely because it is an obvious rule of Art that effects should be made to spring from direct causes—that objects should be attained through means best adapted for their attainment—no one as yet having been weak enough to deny that the peculiar elevation alluded to is *most readily* attained in the poem. Now the object Truth, or the satisfaction of the intellect, and the object Passion, or the excitement of the heart, are, although attainable, to a certain extent, in poetry, far more readily attainable in prose. Truth, in fact, demands a precision, and Passion a *homeliness* (the truly passionate will comprehend me) which are absolutely antagonistic to that Beauty which, I maintain, is the excitement, or pleasurable elevation, of the soul. It by no means

follows from any thing here said, that passion, or even truth, may not be introduced, and even profitably introduced, into a poem—for they may serve in elucidation, or aid the general effect, as do discords in music, by contrast—but the true artist will always contrive, first, to tone them into proper subservience to the predominant aim, and, secondly, to enveil them, as far as possible, in that Beauty which is the atmosphere and the essence of the poem.

Regarding, then, Beauty as my province, my next question referred to the *tone* of its highest manifestation—and all experience has shown that this tone is one of *sadness*. Beauty of whatever kind, in its supreme development, invariably excites the sensitive soul to tears. Melancholy is thus the most legitimate of all the poetical tones.

The length, the province, and the tone, being thus determined, I betook myself to ordinary induction, with the view of obtaining some artistic piquancy which might serve me as a key-note in the construction of the poem—some pivot upon which the whole structure might turn. In carefully thinking over all the usual artistic effects—or more properly *points,* in the theatrical sense—I did not fail to perceive immediately that no one had been so universally employed as that of the *refrain.* The universality of its employment sufficed to assure me of its intrinsic value, and spared me the necessity of submitting it to analysis. I considered it, however, with regard to its susceptibility of improvement, and soon saw it to be in a primitive condition. As commonly used, the *refrain,* or burden, not only is limited to lyric verse, but depends for its impression upon the force of monotone—both in sound and thought. The pleasure is deduced solely from the sense of identity—of repetition. I resolved to diversify, and so heighten, the effect, by adhering, in general, to the monotone of sound, while I continually varied that of thought: that is to say, I determined to produce continuously novel effects, by the variation *of the application* of the *refrain*—the *refrain* itself remaining, for the most part, unvaried.

These points being settled, I next bethought me of the *nature* of my refrain. Since its application was to be repeatedly varied, it was clear that the *refrain* itself must be brief, for there would have been an insurmountable difficulty in frequent variations of application in any sentence of length. In proportion to the brevity of the sentence, would, of course, be the facility of the variation. This led me at once to a single word as the best *refrain.*

The question now arose as to the *character* of the word. Having made up my mind to a *refrain,* the division of the poem into stanzas was, of course, a corollary: the *refrain* forming the close of each stanza. That such a close, to have force, must be sonorous and susceptible of protracted emphasis, admitted no doubt: and these considerations inevitably led me to the long *o* as the most sonorous vowel, in connection with *r* as the most producible consonant.

The sound of the *refrain* being thus determined, it became necessary to select a word embodying this sound, and at the same time in the fullest possible keeping with that melancholy which I had predetermined as the tone of the poem. In such a search it would have been absolutely impossible to overlook the word "Nevermore." In fact, it was the very first which presented itself.

The next *desideratum* was a pretext for the continuous use of the one word "nevermore." In observing the difficulty which I at once found in inventing a sufficiently plausible reason for its continuous repetition, I did not fail to perceive that this difficulty arose solely from the pre-assumption that the word was to be so continuously or monotonously spoken by a *human* being—I did not fail to perceive, in short, that the difficulty lay in the reconciliation of this monotony with the exercise of reason on the part of the creature repeating the word. Here, then, immediately arose the idea of a *non*-reasoning creature capable of speech; and, very naturally, a parrot, in the first instance, suggested itself, but was superseded forthwith by a Raven, as equally capable of speech, and infinitely more in keeping with the intended *tone*.

I had now gone so far as the conception of a Raven—the bird of ill omen—monotonously repeating the one word, "Nevermore," at the conclusion of each stanza, in a poem of melancholy tone, and in length about one hundred lines. Now, never losing sight of the object *supremeness,* or perfection, at all points, I asked myself—"Of all melancholy topics, what, according to the *universal* understanding of mankind, is the *most* melancholy?" Death—was the obvious reply. "And when," I said, "is this most melancholy of topics most poetical?" From what I have already explained at some length, the answer, here also, is obvious—"When it most closely allies itself to *Beauty:* the death, then, of a beautiful woman is, unquestionably, the most poetical topic in the world—and equally is it beyond doubt that the lips best suited for such topic are those of a bereaved lover."

I had now to combine the two ideas, of a lover lamenting his deceased mistress and a Raven continuously repeating the word "Nevermore."—I had to combine these, bearing in mind my design of varying, at every turn, the *application* of the word repeated; but the only intelligible mode of such combination is that of imagining the Raven employing the word in answer to the queries of the lover. And here it was that I saw at once the opportunity afforded for the effect on which I had been depending—that is to say, the effect of the *variation of application.* I saw that I could make the first query propounded by the lover—the first query to which the Raven should reply "Nevermore"—that I could make this first query a commonplace one—the second less so—the third still less, and so on—until at length the lover, startled from his original *nonchalance* by the melancholy character of the word itself—by its frequent repetition—and by a consideration of the ominous reputation of the fowl that uttered it—is at length

excited to superstition, and wildly propounds queries of a far different character—queries whose solution he had passionately at heart—propounds them half in superstition and half in that species of despair which delights in self-torture—propounds them not altogether because he believes in the prophetic or demoniac character of the bird (which, reason assures him, is merely repeating a lesson learned by rote) but because he experiences a phrenzied pleasure in so modeling his questions as to receive the most intolerable of sorrow. Perceiving the opportunity thus afforded me—or, more strictly, thus forced upon me in the progress of the construction—I first established in mind the climax, or concluding query—that query to which "Nevermore" should be in the last place an answer—that in reply to which this word "Nevermore" should involve the utmost conceivable amount of sorrow and despair.

Here then the poem may be said to have its beginning—at the end, where all works of art should begin—for it was here, at this point of my preconsiderations, that I first put pen to paper in the composition of the stanza:

> "Prophet," said I, "thing of evil! prophet still if bird or devil!
> By that heaven that bends above us—by that God we both adore,
> Tell this soul with sorrow laden, if within the distant Aidenn,
> It shall clasp a sainted maiden whom the angels name Lenore—
> Clasp a rare and radiant maiden whom the angels name Lenore."
> Quoth the raven, "Nevermore."

I composed this stanza, at this point, first that, by establishing the climax, I might the better vary and graduate, as regards seriousness and importance, the preceding queries of the lover—and, secondly, that I might definitely settle the rhythm, the metre, and the length and general arrangement of the stanza—as well as graduate the stanzas which were to precede, so that none of them might surpass this in rhythmical effect. Had I been able, in the subsequent composition, to construct more vigorous stanzas, I should, without scruple, have purposely enfeebled them, so as not to interfere with the climacteric effect.

And here I may as well say a few words of the versification. My first object (as usual) was originality. The extent to which this has been neglected, in versification, is one of the most unaccountable things in the world. Admitting that there is little possibility of variety in mere *rhythm,* it is still clear that the possible varieties of metre and stanza are absolutely infinite—and yet, *for centuries, no man, in verse, has ever done, or ever seemed to think of doing, an original thing.* The fact is, that originality (unless in minds of very unusual force) is by no means a matter, as some suppose, of impulse or intuition. In general, to be found, it must be elaborately sought, and although a positive merit of the highest class, demands in its attainment less of invention than negation.

Of course, I pretend to no originality in either the rhythm or metre of the "Raven." The former is trochaic—the latter is octameter acatalectic, alternating with heptameter catalectic repeated in the *refrain* of the fifth verse, and terminating with tetrameter catalectic. Less pedantically—the feet employed throughout (trochees) consist of a long syllable followed by a short: the first line of the stanza consists of eight of these feet—the second of seven and a half (in effect two-thirds)—the third of eight—the fourth of seven and a half—the fifth the same—the sixth three and a half. Now, each of these lines, taken individually, has been employed before, and what originality the "Raven" has, is in their *combination into stanza;* nothing even remotely approaching this combination has ever been attempted. The effect of this originality of combination is aided by other unusual, and some altogether novel effects, arising from an extension of the application of the principles of rhyme and alliteration.

The next point to be considered was the mode of bringing together the lover and the Raven—and the first branch of this consideration was the *locale*. For this the most natural suggestion might seem to be a forest, or the fields—but it has always appeared to me that a close *circumscription of space* is absolutely necessary to the effect of insulated incident:—it has the force of a frame to a picture. It has an indisputable moral power in keeping concentrated the attention, and, of course, must not be confounded with mere unity of place.

I determined, then, to place the lover in his chamber—in a chamber rendered sacred to him by memories of her who had frequented it. The room is represented as richly furnished—this in mere pursuance of the ideas I have already explained on the subject of Beauty, as the sole true poetical thesis.

The *locale* being thus determined, I had now to introduce the bird— and the thought of introducing him through the window, was inevitable. The idea of making the lover suppose, in the first instance, that the flapping of the wings of the bird against the shutter, is a "tapping" at the door, originated in a wish to increase, by prolonging, the reader's curiosity, and in a desire to admit the incidental effect arising from the lover's throwing open the door, finding all dark, and thence adopting the half-fancy that it was the spirit of his mistress that knocked.

I made the night tempestuous, first, to account for the Raven's seeking admission, and secondly, for the effect of contrast with the (physical) serenity within the chamber.

I made the bird alight on the bust of Pallas, also for the effect of contrast between the marble and the plumage—it being understood that the bust was absolutely *suggested* by the bird—the bust of *Pallas* being chosen, first, as most in keeping with the scholarship of the lover, and, secondly, for the sonorousness of the word, Pallas, itself.

About the middle of the poem, also, I have availed myself of the

force of contrast, with a view of deepening the ultimate impression. For example, an air of the fantastic—approaching as nearly to the ludicrous as was admissible—is given to the Raven's entrance. He comes in "with many a flirt and flutter."

> Not the *least obeisance made he*—not a moment stopped or stayed he,
> *But with mien of lord or lady,* perched above my chamber door.

In the two stanzas which follow, the design is more obviously carried out:—

> Then this ebony bird beguiling my sad fancy into smiling
> By the *grave and stern decorum of the countenance it wore,*
> "Though thy *crest be shorn and shaven* thou," I said, "art sure no
>      craven,
> Ghastly grim and ancient Raven wandering from the nightly shore—
> Tell me what thy lordly name is on the Night's Plutonian shore?"
>      Quoth the Raven, "Nevermore."

> Much I marvelled *this ungainly fowl* to hear discourse so plainly
> Though its answer little meaning—little relevancy bore;
> For we cannot help agreeing that no living human being
> *Ever yet was blessed with seeing bird above his chamber door—*
> *Bird or beast upon the sculptured bust above his chamber door,*
>      With such name as "Nevermore."

The effect of the *dénouement* being thus provided for, I immediately drop the fantastic for a tone of the most profound seriousness:—this tone commencing in the stanza directly following the one last quoted, with the line,

> But the Raven, sitting lonely on that placid bust, spoke only, etc.

From this epoch the lover no longer jests—no longer sees any thing even of the fantastic in the Raven's demeanor. He speaks of him as a "grim, ungainly, ghastly, gaunt, and ominous bird of yore," and feels the "fiery eyes" burning into his "bosom's core." This revolution of thought, or fancy, on the lover's part, is intended to induce a similar one on the part of the reader—to bring the mind into a proper frame for the *dénouement*—which is now brought about as rapidly and as *directly* as possible.

With the *dénouement* proper—with the Raven's reply, "Nevermore," to the lover's final demand if he shall meet his mistress in another world—the poem, in its obvious phase, that of a simple narrative, may be said to have its completion. So far, every thing is within the limits of the accountable—of the real. A raven, having learned by rote the single word "Nevermore," and having escaped from the custody of its owner, is driven at midnight, through the violence of a storm, to seek admission at a window from which a light still gleams—the chamber-window of a student, oc-

cupied half in poring over a volume, half in dreaming of a beloved mistress deceased. The casement being thrown open at the fluttering of the bird's wing, the bird itself perches on the most convenient seat out of the immediate reach of the student, who, amused by the incident and the oddity of the visitor's demeanor, demands of it, in jest and without looking for a reply, its name. The raven addressed, answers with its customary word, "Nevermore"—a word which finds immediate echo in the melancholy heart of the student, who, giving utterance aloud to certain thoughts suggested by the occasion, is again startled by the fowl's repetition of "Nevermore." The student now guesses the state of the case, but is impelled, as I have before explained, by the human thirst for self-torture, and in part by superstition, to propound such queries to the bird as will bring him, the lover, the most of the luxury of sorrow, through the anticipated answer "Nevermore." With the indulgence, to the extreme, of this self-torture, the narration, in what I have termed its first obvious phase, has a natural termination, and so far there has been no overstepping of the limits of the real.

But in subjects so handled, however skillfully, or with however vivid an array of incident, there is always a certain hardness or nakedness, which repels the artistical eye. Two things are invariably required—first, some amount of complexity, or more properly, adaptation; and, secondly, some amount of suggestiveness—some under-current, however indefinite, of meaning. It is this latter, in especial, which imparts to a work of art so much of that *richness* (to borrow from colloquy a forcible term) which we are too fond of confounding with *the ideal*. It is the excess of the suggested meaning—it is the rendering this the upper instead of the under current of the theme—which turns into prose (and that of the very flattest kind) the so called poetry of the so called transcendentalists.

Holding these opinions, I added the two concluding stanzas of the poem—their suggestiveness being thus made to pervade all the narrative which has preceded them. The under-current of meaning is rendered first apparent in the lines—

"Take thy beak from out *my heart,* and take thy form from off my
   door!"
Quoth the Raven, "Nevermore!"

It will be observed that the words, "from out my heart," involve the first metaphorical expression in the poem. They, with the answer, "Nevermore," dispose the mind to seek a moral in all that has been previously narrated. The reader begins now to regard the Raven as emblematical—but it is not until the very last line of the very last stanza, that the intention of making him emblematical of *Mournful and Never-ending Remembrance* is permitted distinctly to be seen:

And the Raven, never flitting, still is sitting, still is sitting,
On the pallid bust of Pallas, just above my chamber door;
And his eyes have all the seeming of a demon's that is dreaming,
And the lamplight o'er him streaming throws his shadow on the floor;
And my soul *from out that shadow* that lies floating on the floor
    Shall be lifted—nevermore.


## TOPICS FOR DISCUSSION

1   Where in the introductory paragraphs is Poe's central thesis stated? How do all the aspects of composition which follow relate to this statement?

2   Distinguish among a poem, a long poem, and a brief poetical effect. Do these seem significant distinctions?

3   What is Poe's aim in poetry? How does this aim dictate the method of composition?

4   What do the following foreign words mean: *dénouement* (page 147, paragraph 2; page 154, paragraphs 3, 4, and 5); *histrio* (page 148, paragraph 1); *desideratum* (page 148, paragraph 3; page 152, paragraph 2); *modus operandi* (page 148, paragraph 3); *per se* (page 148, paragraph 4); *ceteris paribus* (page 148, paragraph 6); and *nonchalance* (page 151, paragraph 4)? Were they understandable in context? Could any *exact* English synonym have been substituted? How many of these words have been absorbed into the English language?

5   How is the philosophy of composition here presented adaptable to prose exposition? What elements are not relevant to exposition?

6   In what ways do Highet ("The First Few Words") and Poe appear to agree regarding the act of composition?


## ...AND COMPOSITION

7   Comment on the effect of "The Raven" on you, using the critical terms of Poe if you choose.

8   Write a paragraph using the word "nevermore" several times, aiming for the effect Poe achieved. Write another paragraph using the word "nevermore" achieving as contrary an effect as possible.

9   Compare the approaches to composition, with emphasis on language, of C. S. Lewis ("At the Fringe of Language") and Poe.

# The Making of a Poem

Why is it that nowadays, when poetry brings in little prestige and less
money, people are still found who devote their lives to the apparently
unrewarding occupation of making poems? Is the poet a quaint anachro-
nism in the modern world—a pathetic shadow of the primitive bard who,
unable for some reason to take active part in the life of his tribe, won
himself an honorable place in the community by singing of the exploits
of hunters and warriors?

Certainly a poem is still a cry from solitude, an attempt the poet has
made to break out of individual isolation and set down his experience in
such a way that it can be shared by his fellow beings. And he still uses the
power of incantation, of rhyme, rhythm and repetition, which the primitive
bard employed to bind the social group together in a common emotion.
But, while he is writing a poem, he is not aware of a need to communicate.
He has two conscious motives: to create an object in words, and to explore
reality and make sense of his own experience.

He wishes this object to be both self-contained and elegant—elegant
in the sense that a mathematician will call an equation "elegant." The
poem must stand up after the poet has got out from underneath it; it must
apply beyond the individual experience out of which it arose and carry
meaning beyond the poet's own time and social environment.

This durability can only be achieved through a special way of using
language. Deep thought and passionate feeling will not of themselves create
poetry. Poets are not philosophers, and good poems can be composed—
they usually are—from the commonplaces of human experience. The
poet's instrument is language and, unlike those of the scientist, it is not
an instrument of precision. He has to make something out of the words
we all use—out of the vague, stale, wasteful language of common speech.
He will do this, partly by the use of metaphor and image and partly by
concentration of language—the packing of the greatest possible amount of

meaning into the smallest possible space. When Marlowe's Faustus sees Helen, he cries out:

> Was this the face that launch'd a thousand ships,
> And burnt the topless towers of Ilium?

He is expressing the same emotion as the man who says, "That baby's got everything. I could go for her in a big way," but he is expressing it in an infinitely more concentrated, colourful and vital manner. Or again, when Robert Burns wrote

> Oh, wert thou in the cauld blast,
>     On yonder lea, on yonder lea;
> My plaidie to the angry airt,
>     I'd shelter thee, I'd shelter thee.

he made articulate, once and for all, through a simple picture given in the simplest words, the inarticulate tenderness of every lover wishing to protect his beloved.

The poet's medium is words, and his material is experience—his own states of mind or those of others into which he can sympathetically enter. He explores these states of mind, feeling his way with the sensitive instruments of his language. He may even, though he seldom consciously makes the poem for this purpose, change a state of mind by thus exploring and expressing it: a love lyric, an elegy, a satire will work out of his system, or at least temporarily assuage, the pangs of unrequited love, the weight of grief for a dead friend, the nagging heartburn of hatred.

As a poet grows older, his states of mind are likely to become more complex. That is why lyric poems—which are single-minded, single-mooded, transparent and uncomplicated—have mostly been written by young men; and for a similar reason, in our own elaborate civilization, pure lyric poetry has yielded place to a poetry of irony and complexity. Time, too, has changed the way poets think about their craft. On the whole, the classical poet would have claimed no more—though he often *did* much more—than that his poetry was an "imitation" of life, that he was representing reality, and in such a way as to give instruction through pleasure. Since the great romantics, poets have come to think of their work not as an imitation of reality, but as a re-creation of it. They seek to interpret reality by creating an object of a different order of reality.

The common factor between the classical and the post-classical poet is the imparting of knowledge. "Knowledge?" you may say. "But isn't that the province of the scientist nowadays?" Yes and no. Both science and poetry stem from magic, man's earliest method of trying to gain knowledge of Nature and power over it. The scientist and the poet are still concerned with the exploring of reality to that end. The poet's descriptions, unlike the scientist's, are not capable of proof, only of assent; but this does not mean that they are not contributions to knowledge. Let us take two

looks at the common wild daffodil; the first through the eyes of a botanist, the second through the eyes of Wordsworth.

> Narcissus, pseudo-narcissus: flower stalk hollow, two-edged, bearing near its summit a membranous sheath and a single flower; nectary notched and curled at the margin, as long as the sepals and petals.

> I wandered lonely as a cloud
> That floats on high, o'er vales and hills,
> When all at once I saw a crowd,
> A host of golden daffodils;
> Beside the lake, beneath the trees,
> Fluttering and dancing in the breeze.

The botanist distinguishes, classifies and generalizes: his description is objective; and it can be proved, for all daffodils of this kind will be found to conform to it. Wordsworth's description is of a different order. His lines make us say, "Yes, that's what daffodils look like," or, "Yes, that's what it feels like to look at daffodils." The poet describes objects in the light of his own feeling about them. "But what's this to do with knowledge?" you may argue. I should reply, "Enlightenment about one's own feelings is as valuable as any other knowledge."

Though the poet differs from the scientist in the method and field of his work, both start from one basic assumption—that there is pattern, or law, in the cosmos. A poem is a microcosm in which the apparent chaos of life is made manageable, given order and pattern. Both scientist and poet, therefore, are deeply concerned with relationships—the scientist objectively and the poet in the light of his own feelings. The poet, like the scientist, must try to see things as they really are; but nothing "really is" in isolation, pure and self-sufficient: reality involves relationship; and as soon as you have relationship, you have—for human beings—feeling. The poet cannot see things as they really are, cannot be precise about them, *unless he is precise about the feelings which attach him to them.*

This precision he achieves through image, metaphor, analogy and his special way of using language. But scientists, too, unless they can employ the language of mathematics, must often work by analogy and do often use metaphorical language. The poet Burns says,

> O, my Luve is like a red, red rose,
> That's newly sprung in June;

or Gerard Manley Hopkins says,

> O the mind, mind has mountains;
>     cliffs of fall
> Frightful, sheer, no-man-
>     fathomed,

to describe accurately the feeling of love or the feeling of spiritual despair.

"Let me compare my love to a June rose," Burns is in effect saying, "and see what follows." The natural philosopher Descartes did exactly the same. He proposed, "Let us compare the universe with a clock, and see where we go from there." And modern neurologists believe they may be able to learn from an automatic brain something about the workings of the human brain. This, too, is a method of analogy, an attempt to learn about the unknown through the known. We know what a June rose and a mountain precipice look like. So Burns and Hopkins use them to convey to us an exaltation of love, an abyss of despair, which we may have experienced but cannot ourselves express or even perhaps fully *know* till the "no-man-fathomed" experience has clothed itself in rose or precipice. So the word is made flesh.

The poet, then, like the experimental scientist, is an explorer. He needs to find things out for himself and record them. For him, as a poet, all human experience—however common, however trivial—is virgin soil; each poem is a fresh experiment in the chemistry of the human soul. How does he set about these experiments, these explorations which, like those of the land and sea discoverers, are so often gropings in the dark toward an unknown destination? I can only speak authoritatively for one poet—myself. But I believe many poets today would give a fairly similar account of what is involved in the making of a poem.

First, I do not sit down at my desk to put into verse something that is already clear in my mind. If it were clear in my mind, I should have no incentive or need to write about it, for I am an explorer, not a journalist, a propagandist or a statistician. For me a poem begins with a vague feeling, part excitement, part apprehension, which I can sometimes localize in my solar plexus. A feeling, it may be, comparable with that of a woman just before her confinement begins.

My poetry phases—I tend to write a good deal of verse for two years and for the next year or so to write none and have little desire to write any—are often preceded by some emotional churning-up. But the poems I write during these periods are not necessarily related to the cause of the disturbance. For instance, though I did write some "war poems" in 1939–45, the main effect upon me of the emotional disturbance of war was that, for the first time in my life, I was able to use in poetry my memories of childhood and adolescence. It was as though a seismic upheaval had thrown up to the surface of my mind strata of experience previously inaccessible to me as a poet.

During these creative phases I see the raw material of poems every-where; everything, around me or in my memory, assumes a sort of poetic potency, and I feel an intermittent but confident exhilaration. This mood of vague, undirected excitement will often throw up a line of poetry, which seems to come out of the blue. I brood upon this line, trying to discover in what direction it is pointing, to what experience it refers, and to what sort of poem it is a clue. During the war, for example, a line came into

my head—"the flags, the roundabouts, the gala day"—which turned out to be the germ of a sequence of nine sonnets about childhood and youth. This line, at the start, had the fascination of a riddle for me. Only gradually, meditating upon its quality of childish gusto and eager anticipation, did I realize what it was trying to tell me. Even a single word, "gala," helped. I had never heard this word used as an adjective except by my Irish relatives; and the sonnet in which that line was finally used contains also two key memories of my childhood days in Ireland.

Sometimes, of course, these clue lines or *données* emerge not quite out of the blue, but from some area of experience I am already preoccupied with. Recently, for instance, I had been thinking a lot about possessions— the way, in youth, some of us tend to be high-minded and haughty about our elders' love for acquiring objects, whereas when we ourselves grow older, our attitude changes and our material possessions become not merely status symbols but extensions and supports of our own personalities. These vague and far from original ruminations suddenly produced the phrase "streamlined whales and hulls." The phrase fairly rapidly developed into:

Think of streamlined whales and hulls
Accumulating barnacles
By moving long enough immersed
In their own element . . .

That original phrase directed my rather abstract thoughts about possessions into a marine allegory, *Travelling Light*. It also hinted at the right meter for the poem just as "the flags, the roundabouts, the gala day" had suggested the normal sonnet meter.

If I am lucky enough to be given such a clue line—this *donnée*, together with the initial excitement of conceiving a poem, are all that I personally understand by the word "inspiration"—I use it as a bait. That is to say, I drop it back into the unconscious, and in a state of "wise passivity" wait for what it may catch. Other phrases, images, ideas and associations attach themselves to the bait, and I carefully reel them in. Thus, gradually, the potential subject matter of a poem is accumulated. But much of it will have to be discarded and will not figure in the finished poem. The selection of material—the deciding what is and what is not finally relevant—will be done partly, as we shall see, by the form of the poem (Paul Valéry said that we use strict form in a poem so as to prevent ourselves "saying everything" in it), but chiefly by the theme.

The theme of a poem is the meaning of its subject matter for me. When I have discovered the meaning *to me* of the various fragments of experience which are constellating in my mind, I have begun to make sense of such experience and to realize a pattern in it; and often I have gone some way with a poem before I am able to grasp the theme which lies hidden in the material that has accumulated.

There is a parallel here with scientific discovery. The scientist has at

his disposal a mass of verified data. Out of the mass may emerge, through an imaginative leap of his mind, a hypothesis which relates all these data and makes sense of them. The scientist's hypothesis, if satisfactory, becomes a scientific "law." It is the equivalent of the poet's theme. At a certain crucial stage both poet and scientist are groping in the dark, hardly knowing—it may be—in what direction their data are tending, till a flash of imagination lights up the pattern for them. We have evidence, in the lives of the great scientific discoverers, how often this flash comes when the mind is asleep or occupied with other matters. But it would not have come, any more than a theme comes to the poet, without a great deal of preliminary work in the sifting and assessing of data and experience.

I would like to illustrate with a poem of mine called *The Gate*. It is one of several written in a state of creative exhilaration stimulated by my first visit to the United States a few years ago. I have chosen it partly because its data—which are all given in the first six lines of the poem— were apparently simple and straightforward and were already contained within a frame; for the poem arose out of a picture, painted by a friend of mine—a picture to which I responded with pleasure and excitement, but also with a sense that it held for me a special and mysterious meaning I must try to explore through poetry.

### The Gate

In the foreground, clots of cream-white flowers (meadowsweet?
Guelder? Cow parsley?) : a patch of green: then a gate
Dividing the green from a brown field; and beyond,
By steps of mustard and sainfoin-pink, the distance
Climbs right-handed away
Up to an olive hilltop and the sky.

The gate it is, dead-centre, ghost-amethyst-hued,
Fastens the whole together like a brooch.
It is all arranged, all there, for the gate's sake
Or for what may come through the gate. But those white flowers,
Craning their necks, putting their heads together,
Like a crowd that holds itself back from surging forward,
Have their own point of balance—poised, it seems,
On the airy brink of whatever it is they await.

And I, gazing over their heads from outside the picture,
Question what we are waiting for: not summer—
Summer is here in charlock, grass and sainfoin.
A human event? But there's no path to the gate,
Nor does it look as if it was meant to open.
The ghost of one who often came this way
When there was a path? I do not know. But I think,
If I could go deep into the heart of the picture

From the flowers' point of view, all I would ask is
Not that the gate should open, but that it should
Stay there, holding the coloured folds together.
We expect nothing (the flowers might add), we only
Await: this pure awaiting—
It is the kind of worship we are taught.

This poem was written more or less straight ahead. More often I compose a bit here, a bit there, like a painter. The first stanza objectively sets out the facts—the colour and detail of the pictured landscape. In the second stanza, the eye pans up to its dominant features—the flowers in the foreground and the gate in the center focusing the whole landscape together. At this point I still had no idea *why* the picture had such attractive mystery for me, or what it was trying to convey. However, in this second stanza I concentrated upon its main features subjectively—my sense that the whole picture was somehow there *for the sake of* the gate, the central mystery, and my sense that the foreground flowers stood in an attentive pose, waiting for something to happen.

But I still had not discovered the theme of the growing poem. So, in stanza three, I tried putting a number of questions to the picture. Just *what* are the flowers, and myself, the outside observer, waiting for? Several possible answers were given, and each of them in turn rejected; but the first seven lines of this stanza are constructed out of the several rejections, in such a way that their logical negatives create something emotionally positive. And then, at last, I saw what the landscape—and the poem—was saying to me. I saw it by moving from outside the picture and looking at the gate "from the flowers' point of view." In my tiny way I had done what Copernicus did when, with a superb imaginative leap, leaving the earth and placing himself in the sun, he found that the orbits of the planets looked simpler from that point of view.

What the picture was saying to me, I discovered, is first that the flowers expect nothing, their task being one of "pure awaiting," a kind of worship; and second, that they, and I, are not concerned with a divine revelation (the gate opening), but only that the gate should stay there—in other words, that we should retain the sense of some power at the center of things, holding them together. This idea had been foreshadowed (line eight) in purely visual or aesthetic terms. It was not till I reached the final stanza that I became aware of its deeper significance and realized that the poem was a religious poem. It is also obviously the poem of an agnostic— one who is, in a sense, "outside the picture"—but an agnostic whose upbringing was Christian. The "olive hilltop," with its echo of Mount Olivet, may conceivably have started the poem in the religious direction which, unforeseen by me, it was to take; and the "ghost-amethyst" colour of the gate certainly led me along to "The ghost of one who often came this way"—that is, the once-felt presence of deity in the human scene.

A few technical points: The poem has no end rhymes, but the two most important words in it rhyme and are repeated—"gate" six times and "wait" ("await," "awaiting") four times. The stanzas are carefully organized, the first corresponding metrically with the last, the second with the third. The pause between third and fourth stanza, which should be observed in reading the poem aloud, throws the greatest possible emphasis on "From the flowers' point of view," highlighting the change of position which is to reveal the theme. Finally, the rhythms are as flexible as I could make them, within a regular meter, so as to reflect the inquiring and tentative nature of the poem's thought process.

Talking about the poem in this detached way, I have given the impression perhaps that a poem "writes itself." Nothing could be further from the truth—in my case, at any rate. Certainly, in the first phase of composition, the "fishing" phase, the intellect is relatively inactive; one accepts, in a trancelike state, everything that comes up. But there follows a phase of the most arduous intellectual activity, when the gathered material has to be criticized in the light of the growing poem and of whatever inkling I may have about its theme. Since the two phases constantly overlap, it is almost impossible to give a blow-by-blow commentary on the making of a poem. All I can say is that my mind moves gradually over from passive to active, as it tries to perform the two functions of making and of exploring.

They are inseparable functions, because the technical patternmaking of the poem must go hand in hand and step by step with the search for a theme, the exploration of reality. What we aim at in pattern is a perfect consonance of image, rhythm and phrasing which will present the theme *whole,* with nothing irrelevant or superfluous, nothing diluted or scamped. A poem must indeed grow organically. I cannot tell *in advance* what shape it should take. But, once I have an idea of its shape, I must take great care in the shaping.

For this reason I find it particularly important to go slowly and tentatively in the early stages of composition, so as to avoid imposing the wrong shape on a poem—or, putting it another way, so as to keep open a number of avenues until I am fairly sure which is the right one for the poem to move along. Impatience, haste and glibness are great dangers to the poet who has acquired some technical facility, for they tempt him to let his poem take the easiest way—and this often turns out to be a blind alley. Just as an obstetrician may deliberately slow down a birth in the interests of the child, or a cook will keep a dish constantly stirred to prevent it "setting" too quickly, so I try to keep a poem in solution during the early stages. I have several expedients for this: composing the first draft in very small, faint pencil writing, for instance, and putting down a great number of alternative words, so that the whole thing looks tentative and provisional.

The dangers of haste, of letting a poem "set" too soon in a certain form, can be illustrated by *The New-Born,* which I wrote at the same

period as *The Gate*. Excited by the birth of my son, I jotted down some notes, as follows:

> Baby—blank sheet (heat) but invisible writing
> see here/original sin, eternal hope
> naked as a nut/castaway
> nine-month nonentity/this manikin.

Rashly and overconfidently I dashed on. The following lines, with a great many variations which I will not print, were produced:

> This manikin who just now
> Found his rough path into the world
> And as a perfect miniature lies unshelled
> From foot to brow
>
> Was but an hour ago
> A wish, a dread, a shape that we
> Had felt through its nine-month nonentity
> Quicken, and grow.
>
> Heaved hither on mounting waves
> Of agony, tossed up today
> On earth, he lies limp as a castaway
> And nothing craves
>
> But the long sleep birth ended. . . .

But there the poem stalled. It had been misfiring badly from the start—those stanzas are atrociously feeble—so there was nothing to do but get out, lift the hood and look for the cause of the trouble. I decided, eventually, that I had chosen the wrong form. I needed one which, because it was more elaborate, would help me to distance myself from my still raw paternal emotions. Perhaps if I replaced the four-line stanza with one of ten lines, in strict metrical form, would it do the trick? The first two stanzas now went much better:

> This manikin who just now
> Broke prison and stepped free
> Into his own identity—
> Hand, foot and brow
> A finished work, a breathing miniature—
> Was still, one night ago,
> A hope, a dread, a mere shape we
> Had lived with, only sure
> Something would grow
> Out of its coiled, nine-month nonentity.
>
> Heaved hither on quickening throes,
> Tossed up on earth today,
> He sprawls limp as a castaway

And nothing knows
Beside the warm sleep of his origin.
Soon lips and hands shall grope
To try the world, this speck of clay
And spirit shall begin
To feed on hope,
To learn how truth blows cold and loves betray.

By using a form technically much more difficult than the original one, I had made it easier for myself to discover exactly what I wanted to say and to get deeper into the experience I was writing about. For example, the last two lines of the first draft are evidently much inferior to "And nothing knows/Beside the warm sleep of his origin," which concentrates two ideas in one phrase—that the baby knows nothing *except* his sleep in the womb, and that he knows nothing as he lies there *at the side of* his sleeping mother.

A third stanza, in which I extended the metaphor of the baby as a blank sheet written over with invisible ink "Which the day's heat/Will show," also ran well. But then, to my consternation, the poem stalled again. It took me a long time to find out what was wrong. But at last I perceived that, half-consciously, I had been edging the poem in the direction of that preliminary note, "original sin, eternal hope." And I do not believe in original sin—or not positively enough to make it a theme of a poem. In trying to do so, I had been insincere, and properly punished for it. So I restarted at the point where I had broken down, and two more stanzas were added, beginning:

This morsel of man I've held—
What potency it has,
Though strengthless still and naked as
A nut unshelled!

I have been discussing the kind of poems in which, as a maker, one is at full stretch. After finishing such a poem I feel exhausted, as if I had solved a diabolically difficult puzzle—usually, looking back at the poem later, I see that I failed to solve it. But there are other levels of poetry, more superficial, yet not valueless, at which the poet can work; and again, working upon a relatively "light" poem, I have occasionally found myself breaking through to a level of deeper significance. What is essential is to develop the sort of tact or flair which enables one to know how much weight of meaning and how dense a verbal texture each incipient poem will bear, so that one neither overloads it nor underplays it. Each poet must learn to recognize his limitations, yet be able to seize the rare chance of being possessed by a spirit that transcends them and makes him write better than he knows how.

Each new poem I begin is an attempt at making and exploring. Each finished one is, in effect, a way of praising life, a sacrifice in life's honor.

I need devotion, discipline, sincerity, skill, and above all, patience, if the poem is to come to anything; but I also need something I cannot cultivate —call it luck. And when I see how rarely my own sacrifices are acceptable, I must say as I did in my poem, *Final Instructions:*

> You are called only to make the sacrifice:
> Whether or no he enters into it
> Is the god's affair; and whatever the handbooks say,
> You can neither command his presence nor explain it—
> All you can do is to make it possible.
> If the sacrifice catches fire of its own accord
> On the altar, well and good. But do not
> Flatter yourself that discipline and devotion
> Have wrought the miracle: they have only allowed it.

## TOPICS FOR DISCUSSION

1    Where in the introductory paragraphs does Lewis state directly his general thesis? What is this thesis?

2    Why does Lewis devote so much of his essay to a treatment of the similarity between scientific and poetic explorations of reality?

3    How is the personal account of Lewis's writing a reflection of poetry as an exploration of reality?

4    What are the stages of composition for Lewis? How do these correspond to those suggested by Poe?

5    What is a *donnée,* and how is it used?

6    On first reading did you find "The Gate" a religious poem? Did Lewis's explication convince you?

7    Why does the "technical patternmaking of the poem . . . go hand in hand and step by step with the search for a theme, the exploration of reality"?

## ...AND COMPOSITION

8    Introduce a problem as Lewis does, using only rhetorical questions.

9    Compare and contrast the steps in writing a poem described in the Poe and the Lewis selections.

10    Write your own commentary on "The Gate."

**HERMAN MELVILLE (1819–1891)** himself sailed the farthest seas and lived far out from the America his tame neighbors knew. And in his books the imaginative reach is even more impressive than any physical wandering. *Moby Dick* stands as one of the world's greatest books. The passage below demonstrates something of its intensity and ambition. Following this passage is a long, lyrical appreciation of the book by D. H. Lawrence, who saw in it a reflection of his own judgments on modern civilization.

# The Whiteness of the Whale

What the white whale was to Ahab, has been hinted; what, at times, he was to me, as yet remains unsaid.

Aside from those more obvious considerations touching Moby Dick, which could not but occasionally awaken in any man's soul some alarm, there was another thought, or rather vague, nameless horror concerning him, which at times by its intensity completely overpowered all the rest; and yet so mystical and well nigh ineffable was it, that I almost despair of putting it in a comprehensible form. It was the whiteness of the whale that above all things appalled me. But how can I hope to explain myself here; and yet, in some dim, random way, explain myself I must, else all these chapters might be naught.

Though in many natural objects, whiteness refiningly enhances beauty, as if imparting some special virtue of its own, as in marbles, japonicas, and pearls; and though various nations have in some way recognised a certain royal pre-eminence in this hue; even the barbaric, grand old kings of Pegu placing the title "Lord of the White Elephants" above all their other magniloquent ascriptions of dominion; and the modern kings of Siam unfurling the same snow-white quadruped in the royal standard; and the Hanoverian flag bearing the one figure of a snow-white charger; and the great Austrian Empire, Cæsarian, heir to overlording Rome, having for the imperial color the same imperial hue; and though this pre-eminence in it applies to the human race itself, giving the white man ideal mastership over every dusky tribe; and though, besides, all this whiteness has been even made significant of gladness, for among the Romans a white stone marked a joyful day; and though in other mortal sympathies and symbolizings, this same hue is made the emblem of many touching, noble things— the innocence of brides, the benignity of age; though among the Red Men of America the giving of the white belt of wampum was the deepest pledge of honor; though in many climes, whiteness typifies the majesty of Justice in the ermine of the Judge, and contributes to the daily state of kings and

queens drawn by milk-white steeds; though even in the higher mysteries of the most august religions it has been made the symbol of the divine spotlessness and power; by the Persian fire worshippers, the white forked flame being held the holiest on the altar; and in the Greek mythologies, Great Jove himself being made incarnate in a snow-white bull; and though to the noble Iroquois, the midwinter sacrifice of the sacred White Dog was by far the holiest festival of their theology, that spotless, faithful creature being held the purest envoy they could send to the Great Spirit with the annual tidings of their own fidelity; and though directly from the Latin word for white, all Christian priests derive the name of one part of their sacred vesture, the alb or tunic, worn beneath the cassock; and though among the holy pomps of the Romish faith, white is specially employed in the celebration of the Passion of our Lord; though in the Vision of St. John, white robes are given to the redeemed, and the four-and-twenty elders stand clothed in white before the great white throne, and the Holy One that sitteth there white like wool; yet for all these accumulated associations, with whatever is sweet, and honorable, and sublime, there yet lurks an elusive something in the innermost idea of this hue, which strikes more of panic to the soul than that redness which affrights in blood.

This elusive quality it is, which causes the thought of whiteness, when divorced from more kindly associations, and coupled with any object terrible in itself, to heighten that terror to the furthest bounds. Witness the white bear of the poles, and the white shark of the tropics; what but their smooth, flaky whiteness makes them the transcendent horrors they are? That ghastly whiteness it is which imparts such an abhorrent mildness, even more loathsome than terrific, to the dumb gloating of their aspect. So that not the fierce-fanged tiger in his heraldic coat can so stagger courage as the white-shrouded bear or shark.[1]

Bethink thee of the albatross, whence come those clouds of spiritual wonderment and pale dread, in which that white phantom sails in all

---

[1] With reference to the Polar bear, it may possibly be urged by him who would fain go still deeper into this matter, that it is not the whiteness, separately regarded, which heightens the intolerable hideousness of that brute; for, analysed, that heightened hideousness, it might be said, only rises from the circumstance, that the irresponsible ferociousness of the creature stands invested in the fleece of celestial innocence and love; and hence, by bringing together two such opposite emotions in our minds, the Polar bear frightens us with so unnatural a contrast. But even assuming all this to be true; yet, were it not for the whiteness, you would not have that intensified terror.

As for the white shark, the white gliding ghostliness of repose in that creature, when beheld in his ordinary moods, strangely tallies with the same quality in the Polar quadruped. This peculiarity is most vividly hit by the French in the name they bestow upon that fish. The Romish mass for the dead begins with "Requiem eternam" (eternal rest), whence *Requiem* denominating the mass itself, and any other funeral music. Now, in allusion to the white, silent stillness of death in this shark, and the mild deadliness of his habits, the French call him *Requin*.

imaginations? Not Coleridge first threw that spell; but God's great, un-flattering laureate, Nature.[2]

Most famous in our Western annals and Indian traditions is that of the White Steed of the Prairies; a magnificent milk-white charger, large-eyed, small-headed, bluff-chested, and with the dignity of a thousand monarchs in his lofty, overscorning carriage. He was the elected Xerxes of vast herds of wild horses, whose pastures in those days were only fenced by the Rocky Mountains and the Alleghanies. At their flaming head he westward trooped it like that chosen star which every evening leads on the hosts of light. The flashing cascade of his mane, the curving comet of his tail, invested him with housings more resplendent than gold and silver-beaters could have furnished him. A most imperial and archangelical apparition of that unfallen, western world, which to the eyes of the old trappers and hunters revived the glories of those primeval times when Adam walked majestic as a god, bluff-browed and fearless as this mighty steed. Whether marching amid his aides and marshals in the van of countless cohorts that endlessly streamed it over the plains, like an Ohio; or whether with his circumambient subjects browsing all around at the horizon, the White Steed gallopingly reviewed them with warm nostrils reddening through his cool milkiness; in whatever aspect he presented himself, always to the bravest Indians he was the object of trembling reverence and awe. Nor can it be questioned from what stands on legendary record

[2] I remember the first albatross I ever saw. It was during a prolonged gale, in waters hard upon the Antarctic seas. From my forenoon watch below, I ascended to the overclouded deck; and there, dashed upon the main hatches, I saw a regal, feathery thing of unspotted whiteness, and with a hooked, Roman bill sublime. At intervals, it arched forth its vast archangel wings, as if to embrace some holy ark. Wondrous flutterings and throbbings shook it. Though bodily unharmed, it uttered cries, as some king's ghost in supernatural distress. Through its inexpressible, strange eyes, methought I peeped to secrets which took hold of God. As Abraham before the angels, I bowed myself; the white thing was so white, its wings so wide, and in those for ever exiled waters, I had lost the miserable warping memories of traditions and of towns. Long I gazed at that prodigy of plumage. I cannot tell, can only hint, the things that darted through me then. But at last I awoke; and turning, asked a sailor what bird was this. A goney, he replied. Goney! I never had heard that name before; is it conceivable that this glorious thing is utterly unknown to men ashore! never! But some time after, I learned that goney was some seaman's name for albatross. So that by no possibility could Coleridge's wild Rhyme have had aught to do with those mystical impressions which were mine, when I saw that bird upon our deck. For neither had I then read the Rhyme, nor knew the bird to be an albatross. Yet, in saying this, I do but indirectly burnish a little brighter the noble merit of the poem and the poet.

I assert, then, that in the wondrous bodily whiteness of the bird chiefly lurks the secret of the spell; a truth the more evinced in this, that by a solecism of terms there are birds called grey albatrosses; and these I have frequently seen, but never with such emotion as when I beheld the Antarctic fowl.

But how had the mystic thing been caught? Whisper it not, and I will tell; with a treacherous hook and line, as the fowl floated on the sea. At last the Captain made a postman of it; tying a lettered, leathern tally round its neck, with the ship's time and place; and then letting it escape. But I doubt not, that leathern tally, meant for man, was taken off in Heaven, when the white fowl flew to join the wing-folding, the invoking, and adoring cherubim!

of this noble horse, that it was his spiritual whiteness chiefly, which so clothed him with divineness; and that this divineness had that in it which, though commanding worship, at the same time enforced a certain nameless terror.

But there are other instances where this whiteness loses all that accessory and strange glory which invests it in the White Steed and Albatross.

What is it that in the Albino man so peculiarly repels and often shocks the eye, as that sometimes he is loathed by his own kith and kin! It is that whiteness which invests him, a thing expressed by the name he bears. The Albino is as well made as other men—has no substantive deformity—and yet this mere aspect of all-pervading whiteness makes him more strangely hideous than the ugliest abortion. Why should this be so?

Nor, in quite other aspects, does Nature in her least palpable but not the less malicious agencies, fail to enlist among her forces this crowning attribute of the terrible. From its snowy aspect, the gauntleted ghost of the Southern Seas has been denominated the White Squall. Nor, in some historic instances, has the art of human malice omitted so potent an auxiliary. How wildly it heightens the effect of that passage in Froissart, when, masked in the snowy symbol of their faction, the desperate White Hoods of Ghent murder their bailiff in the market-place!

Nor, in some things, does the common, hereditary experience of all mankind fail to bear witness to the supernaturalism of this hue. It cannot well be doubted, that the one visible quality in the aspect of the dead which most appals the gazer, is the marble pallor lingering there; as if indeed that pallor were as much like the badge of consternation in the other world, as of mortal trepidation here. And from that pallor of the dead, we borrow the expressive hue of the shroud in which we wrap them. Nor even in our superstitions do we fail to throw the same snowy mantle round our phantoms; all ghosts rising in a milk-white fog—Yea, while these terrors seize us, let us add that even the king of terrors, when personified by the evangelist, rides on his pallid horse.

Therefore, in his other moods, symbolize whatever grand or gracious thing he will by whiteness, no man can deny that in its profoundest idealized significance it calls up a peculiar apparition to the soul.

But though without dissent this point be fixed, how is mortal man to account for it? To analyze it, would seem impossible. Can we, then, by the citation of some of those instances wherein this thing of whiteness—though for the time either wholly or in great part stripped of all direct associations calculated to import to it aught fearful, but nevertheless, is found to exert over us the same sorcery, however modified;—can we thus hope to light upon some chance clue to conduct us to the hidden cause we seek?

Let us try. But in a matter like this, subtlety appeals to subtlety, and

without imagination no man can follow another into these halls. And though, doubtless, some at least of the imaginative impressions about to be presented may have been shared by most men, yet few perhaps were entirely conscious of them at the time, and therefore may not be able to recall them now.

Why to the man of untutored ideality, who happens to be but loosely acquainted with the peculiar character of the day, does the bare mention of Whitsuntide marshal in the fancy such long, dreary, speechless processions of slow-pacing pilgrims, down-cast and hooded with new-fallen snow? Or to the unread, unsophisticated Protestant of the Middle American States, why does the passing mention of a White Friar or a White Nun, evoke such an eyeless statue in the soul?

Or what is there apart from the traditions of dungeoned warriors and kings (which will not wholly account for it) that makes the White Tower of London tell so much more strongly on the imagination of an untravelled American, than those other storied structures, its neighbors—the Byward Tower, or even the Bloody? And those sublimer towers, the White Mountains of New Hampshire, whence, in peculiar moods, comes that gigantic ghostliness over the soul at the bare mention of that name, while the thought of Virginia's Blue Ridge is full of a soft, dewy, distant dreaminess? Or why, irrespective of all latitudes and longitudes, does the name of the White Sea exert such a spectralness over the fancy, while that of the Yellow Sea lulls us with mortal thoughts of long lacquered mild afternoons on the waves, followed by the gaudiest and yet sleepiest of sunsets? Or, to choose a wholly unsubstantial instance, purely addressed to the fancy, why, in reading the old fairy tales of Central Europe, does "the tall pale man" of the Hartz forests, whose changeless pallor unrustlingly glides through the green of the groves—why is this phantom more terrible than all the whooping imps of the Blocksburg?

Nor is it, altogether, the remembrance of her cathedral-toppling earthquakes; nor the stampedoes of her frantic seas; nor the tearlessness of arid skies that never rain; nor the sight of her wide field of leaning spires, wrenched cope-stones, and crosses all adroop (like canted yards of anchored fleets); and her suburban avenues of house-walls lying over upon each other, as a tossed pack of cards;—it is not these things alone which make tearless Lima, the strangest, saddest city thou can'st see. For Lima has taken the white veil; and there is a higher horror in this whiteness of her woe. Old as Pizarro, this whiteness keeps her ruins for ever new; admits not the cheerful greenness of complete decay; spreads over her broken ramparts the rigid pallor of an apoplexy that fixes its own distortions.

I know that, to the common apprehension, this phenomenon of whiteness is not confessed to be the prime agent in exaggerating the terror of objects otherwise terrible; nor to the unimaginative mind is there aught of terror in those appearances whose awfulness to another mind almost solely

consists in this one phenomenon, especially when exhibited under any form at all approaching to muteness or universality. What I mean by these two statements may perhaps be respectively elucidated by the following examples.

First: The mariner, when drawing nigh the coasts of foreign lands, if by night he hear the roar of breakers, starts to vigilance, and feels just enough of trepidation to sharpen all his faculties; but under precisely similar circumstances, let him be called from his hammock to view his ship sailing through a midnight sea of milky whiteness—as if from encircling headlands shoals of combed white bears were swimming round him, then he feels a silent, superstitious dread; the shrouded phantom of the whitened waters is horrible to him as a real ghost; in vain the lead assures him he is still off soundings; heart and helm they both go down; he never rests till blue water is under him again. Yet where is the mariner who will tell thee, "Sir, it was not so much the fear of striking hidden rocks, as the fear of that hideous whiteness that so stirred me"?

Second: To the native Indian of Peru, the continual sight of the snow-howdahed Andes conveys naught of dread, except, perhaps, in the mere fancying of the eternal frosted desolateness reigning at such vast altitudes, and the natural conceit of what a fearfulness it would be to lose oneself in such inhuman solitude. Much the same is it with the backwoodsman of the West, who with comparative indifference views an unbounded prairie sheeted with driven snow, no shadow of tree or twig to break the fixed trance of whiteness. Not so the sailor, beholding the scenery of the Antarctic seas; where at times, by some infernal trick of legerdemain in the powers of frost and air, he, shivering and half shipwrecked, instead of rainbows speaking hope and solace to his misery, views what seems a boundless churchyard grinning upon him with its lean ice monuments and splintered crosses.

But thou sayest, methinks this white-lead chapter about whiteness is but a white flag hung out from a craven soul; thou surrenderest to a hypo, Ishmael.

Tell me, why this strong young colt, foaled in some peaceful valley of Vermont, far removed from all beasts of prey—why is it that upon the sunniest day, if you but shake a fresh buffalo robe behind him, so that he cannot even see it, but only smells its wild animal muskiness—why will he start, snort, and with bursting eyes paw the ground in phrensies of affright? There is no remembrance in him of any gorings of wild creatures in his green northern home, so that the strange muskiness he smells cannot recall to him anything associated with the experience of former perils; for what knows he, this New England colt, of the black bisons of distant Oregon?

No; but here thou beholdest even in a dumb brute, the instinct of the knowledge of the demonism in the world. Though thousands of miles from Oregon, still when he smells that savage musk, the rending, goring bison

herds are as present as to the deserted wild foal of the prairies, which this
instant they may be trampling into dust.

Thus, then, the muffled rollings of a milky sea; the bleak rustlings
of the festooned frosts of mountains; the desolate shiftings of the wind-
rowed snows of prairies; all these, to Ishmael, are as the shaking of that
buffalo robe to the frightened colt!

Though neither knows where lie the nameless things of which the
mystic sign gives forth such hints; yet with me, as with the colt, somewhere
those things must exist. Though in many of its aspects this visible world
seems formed in love, the invisible spheres were formed in fright.

But not yet have we solved the incantation of this whiteness, and
learned why it appeals with such power to the soul; and more strange and
far more portentous—why, as we have seen, it is at once the most meaning
symbol of spiritual things, nay, the very veil of the Christian's Deity; and
yet should be as it is, the intensifying agent in things the most appalling
to mankind.

Is it that by its indefiniteness it shadows forth the heartless voids and
immensities of the universe, and thus stabs us from behind with the
thought of annihilation, when beholding the white depths of the milky
way? Or is it, that as in essence whiteness is not so much a color as the
visible absence of color; and at the same time the concrete of all colors;
is it for these reasons that there is such a dumb blankness, full of meaning,
in a wide landscape of snows—a colorless, all-color of atheism from which
we shrink? And when we consider that other theory of the natural philosophers, that all other earthly hues—every stately or lovely emblazoning—
the sweet tinges of sunset skies and woods; yea, and the gilded velvets of
butterflies, and the butterfly cheeks of young girls; all these are but subtile
deceits, not actually inherent in substances, but only laid on from without;
so that all deified Nature absolutely paints like the harlot, whose allurements cover nothing but the charnel-house within; and when we proceed
further and consider that the mystical cosmetic which produces every one
of her hues, the great principle of light, for ever remains white or colorless
in itself, and if operating without medium upon matter, would touch all
objects, even tulips and roses, with its own blank tinge—pondering all this,
the palsied universe lies before us a leper; and like wilful travellers in
Lapland, who refuse to wear colored and coloring glasses upon their eyes,
so the wretched infidel gazes himself blind at the monumental white shroud
that wraps all the prospect around him. And of all these things the Albino
whale was the symbol. Wonder ye then at the fiery hunt?

TOPICS FOR DISCUSSION

1  Is it possible to define exactly what the whiteness of the whale means to Ishmael?

2  For what organizational reason are all the examples of the kindly aspects of whiteness strung out like a catalog in a single sentence in paragraph 3? What is gained by the heavy repetition of "though"?

3  In what way does the example of the Vermont colt come closest to being an exact definition?

4  What characteristics does "God's great, unflattering laureate, Nature," take on by the end of the chapter?

5  What is gained by the abundant use of the rhetorical question?

6  Why is "dumb blankness" the most appalling characteristic of all?

... AND COMPOSITION

7  What are all the connotations of the color red that come to your mind? Explore them and arrange them in climactic order of interest or of importance or of color intensity as you relate color intensity to connotation.

8  Imitate the following sentence: "What the white whale was to Ahab, has been hinted; what, at times, he was to me, as yet remains unsaid."

**D. H. LAWRENCE (1885–1930)** saw the twentieth century as blighted: machinery, mechanical thought, and grim purposes were killing the spirit in man. In letters, essays, short stories, books of travel, and novels he championed a full emotional life. His work partook of the new interest in psychology, the subconscious, the conviction that simple dominance over nature had isolated and endangered mankind. His commitment to emotion as guide, and in particular his direct treatment of sex, has made his work a center of lasting controversy. His independence, his headlong perceptivity and appreciation of vivid writers like Melville, and his constant linking of experience to the emotional concerns of modern man are displayed in the following essay.

# Herman Melville's Moby Dick

*Moby Dick, or the White Whale.*
A hunt. The last great hunt.
For what?
For Moby Dick, the huge white sperm whale: who is old, hoary, monstrous, and swims alone; who is unspeakably terrible in his wrath, having so often been attacked; and snow-white.
Of course he is a symbol.
Of what?
I doubt if even Melville knew exactly. That's the best of it.
He is warm-blooded, he is lovable. He is lonely Leviathan, not a Hobbes sort. Or is he?
But he is warm-blooded, and lovable. The South Sea Islanders, and Polynesians, and Malays, who worship shark, or crocodile, or weave endless frigate-bird distortions, why did they never worship the whale? So big!
Because the whale is not wicked. He doesn't bite. And their gods had to bite.
He's not a dragon. He is Leviathan. He never coils like the Chinese dragon of the sun. He's not a serpent of the waters. He is warm-blooded, a mammal. And hunted, hunted down.
It is a great book.
At first you are put off by the style. It reads like journalism. It seems spurious. You feel Melville is trying to put something over you. It won't do.
And Melville really is a bit sententious: aware of himself, self-conscious, putting something over even himself. But then it's not easy to get into the swing of a piece of deep mysticism when you just set out with a story.
Nobody can be more clownish, more clumsy and sententiously in bad taste, than Herman Melville, even in a great book like *Moby Dick*. He preaches and holds forth because he's not sure of himself. And he holds forth, often, so amateurishly.

The artist was so *much* greater than the man. The man is rather a tiresome New Englander of the ethical mystical-transcendentalist sort: Emerson, Longfellow, Hawthorne, etc. So unrelieved, the solemn ass even in humour. So hopelessly *au grand serieux,* you feel like saying: Good God, what does it matter? If life is a tragedy, or a farce, or a disaster, or anything else, what do I care! Let life be what it likes. Give me a drink, that's what I want just now.

For my part, life is so many things I don't care what it is. It's not my affair to sum it up. Just now it's a cup of tea. This morning it was wormwood and gall. Hand me the sugar.

One wearies of the *grand serieux*. There's something false about it. And that's Melville. Oh, dear, when the solemn ass brays! brays! brays!

But he was a deep, great artist, even if he was rather a sententious man. He was a real American in that he always felt his audience in front of him. But when he ceases to be American, when he forgets all audience, and gives us his sheer apprehension of the world, then he is wonderful, his book commands a stillness in the soul, an awe.

In his "human" self, Melville is almost dead. That is, he hardly reacts to human contacts any more: or only ideally: or just for a moment. His human-emotional self is almost played out. He is abstract, self-analytical and abstracted. And he is more spell-bound by the strange slidings and collidings of Matter than by the things men do. In this he is like Dana. It is the material elements he really has to do with. His drama is with them. He was a futurist long before futurism found paint. The sheer naked slidings of the elements. And the human soul experiencing it all. So often, it is almost over the border: psychiatry. Almost spurious. Yet so great.

It is the same old thing as in all Americans. They keep their old-fashioned ideal frock-coat on, and an old-fashioned silk hat, while they do the most impossible things. There you are: you see Melville hugged in bed by a huge tattooed South Sea Islander, and solemnly offering burnt offering to this savage's little idol, and his ideal frock-coat just hides his shirt-tails and prevents us from seeing his bare posterior as he salaams, while his ethical silk hat sits correctly over his brow the while. That is so typically American: doing the most impossible things without taking off their spiritual get-up. Their ideals are like armour which has rusted in, and will never more come off. And meanwhile in Melville his bodily knowledge moves naked, a living quick among the stark elements. For with sheer physical, vibrational sensitiveness, like a marvellous wireless-station, he registers the effects of the outer world. And he records also, almost beyond pain or pleasure, the extreme transitions of the isolated, far-driven soul, the soul which is now alone, without any real human contact.

The first days in New Bedford introduce the only human being who really enters into the book, namely, Ishmael, the "I" of the book. And then the moment's hearts-brother, Queequeg, the tattooed, powerful South

Sea harpooner, whom Melville loves as Dana loves "Hope." The advent of Ishmael's bedmate is amusing and unforgettable. But later the two swear "marriage," in the language of the savages. For Queequeg has opened again the flood-gates of love and human connection in Ishmael.

"As I sat there in that now lonely room, the fire burning low, in that mild stage when, after its first intensity has warmed the air, it then only glows to be looked at; the evening shades and phantoms gathering round the casements, and peering in upon us silent, solitary twain: I began to be sensible of strange feelings. I felt a melting in me. No more my splintered hand and maddened heart was turned against the wolfish world. This soothing savage had redeemed it. There he sat, his very indifference speaking a nature in which there lurked no civilized hypocrisies and bland deceits. Wild he was; a very sight of sights to see; yet I began to feel myself mysteriously drawn towards him."[1]—So they smoke together, and are clasped in each other's arms. The friendship is finally sealed when Ishmael offers sacrifice to Queequeg's little idol, Gogo.

"I was a good Christian, born and bred in the bosom of the infallible Presbyterian Church. How then could I unite with the idolater in worshipping his piece of wood? But what is worship?—to do the will of God— *that* is worship. And what is the will of God?—to do to my fellowman what I would have my fellowman do to me—*that* is the will of God."— Which sounds like Benjamin Franklin, and is hopelessly bad theology. But it is real American logic. "Now Queequeg is my fellowman. And what do I wish that this Queequeg would do to me. Why, unite with me in my particular Presbyterian form of worship. Consequently, I must unite with him; ergo, I must turn idolater. So I kindled the shavings; helped prop up the innocent little idol; offered him burnt biscuit with Queequeg; salaamed before him twice or thrice; kissed his nose; and that done, we undressed and went to bed, at peace with our own consciences and all the world. But we did not go to sleep without some little chat. How it is I know not; but there is no place like bed for confidential disclosures between friends. Man and wife, they say, open the very bottom of their souls to each other; and some old couples often lie and chat over old times till nearly morning. Thus, then, lay I and Queequeg—a cozy, loving pair—"

You would think this relation with Queequeg meant something to Ishmael. But no. Queequeg is forgotten like yesterday's newspaper. Human things are only momentary excitements or amusements to the American Ishmael. Ishmael, the hunted. But much more, Ishmael the hunter. What's a Queequeg? What's a wife? The white whale must be hunted down. Queequeg must be just "KNOWN," then dropped into oblivion.

And what in the name of fortune is the white whale?

---

[1] ED. NOTE: In his quotations in this essay, Lawrence has not always strictly followed Melville's text.

Elsewhere Ishmael says he loved Queequeg's eyes: "large, deep eyes, fiery black and bold." No doubt, like Poe, he wanted to get the "clue" to them. That was all.

The two men go over from New Bedford to Nantucket, and there sign on to the Quaker whaling ship, the *Pequod.* It is all strangely fantastic, phantasmagoric. The voyage of the soul. Yet curiously a real whaling voyage, too. We pass on into the midst of the sea with this strange ship and its incredible crew. The Argonauts were mild lambs in comparison. And Ulysses went *defeating* the Circes and overcoming the wicked hussies of the isles. But the *Pequod's* crew is a collection of maniacs fanatically hunting down a lonely, harmless white whale.

As a soul history, it makes one angry. As a sea yarn, it is marvellous: there is always something a bit over the mark, in sea yarns. Should be. Then again the masking up of actual seaman's experience with sonorous mysticism sometimes gets on one's nerves. And again, as a revelation of destiny the book is too deep even for sorrow. Profound beyond feeling.

You are some time before you are allowed to see the captain, Ahab: the mysterious Quaker. Oh, it is a God-fearing Quaker ship.

Ahab, the captain. The captain of the soul.

I am the master of my fate.
I am the captain of my soul!

Ahab!
"Oh, captain, my captain, our fearful trip is done."

The gaunt Ahab, Quaker, mysterious person, only shows himself after some days at sea. There's a secret about him? What?

Oh, he's a portentous person. He stumps about on an ivory stump, made from sea-ivory. Moby Dick, the great white whale, tore off Ahab's leg at the knee, when Ahab was attacking him.

Quite right, too. Should have torn off both his legs, and a bit more besides.

But Ahab doesn't think so. Ahab is now a monomaniac. Moby Dick is his monomania. Moby Dick must *die,* or Ahab can't live any longer. Ahab is atheist by this.

All right.

This *Pequod,* ship of the American soul, has three mates.

1  Starbuck: Quaker, Nantucketer, a good responsible man of reason, forethought, intrepidity, what is called a dependable man. At the bottom, *afraid.*
2  Stubb: "Fearless as fire, and as mechanical." Insists on being reckless and jolly on every occasion. Must be afraid too, really.
3  Flask: Stubborn, obstinate, without imagination. To him "the wondrous whale was but a species of magnified mouse, or water-rat——"

There you have them: a maniac captain and his three mates, three splendid seamen, admirable whalemen, first class men at their job.

America!

It is rather like Mr. Wilson and his admirable, "efficient" crew, at the Peace Conference. Except that none of the Pequodders took their wives along.

A maniac captain of the soul, and three eminently practical mates.

America!

Then such a crew. Renegades, castaways, cannibals: Ishmael, Quakers.

America!

Three giant harpooners, to spear the great white whale.

1   Queequeg, the South Sea Islander, all tattooed, big and powerful.
2   Tashtego, the Red Indian of the sea-coast, where the Indian meets the sea.
3   Daggoo, the huge black negro.

There you have them, three savage races, under the American flag, the maniac captain, with their great keen harpoons, ready to spear the *White* whale.

And only after many days at sea does Ahab's own boatcrew appear on deck. Strange, silent, secret, black-garbed Malays, fire-worshipping Parsees. These are to man Ahab's boat, when it leaps in pursuit of that whale.

What do you think of the ship *Pequod,* the ship of the soul of an American?

Many races, many peoples, many nations, under the Stars and Stripes. Beaten with many stripes.

Seeing stars sometimes.

And in a mad ship, under a mad captain, in a mad, fanatic's hunt.

For what?

For Moby Dick, the great white whale.

But splendidly handled. Three splendid mates. The whole thing practical, eminently practical in its working. American industry!

And all this practicality in the service of a mad, mad chase.

Melville manages to keep it a real whaling ship, on a real cruise, in spite of all fantastics. A wonderful, wonderful voyage. And a beauty that is so surpassing only because of the author's awful flounderings in mystical waters. He wanted to get metaphysically deep. And he got deeper than metaphysics. It is a surpassingly beautiful book. With an awful meaning. And bad jolts.

It is interesting to compare Melville with Dana, about the albatross. Melville a bit sententious.—"I remember the first albatross I ever saw. It was during a prolonged gale in waters hard upon the Antarctic seas. From my forenoon watch below I ascended to the over-crowded deck,

and there, lashed upon the main hatches, I saw a regal feathered thing of unspotted whiteness, and with a hooked Roman bill sublime. At intervals it arched forth its vast, archangel wings.—Wondrous throbbings and flutterings shook it. Though bodily unharmed, it uttered cries, as some King's ghost in supernatural distress. Through its inexpressible strange eyes methought I peeped to secrets now below the heavens—the white thing was so white, its wings so wide, and in those for ever exiled waters, I had lost the miserable warping memories of traditions and of towns.—I assert then, that in the wondrous bodily whiteness of the bird chiefly lurks the secret of the spell—"

Melville's albatross is a prisoner, caught by a bait on a hook.

Well, I have seen an albatross, too: following us in waters hard upon the Antarctic, too, south of Australia. And in the Southern winter. And the ship, a P. and O. boat, nearly empty. And the lascar crew shivering.

The bird with its long, long wings following, then leaving us. No one knows till they have tried, how lost, how lonely those Southern waters are. And glimpses of the Australian coast.

It makes one feel that our day is only a day. That in the dark of the night ahead other days stir fecund, when we have lapsed from existence.

Who knows how utterly we shall lapse.

But Melville keeps up his disquisition about "whiteness." The great abstract fascinated him. The abstract where we end, and cease to be. White or black. Our white, abstract end!

Then again it is lovely to be at sea on the *Pequod,* with never a grain of earth to us.

"It was a cloudy, sultry afternoon; the seamen were lazily lounging about the decks, or vacantly gazing over into the lead-coloured waters. Queequeg and I were mildly employed weaving what is called a sword-mat, for an additional lashing to our boat. So still and subdued and yet somehow preluding was all the scene, and such an incantation of reverie lurked in the air that each silent sailor seemed resolved into his own invisible self.—"

In the midst of this preluding silence came the first cry: "There she blows! there! there! there! She blows!"—And then comes the first chase, a marvellous piece of true sea-writing, the sea, and sheer sea-beings on the chase, sea-creatures chased. There is scarcely a taint of earth,—pure sea-motion.

" 'Give way men,' whispered Starbuck, drawing still further aft the sheet of his sail; 'there is time to kill fish yet before the squall comes. There's white water again!—Close to!—Spring!' Soon after, two cries in quick succession on each side of us denoted that the other boats had got fast; but hardly were they overheard, when with a lightning-like hurtling whisper Starbuck said: 'Stand up!' and Queequeg, harpoon in hand, sprang to his feet.—Though not one of the oarsmen was then facing the life and death peril so close to them ahead, yet their eyes on the intense

countenance of the mate in the stern of the boat, they knew that the imminent instant had come; they heard, too, an enormous wallowing sound, as of fifty elephants stirring in their litter. Meanwhile the boat was still booming through the mist, the waves curbing and hissing around us like the erected crests of enraged serpents.

" 'That's his hump. *There! There,* give it to him!' whispered Starbuck. —A short rushing sound leapt out of the boat; it was the darted iron of Queequeg. Then all in one welded motion came a push from astern, while forward the boat seemed striking on a ledge; the sail collapsed and exploded; a gush of scalding vapour shot up near by; something rolled and tumbled like an earthquake beneath us. The whole crew were half-suffocated as they were tossed helter-skelter into the white curling cream of the squall. Squall, whale, and harpoon had all blended together; and the whale, merely grazed by the iron, escaped—"

Melville is a master of violent, chaotic physical motion, he can keep up a whole wild chase without a flaw. He is as perfect at creating stillness. The ship is cruising on the Carrol Ground, south of St. Helena.—"It was while gliding through these latter waters that one serene and moonlight night, when all the waves rolled by like scrolls of silver; and by their soft, suffusing seethings, made what seemed a silvery silence, not a solitude; on such a silent night a silvery jet was seen far in advance of the white bubbles at the bow—"

Then there is the description of Brit. "Steering northeastward from the Crozello we fell in with vast meadows of brit, the minute, yellow substance upon which the right whale largely feeds. For leagues and leagues it undulated round us, so that we seemed to be sailing through boundless fields of ripe and golden wheat. On the second day, numbers of right whales were seen, secure from the attack of a sperm whaler like the *Pequod*. With open jaws they sluggishly swam through the brit, which, adhering to the fringed fibres of that wondrous Venetian blind in their mouths, was in that manner separated from the water that escaped at the lip. As moving mowers who, side by side, slowly and seethingly advance their scythes through the long wet grass of the marshy meads; even so these monsters swam, making a strange, grassy, cutting sound; and leaving behind them endless swaths of blue on the yellow sea. But it was only the sound they made as they parted the brit which at all reminded one of mowers. Seen from the mastheads, especially when they paused and were stationary for a while, their vast black forms looked more like masses of rock than anything else—"

This beautiful passage brings us to the apparition of the squid.

"Slowly wading through the meadows of brit, the *Pequod* still held her way northeastward towards the island of Java; a gentle air impelling her keel, so that in the surrounding serenity her three tall, tapering masts mildly waved to that languid breeze, as three mild palms on a plain. And

still, at wide intervals, in the silvery night, that lonely, alluring jet would be seen.

"But one transparent-blue morning, when a stillness almost preternatural spread over the sea, however unattended with any stagnant calm; when the long burnished sunglade on the waters seemed a golden finger laid across them, enjoining secrecy; when all the slippered waves whispered together as they softly ran on; in this profound hush of the visible sphere a strange spectre was seen by Daggoo from the mainmast head.

"In the distance, a great white mass lazily rose, and rising higher and higher, and disentangling itself from the azure, at last gleamed before our prow like a snow-slide, new slid from the hills. Thus glistening for a moment, as slowly it subsided, and sank. Then once more arose, and silently gleamed. It seemed not a whale; and yet, is this Moby Dick? thought Daggoo—"

The boats were lowered and pulled to the scene.

"In the same spot where it sank, once more it slowly rose. Almost forgetting for the moment all thoughts of Moby Dick, we now gazed at the most wondrous phenomenon which the secret seas have hitherto revealed to mankind. A vast pulpy mass, furlongs in length and breadth, of a glancing cream-colour, lay floating on the water, innumerable long arms radiating from its centre, and curling and twisting like a nest of anacondas, as if blindly to clutch at any hapless object within reach. No perceptible face or front did it have; no conceivable token of either sensation or instinct; but undulated there on the billows, an unearthly, formless, chance-like apparition of life. And with a low sucking it slowly disappeared again."

The following chapters, with their account of whale-hunts, the killing, the stripping, the cutting up, are magnificent records of actual happening. Then comes the queer tale of the meeting of the *Jeroboam,* a whaler met at sea, all of whose men were under the domination of a religious maniac, one of the ship's hands. There are detailed descriptions of the actual taking of the sperm oil from a whale's head. Dilating on the smallness of the brain of a sperm whale, Melville significantly remarks—"for I believe that much of a man's character will be found betokened in his backbone. I would rather feel your spine than your skull, whoever you are—" And of the whale, he adds:

"For, viewed in this light, the wonderful comparative smallness of his brain proper is more than compensated by the wonderful comparative magnitude of his spinal cord."

In among the rush of terrible, awful hunts come touches of pure beauty.

"As the three boats lay there on that gently rolling sea, gazing down into its eternal blue noon; and as not a single groan or cry of any sort, nay not so much as a ripple or a thought, came up from its depths; what lands-

man would have thought that beneath all that silence and placidity the utmost monster of the seas was writhing and wrenching in agony!"

Perhaps the most stupendous chapter is the one called *The Grand Armada,* at the beginning of Volume III. The *Pequod* was drawing through the Sunda Straits towards Java when she came upon a vast host of sperm whales. "Broad on both bows, at a distance of two or three miles, and forming a great semi-circle embracing one-half of the level horizon, a continuous chain of whale-jets were up-playing and sparkling in the noon-day air." Chasing this great herd, past the Straits of Sunda, themselves chased by Javan pirates, the whalers race on. Then the boats are lowered. At last that curious state of inert irresolution came over the whales, when they were, as the seamen say, gallied. Instead of forging ahead in huge martial array they swam violently hither and thither, a surging sea of whales, no longer moving on. Starbuck's boat, made fast to a whale, is towed in amongst this howling Leviathan chaos. In mad career it cockles through the boiling surge of monsters, till it is brought into a clear lagoon in the very centre of the vast, mad, terrified herd. There a sleek, pure calm reigns. There the females swam in peace, and the young whales came snuffing tamely at the boat, like dogs. And there the astonished seamen watched the love-making of these amazing monsters, mammals, now in rut far down in the sea.—"But far beneath this wondrous world upon the surface, another and still stranger world met our eyes, as we gazed over the side. For, suspended in these watery vaults, floated the forms of the nursing mothers of the whales, and those that by their enormous girth seemed shortly to become mothers. The lake, as I have hinted, was to a considerable depth exceedingly transparent; and as human infants while sucking will calmly and fixedly gaze away from the breast, as if leading two different lives at a time; and while yet drawing mortal nourishment, be still spiritually feasting upon some unearthly reminiscence, even so did the young of these whales seem looking up towards us, but not at us, as if we were but a bit of gulf-weed in their newborn sight. Floating on their sides, the mothers also seemed quietly eyeing us.—Some of the subtlest secrets of the seas seemed divulged to us in this enchanted pond. We saw young Leviathan amours in the deep. And thus, though surrounded by circle upon circle of consternation and affrights, did these inscrutable creatures at the centre freely and fearlessly indulge in all peaceful concernments; yea, serenely revelled in dalliance and delight—"

There is something really overwhelming in these whale-hunts, almost superhuman or inhuman, bigger than life, more terrific than human activity. The same with the chapter on ambergris: it is so curious, so real, yet so unearthly. And again in the chapter called *The Cassock*—surely the oddest piece of phallicism in all the world's literature.

After this comes the amazing account of the Try-works, when the

ship is turned into the sooty, oily factory in mid-ocean, and the oil is extracted from the blubber. In the night of the red furnace burning on deck, at sea, Melville has his startling experience of reversion. He is at the helm, but has turned to watch the fire: when suddenly he feels the ship rushing backward from him, in mystic reversion.—"Uppermost was the impression, that whatever swift, rushing thing I stood on was not so much bound to any haven ahead, as rushing from all havens astern. A stark, bewildered feeling, as of death, came over me. Convulsively my hands grasped the tiller, but with the crazy conceit that the tiller was, somehow, in some enchanted way, inverted. My God! What is the matter with me, I thought!"

This dream-experience is a real soul-experience. He ends with an injunction to all men, not to gaze on the red fire when its redness makes all things look ghastly. It seems to him that his gazing on fire has evoked this horror of reversion, undoing.

Perhaps it had. He was water-born.

After some unhealthy work on the ship, Queequeg caught a fever and was like to die.—"How he wasted and wasted in those few, long-lingering days, till there seemed but little left of him but his frame and tattooing. But as all else in him thinned, and his cheek-bones grew sharper, his eyes, nevertheless, seemed growing fuller and fuller; they took on a strangeness of lustre; and mildly but deeply looked out at you there from his sickness, a wondrous testimony to that immortal health in him which could not die, or be weakened. And like circles on the water, which, as they grow fainter, expand; so his eyes seemed rounding and rounding, like the circles of Eternity. An awe that cannot be named would steal over you as you sat by the side of this waning savage—"

But Queequeg did not die—and the *Pequod* emerges from the Eastern Straits, into the full Pacific. "To my meditative Magian rover, this serene Pacific once beheld, must ever after be the sea of his adoption. It rolls the utmost waters of the world—"

In this Pacific the fights go on.—"It was far down the afternoon; and when all the spearings of the crimson fight were done; and floating in the lovely sunset sea and sky, sun and whale both died stilly together; then such a sweetness and such a plaintiveness, such inwreathing orisons curled up in that rosy air, that it almost seemed as if far over from the deep green convent valleys of the Manila isles, the Spanish land-breeze had gone to sea, freighted with these vesper hymns.—Soothed again, but only soothed to deeper gloom, Ahab, who has steered off from the whale, sat intently watching his final wanings from the now tranquil boat. For that strange spectacle, observable in all sperm whales dying—the turning of the head sunwards, and so expiring—that strange spectacle, beheld of such a placid evening, somehow to Ahab conveyed wondrousness unknown before. 'He

turns and turns him to it; how slowly, but how steadfastly, his home-rendering and invoking brow, with his last dying motions. He too worships fire; . . .' "

So Ahab soliloquizes: and so the warm-blooded whale turns for the last time to the sun, which begot him in the waters.

But as we see in the next chapter, it is the Thunder-fire which Ahab really worships: that living sundering fire of which he bears the brand, from head to foot.—It is storm, the electric storm of the *Pequod*, when the corposants burn in high, tapering flames of supernatural pallor upon the masthead, and when the compass is reversed. After this all is fatality. Life itself seems mystically reversed. In these hunters of Moby Dick there is nothing but madness and possession. The captain, Ahab, moves hand in hand with the poor imbecile negro boy, Pip, who has been so cruelly demented, left swimming alone in the vast sea. It is the imbecile child of the sun hand in hand with the northern monomaniac, captain and master.

The voyage surges on. They meet one ship, then another. It is all ordinary day-routine, and yet all is a tension of pure madness and horror, the approaching horror of the last fight. "Hither and thither, on high, glided the snow-white wings of small unspecked birds; these were the gentle thoughts of the feminine air; but to and fro in the deeps, far down in the bottomless blue, rushed mighty leviathans, sword-fish and sharks; and these were the strong, troubled, murderous thinkings of the masculine sea—" On this day Ahab confesses his weariness, the weariness of his burden. "But do I look very old, so very, very old, Starbuck? I feel deadly faint, and bowed, and humped, as though I were Adam staggering beneath the piled centuries since Paradise—" It is the Gethsemane of Ahab, before the last fight: the Gethsemane of the human soul seeking the last self-conquest, the last attainment of extended consciousness—infinite consciousness.

At last they sight the whale. Ahab sees him from his hoisted-perch at the masthead.—"From this height the whale was now seen some mile or so ahead, at every roll of the sea revealing his high, sparkling hump, and regularly jetting his silent spout into the air."

The boats are lowered, to draw near the white whale. "At length the breathless hunter came so nigh his seemingly unsuspectful prey that his entire dazzling hump was distinctly visible, sliding along the sea as if an isolated thing, and continually set in a revolving ring of finest, fleecy, greenish foam. He saw the vast involved wrinkles of the slightly projecting head, beyond. Before it, far out on the soft, Turkish rugged waters, went the glistening white shadow from his broad, milky forehead, a musical rippling playfully accompanying the shade; and behind, the blue waters interchangeably flowed over the moving valley of his steady wake; and on either side bright bubbles arose and danced by his side. But these were broken again by the light toes of hundreds of gay fowl softly feathering the sea, alternate with their fitful flight; and like to some flagstaff rising from

the pointed hull of an argosy, the tall but shattered pole of a recent lance projected from the white whale's back; and at intervals one of the clouds of soft-toed fowls hovering, and to and fro shimmering like a canopy over the fish, silently perched and rocked on this pole, the long tail-feathers streaming like pennons.

"A gentle joyousness—a mighty mildness of repose in swiftness, invested the gliding whale—"

The fight with the whale is too wonderful, and too awful, to be quoted apart from the book. It lasted three days. The fearful sight, on the third day, of the torn body of the Parsee harpooner, lost on the previous day, now seen lashed on to the flanks of the white whale by the tangle of harpoon lines, has a mystic dream-horror. The awful and infuriated whale turns upon the ship, symbol of this civilized world of ours. He smites her with a fearful shock. And a few minutes later, from the last of the fighting whale boats comes the cry: " 'The ship! Great God, where is the ship?'—Soon they, through the dim, bewildering mediums, saw her sidelong fading phantom, as in the gaseous Fata Morgana; only the uppermost masts out of the water; while fixed by infatuation, or fidelity, or fate, to their once lofty perches, the pagan harpooners still maintained their sinking lookouts on the sea. And now concentric circles seized the lone boat itself, and all its crew, and each floating oar, and every lance-pole, and spinning, animate and inanimate, all round and round in one vortex, carried the smallest chip of the *Pequod* out of sight—"

The bird of heaven, the eagle, St. John's bird, the Red Indian bird, the American, goes down with the ship, nailed by Tashtego's hammer, the hammer of the American Indian. The eagle of the spirit. Sunk!

"Now small fowls flew screaming over the yet yawning gulf; a sullen white surf beat against its steep sides; then all collapsed; and then the great shroud of the sea rolled on as it rolled five thousand years ago."

So ends one of the strangest and most wonderful books in the world, closing up its mystery and its tortured symbolism. It is an epic of the sea such as no man has equalled; and it is a book of exoteric symbolism of profound significance, and of considerable tiresomeness.

But it is a great book, a very great book, the greatest book of the sea ever written. It moves awe in the soul.

The terrible fatality.

Fatality.

Doom.

Doom! Doom! Doom! Something seems to whisper it in the very dark trees of America. Doom!

Doom of what?

Doom of our white day. We are doomed, doomed. And the doom is in America. The doom of our white day.

Ah, well, if my day is doomed, and I am doomed with my day, it is

something greater than I which dooms me, so I accept my doom as a sign of the greatness which is more than I am.

Melville knew. He knew his race was doomed. His white soul, doomed. His great white epoch, doomed. Himself, doomed. The idealist, doomed. The spirit, doomed.

The reversion. "Not so much bound to any haven ahead, as rushing from all havens astern."

That great horror of ours! It is our civilization rushing from all havens astern.

The last ghastly hunt. The White Whale.

What then is Moby Dick?—He is the deepest blood-being of the white race. He is our deepest blood-nature.

And he is hunted, hunted, hunted by the maniacal fanaticism of our white mental consciousness. We want to hunt him down. To subject him to our will. And in this maniacal conscious hunt of ourselves we get dark races and pale to help us, red, yellow, and black, east and west, Quaker and fire-worshipper, we get them all to help us in this ghastly maniacal hunt which is our doom and our suicide.

The last phallic being of the white man. Hunted into the death of upper consciousness and the ideal will. Our blood-self subjected to our will. Our blood-consciousness sapped by a parasitic mental or ideal consciousness.

Hot-blooded sea-born Moby Dick. Hunted by monomaniacs of the idea.

Oh God, oh God, what next, when the *Pequod* has sunk?

She sank in the war, and we all are flotsam.

Now what next?

Who knows? *Quien sabe? Quien sabe, señor?*

Neither Spanish nor Saxon America has any answer.

The *Pequod* went down. And the *Pequod* was the ship of the white American soul. She sank, taking with her Negro and Indian and Polynesian, Asiatic and Quaker and good, businesslike Yankees and Ishmael: she sank all the lot of them.

*Boom!* as Vachel Lindsay would say.

To use the words of Jesus, IT IS FINISHED.

*Consummatum est!*

But *Moby Dick* was first published in 1851. If the Great White Whale sank the ship of the Great White Soul in 1851, what's been happening ever since?

Post mortem effects, presumably.

Because, in the first centuries, Jesus was Cetus, the Whale. And the Christians were the little fishes. Jesus, the Redeemer, was Cetus, Leviathan. And all the Christians all his little fishes.

## TOPICS FOR DISCUSSION

1 In what ways has Lawrence both retold the story and analyzed special features of it at the same time? Do the long quotations from the novel seem to support or contradict the conclusions of Lawrence?

2 Trace the development of Moby Dick from a "lovable but hunted creature to the blood self."

3 How does Lawrence's own philosophy reveal itself? Does this add color to the study of the novel or only confuse and irritate the reader?

4 Find instances of unusual sentence structure, paragraphing, and punctuation. What special effect do these have on the tone of the essay?

5 Does Lawrence's complaint at Melville's "sententiousness" make his ultimate praise of the novel seem all the more deserved, or is it so cleverly done that the final praise cannot recoup the losses?

## ...AND COMPOSITION

6 Write a review of a book, an essay, or a movie, paraphrasing enough of it so that the main lines are made clear and analyzing special features of it, coming to a judicious conclusion.

7 Write a Lawrence-like attack on a political figure's sententiousness.

8 Challenge or support Lawrence's interpretation of *Moby Dick,* basing your opinions on the selection "The Whiteness of the Whale" or on your own reading of the complete text.

GEORGE ORWELL [ERIC BLAIR] (1903–1950)   pursuing that conviction he
held about directness and clarity (see page 8), here outlines a nightmare
about language: its present tendencies could evolve toward such poverty
and rigidity that freedom would be impossible, since thought would be
inhibited. In that nightmare to come, no one could effectually oppose
the trend, even when he could "bellyfeel" that it was "doubleplusungood."

# The Principles of Newspeak

Newspeak was the official language of Oceania and had been devised to meet the ideological needs of Ingsoc, or English Socialism. In the year 1984 there was not as yet anyone who used Newspeak as his sole means of communication, either in speech or writing. The leading articles in the *Times* were written in it, but this was a tour de force which could only be carried out by a specialist. It was expected that Newspeak would have finally superseded Oldspeak (or Standard English, as we should call it) by about the year 2050. Meanwhile it gained ground steadily, all Party members tending to use Newspeak words and grammatical constructions more and more in their everyday speech. The version in use in 1984, and embodied in the Ninth and Tenth Editions of the Newspeak dictionary, was a provisional one, and contained many superfluous words and archaic formations which were due to be suppressed later. It is with the final, perfected version, as embodied in the Eleventh Edition of the dictionary, that we are concerned here.

The purpose of Newspeak was not only to provide a medium of expression for the world-view and mental habits proper to the devotees of Ingsoc, but to make all other modes of thought impossible. It was intended that when Newspeak had been adopted once and for all and Oldspeak forgotten, a heretical thought—that is, a thought diverging from the principles of Ingsoc—should be literally unthinkable, at least so far as thought is dependent on words. Its vocabulary was so constructed as to give exact and often very subtle expression to every meaning that a Party member could properly wish to express, while excluding all other meanings and also the possibility of arriving at them by indirect methods. This was done partly by the invention of new words, but chiefly by eliminating undesirable words and by stripping such words as remained of unorthodox meanings, and so far as possible of all secondary meanings whatever. To give a single example. The word *free* still existed in Newspeak, but it could only be used in such statements as "This dog is free from lice" or "This field is free from weeds." It could not be used in its old sense of "politically free" or "intellectually free," since political and intellectual freedom no longer existed even as concepts, and were therefore of necessity nameless.

Quite apart from the suppression of definitely heretical words, reduction of vocabulary was regarded as an end in itself, and no word that could be dispensed with was allowed to survive. Newspeak was designed not to extend but to *diminish* the range of thought, and this purpose was indirectly assisted by cutting the choice of words down to a minimum.

Newspeak was founded on the English language as we now know it, though many Newspeak sentences, even when not containing newly created words, would be barely intelligible to an English-speaker of our own day. Newspeak words were divided into three distinct classes, known as the A vocabulary, the B vocabulary (also called compound words), and the C vocabulary. It will be simpler to discuss each class separately, but the grammatical peculiarities of the language can be dealt with in the section devoted to the A vocabulary, since the same rules held good for all three categories.

### THE A VOCABULARY

The A vocabulary consisted of the words needed for the business of everyday life—for such things as eating, drinking, working, putting on one's clothes, going up and down stairs, riding in vehicles, gardening, cooking, and the like. It was composed almost entirely of words that we already possess—words like *hit, run, dog, tree, sugar, house, field*—but in comparison with the present-day English vocabulary, their number was extremely small, while their meanings were far more rigidly defined. All ambiguities and shades of meaning had been purged out of them. So far as it could be achieved, a Newspeak word of this class was simply a staccato sound expressing *one* clearly understood concept. It would have been quite impossible to use the A vocabulary for literary purposes or for political or philosophical discussion. It was intended only to express simple, purposive thoughts, usually involving concrete objects or physical actions.

The grammar of Newspeak had two outstanding peculiarities. The first of these was an almost complete interchangeability between different parts of speech. Any word in the language (in principle this applied even to very abstract words such as *if* or *when*) could be used either as verb, noun, adjective, or adverb. Between the verb and the noun form, when they were of the same root, there was never any variation, this rule of itself involving the destruction of many archaic forms. The word *thought,* for example, did not exist in Newspeak. Its place was taken by *think,* which did duty for both noun and verb. No etymological principle was involved here; in some cases it was the original noun that was chosen for retention, in other cases the verb. Even where a noun and verb of kindred meaning were not etymologically connected, one or other of them was frequently suppressed. There was, for example, no such word as *cut,* its meaning being sufficiently covered by the noun-verb *knife.* Adjectives were formed by adding the suffix *-ful* to the noun-verb, and adverbs by adding *-wise*.

Thus, for example, *speedful* meant "rapid" and *speedwise* meant "quickly." Certain of our present-day adjectives, such as *good, strong, big, soft,* were retained, but their total number was very small. There was little need for them, since almost any adjectival meaning could be arrived at by adding *-ful* to a noun-verb. None of the now-existing adverbs was retained, except for a very few already ending in *-wise;* the *-wise* termination was invariable. The word *well,* for example, was replaced by *goodwise.*

In addition, any word—this again applied in principle to every word in the language—could be negatived by adding the affix *un-,* or could be strengthened by the affix *plus-,* or, for still greater emphasis, *doubleplus-.* Thus, for example, *uncold* meant "warm," while *pluscold* and *doubleplus-cold* meant, respectively, "very cold" and "superlatively cold." It was also possible, as in present-day English, to modify the meaning of almost any word by prepositional affixes such as *ante-, post-, up-, down-,* etc. By such methods it was found possible to bring about an enormous diminution of vocabulary. Given, for instance, the word *good,* there was no need for such a word as *bad,* since the required meaning was equally well—indeed, better—expressed by *ungood.* All that was necessary, in any case where two words formed a natural pair of opposites, was to decide which of them to suppress. *Dark,* for example, could be replaced by *unlight,* or *light* by *undark,* according to preference.

The second distinguishing mark of Newspeak grammar was its regularity. Subject to a few exceptions which are mentioned below, all inflections followed the same rules. Thus, in all verbs the preterite and the past participle were the same and ended in *-ed.* The preterite of *steal* was *stealed,* the preterite of *think* was *thinked,* and so on throughout the language, all such forms as *swam, gave, brought, spoke, taken,* etc., being abolished. All plurals were made by adding *-s* or *-es* as the case might be. The plurals of *man, ox, life* were *mans, oxes, lifes.* Comparison of adjectives was invariably made by adding *-er, -est (good, gooder, goodest),* irregular forms and the *more, most* formation being suppressed.

The only classes of words that were still allowed to inflect irregularly were the pronouns, the relatives, the demonstrative adjectives, and the auxiliary verbs. All of these followed their ancient usage, except that *whom* had been scrapped as unnecessary, and the *shall, should* tenses had been dropped, all their uses being covered by *will* and *would.* There were also certain irregularities in word-formation arising out of the need for rapid and easy speech. A word which was difficult to utter, or was liable to be incorrectly heard, was held to be ipso facto a bad word; occasionally therefore, for the sake of euphony, extra letters were inserted into a word or an archaic formation was retained. But this need made itself felt chiefly in connection with the B vocabulary. *Why* so great an importance was attached to ease of pronunciation will be made clear later in this essay.

## THE B VOCABULARY

The B vocabulary consisted of words which had been deliberately constructed for political purposes: words, that is to say, which not only had in every case a political implication, but were intended to impose a desirable mental attitude upon the person using them. Without a full understanding of the principles of Ingsoc it was difficult to use these words correctly. In some cases they could be translated into Oldspeak, or even into words taken from the A vocabulary, but this usually demanded a long paraphrase and always involved the loss of certain overtones. The B words were a sort of verbal shorthand, often packing whole ranges of ideas into a few syllables, and at the same time more accurate and forcible than ordinary language.

The B words were in all cases compound words.[1] They consisted of two or more words, or portions of words, welded together in an easily pronounceable form. The resulting amalgam was always a noun-verb, and inflected according to the ordinary rules. To take a single example: the word *goodthink,* meaning, very roughly, "orthodoxy," or, if one chose to regard it as a verb, "to think in an orthodox manner." This inflected as follows: noun-verb, *goodthink;* past tense and past participle, *goodthinked;* present participle, *goodthinking;* adjective, *goodthinkful;* adverb, *goodthinkwise;* verbal noun, *goodthinker.*

The B words were not constructed on any etymological plan. The words of which they were made up could be any parts of speech, and could be placed in any order and mutilated in any way which made them easy to pronounce while indicating their derivation. In the word *crimethink* (thought-crime), for instance, the *think* came second, whereas in *thinkpol* (Thought Police) it came first, and in the latter word *police* had lost its second syllable. Because of the greater difficulty in securing euphony, irregular formations were commoner in the B vocabulary than in the A vocabulary. For example, the adjectival forms of *Minitrue, Minipax,* and *Miniluv* were, respectively, *Minitruthful, Minipeaceful,* and *Minilovely,* simply because *-trueful, -paxful,* and *loveful* were slightly awkward to pronounce. In principle, however, all B words could inflect, and all inflected in exactly the same way.

Some of the B words had highly subtilized meanings, barely intelligible to anyone who had not mastered the language as a whole. Consider, for example, such a typical sentence from a *Times* leading article as *Oldthinkers unbellyfeel Ingsoc.* The shortest rendering that one could make of this in Oldspeak would be: "Those whose ideas were formed before the Revolution cannot have a full emotional understanding of the principles of English Socialism." But this is not an adequate translation. To begin

[1] Compound words, such as *speakwrite,* were of course to be found in the A vocabulary, but these were merely convenient abbreviations and had no special ideological color.

with, in order to grasp the full meaning of the Newspeak sentence quoted above, one would have to have a clear idea of what is meant by *Ingsoc*. And, in addition, only a person thoroughly grounded in Ingsoc could appreciate the full force of the word *bellyfeel*, which implied a blind, enthusiastic acceptance difficult to imagine today; or of the word *oldthink*, which was inextricably mixed up with the idea of wickedness and decadence. But the special function of certain Newspeak words, of which *oldthink* was one, was not so much to express meanings as to destroy them. These words, necessarily few in number, had had their meanings extended until they contained within themselves whole batteries of words which, as they were sufficiently covered by a single comprehensive term, could now be scrapped and forgotten. The greatest difficulty facing the compilers of the Newspeak dictionary was not to invent new words, but, having invented them, to make sure what they meant: to make sure, that is to say, what ranges of words they canceled by their existence.

As we have already seen in the case of the word *free*, words which had once borne a heretical meaning were sometimes retained for the sake of convenience, but only with the undesirable meanings purged out of them. Countless other words such as *honor, justice, morality, internationalism, democracy, science,* and *religion* had simply ceased to exist. A few blanket words covered them, and, in covering them, abolished them. All words grouping themselves round the concepts of liberty and equality, for instance, were contained in the single word *crimethink,* while all words grouping themselves round the concepts of objectivity and rationalism were contained in the single word *oldthink.* Greater precision would have been dangerous. What was required in a Party member was an outlook similar to that of the ancient Hebrew who knew, without knowing much else, that all nations other than his own worshipped "false gods." He did not need to know that these gods were called Baal, Osiris, Moloch, Ashtaroth, and the like; probably the less he knew about them the better for his orthodoxy. He knew Jehovah and the commandments of Jehovah; he knew, therefore, that all gods with other names or other attributes were false gods. In somewhat the same way, the Party member knew what constituted right conduct, and in exceedingly vague, generalized terms he knew what kinds of departure from it were possible. His sexual life, for example, was entirely regulated by the two Newspeak words *sexcrime* (sexual immorality) and *goodsex* (chastity). *Sexcrime* covered all sexual misdeeds whatever. It covered fornication, adultery, homosexuality, and other perversions, and, in addition, normal intercourse practiced for its own sake. There was no need to enumerate them separately, since they were all equally culpable, and, in principle, all punishable by death. In the C vocabulary, which consisted of scientific and technical words, it might be necessary to give specialized names to certain sexual aberrations, but the ordinary citizen

had no need of them. He knew what was meant by *goodsex*—that is to say, normal intercourse between man and wife, for the sole purpose of begetting children, and without physical pleasure on the part of the woman; all else was *sexcrime*. In Newspeak it was seldom possible to follow a heretical thought further than the perception that it *was* heretical; beyond that point the necessary words were nonexistent.

No word in the B vocabulary was ideologically neutral. A great many were euphemisms. Such words, for instance, as *joycamp* (forced-labor camp) or *Minipax* (Ministry of Peace, i.e., Ministry of War) meant almost the exact opposite of what they appeared to mean. Some words, on the other hand, displayed a frank and contemptuous understanding of the real nature of Oceanic society. An example, was *prolefeed,* meaning the rubbishy entertainment and spurious news which the Party handed out to the masses. Other words, again, were ambivalent, having the connotation "good" when applied to the Party and "bad" when applied to its enemies. But in addition there were great numbers of words which at first sight appeared to be mere abbreviations and which derived their ideological color not from their meaning but from their structure.

So far as it could be contrived, everything that had or might have political significance of any kind was fitted into the B vocabulary. The name of every organization, or body of people, or doctrine, or country, or institution, or public building, was invariably cut down into the familiar shape; that is, a single easily pronounced word with the smallest number of syllables that would preserve the original derivation. In the Ministry of Truth, for example, the Records Department, in which Winston Smith worked, was called *Recdep,* the Fiction Department was called *Ficdep,* the Teleprograms Department was called *Teledep,* and so on. This was not done solely with the object of saving time. Even in the early decades of the twentieth century, telescoped words and phrases had been one of the characteristic features of political language; and it had been noticed that the tendency to use abbreviations of this kind was most marked in totalitarian countries and totalitarian organizations. Examples were such words as *Nazi, Gestapo, Comintern, Inprecorr, Agitprop.* In the beginning the practice had been adopted as it were instinctively, but in Newspeak it was used with a conscious purpose. It was perceived that in thus abbreviating a name one narrowed and subtly altered its meaning, by cutting out most of the associations that would otherwise cling to it. The words *Communist International,* for instance, call up a composite picture of universal human brotherhood, red flags, barricades, Karl Marx, and the Paris Commune. The word Comintern, on the other hand, suggests merely a tightly knit organization and a well-defined body of doctrine. It refers to something almost as easily recognized, and as limited in purpose, as a chair or a table. *Comintern* is a word that can be uttered almost without

taking thought, whereas *Communist International* is a phrase over which one is obliged to linger at least momentarily. In the same way, the associations called up by a word like *Minitrue* are fewer and more controllable than those called up by *Ministry of Truth*. This accounted not only for the habit of abbreviating whenever possible, but also for the almost exaggerated care that was taken to make every word easily pronounceable.

In Newspeak, euphony outweighed every consideration other than exactitude of meaning. Regularity of grammar was always sacrificed to it when it seemed necessary. And rightly so, since what was required, above all for political purposes, were short clipped words of unmistakable meaning which could be uttered rapidly and which roused the minimum of echoes in the speaker's mind. The words of the B vocabulary even gained in force from the fact that nearly all of them were very much alike. Almost invariably these words—*goodthink, Minipax, prolefeed, sexcrime, joycamp, Ingsoc, bellyfeel, thinkpol,* and countless others—were words of two or three syllables, with the stress distributed equally between the first syllable and the last. The use of them encouraged a gabbling style of speech, at once staccato and monotonous. And this was exactly what was aimed at. The intention was to make speech, and especially speech on any subject not ideologically neutral, as nearly as possible independent of consciousness. For the purposes of everyday life it was no doubt necessary, or sometimes necessary, to reflect before speaking, but a Party member called upon to make a political or ethical judgment should be able to spray forth the correct opinions as automatically as a machine gun spraying forth bullets. His training fitted him to do this, the language gave him an almost foolproof instrument, and the texture of the words, with their harsh sound and a certain willful ugliness which was in accord with the spirit of Ingsoc, assisted the process still further.

So did the fact of having very few words to choose from. Relative to our own, the Newspeak vocabulary was tiny, and new ways of reducing it were constantly being devised. Newspeak, indeed, differed from almost all other languages in that its vocabulary grew smaller instead of larger every year. Each reduction was a gain, since the smaller the area of choice, the smaller the temptation to take thought. Ultimately it was hoped to make articulate speech issue from the larynx without involving the higher brain centers at all. This aim was frankly admitted in the Newspeak word *duckspeak,* meaning "to quack like a duck." Like various other words in the B vocabulary, *duckspeak* was ambivalent in meaning. Provided that the opinions which were quacked out were orthodox ones, it implied nothing but praise, and when the *Times* referred to one of the orators of the Party as a *doubleplusgood duckspeaker* it was paying a warm and valued compliment.

## THE C VOCABULARY

The C vocabulary was supplementary to the others and consisted entirely of scientific and technical terms. These resembled the scientific terms in use today, and were constructed from the same roots, but the usual care was taken to define them rigidly and strip them of undesirable meanings. They followed the same grammatical rules as the words in the other two vocabularies. Very few of the C words had any currency either in everyday speech or in political speech. Any scientific worker or technician could find all the words he needed in the list devoted to his own specialty, but he seldom had more than a smattering of the words occurring in the other lists. Only a very few words were common to all lists, and there was no vocabulary expressing the function of Science as a habit of mind, or a method of thought, irrespective of its particular branches. There was, indeed, no word for "Science," any meaning that it could possibly bear being already sufficiently covered by the word *Ingsoc*.

From the foregoing account it will be seen that in Newspeak the expression of unorthodox opinions, above a very low level, was well-nigh impossible. It was of course possible to utter heresies of a very crude kind, a species of blasphemy. It would have been possible, for example, to say *Big Brother is ungood*. But this statement, which to an orthodox ear merely conveyed a self-evident absurdity, could not have been sustained by reasoned argument, because the necessary words were not available. Ideas inimical to Ingsoc could only be entertained in a vague wordless form, and could only be named in very broad terms which lumped together and condemned whole groups of heresies without defining them in doing so. One could, in fact, only use Newspeak for unorthodox purposes by illegitimately translating some of the words back into Oldspeak. For example, *All mans are equal* was a possible Newspeak sentence, but only in the same sense in which *All men are redhaired* is a possible Oldspeak sentence. It did not contain a grammatical error, but it expressed a palpable untruth, i.e., that all men are of equal size, weight, or strength. The concept of political equality no longer existed, and this secondary meaning had accordingly been purged out of the word *equal*. In 1984, when Oldspeak was still the normal means of communication, the danger theoretically existed that in using Newspeak words one might remember their original meanings. In practice it was not difficult for any person well grounded in *doublethink* to avoid doing this, but within a couple of generations even the possibility of such a lapse would have vanished. A person growing up with Newspeak as his sole language would no more know that *equal* had once had the secondary meaning of "politically equal," or that *free* had once meant "intellectually free," than, for instance, a person who had never heard of

chess would be aware of the secondary meanings attaching to *queen* and *rook*. There would be many crimes and errors which it would be beyond his power to commit, simply because they were nameless and therefore unimaginable. And it was to be foreseen that with the passage of time the distinguishing characteristics of Newspeak would become more and more pronounced—its words growing fewer and fewer, their meanings more and more rigid, and the chance of putting them to improper uses always diminishing.

When Oldspeak had been once and for all superseded, the last link with the past would have been severed. History had already been rewritten, but fragments of the literature of the past survived here and there, imperfectly censored, and so long as one retained one's knowledge of Oldspeak it was possible to read them. In the future such fragments, even if they chanced to survive, would be unintelligible and untranslatable. It was impossible to translate any passage of Oldspeak into Newspeak unless it either referred to some technical process or some very simple everyday action, or was already orthodox (*goodthinkful* would be the Newspeak expression) in tendency. In practice this meant that no book written before approximately 1960 could be translated as a whole. Prerevolutionary literature could only be subjected to ideological translation—that is, alteration in sense as well as language. Take for example the well-known passage from the Declaration of Independence:

> We hold these truths to be self-evident, that all men are created equal, that they are endowed by their Creator with certain inalienable rights, that among these are life, liberty and the pursuit of happiness. That to secure these rights, Governments are instituted among men, deriving their powers from the consent of the governed. That whenever any form of Government becomes destructive of those ends, it is the right of the People to alter or abolish it, and to institute new Government. . . .

It would have been quite impossible to render this into Newspeak while keeping to the sense of the original. The nearest one could come to doing so would be to swallow the whole passage up in the single word *crimethink*. A full translation could only be an ideological translation, whereby Jefferson's words would be changed into a panegyric on absolute government.

A good deal of the literature of the past was, indeed, already being transformed in this way. Considerations of prestige made it desirable to preserve the memory of certain historical figures, while at the same time bringing their achievements into line with the philosophy of Ingsoc. Various writers, such as Shakespeare, Milton, Swift, Byron, Dickens, and some others were therefore in process of translation; when the task had been completed, their original writings, with all else that survived of the literature of the past, would be destroyed. These translations were a slow and difficult

business, and it was not expected that they would be finished before the first or second decade of the twenty-first century. There were also large quantities of merely utilitarian literature—indispensable technical manuals and the like—that had to be treated in the same way. It was chiefly in order to allow time for the preliminary work of translation that the final adoption of Newspeak had been fixed for so late a date as 2050.

## TOPICS FOR DISCUSSION

1   Is what the speaker says the actual subject of the essay?

2   Characterize the speaker of the essay. What is the nature of the society to which he apparently belongs and to which he gives such an oddly poised attention?

3   How does the author of the essay separate himself from the speaker? How do you know that the intent of the essay is ironic?

4   Irony usually calls attention to discrepancy or to contrasts between what is and what should be, between what is pretended to be and what actually is, or between what is valuable and what is valueless. The critical problem in such an indirect method of approach is to establish the two elements of the subject and still maintain the emphasis and subtlety of the ironic. What are the two standards here presented?

5   The essay is generally a statement in a neutral voice, without feeling, of the technical and semitechnical aspects of the new language. What does this tone add to the effect of the essay?

6   How can you tell that some kinds of Newspeak are already in use in our contemporary society?

7   The treatments of the A, B, and C vocabularies are uneven in length. Is there any reason for this?

## ...AND COMPOSITION

8   Find in a recent magazine article, newspaper editorial, or official publication evidences of Newspeak and comment on them.

9   Write a paragraph in Newspeak on an important problem and manage it so that the language subverts the pretended message. Rewrite the paragraph in vital, meaningful language, remembering Orwell's other essay, "Politics and the English Language."

10   Compare Orwell's understanding of the power of words with that of Mencken.

**JAMES JOYCE (1882–1941)**  was beleaguered by meanings all his life and
made successive moves to cleanse himself, horrifiedly examining his tracks
as he went. From his education in Jesuit schools in Dublin, he retreated
by way of higher education in modern languages, moved to the Continent
to teach and to write, and after a short return and some cleansing by
means of short stories about Dublin life sought permanent exile in Europe.
His writings moved also, through more realistic early stories, to increasing
complexity and symbolism, and finally to the world's record for allusion
and ambiguity, *Finnegan's Wake*, the source of the following passage.
Language always has this potential ambiguity; Joyce brings into flickering
consciousness meanings which lurk for most of us at the subliminal level.

# Shem

Shem is as short for Shemus as Jem is joky for Jacob. A few tough-
necks are still getatable who pretend that aboriginally he was of respectable
stemming (he was an outlex between the lines of Ragonar Blaubarb and
Horrild Hairwire and an inlaw to Capt. the Hon. and Rev. Mr. Bbyrdwood
de Trop Blogg was among his most distant connections) but every honest
to goodness man in the land of the space of today knows that his back life
will not stand being written about in black and white. Putting truth and
untruth together a shot may be made at what this hybrid actually was like
to look at.

Shem's bodily getup, it seems, included an adze of a skull, an eight of
a larkseye, the whoel of a nose, one numb arm up a sleeve, fortytwo hairs
off his uncrown, eighteen to his mock lip, a trio of barbels from his
megageg chin (sowman's son), the wrong shoulder higher than the right,
all ears, an artificial tongue with a natural curl, not a foot to stand on, a
handful of thumbs, a blind stomach, a deaf heart, a loose liver, two fifths
of two buttocks, one gleetsteen avoirdupoider for him, a manroot of all
evil, a salmonkelt's thinskin, eelsblood in his cold toes, a bladder tristended,
so much so that young Master Shemmy on his very first debouch at the
very dawn of protohistory seeing himself such and such, when playing with
thistlewords in their garden nursery, Griefotrofio, at Phig Streat III, Shuvlin,
Old Hoeland, (would we go back there now for sounds, pillings and sense?
would we now for annas and annas? would we for full-score eight and a
liretta? for twelve blocks one bob? for four testers one groat? not for a
dinar! not for jo!) dictited to of all his little brothron and sweetstureens
the first riddle of the universe: asking, when is a man not a man?: telling
them take their time, yungfries, and wait till the tide stops (for from the
first his day was a fortnight) and offering the prize of a bittersweet crab,
a little present from the past, for their copper age was yet unminted, to
the winner. One said when the heavens are quakers, a second said when

Bohemeand lips, a third said when he, no, when hold hard a jiffy, when he is a gnawstick and detarmined to, the next one said when the angel of death kicks the bucket of life, still another said the wine's at witsends, and still another when lovely wooman stoops to conk him, one of the littliest said me, me, Sem, when pappa papared the harbour, one of the wittiest said, when he yeat ye abblokooken and he zmear hezelf zo zhooken, still one said when you are old I'm grey fall full wi sleep, and still another when wee deader walkner, and another when he is just only after having being semisized, another when yea, he hath no mananas, and one when dose pigs they begin now that they will flies up intil the looft. All were wrong, so Shem himself, the doctator, took the cake, the correct solution being—all give it up?—; when he is a—yours till the rending of the rocks,—Sham.

Shem was a sham and a low sham and his lowness creeped out first via foodstuffs. So low was he that he preferred Gibsen's teatime salmon tinned, as inexpensive as pleasing, to the plumpest roeheavy lax or the friskiest parr or smolt troutlet that ever was gaffed between Leixlip and Island Bridge and many was the time he repeated in his botulism that no junglegrown pineapple ever smacked like the whoppers you shook out of Ananias' cans, Findlater and Gladstone's, Corner House, Englend. None of your inchthick blueblooded Balaclava fried-at-belief-stakes or juicejelly legs of the Grex's molten mutton or greasilygristly grunters' goupons or slice upon slab of luscious goosebosom with lump after load of plum-pudding stuffiny all aswim in a swamp of bogoakgravy for that greeken-hearted yude! Rosbif of Old Zealand! he could not attouch it. See what happens when your somatophage merman takes his fancy to our virgitarian swam? He even ran away with hunself and became a farsoonerite, saying he would far sooner muddle through the hash of lentils in Europe than meddle with Irrland's split little pea. Once when among those rebels in a state of hopelessly helpless intoxication the piscivore strove to lift a czitround peel to either nostril, hiccupping, apparently impromptued by the hibat he had with his glottal stop, that he kukkakould flowrish for ever by the smell, as the czitr, as the kcedron, like a scedar, of the founts, on mountains, with limon on, of Lebanon. O! the lowness of him was beneath all up to that sunk to! No likedbylike firewater or firstserved firstshot or gulletburn gin or honest brewbarrett beer either. O dear no! Instead the tragic jester sobbed himself wheywhingingly sick of life on some sort of a rhubarbarous maundarin yellagreen funkleblue windigut diodying applejack squeezed from sour grapefruice and, to hear him twixt his sedimental cupslips when he had gulfed down mmmmuch too mmmmany gourds of it retching off to almost as low withswillers, who always knew notwithstand-ing when they had had enough and were rightly indignant at the wretch's hospitality when they found to their horror they could not carry another drop, it came straight from the noble white fat, jo, openwide sat, jo, jo, her why hide that, jo jo jo, the winevat, of the most serene magyansty az

archdiochesse, if she is a duck, she's a douches, and when she has a feherbour snot her fault, now is it? artstouchups, funny you're grinning at, fancy you're in her yet, Fanny Urinia.

Aint that swell, hey? Peamengro! Talk about lowness! Any dog's quantity of it visibly oozed out thickly from this dirty little blacking beetle for the very fourth snap the Tulloch-Turnbull girl with her coldblood kodak shotted the as yet unremuneranded national apostate, who was cowardly gun and camera shy, taking what he fondly thought was a short cut to Caer Fere, Soak Amerigas, vias the shipsteam *Pridewin,* after having buried a hatchet not so long before, by the wrong goods exeunt, nummer desh to tren, into Patatapapaveri's, fruiterers and musical florists, with his *Ciaho, chavi! Sar shin, shillipen?* she knew the vice out of bridewell was a bad fast man by his walk on the spot.

[Johns is a different butcher's. Next place you are up town pay him a visit. Or better still, come tobuy. You will enjoy cattlemen's spring meat. Johns is now quite divorced from baking. Fattens, kills, flays, hangs, draws, quarters and pieces. Feel his lambs! Ex! Feel how sheap! Exex! His liver too is great value, a spatiality! Exexex! COMMUNICATED.]

Around that time, moravar, one generally, for luvvomony hoped or at any rate suspected among morticians that he would early turn out badly, develop hereditary pulmonary T.B., and do for himself one dandy time, nay, of a pelting night blanketed creditors, hearing a coarse song and splash off Eden Quay sighed and rolled over, sure all was up, but, though he fell heavily and locally into debit, not even then could such an antinomian be true to type. He would not put fire to his cerebrum; he would not throw himself in Liffey; he would not explaud himself with pneumantics; he refused to saffrocake himself with a sod. With the foreign devil's leave the fraid born fraud diddled even death. *Anzi,* cabled (but shaking the worth out of his maulth: Guardacosta leporello? Szasas Kraicz!) from his Nearapoblican asylum to his jonathan for a brother: Here tokay, gone tomory, we're spluched, do something, Fireless. And had answer: Inconvenient, David.

You see, chaps, it will trickle out, freaksily of course, but the tom and the shorty of it is: he was in his bardic memory low. All the time he kept on treasuring with condign satisfaction each and every crumb of trektalk, covetous of his neighbour's word, and if ever, during a Munda conversazione commoted in the nation's interest, delicate tippits were thrown out to him touching his evil courses by some wellwishers, vainly pleading by scriptural arguments with the opprobrious papist about trying to brace up for the kidos of the thing, Scally wag, and be a men instead of a dem scrounger, dish it all, such as: Pray, what is the meaning, sousy, of that continental expression, if you ever came acrux it, we think it is a word transpiciously like *canaille?*: or: Did you anywhere, kennel, on your gullible's travels or during your rural troubadouring, happen to stumble

upon a certain gay young nobleman whimpering to the name of Low Swine who always addresses women out of the one corner of his mouth, lives on loans and is furtivefree yours of age? without one sigh of haste like the supreme prig he was, and not a bit sorry, he would pull a vacant landlubber's face, root with earwaker's pensile in the outer of his lauscher and then, lisping, the prattlepate parnella, to kill time, and swatting his deadbest to think what under the canopies of Jansens Chrest would any decent son of an Albiogenselman who had bin to an university think, let a lent hit a hint and begin to tell all the intelligentsia admitted to that tamileasy samtalaisy conclamazzione (since, still and before physicians, lawyers merchant, belfry pollititians, agricolous manufraudurers, sacrestanes of the Pure River Society, philanthropicks lodging on as many boards round the panesthetic at the same time as possible) the whole lifelong swrine story of his entire low cornaille existence, abusing his deceased ancestors wherever the sods were and one moment tarabooming great blunderguns (poh!) about his farfamed fine Poppamore, Mr Humhum, whom history, climate and entertainment made the first of his sept and always up to debt, though Eavens ears ow many fines he faces, and another moment visanvrerssas, cruaching three jeers (pah!) for his rotten little ghost of a Peppybeg, Mr Himmyshimmy, a blighty, a reeky, a lighty, a scrapy, a babbly, a ninny, dirty seventh among thieves and always bottom sawyer, till nowan knowed how howmely howme could be, giving unsolicited testimony on behalf of the absent, as glib as eaveswater to those present (who meanwhile, with increasing lack of interest in his semantics, allowed various subconscious smickers to drivel slowly across their fichers), unconsciously explaining, for inkstands, with a meticulosity bordering on the insane, the various meanings of all the different foreign parts of speech he misused and cuttlefishing every lie unshrinkable about all the other people in the story, leaving out, of course, foreconsciously, the simple worf and plague and poison they had cornered him about until there was not a snoozer among them but was utterly undeceived in the heel of the reel by the recital of the rigmarole.

## TOPICS FOR DISCUSSION

1  In the midst of apparent confusion, Joyce has included many, clear, simple sentences. Find a topic sentence for each paragraph.

2  Despite the appearance of disorder, this selection is very simply organized; outline it. What are the principal topics it takes up? In what order are these topics presented?

3  Through the portrait of Shem, Joyce characterizes the writer as one who asks "the first riddle of the universe: . . . when is a man

not a man?" What answers are advanced and rejected by Shem? How is his, the writer's, answer particularly ironic?

4  The style in this selection is most obviously distinguished by its heavily allusive texture and by its insistent punning in several languages. How many allusions can you identify? Are they merely cute, or are they functional? Are such puns as "One said when the heavens are quakers . . ." just puns, or are they metaphors?

5  What principles guide Joyce in his seemingly eccentric spelling and punctuation?

## . . . AND COMPOSITION

6  Write a paragraph describing the physical appearance of a man in a style which tries to be what it suggests, just as Shem is described in language which is Shem-like.

7  How many puns can you work into a single sentence?

8  *Finnegan's Wake* was published in the 1930s; if its experimental style is going to have any effect on our language, these effects should be manifest by now. On the basis of this selection, can you trace any influences on other writers in this book (e.g., Stein, Faulkner, White), or on other writers you are familiar with, or on other areas of writing (e.g., advertising)?

PART *2*

*Issues:*
*Styles*
*in*
*Persuasion*

A writer's resources liberate him, and he may exercise from sheer exuberance the opportunities which open as he avails himself of spontaneous dialogue with his material. The product of such creative activity may be shimmering and hard to classify, a new object in and of itself, as was demonstrated in Part I in the Joyce and the Melville pieces.

Often, however, some kind of felt opposition determines the strategy of the composition. The writer, being helplessly unique, no matter how much he may try to approximate a social norm or recognized type, often finds himself taking a persuasive stance. He finds himself possessed of a point of view which has some chance of acceptance but which can benefit from composition designed for the purposeful and managed enlightenment of others. This kind of writing makes up Part 2, and for convenience the pieces are grouped around currently—and perhaps permanently—absorbing issues: education, freedom, science, belief. Represented are significant, perennial points of view, which students are invited to recognize. There are slant and ironic views, teasing and puzzling approaches. Unclaimed opportunities await writers on all these issues, and on some of them student writers may hope to make satisfactory closures. But no one is likely to say the last word, even later—many books from now.

**ALFRED NORTH WHITEHEAD (1861–1947)** one of the most distinguished
intellectuals of our time, was most noted in mathematics and philosophy,
but the direction and scope of his interests led him into education
and literature. He identified modern trends and crises in broad perspective,
as in his characteristically ambitious book *Science and the Modern World*.
After a teaching career of almost forty years in Britain, he moved in 1924
to the United States, for a full second career and universal acclaim.

# The Aims of Education

Culture is activity of thought, and receptiveness to beauty and humane
feeling. Scraps of information have nothing to do with it. A merely well-
informed man is the most useless bore on God's earth. What we should
aim at producing is men who possess both culture and expert knowledge
in some special direction. Their expert knowledge will give them the
ground to start from, and their culture will lead them as deep as philosophy
and as high as art. We have to remember that the valuable intellectual
development is self-development, and that it mostly takes place between
the ages of sixteen and thirty. As to training, the most important part is
given by mothers before the age of twelve. A saying due to Archbishop
Temple illustrates my meaning. Surprise was expressed at the success
in after-life of a man, who as a boy at Rugby had been somewhat undistinguished. He answered, "It is not what they are at eighteen, it is what
they become afterwards that matters."

In training a child to activity of thought, above all things we must
beware of what I will call "inert ideas"—that is to say, ideas that are
merely received into the mind without being utilised, or tested, or thrown
into fresh combinations.

In the history of education, the most striking phenomenon is that schools of learning, which at one epoch are alive with a ferment of genius, in a succeeding generation exhibit merely pedantry and routine. The reason is, that they are overladen with inert ideas. Education with inert ideas is not only useless: it is, above all things, harmful—*Corruptio optimi, pessima.* Except at rare intervals of intellectual ferment, education in the past has been radically infected with inert ideas. That is the reason why uneducated clever women, who have seen much of the world, are in middle life so much the most cultured part of the community. They have been saved from this horrible burden of inert ideas. Every intellectual revolution which has ever stirred humanity into greatness has been a passionate protest against inert ideas. Then, alas, with pathetic ignorance of human psychology, it has proceeded by some educational scheme to bind humanity afresh with inert ideas of its own fashioning.

Let us now ask how in our system of education we are to guard against this mental dryrot. We enunciate two educational commandments, "Do not teach too many subjects," and again, "What you teach, teach thoroughly."

The result of teaching small parts of a large number of subjects is the passive reception of disconnected ideas, not illumined with any spark of vitality. Let the main ideas which are introduced into a child's education be few and important, and let them be thrown into every combination possible. The child should make them his own, and should understand their application here and now in the circumstances of his actual life. From the very beginning of his education, the child should experience the joy of discovery. The discovery which he has to make, is that general ideas give an understanding of that stream of events which pours through his life, which is his life. By understanding I mean more than a mere logical analysis, though that is included. I mean "understanding" in the sense in which it is used in the French proverb, "To understand all, is to forgive all." Pedants sneer at an education which is useful. But if education is not useful, what is it? Is it a talent, to be hidden away in a napkin? Of course, education should be useful, whatever your aim in life. It was useful to Saint Augustine and it was useful to Napoleon. It is useful, because understanding is useful.

I pass lightly over that understanding which should be given by the literary side of education. Nor do I wish to be supposed to pronounce on the relative merits of a classical or a modern curriculum. I would only remark that the understanding which we want is an understanding of an insistent present. The only use of a knowledge of the past is to equip us for the present. No more deadly harm can be done to young minds than by depreciation of the present. The present contains all that there is. It is holy ground; for it is the past, and it is the future. At the same time it must be observed that an age is no less past if it existed two hundred years ago than if it existed two thousand years ago. Do not be deceived by the

pedantry of dates. The ages of Shakespeare and of Molière are no less past than are the ages of Sophocles and of Virgil. The communion of saints is a great and inspiring assemblage, but it has only one possible hall of meeting, and that is, the present; and the mere lapse of time through which any particular group of saints must travel to reach that meeting-place, makes very little difference.

Passing now to the scientific and logical side of education, we remember that here also ideas which are not utilised are positively harmful. By utilising an idea, I mean relating it to that stream, compounded of sense perceptions, feelings, hopes, desires, and of mental activities adjusting thought to thought, which forms our life. I can imagine a set of beings which might fortify their souls by passively reviewing disconnected ideas. Humanity is not built that way—except perhaps some editors of newspapers.

In scientific training, the first thing to do with an idea is to prove it. But allow me for one moment to extend the meaning of "prove"; I mean— to prove its worth. Now an idea is not worth much unless the propositions in which it is embodied are true. Accordingly an essential part of the proof of an idea is the proof, either by experiment or by logic, of the truth of the propositions. But it is not essential that this proof of the truth should constitute the first introduction to the idea. After all, its assertion by the authority of respectable teachers is sufficient evidence to begin with. In our first contact with a set of propositions, we commence by appreciating their importance. That is what we all do in after-life. We do not attempt, in the strict sense, to prove or to disprove anything, unless its importance makes it worthy of that honour. These two processes of proof, in the narrow sense, and of appreciation, do not require a rigid separation in time. Both can be proceeded with nearly concurrently. But in so far as either process must have the priority, it should be that of appreciation by use.

Furthermore, we should not endeavor to use propositions in isolation. Emphatically I do not mean, a neat little set of experiments to illustrate Proposition I and then the proof of Proposition I, a neat little set of experiments to illustrate Proposition II and then the proof of Proposition II, and so on to the end of the book. Nothing could be more boring. Interrelated truths are utilised *en bloc,* and the various propositions are employed in any order, and with any reiteration. Choose some important applications of your theoretical subject; and study them concurrently with the systematic theoretical exposition. Keep the theoretical exposition short and simple, but let it be strict and rigid so far as it goes. It should not be too long for it to be easily known with thoroughness and accuracy. The consequences of a plethora of half-digested theoretical knowledge are deplorable. Also the theory should not be muddled up with the practice. The child should have no doubt when it is proving and when it is utilising. My point is that what is proved should be utilised, and that what is utilised

should—so far as is practicable—be proved. I am far from asserting that proof and utilisation are the same thing.

At this point of my discourse, I can most directly carry forward my argument in the outward form of a digression. We are only just realising that the art and science of education require a genius and a study of their own; and that this genius and this science are more than a bare knowledge of some branch of science or of literature. This truth was partially perceived in the past generation; and headmasters, somewhat crudely, were apt to supersede learning in their colleagues by requiring left-hand bowling and a taste for football. But culture is more than cricket, and more than football, and more than extent of knowledge.

Education is the acquisition of the art of the utilisation of knowledge. This is an art very difficult to impart. Whenever a text-book is written of real educational worth, you may be quite certain that some reviewer will say that it will be difficult to teach from it. Of course it will be difficult to teach from it. If it were easy, the book ought to be burned; for it cannot be educational. In education, as elsewhere, the broad primrose path leads to a nasty place. This evil path is represented by a book or a set of lectures which will practically enable the student to learn by heart all the questions likely to be asked at the next external examination. And I may say in passing that no educational system is possible unless every question directly asked of a pupil at any examination is either framed or modified by the actual teacher of that pupil in that subject. The external assessor may report on the curriculum or on the performance of the pupils, but never should be allowed to ask the pupil a question which has not been strictly supervised by the actual teacher, or at least inspired by a long conference with him. There are a few exceptions to this rule, but they are exceptions, and could easily be allowed for under the general rule.

We now return to my previous point, that theoretical ideas should always find important applications within the pupil's curriculum. This is not an easy doctrine to apply, but a very hard one. It contains within itself the problem of keeping knowledge alive, of preventing it from becoming inert, which is the central problem of all education.

The best procedure will depend on several factors, none of which can be neglected, namely, the genius of the teacher, the intellectual type of the pupils, their prospects in life, the opportunities offered by the immediate surroundings of the school, and allied factors of this sort. It is for this reason that the uniform external examination is so deadly. We do not denounce it because we are cranks, and like denouncing established things. We are not so childish. Also, of course, such examinations have their use in testing slackness. Our reason of dislike is very definite and very practical. It kills the best part of culture. When you analyse in the light of experience the central task of education, you find that its successful accomplishment depends on a delicate adjustment of many variable factors.

The reason is that we are dealing with human minds, and not with dead matter. The evocation of curiosity, of judgment, of the power of mastering a complicated tangle of circumstances, the use of theory in giving foresight in special cases—all these powers are not to be imparted by a set rule embodied in one schedule of examination subjects.

I appeal to you, as practical teachers. With good discipline, it is always possible to pump into the minds of a class a certain quantity of inert knowledge. You take a text-book and make them learn it. So far, so good. The child then knows how to solve a quadratic equation. But what is the point of teaching a child to solve a quadratic equation? There is a traditional answer to this question. It runs thus: The mind is an instrument, you first sharpen it, and then use it; the acquisition of the power of solving a quadratic equation is part of the process of sharpening the mind. Now there is just enough truth in this answer to have made it live through the ages. But for all its half-truth, it embodies a radical error which bids fair to stifle the genius of the modern world. I do not know who was first responsible for this analogy of the mind to a dead instrument. For aught I know, it may have been one of the seven wise men of Greece, or a committee of the whole lot of them. Whoever was the originator, there can be no doubt of the authority which it has acquired by the continuous approval bestowed upon it by eminent persons. But whatever its weight of authority, whatever the high approval which it can quote, I have no hesitation in denouncing it as one of the most fatal, erroneous, and dangerous conceptions ever introduced into the theory of education. The mind is never passive; it is a perpetual activity, delicate, receptive, responsive to stimulus. You cannot postpone its life until you have sharpened it. Whatever interest attaches to your subject-matter must be evoked here and now; whatever powers you are strengthening in the pupil, must be exercised here and now; whatever possibilities of mental life your teaching should impart, must be exhibited here and now. That is the golden rule of education, and a very difficult rule to follow.

The difficulty is just this: the apprehension of general ideas, intellectual habits of mind, and pleasurable interest in mental achievement can be evoked by no form of words, however accurately adjusted. All practical teachers know that education is a patient process of the mastery of details, minute by minute, hour by hour, day by day. There is no royal road to learning through an airy path of brilliant generalisations. There is a proverb about the difficulty of seeing the wood because of the trees. That difficulty is exactly the point which I am enforcing. The problem of education is to make the pupil see the wood by means of the trees.

The solution which I am urging, is to eradicate the fatal disconnection of subjects which kills the vitality of our modern curriculum. There is only one subject-matter for education, and that is Life in all its manifestations. Instead of this single unity, we offer children—Algebra, from which nothing

follows; Geometry, from which nothing follows; Science, from which nothing follows; History, from which nothing follows; a Couple of Languages, never mastered; and lastly, most dreary of all, Literature, represented by plays of Shakespeare, with philological notes and short analyses of plot and character to be in substance committed to memory. Can such a list be said to represent Life, as it is known in the midst of the living of it? The best that can be said of it is, that it is a rapid table of contents which a deity might run over in his mind while he was thinking of creating a world, and had not yet determined how to put it together.

Let us now return to quadratic equations. We still have on hand the unanswered question. Why should children be taught their solution? Unless quadratic equations fit into a connected curriculum, of course there is no reason to teach anything about them. Furthermore, extensive as should be the place of mathematics in a complete culture, I am a little doubtful whether for many types of boys algebraic solutions of quadratic equations do not lie on the specialist side of mathematics. I may here remind you that as yet I have not said anything of the psychology or the content of the specialism, which is so necessary a part of an ideal education. But all that is an evasion of our real question, and I merely state it in order to avoid being misunderstood in my answer.

Quadratic equations are part of algebra, and algebra is the intellectual instrument which has been created for rendering clear the quantitative aspects of the world. There is no getting out of it. Through and through the world is infected with quantity. To talk sense, is to talk in quantities. It is no use saying that the nation is large,—How large? It is no use saying that radium is scarce,—How scarce? You cannot evade quantity. You may fly to poetry and to music, and quantity and number will face you in your rhythms and your octaves. Elegant intellects which despise the theory of quantity, are but half developed. They are more to be pitied than blamed. The scraps of gibberish, which in their school-days were taught to them in the name of algebra, deserve some contempt.

This question of the degeneration of algebra into gibberish, both in word and in fact, affords a pathetic instance of the uselessness of reforming educational schedules without a clear conception of the attributes which you wish to evoke in the living minds of the children. A few years ago there was an outcry that school algebra was in need of reform, but there was a general agreement that graphs would put everything right. So all sorts of things were extruded, and graphs were introduced. So far as I can see, with no sort of idea behind them, but just graphs. Now every examination paper has one or two questions on graphs. Personally, I am an enthusiastic adherent of graphs. But I wonder whether as yet we have gained very much. You cannot put life into any schedule of general education unless you succeed in exhibiting its relation to some essential characteristic of all intelligent or emotional perception. It is a hard saying, but

it is true; and I do not see how to make it any easier. In making these little formal alterations you are beaten by the very nature of things. You are pitted against too skilful an adversary, who will see to it that the pea is always under the other thimble.

Reformation must begin at the other end. First, you must make up your mind as to those quantitative aspects of the world which are simple enough to be introduced into general education; then a schedule of algebra should be framed which will about find its exemplification in these applications. We need not fear for our pet graphs, they will be there in plenty when we once begin to treat algebra as a serious means of studying the world. Some of the simplest applications will be found in the quantities which occur in the simplest study of society. The curves of history are more vivid and more informing than the dry catalogues of names and dates which comprise the greater part of that arid school study. What purpose is effected by a catalogue of undistinguished kings and queens? Tom, Dick, or Harry, they are all dead. General resurrections are failures, and are better postponed. The quantitative flux of the forces of modern society is capable of very simple exhibition. Meanwhile, the idea of the variable, of the function, of rate of change, of equations and their solution, of elimination, are being studied as an abstract science for their own sake. Not, of course, in the pompous phrases with which I am alluding to them here, but with that iteration of simple special cases proper to teaching.

If this course be followed, the route from Chaucer to the Black Death, from the Black Death to modern Labour troubles, will connect the tales of the mediæval pilgrims with the abstract science of algebra, both yielding diverse aspects of that single theme, Life. I know what most of you are thinking at this point. It is that the exact course which I have sketched out is not the particular one which you would have chosen, or even see how to work. I quite agree. I am not claiming that I could do it myself. But your objection is the precise reason why a common external examination system is fatal to education. The process of exhibiting the applications of knowledge must, for its success, essentially depend on the character of the pupils and the genius of the teacher. Of course I have left out the easiest applications with which most of us are more at home. I mean the quantitative sides of sciences, such as mechanics and physics.

Again, in the same connection we plot the statistics of social phenomena against the time. We then eliminate the time between suitable pairs. We can speculate how far we have exhibited a real causal connection, or how far a mere temporal coincidence. We notice that we might have plotted against the time one set of statistics for one country and another set for another country, and thus, with suitable choice of subjects, have obtained graphs which certainly exhibited mere coincidence. Also other graphs exhibit obvious causal connections. We wonder how to discriminate. And so are drawn on as far as we will.

But in considering this description, I must beg you to remember what I have been insisting on above. In the first place, one train of thought will not suit all groups of children. For example, I should expect that artisan children will want something more concrete and, in a sense, swifter than I have set down here. Perhaps I am wrong, but that is what I should guess. In the second place, I am not contemplating one beautiful lecture stimulating, once and for all, an admiring class. That is not the way in which education proceeds. No; all the time the pupils are hard at work solving examples, drawing graphs, and making experiments, until they have a thorough hold on the whole subject. I am describing the interspersed explanations, the directions which should be given to their thoughts. The pupils have got to be made to feel that they are studying something, and are not merely executing intellectual minuets.

Finally, if you are teaching pupils for some general examination, the problem of sound teaching is greatly complicated. Have you ever noticed the zig-zag moulding round a Norman arch? The ancient work is beautiful, the modern work is hideous. The reason is, that the modern work is done to exact measure, the ancient work is varied according to the idiosyncrasy of the workman. Here it is crowded, and there it is expanded. Now the essence of getting pupils through examinations is to give equal weight to all parts of the schedule. But mankind is naturally specialist. One man sees a whole subject, where another can find only a few detached examples. I know that it seems contradictory to allow for specialism in a curriculum especially designed for a broad culture. Without contradictions the world would be simpler, and perhaps duller. But I am certain that in education wherever you exclude specialism you destroy life.

We now come to the other great branch of a general mathematical education, namely Geometry. The same principles apply. The theoretical part should be clear-cut, rigid, short, and important. Every proposition not absolutely necessary to exhibit the main connection of ideas should be cut out, but the great fundamental ideas should be all there. No omission of concepts, such as those of Similarity and Proportion. We must remember that, owing to the aid rendered by the visual presence of a figure, Geometry is a field of unequalled excellence for the exercise of the deductive faculties of reasoning. Then, of course, there follows Geometrical Drawing, with its training for the hand and eye.

But, like Algebra, Geometry and Geometrical Drawing must be extended beyond the mere circle of geometrical ideas. In an industrial neighbourhood, machinery and workshop practice form the appropriate extension. For example, in the London Polytechnics this has been achieved with conspicuous success. For many secondary schools I suggest that surveying and maps are the natural applications. In particular, plane-table surveying should lead pupils to a vivid apprehension of the immediate application of geometric truths. Simple drawing apparatus, a surveyor's chain, and

a surveyor's compass, should enable the pupils to rise from the survey and mensuration of a field to the construction of the map of a small district. The best education is to be found in gaining the utmost information from the simplest apparatus. The provision of elaborate instruments is greatly to be deprecated. To have constructed the map of a small district, to have considered its roads, its contours, its geology, its climate, its relation to other districts, the effects on the status of its inhabitants, will teach more history and geography than any knowledge of Perkin Warbeck or of Behren's Straits. I mean not a nebulous lecture on the subject, but a serious investigation in which the real facts are definitely ascertained by the aid of accurate theoretical knowledge. A typical mathematical problem should be: Survey such and such a field, draw a plan of it to such and such a scale, and find the area. It would be quite a good procedure to impart the necessary geometrical propositions without their proofs. Then, concurrently in the same term, the proofs of the propositions would be learnt while the survey was being made.

Fortunately, the specialist side of education presents an easier problem than does the provision of a general culture. For this there are many reasons. One is that many of the principles of procedure to be observed are the same in both cases, and it is unnecessary to recapitulate. Another reason is that specialist training takes place—or should take place—at a more advanced stage of the pupil's course, and thus there is easier material to work upon. But undoubtedly the chief reason is that the specialist study is normally a study of peculiar interest to the student. He is studying it because, for some reason, he wants to know it. This makes all the difference. The general culture is designed to foster an activity of mind; the specialist course utilises this activity. But it does not do to lay too much stress on these neat antitheses. As we have already seen, in the general course foci of special interest will arise; and similarly in the special study, the external connections of the subject drag through outwards.

Again, there is not one course of study which merely gives general culture, and another which gives special knowledge. The subjects pursued for the sake of a general education are special subjects specially studied; and, on the other hand, one of the ways of encouraging general mental activity is to foster a special devotion. You may not divide the seamless coat of learning. What education has to impart is an intimate sense for the power of ideas, for the beauty of ideas, and for the structure of ideas, together with a particular body of knowledge which has peculiar reference to the life of the being possessing it.

The appreciation of the structure of ideas is that side of a cultured mind which can only grow under the influence of a special study. I mean that eye for the whole chessboard, for the bearing of one set of ideas on another. Nothing but a special study can give any appreciation for the exact formulation of general ideas, for their relations when formulated, for

their service in the comprehension of life. A mind so disciplined should be both more abstract and more concrete. It has been trained in the comprehension of abstract thought and in the analysis of facts.

Finally, there should grow the most austere of all mental qualities; I mean the sense for style. It is an æsthetic sense, based on admiration for the direct attainment of a foreseen end, simply and without waste. Style in art, style in literature, style in science, style in logic, style in practical execution have fundamentally the same æsthetic qualities, namely, attainment and restraint. The love of a subject in itself and for itself, where it is not the sleepy pleasure of pacing a mental quarter-deck, is the love of style as manifested in that study.

Here we are brought back to the position from which we started, the utility of education. Style, in its finest sense, is the last acquirement of the educated mind; it is also the most useful. It pervades the whole being. The administrator with a sense for style hates waste; the engineer with a sense for style economises his material; the artisan with a sense for style prefers good work. Style is the ultimate morality of mind.

But above style, and above knowledge, there is something, a vague shape like fate above the Greek gods. That something is Power. Style is the fashioning of power, the restraining of power. But, after all, the power of attainment of the desired end is fundamental. The first thing is to get there. Do not bother about your style, but solve your problem, justify the ways of God to man, administer your province, or do whatever else is set before you.

Where, then, does style help? In this, with style the end is attained without side issues, without raising undesirable inflammations. With style you attain your end and nothing but your end. With style the effect of your activity is calculable, and foresight is the last gift of gods to men. With style your power is increased, for your mind is not distracted with irrelevancies, and you are more likely to attain your object. Now style is the exclusive privilege of the expert. Whoever heard of the style of an amateur painter, of the style of an amateur poet? Style is always the product of specialist study, the peculiar contribution of specialism to culture.

English education in its present phase suffers from a lack of definite aim, and from an external machinery which kills its vitality. Hitherto in this address I have been considering the aims which should govern education. In this respect England halts between two opinions. It has not decided whether to produce amateurs or experts. The profound change in the world which the nineteenth century has produced is that the growth of knowledge has given foresight. The amateur is essentially a man with appreciation and with immense versatility in mastering a given routine. But he lacks the foresight which comes from special knowledge. The object of this address is to suggest how to produce the expert without loss of the essential virtues of the amateur. The machinery of our secondary education is rigid where

it should be yielding, and lax where it should be rigid. Every school is bound on pain of extinction to train its boys for a small set of definite examinations. No headmaster has a free hand to develop his general education or his specialist studies in accordance with the opportunities of his school, which are created by its staff, its environment, its class of boys, and its endowments. I suggest that no system of external tests which aims primarily at examining individual scholars can result in anything but educational waste.

Primarily it is the schools and not the scholars which should be inspected. Each school should grant its own leaving certificates, based on its own curriculum. The standards of these schools should be sampled and corrected. But the first requisite for educational reform is the school as a unit, with its approved curriculum based on its own needs, and evolved by its own staff. If we fail to secure that, we simply fall from one formalism into another, from one dung-hill of inert ideas into another.

In stating that the school is the true educational unit in any national system for the safeguarding of efficiency, I have conceived the alternative system as being the external examination of the individual scholar. But every Scylla is faced by its Charybdis—or, in more homely language, there is a ditch on both sides of the road. It will be equally fatal to education if we fall into the hands of a supervising department which is under the impression that it can divide all schools into two or three rigid categories, each type being forced to adopt a rigid curriculum. When I say that the school is the educational unit, I mean exactly what I say, no larger unit, no smaller unit. Each school must have the claim to be considered in relation to its special circumstances. The classifying of schools for some purposes is necessary. But no absolutely rigid curriculum, not modified by its own staff, should be permissible. Exactly the same principles apply, with the proper modifications, to universities and to technical colleges.

When one considers in its length and in its breadth the importance of this question of the education of a nation's young, the broken lives, the defeated hopes, the national failures, which result from the frivolous inertia with which it is treated, it is difficult to restrain within oneself a savage rage. In the conditions of modern life the rule is absolute, the race which does not value trained intelligence is doomed. Not all your heroism, not all your social charm, not all your wit, not all your victories on land or at sea, can move back the finger of fate. To-day we maintain ourselves. To-morrow science will have moved forward yet one more step, and there will be no appeal from the judgment which will then be pronounced on the uneducated.

We can be content with no less than the old summary of educational ideal which has been current at any time from the dawn of our civilisation. The essence of education is that it be religious.

Pray, what is religious education?

A religious education is an education which inculcates duty and reverence. Duty arises from our potential control over the course of events. Where attainable knowledge could have changed the issue, ignorance has the guilt of vice. And the foundation of reverence is this perception, that the present holds within itself the complete sum of existence, backwards and forwards, that whole amplitude of time, which is eternity.

## TOPICS FOR DISCUSSION

1  What do phrases like "scraps of information" and "useless bore" in paragraph 1 tell you about the direction this article is likely to take?

2  What are "inert ideas"? How much of your education has been of this type? Do you believe you were ever responsible for its remaining "inert"? How can ideas be kept from becoming "inert"?

3  Why is the method of thinking a more important educational objective than the materials of thinking? How can, for example, the knowledge of a dead date, say the Magna Charta, be made useful to one student and totally useless to another?

4  In what ways does the external examination system violate Whitehead's theories of education? Have you been subjected to an external examination system? What effect do you think it has?

5  Why does anyone learn to solve quadratic equations? Does Whitehead believe everyone should?

6  What evidence is there in this article that Whitehead manifests in himself what he advocates in the education of others?

7  The author says: "The best education is to be found in gaining the utmost information from the simplest apparatus." How would this procedure forward the kind of education advocated in the article?

## ... AND COMPOSITION

8  "Style is the ultimate morality of mind." Write an essay interpreting this statement.

9  Recount an experience in which ideas were placed in exciting new combinations for you.

10  "The essence of education is that it be religious." Develop Whitehead's idea further, touching on the special connotation of "religious."

JOHN WAIN (1925–    )   during the fifties and sixties has
been popularly identified with the "angry young men" in British life and with
the "movement" in English poetry. Educated at Oxford, he taught at the
University of Reading till 1955 and now pursues his career as critic,
poet, and novelist. Through his writing he has come to exemplify a stance
characteristic of his generation: staunchly critical, not to be put off
by shibboleths, determined to move away from the tradition. The
following essay demonstrates something of that stance.

# Education: For Assent or Dissent?

In attitudes to education, as in most things, the world is divided. Many people in the West seem to believe that an educated person is somehow unworthy—little better than a traitor to the whole idea of education— unless he ranges himself pretty determinedly against the forces that propel his society along. This gives rise to the question: Can education legitimately aim at molding people into agreement with the basic assumptions of the society they live in, or is the only honorable role for the educated man that of rebel and disputant? Mr. David Riesman in a recent article has said roundly that "the relation of education to later life should be a dialectical and critical one." And speaking of the kind of student who makes the most favorable impression on faculty members and finds himself recommended for fellowships, jobs and so on, he notes that the most favored ones were "a bit rebellious, a bit offbeat . . . these were the students apt to appeal to a faculty member who had not entirely repressed a rebelliousness of his own that had led him to be a teacher in the first place."

The assumption here, that a main motive for devoting one's life to education is or can be "rebelliousness," is a widespread one in the West, though it must be virtually unknown in the Communist world, where the educational machine is seen as an assemblyline for producing good Communist citizens. But there are people in the West, also, who do not see education chiefly in terms of inciting people to challenge the society they live in, to overturn its assumptions, to rebel against its conventions. The word "convention" means a coming together, and in every society there are important areas of thought and feeling on which men have come together. What is education primarily useful for? To strengthen this cohesion, to bind a society more closely together by presenting its basic assumptions in an acceptable form or to weaken them by encouraging rebellion in every sphere and over every issue? Is the rebel thinking too much of himself and too little of others? Are there some things more important than the purity of one's spotless little intellectual integrity? We must be careful—the answer may be "No."

Some societies, both today and in the past, have gone so far along the road toward an official orthodox education that the very question we are discussing would seem to them meaningless. In the Middle Ages European education was dominated by the Roman Catholic Church; theology was queen of the sciences in every scheme of learning, and the question of an unorthodox—or antiorthodox—teaching never arose.

As a matter of fact, the Middle Ages offer an interesting point of comparison with totalitarian modern societies. Their literary and scientific culture was based on the Greek and Latin past; when the highly trained, subtle, disputatious medieval scholar engaged in historical or literary teaching, he was working with material which dated from before the rise of his own society with its all-pervading Christian beliefs and assumptions. This set a problem which, during the medieval centuries, called forth some heroic solutions. A medieval scholar who loved, say Vergil—who responded to the majesty and beauty of Vergil's language and the nobility of his vision—was faced with the awkward fact that Vergil, having lived before Christ, was not a Christian writer, and therefore could not be used as an instrument of direct Christian teaching. If the medieval Christian scholars had been narrowly Philistine, they would have turned away from Vergil and concentrated entirely on their own Christian, Neo-Latin culture. In fact, they did nothing of the kind; all the great Greek and Latin writers, insofar as the Middle Ages knew of their existence, were handed down with the utmost care, and every scrap of information about them was lovingly gathered.

To do this with the official backing of the Church was, of course, a matter of giving a Christian slant to the interpretation of the pagan classics, and this was accordingly done. Some of the interpretations we read about in a book like Comparetti's *Vergil in the Middle Ages* remind one of nothing so much as the efforts of present-day Soviet professors to prove that Shakespeare or Goethe was progressive—that is, a Communist before his time. Their motive is a very strong one; being sensitive, intelligent readers, they want to go on being allowed to study these great poets and to spread a knowledge of them among their students; if this means dragging them across the ideological barrier, then drag they will. It is a mistake to mock at these men. If the Middle Ages had not performed the same service for Vergil and Ovid, not only would medieval culture have been much the poorer, but the works of these poets might have disappeared forever.

The medieval church was no very hard taskmaster. In the absence of any strict standards of historical criticism a scholar could get away with some very odd interpretations, if he had a strong enough motive to make him present his case vehemently. Thus, it was confidently asserted that the ancients were familiar with the *Old Testament,* so that they were already halfway to Christianity. Following on from this, the annotators pounced

on everything that would bear a Christian interpretation. Vergil's *Fourth Eclogue,* for instance, celebrates the prospective birth of a child to Pollio's wife, a government official who was one of Vergil's early protectors. The poem pictures a new golden age of security and happiness which will date from this birth, and not unnaturally the early Christian commentators took this as a prophetic reference to the coming of the Messiah. It followed that Vergil must have been gifted with mystical powers of prophecy; and if he had them, might not others?

The important thing about the campaign is that it worked. Modern scholars are often puzzled to discern the exact degree of sincerity behind the medieval policy of reading all literary texts as if they were allegories, and making them yield the "right" meaning. Certainly they developed great skill at this kind of interpretation, and the exercise of that skill must have been a satisfaction in itself. But did the average medieval scholar, sitting down to expound a poem like the *Aeneid* or Ovid's *Metamorphoses* by splitting it up prismatically into a series of allegories, really believe that he was unwrapping a series of packages that had been deliberately tied by the author? Or did he not care about the author one way or another? Of course, the Middle Ages lacked the sense of history, as we now know it; they probably did not realize that an ancient Greek or Roman had an imagination attuned to a very different way of life from theirs, so different that the first step toward understanding his work would be to try to feel oneself back into his times. All they knew was that the ancients were pagan and must be made to yield a Christian message. Or was it all they knew? Did some of the more sensitive among them realize, as they compiled their vast commentaries in which every detail of the text had its allegorical solution, like a puzzle, that their labors were essentially irrelevant, that they erected a superstructure of their own on the base provided by the author's words?

I fancy this thought must have strayed into their minds now and again, just as it must stray into the minds of Communist critics whose lifework is to provide every literary classic with a protective awning of socialist realism. Sometimes very subtle and perceptive work can be produced even under these conditions; I have read Marxist analyses of Shakespearean plays which certainly provide interesting sidelights; the young English art critic, Mr. John Berger, is not so utterly insensitive to painting as you would think from reading his bald statement that "We can only make sense of art if we judge it by the criterion of whether or not it helps men to claim their social rights." This is exactly on a level with the medieval view that, since Christian truth is the only truth, any writing which cannot be made to yield a direct Christian message is simply falsehood. And yet medieval literary criticism is often profoundly interesting. My own view, by the way, is the exact inversion of the medieval one; I think that if Christianity is true, then every good poem or novel is "Christian." And if Marxism, with

its economic explanations and its relentless emphasis on the class struggle, really offered a satisfying explanation of human history, then all good writing would be Marxist writing; it would relate, in its own way, to the truth as Marx proclaimed it.

Much has been written in the West about Soviet education, and violent arguments have sprung up between those who warn us that it is already ahead of our own and those who, at the opposite extreme, maintain that the Soviet Union, not being interested in the cultivation of intellectual freedom and the spirit of inquiry, has no such thing as education, in our Western sense, anywhere within its borders. The first group points to the colossal Soviet expenditure on schools and colleges; the second to the heavily slanted doctrinaire nature of Soviet teaching.

Without wishing to open old wounds—for I have been involved in some of these arguments myself—I think it can be fairly said that Soviet education, admirably thorough as it is and enviably confident in the rightness of its own methods, is pre-eminently aimed at teaching its people to *know the answers*. All the answers: about medicine, about mathematics, about agriculture, about philosophy, about literature and about history and politics. The Soviet rulers do not encourage specialization, at any rate for undergraduates. They do not want historians or literary critics, they do not even want surgeons and engineers, who get on with the job according to their own lights, without much idea of wider social implications of what they are doing. Their attitude is that all work is Communist work. A dam built by a Soviet engineer is not just a dam, it is a Communist dam. And so on down the line, until even the simplest tonsillectomy performed by a Soviet surgeon is a Communist tonsillectomy. Just as all literature, art and music produced by Soviet artists are required to be propaganda for the Soviet way of life, so all work is understood to be motivated first by a desire to serve that way of life and only second by love of the work itself.

This attitude, as everyone knows, is intensively fostered by Soviet teaching. The place occupied in eighteenth-century England by a simple assent to the *Thirty-Nine Articles,* which were adopted by the English clergy in 1563 to unify Anglican worship, is occupied in the Soviet Union by a trio of formidable indoctrination courses, compulsory for all students, in whatever faculty, throughout the fifteen republics of the U.S.S.R. Thanks to the University of Michigan, we can now study the syllabuses for these courses; in a thick pamphlet, *Administration of Teaching in Social Sciences in the U.S.S.R.,* they have published in English translation the requirements for three basic, compulsory courses: History of the Communist Party of the U.S.S.R., Political Economy, and Dialectical and Historical Materialism. The material is offered without comment, save for a short introduction by Michigan President Harlan H. Hatcher, setting out the circumstances— what the syllabuses are, how they were obtained, and so on. One sentence

from this introduction leaps into relief: "Compulsory for all students, these courses constitute about 8 to 10 per cent of the total instructional program of Soviet universities, technical schools, medical colleges and other institutions of higher education."

Obviously a system which compels every trained person, from a marine biologist to a lawyer, to spend one hour out of every ten during his or her college years in getting by heart the official doctrines of the state is determined on one thing at least: no one among the intelligentsia is going to be able to plead ignorance on any question of dogma. If anyone fails to live up to the full doctrinal requirements, the responsibility is entirely on his own shoulders, since his professional career was not at liberty to begin until he had shown himself word perfect in the orthodoxy..

All this, in general terms, one knew already. From conversations with Soviet students and bureaucrats, I had come away with the impression of a flawlessly rehearsed catechism. What the Michigan pamphlet does is to reveal, step by step, how the indoctrination is done. Each subject is divided into topics; every topic has its official allotment of time and its list of required reading. And the conclusions that must be reached are formulated in advance, there in the syllabus. Here, for example, is Topic 22 of the Political Economy course: "Completion of Territorial Division of World Among Great Powers and Struggle for its Redivision. Formation and Basic Features of Imperialism's Colonial System."

> 1. Imperialism as system of financial enslavement and colonial oppression. Completion of territorial division of world toward beginning of twentieth century. Struggle for redivision of divided world. Struggle of imperialists for world domination. Wars and militarization of natural economy in capitalist countries.
> 2. Formation of imperialism's colonial system. Colonies and semi-colonies. Role of colonies in era of imperialism. Colonies as spheres for investing capital. Colonies as markets for sales and as appendages supplying metropolitan countries with agricultural raw materials. One-sided character of development of national economy in colonial countries. Colonies as strategic military bases of imperialism.

And so on through two more articles.

That second section, when I read it, gave me a clue to the real nature of several conversations I had had in Moscow earlier in the year. Whenever imperialism was mentioned, the same arguments came out, no matter to whom you were talking. The basic position was, in each case, that there is only one kind of imperialism—that is, planting your flag on the soil of another country and then proceeding to exploit that country. No distinction was admitted between old-style exploitation and modern mandate or protectorate systems; nor between countries which were being progressively educated toward self-government and those being held down by force. It

was all imperialism—whereas the Soviet annexation of, say, Latvia, was not imperialism because it didn't involve running up the Soviet flag. And having read Topic 22, I see it all. If one urged that the British action in Cyprus was motivated not by a wish to exploit the Cypriots, but by an obligation to NATO, that had been forestalled under the heading, "Colonies as strategic military bases of imperialism."

I give this small and commonplace example to bring out the main point—that the Soviet educational system is succeeding in the basic task its rulers have imposed on it, which is to rehearse its entire *bourgeoisie* in an elaborate question-and-answer system of apologetics.

This is a form of education for orthodoxy which is easy enough to reject as undesirable; one can't imagine any thoughtful person actually *wishing* to go in with such a system—though, no doubt, once enclosed in it most people would resign themselves and keep their mouths shut.

When I proposed for examination the question with which I started, about education for assent or dissent, I naturally had no intention of seriously recommending a giant processing machine such as the Soviet Union has evolved. It isn't—in the West—necessary to muster all the arguments against such a system but, if I had to choose one argument that contains all the others, I would merely point out that education is essentially a process of *launching*. An education, of whatever kind, has failed if it has not managed to stimulate in the student that kind of intellectual curiosity which will naturally lead him, year by year, to extend his knowledge. And also, it should give him the necessary basic information to build on; not only factual information but skills of a kind that do not show themselves in a parade of facts. How to find the knowledge he wants; how to marshal information; how to consider a subject dispassionately, brushing away the dust and cobwebs that naturally will form over any subject that has lain in his mind for a few years, among the lumber of his own prejudices and personal emphases. All this the student needs before he can begin. And he begins on the day he leaves college, just as the aviator begins on the day he first flies on his own.

By this test, the Soviet system of education fails. Its aim is not to launch people on a lifetime of original and developing thought, but to process them. By providing everyone with a shared background of information and argument, they may paper over the cracks in the Communist system and in some cases actually cement them. But there is nothing here that can call itself education.

This kind of defect in the education of a totalitarian country is so glaringly obvious that one is sometimes driven close to the opposite extreme. It is tempting, after a look at the results of Communist orthodoxy in education, to throw the whole thing up and say that the sole duty of an educated person is to question, to probe, to protest, to rebel. Tempting, but in the end not satisfying.

All societies try to perpetuate themselves; we cannot deny them this right. Unless we take the extreme position represented by, "Communism is evil. Therefore anything that helps to strengthen a Communist society is evil. Therefore Communist education is evil," we can hardly quarrel with Russia or China for wanting to slant their educational systems toward orthodoxy. The West, naturally, does it too. In England, to take the example I know best, the state schools faithfully reflect the involvement of Church and Government, which we symbolize by placing the Queen at the head of the Church of England. England is thus an officially Christian country, in that the reigning monarch is identified with the established Church. Proceeding downward in a direct cause-and-effect chain, we get the compulsory religious teaching in schools. Every state-run school has to have religious instruction; it is the only compulsory subject, whereas there is no law which compels a school to teach, say, arithmetic. And every such school must assemble teachers and pupils together once every day for religious worship. Both the instruction and the worship must be undenominational; there must be nothing to stir up the fierce warfare of the sects. But religion there must be. If a child's parents object—if they are Roman Catholics, or Orthodox Jews or convinced atheists—the child is excused from these activities. But the school is not excused from the duty to provide them.

A Communist, then, could point out that we in England slant our education toward Christianity, which from his point of view is either a mere deception, aimed at keeping the poor in a proper state of resignation and holding back the wheels of change, or else a pitiable illusion. And however we chose to answer him, we could not deny that England has, in recent centuries, insisted on a definite show of orthodoxy from those entrusted with responsibility. The settlement of 1688—which came at the end of a long series of dangers and disasters provided largely by Roman Catholic powers on the one hand and the extreme revolutionary forms of Protestantism on the other—found a solution in the *Thirty-Nine Articles*. The Church of England, as a middle way, was deliberately used as a political instrument. From the 1680's until within living memory, it was impossible to hold a responsible position in England without assenting to the *Thirty-Nine Articles*—in other words, belonging to the Church of England. Without that assent, no one could hold government office, be a member of Parliament, study at Oxford or Cambridge or hold a commission in the army or navy.

What is more, this system remained firmly in place until the historical circumstances that produced it had finally withered away. It was never overthrown by determined opposition from below; it simply faded away of its own accord when it became out-of-date. One of the last people to run up against it, incidentally, was H. G. Wells. As a boy, already sceptical in his views, he wanted to become a pupil-teacher in order to carry on with

his education. The *Thirty-Nine Articles* were demanded; he writhed, raged, but gave in for the sake of going on increasing his knowledge. As a result he hated religions, churches and priests till his dying hour.

It is beyond my competence to settle, or even profitably discuss, the question, Was England right in taking this action, or wrong? I can see, of course, that the country entered a period of political stability in the 1680's such as the world has seldom seen and continued in it until the twentieth century. And it seems reasonable to guess that the price that had to be paid for this stability was the *Thirty-Nine Articles.* But, as I say, the question lies outside my competence. The stability may have had other causes. What matters for our present purpose is that England, a country always known as a stronghold of political freedom, did find it necessary for more than 200 years to impose on its citizens, or on such of them as sought to win authority and influence, a kind of loyalty oath.

This decision, however, did not bear very directly on English education. You had to be "Church of England" to get into Oxford or Cambridge, but once there you were not required to organize your studies along orthodox lines. And if you were a dissenter, there was, after the 1820's, the University of London offering first-class instruction—and there were always the dissenting academies, which play an honorable part in English educational history. In other words, it was admitted that orthodoxy could not, in education, be forced on the student at every step. Compromise reigned; the comparison with modern Russia or China or Nazi Germany very soon breaks down. Shelley was sent down from Oxford for writing a pamphlet called *The Necessity of Atheism;* but if he had restrained his impatience for print and merely *talked* about this necessity, he would have been left in peace.

The battle, in short, was never violently joined. Since the Church was at the heart of English institutional life, successive governments protected themselves by the simple bargain of requiring assent to the *Thirty-Nine Articles* from those who directed or studied at the country's chief centers of learning; but they did nothing to hinder the setting-up of rival centers, nor did they indulge in witch-hunting among the accepted. Both orthodox and unorthodox proceeded along the same traditional lines. They saw education as a matter of imparting a traditional body of wisdom. The three classical languages—Latin, Greek and Biblical Hebrew—would enable a man to study in the original most of the texts on which the culture and ethics of Western society were based. Then there were principal modern languages. Then there was history—mostly European history, since Europe was effectively "the world" until the twentieth century, just as "philosophy" meant Western philosophy.

It was all rather like the process whereby old birds teach young birds to fly. The student was introduced to the texts in which the society's basic values were enshrined, and the implication was that if he made a mess of

his life, or failed to be of use to the community, the responsibility would be his own.

Until the rise of mass communications, this system worked reasonably well. The target was a limited one; no attempt was made to educate an entire population, since it was assumed that decisions would be made by the educated class and that values could be spread downward, like butter soaking through a baked potato. Not until toward the end of the nineteenth century did successive shocks begin to weaken the traditional structure. First came industrialism with its demand for universal literacy. No industrial society can be run by an illiterate working class. England, which became fully industrialized very early, was correspondingly early (1871) with compulsory free education, resulting in virtually 100 per cent literacy. The ruling class of that time, like the Soviet ruling class of the present day, indulged in a good deal of boasting about its paternal generosity in teaching the people to read and write, but the more astute among them must have known that if they did not provide the funds for this instruction they would fall behind—in the race for trade—nations who *would* provide it.

From that hour the older education was doomed. A literate people means a mass press, challenging the values instilled by education with sensational and get-rich-quick values of its own. And within forty or fifty years the press was itself challenged by radio, cinema and, later, television. In every country where the entertainment and advertising industries are allowed a free hand, they spend money which makes the country's education budget look pitiable. They offer salaries to bright men which make the teacher's way of life, by comparison, reek of masochism. And they batter the minds of the people into insensibility before the vitalizing suggestions of literature, art or philosophy can begin to do their work.

It is at this point that we meet again, and in a sharper form, the initial question. Education for assent or dissent? For conformity or rebellion? In the East there is no problem because both sides have been drawn into one central mass. The entertainment industry, the press and the advertising copy writers have all been processed into the same solid block that contains the teacher and the writer. And Western visitors who feel disgust at the blatancy of their own admen and journalists often come back from Russia or China full of respect for the relative quietness and single-mindedness in the Communist atmosphere. Personally I didn't. The bludgeoned conformity aroused my pity; the holier-than-thou attitude of official communism, my impatience. This is not the way out. Better singing commercials than culture squads raising hymns to Lenin by numbers.

And neither can that initial question admit of any simple answer. Should a society educate its members for assent? Assent *to what?* The claim that a society can teach only the values that it has implies that those values are widely recognized and can be stated easily. In the Communist world,

this is true, at least as far as the official values are concerned. But in a free society, values are continually forming, evolving, emerging into consciousness. If we say, for instance, that the twin sources of Western civilization are still, in spite of all modern changes, Christianity and the classics, that does not close the discussion. It opens it. We see the Christian thread running through various attempts at social justice—welfare states and the like. And we see the classical thread running through the efforts to preserve intellectual freedom—the gift of the Greek—and impartial, universally recognized laws—the gift of the Roman. But having noted these broad outlines we are no nearer to answering the enormous number of questions thrust on us by day-to-day life which all resolve themselves into one basic question: Given that our values are these, how do we apply them in this situation? And this? And that which is coming toward us? For liberal democracy, unlike Communism, has no answer book; we do not claim, as the Communists do, that the truth is immediately obvious. John Donne has told us in his *Third Satire* that

> On a huge hill,
> Cragged and steep, Truth stands, and he that will
> Reach her, about must, and about must go,

and we believe him and are willing to go about and about, toiling up to where Truth stands.

And this, of course, puts a great strain on the teacher. In our kind of society the teacher—any kind of teacher, from kindergarten to graduate school—is in an almost impossible position. In a society inclined to be skeptical about the practical use of education, except insofar as it channels the young into well-paid jobs, the teacher, who has no well-paid job, has to stand as a witness that education does confer riches and happiness. However modest he is, sooner or later he has to make the claim, "I have something to give your children. It will not bring them big incomes and security; it will not solve their immediate personal problems. But I am offering it, and I advise you to accept it on their behalf." And if society, still skeptical, with an eye on the teacher's low salary, few possessions, modest living quarters, answers with the sneer, "You mean it will make them more like *you?*" then the teacher must find within himself, somewhere, the courage to say "Yes." And let it go at that. Conscious as he is of his own inadequacies and limitations, of the many sacrifices he has accepted, of his own unsatisfied wants and irrational loves and hatreds, he must appear before the world as the representative of the free human mind. It is an almost impossible demand to make of anyone. And yet thousands accept it, and undertake the impossible, in every free country.

And having accepted it, they find themselves in the front line of attack. A society teaches the values that it has, only by feeling its way concretely

toward those values through the experience of living men and women. Both assent and dissent become merged in inquiry. For if we assent to the principle of intellectual freedom, we commit ourselves to fearless questioning. If we assent to the principle of the sacredness of the individual, we commit ourselves to the personal judgment. If we throw away the authority of the intellectual policeman on the corner, and substitute the right of appeal to the community of reasonable beings, we commit ourselves to respect for other people.

On either side of the fence, what we find is an education for assent. On the one side, assent to an authority which hands down values from above, can alter them at will and dictate exactly by what means they are to be put into practice. On the other, assent to a tradition of inquiry, of bringing even the least palatable truths into the open and of making the practical application of those truths a matter for the individual conscience.

On the one side, assent to the tabulated and formally announced doctrines of a society. On the other, assent to the inner laws by whose authority the society came into being and which, thwarted and fouled as they may be by individual acts of selfishness, still make themselves felt—as long as there is an education which frees the mind. To be free is, often, to be baffled by indecision; but a society whose education aims at banishing indecision will sooner or later find that truth, sanity and even loyalty have been banished as well.

## TOPICS FOR DISCUSSION

1   Note how often the author poses questions. Does he answer all the questions he asks? How is the entire essay an answer to his initial question in the first paragraph?

2   What purposes may be served by asking questions?

3   In what ways are the Christian allegorists of the Middle Ages similar to the Marxist interpreters of modern times? Does Wain seem equally sympathetic to these two orthodoxies? What objections might a Marxist raise to the terminology Wain uses in discussing the "Communist world"?

4   How is orthodoxy in England through the official church justified despite many historical injustices perpetrated in its name? Is Wain totally convinced? Are you convinced that the stability he identifies was worth the means used to assure it?

5   How is the section on the teacher integrated into the total theme?

6   Is there a paradox in the final answer to the initial question of paragraph 1?

## ...AND COMPOSITION

7   Describe a social value in which you believe. Do you think social values should be taught in all public schools? Were many of them taught to you in such schools?

8   Write a paper based on an initial question and developed through a set of subsequent questions which you answer.

9   When does orthodoxy threaten free inquiry? Write an essay on kinds of orthodoxy or conditions under which orthodoxy might tolerate or even encourage free inqury.

**DAVID RIESMAN (1909–    )** a famous sociologist at Harvard, with two
collaborators published *The Lonely Crowd: A Study in the Changing
American Character.* This very influential book analyzes the life we lead and
the kind of people we are becoming. The modern being so vividly
asserted there may be alienated, rootless, deprived, but he has certain
advantages, too. Mr. Riesman's concern about the "changing
American character" focuses in the following article on a
particularly fascinating group, our college population—you.

# Where Is the College Generation Headed?

The conflict of the generations is neither a new nor a particularly
American story, but it is perhaps exacerbated by the self-consciousness
and the partial segregation of teen-age culture, to such an extent that both
old and young are exceptionally vulnerable to their mutual criticism. I
do not care to add to the complacency of my agemates who, from their
clubs, pulpits, and other rostrums, attack the alleged "softness" of the
young, whom they have themselves brought up, while failing to see the
difficulties young people face today precisely because the manifest hardships
with which earlier Americans coped have been, for millions, attenuated.
These hardships cannot be artificially restored, at least for people over
twelve; however, I believe that college students are now beginning to find
new ways to become active politically, and hence responsible humanly.

It is easy to underestimate the importance of this in America, where
students until recently did not play the role in politics that they do in
Latin America, Turkey, Korea, or Japan. For, the cadres of the disinherited
who once helped power political change in this country are diminished in
numbers and even more diminished in leadership, now that nearly every
bright, motivated boy gets funneled into college if he wants to go. Thus,
our expanding colleges absorb increasingly large fractions of the available
idealism and dynamism of our society. And at the same time, as I shall
try to show, many students are not attracted by the traditional goals of
commercial or professional ambition; the best of them have no love for the
status quo. Rejecting careerism, they often choose familism instead. But
shaken out of this, either by the open discrimination felt by Negroes or
the subtler dissatisfaction with contemporary life felt by whites, they comprise a privileged minority, ignorant of its strength, yet capable of change.

College students today often act as if they believed that work in large
organizations, and beyond that, work in general, could not be basically
satisfying (or, at times, even honest), but is primarily a way to earn a living,
to find a place in the social order, and to meet nice or not-so-nice people.
This is a conclusion which is partly projected upon the occupational scene

as the result of their experience with the curriculum in college and university, and also as the result of experience with college and university as organizations which are viewed as bureaucratic, monolithic, and unchangeable by many students.

I do not think it is the primary task of education to prepare students for later occupational roles, or, indeed, any narrowly specialized roles, nor to teach them to enjoy work regardless of its quality and meaning. Rather, the relation of education to later life should be a dialectical and critical one. If, however, one result of going to college is to become alienated from work per se and defeatist about the possibility of altering one's relation to it, then it seems to me one ought to re-examine academic institutions themselves and see whether anything in them, or in one's own attitudes, or in both might be changed.

In the spring of 1955, several hundred interviews were done (at the behest of *Time* magazine) with seniors at twenty colleges throughout the country, most of them colleges of distinction. The seniors were supposed to be reasonably representative, but what this was taken to mean and how it was applied at different colleges and universities varied greatly. A good many student leaders were chosen, a good many bright people, but hardly any women were included (a questionnaire circulated by *Mademoiselle* gave me somewhat comparable data concerning college women). When I first examined the interviews, and now again when I have once more gone over them, I have been struck by what appears to be a not quite conscious ambivalence toward work in large organizations. Nevertheless, the majority are planning to enter large organizations in pursuit of their careers: big corporations, big governments, big law offices, and so on. Only a few seek independence in their work, either in terms of old-fashioned ideals of entrepreneurship or in terms of the desire to become a foreign correspondent, to enter politics, or to follow some other individualistic or exotic calling. (Moreover, hardly anyone expresses resentment against his prospective army service on the ground that the army is a large organization; there is no eagerness for service, but rather resignation to it as one of the givens of life.)

And yet, when these young people are asked about their lives outside of work, a very different picture emerges. There, bigness and scale are definitely not valued. Only a tiny fraction want to head for the metropolis, even if their careers might make such a location convenient. They want the suburbs—not later, after some bachelor independence in the big city, but now, on graduation. The great majority either are already married or plan to get married soon (even if there is no special one in mind at the moment); they plan to start having children at once and to begin building a community-centered life in the suburbs. They envisage a two-car, but usually not a two-career, family, in which the prospective wife will be active in the parent-teacher association, with assistance from the husband,

and in which both spouses will concern themselves with a manageable bit of real estate in a suburban neighborhood in which they can at once be active and hope to make a difference. It does not occur to them that they might be gifted and energetic enough to make a difference even in a big city. Rather, they want to be able to work through a face-to-face group—the postcollegiate fraternity of the small suburbs.

Correspondingly, the very emphasis on family life, which is one of the striking and, in so many ways, attractive qualities of young people today, is an implicit rejection of large organization. The suburban family, with its garden, its barbecue, its lack of privacy in the open-plan house, is itself a manifesto of decentralization, even though it makes use of centralized services such as television, clinics, chain stores, and *House Beautiful.* The wish to build a nest, even if a somewhat transient one, is a striking feature of the interviews, in contrast with the wish to build a fortune or a career, which might have dominated some comparable interviews a generation earlier.

This pattern—the acceptance of large organizations, combined with tacit and uncrystallized resistance to them—appears not only in the respondents' emphasis on the family but also in what they say about their plans and attitudes toward their future work. I get a sense from the material, and from other comparable data, of a certain withdrawal of emotional adherence from work. To be sure, it has become fashionable to speak of one's work or other activities in deprecatory terms and to adopt a pose of relative indifference to the larger goals of an organization. In an era of political, economic, and cultural salesmanship, such deprecation is a way of guarding against being exploited for ends outside one's self. It is as if one had constantly to conduct psychological warfare against an outside enemy. But, as in any such process, students become to some extent the victims of their own defenses. They come to believe that work cannot really be worth doing for its own sake, whether or not it is done on behalf of a large, impersonal organization. They fear overcommitment to their work even while they are at the workplace. In the course of getting rid of earlier collegiate or rah-rah enthusiasm, these young people have come to feel that work is not worth even their part-time devotion, and perhaps that nothing, except family, deserves their wholehearted allegiance.

We see the same attitudes, of course, among the junior echelons now engaged in work. One hears them talk of their benevolent company as "a mink-lined rat trap," or speak of "the rat race," or refer to fights over principles as "ruckuses" or "blowups"—if somebody cares, he is said to "blow his top." In a number of business novels, of which *The Man in the Gray Flannel Suit* is representative, it is taken for granted that a sensible fellow, and, indeed, an honest one, will prefer suburban domesticity and a quiet niche to ulcerous competition for large business stakes, despite the view from the top and the interesting climb.

Attitudes such as these are of course an aspect of a general cultural shift, not confined to students and not confined to those who seek employment in large organizations; similar attitudes turn up in some measure even among those who, studiously avoiding such organizations, look for a professional career in which they hope to be their own masters. Scholars, for example, are not immune to distaste for their work, nor are architects or physicians. But, while I do not intend to imply that a life without any boredom is conceivable, except for a very stupid person, still, I think we are witnessing a silent revolution against work on the part of even those relatively privileged groups who have been free to choose their work and to exercise some freedom in the doing of it. This reflects, in part, the fact that much work is meaningless per se, save as a source of income, prestige, and sociability, but it also indicates, as I have already implied, that people too readily accept their work as it comes, without the hope of making it more meaningful.

Not all large organizations are alike, despite the sorts of institutional similarities investigated by sociologists, and, of course, not all positions in them are alike. Many, although their top executives clamor for creativity and independence of mind, largely manage to process these qualities out of "their" people in the lower ranks. Others stockpile talent and expect it to keep as gold keeps at Fort Knox. Still others make products or provide services which are either antisocial or useless. But here and there one finds companies which face real and not contrived problems and apply to them an intelligence which is often remarkably disinterested and, in the best sense of the term, "academic." Young people in search of challenge and development would do well to seek out such relatively productive climates, rather than to assume offhand that these (as is true of so many brand-name products) are all alike except for the advertising and the label. And this search is necessary precisely because many of the motives which impelled work in the older generation have fortunately become attenuated, motives such as money for its own sake, power, and fame—goals, that is, whose emptiness became evident with their attainment. Our industrial and commercial plant no longer "needs" such compulsive attachments to work, which are based not on any genuine creative impulse but on the drying up of other alternatives and on the pressure of extrinsic standards of value.

There is a further issue concerning work in large organizations where, again, differentiation is required. I refer to the conception that work in organizations requires surrender of independence of judgment, if not of integrity. When I was in college, there was a prevalent feeling among the more sensitive that this was true only of business and commercial organizations, not of governmental or philanthropic ones, and young men debated whether they would enter Wall Street and make money, or enter government or teaching and be saved. This dichotomy has in large measure vanished, although traces of it do survive among the less cynical. For instance, I

have known many graduate students in social psychology who believe that if they teach, they can be honest, but that if they work in market research, they will serve manipulation and corruption and will have no power over their own work. Such judgments oversimplify the ethical dilemmas of any calling and are, in addition, snobbish; one can find hucksterism (often hypocritically veiled) among academic people in search of reputations, grants, and promotions, as well as among market researchers and other businessmen.

Indeed, I am inclined to think that, at present, many observant young people do not need to be persuaded of this; many are actually overpersuaded to the point of believing that every occupation is a racket and that at best some of the racketeers are less pious about it than others. And this, I suspect, is one of the reasons they tend to withdraw emotional allegiance from their work—with the impression that they have no control over it anyway, that all is in the hands of the mysterious men upstairs who run the show. If there is greater wisdom in their belief that all occupations, like all forms of power, are corrupting in some degree, there is also greater resignation, greater passivity and fatalism.

Where are such attitudes learned and confirmed? Even at some of the leading colleges, the more intellectual colleges, the colleges which produce literary magazines, the relation of students to the curriculum has a certain alienated quality, in the sense that the students do not believe they have any control over their own education.

In the last few years I have visited a number of colleges of high quality, colleges which turn out eminent professional men, scholars, and scientists, and I have made it my business to talk with students informally, to read their student newspapers and, where possible, student council reports. At a number of these institutions, the livelier students complain of the educational fare they are getting, of the very little contact the curriculum makes with the problems that are meaningful to them. Sometimes they feel that opportunities for a civilized and intellectual life on campus are wanting—for example, that there are few inviting places to study or to talk, that social pressures in dormitories force any intellectual life out of the group setting, that student publications are either dominated by the school administration or devoted to campus news and trivia, that the bookstore is inadequate, or that the library is geared to meet research needs rather than to attract undergraduate browsers. They often feel that they have no access to the faculty for other than merely routine matters. Sometimes students complain about the prerequisites of a department, which serve its monopolistic aims or protect its mediocre teachers from boycott rather than serve any defensible pedagogic aims.

Yet, when I ask students what they have done about these things, they are surprised at the very thought that they could do anything. They think I am joking when I suggest that, if things came to the worst, they

could picket! They think I am wholly unrealistic when I say that many on the faculty might welcome student initiative in revising the curriculum, or that it might be possible to raise modest sums of money among alumni or others to bring visiting lecturers or poets to the campus, or to furnish commodious rooms for interest-group meetings. When I tell them that the Harvard house plan came about in considerable measure because of the report of a student council committee in 1926 which caught the attention of the philanthropist Edward Harkness, they shrug. That must have been a golden era, they say; nothing like that could happen now. Of course, as long as they think that, they will conduct themselves accordingly.

Why is it that students, often so precocious about many things—about each other, about sex, about their families, and occasionally even about national and world affairs—are comparatively inattentive to what concerns them as closely as does their curriculum?

For one thing, it seems to me that students do not want to believe that their activities might make a difference, because, in a way, they profit from their lack of commitment to what they are doing. I do not mean that they are not industrious students; they go through the required motions of working, but they seldom get really involved with the content of their courses. It is here that the better, more conscientious students sabotage their own education and restrict production; true enough, they turn out the credits and the grades, but they do not believe that it really matters in any fundamental sense what they think and feel.

When I have discussed this with students, they have often told me that it doesn't pay to be too interested in anything, because then one is tempted to spend too much time on it, at the expense of what optimal distribution of effort which will produce the best grades—and after all, they do have to get into medical school, keep their scholarship, and "please the old man." Now, I am convinced that grades contaminate education— they are a kind of currency which, like money, gets in the way of students' discovering their intellectual interests—but here, too, the students in their realism are being somewhat unrealistic. They assume, for one thing, that it is hopeless to try to alter the curriculum so that it might penalize them less for serious interest in one topic at the expense of others, or so that there might be more emphasis on reading and discussion and more oppor- tunity for independent thinking. And here, also, the students have a dis- torted image of what will actually make an impression on their teachers either now or later. On this point, I have some evidence to back me up.

After I had tried in vain for some time to persuade graduate students at Chicago that they could be more independent in their course and thesis work without any heroism, any martyrdom, there was a thesis done by a student which documented my arguments. The student went around to the departments and asked them which students in recent years they had recommended for jobs or advanced training or fellowships and which they

had not. Then he interviewed some of these students in various categories of faculty blessing or disapproval, looked at their grades, and so on. He concluded that those students frequently fared best who were not too obedient, who did not get an undiluted, uncomplicated, straight-A record. (The straight-A students, in fact, sometimes slipped away without anyone's noticing.)

The students who were most successful were a bit rebellious, a bit offbeat, though not entirely "goof-offs"; these were the students likely to appeal to a faculty member who had not entirely repressed a rebelliousness of his own that had led him to be a teacher in the first place, a faculty member who was looking for signs of life, even if they gave him a bit of trouble at times. To be sure, such a student had to do well in something to earn this response, but he was often better off to have written a brilliant paper or two than to have divided his time, as an investment banker his money, among a variety of subjects. Those students who were the most self-consciously opportunistic and realistic in allocating their time and emotion were in fact sacrificing themselves unprofitably, suffering not only now, during the studies which they regarded as an anteroom to life, but later on as well.

Now, not all departments at Chicago were alike in this matter; some gave more play to defiance and deviation than others. Moreover, this study encompassed only the social science departments. No doubt departments and institutions differ very much in this respect. But that is just the point I want to emphasize: by concluding prematurely that all organizations are alike, that all demand the same kinds of conformity, students not only surrender the chance to experience an atmosphere that is freer and more conducive to their own development but perpetuate a myth that then controls their passage through jobs in later life. If the University of Chicago or even one's department itself cannot be changed from below, how can one expect to change General Motors, or *Look* magazine, or the big hospitals of San Francisco? And if that is so, then why not settle for the fringe benefits, for a position of moderate respectability and adequate, if not dazzling, salary?

At work here is a characteristic social pattern in which individuals, hesitant to reveal feelings they have scarcely voiced to themselves, are misled about what in effect could be done if they expressed themselves, thereby discovering others who might share their views. (Sociologists refer to this process as "pluralistic ignorance.") Leadership, of course, whether in politics or in other affairs, often serves to help a group change its apparent mood to conform to its actual or potential but repressed views, but leadership also may, and frequently does, serve to continue enforcing the repression. Even in a large organization, radical and what were previously regarded as "impossible" changes come about almost instantane-

ously once people discover that views they had previously regarded as unacceptable or idiosyncratic are in fact widely shared.

The students know that there are many decisions out of their conceivable control, decisions upon which their lives and fortunes truly depend. But what I am contending is that this truth, this insight, is overgeneralized, and that, being believed, it becomes more and more "true." Not only do we fail to spot those instances in which intervention might change things quite substantially, but we fail to develop the competence and the confidence in ourselves that are necessary to any large endeavor. In that sense, despite our precociousness, we fail to grow up; we remain the children of organization, not the masters of it.

For Americans, there is something paradoxical about this development. Americans in the past have not been overimpressed by mechanical achievements. Workers in a steel mill are not awed by the giant rollers, and we take for granted that we are not awed by any large physical construction made by our hands and brains. Contrary to the prevalent impression abroad that we are slaves to our machines, we are actually relatively uninvolved with them, and we surely do not feel dominated by them. But it seems to be different with the organizational machines. These are as much the product of our thinking and our imagination as any technological feat; yet as Erich Fromm has said, we worship like idolaters the product we have created, an image not of stone but of other images.

It is a commonplace observation that in organizational life we use arguments to convince others which we think will appeal to them, even though they do not convince us. We try to persuade people to behave justly to Negroes because "discrimination makes the United States look bad in the Cold War," as if that were why we ourselves behaved decently. Or we persuade businessmen to give money to colleges for all sorts of public relations reasons, playing on their fear of radicalism or federal control or whatnot, whereas we ourselves devote our lives to education for quite different reasons. All arguments of this nature have two qualities: they patronize the other person and they perpetuate "pluralistic ignorance." It can be contended that there may be occasions when we must appeal to others as they are, not as we should like them to be; when there is not time for idealism. But, in our realism, we often make mistakes about what others will actually respond to, and we sacrifice the integrity and clarity of our argument to our false image of what will go over. The result: we conclude that one cannot be honest while working for an organization, that one can be honest only when one is at home with one's family in the suburbs.

There is another result as well; namely, that we often end up in doubt as to what we ourselves think. We come to believe what we say to others and thus become "more sincere" in the subjective sense, but at the price

of becoming still more confused as to what is actually so: we are the first victims of our own propaganda. No wonder we end up without emotional ties to what we do, for it is no longer we who do it, but some limited part of ourselves, playing a role. Not recognizing that we in some measure have done this to ourselves, we attribute to organizations the power and the primacy we have lost. And then, as I have said, we strike back, not directly, but by a kind of emotional attrition in which we lend to our work willingness without enthusiasm, conscientiousness without creativity.

I am sure that many college students who are not only serious but dedicated know that as well as I do. Such students have managed to make college serve their purposes and have in this way gained some rational confidence that they will be able to do the same in the organizations they will enter later, whether these are universities, business concerns, or the many voluntary organizations through which we Americans carry out much of our communal work. What I have principally sought to do in these remarks is to encourage greater and more differentiated realism than many young people already possess, a realism which does not take for granted the social structures which seem so impressive but which looks for the points of leverage where one's own effort, joined to that of others similarly freed from mythology, might make a difference. In many situations, there is more leeway than students think, and college is a good place to find this out.

Three years later, I have naturally asked myself to what extent the foregoing remarks still strike me as true. I had in 1955 and 1957 paid very brief visits to several of the Southern Negro colleges that have since been in the forefront of sit-in demonstrations; at that time they seemed to me, as to some of their own faculty members, acquiescent and cautious, preparing students to enter the army uncomplainingly, the "Black Bourgeoisie" un-thinkingly. Of course, the students were aware of the struggles over integration, but for them the issues remained somewhat abstract, particularly as many of them had chosen the shelter of a segregated college, as in their prospective occupations—teaching, the ministry, Negro business—many would choose the still segregated occupations.

As so often, appearances were deceptive; some of these students carried out the first sit-ins and refused to become daunted or disorganized when either their own pressured administrations or reactive whites sought to end the picketing and protests; a brave few, in active civil disobedience, have chosen jail rather than bail. Relatively immune to the economic boycotts that can hamstring their parents, and free, too, of the traditional Negro leadership in their communities, they have discovered their organizational powers and talents. This has been bracing and highly educative.

Meanwhile, among white students in the North, sympathetic picketing of the chain stores was rapidly organized, and many campuses had their first taste of political life in twenty years. The young people I have been

describing are markedly tolerant; in the 1955 interviews, hardly any exhibited bigotry (at the Southern universities many said that once the old folks are gone, the race problem will die with them). Moreover, tolerance appears to them a virtue that is civic and personal, tied into one's own immediate human reactions and relations; to be tolerant to classmates, one does not have to fight city hall, though one may sometimes have to fight alumni guardians of the more collegiate fraternities.

Furthermore, the simplicity of the race issue, the near lack of rational or civilized defense of segregation and discrimination, allows Northern students to extrapolate public activity on the basis of private decency, without feeling themselves to be involved in "politics" or in ideology. True, the planned picketing has involved these highly individualistic students in more organization and decision making than appeals to most of them; the term "politician" is as much one of contempt on the better campuses as it is generally in American life. Even so, many students have discovered, though less dramatically than the Southern Negro students, that they are capable of action in areas outside the usual complaints about library hours, dormitory food, and parking, and that even such seemingly large outfits as Woolworth's are not invulnerable.

So, too, there have recently been some energetic student actions in the area of curriculum. In the spring of 1958, students at the University of Wisconsin submitted a petition to the administration requesting more challenge and stimulation in their courses and in their educational program generally. During the same period, undergraduates at Chicago mobilized to defend the general education program against attempts to subordinate it to the requirements of the graduate departments. A group of students at Wesleyan last year arranged a series of discussions on education, geared to the problems and opportunities faced by a liberal arts college; apparently the students helped influence curricular change. While, in some instances, students could graduate before realizing that what they did had any impact, others learned from their experiences that institutions are man-made and subject to change.

It is understandably seldom that such sporadic and ad hoc actions have been carried over into political controversies on the national scene. There have been occasional protests against compulsory ROTC, based as much on the unintellectual waste of time of the programs as on any explicit antimilitarist views. The student political party (Slate) at Berkeley was a factor in last year's protest against the Un-American Activities Committee hearings in San Francisco—a brave protest, since many students fear it will go on their records in an FBI dossier. And, increasingly, the issues of peace and disarmament have found a student audience. Students are picketing weekly on Boston Common under the auspices of the Committee for a Sane Nuclear Policy and are encountering, as they did to only a minor degree in picketing the chain stores, violent and jeering attacks

as Reds or yellow appeasers. Challenge at Michigan and Yale, Concern at Ohio Wesleyan, Tocsin at Harvard are among the groups that have sprung up to discuss peace and other political questions. Only a very small minority are involved—but then only a small minority were involved in the supposedly activist 1930s. Probably some of these organizations will last only for the college lifetimes of a handful of committed students.

Indeed, the very fact that academic values have triumphed on many campuses puts heavy competition in the way of all extracurricular activity, including politics. I recall one student who recently felt he had to choose between active participation in organizing a student chapter of SANE and writing a senior distinction thesis; he believed that if he did not do the latter, he would not get into graduate school (not an unrealistic fear) and would jeopardize his whole career (in my judgment, a less realistic fear). Perhaps more important, the professors have taught, especially the better students, that all questions are complex, all ideologies suspect, and all larger passions fanatical; the fear of being naïve prevents many young people from feeling confidence in any action or reaction. (Some of these same adults then criticize the students for apathy!) Questions of foreign policy and disarmament *are* complex—in a way that the race question is not—and students have in the past feared to take a position that expert or "classified" knowledge might explode. Once they begin, however, these same academic values lead them to a seriousness illustrated by the Tocsin students, who have organized seminars on technical problems of disarmament and, as the phrase goes, "done their homework" in Kahn, Kissinger, King-Hall, the *Bulletin of the Atomic Scientists,* and so on.

The long-buried idealism of many gifted and sensitive students has come out most strongly, however, in their response to President Kennedy's proposal of a Peace Corps. It is exciting to watch a group of them examining in detail what American students might contribute to secondary education in Nigeria and what qualities of judgment, self-reliance, pertinacity, and technique such students would need to be of real help. I have seen students who seemed, even in their own eyes, cool customers, ready to ride the organizational escalator, discover in themselves unexpected resources of dedication when beckoned by a chance to serve in an underdeveloped country. To be sure, such service appears to many students as quite unpolitical, outside the polemical orbit of American domestic struggles; and one could argue that there are escapist elements in this choice, this interpretation. But one has to start somewhere, and when one is emerging from privatism, the first movements are apt to be tentative.

We must still ask whether there will be any carry-over from these campus stirrings into the attitudes that college graduates take toward their work: will they continue to regard it as mere "bread," needful for existence, but not a locus either for defining the self or changing the world? If one is apathetic about one's work, it is hard to prevent this apathy from

spreading to other areas, even to those on which one had originally thought to build one's life: domesticity, the arts, and personal relations. But, conversely, the vitality and sense for relevant accomplishment that students may gain in college should spread to their academic work and thence to their lifework. For, in the more selective colleges at present, as I have already indicated, there is very little left of the collegiate or teen-ager high jinks of the former *jeunesse dorée;* it is in the high schools now that these ersatz values reign. Thus, college is already, not always happily, an aspect of adult life, not simply a playful preparation, and experience there is no longer compartmentalized as a childish thing.


## TOPICS FOR DISCUSSION

1  Commitment and action are attributes Riesman would like to find in the college generation. Where does he find endeavors which demonstrate these attributes? Would Whitehead ("The Aims of Education") feel that these were worthy endeavors? Would Wain ("Education: For Assent or Dissent?") consider them merely rebelliousness? Would Thoreau ("Civil Disobedience") find them worthy examples of civil disobedience?

2  What is "privatism"? What is "pluralistic ignorance"? What do these terms have to do with involvement in professional or academic problems?

3  Do you believe with Riesman that the high jinks formerly associated with college students can now be found only in the high schools?


## ...AND COMPOSITION

4  Using ideas derived from Whitehead, Wain, and Riesman, discuss your intentions for your college years, and after.

5  Specify a few definite changes you would advocate in the academic program of your college.

6  Are you involved in, or do you see any evidence of, campus political activity around you? Write an essay on the most lively political activity you have experienced in college.

JONATHAN SWIFT (1667–1745)   excites admiration in those who read
him alertly and see how well he writes. Trenchant, piercingly perceptive,
he advances through an argument or through an apparently random narrative
by means so relentlessly controlled that the least waver on the part of
the reader may leave him a victim to the poised satire. In Swift's
writing, judgment hovers over every topic. Gulliver's Travels
can entertain a child or devastate the pretensions of the great.
The following episodes from "A Voyage to Laputa" illustrate the advance
of the narrative—and the effects of its multiple ironies.

# The Grand Academy of Lagado

This academy is not an entire single building, but a continuation of
several houses on both sides of a street, which, growing waste, was pur-
chased, and applied to that use. I was received very kindly by the warden,
and went for many days to the academy. Every room hath in it one or more
projectors; and, I believe, I could not be in fewer than five hundred rooms.

The first man I saw was of a meagre aspect, with sooty hands and face,
his hair and beard long, ragged and singed in several places. His clothes,
shirt, and skin were all of the same colour. He had been eight years upon
a project for extracting sun-beams out of cucumbers, which were to be put
into vials hermetically sealed, and let out to warm the air in raw inclement
summers. He told me, he did not doubt, in eight years more, he should
be able to supply the governor's gardens with sunshine at a reasonable rate;
but he complained that his stock was low, and entreated me to give him
something as an encouragement to ingenuity, especially since this had been
a· very dear season for cucumbers. I made him a small present, for my
lord had furnished me with money on purpose, because he knew their
practice of begging from all who go to see them.

I saw another at work to calcine ice into gunpowder, who likewise
shewed me a treatise he had written concerning the malleability of fire,
which he intended to publish.

There was a most ingenious architect, who had contrived a new method
for building houses, by beginning at the roof, and working downwards to
the foundation, which he justified to me, by the like practice of those two
prudent insects, the bee and the spider.

There was a man born blind, who had several apprentices in his own
condition: their employment was to mix colours for painters, which their
master taught them to distinguish by feeling and smelling. It was, indeed,
my misfortune to find them, at that time, not very perfect in their lessons,
and the professor himself happened to be generally mistaken: this artist
is much encouraged and esteemed by the whole fraternity.

In another apartment, I was highly pleased with a projector who had found a device of plowing the ground with hogs, to save the charges of ploughs, cattle, and labour. The method is this: in an acre of ground you bury, at six inches distance, and eight deep, a quantity of acorns, dates, chestnuts, and other mast, or vegetables, whereof these animals are fondest: then you drive six hundred, or more of them, into the field, where, in few days, they will root up the whole ground in search of their food, and make it fit for sowing; it is true, upon experiment, they found the charge and trouble very great, and they had little or no crop. However, it is not doubted that this invention may be capable of great improvement.

I went into another room, where the walls and ceiling were all hung round with cobwebs, except a narrow passage for the artist to go in and out. At my entrance he called aloud to me not to disturb his webs. He lamented the fatal mistake the world had been so long in of using silk-worms, while we had such plenty of domestic insects, who infinitely excelled the former, because they understood how to weave, as well as spin. And he proposed farther, that, by employing spiders, the charge of dying silks would be wholly saved; whereof I was fully convinced, when he shewed me a vast number of flies most beautifully coloured, wherewith he fed his spiders, assuring us that the webs would take a tincture from them; and, as he had them of all hues, he hoped to fit every body's fancy, as soon as he could find proper food for the flies, of certain gums, oils, and other glutinous matter, to give a strength and consistence to the threads.

There was an astronomer, who had undertaken to place a sundial upon the great weathercock on the town house, by adjusting the annual and diurnal motions of the earth and sun, so as to answer and coincide with all accidental turnings of the wind.

I visited many other apartments, but shall not trouble my reader with all the curiosities I observed, being studious of brevity.

I had hitherto seen only one side of the academy, the other being appropriated to the advancers of speculative learning, of whom I shall say something, when I have mentioned one illustrious person more, who is called among them the universal artist. He told us he had been thirty years employing his thoughts for the improvement of human life. He had two large rooms full of wonderful curiosities, and fifty men at work. Some were condensing air into a dry tangible substance, by extracting the nitre, and letting the aqueous or fluid particles percolate; others softening marble for pillows and pincushions; others petrifying the hoofs of a living horse, to preserve them from foundering. The artist himself was at that time busy upon two great designs; the first to sow land with chaff, wherein he affirmed the true seminal virtue to be contained, as he demonstrated by several experiments which I was not skillful enough to comprehend. The other was, by a certain composition of gums, minerals, and vegetables, outwardly applied, to prevent the growth of wool upon two young lambs; and he

hoped, in a reasonable time, to propagate the breed of naked sheep all over the kingdom.

We crossed a walk to the other part of the academy, where, as I have already said, the projectors in speculative learning resided.

The first professor I saw was in a very large room, with forty pupils about him. After salutation, observing me to look earnestly upon a frame which took up the greatest part of both the length and breadth of the room, he said, perhaps I might wonder to see him employed in a project for improving speculative knowledge by practical and mechanical operations. But the world would soon be sensible of its usefulness; and he flattered himself that a more noble exalted thought never sprang in any other man's head. Every one knew how laborious the usual method is of attaining to arts and sciences; whereas, by his contrivance, the most ignorant person, at a reasonable charge, and with a little bodily labour may write books in philosophy, poetry, politics, law, mathematics, and theology, without the least assistance from genius or study. He then led me to the frame, about the sides whereof all his pupils stood in ranks. It was twenty feet square, placed in the middle of the room. The superficies was composed of several bits of wood, about the bigness of a die, but some larger than others. They were all linked together by slender wires. These bits of wood were covered on every square with paper pasted on them; and on these papers were written all the words of their language in their several moods, tense, and declensions; but without any order. The professor then desired me to observe, for he was going to set his engine at work. The pupils, at his command, took each of them hold of an iron handle, whereof there were forty fixed round the edges of the frame; and, giving them a sudden turn, the whole disposition of the words was entirely changed. He then commanded six and thirty of the lads to read the several lines softly, as they appeared upon the frame; and, where they found three or four words together that might make part of a sentence, they dictated to the four remaining boys who were scribes. This work was repeated three or four times, and at every turn, the engine was so contrived, that the words shifted into new places, as the square bits of wood moved upside down.

Six hours a day the young students were employed in this labour, and the professor shewed me several volumes in large folio already collected, of broken sentences, which he intended to piece together, and, out of those rich materials, to give the world a complete body of all arts and sciences; which, however, might be still improved, and much expedited, if the public would raise a fund for making and employing five hundred such frames in Lagado, and oblige the managers to contribute in common their several collections.

He assured me that this invention had employed all his thoughts from his youth; that he had emptied the whole vocabulary into his frame, and made the strictest computation of the general proportion there is in books

between the numbers of particles, nouns, and verbs, and other parts of speech.

I made my humblest acknowledgment to this illustrious person for his great communicativeness; and promised, if ever I had the good fortune to return to my native country, that I would do him justice, as the sole inventor of this wonderful machine. . . . I told him, although it were the custom of our learned in Europe to steal inventions from each other, who had thereby, at least, this advantage, that it became a controversy which was the right owner, yet I would take such caution, that he should have the honour entire, without a rival.

We next went to the school of languages, where three professors sat in consultation upon improving that of their own country.

The first project was to shorten discourse by cutting polysyllables into one, and leaving out verbs and particles; because, in reality, all things imaginable are but nouns.

The other project was a scheme for entirely abolishing all words whatsoever; and this was urged as a great advantage in point of health, as well as brevity. For it is plain, that every word we speak is, in some degree, a diminution of our lungs by corrosion; and consequently contributes to the shortening of our lives. An expedient was therefore offered, that since words are only names for things, it would be more convenient for all men to carry about them such things as were necessary to express the particular business they are to discourse on. And this invention would certainly have taken place, to the great ease as well as health of the subject, if the women, in conjunction with the vulgar and illiterate, had not threatened to raise a rebellion, unless they might be allowed the liberty to speak with their tongues after the manner of their forefathers; such constant irreconcilable enemies to science are the common people. However, many of the most learned and wise adhere to the new scheme of expressing themselves by things; which hath only this inconvenience attending it, that if a man's business be very great, and of various kinds he must be obliged, in proportion, to carry a greater bundle of things upon his back, unless he can afford one or two strong servants to attend him. I have often beheld two of those sages almost sinking under the weight of their packs, like pedlars among us; who, when they met in the streets, would lay down their loads, open their sacks, and hold conversation for an hour together; then put up their implements, help each other resume their burthens, and take their leave.

But, for short conversations, a man may carry implements in his pockets, and under his arms, enough to supply him; and in his house he cannot be at a loss. Therefore the room where company meet, who practise this art, is full of all things ready at hand, requisite to furnish matter for this kind of artificial converse.

Another great advantage, proposed by this invention, was, that it would serve as an universal language, to be understood in all civilized

nations, whose goods and utensils are generally of the same kind, or nearly resembling, so that their uses might easily be comprehended. And thus ambassadors would be qualified to treat with foreign princes, or ministers of state, to whose tongues they were utter strangers.

I was at the mathematical school, where the master taught his pupils after a method scarce imaginable to us in Europe. The proposition and demonstration were fairly written on a thin wafer, with ink composed of a cephalic tincture. This the student was to swallow upon a fasting stomach, and for three days following eat nothing but bread and water. As the wafer digested, the tincture mounted to his brain, bearing the proposition along with it. But the success had not hitherto been answerable, partly by some error in the quantum or composition, and partly by the perverseness of lads; to whom this bolus is so nauseous, that they generally steal aside, and discharge it upwards, before it can operate; neither have been yet persuaded to use so long an abstinence as the prescription requires.

In the school of political projectors, I was but ill entertained; the professors appearing, in my judgment, wholly out of their senses; which is a scene that never fails to make me melancholy. These unhappy people were proposing schemes for persuading monarchs to choose favourites upon the score of their wisdom, capacity, and virtue; of teaching ministers to consult the public good; of rewarding merit, great abilities, and eminent services; of instructing princes to know their true interest, by placing it on the same foundation with that of their people; of choosing for employment persons qualified to exercise them; with many other wild impossible chimæras, that never entered before into the heart of man to conceive; and confirmed in me the old observation, that there is nothing so extravagant and irrational which some philosophers have not maintained for truth.

But, however, I shall so far do justice to this part of the academy, as to acknowledge that all of them were not so visionary. There was a most ingenious doctor, who seemed to be perfectly versed in the whole nature and system of government. This illustrious person had very usefully employed his studies in finding out effectual remedies for all diseases and corruptions to which the several kinds of public administration are subject, by the vices or infirmities of those who govern, as well as by the licentiousness of those who are to obey. For instance, whereas all writers and reasoners have agreed that there is a strict universal resemblance between the natural and the political body; can there be anything more evident, than that the health of both must be preserved, and the diseases curbed by the same prescriptions. It is allowed that senates and great councils are often troubled with redundant, ebullient, and other peccant humours; with many diseases of the head, and more of the heart; with strong con-

vulsions, with grievous contractions of the nerves and sinews in both hands, but especially the right; with spleen, flatus, vertigos, and deliriums; with scrophulous tumours full of fœtid purulent matter; with foul frothy ructations, with canine appetites and crudeness of digestion, besides many others needless to mention. This doctor therefore proposed, that, upon the meeting of a senate, certain physicians should attend at the three first days of their sitting, and, at the close of each day's debate, feel the pulses of every senator; after which, having maturely considered, and consulted upon the nature of the several maladies, and the methods of cure, they should on the fourth day return to the senate-house, attended by their apothecaries stored with proper medicines; and, before the members sat, administer to each of them lenitives, aperitives, abstersives, corrosives, restringents, palliatives, laxatives, cephalalgics, icterics, apophlegmatics, acoustics, as their several cases required; and, according as these medicines should operate, repeat, alter, or admit them at the next meeting.

This project could not be of any great expense to the public, and would, in my poor opinion, be of much use for the dispatch of business in those countries where senates have any share in the legislative power; beget unanimity, shorten debates, open a few mouths which are now closed, and close many more which are now open; curb the petulancy of the young, and correct the positiveness of the old, rouse the stupid, and damp the pert.

Again: because it is a general complaint, that the favourites of princes are troubled with short and weak memories, the same doctor proposed, that whoever attended a first minister, after having told his business with the utmost brevity, and in the plainest words, should, at his departure, give the said minister a tweak by the nose, or a kick in the belly, or tread on his corns, or lug him thrice by both ears, or run a pin into his breech, or pinch his arm black and blue, to prevent forgetfulness; and at every levee day, repeat the same operation, till the business were done, or absolutely refused.

He likewise directed, that every senator in the great council of a nation, after he had delivered his opinion, and argued in the defence of it, should be obliged to give his vote directly contrary; because, if that were done, the result would infallibly terminate in the good of the public.

When parties in a state are violent, he offered a wonderful contrivance to reconcile them. The method is this: you take an hundred leaders of each party; you dispose them into couples of such whose heads are nearest of a size; then let two nice operators saw off the occiput of each couple at the same time, in such a manner that the brain may be equally divided. Let the occiputs thus cut off be interchanged, applying each to the head of his opposite party-man. It seems indeed, to be a work that requireth some exactness, but the professor assured us that, if it were dexterously performed, the cure would be infallible. For he argued thus; that the two

half brains being left to debate the matter between themselves, within the space of one skull, would soon come to a good understanding, and produce that moderation, as well as regularity of thinking, so much to be wished for in the heads of those who imagine they come into the world only to watch and govern its motion: and as to the difference of brains in quantity or quality, among those who are directors in faction, the doctor assured us, from his own knowledge, that it was a perfect trifle.

I heard a very warm debate between two professors, about the most commodious and effectual ways and means of raising money without grieving the subject. The first affirmed the justest method would be to lay a certain tax upon vices and folly: and the sum fixed upon every man to be rated after the fairest manner by a jury of his neighbours. The second was of an opinion directly contrary, to tax those qualities of body and mind for which men chiefly value themselves; the rate to be more or less according to the degrees of excelling: the decision whereof should be left entirely to their own breast. The highest tax was upon men who are the greatest favourites of the other sex, and the assessments according to the number and natures of the favours they have received; for which they are allowed to be their own vouchers. Wit, valour, and politeness were likewise proposed to be largely taxed, and collected in the same manner, by every person giving his own word for the quantum of what he possessed. But as to honour, justice, wisdom and learning, they should not be taxed at all; because they are qualifications of so singular a kind that no man will either allow them in his neighbour or value them in himself.

The women were proposed to be taxed according to their beauty, and skill in dressing; wherein they had the same privilege with the men, to be determined by their own judgment. But constancy, chastity, good sense, and good nature were not rated, because they would not bear the charge of collecting.

To keep senators in the interest of the crown, it was proposed that the members should raffle for employments; every man first taking an oath, and giving security that he would vote for the court, whether he won or no; after which the losers had, in their turn, the liberty of raffling upon the next vacancy. Thus hope and expectation would be kept alive; none would complain of broken promises, but impute their disappointments wholly to Fortune, whose shoulders are broader and stronger than those of a ministry.

Another professor shewed me a large paper for instructions for discovering plots and conspiracies against the government.

The whole discourse was written with great acuteness, containing many observations both curious and useful for politicians; but, as I conceived, not altogether complete. This I ventured to tell the author, and offered, if he pleased, to supply him with some additions. He received my proposition with more compliance than usual among writers, especially those of

the projecting species; professing he would be glad to receive farther information.

I told him, that in the kingdom of Tribnia, by the natives called Langden, where I had sojourned some time in my travels, the bulk of the people consist, in a manner, wholly of discoverers, witnesses, informers, accusers, prosecutors, evidences, swearers, together with their several subservient and subaltern instruments, all under the colours, the conduct, and pay of ministers of state, and their deputies. The plots in that kingdom are usually the workmanship of those persons, who desire to raise their own characters of profound politicians; to restore new vigour to a crazy administration; to stifle or divert general discontents; to fill their pockets with forfeitures; and raise or sink the opinion of the public credit, as either shall best answer their private advantage. It is first agreed and settled among them, what suspected persons shall be accused of a plot; then effectual care is taken to secure all their letters and papers, and put the criminals in chains. These papers are delivered to a set of artists, very dexterous in finding out the mysterious meanings of words, syllables, and letters: for instance, they can discover a flock of geese to signify a senate; a lame dog, an invader; the plague, a standing army; a buzzard, a prime minister; the gout, a high priest; a gibbet, a secretary of state; a sieve, a court lady; a broom, a revolution; a mouse-trap, an employment; a bottomless pit, a treasury; a sink, a court; a cap and bells, a favourite; a broken reed, a court of justice; an empty tun, a general; a running sore, the administration.

Where this method fails, they have two others more effectual, which the learned among them call acrostics and anagrams. First, they can decipher all initial letters into political meanings. Thus *N* shall signify a plot, *B* a regiment of horse, *L* a fleet at sea: or, secondly, by transposing the letters of the alphabet in any suspected paper, they can lay open the deepest designs of a discontented party. So, for example, if I should say in a letter to a friend, our brother Tom has just got the piles, a skilful decipherer would discover that the same letters which compose that sentence, may be analysed in the following words: Resist—a plot is brought home—the tour. And this is the anagrammatic method.

The professor made me great acknowledgments for communicating these observations, and promised to make honourable mention of me in his treatise.

I saw nothing in this country that could invite me a longer continuance, and began to think of returning home to England.

## TOPICS FOR DISCUSSION

1  What common element do you find in all the episodes of the first twenty-one paragraphs, pp. 242-246? Why is it more effective

to present many examples of this common element than merely to supply one very detailed example?

2  What common element unifies the last twelve paragraphs, pp. 247-249? Does there seem to be a change in tone in the last part of the selection?

3  Does the narrator's apparent interest and generally noncritical attitude help to develop the satiric punch? What things does the narrator stir himself to criticize? Does his open criticism identify the author's sentiments?

4  Why are long lists of good things or bad things effective in satire?

5  In what ways is the Lagado Academy not merely an imaginary place? What specific complaints does Swift express about his own society?

## ...AND COMPOSITION

6  Write an attack on something you find objectionable, using only praise.

7  Of what modern academies of Lagado have you knowledge?

8  For the treatment of political problems, do you prefer the direct, earnest approach of Thoreau ("Civil Disobedience") or the indirect, satiric approach of Swift? Why?

**LEARNED HAND (1872–1961)**   in his long career as judge built up a
great body of influential decisions. Involved in complex cases, he had
to perceive fine and crucial distinctions, and he was led to examine carefully
the assumptions of his society. He helped that society to see that inherited
values must be understood and fitted into developing situations. One
of those inherited values, liberty, is the topic of the essay below. You may be
interested in discovering whether being judicious requires neutrality, whether
judging implies that prior to striking a balance one must remain noncommittal.

# *Liberty*

I have chosen for the subject of my talk, "Liberty." When I say that
I chose it, I am not speaking quite the truth; rather it chose itself. I was
so acutely aware of the quicksands and wastes which await the explorer
in that region that I tried to avoid an expedition into it. Perhaps a judge
is especially aware of these; his colleagues are constantly assuring him that
all he needs is to avoid license and anarchy on the one hand, and tyranny
and despotism on the other; if he will only stick to that simple admonition
he is sure to arrive. That is not very encouraging as a starter; but what
gives the task its real difficulty is that the word is so charged with passion.
About none is written a more fiery record of suffering and heroism; it is the
center and the kernel of that inner life for which men will fight and die
who will fight and die for anything. Furthermore, and perhaps for that
reason, it has been the rallying cry of those who hold quite opposite
beliefs; one can say of it after Lincoln: "Both sides pray to it and each
invokes its aid against the other." Few stop to ask what they mean, and
those who do soon find the answer baffling and uncertain. Why then
should I venture to talk about it here tonight? Only because I could not

help it. In such a world as this, so wretched and so riven, where men and women are suffering misery, mutilation, and death in the name of Liberty—whatever it may be—how can anyone be content who does not try to come to at least a tentative conclusion with himself about it? And so, although I am conscious of the small chance of success where so many have failed, I shall ask you to bear with me as I too try my luck with this Sphinx, whom like her prototype if I answer I answer at my peril.

I do not know how it is with you, but my own first spontaneous response to the word is negative; I think that I am free when I can do what I want; this tiny protoplasmal center of radiant energy demands that alien impacts shall not thwart its insistences and its self-assertions. What are these? We can start with a dictum attributed to Lawrence Henderson that they consist in the performance of our accustomed rituals. (Those of you who have read Trotter's *Instinct of the Herd* will perhaps remember analogues drawn from the accepted social observances of man's best friend, the Dog, which I forbear to quote.) Henderson's definition would be entirely satisfactory to anthropologists, who, very properly, refuse to play favorites among the conventions of mankind. It is as authentic a denial of freedom to compel a Bushman to look at his mother-in-law during the period of his wife's gestation, as it is to deny Colonel Lindbergh the privilege of assuring us of the speedy and certain collapse of Great Britain. Each has a vested right in his freedom grounded in the deepest of foundations, the current liturgies of the society to which he belongs. Since, so conceived, Liberty is negative, one freedom is as good as another; there is no objective standard except for blind partisans of the status quo whatever it may be. The rite of burying the aged alive, whatever the aged may say against it, has equal sanction with that of providing a college education for those who are not fit to receive one.

Let us then look for an objective standard. Surely we can safely begin with the satisfaction of our primitive needs. We must eat, sleep, be clothed and sheltered, and have our mates and our children. It is irrelevant that the Universe so often denies us these; we are considering hindrances by our fellows. Shall we say then that, so far as they deny us such goods, they deny our Liberty? "Do not waste our time in trivialities," you will answer, "we must of course yield these in part, and other desires scarcely less imperious; but by doing so we create civilized society so that our life shall not be 'short, brutish, and nasty.' Why go over that old stuff again? It was what Holmes meant when he said he liked to pay taxes because he felt he was buying civilization." No doubt; but if we press the inquiry a little further it gets more real. To say that we must compromise leaves all practical questions unanswered. Kant may have been right when he said that our conduct must be such that it can be made a universal rule; but that does not help us to find any particular rule; perhaps there are not any. If we declare that a freeman will yield so far, but only so far, as,

having with entire detachment weighed his own good against his neighbor's, he finds the neighbor's better, that does not tell us how he is to decide which of the two is in fact the better. Of course there is the initial obstacle that entire detachment is an obvious fiction. To proceed at all we must set up some persons in our society with authority—like Plato's "Guardians" for instance, to whom we can depute the weighing of one good against another. The outlook has never been very propitious that we can find any such guardians, but for my purposes it is not important; for if we secured absolute detachment and impartiality, we should have got no further than to face the real problem.

Let me start with an example drawn from Plato's own city; not because we need doubt the answer, but because it illustrates the incommensurability of the elements that must be measured. When at times I hear, as we all do, some cultivated snob vaporing about the perfection of life in Athens, say from 480 to 430 B.C., and how it was the apex of civilization, someone is sure to interject that it was not so at all; rather that Athens was a hideous nightmare; that these supposed specimens of ultimate human perfection were shameless exploiters of a far greater number of other men whose misery, when matched against their own splendors, makes Stygian blackness to the eyes of all just and humane persons. When such a Thersites disturbs the complacency of the cultivated snob, sometimes I feel like siding with the snob—even now when the dawn of social justice has broken into bright unclouded day. I should not do so by way of challenge to the challenger's conclusion, but I should ask him to tell me the process by which he reached it. I should say that of course I recognized that the exploitation of the weak, taken by itself, was undiluted evil; and that in its more aggravated form we need not even discuss it—for instance, the often lamented lot of those unfortunate men who were worked to death in the mines of Laurium no doubt outweighed an infinity of noble employment of leisure. I should ask him to put aside such concrete incidents disturbing to philosophic speculation and consider the issue abstractly. Supposing that an ethical or hedonistic calculus were possible, and supposing that there were no other means than the exploitation of the exploited by which the lives of the Athenian citizens could have been what they were, and supposing that these were as perfect as both he and the cultivated snob seemed to agree they were; how he could guess which way the beam would tip if one put the lives of the citizens in one scale and the good things of which they deprived their slaves in the other. I should tell him that, though I was sure of the answer, I had always been a little baffled to know how such a balance could be struck; but that, like Socrates, I was confident that he must know, since he seemed so certain. And if he, rightly angry at this offensively insincere humility, were to answer, as I suspect he might, that injustice could never be right, and that there were some things which everyone knew, among which was that oppression and justice

were inherently antithetical, I should not feel that he had thoroughly illuminated all the dark places.

At any rate I know that, whatever he said, he could not tell me how to strike such a balance. While each of us can do it for himself here and now, he finds trouble even for himself when he includes his own future; and when we come to deal with a community, a community of say one hundred and thirty million persons, how can we possibly proceed? What we do in fact is to assume that all are alike; that what is a good for A is a good for B, and that A's preference—A's better—will be B's. Perhaps one cannot conduct a democracy on any other assumption; but not only is it not true in fact; but whatever its truth, it is impossible to make people believe it. They will do so in the abstract, but they fall into endless dispute in application, and the effort is apt to end either in mutual paralysis of action, or a seizure of power by a part. The resulting confusion and discord have therefore often suggested this solution: instill in all a faith that each achieves his personal and individual best by submerging himself in common aspirations, a common fate, a common self. There would be no denial of Liberty in that; nobody would feel himself under alien domination; each would realize himself in all, and all in each.

"Old stuff again," you will say, "it sounds good but you know it cannot be done; people are too different, and that is all there is to it. Once you try to make them alike you have more trouble on your hands than when you started." On the contrary I am disposed to believe that perhaps it can be done, for a time anyway, and for a very large proportion at least of a large community. Certainly I am not so sure as I used to be that it cannot be done. There are more and more signs about us that our increasingly efficient and pervasive apparatus of mass suggestion is planing off individual differences, and making us more and more facile for mass manipulation. We need not look to Russia and Germany, or to their pathetic Italian imitator; we need not leave home at all. Indeed, something of the kind was possible long before the days of the tabloid, the radio, the moving picture, and the motor car. Sparta was an instance; so was Rome for a while; and Islam in the 8th Century, Spain in the 16th, and France in the 18th. And it has always been possible to create nonpolitical groups with corporate selves. Man is a gregarious animal, extremely sensitive to authority; if it will only indoctrinate him thoroughly in his childhood and youth, he can be made to espouse any kind of orthodoxy—whether of belief or feeling. There were philosophical prophets of the Absolute Collective Self long before Hegel and Fichte. In his early manhood Plato had seen the Athenian democracy crumble from faction; he concluded that only under the Spartan model could mankind achieve that justice which was the end of society as it was of the individual. Again and again the same theme has recurred thereafter.

Now, as a practical means of realizing common purposes nothing

comparable exists, as we are now learning to our cost. Lord Lothian shortly before his death—and very near, I think, to where we now are—forcibly admonished us of this. "You cannot match the power of such a people as the Germans, unless you are willing to sink your separate interests in your common cause and accept sacrifices such as they accept by means of a faith of equal fervor." Hitler is quite right in predicting the doom of democracies as he understands democracies; I wish it were more certain that he misunderstands them. A society in which each is willing to surrender only that for which he can see a personal equivalent, is not a society at all; it is a group already in process of dissolution, and no one need concern himself to stay its inevitable end; it would be a hard choice between it and a totalitarian society. No Utopia, nothing but Bedlam, will automatically emerge from a regime of unbridled individualism, be it ever so rugged.

What then, you will ask, am I really talking about? If it be true that any orthodoxy can be implanted in us, provided we are caught and schooled while young, or provided even in our later years that we are subjected to the everlasting iteration of sacred rubrics, in school, in press, in moving picture, and by radio; and if, when we have been so "conditioned," we feel authority to be no restraint but rather a means toward the realization of our deeper self; and if something of the sort is essential to survival in a robbers' world, where the strong are sure to win; if all these things be true, why should we boggle about any other Liberty; what more do we need? That other societies so organized have been predatory, does not mean that we need be predacious; our communal self can become the chalice for a more exquisite liquor of civilization than the troubled world has yet seen. In our Father's house are many mansions; we will occupy one where life shall be seemly and noble and forbearing and happy and gay; yet strong enough withal to resist any aggression.

Some day such a vision may come true; the future may have in store aeons of beatitude in which men shall find utter self-realization and utter self-expression in the utter self-surrender of the hive; I do not forget the words of the collect: "Whose service is perfect freedom." Be that as it may, it is not on the score of its impracticability that I do not welcome that prospect; but because I believe that its realization would suppress the most precious part of our nature. To put it very badly, and perhaps a little contentiously, it is man's inherent willfulness that I would preserve, and in which I wish to set the stronghold of that Liberty I prize; that stone which social reformers have always rejected I would make the head of the corner.

I cannot tell why to me personally such a society seems stifling; I only know that although with Epictetus I can say: "If I were an ant, I should play the part of an ant," in fact I am not an ant, and if I try to play the part of an ant I know that I shall end in the care of a psychoanalyst. I will own that when on occasion I visit my simian cousins in captivity, the spectacle does not refresh me. Not only have they a distressing lack of

reserve, but their restlessness affects me with a homeopathic uneasiness. Kipling seems right, and I wince that we have so many family traits in common. My kinship with them becomes even more distasteful when I pass to the cages of the great cats, who lie there serenely with their steady yellow eyes, calm, self-secure, fearing nothing. Why must my cousins and I be so agitated; why this ceaseless, errant curiosity; pausing only for an instant and then off to something new? It is all very trying; and yet here will I pitch my tent. James Harvey Robinson used to say that we rose from the ape because like him we kept "monkeying around," always meddling with everything about us. True, there is a difference, because although the ape meddles, he forgets, and we have learned, first to meddle and remember, and then to meddle and record. But without the meddling nothing would have happened of all that glorious array of achievement: battleships, aeroplanes, relativity, the proton, neutron, and electron, T.N.T., poison gas, sulfathiazole, the Fifth Symphony, *The Iliad, The Divine Comedy, Hamlet, Faust, The Critique of Pure Reason, Das Kapital,* The Constitution of the United States, The Congress of Industrial Organizations, Huey Long, and The New Deal. All these from just "monkeying around"!

My thesis is that any organization of society which depresses free and spontaneous meddling is on the decline, however showy its immediate spoils; I maintain that in such a society Liberty is gone, little as its members may know it; that the Nirvana of the individual is too high a price for a collective Paradise. I maintain this primarily as an authentic demand of the spirit—*animula vagula blandula . . . quae nunc abibis in loca*—and I maintain it too as practical sagacity. Because, once you get people believing that there is an authoritative well of wisdom to which they can turn for absolutes, you have dried up the springs on which they must in the end draw even for the things of this world. As soon as we cease to pry about at random, we shall come to rely upon accredited bodies of authoritative dogma; and as soon as we come to rely upon accredited bodies of authoritative dogma, not only are the days of our Liberty over, but we have lost the password that has hitherto opened to us the gates of success as well. Even in that very technology on which they so much pride themselves, the totalitarians in the end will fail; for they stand upon the shoulders of generations of free inquiry. No doubt they will try to keep their hands off materially profitable activities; but they will finally learn that you cannot put men's minds in watertight compartments; you cannot have a nation, each one of whom is half slave and half free, any more than you can have a nation in which half are wholly slave and half are wholly free. Where heterodoxy in what men prize most is a crime, fresh thinking about anything will disappear. Even the loaves and fishes will not be multiplied.

As I predicted, I have brought down a very small quarry. We started to find some positive content for Liberty, and all we have discovered is

that it does not follow because we are not conscious of constraint that we are not constrained. Yet little as that seems, it is not I think an altogether contemptible result, for behind it lies a faith. It is the faith that our collective fate in the end depends upon the irrepressible fertility of the individual, and the finality of what he chooses to call good. It is the faith that neither principalities, nor powers, nor things present, nor things to come, can rightfully suppress that fertility or deny that good. It is the faith in the indefectible significance of each one of us, inherited, if I understand it aright, from One who lived and died some 1900 years ago in Palestine. It is a faith not easy to live by, whose credo is full of hard sayings. If you accept it, it may cast you for the role of Prometheus, a part of whose lines, you will remember, contain a good deal about defying the Powers of this World. Those powers are ruthless, competent, and strong; and among the properties in the play there are real lightning and a real eagle; make no mistake about that. Moreover, the audience is likely to be very small; indeed it is not improbable that there will be none at all. The only curtain calls you will get are those you give yourself. But the lead is a man's part, and perhaps some of us can fill it. Who can tell?

## TOPICS FOR DISCUSSION

1   What are the main divisions of this essay? How does Hand guide his reader across these divisions?

2   Why are the two questions which begin paragraph 2, p. 255, effective as a transition between sections of the argument?

3   What is discounted as unreliable before Hand comes to his own contribution regarding liberty? Why does he take so much time to do so? Is anything to be gained by removing opposition or alternatives before making a commitment to a thesis? What is his thesis?

4   The use of "you" in the essay might be explained by the public speech which occasioned the piece, but it serves a much more useful function as well. What does it do for the reader? Do the moments of unresponsive questions from the "you" make the final argument any stronger? Is this a matter of logic or of rhetoric?

5   Judging from the allusions, ancient and modern, how well-educated a man would you consider Hand? Does the range of allusion give any additional strength to his argument? Can you identify specifically all the allusions and understand clearly their function in the essay? Do some of them betray a bias?

**6** What does Hand mean in the following? "Hitler is quite right in predicting the doom of democracies as he understands democracies. . . . A society in which each is willing to surrender only that for which he can see a personal equivalent, is not a society at all; it is a group already in process of dissolution, and no one need concern himself to stay its inevitable end; it would be a hard choice between it and a totalitarian society."

## . . . AND COMPOSITION

**7** Are there competing liberties that must compromise themselves to continue their existence? Discuss.

**8** Is it true that to preserve a society of free inquiry one must give up some liberty? Be specific. Can this individual sacrifice ultimately harm the society? How?

**9** What are some orthodoxies implanted in us from our youth? Discuss.

**10** How can individual inquiry or meddling topple a tyranny? What alternatives are there to war, domestic or foreign?

**11** Orwell ("Politics and the English Language") called "liberty" a "meaningless" word; did Hand make it any less meaningless by his analysis?

HENRY DAVID THOREAU (1817–1862) distilled from ideas current at his place and time the kind of individualism most natural to Americans. At Walden Pond he lived it, and in his writings he weighed it and worked out its implications. "Civil Disobedience" has directly influenced world affairs, notably in India with Gandhi's program, and of course in the freedom movements which mark our time. Thoreau's writing demonstrates poise, bite, and continuous awareness. In conduct and in writing he points to standards fit for heroes.

# Civil Disobedience

I heartily accept the motto,—"That government is best which governs least"; and I should like to see it acted up to more rapidly and systematically. Carried out, it finally amounts to this, which also I believe,—"That government is best which governs not at all"; and when men are prepared for it, that will be the kind of government which they will have. Government is at best but an expedient; but most governments are usually, and all governments are sometimes, inexpedient. The objections which have been brought against a standing army, and they are many and weighty, and deserve to prevail, may also at last be brought against a standing government. The standing army is only an arm of the standing government. The government itself, which is only the mode which the people have chosen to execute their will, is equally liable to be abused and perverted before the people can act through it. Witness the present Mexican war, the work of comparatively a few individuals using the standing government as their tool; for, in the outset, the people would not have consented to this measure.

This American government,—what is it but a tradition, though a recent one, endeavoring to transmit itself unimpaired to posterity, but each instant losing some of its integrity? It has not the vitality and force of a single living man; for a single man can bend it to his will. It is a sort of wooden gun to the people themselves. But it is not the less necessary for this; for the people must have some complicated machinery or other, and hear its din, to satisfy that idea of government which they have. Governments show thus how successfully men can be imposed on, even impose on themselves, for their own advantage. It is excellent, we must all allow. Yet this government never of itself furthered any enterprise, but by the alacrity with which it got out of its way. *It* does not keep the country free. *It* does not settle the West. *It* does not educate. The character inherent in the American people has done all that has been accomplished; and it would have done somewhat more, if the government had not sometimes got in its way. For government is an expedient by which men would fain succeed in letting one another alone; and, as has been said, when it is most expedient, the

governed are most let alone by it. Trade and commerce, if they were not made of india-rubber, would never manage to bounce over the obstacles which legislators are continually putting in their way; and, if one were to judge these men wholly by the effects of their actions and not partly by their intentions, they would deserve to be classed and punished with those mischievous persons who put obstructions on the railroads.

But, to speak practically and as a citizen, unlike those who call themselves no-government men, I ask for, not at once no government, but *at once* a better government. Let every man make known what kind of government would command his respect, and that will be one step toward obtaining it.

After all, the practical reason why, when the power is once in the hands of the people, a majority are permitted, and for a long period continue, to rule is not because they are most likely to be in the right, nor because this seems fairest to the minority, but because they are physically the strongest. But a government in which the majority rule in all cases cannot be based on justice, even as far as men understand it. Can there be a government in which majorities do not virtually decide right and wrong, but conscience?—in which majorities decide only those questions to which the rule of expediency is applicable? Must the citizen ever for a moment, or in the least degree, resign his conscience to the legislator? Why has every man a conscience, then? I think that we should be men first, and subjects afterward. It is not desirable to cultivate a respect for the law, so much as for the right. The only obligation which I have a right to assume is to do at any time what I think right. It is truly enough said that a corporation has no conscience; but a corporation of conscientious men is a corporation *with* a conscience. Law never made men a whit more just; and, by means of their respect for it, even the well-disposed are daily made the agents of injustice. A common and natural result of an undue respect for law is, that you may see a file of soldiers, colonel, captain, corporal, privates, powder-monkeys, and all, marching in admirable order over hill and dale to the wars, against their wills, ay, against their common sense and consciences, which makes it very steep marching indeed, and produces a palpitation of the heart. They have no doubt that it is a damnable business in which they are concerned; they are all peaceably inclined. Now, what are they? Men at all? or small movable forts and magazines, at the service of some unscrupulous man in power? Visit the Navy-Yard, and behold a marine, such a man as an American government can make, or such as it can make a man with its black arts,—a mere shadow and reminiscence of humanity, a man laid out alive and standing, and already, as one may say, buried under arms with funeral accompaniments, though it may be,—

> Not a drum was heard, not a funeral note,
>     As his corse to the rampart we hurried;

> Not a soldier discharged his farewell shot
>     O'er the grave where our hero we buried.

The mass of men serve the state thus, not as men mainly, but as machines, with their bodies. They are the standing army, and the militia, jailers, constables, *posse comitatus,* etc. In most cases there is no free exercise whatever of the judgment or of the moral sense; but they put themselves on a level with wood and earth and stones; and wooden men can perhaps be manufactured that will serve the purpose as well. Such command no more respect than men of straw or a lump of dirt. They have the same sort of worth only as horses and dogs. Yet such as these even are commonly esteemed good citizens. Others—as most legislators, politicians, lawyers, ministers, and office-holders—serve the state chiefly with their heads; and, as they rarely make any moral distinctions, they are as likely to serve the devil, without *intending* it, as God. A very few,—as heroes, patriots, martyrs, reformers in the great sense, and *men*—serve the state with their consciences also, and so necessarily resist it for the most part; and they are commonly treated as enemies by it. A wise man will only be useful as a man, and will not submit to be "clay," and "stop a hole to keep the wind away," but leave that office to his dust at least:—

> I am too high-born to be propertied,
> To be a secondary at control,
> Or useful serving-man and instrument
> To any sovereign state throughout the world.

He who gives himself entirely to his fellow-men appears to them useless and selfish; but he who gives himself partially to them is pronounced a benefactor and philanthropist.

How does it become a man to behave toward this American government to-day? I answer, that he cannot without disgrace be associated with it. I cannot for an instant recognize that political organization as *my* government which is the *slave's* government also.

All men recognize the right of revolution; that is, the right to refuse allegiance to, and to resist, the government, when its tyranny or its inefficiency are great and unendurable. But almost all say that such is not the case now. But such was the case, they think, in the Revolution of '75. If one were to tell me that this was a bad government because it taxed certain foreign commodities brought to its ports, it is most probable that I should not make an ado about it, for I can do without them. All machines have their friction; and possibly this does enough good to counterbalance the evil. At any rate, it is a great evil to make a stir about it. But when the friction comes to have its machine, and oppression and robbery are organized, I say, let us not have such a machine any longer. In other words, when a sixth of the population of a nation which has undertaken to be the refuge of liberty are slaves, and a whole country is unjustly overrun

and conquered by a foreign army, and subjected to military law, I think that it is not too soon for honest men to rebel and revolutionize. What makes this duty the more urgent is the fact that the country so overrun is not our own, but ours is the invading army.

Paley, a common authority with many on moral questions, in his chapter on the "Duty of Submission to Civil Government," resolves all civil obligation into expediency; and he proceeds to say "that so long as the interest of the whole society requires it, that is, so long as the established government cannot be resisted or changed without public inconveniency, it is the will of God . . . that the established government be obeyed,—and no longer. This principle being admitted, the justice of every particular case of resistance is reduced to a computation of the quantity of the danger and grievance on the one side, and of the probability and expense of redressing it on the other." Of this, he says, every man shall judge for himself. But Paley appears never to have contemplated those cases to which the rule of expediency does not apply, in which a people, as well as an individual, must do justice, cost what it may. If I have unjustly wrested a plank from a drowning man, I must restore it to him though I drown myself. This, according to Paley, would be inconvenient. But he that would save his life, in such a case, shall lose it. This people must cease to hold slaves, and to make war on Mexico, though it cost them their existence as a people.

In their practice, nations agree with Paley; but does any one think that Massachusetts does exactly what is right at the present crisis?

> A drab of state, a cloth-o'-silver slut,
> To have her train borne up, and her soul trail in the dirt.

Practically speaking, the opponents to a reform in Massachusetts are not a hundred thousand politicians at the South, but a hundred thousand merchants and farmers here, who are more interested in commerce and agriculture than they are in humanity, and are not prepared to do justice to the slave and to Mexico, *cost what it may*. I quarrel not with far-off foes, but with those who, near at home, coöperate with, and do the bidding of, those far away, and without whom the latter would be harmless. We are accustomed to say, that the mass of men are unprepared; but improvement is slow, because the few are not materially wiser or better than the many. It is not so important that many should be as good as you, as that there be some absolute goodness somewhere; for that will leaven the whole lump. There are thousands who are *in opinion* opposed to slavery and to the war, who yet in effect do nothing to put an end to them; who, esteeming themselves children of Washington and Franklin, sit down with their hands in their pockets, and say that they know not what to do, and do nothing; who even postpone the question of freedom to the question of free trade, and quietly read the prices-current along with the latest advices from

Mexico, after dinner, and, it may be, fall asleep over them both. What is the price-current of an honest man and patriot to-day? They hesitate, and they regret, and sometimes they petition; but they do nothing in earnest and with effect. They will wait, well disposed, for others to remedy the evil, that they may no longer have it to regret. At most, they give only a cheap vote, and a feeble countenance and God-speed, to the right, as it goes by them. There are nine hundred and ninety-nine patrons of virtue to one virtuous man. But it is easier to deal with the real possessor of a thing than with the temporary guardian of it.

All voting is a sort of gaming, like checkers or backgammon, with a slight moral tinge to it, a playing with right and wrong, with moral questions; and betting naturally accompanies it. The character of the voters is not staked. I cast my vote, perchance, as I think right; but I am not vitally concerned that that right should prevail. I am willing to leave it to the majority. Its obligation, therefore, never exceeds that of expediency. Even voting *for the right* is *doing* nothing for it. It is only expressing to men feebly your desire that it should prevail. A wise man will not leave the right to the mercy of chance, nor wish it to prevail through the power of the majority. There is but little virtue in the action of masses of men. When the majority shall at length vote for the abolition of slavery, it will be because they are indifferent to slavery, or because there is but little slavery left to be abolished by their vote. *They* will then be the only slaves. Only *his* vote can hasten the abolition of slavery who asserts his own freedom by his vote.

I hear of a convention to be held at Baltimore, or elsewhere, for the selection of a candidate for the Presidency, made up chiefly of editors, and men who are politicians by profession; but I think, what is it to any independent, intelligent, and respectable man what decision they may come to? Shall we not have the advantage of his wisdom and honesty, nevertheless? Can we not count upon some independent votes? Are there not many individuals in the country who do not attend conventions? But no: I find that the respectable man, so called, has immediately drifted from his position, and despairs of his country, when his country has more reason to despair of him. He forthwith adopts one of the candidates thus selected as the only *available* one, thus proving that he is himself *available* for any purposes of the demagogue. His vote is of no more worth than that of any unprincipled foreigner or hireling native, who may have been bought. O for a man who is a *man,* and, as my neighbor says, has a bone in his back which you cannot pass your hand through! Our statistics are at fault: the population has been returned too large. How many *men* are there to a square thousand miles in this country? Hardly one. Does not America offer any inducement for men to settle here? The American has dwindled into an Odd Fellow,—one who may be known by the development of his organ of gregariousness, and a manifest lack of intellect and cheerful self-

reliance; whose first and chief concern, on coming into the world, is to see that the alms-houses are in good repair; and, before yet he has lawfully donned the virile garb, to collect a fund for the support of the widows and orphans that may be; who, in short, ventures to live only by the aid of the Mutual Insurance company, which has promised to bury him decently.

It is not a man's duty, as a matter of course, to devote himself to the eradication of any, even the most enormous, wrong; he may still properly have other concerns to engage him; but it is his duty, at least, to wash his hands of it, and, if he gives it no thought longer, not to give it practically his support. If I devote myself to other pursuits and contemplations, I must first see, at least, that I do not pursue them sitting upon another man's shoulders. I must get off him first, that he may pursue his contemplations too. See what gross inconsistency is tolerated. I have heard some of my townsmen say, "I should like to have them order me out to help put down an insurrection of the slaves, or to march to Mexico;—see if I would go"; and yet these very men have each, directly by their allegiance, and so indirectly, at least, by their money, furnished a substitute. The soldier is applauded who refuses to serve in an unjust war by those who do not refuse to sustain the unjust government which makes the war; is applauded by those whose own act and authority he disregards and sets at naught; as if the state were penitent to that degree that it hired one to scourge it while it sinned, but not to that degree that it left off sinning for a moment. Thus, under the name of Order and Civil Government, we are all made at last to pay homage to and support our own meanness. After the first blush of sin comes its indifference; and from immoral it becomes, as it were, *un*moral, and not quite unnecessary to that life which we have made.

The broadest and most prevalent error requires the most disinterested virtue to sustain it. The slight reproach to which the virtue of patriotism is commonly liable, the noble are most likely to incur. Those who, while they disapprove of the character and measures of a government, yield to it their allegiance and support are undoubtedly its most conscientious supporters, and so frequently the most serious obstacles to reform. Some are petitioning the State to dissolve the Union, to disregard the requisitions of the President. Why do they not dissolve it themselves,—the union between themselves and the State,—and refuse to pay their quota into its treasury? Do not they stand in the same relation to the State that the State does to the Union? And have not the same reasons prevented the State from resisting the Union which have prevented them from resisting the State?

How can a man be satisfied to entertain an opinion merely, and enjoy *it?* Is there any enjoyment in it, if his opinion is that he is aggrieved? If you are cheated out of a single dollar by your neighbor, you do not rest satisfied with knowing that you are cheated, or with saying that you are

cheated, or even with petitioning him to pay you your due; but you take effectual steps at once to obtain the full amount, and see that you are never cheated again. Action from principle, the perception and the performance of right, changes things and relations; it is essentially revolutionary, and does not consist wholly with anything which was. It not only divides States and churches, it divides families; ay, it divides the *individual,* separating the diabolical in him from the divine.

Unjust laws exist: shall we be content to obey them, or shall we endeavor to ámend them, and obey them until we have succeeded, or shall we transgress them at once? Men generally, under such a government as this, think that they ought to wait until they have persuaded the majority to alter them. They think that, if they should resist, the remedy would be worse than the evil. But it is the fault of the government itself that the remedy *is* worse than the evil. *It* makes it worse. Why is it not more apt to anticipate and provide for reform? Why does it not cherish its wise minority? Why does it cry and resist before it is hurt? Why does it not encourage its citizens to be on the alert to point out its faults, and *do* better than it would have them? Why does it always crucify Christ, and excommunicate Copernicus and Luther, and pronounce Washington and Franklin rebels?

One would think, that a deliberate and practical denial of its authority was the only offense never contemplated by government; else, why has it not assigned its definite, its suitable and proportionate penalty? If a man who has no property refuses but once to earn nine shillings for the State, he is put in prison for a period unlimited by any law that I know, and determined only by the discretion of those who placed him there; but if he should steal ninety times nine shillings from the State, he is soon permitted to go at large again.

If the injustice is part of the necessary friction of the machine of government, let it go, let it go: perchance it will wear smooth,—certainly the machine will wear out. If the injustice has a spring, or a pulley, or a rope, or a crank, exclusively for itself, then perhaps you may consider whether the remedy will not be worse than the evil; but if it is of such a nature that it requires you to be the agent of injustice to another, then, I say, break the law. Let your life be a counter friction to stop the machine. What I have to do is to see, at any rate, that I do not lend myself to the wrong which I condemn.

As for adopting the ways which the State has provided for remedying the evil, I know not of such ways. They take too much time, and a man's life will be gone. I have other affairs to attend to. I came into this world, not chiefly to make this a good place to live in, but to live in it, be it good or bad. A man has not everything to do, but something; and because he cannot do *everything,* it is not necessary that he should do *something* wrong. It is not my business to be petitioning the Governor or the Legisla-

ture any more than it is theirs to petition me; and if they should not hear my petition, what should I do then? But in this case the State has provided no way: its very Constitution is the evil. This may seem to be harsh and stubborn and unconciliatory; but it is to treat with the utmost kindness and consideration the only spirit that can appreciate or deserves it. So is all change for the better, like birth and death, which convulse the body.

I do not hesitate to say, that those who call themselves Abolitionists should at once effectually withdraw their support, both in person and property, from the government of Massachusetts, and not wait till they constitute a majority of one, before they suffer the right to prevail through them. I think that it is enough if they have God on their side, without waiting for that other one. Moreover, any man more right than his neighbors constitutes a majority of one already.

I meet this American government, or its representative, the State government, directly, and face to face, once a year—no more—in the person of its tax-gatherer; this is the only mode in which a man situated as I am necessarily meets it; and it then says distinctly, Recognize me; and the simplest, the most effectual, and, in the present posture of affairs, the indispensablest mode of treating with it on this head, of expressing your little satisfaction with and love for it, is to deny it then. My civil neighbor, the tax-gatherer, is the very man I have to deal with,—for it is, after all, with men and not with parchment that I quarrel,—and he has voluntarily chosen to be an agent of the government. How shall he ever know well what he is and does as an officer of the government, or as a man, until he is obliged to consider whether he shall treat me, his neighbor, for whom he has respect, as a neighbor and well-disposed man, or as a maniac and disturber of the peace, and see if he can get over this obstruction to his neighborliness without a ruder and more impetuous thought or speech corresponding with his action. I know this well, that if one thousand, if one hundred, if ten men whom I could name,—if ten *honest* men only,— ay, if *one* HONEST man, in this State of Massachusetts, *ceasing to hold slaves,* were actually to withdraw from this copartnership, and be locked up in the county jail therefor, it would be the abolition of slavery in America. For it matters not how small the beginning may seem to be: what is once well done is done forever. But we love better to talk about it: that we say is our mission. Reform keeps many scores of newspapers in its service, but not one man. If my esteemed neighbor, the State's ambassador, who will devote his days to the settlement of the question of human rights in the Council Chamber, instead of being threatened with the prisons of Carolina, were to sit down the prisoner of Massachusetts, that State which is so anxious to foist the sin of slavery upon her sister,—though at present she can discover only an act of inhospitality to be the ground of a quarrel with her,—the Legislature would not wholly waive the subject the following winter.

Under a government which imprisons any unjustly, the true place for a just man is also a prison. The proper place to-day, the only place which Massachusetts has provided for her freer and less desponding spirits, is in her prisons, to be put out and locked out of the State by her own act, as they have already put themselves out by their principles. It is there that the fugitive slave, and the Mexican prisoner on parole, and the Indian come to plead the wrongs of his race should find them; on that separate, but more free and honorable ground, where the State places those who are not *with* her, but *against* her,—the only house in a slave State in which a free man can abide with honor. If any think that their influence would be lost there, and their voices no longer afflict the ear of the State, that they would not be as an enemy within its walls, they do not know by how much truth is stronger than error, nor how much more eloquently and effectively he can combat injustice who has experienced a little in his own person. Cast your whole vote, not a strip of paper merely, but your whole influence. A minority is powerless while it conforms to the majority; it is not even a minority then; but it is irresistible when it clogs by its whole weight. If the alternative is to keep all just men in prison, or give up war and slavery, the State will not hesitate which to choose. If a thousand men were not to pay their tax-bills this year, that would not be a violent and bloody measure, as it would be to pay them, and enable the State to commit violence and shed innocent blood. This is, in fact, the definition of a peaceable revolution, if any such is possible. If the tax-gatherer, or any other public officer, asks me, as one has done, "But what shall I do?" my answer is, "If you really wish to do anything, resign your office." When the subject has refused allegiance, and the officer has resigned his office, then the revolution is accomplished. But even suppose blood should flow. Is there not a sort of blood shed when the conscience is wounded? Through this wound a man's real manhood and immortality flow out, and he bleeds to an everlasting death. I see this blood flowing now.

I have contemplated the imprisonment of the offender, rather than the seizure of his goods,—though both will serve the same purpose,—because they who assert the purest right, and consequently are most dangerous to a corrupt State, commonly have not spent much time in accumulating property. To such the State renders comparatively small service, and a slight tax is wont to appear exorbitant, particularly if they are obliged to earn it by special labor with their hands. If there were one who lived wholly without the use of money, the State itself would hesitate to demand it of him. But the rich man—not to make any invidious comparison—is always sold to the institution which makes him rich. Absolutely speaking, the more money, the less virtue; for money comes between a man and his objects, and obtains them for him; and it was certainly no great virtue to obtain it. It puts to rest many questions which he would otherwise be taxed to answer; while the only new question which it puts is the hard but super-

fluous one, how to spend it. Thus his moral ground is taken from under his feet. The opportunities of living are diminished in proportion as what are called the "means" are increased. The best thing a man can do for his culture when he is rich is to endeavor to carry out those schemes which he entertained when he was poor. Christ answered the Herodians according to their condition. "Show me the tribute-money," said he;—and took one penny out of his pocket;—if you use money which has the image of Caesar on it and which he has made current and valuable, that is, *if you are men of the State,* and gladly enjoy the advantages of Caesar's government, then pay him back some of his own when he demands it. "Render therefore to Caesar that which is Caesar's, and to God those things which are God's,"—leaving them no wiser than before as to which was which; for they did not wish to know.

When I converse with the freest of my neighbors, I perceive that, whatever they may say about the magnitude and seriousness of the question, and their regard for the public tranquillity, the long and the short of the matter is, that they cannot spare the protection of the existing government, and they dread the consequences to their property and families of disobedience to it. For my own part, I should not like to think that I ever rely on the protection of the State. But, if I deny the authority of the State when it presents its tax-bill, it will soon take and waste all my property, and so harass me and my children without end. This is hard. This makes it impossible for a man to live honestly, and at the same time comfortably, in outward respects. It will not be worth the while to accumulate property; that would be sure to go again. You must hire or squat somewhere, and raise but a small crop, and eat that soon. You must live within yourself, and depend upon yourself always tucked up and ready for a start, and not have many affairs. A man may grow rich in Turkey even, if he will be in all respects a good subject of the Turkish government. Confucius said: "If a state is governed by the principles of reason, poverty and misery are subjects of shame; if a state is not governed by the principles of reason, riches and honors are the subjects of shame." No: until I want the protection of Massachusetts to be extended to me in some distant Southern port, where my liberty is endangered, or until I am bent solely on building up an estate at home by peaceful enterprise, I can afford to refuse allegiance to Massachusetts, and her right to my property and life. It costs me less in every sense to incur the penalty of disobedience to the State than it would to obey. I should feel as if I were worth less in that case.

Some years ago, the State met me in behalf of the Church, and commanded me to pay a certain sum toward the support of a clergyman whose preaching my father attended, but never I myself. "Pay," it said, "or be locked up in the jail." I declined to pay. But, unfortunately, another man saw fit to pay it. I did not see why the schoolmaster should be taxed to support the priest, and not the priest the schoolmaster; for I was not the

State's schoolmaster, but I supported myself by voluntary subscription. I did not see why the lyceum should not present its tax-bill, and have the State to back its demand, as well as the Church. However, at the request of the selectmen, I condescended to make some such statement as this in writing:—"Know all men by these presents, that I, Henry Thoreau, do not wish to be regarded as a member of any incorporated society which I have not joined." This I gave to the town clerk; and he has it. The State, having thus learned that I did not wish to be regarded as a member of that church, has never made a like demand on me since; though it said that it must adhere to its original presumption that time. If I had known how to name them, I should then have signed off in detail from all the societies which I never signed on to; but I did not know where to find a complete list.

I have paid no poll-tax for six years. I was put into a jail once on this account, for one night; and, as I stood considering the walls of solid stone, two or three feet thick, the door of wood and iron, a foot thick, and the iron grating which strained the light, I could not help being struck with the foolishness of that institution which treated me as if I were mere flesh and blood and bones, to be locked up. I wondered that it should have concluded at length that this was the best use it could put me to, and had never thought to avail itself of my services in some way. I saw that, if there was a wall of stone between me and my townsmen, there was a still more difficult one to climb or break through before they could get to be as free as I was. I did not for a moment feel confined, and the walls seemed a great waste of stone and mortar. I felt as if I alone of all my townsmen had paid my tax. They plainly did not know how to treat me, but behaved like persons who are underbred. In every threat and in every compliment there was a blunder; for they thought that my chief desire was to stand on the other side of that stone wall. I could not but smile to see how industriously they locked the door on my meditations, which followed them out again without let or hindrance, and *they* were really all that was dangerous. As they could not reach me, they had resolved to punish my body; just as boys, if they cannot come at some person against whom they have a spite, will abuse his dog. I saw that the State was half-witted, that it was timid as a lone woman with her silver spoons, and that it did not know its friends from its foes, and I lost all my remaining respect for it, and pitied it.

Thus the State never intentionally confronts a man's sense, intellectual or moral, but only his body, his senses. It is not armed with superior wit or honesty, but with superior physical strength. I was not born to be forced. I will breathe after my own fashion. Let us see who is the strongest. What force has a multitude? They only can force me who obey a higher law than I. They force me to become like themselves. I do not hear of *men* being *forced* to live this way or that by masses of men. What sort of life were that to live? When I meet a government which says to me, "Your

money or your life," why should I be in haste to give it my money? It may be in a great strait, and not know what to do: I cannot help that. It must help itself; do as I do. It is not worth the while to snivel about it. I am not responsible for the successful working of the machinery of society. I am not the son of the engineer. I perceive that, when an acorn and a chestnut fall side by side, the one does not remain inert to make way for the other, but both obey their own laws, and spring and grow and flourish as best they can, till one, perchance, overshadows and destroys the other. If a plant cannot live according to its nature, it dies; and so a man.

The night in prison was novel and interesting enough. The prisoners in their shirt-sleeves were enjoying a chat and the evening air in the doorway, when I entered. But the jailer said, "Come, boys, it is time to lock up," and so they dispersed, and I heard the sound of their steps returning into the hollow apartments. My room-mate was introduced to me by the jailer as "a first-rate fellow and a clever man." When the door was locked, he showed me where to hang my hat, and how he managed matters there. The rooms were white-washed once a month; and this one, at least, was the whitest, most simply furnished, and probably the neatest apartment in the town. He naturally wanted to know where I came from, and what brought me there; and, when I had told him, I asked him in my turn how he came there, presuming him to be an honest man, of course; and, as the world goes, I believe he was. "Why," said he, "they accuse me of burning a barn; but I never did it." As near as I could discover, he had probably gone to bed in a barn when drunk, and smoked his pipe there; and so a barn was burnt. He had the reputation of being a clever man, had been there some three months waiting for his trial to come on, and would have to wait as much longer; but he was quite domesticated and contented, since he got his board for nothing, and thought that he was well treated.

He occupied one window, and I the other; and I saw that if one stayed there long, his principal business would be to look out the window. I had soon read all the tracts that were left there, and examined where former prisoners had broken out, and where a gate had been sawed off, and heard the history of the various occupants of that room; for I found that even here there was a history and a gossip which never circulated beyond the walls of the jail. Probably this is the only house in the town where verses are composed, which are afterward printed in circular form, but not published. I was shown quite a long list of verses which were composed by some young men who had been detected in an attempt to escape, who avenged themselves by singing them.

I pumped my fellow-prisoner as dry as I could, for fear I should never see him again; but at length he showed me which was my bed, and left me to blow out the lamp.

It was like traveling into a far country, such as I had never expected to behold, to lie there for one night. It seemed to me that I never had

heard the town clock strike before, nor the evening sounds of the village; for we slept with the windows open, which were inside the grating. It was to see my native village in the light of the Middle Ages, and our Concord was turned into a Rhine stream, and visions of knights and castles passed before me. They were the voices of old burghers that I heard in the streets. I was an involuntary spectator and auditor of whatever was done and said in the kitchen of the adjacent village-inn,—a wholly new and rare experience to me. It was a closer view of my native town. I was fairly inside of it. I never had seen its institutions before. This is one of the peculiar institutions; for it is a shire town. I began to comprehend what its inhabitants were about.

In the morning, our breakfasts were put through the hole in the door, in small oblong-square tin pans, made to fit, and holding a pint of chocolate, with brown bread, and an iron spoon. When they called for the vessels again, I was green enough to return what bread I had left; but my comrade seized it, and said that I should lay that up for lunch or dinner. Soon after he was let out to work at haying in a neighboring field, whither he went every day, and would not be back till noon; so he bade me good-day, saying that he doubted if he should see me again.

When I came out of prison,—for some one interfered, and paid that tax,—I did not perceive that great changes had taken place on the common, such as he observed who went in a youth and emerged a tottering and gray-headed man; and yet a change had to my eyes come over the scene,— the town, and State, and country,—greater than any that mere time could effect. I saw yet more distinctly the State in which I lived. I saw to what extent the people among whom I lived could be trusted as good neighbors and friends; that their friendship was for summer weather only; that they did not greatly propose to do right; that they were a distinct race from me by their prejudices and superstitions, as the Chinamen and Malays are; that in their sacrifices to humanity they ran no risks, not even to their property; that after all they were not so noble but they treated the thief as he had treated them, and hoped, by a certain outward observance and a few prayers, and by walking in a particular straight though useless path from time to time, to save their souls. This may be to judge my neighbors harshly; for I believe that many of them are not aware that they have such an institution as the jail in their village.

It was formerly the custom in our village, when a poor debtor came out of jail, for his acquaintances to salute him, looking through their fingers, which were crossed to represent the grating of a jail window, "How do ye do?" My neighbors did not thus salute me, but first looked at me, and then at one another, as if I had returned from a long journey. I was put into jail as I was going to the shoemaker's to get a shoe which was mended. When I was let out the next morning, I proceeded to finish my errand, and, having put on my mended shoe, joined a huckleberry party, who were

impatient to put themselves under my conduct; and in half an hour,—for the horse was soon tackled,—was in the midst of a huckleberry field, on one of our highest hills, two miles off, and then the State was nowhere to be seen.

This is the whole history of "My Prisons."

I have never declined paying the highway tax, because I am as desirous of being a good neighbor as I am of being a bad subject; and as for supporting schools, I am doing my part to educate my fellow-countrymen now. It is for no particular item in the tax-bill that I refuse to pay it. I simply wish to refuse allegiance to the State, to withdraw and stand aloof from it effectually. I do not care to trace the course of my dollar, if I could, till it buys a man or a musket to shoot one with,—the dollar is innocent,—but I am concerned to trace the effects of my allegiance. In fact, I quietly declare war with the State, after my fashion, though I will still make what use and get what advantage of her I can, as is usual in such cases.

If others pay the tax which is demanded of me, from a sympathy with the State, they do but what they have already done in their own case, or rather they abet injustice to a greater extent than the State requires. If they pay the tax from a mistaken interest in the individual taxed, to save his property, or prevent his going to jail, it is because they have not considered wisely how far they let their private feelings interfere with the public good.

This, then, is my position at present. But one cannot be too much on his guard in such a case, lest his action be biased by obstinacy or an undue regard for the opinions of men. Let him see that he does only what belongs to himself and to the hour.

I think sometimes, Why, this people mean well, they are only ignorant; they would do better if they knew how: why give your neighbors this pain to treat you as they are not inclined to? But I think again, This is no reason why I should do as they do, or permit others to suffer much greater pain of a different kind. Again, I sometimes say to myself, When many millions of men, without heat, without ill will, without personal feeling of any kind, demand of you a few shillings only, without the possibility, such is their constitution, of retracting or altering their present demand, and without the possibility, on your side, of appeal to any other millions, why expose yourself to this overwhelming brute force? You do not resist cold and hunger, the winds and the waves, thus obstinately; you quietly submit to a thousand similar necessities. You do not put your head into the fire. But just in proportion as I regard this as not wholly a brute force, but partly a human force, and consider that I have relations to those millions as to so many millions of men, and not of mere brute or inanimate things, I see that appeal is possible, first and instantaneously, from them

to the Maker of them, and, secondly, from them to themselves. But if I put my head deliberately into the fire, there is no appeal to fire or to the Maker of fire, and I have only myself to blame. If I could convince myself that I have any right to be satisfied with men as they are, and to treat them accordingly, and not according, in some respects, to my requisitions and expectations of what they and I ought to be, then, like a good Mussulman and fatalist, I should endeavor to be satisfied with things as they are, and say it is the will of God. And, above all, there is this difference between resisting this and a purely brute or natural force, that I can resist this with some effect; but I cannot expect, like Orpheus, to change the nature of the rocks and trees and beasts.

I do not wish to quarrel with any man or nation. I do not wish to split hairs, to make fine distinctions, or set myself up as better than my neighbors. I seek rather, I may say, even an excuse for conforming to the laws of the land. I am but too ready to conform to them. Indeed, I have reason to suspect myself on this head; and each year, as the tax-gatherer comes round, I find myself disposed to review the acts and position of the general and State governments, and the spirit of the people, to discover a pretext for conformity.

> We must affect our country as our parents,
> And if at any time we alienate
> Our love or industry from doing it honor,
> We must respect effects and teach the soul
> Matter of conscience and religion,
> And not desire of rule or benefit.

I believe that the State will soon be able to take all my work of this sort out of my hands, and then I shall be no better a patriot than my fellow-countrymen. Seen from a lower point of view, the Constitution, with all its faults, is very good; the law and the courts are very respectable; even this State and this American government are, in many respects, very admirable, and rare things, to be thankful for, such as a great many have described them; but seen from a point of view a little higher, they are what I have described them; seen from a higher still, and the highest, who shall say what they are, or that they are worth looking at or thinking of at all?

However, the government does not concern me much, and I shall bestow the fewest possible thoughts on it. It is not many moments that I live under a government, even in this world. If a man is thought-free, fancy-free, imagination-free, that which *is not* never for a long time appearing *to be* to him, unwise rulers or reformers cannot fatally interrupt him.

I know that most men think differently from myself; but those whose

lives are by profession devoted to the study of these or kindred subjects content me as little as any. Statesmen and legislators, standing so completely within the institution, never distinctly and nakedly behold it. They speak of moving society, but have no resting-place without it. They may be men of a certain experience and discrimination, and have no doubt invented ingenious and even useful systems, for which we sincerely thank them; but all their wit and usefulness lie within certain not very wide limits. They are wont to forget that the world is not governed by policy and expediency. Webster never goes behind government, and so cannot speak with authority about it. His words are wisdom to those legislators who contemplate no essential reform in the existing government; but for thinkers, and those who legislate for all time, he never once glances at the subject. I know of those whose serene and wise speculations on this theme would soon reveal the limits of his mind's range and hospitality. Yet, compared with the cheap professions of most reformers, and the still cheaper wisdom and eloquence of politicians in general, his are almost the only sensible and valuable words, and we thank Heaven for him. Comparatively, he is always strong, original, and, above all, practical. Still, his quality is not wisdom, but prudence. The lawyer's truth is not Truth, but consistency or a consistent expediency. Truth is always in harmony with herself, and is not concerned chiefly to reveal the justice that may consist with wrong-doing. He well deserves to be called, as he has been called, the Defender of the Constitution. There are really no blows to be given by him but defensive ones. He is not a leader, but a follower. His leaders are the men of '87. "I have never made an effort," he says, "and never propose to make an effort; I have never countenanced an effort, and never mean to countenance an effort, to disturb the arrangement as originally made, by which the various States came into the Union." Still thinking of the sanction which the Constitution gives to slavery, he says, "Because it was a part of the original compact,—let it stand." Notwithstanding his special acuteness and ability, he is unable to take a fact out of its merely political relations, and behold it as it lies absolutely to be disposed of by the intellect,—what, for instance, it behooves a man to do here in America to-day with regard to slavery,— but ventures, or is driven, to make some such desperate answer as the following, while professing to speak absolutely, and as a private man,— from which what new and singular code of social duties might be inferred? "The manner," says he, "in which the governments of those States where slavery exists are to regulate it is for their own consideration, under their responsibility to their constituents, to the general laws of propriety, humanity, and justice, and to God. Associations formed elsewhere, springing from a feeling of humanity, or any other cause, have nothing whatever to do with it. They have never received any encouragement from me, and they never will."

They who know of no purer sources of truth, who have traced up its stream no higher, stand, and wisely stand, by the Bible and the Constitution, and drink at it there with reverence and humility; but they who behold where it comes trickling into this lake or that pool, gird up their loins once more, and continue their pilgrimage toward its fountain-head.

No man with a genius for legislation has appeared in America. They are rare in the history of the world. There are orators, politicians, and eloquent men, by the thousand; but the speaker has not yet opened his mouth to speak who is capable of settling the much-vexed questions of the day. We love eloquence for its own sake, and not for any truth which it may utter, or any heroism it may inspire. Our legislators have not yet learned the comparative value of free trade and of freedom, of union, and of rectitude, to a nation. They have no genius or talent for comparatively humble questions of taxation and finance, commerce and manufactures and agriculture. If we were left solely to the wordy wit of legislators in Congress for our guidance, uncorrected by the seasonable experience and the effectual complaints of the people, America would not long retain her rank among the nations. For eighteen hundred years, though perchance I have no right to say it, the New Testament has been written; yet where is the legislator who has wisdom and practical talent enough to avail himself of the light which it sheds on the science of legislation?

The authority of government, even such as I am willing to submit to,—for I will cheerfully obey those who know and can do better than I, and in many things even those who neither know nor can do so well,—is still an impure one: to be strictly just, it must have the sanction and consent of the governed. It can have no pure right over my person and property but what I concede to it. The progress from an absolute to a limited monarchy, from a limited monarchy to a democracy, is a progress toward a true respect for the individual. Even the Chinese philosopher was wise enough to regard the individual as the basis of the empire. Is a democracy, such as we know it, the last improvement possible in government? Is it not possible to take a step further towards recognizing and organizing the rights of man? There will never be a really free and enlightened State until the State comes to recognize the individual as a higher and independent power, from which all its own power and authority are derived, and treats him accordingly. I please myself with imagining a State at last which can afford to be just to all men, and to treat the individual with respect as a neighbor; which even would not think it inconsistent with its own repose if a few were to live aloof from it, not meddling with it, nor embraced by it, who fulfilled all the duties of neighbors and fellow-men. A State which bore this kind of fruit, and suffered it to drop off as fast as it ripened, would prepare the way for a still more perfect and glorious State, which also I have imagined, but not yet anywhere seen.

## TOPICS FOR DISCUSSION

1   What is Thoreau's thesis? What kinds of evidence does he present to support his thesis? Is his case convincing in its context—under a government countenancing slavery and carrying war into Mexico? Would his case be equally convincing today? Would it become so again if your country again prosecuted such a war? Never? Maybe? Would his position be valid in some other country?

2   "Right" and "justice" are Thoreau's guides in determining conduct, including conduct in relation to his own government. How can he know what is "right" or "just"? How can you?

3   Would any of the following make new issues or decisive differences in applying Thoreau's doctrines: establishment of civil-rights laws; imminent threats against your government from outside or inside the country; use or threatened use of mass destruction—nuclear bombs, for example?

4   Does Thoreau ever exaggerate his comments in order to shock his reader? Where?

5   Does Thoreau distinguish between civil disobedience and lawlessness?

## ...AND COMPOSITION

6   Write a defense for a pacifist taxpayer who refuses to contribute taxes to national military budgets.

7   Write a rebuttal.

8   How can minority groups with unpopular programs be protected in a democracy (e.g., a religious group refusing to send a child to school, or an antifluoridationist refusing to allow fluorides in his water)?

**WALTER LIPPMANN (1889–   )** has combined scholarship and journalism so effectively, and applied them so steadily to politics, that he has become a reference point in public life, a writer-statesman. To any immediate issue he brings that kind of balance which comes from knowing the danger of solutions which violate the prospects for other solutions. The titles of some of his books indicate his breadth of interest, and something of his approach: *A Preface to Morals, A Preface to Politics, The United States in World Affairs, The Good Society.* The piece which follows, from *The Good Society*, illustrates his specialty: a scholar's informed engagement with current history.

# The Will to Be Free

## I

When the Inquisitors summoned Galileo before them, they told him he must not find that the earth revolves around the sun. Galileo had been observing the heavens through a telescope: he had become convinced that the evidence warranted his conclusion. But the Inquisitors did not look through the telescope. They knew all about astronomy from reading the Bible. So against Galileo's telescope the Inquisitors employed another instrument: the rack. And by the rack, which could inflict pain on the astronomer's body, they undertook to cure the astronomer of his scientific error. Thus they prohibited the exploration of the heavens by the exercise of their physical power.

But the rack is not an instrument for exploring the heavens. A concentration camp is not a political seminar. Burning men at the stake is not a mode of religious revelation. Firing squads are not commissions for observing and analyzing the economic situation. Censorship is not testimony and argument. As regards the intrinsic issues, these exercises of power are nothing but senseless interference, sheer brute irrelevance like the incursion of a herd of wild asses. What Galileo needed was the criticism of other astronomers: what he suffered was the meddling of powerful ignoramuses. Galileo was unfree to be an astronomer because these ignoramuses insisted on weighting the scales with the terror of prisons, torture chambers, and the stake; he had to take his astronomy from men who had never studied it.

The movement which drives human life forward is exemplified by Galileo's impulse to explore the heavens. The forces which hold mankind back, pinned to the ignorance they happen to be in, are exemplified by the Inquisitors insisting that the preponderant force and not the preponderant evidence shall determine whether the sun is the center of our solar system. Thus we may think of the creative, the productive, and the adaptive energies of mankind as struggling to release themselves from the

entanglements and perversions, the exploitation and the smothering, the parasitism and the obfuscation and the discouragement of aggressive, acquisitive, dogmatic, and arbitrary impulses. Men are moved to plant, but the seeds bear fruit with difficulty, so rank are the weeds which choke them. The cutting back of the weeds, the clearing of little spaces in which good things can grow, has been the task of human emancipation. Its method is to restrain arbitrariness. But its object is to disengage the human spirit in order that it may flourish.

Thus liberalism, which in its moral essence is a challenge to all arbitrariness, to all who would use the rack rather than the telescope, is not itself the substantive principle of the good life. The substantive principle is in Galileo's curiosity and his genius; in fostering and protecting curiosity and genius, liberalism is the guardian principle of the good life. It stakes its hopes upon the human spirit released from and purged of all arbitrariness. It does not say what such a spirit can or will or ought to make of men's lives. For men have never yet known but a little of such freedom. And they cannot hope to imagine what they have never yet known. But they have known enough of freedom to know that the arbitrary power of men over men is parasitical, that it perverts, that it sterilizes and corrupts.

Though liberalism has often been identified with indifference, inaction, and nonresistance, it should now be evident that this is mere confusion. A doctrine which is opposed to all arbitrariness must mean the determination to resist arbitrariness, to check it, to cut it down, to crush it, wherever and whenever it appears. It cannot mean, for example, that in the seventeenth century the King was under God and the law, but that in the nineteenth century the owners of property were not, that in the twentieth century majorities, pluralities, mobs, or dictators are not, under God and the law. For liberalism all arbitrary power is evil. It matters not what are the titles or the pretensions or the promises of arbitrary power. It must be resisted and brought under control.

So liberalism is not quietism and weak government. That is the corruption of liberalism. In its vigorous periods liberalism has always meant rebellion against oppression and a determination to police aggression and acquisitiveness. Liberalism, therefore, is not the doctrine of laissez faire, let her rip, and the devil take the hindmost. It does not envisage the demobilization of the police, the repeal of the laws, the disestablishment of legislatures and courts. On the contrary, the effective liberals have always been concerned with the development of the law, with the definition of rights and duties, with the organizing of constitutions, with the absorption of all power to coerce in the hands of duly constituted authorities, with the liquidation or regulation of all kinds of private and petty powers within the community. For the liberal, as distinguished from the anarchist, holds that mere unrestraint does not give the freedom of a voluntary society, that unrestraint merely inaugurates a competitive struggle in which the ruthless

will exploit the rest. He insists that the promise of a voluntary life can be realized only as the law is strong enough to restrain aggressors at home and abroad.

But in the liberal view the reward for restraining the aggressor is that the creative and productive faculties can then begin to work. Suppose that Galileo had been able to study the heavens without having at any time to consider whether he would be punished for his conclusions. Suppose that he had needed only to argue with the theologians and to debate with other astronomers. Suppose that his opponents and his critics had been unable to invoke the threats of prison and the rack, or even of ostracism and the muttering of the mob. Suppose that his relations with his contemporaries had been purged of all the irrelevance of arbitrary power, that he had felt that if he was wrong his only punishment would be the knowledge that he had been wrong. Suppose that those who opposed him could have thrown into the scales only the immaterial weight of tradition, experience, observation, and dialectic. Is there any question that in such a community Galileo's faculties would have been enhanced, that others would have been encouraged to use theirs, that immense energy devoted to the coercive enforcement of a particular dogma would have been available in the search for the truest cosmology?

The essence of the matter is that arbitrariness is a disturbing intrusion in the creative life of mankind. It may be a mere annoyance, like the buzzing of a fly around the nose of a philosopher; or it may be like a great catastrophe, say an earthquake, which stops his work by bringing down the house around his ears. We can appreciate the real energy of freedom if we think of men, working, studying, collaborating, but beset by conquerors, exploiters, adventurers—by men who do not work, but appropriate the work of others; who do not produce, but take tolls; who do not invent, but impose prejudices; who do not create, but coerce those who do. The pursuit of liberty is the affirmation of those who produce the really good things of life.

When a Galileo is coerced by a more powerful but a more ignorant inquisitor, his scientific genius is arbitrarily leveled down to the obscurantism of his masters. It is only by freeing him from the bondage of authority that his superiority as an observer and thinker can be exercised. In our time there are governments which enforce an official culture by exile, proscription, the axe, firing squads, castor oil, and imprisonment in concentration camps: they are using arbitrary force to reduce scholars and artists, and in fact the whole population, to the cultural level of the dominant politicians. The opinion of unqualified men is artificially, by the mere arbitrary intervention of the police, made to prevail over the opinion of men who are specially gifted and have labored to qualify themselves.

The same kind of obscurantism results from the exercise of all privileges. The man who has built himself a castle above the highway in order

that he may exact a toll from the merchants on their way to market acquires wealth not by producing it but by seizing it. His predatory incursions arbitrarily yield the returns which would otherwise go to invention, industry, and thrift. But for his castle and his armed hands he would be poorer than the passing merchant whom he despoils; because he is more powerful but is unrestrained, he reaps a greater reward from highway robbery than other men can make by producing wealth. Thus the ideal of equal rights for all and special privileges for none is inseparable from the pursuit of liberty. A free society is one in which inequalities in the condition of men, in their rewards, and in their social status do not arise out of extrinsic and artificial causes—out of the physical power to coerce, out of legal privilege, out of special prerogative, or out of fraud, sharp practice, necessitous bargaining.

This is no forcible leveling of men to a uniform condition of life. That is the tyrant's way. The libertarian does not demand that all the runners in the race must keep in step and finish together; he asks that they start from scratch and that none shall be permitted to elbow his rival off the track. Then the winner will be the best runner. The winner will not be the competitor who wangled a handicap from the judges, or obtained an advantage which had nothing to do with his ability to run the race. Manifestly, the liberal conception of equality does not promise to make all men equal in riches, influence, honor, and wisdom. On the contrary, its promise is that as the extrinsic inequalities imposed by prerogative and privilege are reduced, the intrinsic superiorities will assert themselves.

This, I believe, is the insight at the heart of the liberal conception of society. I am only too well aware of how imperfectly I have understood it, how imprecisely I have been able to put it into words. But I think it is not misleading to say that some such dim but pregnant apprehension as this has been hammered out on the anvil of long experience, that it is no abstract and *a priori* speculation arrived at in the eighteenth century and declared to mankind by William Ewart Gladstone, but that it is much older, has its roots in centuries of confused struggle with all manner of censorship and inquisition, prerogative and privilege.

In those struggles men gradually perceive that they must disengage creative and productive labor and the friendly adaptability of men to one another from the exactions and interferences of the predatory, acquisitive, parasitic, prejudicial, domineering, and irrational elements of human life. This is the "obvious and simple system of natural liberty" which the classic liberals discerned. Though their history was wrong when they adopted the naive belief that this natural order prevailed in the childhood of the race, though they greatly underestimated the length and the complexity of the struggle, their insight was true and their hearts were in the right place.

We must not deny the prophet because he speaks in parables and ephemeral myths: the classic liberals arrived at a profound and enduring

insight into the difference between the real and the factitious in human affairs. They were on the side of Galileo because by protecting Galileo the knowledge of astronomy is advanced. They knew that to find truth is to add to the real values of human existence. They were against the Inquisitors because they knew that astronomy cannot be advanced by imprisoning astronomers, or by compelling them to obtain a license from the secret police and the minister of propaganda.

The ultimate concern of the liberal is with the enhancement of real values by men who actually observe, reason, meditate, invent, dig, construct—seeking to arrange the world to satisfy human demands. To this end the laws, constitutions, bills of rights, courts, and social philosophies are but the means which allow creative labor to proceed without arbitrary interference.

Thus the challenge to oppression arises from the productive energies of men. The movement toward human emancipation is the rebellion of those who plant and till, dig and make, invent and construct, explore and understand; they cannot work and reap their rewards until they have subdued those who exploit and throttle and dominate their productive labors. Men withdrawn into an ivory tower can be indifferent to oppression and can come to terms with it; but those who must earn their living in the sweat of their brows cannot be indifferent, nor those who have the instinct of workmanship, or are curious and must understand the world and their destiny in it.

Among them the liberators have found their followers—among rebellious slaves, serfs demanding land and peace, merchants crying out against the robber barons, small men resisting the monopolists, industrial workers demanding recognition and status and equality of bargaining power, among artists and men of science and educators and parents crying out against the conscription of all they have created.

Their impulse to create has been their impulse to be free. And as they create it becomes more and more necessary that they should be free. For as men work, and perfect their work by invention and skill, they lift themselves out of the primitive condition in which they lead a meager and selfsufficing existence. The improvement of their skill, the development of their special aptitudes, the use of their particular opportunities, result in the specialization of their labor. Because they do the work they are able to do, they are no longer self-sufficing and must live by the exchange of their products. They enter into the economy of the division of labor.

The division of labor was not invented by economists; it was not invented by the inventors of machinery and steam railroads. The division of labor in an exchange economy is implied in the very essence of productive labor itself. In order that Galileo might study the heavens it was not sufficient that the Inquisitors should let him alone; it was necessary that someone else should grow the food he ate and make the clothes he

wore and grind the lenses through which he observed the heavens. He had to be liberated not only from the oppression of arbitrary authority but from the sterile drudgery of a self-sufficient existence. And because by the division of labor he was liberated from the drudgery, he was able to be an astronomer who necessarily rebelled against authority.

Thus the connection between liberty and the industrial revolution is organic. The impulse to create and the impulse to be free are cumulative: each is to the other both cause and effect. Because men wish to work they insist on freedom from arbitrary interference; because they are free, they work by a division of labor which requires the freedom of certain and equal rights.

This is the reason why all the conceptions which constitute the testament of liberty have been evolved in great societies that have lived by extensive and complicated commerce. They come to us from the Graeco-Roman society, from the merchant cities of the Renaissance, from western Europe, from England, France, the Netherlands, and Italy, from the peoples who first emerged from self-sufficiency and had to establish a common law in which their transactions could be secure. It is no accident that it was the Athenians, living by commerce, rather than the Spartans living by exploitation and war, who conceived the good life; or that the Romans who traded all over the known world should have understood the necessity for law; or that the nation of shopkeepers was the mother of parliaments; or that Yankee traders in Boston fomented the American Revolution and the abolition of slavery. For among a people living by a primitive undifferentiated economy under routine and in isolation, the necessity for constitutional liberty does not exist and can scarcely be conceived.

## II

This truth our contemporary authoritarians, whether of the left or of the right, have failed to grasp. They look upon the great sprawling complex of transactions by which mankind lives, seeing that these transactions are in large part still unregulated by law, and that therefore there is much confusion and injustice, they have turned their backs upon the task of regulation by law and have beguiled themselves with the notion that they can plan this economy systematically and administer it rationally. The exact contrary is the truth. The modern economy is perhaps the least systematic of any that has ever existed. It is world-wide, formless, vast, complicated, and owing to technological progress, in constant change. For that reason it is incapable of being conceived as a system, or of being replaced by another system, or of being managed as an administrative unit.

The hankering for schemes and systems and comprehensive organization is the wistfulness of an immature philosophy which has not come to terms with reality, no less when the conservators of vested interests would

stabilize the modern economy in status quo by protective laws and monopolistic schemes than when the revolutionist makes blueprints of a world composed of planning national economies "coordinated" by a world-planning authority. Neither takes any more account of reality than if he were studying landscape architecture with a view to making a formal garden out of the Brazilian jungle.

For the greater the society, the higher and more variable the standards of life, the more diversified the energies of its people for invention, enterprise, and adaptation, the more certain it is that the social order cannot be planned *ex cathedra* or governed by administrative command. We live in such an immensely diversified civilization that the only intelligible criterion which political thinkers can entertain in regard to it, the only feasible goal which statesmen can set themselves in governing it, is to reconcile the conflicts which spring from this diversity. They cannot hope to comprehend it as a system. For it is not a system. They cannot hope to plan and direct it. For it is not an organization. They can hope only to dispense lawful justice among individuals and associations where their interests conflict, to mitigate the violence of conflict and competition by seeking to make lawful justice more and more equitable.

It requires much virtue to do that well. There must be a strong desire to be just. There must be a growing capacity to be just. There must be discernment and sympathy in estimating the particular claims of divergent interests. There must be moral standards which discourage the quest of privilege and the exercise of arbitrary power. There must be resolution and valor to resist oppression and tyranny. There must be patience and tolerance and kindness in hearing claims, in argument, in negotiation, and in reconciliation.

But these are human virtues; though they are high, they are within the attainable limits of human nature as we know it. They actually exist. Men do have these virtues, all but the most hopelessly degenerate, in some degree. We know that they can be increased. When we talk about them we are talking about virtues that have affected the course of actual history, about virtues that some men have practised more than other men, and no man sufficiently, but enough men in great enough degree to have given mankind here and there and for varying periods of time the intimations of a Good Society.

But the virtues that are required for the overhead administration of a civilization are superhuman; they are attributes of providence and not of mortal men. It is true that there have been benevolent despots and that for a little while in a particular place they have made possible a better life than their subjects were able to achieve without the rule of a firm and authoritative guardian. And no doubt it is still true that a community which does not have the essential discipline of liberty can choose only among alternative disciplines by authority. But if a community must have such

a guardian, then it must resign itself to living a simple regimented existence, must entertain no hopes of the high and diversified standard of life which the division of labor and modern technology make possible. For despots cannot be found who could plan, organize, and direct a complex economy.

To do that would require a comprehensive understanding of the life and the labor and the purposes of hundreds of millions of persons, the gift of prophesying their behavior and omnipotence to control it. These faculties no man has ever possessed. When in theorizing we unwittingly postulate such faculties, we are resting our hopes on a conception of human nature which has no warrant whatever in any actual experience. The collectivist planners are not talking about the human race but about some other breed conceived in their dreams. They postulate qualities of intelligence and of virtue so unlike those which men possess that it would be just as intelligible to make plans for a society in which human beings were born equipped to fly like the angels, to feed on the fragrance of the summer breezes, and endowed with all possible knowledge.

Thus while the liberal philosophy is concerned with the reform of the laws in order to adapt them to the changing needs and standards of the dynamic economy, while the agenda of reform are long and varied, no one must look to liberalism for a harmonious scheme of social reconstruction. The Good Society has no architectural design. There are no blueprints. There is no mold in which human life is to be shaped. Indeed, to expect the blueprint of such a mold is a mode of thinking against which the liberal temper is a constant protest.

To design a personal plan for a new society is a pleasant form of madness; it is in imagination to play at being God and Caesar to the human race. Any such plan must implicitly assume that the visionary or someone else might find the power, or might persuade the masses to give him the power, to shape society to the plan; all such general plans of social reconstruction are merely the rationalization of the will to power. For that reason they are the subjective beginnings of fanaticism and tyranny. In these utopias the best is the enemy of the good, the heart's desire betrays the interests of man. To think in terms of a new scheme for a whole society is to use the idiom of authority, to approach affairs from the underlying premise that they can be shaped and directed as an overhead control, that social relations can be fabricated according to a master plan drawn up by a supreme architect.

The supreme architect, who begins as a visionary, becomes a fanatic, and ends as a despot. For no one can be the supreme architect of society without employing a supreme despot to execute the design. So if men are to seek freedom from the arbitrary dominion of men over men, they must not entertain fantasies of the future in which they play at being the dictators of civilization. It is the bad habit of an undisciplined imagination. The descent from fantasy to fanaticism is easy. Real dictators raised to power

by the fanatics who adore them are only too likely to adopt the fantasy to justify their lust for power.

On the other hand, reasonable and civilized people who would like to make the best of the situation before them, but have no ambition for, or expectation of, the power to reshape a whole society, get no help from these architectural designs. The blueprint, be it as grandiose a work of genius as Plato's *Republic,* cannot hope to fit the specific situation. No *a priori* reasoning can anticipate the precise formulae which will reconcile the infinitely varied interests of men. The reconciliation has to be achieved by the treatment of specific issues and the solution will appear only after the claims and the evidence have been examined and fairly judged. Thus in Plato's great scheme each man was assigned his station and his duties; any architectural plan is necessarily based on the same presumption. But Plato's scheme worked only in Plato's imagination, never in the real world. No such scheme can ever work in the real world. For the scheme implies that men will remain content in the station which the visionary has assigned to them. To formulate such plans is not to design a society for real men. It is to re-create men to fit the design. For in real life men rest content in their station only if their interests have been successfully reconciled: failing that, they do not fit the design until they have been dosed with castor oil, put in concentration camps, or exiled to Siberia.

That is why the testament of liberty does not contain the project of a new social order. It adumbrates a way of life in which men seek to reconcile their interests by perfecting the rules of justice. No scheme which promises to obliterate the differences of interest can be deduced from it, no architectural design of society in which all human problems have been resolved. There is no plan of the future: there is, on the contrary, the conviction that the future must have the shape that human energies, purged in so far as possible of arbitrariness, will give it. Compared with the elegant and harmonious schemes which are propounded by the theoretical advocates of capitalism, communism, fascism, it must seem intellectually unsatisfying, and I can well imagine that many will feel about the liberal society as Emma Darwin felt when she wrote about the *Descent of Man,* "I think it will be very interesting, but that I shall dislike it very much as again putting God further off."

But though it must seem an insufficient ideal both to those who wish to exercise authority and to those who feel the need of leaning upon authority, it is the only practicable ideal of government in the Great Society. When huge masses of men have become dependent upon one another through the division of labor in countless, infinitely complex transactions, their activities cannot be planned and directed by public officials.

Thus it is true that the liberal state is not to be conceived as an earthly providence administering civilization. That is the essence of the matter. To the liberal mind the notion that men can authoritatively plan and impose

a good life upon a great society is ignorant, impertinent, and pretentious. It can be entertained only by men who do not realize the infinite variety of human purposes, who do not appreciate the potentialities of human effort, or by men who do not choose to respect them.

The liberal state is to be conceived as the protector of equal rights by dispensing justice among individuals. It seeks to protect men against arbitrariness, not arbitrarily to direct them. Its ideal is a fraternal association among free and equal men. To the initiative of individuals, secure in their rights and accountable to others who have equal rights, liberalism entrusts the shaping of the human destiny. It offers no encouragement to those who dream of what they could make of the world if they possessed supreme power. In the testament of liberty these ambitions have been assessed: the record of all the Caesars from Alexander to Adolf is visible. The world has known many societies in which each man had his station, his duties, and his ordained destiny, and the record shows that it is beyond the understanding of men to know all human needs, to appreciate all human possibilities, to imagine all human ends, to shape all human relations.

Yet if the ambitions of liberalism are more modest than those of authority, its promise is greater. It relies upon the development of the latent faculties of all men, shaped by their free transactions with one another. Liberalism commits the destiny of civilization, not to a few finite politicians here and there, but to the whole genius of mankind. This is a grander vision than that of those who would be Caesar and would set themselves up as little tin gods over men. It is a hope engendered in the human heart during the long ages in which the slowly emerging impulses of civilization, beset by barbarism, have struggled to be free.

## TOPICS FOR DISCUSSION

1   Distinguish between the characteristics of liberalism and arbitrariness.

2   Is the liberal view of human life, as presented by Lippmann, unduly optimistic?

3   What is privilege? How does it interfere with liberty? Can a free-enterprise economy avoid the free growth of privilege? What privileges exist in our society? What privileges are controlled?

4   Why is a planned society not the aim of liberalism?

5   How is paragraph 2, page 279, developed? Why is it particularly effective?

6   In how many ways is the Galileo story used? What does its recurrent appearance do for the essay, aside from supplying a useful example?

## ...AND COMPOSITION

7  Distinguish between a laissez-faire, a planned, and a liberal state.

8  Although Lippmann speaks of freedom as the product as well as the creator of modern division of labor, how has this division of labor also taken some liberties from man?

9  In what specific ways is Lippmann's argument an answer to Thoreau's tentative anarchism?

JOHN MILTON (1608–1674)  wrote so ambitiously and so brilliantly that we
are too much awed to learn the "how" of his work: *Paradise Lost,*
*Samson Agonistes,* and "Lycidas" make us forget that they are composed—
are compositions. Milton's prose, too, is dazzling, rippling, and full of
invention. In "Areopagitica" he directly attacks his government's action to
require official approval of a written work before it could be published.
In making his case he voices rallying points of freedom which
have become standard in our culture. Do not let awe prevent close, local
observation of how he works, even as you yield to the flow of the language.

# Areopagitica

I cannot praise a fugitive and cloistered virtue, unexercised and un-
breathed, that never sallies out and sees her adversary, but slinks out of
the race, where that immortal garland is to be run for, not without dust
and heat. Assuredly we bring not innocence into the world, we bring
impurity much rather; that which purifies us is trial, and trial is by what
is contrary. That virtue therefore which is but a youngling in the contemplation of evil, and knows not the utmost that vice promises to her followers,
and rejects it, is but a blank virtue, not a pure; her whiteness is but an
excremental whiteness. Which was the reason why our sage and serious
poet Spenser, whom I dare be known to think a better teacher than Scotus
or Aquinas, describing true temperance under the person of Guion, brings
him in with his palmer through the cave of Mammon, and the bower of
earthly bliss, that he might see and know, and yet abstain. Since therefore
the knowledge and survey of vice is in this world so necessary to the
constituting of human virtue, and the scanning of error to the confirmation
of truth, how can we more safely, and with less danger, scout into the
regions of sin and falsity than by reading all manner of tractates and
hearing all manner of reason? And this is the benefit which may be had
of books promiscuously read.

But of the harm that may result hence three kinds are usually reckoned.
First, is feared the infection that may spread; but then all human learning
and controversy in religious points must remove out of the world, yea
the Bible itself; for that ofttimes relates blasphemy not nicely, it describes
the carnal sense of wicked men not unelegantly, it brings in holiest men
passionately murmuring against Providence through all the arguments of
Epicurus: in other great disputes it answers dubiously and darkly to the
common reader. And ask a Talmudist what ails the modesty of his marginal Keri, that Moses and all the prophets cannot persuade him to pronounce the textual Chetiv. For these causes we all know the Bible itself

put by the Papist into the first rank of prohibited books. The ancientest fathers must be next removed, as Clement of Alexandria, and that Eusebian book of Evangelic preparation, transmitting our ears through a hoard of heathenish obscenities to receive the Gospel. Who finds not that Irenaeus, Epiphanius, Jerome, and others discover more heresies than they well confute, and that oft for heresy which is the truer opinion?

Nor boots it to say for these, and all the heathen writers of greatest infection, if it must be thought so, with whom is bound up the life of human learning, that they writ in an unknown tongue, so long as we are sure those languages are known as well to the worst of men, who are both most able and most diligent to instil the poison they suck, first into the courts of princes, acquainting them with the choicest delights and criticisms of sin. As perhaps did that Petronius whom Nero called his Arbiter, the master of his revels, and the notorious ribald of Arezzo, dreaded and yet dear to the Italian courtiers. I name not him for posterity's sake, whom Henry VIII. named in merriment his vicar of hell. By which compendious way all the contagion that foreign books can infuse will find a passage to the people far easier and shorter than an Indian voyage, though it could be sailed either by the north of Cataio eastward, or of Canada westward, while our Spanish licensing gags the English press never so severely.

But on the other side that infection which is from books of controversy in religion is more doubtful and dangerous to the learned than to the ignorant; and yet those books must be permitted untouched by the licenser. It will be hard to instance where any ignorant man hath been ever seduced by papistical book in English, unless it were commended and expounded to him by some of that clergy: and indeed all such tractates, whether false or true, are as the prophecy of Isaiah was to the eunuch, not to be *understood without a guide*. But of our priests and doctors how many have been corrupted by studying the comments of Jesuits and Sorbonists, and how fast they could transfuse that corruption into the people, our experience is both late and sad. It is not forgot, since the acute and distinct Arminius was perverted merely by the perusing of a nameless discourse written at Delft, which at first he took in hand to confute.

Seeing, therefore, that those books, and those in great abundance, which are likeliest to taint both life and doctrine, cannot be suppressed without the fall of learning and of all ability in disputation, and that these books of either sort are most and soonest catching to the learned, from whom to the common people whatever is heretical or dissolute may quickly be conveyed, and that evil manners are as perfectly learnt without books a thousand other ways which cannot be stopped, and evil doctrine not with books can propagate, except a teacher guide, which he might also do without writing, and so beyond prohibiting, I am not able to unfold, how this cautelous enterprise of licensing can be exempted from the number of vain and impossible attempts. And he who were pleasantly disposed could

not well avoid to liken it to the exploit of that gallant man who thought to pound up the crows by shutting his park gate.

Besides another inconvenience, if learned men be the first receivers out of books and dispreaders both of vice and error, how shall the licensers themselves be confided in, unless we can confer upon them, or they assume to themselves above all others in the land, the grace of infallibility and uncorruptedness? And again, if it be true that a wise man, like a good refiner, can gather gold out of the drossiest volume, and that a fool will be a fool with the best book, yea or without book; there is no reason that we should deprive a wise man of any advantage to his wisdom, while we seek to restrain from a fool, that which being restrained will be no hindrance to his folly. For if there should be so much exactness always used to keep that from him which is unfit for his reading, we should in the judgment of Aristotle not only, but of Solomon and of our Saviour, not vouchsafe him good precepts, and by consequence not willingly admit him to good books; as being certain that a wise man will make better use of an idle pamphlet, than a fool will do of sacred Scripture.

'Tis next alleged we must not expose ourselves to temptations without necessity, and next to that, not employ our time in vain things. To both these objections one answer will serve, out of the grounds already laid, that to all men such books are not temptations, nor vanities, but useful drugs and materials wherewith to temper and compose effective and strong medicines, which man's life cannot want. The rest, as children and childish men, who have not the art to qualify and prepare these working minerals, well may be exhorted to forbear, but hindered forcibly they cannot be by all the licensing that Sainted Inquisition could ever yet contrive. Which is what I promised to deliver next: that this order of licensing conduces nothing to the end for which it was framed; and hath almost prevented me by being clear already while thus much hath been explaining. See the ingenuity of Truth, who, when she gets a free and willing hand, opens herself faster than the pace of method and discourse can overtake her.

It was the task which I began with, to show that no nation, or well-instituted state, if they valued books at all, did ever use this way of licensing; and it might be answered, that this is a piece of prudence lately discovered. To which I return, that as it was a thing slight and obvious to think on, so if it had been difficult to find out, there wanted not among them long since who suggested such a course; which they not following, leave us a pattern of their judgment that it was not the not knowing, but the not approving, which was the cause of their not using it.

Plato, a man of high authority, indeed, but least of all for his Commonwealth, in the book of his Laws, which no city ever yet received, fed his fancy by making many edicts to his airy burgomasters, which they who otherwise admire him wish had been rather buried and excused in the genial cups of an Academic night sitting. By which laws he seems to tolerate

no kind of learning but by unalterable decree, consisting most of practical traditions, to the attainment whereof a library of smaller bulk than his own Dialogues would be abundant. And there also enacts, that no poet should so much as read to any private man what he had written, until the judges and law-keepers had seen it, and allowed it. But that Plato meant this law peculiarly to that commonwealth which he had imagined, and to no other, is evident. Why was he not else a lawgiver to himself, but a transgressor, and to be expelled by his own magistrates; both for the wanton epigrams and dialogues which he made, and his perpetual reading of Sophron Mimus and Aristophanes, books of grossest infamy, and also for commending the latter of them, though he were the malicious libeller of his chief friends, to be read by the tyrant Dionysius, who had little need of such trash to spend his time on? But that he knew this licensing of poems had reference and dependence to many other provisos there set down in his fancied republic, which in this world could have no place: and so neither he himself, nor any magistrate or city, ever imitated that course, which, taken apart from those other collateral injunctions, must needs be vain and fruitless. For if they fell upon one kind of strictness, unless their care were equal to regulate all other things of like aptness to corrupt the mind, that single endeavour they knew would be but a fond labour; to shut and fortify one gate against corruption, and be necessitated to leave others round about wide open.

If we think to regulate printing, thereby to rectify manners, we must regulate all recreations and pastimes, all that is delightful to man. No music must be heard, no song be set or sung, but what is grave and Doric. There must be licensing of dancers, that no gesture, motion, or deportment be taught our youth but what by their allowance shall be thought honest; for such Plato was provided of. It will ask more than the work of twenty licensers to examine all the lutes, the violins, and the guitars in every house; they must not be suffered to prattle as they do, but must be licensed what they may say. And who shall silence all the airs and madrigals that whisper softness in chambers? The windows also, and the balconies must be thought on; there are shrewd books, with dangerous frontispieces, set to sale; who shall prohibit them, shall twenty licensers? The villages also must have their visitors to inquire what lectures the bagpipe and the rebeck reads, even to the ballatry and the gamut of every municipal fiddler, for these are the countryman's Arcadias, and his Monte Mayors.

Next, what more national corruption, for which England hears ill abroad than household gluttony: who shall be the rectors of our daily rioting? And what shall be done to inhibit the multitudes that frequent those houses where drunkenness is sold and harboured? Our garments also should be referred to the licensing of some more sober workmasters to see them cut into a less wanton garb. Who shall regulate all the mixed conversation of our youth, male and female together, as is the fashion of this

country? Who shall still appoint what shall be discoursed, what presumed, and no further? Lastly, who shall forbid and separate all idle resort, all evil company? These things will be, and must be; but how they shall be least hurtful, how least enticing, herein consists the grave and governing wisdom of a state.

To sequester out of the world into Atlantic and Utopian polities, which never can be drawn into use, will not mend our condition; but to ordain wisely as in this world of evil, in the midst whereof God hath placed us unavoidably. Nor is it Plato's licensing of books will do this, which necessarily pulls along with it so many other kinds of licensing, as will make us all both ridiculous and weary, and yet frustrate; but those un-written, or at least unconstraining, laws of virtuous education, religious and civil nurture, which Plato there mentions as the bonds and ligaments of the commonwealth, the pillars and the sustainers of every written statute; these they be which will bear chief sway in such matters as these, when all licensing will be easily eluded. Impunity and remissness, for certain, are the bane of a commonwealth; but here the great art lies, to discern in what the law is to bid restraint and punishment, and in what things persuasion only is to work.

If every action, which is good or evil in man at ripe years, were to be under pittance and prescription and compulsion, what were virtue but a name, what praise could be then due to well-doing, what gramercy to be sober, just, or continent? Many there be that complain of divine Providence for suffering Adam to transgress; foolish tongues! When God gave him reason, he gave him freedom to choose, for reason is but choosing; he had been else a mere artificial Adam, such an Adam as he is in the motions. We ourselves esteem not of that obedience, or love, or gift, which is of force: God therefore left him free, set before him a provoking object, ever almost in his eyes; herein consisted his merit, herein the right of his reward, the praise of his abstinence. Wherefore did he create passions within us, pleasures round about us, but that these rightly tempered are the very ingredients of virtue?

They are not skilful considerers of human things, who imagine to remove sin by removing the matter of sin; for, besides that it is a huge heap increasing under the very act of diminishing, though some part of it may for a time be withdrawn from some persons, it cannot from all, in such a universal thing as books are; and when this is done, yet the sin re-mains entire. Though ye take from a covetous man all his treasure, he has yet one jewel left, ye cannot bereave him of his covetousness. Banish all objects of lust, shut up all youth into the severest discipline that can be exercised in any hermitage, ye cannot make them chaste, that came not thither so; such great care and wisdom is required to the right managing of this point. Suppose we could expel sin by this means; look how much

we thus expel of sin, so much we expel of virtue: for the matter of them both is the same; remove that, and ye remove them both alike.

This justifies the high providence of God, who, though he command us temperance, justice, continence, yet pours out before us, even to a profuseness, all desirable things, and gives us minds that can wander beyond all limit and satiety. Why should we then affect a rigour contrary to the manner of God and of nature, by abridging or scanting those means, which books freely permitted are, both to the trial of virtue and the exercise of truth? It would be better done, to learn that the law must needs be frivolous, which goes to restrain things, uncertainly and yet equally working to good and to evil. And were I the chooser, a dram of well-doing should be preferred before many times as much the forcible hindrance of evil-doing. For God sure esteems the growth and completing of one virtuous person more than the restraint of ten vicious.

And albeit whatever thing we hear or see, sitting, walking, travelling, or conversing, may be fitly called our book, and is of the same effect that writings are, yet grant the thing to be prohibited were only books, it appears that this Order hitherto is far insufficient to the end which it intends. Do we not see, not once or oftener, but weekly, that continued court-libel against the Parliament and City, printed, as the wet sheets can witness, and dispersed among us, for all that licensing can do? Yet this is the prime service a man would think, wherein this Order should give proof of itself. If it were executed, you'll say. But certain, if execution be remiss or blindfold now, and in this particular, what will it be hereafter and in other books? If then the Order shall not be vain and frustrate, behold a new labour, Lords and Commons, ye must repeal and proscribe all scandalous and unlicensed books already printed and divulged; after ye have drawn them up into a list, that all may know which are condemned, and which not; and ordain that no foreign books be delivered out of custody, till they have been read over. This office will require the whole time of not a few overseers, and those no vulgar men. There be also books which are partly useful and excellent, partly culpable and pernicious; this work will ask as many more officials, to make expurgations and expunctions, that the commonwealth of learning be not damnified. In fine, when the multitude of books increase upon their hands, ye must be fain to catalogue all those printers who are found frequently offending, and forbid the importation of their whole suspected typography. In a word, that this your Order may be exact and not deficient, ye must reform it perfectly according to the model of Trent and Seville, which I know ye abhor to do.

Yet though ye should condescend to this, which God forbid, the Order still would be but fruitless and defective to that end whereto ye meant it. If to prevent sects and schisms, who is so unread or so uncatechized in story, that hath not heard of many sects refusing books as a hindrance,

and preserving their doctrine unmixed for many ages, only by unwritten traditions? The Christian faith, for that was once a schism, is not unknown to have spread all over Asia, ere any Gospel or Epistle was seen in writing. If the amendment of manners be aimed at, look into Italy and Spain, whether those places be one scruple the better, the honester, the wiser, the chaster, since all the inquisitional rigour that hath been executed upon books.

Another reason, whereby to make it plain that this Order will miss the end it seeks, consider by the quality which ought to be in every licenser. It cannot be denied but that he who is made judge to sit upon the birth or death of books, whether they may be wafted into this world or not, had need to be a man above the common measure, both studious, learned, and judicious; there may be else no mean mistakes in the censure of what is passable or not; which is also no mean injury. If he be of such worth as behooves him, there cannot be a more tedious and unpleasing journey-work, a greater loss of time levied upon his head, than to be made the perpetual reader of unchosen books and pamphlets, ofttimes huge volumes. There is no book that is acceptable unless at certain seasons; but to be enjoined the reading of that at all times, and in a hand scarce legible, whereof three pages would not down at any time in the fairest print, is an imposition which I cannot believe how he that values time and his own studies, or is but of a sensible nostril, should be able to endure. In this one thing I crave leave of the present licensers to be pardoned for so thinking; who doubtless took this office up, looking on it through their obedience to the Parliament, whose command perhaps made all things seem easy and unlaborious to them; but that this short trial hath wearied them out already, their own expressions and excuses to them who make so many journeys to solicit their licence are testimony enough. Seeing therefore those who now possess the employment by all evident signs wish themselves well rid of it; and that no man of worth, none that is not a plain unthrift of his own hours, is ever likely to succeed them, except he mean to put himself to the salary of a press corrector; we may easily foresee what kind of licensers we are to expect hereafter, either ignorant, imperious, and remiss, or basely pecuniary. This is what I had to show, wherein this Order cannot conduce to that end whereof it bears the intention.

## TOPICS FOR DISCUSSION

1  How is impurity made pure through trial?
2  How does Milton use this premise to dismiss the charges of harmful influence through the reading of books?
3  Notice how many arguments Milton advances. Which ones do

you consider most valid? Are they the same ones which might appear most persuasive?

4  Do Milton's arguments support free circulation of all kinds of opinion or just attack the evils of prior licensing of intended publications? Would his arguments convince you that censorship is always evil?

5  What kinds of assistance can be given "virtue" to prepare it for a trial?

6  How does Milton use allusions?

## ... AND COMPOSITION

7  Defend the free press (and intellectual freedom generally) using examples which are reprehensible to you personally (e.g., the American Nazi party, the American Communist party, etc.).

8  How necessary a part of a "good society" is a free press? Describe analytically possible dangers of a free press.

9  Write an argument based on a single premise, as Milton's is, from which all the argument develops.

**C. P. SNOW (1905–     )** lives two lives, as scientist and as
novelist. The two sides of his experience led to his assertion that our culture
is split, that an emergency in our time is this division: our values derive
from a tradition being made obsolete by our discoveries, and the
two kinds of men involved in the tradition, on the one hand, and in the
discovering, on the other, must get together or be responsible for paralyzing
our chances for human development. Many have contended that science
and the humanities are not in fact different in the ways
C. P. Snow declares them to be; but as spokesman for the
two-cultures theory, he has sparked many discussions in recent years.

# The Two Cultures

It is about three years since I made a sketch in print of a problem
which had been on my mind for some time. It was a problem I could
not avoid just because of the circumstances of my life. The only credentials
I had to ruminate on the subject at all came through those circumstances,
through nothing more than a set of chances. Anyone with similar experience would have seen much the same things and I think made very much
the same comments about them. It just happened to be an unusual experience. By training I was a scientist: by vocation I was a writer. That was all.
It was a piece of luck, if you like, that arose through coming from a poor
home.

But my personal history isn't the point now. All that I need say is
that I came to Cambridge and did a bit of research here at a time of
major scientific activity. I was privileged to have a ringside view of one
of the most wonderful creative periods in all physics. And it happened
through the flukes of war—including meeting W. L. Bragg in the buffet

on Kettering station on a very cold morning in 1939, which had a determining influence on my practical life—that I was able, and indeed morally forced, to keep that ringside view ever since. So for thirty years I have had to be in touch with scientists not only out of curiosity, but as part of a working existence. During the same thirty years I was trying to shape the books I wanted to write, which in due course took me among writers.

There have been plenty of days when I have spent the working hours with scientists and then gone off at night with some literary colleagues. I mean that literally. I have had, of course, intimate friends among both scientists and writers. It was through living among these groups and much more, I think, through moving regularly from one to the other and back again that I got occupied with the problem of what, long before I put it on paper, I christened to myself as the "two cultures." For constantly I felt I was moving among two groups—comparable in intelligence, identical in race, not grossly different in social origin, earning about the same incomes—who had almost ceased to communicate at all, who in intellectual, moral and psychological climate had so little in common that instead of going from Burlington House or South Kensington to Chelsea, one might have crossed an ocean.

In fact, one had travelled much further than across an ocean—because after a few thousand Atlantic miles, one found Greenwich Village talking precisely the same language as Chelsea, and both having about as much communication with M.I.T. as though the scientists spoke nothing but Tibetan. For this is not just our problem; owing to some of our educational and social idiosyncrasies, it is slightly exaggerated here, owing to another English social peculiarity it is slightly minimized; by and large this is a problem of the entire West.

By this I intend something serious. I am not thinking of the pleasant story of how one of the more convivial Oxford great dons—I have heard the story attributed to A. L. Smith—came over to Cambridge to dine. The date is perhaps the 1890s. I think it must have been at St. John's, or possibly Trinity. Anyway, Smith was sitting at the right hand of the President—or Vice-Master—and he was a man who liked to include all round him in the conversation, although he was not immediately encouraged by the expressions of his neighbours. He addressed some cheerful Oxonian chit-chat at the one opposite to him, and got a grunt. He then tried the man on his own right hand and got another grunt. Then, rather to his surprise, one looked at the other and said, "Do you know what he's talking about?" "I haven't the least idea." At this, even Smith was getting out of his depth. But the President, acting as a social emollient, put him at his ease, by saying, "Oh, those are mathematicians! We never talk to *them.*"

No, I intend something serious. I believe the intellectual life of the whole of western society is increasingly being split into two polar groups. When I say the intellectual life, I mean to include also a large part of our

practical life, because I should be the last person to suggest the two can at the deepest level be distinguished. I shall come back to the practical life a little later. Two polar groups: at one pole we have the literary intellectuals, who incidentally while no one was looking took to referring to themselves as "intellectuals" as though there were no others. I remember G. H. Hardy once remarking to me in mild puzzlement, some time in the 1930s: "Have you noticed how the word 'intellectual' is used nowadays? There seems to be a new definition which certainly doesn't include Rutherford or Eddington or Dirac or Adrian or me. It does seem rather odd, don't y' know."

Literary intellectuals at one pole—at the other scientists, and as the most representative, the physical scientists. Between the two a gulf of mutual incomprehension—sometimes (particularly among the young) hostility and dislike, but most of all lack of understanding. They have a curious distorted image of each other. Their attitudes are so different that, even on the level of emotion, they can't find much common ground. Non-scientists tend to think of scientists as brash and boastful. They hear Mr. T. S. Eliot, who just for these illustrations we can take as an archetypal figure, saying about his attempts to revive verse-drama, that we can hope for very little, but that he would feel content if he and his co-workers could prepare the ground for a new Kyd or a new Greene. That is the tone, restricted and constrained, with which literary intellectuals are at home: it is the subdued voice of their culture. Then they hear a much louder voice, that of another archetypal figure, Rutherford, trumpeting: "This is the heroic age of science! This is the Elizabethan age!" Many of us heard that, and a good many other statements beside which that was mild; and we weren't left in any doubt whom Rutherford was casting for the role of Shakespeare. What is hard for the literary intellectuals to understand, imaginatively or intellectually, is that he was absolutely right.

And compare "this is the way the world ends, not with a bang but a whimper"—incidentally, one of the least likely scientific prophecies ever made—compare that with Rutherford's famous repartee, "Lucky fellow, Rutherford, always on the crest of the wave." "Well, I made the wave, didn't I?"

The non-scientists have a rooted impression that the scientists are shallowly optimistic, unaware of man's condition. On the other hand, the scientists believe that the literary intellectuals are totally lacking in foresight, peculiarly unconcerned with their brother men, in a deep sense anti-intellectual, anxious to restrict both art and thought to the existential moment. And so on. Anyone with a mild talent for invective could produce plenty of this kind of subterranean back-chat. On each side there is some of it which is not entirely baseless. It is all destructive. Much of it rests on misinterpretations which are dangerous. I should like to deal with two of the most profound of these now, one on each side.

First, about the scientists' optimism. This is an accusation which has been made so often that it has become a platitude. It has been made by some of the acutest non-scientific minds of the day. But it depends upon a confusion between the individual experience and the social experience, between the individual condition of man and his social condition. Most of the scientists I have known well have felt—just as deeply as the non-scientists I have known well—that the individual condition of each of us is tragic. Each of us is alone: sometimes we escape from solitariness, through love or affection or perhaps creative moments, but those triumphs of life are pools of light we make for ourselves while the edge of the road is black: each of us dies alone. Some scientists I have known have had faith in revealed religion. Perhaps with them the sense of the tragic condition is not so strong. I don't know. With most people of deep feeling, however high-spirited and happy they are, sometimes most with those who are happiest and most high-spirited, it seems to be right in the fibres, part of the weight of life. That is as true of the scientists I have known best as of anyone at all.

But nearly all of them—and this is where the colour of hope genuinely comes in—would see no reason why, just because the individual condition is tragic, so must the social condition be. Each of us is solitary: each of us dies alone: all right, that's a fate against which we can't struggle—but there is plenty in our condition which is not fate, and against which we are less than human unless we do struggle.

Most of our fellow human beings, for instance, are underfed and die before their time. In the crudest terms, *that* is the social condition. There is a moral trap which comes through the insight into man's loneliness: it tempts one to sit back, complacent in one's unique tragedy, and let the others go without a meal.

As a group, the scientists fall into the trap less than others. They are inclined to be impatient to see if something can be done: and inclined to think that it can be done, until it's proved otherwise. That is their real optimism, and it's an optimism that the rest of us badly need.

In reverse, the same spirit, tough and good and determined to fight it out at the side of their brother men, has made scientists regard the other culture's social attitudes as contemptible. That is too facile: some of them are, but they are a temporary phase and not to be taken as representative.

I remember being cross-examined by a scientist of distinction. "Why do most writers take on social opinions which would have been thought distinctly uncivilized and *démodé* at the time of the Plantagenets? Wasn't that true of most of the famous twentieth-century writers? Yeats, Pound, Wyndham Lewis, nine out of ten of those who have dominated literary sensibility in our time—weren't they not only politically silly, but politically wicked? Didn't the influence of all they represent bring Auschwitz that much nearer?"

I thought at the time, and I still think, that the correct answer was not to defend the indefensible. It was no use saying that Yeats, according to friends whose judgment I trust, was a man of singular magnanimity of character, as well as a great poet. It was no use denying the facts, which are broadly true. The honest answer was that there is, in fact, a connection, which literary persons were culpably slow to see, between some kinds of early twentieth-century art and the most imbecile expressions of anti-social feeling. That was one reason, among many, why some of us turned our backs on the art and tried to hack out a new or different way for ourselves.

But though many of those writers dominated literary sensibility for a generation, that is no longer so, or at least to nothing like the same extent. Literature changes more slowly than science. It hasn't the same automatic corrective, and so its misguided periods are longer. But it is ill-considered of scientists to judge writers on the evidence of the period 1914–50.

Those are two of the misunderstandings between the two cultures. I should say, since I began to talk about them—the two cultures, that is— I have had some criticism. Most of my scientific acquaintances think that there is something in it, and so do most of the practising artists I know. But I have been argued with by non-scientists of strong down-to-earth interests. Their view is that it is an over-simplification, and that if one is going to talk in these terms there ought to be at least three cultures. They argue that, though they are not scientists themselves, they would share a good deal of the scientific feeling. They would have as little use—perhaps, since they knew more about it, even less use—for the recent literary culture as the scientists themselves. J. H. Plumb, Alan Bullock and some of my American sociological friends have said that they vigorously refuse to be corralled in a cultural box with people they wouldn't be seen dead with, or to be regarded as helping to produce a climate which would not permit of social hope.

I respect those arguments. The number 2 is a very dangerous number: that is why the dialectic is a dangerous process. Attempts to divide any-thing into two ought to be regarded with much suspicion. I have thought a long time about going in for further refinements: but in the end I have decided against. I was searching for something a little more than a dashing metaphor, a good deal less than a cultural map: and for those purposes the two cultures is about right, and subtilizing any more would bring more disadvantages than it's worth.

At one pole, the scientific culture really is a culture, not only in an intellectual but also in an anthropological sense. That is, its members need not, and of course often do not, always completely understand each other: biologists more often than not will have a pretty hazy idea of contemporary physics; but there are common attitudes, common standards and patterns

of behaviour, common approaches and assumptions. This goes surprisingly wide and deep. It cuts across other mental patterns, such as those of religion or politics or class.

Statistically, I suppose slightly more scientists are in religious terms unbelievers, compared with the rest of the intellectual world—though there are plenty who are religious, and that seems to be increasingly so among the young. Statistically also, slightly more scientists are on the Left in open politics—though again, plenty always have called themselves conservatives, and that also seems to be more common among the young. Compared with the rest of the intellectual world, considerably more scientists in this country and probably in the U.S. come from poor families. Yet, over a whole range of thought and behaviour, none of that matters very much. In their working, and in much of their emotional life, their attitudes are closer to other scientists than to non-scientists who in religion or politics or class have the same labels as themselves. If I were to risk a piece of shorthand, I should say that naturally they had the future in their bones.

They may or may not like it, but they have it. That was as true of the conservatives J. J. Thomson and Lindemann as of the radicals Einstein or Blackett: as true of the Christian A. H. Compton as of the materialist Bernal: of the aristocrats Broglie or Russell as of the proletarian Faraday: of those born rich, like Thomas Merton or Victor Rothschild, as of Rutherford, who was the son of an odd-job handyman. Without thinking about it, they respond alike. That is what a culture means.

At the other pole, the spread of attitudes is wider. It is obvious that between the two, as one moves through intellectual society from the physicists to the literary intellectuals, there are all kinds of tones of feeling on the way. But I believe the pole of total incomprehension of science radiates its influence on all the rest. That total incomprehension gives, much more pervasively than we realize, living in it, an unscientific flavour to the whole "traditional" culture, and that unscientific flavour is often, much more than we admit, on the point of turning anti-scientific. The feelings of one pole become the anti-feelings of the other. If the scientists have the future in their bones, then the traditional culture responds by wishing the future did not exist. It is the traditional culture, to an extent remarkably little diminished by the emergence of the scientific one, which manages the western world.

This polarization is sheer loss to us all. To us as people, and to our society. It is at the same time practical and intellectual and creative loss, and I repeat that it is false to imagine that those three considerations are clearly separable. But for a moment I want to concentrate on the intellectual loss.

The degree of incomprehension on both sides is the kind of joke which has gone sour. There are about fifty thousand working scientists in the

country and about eighty thousand professional engineers or applied scientists. During the war and in the years since, my colleagues and I have had to interview somewhere between thirty and forty thousand of these— that is, about twenty-five per cent. The number is large enough to give us a fair sample, though of the men we talked to most would still be under forty. We were able to find out a certain amount of what they read and thought about. I confess that even I, who am fond of them and respect them, was a bit shaken. We hadn't quite expected that the links with the traditional culture should be so tenuous, nothing more than a formal touch of the cap.

As one would expect, some of the very best scientists had and have plenty of energy and interest to spare, and we came across several who had read everything that literary people talk about. But that's very rare. Most of the rest, when one tried to probe for what books they had read, would modestly confess, "Well, I've *tried* a bit of Dickens," rather as though Dickens were an extraordinarily esoteric, tangled and dubiously rewarding writer, something like Rainer Maria Rilke. In fact that is exactly how they do regard him: we thought that discovery, that Dickens had been transformed into the type-specimen of literary incomprehensibility, was one of the oddest results of the whole exercise.

But of course, in reading him, in reading almost any writer whom we should value, they are just touching their caps to the traditional culture. They have their own culture, intensive, rigorous, and constantly in action. This culture contains a great deal of argument, usually much more rigorous, and almost always at a higher conceptual level, than literary persons' arguments—even though the scientists do cheerfully use words in senses which literary persons don't recognize, the senses are exact ones, and when they talk about "subjective," "objective," "philosophy," or "progressive," they know what they mean, even though it isn't what one is accustomed to expect.

Remember, these are very intelligent men. Their culture is in many ways an exacting and admirable one. It doesn't contain much art, with the exception, an important exception, of music. Verbal exchange, insistent argument. Long-playing records. Colour-photography. The ear, to some extent the eye. Books, very little, though perhaps not many would go so far as one hero, who perhaps I should admit was further down the scientific ladder than the people I've been talking about—who, when asked what books he read, replied firmly and confidently: "Books? I prefer to use my books as tools." It was very hard not to let the mind wander—what sort of tool would a book make? Perhaps a hammer? A primitive digging instrument?

Of books, though, very little. And of the books which to most literary persons are bread and butter, novels, history, poetry, plays, almost nothing at all. It isn't that they're not interested in the psychological or moral or

social life. In the social life, they certainly are, more than most of us. In the moral, they are by and large the soundest group of intellectuals we have; there is a moral component right in the grain of science itself, and almost all scientists form their own judgments of the moral life. In the psychological they have as much interest as most of us, though occasionally I fancy they come to it rather late. It isn't that they lack the interests. It is much more that the whole literature of the traditional culture doesn't seem to them relevant to those interests. They are, of course, dead wrong. As a result, their imaginative understanding is less than it could be. They are self-impoverished.

But what about the other side? They are impoverished too—perhaps more seriously, because they are vainer about it. They still like to pretend that the traditional culture is the whole of "culture," as though the natural order didn't exist. As though the exploration of the natural order was of no interest either in its own value or its consequences. As though the scientific edifice of the physical world was not, in its intellectual depth, complexity and articulation, the most beautiful and wonderful collective work of the mind of man. Yet most non-scientists have no conception of that edifice at all. Even if they want to have it, they can't. It is rather as though, over an immense range of intellectual experience, a whole group was tone-deaf. Except that this tone-deafness doesn't come by nature, but by training, or rather the absence of training.

As with the tone-deaf, they don't know what they miss. They give a pitying chuckle at the news of scientists who have never read a major work of English literature. They dismiss them as ignorant specialists. Yet their own ignorance and their own specialization is just as startling. A good many times I have been present at gatherings of people who, by the standards of the traditional culture, are thought highly educated and who have with considerable gusto been expressing their incredulity at the illiteracy of scientists. Once or twice I have been provoked and have asked the company how many of them could describe the Second Law of Thermodynamics. The response was cold: it was also negative. Yet I was asking something which is about the scientific equivalent of: *Have you read a work of Shakespeare's?*

I now believe that if I had asked an even simpler question—such as, what do you mean by mass, or acceleration, which is the scientific equivalent of saying, *Can you read?*—not more than one in ten of the highly educated would have felt that I was speaking the same language. So the great edifice of modern physics goes up, and the majority of the cleverest people in the western world have about as much insight into it as their neolithic ancestors would have had.

Just one more of those questions, that my non-scientific friends regard as being in the worst of taste. Cambridge is a university where scientists and non-scientists meet every night at dinner. About two years ago, one

of the most astonishing experiments in the whole history of science was brought off. I don't mean the sputnik—that was admirable for quite different reasons, as a feat of organization and a triumphant use of existing knowledge. No, I mean the experiment at Columbia by Yang and Lee. It is an experiment of the greatest beauty and originality, but the result is so startling that one forgets how beautiful the experiment is. It makes us think again about some of the fundamentals of the physical world. Intuition, common sense—they are neatly stood on their heads. The result is usually known as the contradiction of parity. If there were any serious communication between the two cultures, this experiment would have been talked about at every High Table in Cambridge. Was it? I wasn't here: but I should like to ask the question.

There seems then to be no place where the cultures meet. I am not going to waste time saying that this is a pity. It is much worse than that. Soon I shall come to some practical consequences. But at the heart of thought and creation we are letting some of our best chances go by default. The clashing point of two subjects, two disciplines, two cultures—of two galaxies, so far as that goes—ought to produce creative chances. In the history of mental activity that has been where some of the break-throughs came. The chances are there now. But they are there, as it were, in a vacuum, because those in the two cultures can't talk to each other. It is bizzare how very little of twentieth-century science has been assimilated into twentieth-century art. Now and then one used to find poets conscientiously using scientific expressions, and getting them wrong—there was a time when "refraction" kept cropping up in verse in a mystifying fashion, and when "polarized light" was used as though writers were under the illusion that it was a specially admirable kind of light.

Of course, that isn't the way that science could be any good to art. It has got to be assimilated along with, and as part and parcel of, the whole of our mental experience, and used as naturally as the rest.

## TOPICS FOR DISCUSSION

1   What is Snow's central thesis? Why does he use a humorous episode to lead into the "serious" subject?

2   How do the two "misinterpretations" serve as the framework for the method of development used for the entire essay?

3   What are the misinterpretations on the part of scientists? On the part of literary people?

4   Why is the word "culture" appropriate?

5   If specialists within the sciences cannot talk to one another, how can nonscientifically trained people understand even basic communications with scientists?

6　What is C. P. Snow's special vantage point in viewing this problem? Do you know of many other people so advantageously placed? What special knowledge do you think you could garner from a college education that would make you available to the communications from both cultures?

## ... AND COMPOSITION

7　What can be done to correct this division of cultures?

8　How is specialization of education responsible for this dilemma? Did Whitehead ("The Aims of Education") offer any suggestions?

9　Have you found most modern literature as conservative, religiously and politically, as Snow suggests scientists have found it?

**HENRY ADAMS (1838–1918)** groped outward from his American heritage
trying to accommodate the two kinds of value here considered—religious
and scientific. The two posed divergent meanings which his background
had not fitted him to understand. In Adams we find an emblem of America:
his family was great; his education was the best—and his confusion was complete.
Or so his books tell us. The style in "The Dynamo and the Virgin" is assertive:
"I am lost," it says. And yet the writer is very sophisticated. How can we identify
the strategies of this writer? What kind of confusion is he so elaborately identifying?

# The Dynamo and the Virgin

Until the Great Exposition of 1900 closed its doors in November, Adams haunted it, aching to absorb knowledge, and helpless to find it. He would have liked to know how much of it could have been grasped by the best-informed man in the world. While he was thus meditating chaos, Langley came by, and showed it to him. At Langley's behest, the Exhibition dropped its superfluous rags and stripped itself to the skin, for Langley knew what to study, and why, and how; while Adams might as well have stood outside in the night, staring at the Milky Way. Yet Langley said nothing new, and taught nothing that one might not have learned from Lord Bacon, three hundred years before; but though one should have known the "Advancement of Science" as well as one knew the "Comedy of Errors," the literary knowledge counted for nothing until some teacher should show how to apply it. Bacon took a vast deal of trouble in teaching King James I and his subjects, American or other, towards the year 1620, that true science was the development or economy of forces; yet an elderly American in 1900 knew neither the formula nor the forces; or even so much as to say to himself that his historical business in the Exposition concerned only the economies or developments of force since 1893, when he began the study at Chicago.

Nothing in education is so astonishing as the amount of ignorance it accumulates in the form of inert facts. Adams had looked at most of the accumulations of art in the storehouses called Art Museums; yet he did not know how to look at the art exhibits of 1900. He had studied Karl Marx and his doctrines of history with profound attention, yet he could not apply them at Paris. Langley, with the ease of a great master of experiment, threw out of the field every exhibit that did not reveal a new application of force, and naturally threw out, to begin with, almost the whole art exhibit. Equally, he ignored almost the whole industrial exhibit. He led his pupil directly to the forces. His chief interest was in new motors to make his airship feasible, and he taught Adams the astonishing complexities of the new Daimler motor, and of the automobile, which, since

1893, had become a nightmare at a hundred kilometres an hour, almost as destructive as the electric tram which was only ten years older; and threatening to become as terrible as the locomotive steam-engine itself, which was almost exactly Adams's own age.

Then he showed his scholar the great hall of dynamos, and explained how little he knew about electricity or force of any kind, even of his own special sun, which spouted heat in inconceivable volume, but which, as far as he knew, might spout less or more, at any time, for all the certainty he felt in it. To him, the dynamo itself was but an ingenious channel for conveying somewhere the heat latent in a few tons of poor coal hidden in a dirty engine-house carefully kept out of sight; but to Adams the dynamo became a symbol of infinity. As he grew accustomed to the great gallery of machines, he began to feel the forty-foot dynamos as a moral force, much as the early Christians felt the Cross. The planet itself seemed less impressive, in its old-fashioned, deliberate, annual or daily revolution, than this huge wheel, revolving within arm's-length at some vertiginous speed, and barely murmuring—scarcely humming an audible warning to stand a hair's-breadth further for respect of power—while it would not wake the baby lying close against its frame. Before the end, one began to pray to it; inherited instinct taught the natural expression of man before silent and infinite force. Among the thousand symbols of ultimate energy, the dynamo was not so human as some, but it was the most expressive.

Yet the dynamo, next to the steam-engine, was the most familiar of exhibits. For Adams's objects its value lay chiefly in its occult mechanism. Between the dynamo in the gallery of machines and the engine-house outside, the break of continuity amounted to abysmal fracture for a historian's objects. No more relation could he discover between the steam and the electric current than between the Cross and the cathedral. The forces were interchangeable if not reversible, but he could see only an absolute *fiat* in electricity as in faith. Langley could not help him. Indeed, Langley seemed to be worried by the same trouble, for he constantly repeated that the new forces were anarchical, and specially that he was not responsible for the new rays, that were little short of parricidal in their wicked spirit towards science. His own rays, with which he had doubled the solar spectrum, were altogether harmless and beneficent; but Radium denied its God—or, what was to Langley the same thing, denied the truths of his Science. The force was wholly new.

A historian who asked only to learn enough to be as futile as Langley or Kelvin, made rapid progress under this teaching, and mixed himself up in the tangle of ideas until he achieved a sort of Paradise of ignorance vastly consoling to his fatigued senses. He wrapped himself in vibrations and rays which were new, and he would have hugged Marconi and Branly had he met them, as he hugged the dynamo; while he lost his arithmetic in trying to figure out the equation between the discoveries and the econ-

omies of force. The economies, like the discoveries, were absolute, super-sensual, occult; incapable of expression in horse-power. What mathematical equivalent could he suggest as the value of a Branly coherer? Frozen air, or the electric furnace, had some scale of measurement, no doubt, if somebody could invent a thermometer adequate to the purpose; but X-rays had played no part whatever in man's consciousness, and the atom itself had figured only as a fiction of thought. In these seven years man had translated himself into a new universe which had no common scale of measurement with the old. He had entered a supersensual world, in which he could measure nothing except by chance collisions of movements imperceptible to his senses, perhaps even imperceptible to his instruments, but perceptible to each other, and so to some known ray at the end of the scale. Langley seemed prepared for anything, even for an indeterminable number of universes interfused—physics stark mad in metaphysics.

Historians undertake to arrange sequences,—called stories, or histories—assuming in silence a relation of cause and effect. These assumptions, hidden in the depths of dusty libraries, have been astounding, but commonly unconscious and childlike; so much so, that if any captious critic were to drag them to light, historians would probably reply, with one voice, that they had never supposed themselves required to know what they were talking about. Adams, for one, had toiled in vain to find out what he meant. He had even published a dozen volumes of American history for no other purpose than to satisfy himself whether, by the severest process of stating, with the least possible comment, such facts as seemed sure, in such order as seemed rigorously consequent, he could fix for a familiar moment a necessary sequence of human movement. The result had satisfied him as little as at Harvard College. Where he saw sequence, other men saw something quite different, and no one saw the same unit of measure. He cared little about his experiments and less about his statesmen, who seemed to him quite as ignorant as himself and, as a rule, no more honest; but he insisted on a relation of sequence, and if he could not reach it by one method, he would try as many methods as science knew. Satisfied that the sequence of men led to nothing and that the sequence of their society could lead no further, while the mere sequence of time was artificial, and the sequence of thought was chaos, he turned at last to the sequence of force; and thus it happened that, after ten years' pursuit, he found himself lying in the Gallery of Machines at the Great Exposition of 1900, his historical neck broken by the sudden irruption of forces totally new.

Since no one else showed much concern, an elderly person without other cares had no need to betray alarm. The year 1900 was not the first to upset school-masters. Copernicus and Galileo had broken many professional necks about 1600; Columbus had stood the world on its head towards 1500; but the nearest approach to the revolution of 1900 was that of 310, when Constantine set up the Cross. The rays that Langley

disowned, as well as those which he fathered, were occult, supersensual, irrational; they were a revelation of mysterious energy like that of the Cross; they were what, in terms of mediæval science, were called immediate modes of the divine substance.

The historian was thus reduced to his last resources. Clearly if he was bound to reduce all these forces to a common value, this common value could have no measure but that of their attraction on his own mind. He must treat them as they had been felt; as convertible, reversible, interchangeable attractions on thought. He made up his mind to venture it; he would risk translating rays into faith. Such a reversible process would vastly amuse a chemist, but the chemist could not deny that he, or some of his fellow physicists, could feel the force of both. When Adams was a boy in Boston, the best chemist in the place had probably never heard of Venus except by way of scandal, or of the Virgin except as idolatry; neither had he heard of dynamos or automobiles or radium; yet his mind was ready to feel the force of all, though the rays were unborn and the women were dead.

Here opened another totally new education, which promised to be by far the most hazardous of all. The knife-edge along which he must crawl, like Sir Lancelot in the twelfth century, divided two kingdoms of force which had nothing in common but attraction. They were as different as a magnet is from gravitation, supposing one knew what a magnet was, or gravitation, or love. The force of the Virgin was still felt at Lourdes, and seemed to be as potent as X-rays; but in America neither Venus nor Virgin ever had value as force—at most as sentiment. No American had ever been truly afraid of either.

This problem in dynamics gravely perplexed an American historian. The Woman had once been supreme; in France she still seemed potent, not merely as a sentiment, but as a force. Why was she unknown in America? For evidently America was ashamed of her, and she was ashamed of herself, otherwise they would not have strewn fig-leaves so profusely all over her. When she was a true force, she was ignorant of fig-leaves, but the monthly-magazine-made American female had not a feature that would have been recognized by Adam. The trait was notorious, and often humorous, but any one brought up among Puritans knew that sex was sin. In any previous age, sex was strength. Neither art nor beauty was needed. Every one, even among Puritans, knew that neither Diana of the Ephesians nor any of the Oriental goddesses was worshipped for her beauty. She was goddess because of her force; she was the animated dynamo; she was reproduction—the greatest and most mysterious of all energies; all she needed was to be fecund. Singularly enough, not one of Adams's many schools of education had ever drawn his attention to the opening lines of Lucretius, though they were perhaps the finest in all Latin literature, where the poet invoked Venus exactly as Dante invoked the Virgin:—

Quae quoniam rerum naturam *sola* gubernas.[1]

The Venus of Epicurean philosophy survived in the Virgin of the Schools:—

Donna, sei tanto grande, e tanto vali,
Che qual vuol grazia, e a te non ricorre,
Sua disianza vuol volar senz' ali.[2]

All this was to American thought as though it had never existed. The true American knew something of the facts, but nothing of the feelings; he read the letter, but he never felt the law. Before this historical chasm, a mind like that of Adams felt itself helpless; he turned from the Virgin to the Dynamo as though he were a Branly coherer. On one side, at the Louvre and at Chartres, as he knew by the record of work actually done and still before his eyes, was the highest energy ever known to man, the creator of four-fifths of his noblest art, exercising vastly more attraction over the human mind than all the steam-engines and dynamos ever dreamed of; and yet this energy was unknown to the American mind. An American Virgin would never dare command; an American Venus would never dare exist.

The question, which to any plain American of the nineteenth century seemed as remote as it did to Adams, drew him almost violently to study, once it was posed; and on this point Langleys were as useless as though they were Herbert Spencers or dynamos. The idea survived only as art. There one turned as naturally as though the artist were himself a woman. Adams began to ponder, asking himself whether he knew of any American artist who had ever insisted on the power of sex, as every classic had always done; but he could think only of Walt Whitman; Bret Harte, as far as the magazines would let him venture; and one or two painters, for the flesh-tones. All the rest had used sex for sentiment, never for force; to them, Eve was a tender flower, and Herodias an unfeminine horror. American art, like the American language and American education, was as far as possible sexless. Society regarded this victory over sex as its greatest triumph, and the historian readily admitted it, since the moral issue, for the moment, did not concern one who was studying the relations of unmoral force. He cared nothing for the sex of the dynamo until he could measure its energy.

Vaguely seeking a clue, he wandered through the art exhibit, and, in his stroll, stopped almost every day before St. Gaudens's General Sherman, which had been given the central post of honor. St. Gaudens himself was

[1] "Since thou art, then, sole mistress of the nature of things."
[2] "So mighty art thou, lady, and so great,
That he, who grace desireth, and comes not
To thee for aidance, fain would have desire
Fly without wings." [H. F. CARY, TRANS.]

in Paris, putting on the work his usual interminable last touches, and listening to the usual contradictory suggestions of brother sculptors. Of all the American artists who gave to American art whatever life it breathed in the seventies, St. Gaudens was perhaps the most sympathetic, but certainly the most inarticulate. General Grant or Don Cameron had scarcely less instinct of rhetoric than he. All the others—the Hunts, Richardson, John La Farge, Stanford White—were exuberant; only St. Gaudens could never discuss or dilate on an emotion, or suggest artistic arguments for giving to his work the forms that he felt. He never laid down the law, or affected the despot, or became brutalized like Whistler by the brutalities of his world. He required no incense; he was no egoist; his simplicity of thought was excessive; he could not imitate, or give any form but his own to the creations of his hand. No one felt more strongly than he the strength of other men, but the idea that they could affect him never stirred an image in his mind.

This summer his health was poor and his spirits were low. For such a temper, Adams was not the best companion, since his own gaiety was not *folle;* but he risked going now and then to the studio on Mont Parnasse to draw him out for a stroll in the Bois de Boulogne, or dinner as pleased his moods, and in return St. Gaudens sometimes let Adams go about in his company.

Once St. Gaudens took him down to Amiens, with a party of Frenchmen, to see the cathedral. Not until they found themselves actually studying the sculpture of the western portal, did it dawn on Adams's mind that, for his purposes, St. Gaudens on that spot had more interest to him than the cathedral itself. Great men before great monuments express great truths, provided they are not taken too solemnly. Adams never tired of quoting the supreme phrase of his idol Gibbon, before the Gothic cathedrals: "I darted a contemptuous look on the stately monuments of superstition." Even in the footnotes of his history, Gibbon had never inserted a bit of humor more human than this, and one would have paid largely for a photograph of the fat little historian, on the background of Notre Dame of Amiens, trying to persuade his readers—perhaps himself—that he was darting a contemptuous look on the stately monument, for which he felt in fact the respect which every man of his vast study and active mind always feels before objects worthy of it; but besides the humor, one felt also the relation. Gibbon ignored the Virgin, because in 1789 religious monuments were out of fashion. In 1900 his remark sounded fresh and simple as the green fields to ears that had heard a hundred years of other remarks, mostly no more fresh and certainly less simple. Without malice, one might find it more instructive than a whole lecture of Ruskin. One sees what one brings, and at that moment Gibbon brought the French Revolution. Ruskin brought reaction against the Revolution. St. Gaudens had passed beyond all. He liked the stately monuments much more than

he liked Gibbon or Ruskin; he loved their dignity; their unity; their scale; their lines; their lights and shadows; their decorative sculpture; but he was even less conscious than they of the force that created it all—the Virgin, the Woman—by whose genius "the stately monuments of superstition" were built, through which she was expressed. He would have seen more meaning in Isis with the cow's horns, at Edfoo, who expressed the same thought. The art remained, but the energy was lost even upon the artist.

Yet in mind and person St. Gaudens was a survival of the 1500s; he bore the stamp of the Renaissance, and should have carried an image of the Virgin round his neck, or stuck in his hat, like Louis XI. In mere time he was a lost soul that had strayed by chance into the twentieth century, and forgotten where it came from. He writhed and cursed at his ignorance, much as Adams did at his own, but in the opposite sense. St. Gaudens was a child of Benvenuto Cellini, smothered in an American cradle. Adams was a quintessence of Boston, devoured by curiosity to think like Benvenuto. St. Gaudens's art was starved from birth, and Adams's instinct was blighted from babyhood. Each had but half of a nature, and when they came together before the Virgin of Amiens they ought both to have felt in her the force that made them one; but it was not so. To Adams she became more than ever a channel of force; to St. Gaudens she remained as before a channel of taste.

For a symbol of power, St. Gaudens instinctively preferred the horse, as was plain in his horse and Victory of the Sherman monument. Doubtless Sherman also felt it so. The attitude was so American that, for at least forty years, Adams had never realized that any other could be in sound taste. How many years had he taken to admit a notion of what Michelangelo and Rubens were driving at? He could not say; but he knew that only since 1895 had he begun to feel the Virgin or Venus as force, and not everywhere even so. At Chartres—perhaps at Lourdes—possibly at Cnidos if one could still find there the divinely naked Aphrodite of Praxiteles—but otherwise one must look for force to the goddesses of Indian mythology. The idea died out long ago in the German and English stock. St. Gaudens at Amiens was hardly less sensitive to the force of the female energy than Matthew Arnold at the Grande Chartreuse. Neither of them felt goddesses as power—only as reflected emotion, human expression, beauty, purity, taste, scarcely even as sympathy. They felt a railway train as power; yet they, and all other artists, constantly complained that the power embodied in a railway train could never be embodied in art. All the steam in the world could not, like the Virgin, build Chartres.

Yet in mechanics, whatever the mechanicians might think, both energies acted as interchangeable forces on man, and by action on man all known force may be measured. Indeed, few men of science measured force in any other way. After once admitting that a straight line was the shortest

distance between two points, no serious mathematician cared to deny any-thing that suited his convenience, and rejected no symbol, unproved or unproveable, that helped him to accomplish work. The symbol was force, as a compass needle or a triangle was force, as the mechanist might prove by losing it, and nothing could be gained by ignoring their value. Symbol or energy, the Virgin had acted as the greatest force the Western world ever felt, and had drawn man's activities to herself more strongly than any other power, natural or supernatural, had ever done; the historian's busi-ness was to follow the track of the energy; to find where it came from and where it went to; its complex source and shifting channels; its values, equivalents, conversions. It could scarcely be more complex than radium; it could hardly be deflected, diverted, polarized, absorbed more perplex-ingly than other radiant matter. Adams knew nothing about any of them, but as a mathematical problem of influence on human progress, though all were occult, all reacted on his mind, and he rather inclined to think the Virgin easiest to handle.

The pursuit turned out to be long and tortuous, leading at last into the vast forests of scholastic science. From Zeno to Descartes, hand in hand with Thomas Aquinas, Montaigne, and Pascal, one stumbled as stupidly as though one were still a German student of 1860. Only with the instinct of despair could one force one's self into this old thicket of ignorance after having been repulsed at a score of entrances more promising and more popular. Thus far, no path had led anywhere, unless perhaps to an exceed-ingly modest living. Forty-five years of study had proved to be quite futile for the pursuit of power; one controlled no more force in 1900 than in 1850, although the amount of force controlled by society had enormously increased. The secret of education still hid itself somewhere behind ignor-ance, and one fumbled over it as feebly as ever. In such labyrinths, the staff is a force almost more necessary than the legs; the pen becomes a sort of blind-man's dog, to keep him from falling into the gutters. The pen works for itself, and acts like a hand, modelling the plastic material over and over again to the form that suits it best. The form is never arbitrary, but is a sort of growth like crystallization, as any artist knows too well; for often the pencil or pen runs into side-paths and shapelessness, loses its relations, stops or is bogged. Then it has to return on its trail, and recover, if it can, its line of force. The result of a year's work depends more on what is struck out than on what is left in; on the sequence of the main lines of thought, than on their play or variety. Compelled once more to lean heavily on this support, Adams covered more thousands of pages with figures as formal as though they were algebra, laboriously striking out, altering, burning, experimenting, until the year had expired, the Exposition had long been closed, and winter drawing to its end, before he sailed from Cherbourg, on January 19, 1901, for home.

## TOPICS FOR DISCUSSION

1 What does Adams mean by "force"?

2 Why had the unmeasurable force of 1900 seemed so metaphysical? Does that same force seem metaphysical now? Is it beyond measurement today?

3 Is the sexual force found in the Virgin and Venus the same as that found in, say, a modern sex goddess of motion pictures? How can the Virgin and Venus be thought to have the same attributes? Do you agree with Adams that the Virgin and Venus were great forces in Western civilization?

4 Are Adams's chivalric sentiments about women dated?

5 What subtle effects are gained from retelling the Gibbon episode?

6 Who are the following: Langley; Kelvin; Branly; Copernicus; Galileo; Herbert Spencer; Walt Whitman; Bret Harte; Herodias; John La Farge; Praxiteles; Thomas Aquinas?

## ...AND COMPOSITION

7 Write an essay on a subject of your choice in which you use an object to symbolize a whole world of meanings, as Adams used the dynamo and the Virgin to symbolize varieties of force.

8 Explore your reactions to nuclear force.

9 If Venus and the Virgin have ceased to be the "greatest force the Western world ever felt," what has replaced them?

**ALBERT EINSTEIN (1879–1955)** a native of Germany who became a citizen of the United States, was a natural resource in the form of an intelligence. He discovered himself to be the location of one of those illuminations which chance or genius now and then lavishes on mankind. After very early insights, particularly his glimpse of a hypothesis of relativity (recognized but not understood except by a very few, but accorded by all to be a vast reordering of human conception), he spent his life in further work in mathematics and in the human concerns which he always related to his endeavors in mathematics and physical theory. At the end of his life his attention was much engaged in the relation between science and human values, and one of his abiding concerns was to guide and control for human welfare the terrible power his discoveries had helped to give to men.

# Science and Religion

It would not be difficult to come to an agreement as to what we understand by science. Science is the century-old endeavor to bring together by means of systematic thought the perceptible phenomena of this world into as thoroughgoing an association as possible. To put it boldly, it is the attempt at the posterior reconstruction of existence by the process of conceptualization. But when asking myself what religion is, I cannot think of the answer so easily. And even after finding an answer which may satisfy me at this particular moment, I still remain convinced that I can never under any circumstances bring together, even to a slight extent, all those who have given this question serious consideration.

At first, then, instead of asking what religion is, I should prefer to ask what characterizes the aspirations of a person who gives me the impression of being religious: a person who is religiously enlightened appears to me to be one who has, to the best of his ability, liberated himself from the fetters of his selfish desires and is preoccupied with thoughts, feelings, and aspirations to which he clings because of their super-personal value. It seems to me that what is important is the force of this super-personal content and the depth of the conviction concerning its overpowering meaningfulness, regardless of whether any attempt is made to unite this content with a Divine Being, for otherwise it would not be possible to count Buddha and Spinoza as religious personalities. Accordingly, a religious person is devout in the sense that he has no doubt of the significance and loftiness of those super-personal objects and goals which neither require nor are capable of rational foundation. They exist with the same necessity and matter-of-factness as he himself. In this sense religion is the age-old endeavor of mankind to become clearly and completely conscious of these values and goals and constantly to strengthen and extend their effects. If one conceives of religion and science according to these definitions then a

conflict between them appears impossible. For science can only ascertain what *is,* but not what should be, and outside of its domain value judgments of all kinds remain necessary. Religion, on the other hand, deals only with evaluations of human thought and action; it cannot justifiably speak of facts and relationships between facts. According to this interpretation, the well-known conflicts between religion and science in the past must all be ascribed to a misapprehension of the situation which has been described.

For example, a conflict arises when a religious community insists on the absolute truthfulness of all statements recorded in the Bible. This means an intervention on the part of religion into the sphere of science; this is where the struggle of the Church against the doctrines of Galileo and Darwin belongs. On the other hand, representatives of science have often made an attempt to arrive at fundamental judgments with respect to values and ends on the basis of scientific method, and in this way have set themselves in opposition to religion. These conflicts have all sprung from fatal errors.

Now, even though the realms of religion and science in themselves are clearly marked off from each other, nevertheless there exist between the two, strong reciprocal relationships and dependencies. Though religion may be that which determines the goal, it has, nevertheless, learned from science, in the broadest sense, what means will contribute to the attainment of the goals it has set up. But science can only be created by those who are thoroughly imbued with the aspiration towards truth and understanding. This source of feeling, however, springs from the sphere of religion. To this there also belongs the faith in the possibility that the regulations valid for the world of existence are rational, that is comprehensible to reason. I cannot conceive of a genuine scientist without that profound faith. The situation may be expressed by an image: science without religion is lame, religion without science is blind.

Though I have asserted above, that in truth a legitimate conflict between religion and science cannot exist, I must nevertheless qualify this assertion once again on an essential point, with reference to the actual content of historical religions. This qualification has to do with the concept of God. During the youthful period of mankind's spiritual evolution, human fantasy created gods in man's own image, who, by the operations of their will were supposed to determine, or at any rate to influence, the phenomenal world. Man sought to alter the disposition of these gods in his own favor by means of magic and prayer. The idea of God in the religions taught at present is a sublimation of that old conception of the gods. Its anthropomorphic character is shown, for instance, by the fact that men appeal to the Divine Being in prayers and plead for the fulfilment of their wishes.

Nobody, certainly, will deny that the idea of the existence of an omnipotent, just and omnibeneficent personal God is able to accord man

solace, help, and guidance; also, by virtue of its simplicity the concept is accessible to the most undeveloped mind. But, on the other hand, there are decisive weaknesses attached to this idea in itself, which have been painfully felt since the beginning of history. That is, if this Being is omnipotent, then every occurrence, including every human action, every human thought, and every human feeling and aspiration is also His work; how is it possible to think of holding men responsible for their deeds and thoughts before such an Almighty Being? In giving out punishment and rewards He would to a certain extent be passing judgment on Himself. How can this be combined with the goodness and righteousness ascribed to Him?

The main source of the present-day conflicts between the spheres of religion and of science lies in this concept of a personal God. It is the aim of science to establish general rules which determine the reciprocal connection of objects and events in time and space. For these rules, or laws of nature, absolutely general validity is required—not proven. It is mainly a program, and faith in the possibility of its accomplishment in principle is only founded on partial success. But hardly anyone could be found who would deny these partial successes and ascribe them to human self-deception. The fact that on the basis of such laws we are able to predict the temporal behavior of phenomena in certain domains with great precision and certainty is deeply embedded in the consciousness of the modern man, even though he may have grasped very little of the contents of those laws. He need only consider that planetary courses within the solar system may be calculated in advance with great exactitude on the basis of a limited number of simple laws. In a similar way, though not with the same precision, it is possible to calculate in advance the mode of operation of an electric motor, a transmission system, or of a wireless apparatus, even when dealing with a novel development.

To be sure, when the number of factors coming into play in a phenomenological complex is too large, scientific method in most cases fails us. One need only think of the weather, in which case prediction even for a few days ahead is impossible. Nevertheless no one doubts that we are confronted with a causal connection whose causal components are in the main known to us. Occurrences in this domain are beyond the reach of exact prediction because of the variety of factors in operation, not because of any lack of order in nature.

We have penetrated far less deeply into the regularities obtaining within the realm of living things, but deeply enough nevertheless to sense at least the rule of fixed necessity. One need only think of the systematic order in heredity, and in the effect of poisons, as for instance alcohol on the behavior of organic beings. What is still lacking here is a grasp of connections of profound generality, but not a knowledge of order in itself.

The more a man is imbued with the ordered regularity of all events,

the firmer becomes his conviction that there is no room left by the side of this ordered regularity for causes of a different nature. For him neither the rule of human nor the rule of Divine Will exists as an independent cause of natural events. To be sure, the doctrine of a personal God interfering with natural events could never be *refuted,* in the real sense, by science, for this doctrine can always take refuge in those domains in which scientific knowledge has not yet been able to set foot.

But I am persuaded that such behavior on the part of the representatives of religion would not only be unworthy but also fatal. For a doctrine which is able to maintain itself not in clear light but only in the dark, will of necessity lose its effect on mankind, with incalculable harm to human progress. In their struggle for the ethical good, teachers of religion must have the stature to give up the doctrine of a personal God, that is, give up that source of fear and hope which in the past placed such vast power in the hands of priests. In their labors they will have to avail themselves of those forces which are capable of cultivating the Good, the True, and the Beautiful in humanity itself. This is, to be sure, a more difficult but an incomparably more worthy task.[1] After religious teachers accomplish the refining process indicated, they will surely recognize with joy that true religion has been ennobled and made more profound by scientific knowledge.

If it is one of the goals of religion to liberate mankind as far as possible from the bondage of egocentric cravings, desires, and fears, scientific reasoning can aid religion in yet another sense. Although it is true that it is the goal of science to discover rules which permit the association and foretelling of facts, this is not its only aim. It also seeks to reduce the connections discovered to the smallest possible number of mutually independent conceptual elements. It is in this striving after the rational unification of the manifold that it encounters its greatest successes, even though it is precisely this attempt which causes it to run the greatest risk of falling a prey to illusions. But whoever has undergone the intense experience of successful advances made in this domain is moved by profound reverence for the rationality made manifest in existence. By way of the understanding he achieves a far-reaching emancipation from the shackles of personal hopes and desires, and thereby attains that humble attitude of mind towards the grandeur of reason incarnate in existence, which, in its profoundest depths, is inaccessible to man. This attitude, however, appears to me to be religious, in the highest sense of the word. And so it seems to me that science not only purifies the religious impulse of the dross of its anthropomorphism, but also contributes to a religious spiritualization of our understanding of life.

The further the spiritual evolution of mankind advances, the more

[1] This thought is convincingly presented in Herbert Samuel's book, "Belief and Action."

certain it seems to me that the path to genuine religiosity does not lie through the fear of life, and the fear of death, and blind faith, but through striving after rational knowledge. In this sense I believe that the priest must become a teacher if he wishes to do justice to his lofty educational mission.

## TOPICS FOR DISCUSSION

1  What are the religious concerns of a person, as identified in the second paragraph? Has this presentation of religion significantly changed by the end of the essay—or does the author merely use and adjust his early presentation?

2  What is the basic difference given between religion and science which excludes the need for conflict between them? Why then has there been conflict? Are there sciences which enter the realm of religion as Einstein sees it? Are there religions which enter the realm of science? Do you think there is a basic conflict between science and religion?

3  How are the rhetorical questions at the top of page 317 used? Is this indirect method more useful than a direct statement? Why would the question method be useful when the topic verges on something likely to be contested by the reader?

4  Does Einstein's treatment of the idea of a personal god represent a meddling of science in the matters of religion? By his definition? By your definition?

5  Can a religious person believe in a miracle without violating the role of science? Can a scientist evaluate a belief in a miracle without infringing on the domain of religion?

## ...AND COMPOSITION

6  Have you encountered conflicts of religious faith and scientific fact?

7  Can you find other scientific authorities who dispute Einstein's rejection of the concept of a personal god?

8  How do you define the religious person?

**LOREN EISELEY (1907–      )** as many readers have discovered, has a rewarding combination of abilities. He is an anthropologist, an educator, and a creative writer of prose and poetry. In whatever he writes he connects his various interests, and they combine into an attitude of wonder. The reaches of time, the changes in mankind and the animals, and the potentials for change in the present all get reverent, imaginative treatment. Mr. Eiseley is especially notable for his ability to select some particular, even some apparently trivial bit of evidence, and then to demonstrate its significance. The article below is a good example of his work. His book *The Immense Journey* is a good source for further sampling.

# The Fire Apes

I

I was the only man in the world who saw him do it. Everybody else was hurrying. Everybody else around that hospital was busy, or flat on his back and beyond seeing. I had a smashed ankle and was using a crutch, so I couldn't hurry. That was the only reason I was on the grounds and allowed to sit on a bench. If it hadn't been for that I would have missed it. I saw what it meant, too. I had the perspective, you see, and the time to think about it. In the end I hardly knew whether to be glad or sorry, but it was a frightening experience, perhaps not so much frightening as weird because I suddenly and preternaturally saw very close to the end—the end of all of us—and it happened because of that squirrel.

The bird-feeding station stood on the lawn before my bench. Whoever had erected it was a bird-lover, not a squirrel enthusiast, that much was certain. It was on top of a section of thin pipe stuck upright in the ground, and over the end of the pipe half of a bread can had been inverted. The thin, smooth pipe and the bread can were to keep squirrels from the little wooden platform and roof where the birds congregated to feed. The feeding platform was attached just above the tin shield that protected it from the squirrels. I could see that considerable thought had gone into the production of this apparatus and that it was carefully placed so that no squirrel could spring across from a nearby tree.

In the space of the morning I watched five squirrels lope easily across the lawn and try their wits on the puzzle. It was clear that they knew the bread was there—the problem was to reach it. Five squirrels in succession clawed their way up the thin pipe only to discover they were foiled by the tin umbrella around which they could not pass. Each squirrel in turn slid slowly and protestingly back to earth, flinched at my distant chuckle, and went away with a careful appearance of total disinterest that preserved his dignity.

There was a sixth squirrel that came after a time, but I was bored by then, and only half watching. God knows how many things a man misses by becoming smug and assuming that matters will take their natural course. I almost drowsed enough to miss it, and if I had, I might have gone away from there still believing in the fixity of species, or the inviolability of the human plane of existence. I might even have died believing some crass anthropocentric dogma about the uniqueness of the human brain.

As it was, I had just one sleepy eye half open, and it was through that that I saw the end of humanity. It was really a very little episode, and if it hadn't been for the squirrel I wouldn't have seen it at all. The thing was: he stopped to think. He stopped right there at the bottom of the pole and looked up and I knew he was thinking. Then he went up.

He went up with a bound that swayed the thin pipe slightly and teetered the loose shield. In practically the next second he had caught the tilted rim of the shield with an outstretched paw, flicked his body on to and over it, and was sitting on the platform where only birds were supposed to be. He dined well there and daintily, and went away in due time in the neat quick fashion by which he had arrived. I clucked at him and he stopped a moment in his leisurely sweep over the grass, holding up one paw and looking at me with the small shrewd glance of the wood people. There are times now when I think it was a momentous meeting and that for just a second in that sunlit glade, the present and the future measured each other, half conscious in some strange way of their destinies. Then he was loping away with the autumn sunlight flickering on his fur, to a tree where I could not follow him. I turned away and limped back to the shadow of my bench.

"He's a smart squirrel, all right," I tried to reassure myself. "He's a super-smart squirrel, but just the same he's only a squirrel. Besides, there are monkeys that can solve better problems than that. A nice bit of natural history, an insight into a one-ounce brain at its best, but what's the significance of—"

It was just then I got it. The chill that had been slowly crawling up my back as I faced that squirrel. You have to remember what I said about perspective. I have been steeped in geological eras; my mind is filled with the osseous debris of a hundred graveyards. Up till now I have dealt with the past. I was one of the planet's undisputed masters. But that squirrel had busy fingers. He was loping away from me into the future.

The chill came with the pictures, and those pictures rose dim and vast, as though evoked from my subconscious memory by that small uplifted paw. They were not pleasant pictures. They had to do with times far off and alien. There was one, I remember, of gasping amphibian heads on the shores of marshes, with all about them the birdless silence of a land into which no vertebrate life had ever penetrated because it could not leave the water. There was another in which great brainless monsters bellowed in

the steaming hollows of a fern forest, while tiny wraith-like mammals eyed them from the underbrush. There was a vast lonely stretch of air, through which occasionally skittered the ill-aimed flight of lizard-like birds. And finally there was a small gibbon-like primate teetering along through a great open parkland, upright on his two hind feet. Once he turned, and I seemed to see something familiar about him, but he passed into the shade.

There were more pictures, but always they seemed to depict great empty corridors, corridors in the sense of a planet's spaces, first empty and then filled with life. Always along those corridors as they filled, were eager watchers, watching from the leaves, watching from the grasses, watching from the woods' edge. Sometimes the watchers ventured out a little way and retreated. Sometimes they emerged and strange changes overtook the corridor.

It was somewhere there at the last on the edge of a dying city that I thought I recognized my squirrel. He was farther out of the woods now, bolder, and a bit more insolent, but he was still a squirrel. The city was dying, that was plain, but the cause was undiscernible. I saw with a slight shock that nothing seemed very important about it. It was dying slowly, in the length of centuries, and all about it the little eyes under the leaves were closing in. It was then that I understood, finally, and no longer felt particularly glad or sorry. The city was forfeit to those little shining brains at the woods' edge. I knew how long they had waited. And we, too, had been at the woods' edge in our time. We could afford to go now. Our vast intellectual corridor might stretch empty for a million years. It did not matter. My squirrel would attend to it. And if not he, then the wood rats. They were all there waiting under the leaves.

## II

I suppose everyone keeps by his night light some collection of tales by which he may frighten himself back to sleep in moments of insomnia. I know that I do. And if you are like me, you have, on occasional midnights, disputed lordship of the planet with intellectual octopi, or seen mankind pushed horribly aside by giant termites. These notions may be sinister at midnight, but the truths of daylight are simpler and more terrible: mankind may perish without assistance from any of these.

The human brain was a beautiful and terrible invention. It is unique. And because it is unique there are many who believe that its achievements will never be possible of duplication in nature, that, in the words of one naturalist, "progress hangs on but a single thread. That thread is the human germ plasm." A French scholar murmurs a little uneasily "man alone in the universe is not finished." Julian Huxley defends the uniqueness of the human species with an impassioned vigor. "Among the actual inhabitants of the earth," he says, "past and present, no other lines could

have been taken which would have produced speech and conceptual thought. . . . It could not have been evolved on earth except in man."

That remark is both wise, in a sense, and foolish. It is the statement of a man who has looked far into the depths of the past and seen nothing so wonderful as man. Yet it betrays also the reluctance of the human imagination as it turns toward the future—its concern with itself, its unwillingness to relinquish the stage. This genuinely profound mind is surely not unaware that an intellectual dinosaur of the dying Cretaceous might well have murmured: "The saurians alone are not finished. What possible things could improve upon us?" The Cretaceous date line would have made it a wise and Huxlian statement. It would have taken ten million years to force its serious alteration. Mr. Huxley is equally safe from refutation, so safe in fact that he sniffs contemptuously at the potential threat offered by our rowdy remaining cousins up in the family tree. "The monkeys," he says, "have quite left behind them that more generalized stage from which a conscious thinking creature could develop."

I am afraid that we are altogether too impressed by the fact that we live on the ground and that our remaining relatives, poor fellows, show a decided preference for trees. It never seems to occur to us that if they didn't stay up there we would jolly well show them what for. As for that "more generalized stage" which Mr. Huxley demands for the appearance of a thinking creature, I am quite sure that he cannot define it in a way which would seriously threaten the reputation of several existing primates.

The only way to become a "generalized stage" is to produce, in the course of time, several divergent smart descendants. No one can say that that faculty has been lost, but the whole monkey group will stay upstairs now till we are gone. And if they don't come down, there is still my squirrel, whose actions at times remind me of a certain ancient human forerunner in the Eocene. That chap wasn't recognized as "generalized" either, until somewhere along the way he began to walk on his hind feet. In the beginning, I'm not at all sure he was as smart as my squirrel.

Now I have said that Mr. Huxley is safe from refutation, geological time being what it is. If it is impossible to refute him until the passage of another sixty million years, it might be more comfortable to assume he has spoken the truth. It might have been, that is, up until last year. It was then that scientists began to scratch actively in the African bone lands. It was then that archeologists began to whisper behind their hands and exchange glances. It concerned, of course, a certain skull. That in itself was bad enough, but what ensued was worse.

He was an ape, they had said in the beginning: "A creature lacking the distinctive temporal expansions which appear to be concomitant with and necessary to articulate man is no true man." Then there had come that frightening insistence on the part of his discoverer that he had used fire and tools.

The little fellow was promptly redescribed. His type was cited in glowing terms as "intelligent, energetic, erect, and delicately proportioned little people." He was credited with speech, and spoken of respectfully as a potential human ancestor. It was more comfortable that way. Otherwise you were confronted with a spectacle like Dunsany's mysterious Abu Laheeb, that strange being squatting over its lonely fire in the marshes— the only beast in the world that made fire like man.

The mythical Abu Laheeb survived by hiding in the papyrus swamps of the upper Nile. *Australopithecus prometheus,* the ape who made fire, was not that fortunate. He disappeared. The reason why concerns Mr. Huxley's philosophy and is in some sense a refutation of it. Men say, in the books, that man is the last hope of life on the planet, the last chance, that is, for brain. In the past, however, when man was yet weak, a cousin tried to take the path he walked upon and almost succeeded. A cousin from the despised roof tree, where the eyes still watch us overhead.

To explain his failure and near success, we must go back millions of years. To explain what will come after our own extinction, we must again read backward—not for biological events which can never be repeated in exactitude, not for signs of the reappearance of forms which have had their day and will never again emerge into the light—but rather to project forward into the future those dread principles which have controlled the movement of life on this planet through untold eons of time, and which will continue to direct its destiny through the untold eons of the future. The destructiveness of man has lent a sparse and impoverished aspect to the animal life of the present day. It implies senescence and decline. Both are illusory. The great life stream awaits only its opportunity—the moment of human disappearance.

### III

There are two sorts of evolutionary movement in the world of life, and one is more mysterious than the other. There are, for example, the slight differences which arise between species, the multiplicity of closely related shrubs, grasses, trees, and animals which can be observed over an acre of ground. All of these forms, plant and animal alike, may be occupying essentially the same environment or small, slightly divergent "microenvironments" within that acre. The diversity is pleasing. It leads us to comment on the infinite richness of life. Much of this burgeoning splendor is, nevertheless, without meaning so far as the grander progression of life is concerned. Some of it is the product of genetic drift which may have little importance even in terms of natural selection. It is diversity without significance, save as it represents the infinite capacities of the cell.

The real mystery, by contrast, lies on a mightier stage. It is the great symphonic movement through the world of the corridors. It is the fish who crawled ashore on his fins, the amphibian who painfully learned to

walk. It is the reptile who invented the egg and thus released land verte-brates from dependence on the water. It is the saurian who flew, and who also learned to control his body temperature until he became a high-speed efficient mammalian machine whose brain did not grow torpid in the chill-ing night. It includes, also, a creature who came down from the trees and took his first tentative step down the long grassland corridor that was to lead him out into the magnificent vistas of conceptual thought.

The advance into those various worlds, into the air and the light out of the depths of the waters consumed millions of years of effort. It was not all an upward movement. Species by thousands died; species went into the ground; species went back to the waters; species clung to the high trees and shrieked down at their human brothers. The smaller movements we understand well—the horse from four toes to one, the age-by-age growth of horns on Triceratops or the titanotheres.

Instead it is the plunge through the forbidden zones that catches the heart with its sheer audacity. In the history of life there have been few such episodes. It is that which makes us lonely. We have entered a new corridor, the cultural corridor. There has been nothing here before us. In it we are utterly alone. In it we are appallingly unique. We look at each other and say, "It can never be done again." It is almost as though in our very bones were felt ancestral memories of the way we have come, and the feeling like magic touches us once more so that we repeat with some-thing like terror in our voices, "It can never be done again."

Now it is one of the strange paradoxes of biology that this feeling of mystery concerning the great biological inventions which have opened the doorways of life has deepened as our knowledge has increased. Long evolutionary lines in a given environmental zone have been worked out, transition forms have been noted, and many sequences leading by imper-ceptible degrees from one form to another have been observed. In the be-ginning, Darwin and his followers assumed confidently that the major gaps which yawned between the phyla—the space, say, between the fish and the amphibian, between the reptile and the bird—would eventually be found to contain transition forms extending in the same imperceptible way from the one form to the other, even though a major life threshold had been crossed.

The lack of such transitional forms was not at first disturbing. Success in the pursuit of ancestral lines over long time-intervals led to the con-clusion that these major gaps were due solely to imperfections in the geological record; that the book of Nature had, so to speak, missing pages, but that the main outlines of the story could easily be read from the pages that remained. It was not until much later that those missing pages were observed to occur with almost monotonous regularity at some dramatic transition point, involving the emergence of a new form of life and its adaptation to either an unentered corridor or a corridor offering possi-

bilities of being intruded upon in some new way. The new type, in other words, seemed to emerge with astounding quickness, considering the generally slow evolutionary pace to be read from many of the remains which the fossil hunters were discovering in the better known strata of the earth.

This situation has led to much speculation. It has led on the part of some to a denial of the reality of evolution, on the part of others to claims for some type of "jumping evolution" in which fantastically complex mutations brought new organic forms into existence at a single step. The confusion created by this situation is perhaps nowhere better expressed than in Lecomte du Nouy's recent book, *The Road to Reason.* He says: "The general fact that paleontology only shows us a few transitional forms and still fewer really primitive forms, is also very disturbing. . . . We do not grasp the origin of any group."

It happens, however, that these widely expressed doubts are often tinged unconsciously with emotionalism. The gaps exist but isolated discoveries reveal that transitional forms are by no means non-existent. They are merely scarce. We have in growing numbers the mammal-like reptiles standing between the reptiles and the mammals. We have a strange, rare creature, Archaeopteryx, lying between the reptiles and the birds. There are other gaps which remain unclosed. These signs are, nevertheless, suggestive. More fossils will be found. Those which we possess, inadequate though they are, do not support the notion of fantastic leaps in nature.

They suggest, instead, that the march across a major barrier into a new sphere of existence is made rapidly if it is made successfully at all. A basic organic change of this nature is estimated by the brilliant modern scholar, G. G. Simpson, to have proceeded at a pace, in some instances, ten or fifteen times more rapid than the later recorded evolution of a given group after it has begun to exploit its new domain. The comparatively hasty crossing, hasty in a geological sense, was made by small groups of animals undergoing extreme selection pressure. As a consequence, there will never be numerous fossils. Archaeopteryx, the bird-reptile, for example, was found in 1861. It still remains a solitary specimen.

Another fact can be noted as we study these records. It is in a sense obvious, yet it has been neglected by many writers obsessed with human uniqueness or with the superiority of the mammalian line in general. It can be laid down almost as a truism. *No successful crossing into a new corridor of life can be effected if that corridor is completely dominated by prior intruders.*

This statement must be made somewhat dogmatically. Apparent exceptions can be observed, but they constitute special cases which do not affect the general principle. It could be noted, for example, that the reptiles made two separate attempts to conquer the air corridor, once by the use of membraneous wings—the giant glider Pteranodon being a popularly known example—and secondly by the evolution of true wings and feathers. Both

attempts were successful for a long period, and both must have competed for a time. Eventually the Pterosaurs disappeared and left the corridor to the birds.

Two facts explain this rather unusual situation. Both forms apparently got across into the airways at approximately the same time, so that neither one had radiated and adapted sufficiently to exclude the other. In addition, the development of flowering plants with accompanying nutritious seeds in the Cretaceous period profoundly stimulated insect evolution. The nutritive possibilities in the air corridor thus increased, but increased in a direction which favored the smaller, speedier, and more effective mechanism, namely, the birds.

From the Cretaceous to the present the birds have dominated the airways, and the smaller environmental niches within the airways so effectively that no other vertebrate has successfully challenged their control. One other animal, it is true, has evolved true flight in the interim, but its position only reveals the reality of our truism. The bats, true mammals, came late to the scene. They made the crossing, but made it surreptitiously in the evening twilight. The vast majority of birds are diurnal. The bats cling to the edge of evening, and such prey as they can find there. Their numbers, in comparison with birds, are scant. Both figuratively and literally, they are creatures of the twilight, dwellers at the unwanted margin. That is why they survive.

What the bats might have been capable of under other circumstances, it is, of course, impossible to conjecture, but the tremendous energies, the unknown capacities which may be held in check while a new form of life surges endlessly against an already closed corridor, is nowhere better illustrated than in the story of the rise of the mammalian world itself. Our interpretation of that rise is apt to be distinctly colored. We think of the mammals, our own ancestral line, as a highly effective group which crowded the reptiles aside. Nothing, in actuality, could be further from the truth.

I remarked on an earlier page that the truths of daylight are often the most terrible, and that the end of the human story does not demand our extermination at the hands of some more intellectual or fantastic form of life. That statement was deliberate. The reptiles are a prime example. For 140 million years, during that period known as the Mesozoic, they were the undisputed masters of this planet. In enormous numbers they radiated into every possible geographic niche. They swam and they flew and they walked. Brainless or not, they survived a period of time far more extended than the life of man, far more extended than the whole Age of Mammals.

Now what is not very generally understood by the lay public is the fact that throughout the greater portion of this 140 million years the mammalian world was in existence. It was in existence, but it was highly inconspicuous. It was small; it hid under bushes; it concealed itself in trees.

It had no giant representatives such as it developed later on after the disappearance of the reptiles. Like the bats on the edge of the bird world, it was existing on tolerance. It was marginal. To have grown larger would have been to invite the attention of the most formidable carnivores the world has ever seen—perfected killing machines with teeth like bear traps.

For a hundred million years those little mammals waited. No one would have dreamed that they, in their turn, might create monsters, and no one, above all, would have imagined that the gray and infinitely complex convolutions of the human brain were locked away in the forebrain of an insectivorous creature no larger than a rat. An observer waiting for some sign of creative emergence among those little animals in the underbrush would have grown weary as years by the million flowed away. He would have sworn that every variation in the game of life had been exploited and played out—that the reptiles were the master form—that the mammals were effective only upon an infinitely small size level.

Yet in the end, that strange end that closed the day of the Ruling Reptiles, the armored giants vanished. They vanished from the seas and the fern forests; their great gliding wings disappeared from the coastal air. Nothing living, so far as we can determine today, threatened them. The mammals were insignificant, envious eyes in the reeds—that was all. We in this remote age may murmur about climatic change or any one of a dozen vague possibilities. Sometimes we consider the notion that species may run through a lifetime, grow old and die, as does an individual organism. We do not know. But this we are unpleasantly aware of: the armored ones went in daylight. Nothing, not even their successors, thrust them aside. It would be millions of years before the shovel heads of the mammalian titanotheres grazed in the valleys that knew the thunder lizard, Triceratops.

The mammals did not destroy the great reptiles; they simply occupied, long after, an empty throne. It was only then that the long suppression of creative energy burst forth in a second marvelous efflorescence, the radiation that created the mammalian world. The story, however, has a moral that is little read: man also is the master of a corridor; there is nothing visible to compete with him. He has destroyed the great mammals and left only the little eyes under the rosebush in the garden. He is safe now to write books about his unique qualities—and he is unique, as unique as the dinosaurs. He will not be menaced from the field's edge, but the eyes are still waiting. Once they waited a hundred million years. They can do so again.

This time it will be a new corridor—the cultural corridor—that they enter, but it will not be as unique as it seems to us, writing as we do that we are the "sole representative of life in its progressive aspect and its sole trustee for any progress in the future."

Once, long ago in Africa, that cousin of whom I spoke made tools and, some think, may have experimented with the forbidden magic of fire itself.

Small and timid and slight of brain, he fades back into the silences of prehistory. He made the crossing at the wrong moment, but he proved we are not so unique as we imagine, that the crossing can be made again, perhaps even from above, out of the old roof tree, where everyone sits with his tail curled safely out of reach.

It is the safety of trees or the safety of being men now. The line is sharp; there is no half-way mark as there was when the first ill-adjusted migrants stumbled into an empty world. There is no longer any room for an ape who lights fires and is not a man.

## IV

Almost everything about this animal, up until recently, has been controversial except the fact that it existed. It has been called an ape. It has been called a man. It has been said to have walked upright. It has been said that this is untrue. It has been claimed that it spoke. It is said not to have spoken.

More complete specimens have lately begun to fall into the hands of the bone hunters, so that some of the questions which tormented earlier workers have been answered. Others, however, have taken their place.

The Australopithecine men-apes of South Africa are a group of small, upright-walking anthropoids who haunted the grasslands of the Vaal River area from five hundred thousand to a million years ago. They are not all alike in detail, but the whole stock is characterized by teeth of a quite human character. The great shearing canines of the existing apes are reduced to human proportions. These animals must have been omnivorous grassland wanderers, pursuing small animals, eating wild seeds, and probably robbing an occasional bird's nest. Around four feet in height, with a brain ranging at 450 to 650 cubic centimeters, their intellectual capacities, though low by human standards, were undoubtedly superior to that of any existing gorilla or chimpanzee.

They are the only grassland bipedal ape, as contrasted with primitive grassland man, of which we have any knowledge. As I pointed out earlier, they have been called apes. More lately there has been a tendency to call them men. Awkwardly enough, however, such datings as we have been able to compute for them are much too late in time to allow for their being the direct ancestors of true men. Some, at least, of the man-apes were the contemporaries, for a brief while, of primitive men.

I suppose that, if the truth were known, one reason why man is so impressed with his own uniqueness is the fact that he is alone today in the grassland corridor. In a few remote parts of Africa, a scant number of lower monkeys venture into waste spaces on the ground. The baboon is one of them His experiment has turned in another direction. His face is doglike. He runs upon all fours.

Of that series of arboreal experimenters who ventured into the first grasslands of the planet during the Miocene epoch and who teetered

diffidently from one tree clump to another, upright on their two hind feet, man alone remains. The grasslands were too open, competition too fierce as the sub-men multiplied, for the long continued survival of unlike forms. We of today see a yawning gulf between ourselves and the old forms in the trees. On the grass the others have vanished. The corridor is filled and the rifle would eliminate any wavering half-soul from the forest twilight who was so rash as to venture among us. It is too late for the crossing, too late until man has gone.

I suppose it is the illusion of uniqueness which for so long caused the student of human evolution to take a scattered series of human fossils and try to arrange them in a single line of ascent leading to modern man. It is still being tried with the new man-apes, but there are two embarrassments: their relative recency, and the diversity of their species. It is simply not possible that they are all on the main line of ascent to ourselves. That the Australopithecines have vanished while many simple arboreal relatives of ours survive is not surprising. The man-apes tried to occupy the same environmental niche as man, and as a consequence man destroyed them.

This does not mean that the Australopithecines are totally unrelated to ourselves. It does mean, however, that the old notion involving one human ancestral form and one only as taking the momentous step of climbing out of the trees and learning to walk upright—thus starting a simple and direct evolutionary movement which culminated in man of today—is a fantastic simplification of events.

Twenty million years ago the grasslands of the world were spreading. The long cooling that was to produce the Ice Age of later times had just begun. The low continents of the age of reptiles were giving way to mountain growths that swung the ancient jungles of the earlier lands far skyward, and brought drought to the inner continental basins. The grasslands spread farther and farther. Over vast areas the jungle disappeared or shrank to parkland.

We know that among the mammals of this period, many diverse orders turned to a grazing existence. Changes in their teeth tell us as much, for the high silica content of grass forces the development of a specialized grazing dentition which will resist wear. Man, of course, is not a grazer, nor were his fore-runners up in the diminishing branches.

That grassland world was, nevertheless, attractive. More and more animals were moving into it; here and there in the parklands, anthropoid apes of forms little known ventured on to the ground. A little like the archaic living gibbon, they may have scurried on their hind feet between isolated clumps of trees, snatching insects and seeds before swinging safely into the branches again. The slow changes that some of these animals were undergoing in habits and foot structure may have taken millions of years.

There must have been many of these apes on the edge of the grasslands. We need not be surprised if more than one type, over the vast Old World land mass, successfully made that crossing. The corridor was open

to aggressive, lively anthropoids who were willing to hunt small animals and insects, and whose diet was unspecialized. The climate was more healthful than that of the parasite-infested jungles. A strange competition began.

It was the competition of an odd lot of animals, the apes of the grassland, uncertainly erect, but with the neurological preference for that posture already developed among the branches of the forest. It was the competition of social animals, and therefore it was the competition of groups. Out of that struggle for food, for mates, and for life, the best adapted, the most clever brained, the most successfully communicative would survive.

I say communicative because somewhere here on the grasslands in an environment infinitely more demanding and dangerous than the safe retreat of the trees, the already extensive but instinctive call range of the old tree world began to be abandoned for conceptual thought and speech. Under mysterious endocrine influences about which we know nothing, man's infancy was becoming prolonged, his brain a plastic thing upon which incipient society was beginning to mark the folkways of the group. The strangest corridor in the history of life on this planet was being entered —the cultural corridor. Its final possessors would be masters of the earth. They would write books. They would describe themselves as unique. They were not.

V

The first of those peculiar human-footed apes to which we have previously referred, was announced to an incredulous world by Professor Raymond Dart in 1924. It took over twenty years to discover more of them and to learn something of their habits. Because it was not believed, at first, that they spoke or made tools, Dart, in spite of his conviction that they were closely associated with the earlier history of the human line, referred to them as "no true men."

This year, at Makapansgat in the Central Transvaal of South Africa, Dart reported *Australopithecus prometheus,* the fire-maker. Reporters, of course, went wild. Scientists scratched their heads and looked dubiously at one another. The new fossil was reported from deposits showing evidence of the use of fire in the shape of charred bone and traces of charcoal. Though no stone weapons were discovered, there were suspicious indications that Prometheus had used the long bones of slain animals as clubs. A series of neatly fractured baboon skulls from which the brain had probably been extracted for food supplied the evidence.

A very simple tool-using capacity on the part of an animal with a 650 cubic centimeter brain capacity is acceptable. That these creatures may have been fire-users has shaken all our established notions of human culture history. The suspicion continues to be entertained in some quarters, and will continue until further reports are available, that perhaps advanced forms of men may be responsible for the fires and the broken cranial case of Prometheus himself. It is known, at least, that there are

somewhat later humanly occupied caves at Makapan. It must not be forgotten, however, that it was Dr. Dart who recognized, over twenty years ago, the importance of the first Australopithecine cranium; it was conservative science that smiled and later had to eat its words.

Whether or not the human-footed apes were fire-users, we know that the animal remains with which they are associated at Makapan place them well within Early Ice Age times. Human relatives they are, but in the narrow sense, at least, they are not men. Men, low-browed, perhaps, but true men, were already in existence. The man-apes, by contrast, are a part of that ancient bipedal horde which millions of years ago came out upon the grasslands. Less massive than their divergent human brothers, they clung to the fringe of the corridor, ran before its terrors, and shared with us that dark and ancient blood from the times before man.

Perhaps at the last, late, much too late, they lit the fires that might have made them man; perhaps even—and that in itself is a weird thought, since no animal alive had done it—they watched trembling behind a bush and learned from men the secret of the fire. Perhaps already in some dim, half-human way they sensed their world was fading. Theirs were the last furred hands and theirs the last half-animal voices to be seen and heard in the cultural corridor before the pathway backward closed forever. When it opens again we shall be gone.

Sometimes at night I think one can feel even the pressure of mice waiting in the walls of old houses. All that concentrated life around us and above us, held in check, surging impatiently, ready for a new experiment, tired of us, waiting our passing, active with the busy mysteries of the cell. Sometimes one catches oneself wondering what the fire-apes were intending when they crossed the barrier, whether they were cut short in a new experiment, something smaller, more delicate, more—something, but not a human something. Something for which human beings must first be gotten out of the way. It is perhaps significant that even we ourselves feel a growing inadequacy. Perhaps that is really the secret. Perhaps we are going away.

ED. NOTE. In granting us permission to reprint his essay, Professor Eiseley has added the following postscript:

The evidence bearing upon the use of fire among the Australopithecine man-apes was challenged by other archaeologists a year or so after Dr. Dart's original report. It was contended by some scientists that there was no valid evidence of the use of tools by the man-apes—let alone fire. As a consequence of this disagreement the whole question has never been satisfactorily settled. In the spring of 1955, Dr. Dart produced remains of *Australopithecus prometheus* from African deposits containing a pebble-tool culture which had previously been supposed to be the product of a more advanced form of man. Since that time Dr. L. S. B. Leakey has definitely extended the range of new varieties of the man-apes into a more remote pre-Pleistocene period. He has also contributed additional evidence of their use of tools. The whole question of the mental powers of the man-apes is thus brought prominently before the scientific world again, irrespective of whether any of them were capable of utilizing, as distinct from making, fire. [L. C. E.]

## TOPICS FOR DISCUSSION

1  In the first paragraph the author says his experience was "frightening." The last sentence in the article says: "Perhaps we are going away." Recurrently, the author's discoveries and thoughts are made to be ominous. Is there some unspoken worry back of this whole essay? Is it haunted by something peculiar to our time? How would you account for the presence—and the present effectiveness—of this ominous tone in the article?

2  How successful is paragraph 1 in opening the essay? Do the simple, matter-of-fact sentence structure and vocabulary prepare one for the seriousness of the essay which follows?

3  Which part of the theory of evolution does Eiseley's episode of the sixth squirrel seem to question? What method of paragraph development is used in the second paragraph of section 2, page 322. Why is this method of development particularly useful in a section designed as a refutation?

4  What do all the "pictures" have in common? Why is a word like "picture," connoting fixity, better here than merely a verb indicating a mental view of the scene? What special impact have the pictures when one remembers that the present episode of the squirrel evokes the pictures of the past as well as being a part of the sequence of them?

5  How is the metaphor of the "corridor" developed? What does it mean, and how does it correspond to the less metaphoric descriptions of evolution one normally reads in biological tracts?

6  What are the major steps in the emergence of a corridor-controlling creature, according to Eiseley's theory?

## ...AND COMPOSITION

7  Unlike many writers in natural science, Eiseley uses many figures of speech in place of scientific abstractions. Find the most effective figures of speech and comment on their special uses.

8  Paraphrase Eiseley's argument without the help of figurative language. Paraphrase it using his basic metaphor.

9  Does this essay make you "see the end of humanity" as Eiseley saw it? Comment on the way man and science might leave the corridor vacant.

PHILIP WYLIE (1902–     )  writes fast and furiously; his varied novels,
articles, and social-comment books usually take off from indignation, as in the
following attack on American "progress." One of his titles pretty well
identifies his typical content and his attitude: *Generation of Vipers*.
He has turned his hand to many things, worked for publishers
and for the movies, and produced a large list of very popular books.

# *Science Has Spoiled My Supper*

I

I am a fan for Science. My education is scientific and I have, in one field, contributed a monograph to a scientific journal. Science, to my mind, is applied honesty, the one reliable means we have to find out truth. That is why, when error is committed in the name of Science, I feel the way a man would if his favorite uncle had taken to drink.

Over the years, I have come to feel that way about what science has done to food. I agree that America can set as good a table as any nation in the world. I agree that our food is nutritious and that the diet of most of us is well-balanced. What America eats is handsomely packaged; it is usually clean and pure; it is excellently preserved. The only trouble with it is this: year by year it grows less good to eat. It appeals increasingly to the eye. But who eats with his eyes? Almost everything used to taste better when I was a kid. For quite a long time I thought that observation was merely another index of advancing age. But some years ago I married a girl whose mother is an expert cook of the kind called "old-fashioned." This gifted woman's daughter (my wife) was taught her mother's venerable skills. The mother lives in the country and still plants an old-fashioned garden. She still buys dairy products from the neighbors and, in so far as possible, she uses the same materials her mother and grandmother did— to prepare meals that are superior. They are just as good, in this Year of Grace, as I recall them from my courtship. After eating for a while at the table of my mother-in-law, it is sad to go back to eating with my friends— even the alleged "good cooks" among them. And it is a gruesome experience to have meals at the best big-city restaurants.

Take cheese, for instance. Here and there, in big cities, small stores and delicatessens specialize in cheese. At such places, one can buy at least some of the first-rate cheeses that we used to eat—such as those we had with pie and in macaroni. The latter were sharp but not too sharp. They were a little crumbly. We called them American cheeses, or even rat cheese; actually they were Cheddars. Long ago, this cheese began to be supplanted by a material called "cheese foods." Some cheese foods and "processed"

cheese are fairly edible; but not one comes within miles of the old kinds—
for flavor.

A grocer used to be very fussy about his cheese. Cheddar was made and
sold by hundreds of little factories. Representatives of the factories had
particular customers, and cheese was prepared by hand to suit the grocers,
who knew precisely what their patrons wanted in rat cheese, pie cheese,
American and other cheeses. Some liked them sharper; some liked them
yellower; some liked anise seeds in cheese, or caraway.

What happened? Science—or what is called science—stepped in. The
old-fashioned cheeses didn't ship well enough. They crumbled, became
moldy, dried out. "Scientific" tests disclosed that a great majority of the
people will buy a less-good-tasting cheese if that's all they can get. "Scientific marketing" then took effect. Its motto is "Give the people the least
quality they'll stand for." In food, as in many other things, the "scientific
marketers" regard quality as secondary so long as they can sell most persons anyhow; what they are after is "durability" or "shippability."

It is not possible to make the very best cheese in vast quantities at a low
average cost. "Scientific sampling" got in its statistically nasty work. It
was found that the largest number of people will buy something that is
bland and rather tasteless. Those who prefer a product of a pronounced
and individualistic flavor have a variety of preferences. Nobody is altogether pleased by bland foodstuff, in other words; but nobody is very
violently put off. The result is that a "reason" has been found for turning
out zillions of packages of something that will "do" for nearly all and isn't
even imagined to be superlatively good by a single soul!

Economics entered. It is possible to turn out in quantity a bland, impersonal, practically imperishable substance more or less resembling, say,
cheese—at lower cost than cheese. Chain groceries shut out the independent stores and "standardization" became a principal means of cutting costs.

Imitations also came into the cheese business. There are American
duplications of most of the celebrated European cheeses, mass-produced
and cheaper by far than the imports. They would cause European food-
lovers to gag or guffaw—but generally the imitations are all that's available
in the supermarkets. People buy them and eat them.

Perhaps you don't like cheese—so the fact that decent cheese is hardly
ever served in America any more, or used in cooking, doesn't matter to
you. Well, take bread. There has been (and still is) something of a hulla-
baloo about bread. In fact, in the last few years, a few big bakeries have
taken to making a fairly good imitation of real bread. It costs much more
than what is nowadays called bread, but it is edible. Most persons, however, now eat as "bread" a substance so full of chemicals and so barren of
cereals that it approaches a synthetic.

Most bakers are interested mainly in how a loaf of bread looks. They
are concerned with how little stuff they can put in it—to get how much

money. They are deeply interested in using chemicals that will keep bread from molding, make it seem "fresh" for the longest possible time, and so render it marketable and shippable. They have been at this monkeyshine for a generation. Today a loaf of "bread" looks deceptively real; but it is made from heaven knows what and it resembles, as food, a solidified bubble bath. Some months ago I bought a loaf of the stuff and, experimentally, began pressing it together, like an accordion. With a little effort, I squeezed the whole loaf to a length of about one inch.

Yesterday, at the home of my mother-in-law, I ate with country-churned butter and home-canned wild strawberry jam several slices of actual bread, the same thing we used to have every day at home. People who have eaten actual bread will know what I mean. They will know that the material commonly called bread is not even related to real bread, except in name.

II

For years, I couldn't figure out what had happened to vegetables. I knew, of course, that most vegetables, to be enjoyed in their full deliciousness, must be picked fresh and cooked at once. I knew that vegetables cannot be overcooked and remain even edible, in the best sense. They cannot stand on the stove. That set of facts makes it impossible, of course, for any American restaurant—or, indeed, any city-dweller separated from supply by more than a few hours—to have decent fresh vegetables. The Parisians manage by getting their vegetables picked at dawn and rushed in farmers' carts to market, where no middleman or marketman delays produce on its way to the pot.

Our vegetables, however, come to us through a long chain of command. There are merchants of several sorts—wholesalers before the retailers, commission men, and so on—with the result that what were once edible products become, in transit, mere wilted leaves and withered tubers.

Homes and restaurants do what they can with this stuff—which my mother-in-law would discard on the spot. I have long thought that the famed blindfold test for cigarettes should be applied to city vegetables. For I am sure that if you puréed them and ate them blindfolded, you couldn't tell the beans from the peas, the turnips from the squash, the Brussels sprouts from the broccoli.

It is only lately that I have found how much science has to do with this reduction of noble victuals to pottage. Here the science of genetics is involved. Agronomists and the like have taken to breeding all sorts of vegetables and fruits—changing their original nature. This sounds wonderful and often is insane. For the scientists have not as a rule taken any interest whatsoever in the taste of the things they've tampered with!

What they've done is to develop "improved" strains of things for every purpose but eating. They work out, say, peas that will ripen all at once. The farmer can then harvest his peas and thresh them and be done with

them. It is extremely profitable because it is efficient. What matter if such peas taste like boiled paper wads?

Geneticists have gone crazy over such "opportunities." They've developed string beans that are straight instead of curved, and all one length. This makes them easier to pack in cans, even if, when eating them, you can't tell them from tender string. Ripening time and identity of size and shape are, nowadays, more important in carrots than the fact that they taste like carrots. Personally, I don't care if they hybridize onions till they are as big as your head and come up through the snow; but, in doing so, they are producing onions that only vaguely and feebly remind you of onions. We are getting some varieties, in fact, that have less flavor than the water off last week's leeks. Yet, if people don't eat onions because they taste like onions, what in the name of Luther Burbank do they eat them for?

The women's magazines are about one third dedicated to clothes, one third to mild comment on sex, and the other third to recipes and pictures of handsome salads, desserts, and main courses. "Institutes" exist to experiment and tell housewives how to cook attractive meals and how to turn leftovers into works of art. The food thus pictured looks like famous paintings of still life. The only trouble is it's tasteless. It leaves appetite unquenched and merely serves to stave off famine.

I wonder if this blandness of our diet doesn't explain why so many of us are overweight and even dangerously so. When things had flavor, we knew what we were eating all the while—and it satisfied us. A teaspoonful of my mother-in-law's wild strawberry jam will not just provide a gastronome's ecstasy: it will entirely satisfy your jam desire. But, of the average tinned or glass-packed strawberry jam, you need half a cupful to get the idea of what you're eating. A slice of my mother-in-law's apple pie will satiate you far better than a whole bakery pie.

That thought is worthy of investigation—of genuine scientific investigation. It is merely a hypothesis, so far, and my own. But people—and their ancestors—have been eating according to flavor for upwards of a billion years. The need to satisfy the sense of taste may be innate and important. When food is merely a pretty cascade of viands, with the texture of boiled cardboard and the flavor of library paste, it may be the instinct of *genus homo* to go on eating in the unconscious hope of finally satisfying the ageless craving of the frustrated taste buds. In the days when good-tasting food was the rule in the American home, obesity wasn't such a national curse.

How can you feel you've eaten if you haven't tasted, and fully enjoyed tasting? Why (since science is ever so ready to answer the beck and call of mankind) don't people who want to reduce merely give up eating and get the nourishment they must have in measured doses shot into their arms at hospitals? One ready answer to that question suggests that my

theory of overeating is sound: people like to taste! In eating, they try to satisfy that like.

The scientific war against deliciousness has been stepped up enormously in the last decade. Some infernal genius found a way to make biscuit batter keep. Housewives began to buy this premixed stuff. It saved work, of course. But any normally intelligent person can learn, in a short period, how to prepare superb baking powder biscuits. I can make better biscuits, myself, than can be made from patent batters. Yet soon after this fiasco became an American staple, it was discovered that a half-baked substitute for all sorts of breads, pastries, rolls, and the like could be mass-manufactured, frozen—and sold for polishing off in the home oven. None of these two-stage creations is as good as even a fair sample of the thing it imitates. A man of taste, who had eaten one of my wife's cinnamon buns, might use the premixed sort to throw at starlings—but not to eat! Cake mixes, too, come ready-prepared—like cement and not much better-tasting compared with true cake.

It is, however, "deep-freezing" that has really rung down the curtain on American cookery. Nothing is improved by the process. I have yet to taste a deep-frozen victual that measures up, in flavor, to the fresh, unfrosted original. And most foods, cooked or uncooked, are destroyed in the deep freeze for all people of sense and sensibility. Vegetables with crisp and crackling texture emerge as mush, slippery and stringy as hair nets simmered in Vaseline. The essential oils that make peas peas—and cabbage cabbage—must undergo fission and fusion in freezers. Anyhow, they vanish. Some meats turn to leather. Others to wood pulp. Everything, pretty much, tastes like the mosses of tundra, dug up in midwinter. Even the appearance changes, oftentimes. Handsome comestibles you put down in the summer come out looking very much like the corpses of woolly mammoths recovered from the last Ice Age.

Of course, all this scientific "food handling" tends to save money. It certainly preserves food longer. It reduces work at home. But these facts, and especially the last, imply that the first purpose of living is to avoid work—at home, anyhow.

Without thinking, we are making an important confession about ourselves as a nation. We are abandoning quality—even, to some extent, the quality of people. The "best" is becoming too good for us. We are suckling ourselves on machine-made mediocrity. It is bad for our souls, our minds, and our digestion. It is the way our wiser and calmer forebears fed, not people, but hogs: as much as possible and as fast as possible, with no standard of quality.

The Germans say, *"Mann ist was er isst*—Man is what he eats."* If this be true, the people of the U.S.A. are well on their way to becoming a faceless mob of mediocrities, of robots. And if we apply to other attributes the criteria we apply these days to appetite, that is what would happen!

We would not want bright children any more; we'd merely want them to look bright—and get through school fast. We wouldn't be interested in beautiful women—just a good paint job. And we'd be opposed to the most precious quality of man: his individuality, his differentness from the mob.

There are some people—sociologists and psychologists among them—who say that is exactly what we Americans are doing, are becoming. Mass man, they say, is on the increase. Conformity, standardization, similarity—all on a cheap and vulgar level—are replacing the great American ideas of colorful liberty and dignified individualism. If this is so, the process may well begin, like most human behavior, in the home—in those homes where a good meal has been replaced by something-to-eat-in-a-hurry. By something not very good to eat, prepared by a mother without very much to do, for a family that doesn't feel it amounts to much anyhow.

I call, here, for rebellion.

## TOPICS FOR DISCUSSION

1   What is it about American food that Wylie does not like? What does he use as a standard of excellence? Is it likely that this standard of excellence could exist in the city?

2   By what method does Wylie develop his criticism? What specific examples does he use?

3   What variety of effects are produced with his "Take cheese, for instance"?

4   What does the conversational style contribute to the tone of the essay? What specific examples of this style can you find? How might the essay have been altered by a more formal approach?

5   Can the malpractice of American restaurants be attributed to the "scientific war against deliciousness," or does Wylie lump together bad cooking and scientific developments?

6   Is Wylie really concerned with just food, or is food his occasion for some kind of larger attack? In the last several paragraphs, for instance, does he change direction, or is he consistent?

## ...AND COMPOSITION

7   Write an essay attacking Wylie's point of view, illustrating the advantages of scientific developments in food and of scientific developments generally.

8   Could one justly blame urbanization more than science for the changes in culinary practice?

9   Write an essay based on Wylie's thesis, using a formal style and different examples.

**WILLIAM BARRETT (1913–    )** speaks for general understanding of existentialism—that word so frequently used in discussions about our times. His *What Is Existentialism?* (1947) and *Irrational Man* (1958) are two direct presentations of the topic. In his varied career he has combined the academic—at the University of Illinois, Brown University, and New York University—and the literary, which has brought him into prominence as an editor of *The Partisan Review* and as a literary reviewer for *The Atlantic*.

# *Existentialism as a Symptom of Man's Contemporary Crisis*

Nowadays we speak quite easily and naturally of the crisis through which our civilization is passing. Without questioning the assumption that we are in the midst of a crisis, I should like to ask whether this feeling of crisis is not something inseparable from human life in any historical period. The more closely we examine the past, the more we find that it, too, is uneasy with its own sense of historical crisis and urgency. Sometimes, in retrospect, these crises look illusory, for mankind has survived some of its worst apprehensions; and then we have to remind ourselves that these men and women of the past felt that bygone crisis in their bones, with the same intimate uneasiness with which we feel ours. We begin to suspect that to live itself is to exist in crisis (more or less actual at any moment), and that only in periods of real historic somnolence and lethargy—real decadence, in short—has mankind been without a sense of crisis. No doubt, there are important differences of degree, and one age may be more plainly a period of breakdown than another; it would be folly to neglect such differences of degree, but the thought that crisis, or the sense of it is a

permanent part of human life, does fortify us to see our own contemporary crisis in a much broader light—as a total human condition.

This thought will explain why I prefer to discuss existential philosophy as a symptom, rather than a solution, of our present crisis. For to the degree that we see our crisis as a total and concrete condition, to that degree we shall doubt that any philosophy, no matter how ambitious, can propose itself as the unique path of salvation. Anyone who has had any personal experience of a spiritual crisis will know that recovery does not come through the acquisition of any new abstract ideas. The progress from health to sickness is a change of being, rather than a change in thought. So, if we agree that our civilization is spiritually sick, we should also expect that the recovery will not come through any single set of ideas, or philosophy, but only through a transformation of our whole existence—thus requiring social, economic, and religious change. A new philosophy would be only a necessary *part* of this total change.

Moreover, it is the very characteristic of Existentialism as a philosophy that it must look with irony upon any system of thought that proposes itself as *the* solution for all of life's crises. Let us remember that Kierkegaard, the founder of Existentialism, began to philosophize with the purpose of discovering difficulties, rather than offering easy and readymade solutions. Existentialism as a philosophy attempts to make man aware of certain basic realities of his life. In this sense it seeks to increase, rather than minimize, our human difficulties. The business of finding solutions must come only after a man is aware of the whole depth, import, and, therefore, difficulty, of his human life.

I

This preliminary definition of existential philosophy will be understood better, if we contrast it with the usual kinds of philosophy now taught in our academies. The various schools of philosophy are distinguished from each other by different beliefs. Thus it comes about that a philosophy is understood as a set of beliefs, or propositions, to which a man gives intellectual assent. A man is said to have a philosophy, then, if he has a system of propositions which he holds to be true on purely intellectual or rational grounds. This is the understanding of philosophy that has prevailed particularly in our period of the departmentalization of all human knowledge. But Existentialism seeks to restore a much more primitive sense of the word, "philosophy," than this: namely, the ancient sense of philosophy as a concrete way of life, rather than an abstract set of propositions. Nietzsche, also an Existentialist, pointed out that for ancient man, and even the modern Oriental, the business of achieving a philosophy is one that engaged the whole man, his total being, and was not pursued simply as one specialized department of knowledge among others. Kierkegaard attacked the Hegelian professors of his time as being philosophers

without any real philosophic existence: they had a system of propositions to teach, but the system itself was a means of forgetting the concrete realities of human life. For us in America today the philosopher is merely a "professional" savant among many others.

Existentialism, on the contrary, understands philosophy as a thing that is to be lived, and not merely a body of knowledge to be taught to pupils. I have said that Existentialism attempts to bring to human consciousness the basic, even banal, realities of human life: realities such as death, anxiety, choice, love, freedom, guilt, conscience, the willing acceptance of anxiety, etc., etc. In American academic philosophy today these are not the prevailing concepts: philosophers discuss concepts relating to science, knowledge, logic. Existential concepts are thought to belong to literature, perhaps to poetry. This rejection is an evidence of how far one particular tradition among the intellectual elite of our society has tended to set knowledge above life. If the philosopher exists professionally as a member of a department in a university, and if he accepts his role as one that deals with one special department of knowledge among others, then he is inevitably drawn to devote himself to those very special and technical problems that seem to be the peculiar province of the "expert." Our technological civilization has tended more and more to worship the expert, and the philosopher, assimilated to his civilization, strives more and more to justify his own professional existence by a high technical competence in the special problems of logic and philosophical analysis. The result is that a great deal of modern philosophy has tended to become divorced from life. Hence it is only natural that Existentialism, which struggles against this tendency, is looked on somewhat askance by a great many American philosophers.

All this has been by way of explaining why it seemed preferable to discuss Existentialism as a symptom, rather than a solution, of our contemporary crisis. But there has also been in the background of my remarks another, and much more drastic point, which will be substantiated by my further discussion, but can be announced now: the point, quite simply, that there is never a solution to any of life's crises. This is one of the cardinal points in existential philosophy itself. The word, "solution," belongs to the vocabulary of science and engineering, suggesting some kind of blueprint that would immediately deliver us from the pain and muddle of suffering, when, in fact, we know that our really deep crises in life are precisely those that we have to live through. Our deepest personal problems do not in the least resemble any problem of engineering, and it is the same, we suggest, with the sickness of civilization, even though the "cure" of a sick civilization might require vast exploits of engineering.

II

That movement in thought should be a symptom of its time, is not in the least a condemnation of this movement as a wild or trivial aberra-

tion. I am using the word, "symptom," in its simple and unprejudiced sense of a sign—something that instructs us about the state of the organism from which it arises. Thus Existentialism has a great deal to teach us—which we might otherwise not know—about the condition of the Western civilization that has brought it to birth.

Most Americans connect Existentialism with the current French movement, and particularly with the name of its most brilliant publicist, Jean Paul Sartre. Sartre's is an agile and energetic mind, but his doctrine represents, I believe, a dilution of existential philosophy, and in any case does not take us back to its original sources. These lie in the nineteenth century, and the great innovators are Kierkegaard and Nietzsche—though the latter, unlike Kierkegaard, is not fully aware of his existential point of departure. Existential themes are treated in the fiction of Tolstoi and Dostoievski. In this century the two most important existential philosophers have been the German professors, Martin Heidegger and Karl Jaspers. To these names we might add the considerable figure of the Spanish philosopher, José Ortega y Gasset, who has described his philosophy as one of "vital reason," though it is fundamentally existential in its directions. These names should indicate that Existentialism is not a momentary intellectual fad, derived from the French, but a much wider and deeper movement in Western thought, having roots indeed in the profound upheavals of this civilization during the past two centuries. To see what these roots are, we may find it more convenient to turn, not to an abstruse text in philosophy, but to a work of literature that takes a simpler and more direct grasp of the issues involved: Tolstoi's great story, "The Death of Ivan Ilyich," which by this time has become something of a basic scripture for existential thought.

The plot of Tolstoi's story is slight and almost negligible. Ivan Ilyich is an amiable and undistinguished bourgeois, who has spent his whole life trying to be like everyone else in his social class: a successful and happy man, where happiness means only the absence of suffering. But one day Ivan Ilyich feels a pain in his side, which resists all treatment by doctors, and as his illness progresses, he suddenly realizes that he is going to die. For the first time in his life death becomes a reality for him. In the face of this awful presence, all his disguises fall away: confronting death for the first time in his life, he is also confronting himself for the first time. Hitherto in his life he had hid from himself amid the routine mechanisms of all his social, official, and familial functions. Now, as he is about to die, he asks himself the questions: Who am I? What has been the meaning of my life? In the end Ivan Ilyich dies content, because he has reached the point of knowing that the life he lived was empty, futile, and meaningless.

What Tolstoi is saying here, to put it now as a general thesis, is that modern life has alienated the individual from himself. The materialistic and rationalistic nineteenth century, with its emphasis upon all the bourgeois routines of life, has so externalized the individual that he has lost the

feeling and the passion for his own personal existence. Modern man, Tolstoi is saying, has lost the meaning of life, and, as with Ivan Ilyich, it will take nothing less than the presence of death to restore this sense of life.

The sense of decadence haunts the nineteenth century, even at the moments of its most splendid optimism. There is a widespread uneasiness that life has lost its passion, intensity, and meaning; that there has been some secret decline in human vitality. Kierkegaard puts it as eloquently and compactly as one could wish:

> Let others complain that times are bad; I complain that they are petty because they lack passion. Men's thoughts are as flimsy as thin ice and men themselves as insignificant as the thin snow that covers it. Their thoughts are too petty to be sinful. A worm might consider such thoughts to be sinful, but not a man created in the image of God. Their pleasures are circumspect and boring; their passions, sleep; these materialistic souls fulfill their duties, but they collect their usury for it; they believe that although our Lord keeps His accounts in good order, they can hand Him counterfeit. Out with them! This is why my soul always hearkens back to Shakespeare and the Old Testament. There one feels that those who speak are men; there they hate; there they love; there they kill the enemy, curse their descendants for generations to come, there they sin.

This passage might almost have been written by Nietzsche, who launches his plea from the diametrically opposite anti-christian pole. Modern man, says Nietzsche, lacks a goal, and his existence is, therefore, purposeless and nihilistic. Similar themes appear also in such diverse writers as Stendhal and Burckhardt.

The twentieth century has no reason to forget these fears. Our technological civilization has become even more involved with elaborate apparatus to catch and smother the individual. We have gone beyond the nineteenth century in the development of a fantastic mass culture—in radio, movies, and television—that stamps out all individual differences. Modern society has become more and more a mass society. Cities grow larger, crowds become more and more potent factors, and the individual threatened more than ever by anonymity in the mass. The image of modern man lies in T. S. Eliot's line: "Men and bits of paper, whirled by the cold wind."[1] These fears of the nineteenth century turn out to be prophetic for us: amid this general purposelessness of life, this mass drifting, we set ourselves the task of recapturing the sense and the meaning of life.

## III

When Tolstoi speaks of a loss of the meaning of life, he is not referring to a loss of some rational explanation. Nor is the meaning that is to be restored an intellectual one, some new fact or discovery of the mind. On

---

[1] T. S. Eliot, "Burnt Norton," *Collected Poems of T. S. Eliot*, 1909–1935, Harcourt, Brace & Company, New York, 1936, p. 217.

the contrary, the disorder in modern man that Tolstoi's story speaks of is a disorder in the more primitive and irrational, or non-rational, parts of man's being. Existentialism as a philosophy seeks to deal with these irrational parts of our existence in a way that philosophy has never done before, and by so doing gives reason itself a new place in the human hierarchy.

This is why existential philosophy has been frequently—and, I think, unjustly—criticized as anti-rational. One is not against reason, if one insists that the irrational is an inseparable part of life, and that it is precisely with the irrational parts of our being that modern civilization fails to deal adequately. This so-called "anti-rational" tendency in modern philosophy has now had a long history, from Rousseau to Bergson, Whitehead, and Heidegger in our century, and it embraces too many great names to be dismissed out of hand. Any future rationalism worth its salt will have to assimilate a great deal from these thinkers, and we ourselves would be less than rational, if we did not make an earnest effort to understand in detail how the irrational enters human life.

We gain some idea of the irrational character of life, if we turn back again to Tolstoi's "Ivan Ilyich." As death appears to Ivan Ilyich, it presents itself as something altogether unreasonable and incomprehensible. Immersed in the comfortable structure of his life, he sees this strange and dark intruder creep in to destroy everything. Yes, death is a banal fact, and we know that all men have to die; Ivan Ilyich knows all this with his head, but his heart cannot grasp the incomprehensible fact that he, Ivan Ilyich, should have to die. This bewilderment may strike us as childish, but it is Tolstoi's means of showing us how the irrational, like death, may fall upon us in the most incalculable and unpredictable way, upsetting all our plans for life.

Kierkegaard has expounded the presence of the irrational in another area of human life—in the act of choice or decision. We do not doubt that some decisions are more rational than others, and we may even speak of a decision as being the only rational choice under the circumstances. But is a rational choice one from which the irrational is ever completely excluded? Is any choice, however rational it be, free from the uncertain contingencies of risk and adventure? Of course, there are certain trivial choices that we make every day, and that we may reverse the next day, if we are proved wrong. But these are choices that do not commit us deeply, that leave us relatively disengaged from the consequences. As soon, however, as a choice cuts deeply; as soon as it commits our whole life in a certain direction; so soon, then, do the immense difficulties appear, the balance of probabilities becomes harder, and each alternative appears, however we may canvass its possibilities, as a leap into the unknown.

The choice that personally involved Kierkegaard happened to be the question whether or not to marry. Engaged to a young woman in Copenhagen, he desired marriage intensely, but he felt in himself also a certain religious mission that would prevent him from giving himself completely

in marriage. The particular psychological facts involved here are important for an understanding of Kierkegaard's biography, but the peculiarly personal difficulties should not obscure for us the fact that the pathos of choice Kierkegaard faced is universal. There are, in short, choices in life that are irreversible. Kierkegaard could not have made an *experimental* choice of marriage, in the expectation that if it "did not work out"—to use the expression that has become common among us these days—he could return to his religious vocation and its tasks, for the vocation might have been lost through his marriage. On the other hand, if he renounced marriage experimentally, he could not hope to return to the young lady, should the other alternative not work out. She might not be there (as in fact she was not) when he returned. Love has to be seized at the moment it is offered; our indecision pollutes and destroys it.

All of this points to the fact that the situation of human choice is not at all a situation of scientific experiment. A situation is experimental in science when certain scientific controls have been established, so that through these controls we can repeat the experiment at any time and place we choose, and indeed repeat it indefinitely. The more precisely scientific the experiment becomes, the more its features of accidental particularity become refined away, and the easier it becomes to repeat it in all its detail. But our fundamental choices in life do not permit us this degree of control, because they do not permit us this degree of detachment. We have to choose here and now, and for the rest of our life, and the alternative we renounce is lost forever. We could be completely experimental about our own lives only if we were immortal, and so could repeat any situation or choice indefinitely.

But as death is real and our lives finite, every choice is also a renunciation, and this is why Kierkegaard speaks of the *pathos* of human choice. It was this sacrificial and pathetic aspect of choice that led Kierkegaard to his great polemic against the excessively rational philosophy of Hegel. The old adage puts the matter quite simply and adequately, "You cannot eat your cake and have it, too"; but Hegel devised a sophisticated dialectic by which it was possible to bring together two conflicting alternatives, thesis and antithesis, into a higher synthesis, so that the speculative philosopher, triumphing over life, could both have his cake and eat it, too. Such a reconciling of opposites is indeed possible in knowledge, where a more inclusive theory may embrace two conflicting alternatives; but it is not possible in life, where the suffering of renunciation cannot be altogether eliminated by reason. This opposition between knowledge and life has been one of the chief themes of Existentialism, as well as of a great deal of modern philosophy and literature.

IV

These two brief illustrations of the irrational—death and human choice —which cannot be altogether expunged from our existence, also illustrate

that science, and scientific experiment, cannot take over the whole of life. The fear that science might devour the whole of human life has been a very powerful current of thought in the West, from William Blake onward. Indeed, from the Enlightenment in the eighteenth century to the present day, two deeply opposed attitudes toward science have dominated Western thinking: along with the great hope in science and its possibilities of human liberation, there has developed a great fear that science would somehow mechanize and impoverish human life. This fear of science cannot be dismissed simply as a crude popular superstition, for it embraces too many great names of our culture: Blake, Wordsworth, Kierkegaard, Nietzsche, Dostoievski, Tolstoi, Bergson. Our task, rather, should be to disengage the philosophical traits that characterize this fear of science at its deepest level.

One of the best expressions of the fear of science is found in the first part of Dostoievski's great novel, *Notes from Underground*. The hero is afraid of the scientific society of the future, in which human life can be rationally controlled and ordered, down to the very last detail. When human life is so scientifically precise and predictable, nobody would want to live it. Dostoievski's hero would prefer to smash this machine that would seek to contain him—out of sheer spite, as he puts it—to show that his human will in its liberty transcends the mathematically predictable, even if he has to show this in a destructive way. We come back thus to our principal point: what Dostoievski is saying, through his tormented and oppressed little hero, is that human life must be more than pure reason, and to attempt to reduce it to the latter is to destroy it, even if we make that reduction in the name of universal enlightenment.

It would be a mistake to consider the Underground Man as merely a sick and neurotic individual produced by the stresses of modern society. He is that, of course, but he is also a universal human character. We are all the Underground Man, to some degree or other. He is that dark side of our being, with which we must try to live in peace, and if we take lightly his fulminations against a human regime completely controlled by science and reason, we do so at our own risk.

As he is thus universal, the Underground Man reappears, and perhaps I may drive home my point by turning to the rather extraordinary position advanced in the nineteen hundred and twenties by I. A. Richards, the British critic and psychologist—a position that seems to me to express the extreme of hope that science will master life. (In justice to Richards, however, we must point out that at the time he was much more enamored of the possibilities of psychology than he is today.) Richards contended nothing less than this: that we can anticipate the time when psychological science will have advanced to the point where we can have, if we choose, whatever minds we desire. In the perfectly scientific utopia, in short, you could order your personality at a psychological laboratory the way you might order a prescription at a druggist's. Select your label, follow the

prescription carefully, and you will have the personality, or the mind, that you want. Science which has performed so many miracles in the transformation of matter, and has found synthetic substitutes for almost everything, would here have found at last a substitute for life itself. In this psychological utopia it would be possible for a man to have a certain character without living through the risks, anxieties, and uncertain struggles that make it. We need not live to become a certain kind of being; science would provide it readymade.

We notice that this possibility that once inspired Richards with such hopes, is precisely the possibility against which Dostoievski's Underground Man rebels. Sick and resentful though he may be, the Underground Man at least insists upon having his own human life, rather than some mechanized substitute for it. The science of psychology has gone on developing since Richards's remark, but it is now further from maintaining any such utopian claims as once enchanted him. Among some circles in America, psychoanalysis may be regarded as a kind of magic, but not by the analysts themselves. Some people tend to think of psychoanalysis as a process in which the analyst, somewhat like a mechanic, overhauls the patient and gives him a new engine or set of works. But the serious analyst, while hoping to transform the neurotic patient's fundamental orientations toward life, insists that the patient can solve his problems only in actual life and not in the psychoanalytic session. Life has to be lived, there is no substitute for living—not even psychoanalysis.

Existential philosophy, in its insistence that the categories of life cannot be reduced to science, carries this point further. It may seem a rather trivial platitude to say that there can be no substitute for living, but the saying may not strike us as so platitudinous when we reflect upon the vast mechanized passivity that our civilization imposes upon so many of its members. In such circumstances the living rediscovery of certain banalities may represent an immense task and an immense triumph. Some of the greatest chapters in the history of philosophy are its discoveries of what lay obvious, but unnoticed, before every man's eyes. We may recall the great saying of Heraclitus, at the very dawn of philosophy in the sixth century B.C.: "Man is estranged from that with which he is most familiar, and he must continuously seek to rediscover it." This saying might serve as a very good motto for Existentialism. Among other things, it may make clear why the modern Existentialist, Heidegger, finds these early pre-Socratic Greeks his real forebears in the effort to confront human life and the whole life of nature with a primitive directness. The ancestry of existential philosophy thus turns out to be very ancient. I come back thus to a point made at the beginning, which should now be considerably clearer in its import: Existentialism, a modern movement in philosophy, is, in fact, an effort to recapture an old and very primitive sense of philosophy. Philosophy, here, is not the mere putting together of certain abstract propositions into a system; it is rather the concrete effort of the living individual to

relate himself to his own life and the life of others around him. Quite literally, philosophy is a task that each individual has to perform for himself.

## V

In this search for the primitive, Existentialism is in line with the most considerable movements in art and literature in this century. The word, "primitive," here is bound to arouse misunderstandings, if it is associated with the life of savages, barbarians, or big game hunters. Primitivism suggests to some the beat of tom-toms, Tahiti, maidens in sarongs, Gauguin; in short, an escape from modern civilization into the illusory simplicities of some South Sea island. These forms of primitivism have abounded, but they have always ended in a blind alley, because the desire for escape is itself a very non-primitive state of being. I am using the word, "primitive," in a much more basic—I almost wrote primitive—sense: the primitive is the primary; and the valid search for the primitive is a search for the sources of our being which a too routinized civilization tends to obscure. In this sense, nearly all the art and literature that matter in the past half century have been primitive.

Modern painting and sculpture, for example, have really succeeded in creating a new kind of vision. In these works we stand in a new and more direct relation to colors, shapes, and forms. It is a vision of things at once simpler and more complex than the Western art of the past. In its distorting simplifications, bold arbitrary forms, it often resembles primitive art, from which indeed it has consciously drawn inspiration in certain cases, though it could not exist without the whole tradition of Western art. Moreover, the artist himself seems to stand in a new and direct relation to the very materials of his art: he seeks naively to assert the presence of his paint, stone, or metal, and his art is no longer a device to conceal or transcend this presence.

In literature, in writers such as D. H. Lawrence, James Joyce, and Thomas Mann, we find similar and diverging efforts to deal with the primitive. In his Joseph stories, Mann seeks to restore the primitive mythic consciousness to literature. James Joyce, in his last work, uses the most sophisticated literary technique, drawing upon the whole past of Western literature for its resources, in order to render the most unconscious, inarticulate, and primitive parts of human experience. Of these writers perhaps Lawrence is the most explicitly programmatic in his search for the primitive simplicities that he believes modern life to have lost. The organic unity of being that Lawrence seeks through sexual experience, is something that existential philosophers have sought in other directions. As T. S. Eliot reminds us, Lawrence was a man with an intense spiritual vocation, and his interest in sex was not at all a message of sex-for-sex's sake. Nevertheless, his proposed solution to the sickness of modern civilization seems to us today to be rather onesided. His perception of the sickness was real enough, but his prescription for cure represents a kind of impatient rush

toward a solution. We are reminded, again, that when a sickness is total, the recovery can come only through development along many avenues of being at once.

This list could be swelled indefinitely to show that this struggle for rebirth is one of the great themes of modern culture. I have appended these brief indications to my main discussion only to point to the total historical context in which we must try to see the development of modern existential philosophy; and to suggest that this philosophy is not an eccentric movement, but lies in the main stream of modern culture. Existentialism makes clearer the human tasks that our epoch confronts. Unless we realize what the tasks are, we can hardly work significantly toward any solution at all.

## TOPICS FOR DISCUSSION

1   Why has existentialism been better represented by poets, novelists, and short-story writers than by professional philosophers? Do you think the nature of the concept will always make this so?

2   What is the distinction between knowledge and life? How does this counter the charge of existentialism as antirational?

3   In what ways has modern science intensified the crisis of man's existence? Is this understanding of science compatible with that of C. P. Snow ("The Two Cultures")? Is it similar to your attitudes toward science?

4   How must the word "primitive" be understood in this essay?

5   Has your impression of existentalism been altered by reading this essay? Prior to reading this essay, where did you get your information regarding this philosophy?

6   By what means does section 1 further clarify the definition of existential philosophy? How is this distinction crucial to understanding existential philosophy as a symptom of man's sickness rather than a cure for it?

## ... AND COMPOSITION

7   In the context of this essay, write a short paper on some reading in one of the following: Kierkegaard, Nietzsche, Dostoevski, Tolstoi, Blake, Bergson, or Sartre.

8   "We begin to suspect that to live itself is to exist in crisis. . . ." Comment.

9   Although existentialism offers no systematic solution to man's crisis, it offers a tentative kind of hope. Consider the way this philosophy can help make life palatable.

**BERTRAND RUSSELL (1872–    )** in his long, active life has taught at
Cambridge, California, Harvard, Peking, and elsewhere, and has
combined mathematics, philosophy, social reform, and even writing fiction
in his career. Early in that career he distinguished himself in mathematics and
with Alfred North Whitehead published an influential book, *Principia
Mathematica.* Since the time of World War I, when his pacifist
stand brought prison and notoriety, he has championed unpopular
causes. In recent years he has provided counsel, prestige, and
fiery partisanship to campaigns for nuclear disarmament.

# A Free Man's Worship

To Dr. Faustus in his study Mephistopheles told the history of the
Creation, saying:

"The endless praises of the choirs of angels had begun to grow weari-
some; for, after all, did he not deserve their praise? Had he not given them
endless joy? Would it not be more amusing to obtain undeserved praise,
to be worshipped by beings whom he tortured? He smiled inwardly, and
resolved that the great drama should be performed.

"For countless ages the hot nebula whirled aimlessly through space.
At length it began to take shape, the central mass threw off planets, the
planets cooled, boiling seas and burning mountains heaved and tossed, from
black masses of cloud hot sheets of rain deluged the barely solid crust. And
now the first germ of life grew in the depths of the ocean, and developed
rapidly in the fructifying warmth into vast forest trees, huge ferns springing
from the damp mould, sea monsters breeding, fighting, devouring, and
passing away. And from the monsters, as the play unfolded itself, Man
was born, with the power of thought, the knowledge of good and evil,
and the cruel thirst for worship. And Man saw that all is passing in this
mad, monstrous world, that all is struggling to snatch, at any cost, a few
brief moments of life before Death's inexorable decree. And Man said:
'There is a hidden purpose, could we but fathom it, and the purpose is
good; for we must reverence something, and in the visible world there
is nothing worthy of reverence.' And Man stood aside from the struggle,
resolving that God intended harmony to come out of chaos by human
efforts. And when he followed the instincts which God had transmitted to
him from his ancestry of beasts of prey, he called it Sin, and asked God
to forgive him. But he doubted whether he could be justly forgiven, until
he invented a divine Plan by which God's wrath was to have been appeased.
And seeing the present was bad, he made it yet worse, that thereby the
future might be better. And he gave God thanks for the strength that
enabled him to forgo even the joys that were possible. And God smiled;

and when he saw that Man had become perfect in renunciation and worship, he sent another sun through the sky, which crashed into Man's sun; and all returned again to nebula.

" 'Yes,' he murmured, 'it was a good play; I will have it performed again.' "

Such, in outline, but even more purposeless, more void of meaning, is the world which Science presents for our belief. Amid such a world, if anywhere, our ideals henceforward must find a home. That Man is the product of causes which had no prevision of the end they were achieving; that his origin, his growth, his hopes and fears, his loves and his beliefs, are but the outcome of accidental collocations of atoms; that no fire, no heroism, no intensity of thought and feeling, can preserve an individual life beyond the grave; that all the labours of the ages, all the devotion, all the inspiration, all the noonday brightness of human genius, are destined to extinction in the vast death of the solar system, and that the whole temple of Man's achievement must inevitably be buried beneath the debris of a universe in ruins—all these things, if not quite beyond dispute, are yet so nearly certain, that no philosophy which rejects them can hope to stand. Only within the scaffolding of these truths, only on the firm foundation of unyielding despair, can the soul's habitation henceforth be safely built.

How, in such an alien and inhuman world, can so powerless a creature as Man preserve his aspirations untarnished? A strange mystery it is that Nature, omnipotent but blind, in the revolutions of her secular hurryings through the abysses of space, has brought forth at last a child, subject still to her power, but gifted with sight, with knowledge of good and evil, with the capacity of judging all the works of his unthinking Mother. In spite of Death, the mark and seal of the parental control, Man is yet free, during his brief years, to examine, to criticise, to know, and in imagination to create. To him alone, in the world with which he is acquainted, this freedom belongs; and in this lies his superiority to the resistless forces that control his outward life.

The savage, like ourselves, feels the oppression of his impotence before the powers of Nature; but having in himself nothing that he respects more than Power, he is willing to prostrate himself before his gods, without inquiring whether they are worthy of his worship. Pathetic and very terrible is the long history of cruelty and torture, of degradation and human sacrifice endured in the hope of placating the jealous gods: surely, the trembling believer thinks, when what is most precious has been freely given, their lust for blood must be appeased, and more will not be required. The religion of Moloch—as such creeds may be generically called—is in essence the cringing submission of the slave, who dare not, even in his heart, allow the thought that his master deserves no adulation. Since the independence of ideals is not yet acknowledged, Power may be freely worshipped, and receive an unlimited respect, despite its wanton infliction of pain.

But gradually, as morality grows bolder, the claim of the ideal world begins to be felt; and worship, if it is not to cease, must be given to gods of another kind than those created by the savage. Some, though they feel the demands of the ideal, will still consciously reject them, still urging that naked Power is worthy of worship. Such is the attitude inculcated in God's answer to Job out of the whirlwind; the divine power and knowledge are paraded, but of the divine goodness there is no hint. Such also is the attitude of those who, in our own day, base their morality upon the struggle for survival, maintaining that the survivors are necessarily the fittest. But others, not content with an answer so repugnant to the moral sense, will adopt the position which we have become accustomed to regard as specially religious, maintaining that, in some hidden manner, the world of fact is really harmonious with the world of ideals. Thus Man creates God, all-powerful and all-good, the mystic unity of what is and what should be.

But the world of fact, after all, is not good; and, in submitting our judgment to it, there is an element of slavishness from which our thoughts must be purged. For in all things it is well to exalt the dignity of Man, by freeing him as far as possible from the tyranny of non-human Power. When we have realised that Power is largely bad, that Man, with his knowledge of good and evil, is but a helpless atom in a world which has no such knowledge, the choice is again presented to us: Shall we worship Force, or shall we worship Goodness? Shall our God exist and be evil, or shall he be recognised as the creation of our own conscience?

The answer to this question is very momentous, and affects profoundly our whole morality. The worship of Force, to which Carlyle and Neitzsche and the creed of Militarism have accustomed us, is the result of failure to maintain our own ideals against a hostile universe: it is itself a prostrate submission to evil, a sacrifice of our best to Moloch. If strength indeed is to be respected, let us respect rather the strength of those who refuse that false "recognition of facts" which fails to recognise that facts are often bad. Let us admit that, in the world we know, there are many things that would be better otherwise, and that the ideals to which we do and must adhere are not realised in the realm of matter. Let us preserve our respect for truth, for beauty, for the ideal of perfection which life does not permit us to attain, though none of these things meet with the approval of the unconscious universe. If Power is bad, as it seems to be, let us reject it from our hearts. In this lies Man's true freedom: in determination to worship only the God created by our own love of the good, to respect only the heaven which inspires the insight of our best moments. In action, in desire, we must submit perpetually to the tyranny of outside forces; but in thought, in aspiration, we are free, free from our fellow-men, free from the petty planet on which our bodies impotently crawl, free even, while we live, from the tyranny of death. Let us learn, then, that energy of faith which enables us to live constantly in the vision of the good; and let us descend in action, into the world of fact, with that vision always before us.

When first the opposition of fact and ideal grows fully visible, a spirit of fiery revolt, of fierce hatred of the gods, seems necessary to the assertion of freedom. To defy with Promethean constancy a hostile universe, to keep its evil always in view, always actively hated, to refuse no pain that the malice of Power can invent, appears to be the duty of all who will not bow before the inevitable. But indignation is still a bondage, for it compels our thoughts to be occupied with an evil world; and in the fierceness of desire from which rebellion springs there is a kind of self-assertion which it is necessary for the wise to overcome. Indignation is a submission of our thoughts, but not of our desires; the Stoic freedom in which wisdom consists is found in the submission of our desires, but not of our thoughts. From the submission of our desires springs the virtue of resignation; from the freedom of our thoughts springs the whole world of art and philosophy, and the vision of beauty by which, at last, we half reconquer the reluctant world. But the vision of beauty is possible only to unfettered contemplation, to thoughts not weighted by the load of eager wishes; and thus Freedom comes only to those who no longer ask of life that it shall yield them any of those personal goods that are subject to the mutations of Time.

Although the necessity of renunciation is evidence of the existence of evil, yet Christianity, in preaching it, has shown a wisdom exceeding that of the Promethean philosophy of rebellion. It must be admitted that, of the things we desire, some, though they prove impossible, are yet real goods; others, however, as ardently longed for, do not form part of a fully purified ideal. The belief that what must be renounced is bad, though sometimes false, is far less often false than untamed passion supposes; and the creed of religion, by providing a reason for proving that it is never false, has been the means of purifying our hopes by the discovery of many austere truths.

But there is in resignation a further good element: even real goods, when they are unattainable, ought not to be fretfully desired. To every man comes, sooner or later, the great renunciation. For the young, there is nothing unattainable; a good thing desired with the whole force of a passionate will and yet impossible, is to them not credible. Yet, by death, by illness, by poverty, or by the voice of duty, we must learn, each one of us, that the world was not made for us, and that, however beautiful may be the things we crave, Fate may nevertheless forbid them. It is the part of courage, when misfortune comes, to bear without repining the ruin of our hopes, to turn away our thoughts from vain regrets. This degree of submission to Power is not only just and right; it is the very gate of wisdom.

But passive renunciation is not the whole of wisdom; for not by renunciation alone can we build a temple for the worship of our own ideals. Haunting foreshadowings of the temple appear in the realm of imagination, in music, in architecture, in the untroubled kingdom of reason, and in the

golden sunset magic of lyrics, where beauty shines and glows, remote from the touch of sorrow, remote from the fear of change, remote from the failures and disenchantments of the world of fact. In the contemplation of these things the vision of heaven will shape itself in our hearts, giving at once a touchstone to judge the world about us, and an inspiration by which to fashion to our needs whatever is not incapable of serving as a stone in the sacred temple.

Except for those rare spirits that are born without sin, there is a cavern of darkness to be traversed before that temple can be entered. The gate of the cavern is despair, and its floor is paved with the gravestones of abandoned hopes. There Self must die; there the eagerness, the greed of untamed desire must be slain, for only so can the soul be freed from the empire of Fate. But out of the cavern the Gate of Renunciation leads again to the daylight of wisdom, by whose radiance a new insight, a new joy, a new tenderness, shine forth to gladden the pilgrim's heart.

When, without the bitterness of impotent rebellion, we have learnt both to resign ourselves to the outward rule of Fate and to recognise that the non-human world is unworthy of our worship, it becomes possible at last so to transform and refashion the unconscious universe, so to transmute it in the crucible of the imagination, that a new image of shining gold replaces the old idol of clay. In all the multiform facts of the world—in the visual shapes of trees and mountains and clouds, in the events of the life of Man, even in the very omnipotence of Death—the insight of creative idealism can find the reflection of a beauty which its own thoughts first made. In this way mind asserts its subtle mastery over the thoughtless forces of Nature. The more evil the material with which it deals, the more thwarting to untrained desire, the greater is its achievement in inducing the reluctant rock to yield up its hidden treasures, the prouder its victory in compelling the opposing forces to swell the pageant of its triumph. Of all the arts, Tragedy is the proudest, the most triumphant; for it builds its shining citadel in the very centre of the enemy's country, on the very summit of his highest mountain; from its impregnable watch-towers, his camps and arsenals, his columns and forts, are all revealed; within its walls the free life continues, while the legions of Death and Pain and Despair, and all the servile captains of tyrant Fate, afford the burghers of that dauntless city new spectacles of beauty. Happy those sacred ramparts, thrice happy the dwellers on that all-seeing eminence. Honour to those brave warriors who, through countless ages of warfare, have preserved for us the priceless heritage of liberty, and have kept undefiled by sacrilegious invaders the home of the unsubdued.

But the beauty of Tragedy does but make visible a quality which, in more or less obvious shapes, is present always and everywhere in life. In the spectacle of Death, in the endurance of intolerable pain, and in the irrevocableness of a vanished past, there is a sacredness, an overpowering

awe, a feeling of the vastness, the depth, the inexhaustible mystery of existence, in which, as by some strange marriage of pain, the sufferer is bound to the world by bonds of sorrow. In these moments of insight, we lose all eagerness of temporary desire, all struggling and striving for petty ends, all care for the little trivial things, that, to a superficial view, make up the common life of day by day; we see, surrounding the narrow raft illumined by the flickering light of human comradeship, the dark ocean on whose rolling waves we toss for a brief hour; from the great night without, a chill blast breaks in upon our refuge; all the loneliness of humanity amid hostile forces is concentrated upon the individual soul, which must struggle alone, with what of courage it can command, against the whole weight of a universe that cares nothing for its hopes and fears. Victory, in this struggle with the powers of darkness, is the true baptism into the glorious company of heroes, the true initiation into the overmastering beauty of human existence. From that awful encounter of the soul with the outer world, renunciation, wisdom, and charity are born; and with their birth a new life begins. To take into the inmost shrine of the soul the irresistible forces whose puppets we seem to be—Death and change, the irrevocableness of the past, and the powerlessness of Man before the blind hurry of the universe from vanity to vanity—to feel these things and know them is to conquer them.

This is the reason why the Past has such magical power. The beauty of its motionless and silent pictures is like the enchanted purity of late autumn, when the leaves, though one breath would make them fall, still glow against the sky in golden glory. The Past does not change or strive; like Duncan, after life's fitful fever it sleeps well; what was eager and grasping, what was petty and transitory, has faded away, the things that were beautiful and eternal shine out of it like stars in the night. Its beauty, to a soul not worthy of it, is unendurable; but to a soul which has conquered Fate it is the key of religion.

The life of Man, viewed outwardly, is but a small thing in comparison with the forces of Nature. The slave is doomed to worship Time and Fate and Death, because they are greater than anything he finds in himself, and because all his thoughts are of things which they devour. But, great as they are, to think of them greatly, to feel their passionless splendour, is greater still. And such thought makes us free men; we no longer bow before the inevitable in Oriental subjection, but we absorb it, and make it a part of ourselves. To abandon the struggle for private happiness, to expel all eagerness of temporary desire, to burn with passion for eternal things—this is emancipation, and this is the free man's worship. And this liberation is effected by a contemplation of Fate; for Fate itself is subdued by the mind which leaves nothing to be purged by the purifying fire of Time.

United with his fellow-men by the strongest of all ties, the tie of a

common doom, the free man finds that a new vision is with him always, shedding over every daily task the light of love. The life of Man is a long march through the night, surrounded by invisible foes, tortured by weariness and pain, towards a goal that few can hope to reach, and where none may tarry long. One by one, as they march, our comrades vanish from our sight, seized by the silent orders of omnipotent Death. Very brief is the time in which we can help them, in which their happiness or misery is decided. Be it ours to shed sunshine on their path, to lighten their sorrows by the balm of sympathy, to give them the pure joy of a never-tiring affection, to strengthen failing courage, to instil faith in hours of despair. Let us not weigh in grudging scales their merits and demerits, but let us think only of their need—of the sorrows, the difficulties, perhaps the blindnesses, that make the misery of their lives; let us remember that they are fellow-sufferers in the same darkness, actors in the same tragedy with ourselves. And so, when their day is over, when their good and their evil have become eternal by the immortality of the past, be it ours to feel that, where they suffered, where they failed, no deed of ours was the cause; but wherever a spark of the divine fire kindled in their hearts, we were ready with encouragement, with sympathy, with brave words in which high courage glowed.

Brief and powerless is Man's life; on him and all his race the slow, sure doom falls pitiless and dark. Blind to good and evil, reckless of destruction, omnipotent matter rolls on its relentless way; for Man, condemned to-day to lose his dearest, to-morrow himself to pass through the gate of darkness, it remains only to cherish, ere yet the blow falls, the lofty thoughts that ennoble his little day; disdaining the coward terrors of the slave of Fate, to worship at the shrine that his own hands have built; undismayed by the empire of chance, to preserve a mind free from the wanton tyranny that rules his outward life; proudly defiant of the irresistible forces that tolerate, for a moment, his knowledge and his condemnation, to sustain alone, a weary but unyielding Atlas, the world that his own ideals have fashioned despite the trampling march of unconscious Power.

## TOPICS FOR DISCUSSION

1  The author is famous in the fields of mathematics and philosophy. His essay abounds in "poetic" language—figures of speech, analogies, allusions, emotional terminology. How do you account for this apparent disjunction? Is the strategy of the essay based on some kind of logical progression? Can you find a basis in reason for the elation the author expresses about the possibilities in man?

2   "How, in such an alien and inhuman world, can so powerless a
creature as Man preserve his aspirations untarnished?" asks
Russell early in his essay. His answer is the presentation and
analysis of alternatives: "Shall we worship Force, or shall we
worship Goodness?" What are the characteristics of the alternatives? How is a third alternative removed from consideration in
paragraphs 1 and 2, page 353? Do you agree that the two
alternatives remaining, force and goodness, are the only ones?
Why is it important that only two alternatives remain?

3   What, for Russell, is the beauty of tragedy? How can misery
bring wisdom?

4   Why does the author consider a bitter rebellion against the world
of fact still a submission to that world?

5   What special effects are achieved in the inverted word order of
the following sentence from page 352? "A strange mystery it
is that Nature, omnipotent but blind, in the revolutions of her
secular hurryings through the abysses of space, has brought
forth at last a child, subject still to her power, but gifted with
sight, with knowledge of good and evil, with the capacity of
judging all the works of his unthinking Mother." Can you find
other examples of such patterns throughout the essay? Do most
of them have a special purpose?

6   What images are frequently used to describe the world of the
mind? Individually they might not be noticed, but in combination do they suggest any traditional form of worship? Note
particularly pages 355-357.

7   How often and in what ways does Russell summarize his argument before proceeding to his next point?

## ...AND COMPOSITION

8   Write an essay presenting two and only two alternatives as a
solution to a problem.

9   The Prometheus myth is introduced on page 354. Review this
myth in any encyclopedia or mythology text and write an essay
on it, including in your discussion the general content of the
myth, its relevance to Russell's thesis, and the effect of this
allusion to Prometheus.

10   Imitate the following sentence: "To abandon the struggle for
private happiness, to expel all eagerness of temporary desire, to
burn with passion for eternal things—this is emancipation, and
this is the free man's worship."

PERCY BYSSHE SHELLEY (1792–1822)   was expelled from Oxford in 1811
for writing and publishing the following tract—considerately, he had sent
copies to heads of the colleges and to church leaders all over England. Shelley
was fervent and given to verbal luxury, but in this essay he held himself
to making a strict sequence of points. As everyone knows, this college writer
soon developed into a prodigious author, with works like *Prometheus Unbound*
(a verse drama), "Ode to the West Wind" (a lyric poem), and "A
Defense of Poetry" (a famous document in literary criticism).

# The Necessity of Atheism

A close examination of the validity of the proofs adduced to support
any proposition, has ever been allowed to be the only sure way of attaining
truth, upon the advantages of which it is unnecessary to descant: our
knowledge of the existence of a Deity is a subject of such importance, that
it cannot be too minutely investigated; in consequence of this conviction,
we proceed briefly and impartially to examine the proofs which have been
adduced. It is necessary first to consider the nature of Belief.

When a proposition is offered to the mind, it perceives the agreement
or disagreement of the ideas of which it is composed. A perception of
their agreement is termed belief, many obstacles frequently prevent this
perception from being immediate, these the mind attempts to remove in
order that the perception may be distinct. The mind is active in the investigation, in order to perfect the state of perception which is passive; the
investigation being confused with the perception has induced many falsely
to imagine that the mind is active in belief, that belief is an act of volition,
in consequence of which it may be regulated by the mind. Pursuing, continuing this mistake they have attached a degree of criminality to disbelief
of which in its nature it is incapable; it is equally so of merit.

The strength of belief like that of every other passion is in proportion
to the degrees of excitement.

The degrees of excitement are three.

The senses are the sources of all knowledge to the mind, consequently
their evidence claims the strongest assent.

The decision of the mind founded upon our own experience, derived
from these sources, claims the next degree.

The experience of others which addresses itself to the former one,
occupies the lowest degree.—

Consequently no testimony can be admitted which is contrary to
reason, reason is founded on the evidence of our senses.

Every proof may be referred to one of these three divisions; we are

naturally led to consider what arguments we receive from each of them to convince us of the existence of a Deity.

1st. The evidence of the senses.—If the Deity should appear to us, if he should convince our senses of his existence; this revelation would necessarily command belief;—Those to whom the Deity has thus appeared have the strongest possible conviction of his existence.

Reason claims the 2nd. place, it is urged that man knows that whatever is, must either have had a beginning or existed from all eternity, he also knows that whatever is not eternal must have had a cause.—Where this is applied to the existence of the universe, it is necessary to prove that it was created, until that is clearly demonstrated, we may reasonably suppose that it has endured from all eternity.—In a case where two propositions are diametrically opposite, the mind believes that which is less incomprehensible, it is easier to suppose that the Universe has existed from all eternity, than to conceive a being capable of creating it; if the mind sinks beneath the weight of one, is it an alleviation to increase the intolerability of the burden?—The other argument which is founded on a man's knowledge of his own existence stands thus.—A man knows not only he now is, but that there was a time when he did not exist, consequently there must have been a cause.—But what does this prove? we can only infer from effects causes exactly adequate to those effects;—But there certainly is a generative power which is effected by particular instruments; we cannot prove that it is inherent in these instruments, nor is the contrary hypothesis capable of demonstration; we admit that the generative power is incomprehensible, but to suppose that the same effect is produced by an eternal, omniscient, Almighty Being, not only leaves the cause in the same obscurity, but renders it more incomprehensible.

The 3rd. and last degree of assent is claimed by Testimony—it is required that it should not be contrary to reason.—The testimony that the Deity convinces the senses of men of his existence can only be admitted by us, if our mind considers it less probable that these men should have been deceived, than that the Deity should have appeared to them—our reason can never admit the testimony of men, who not only declare that they were eye-witnesses of miracles but that the Deity was irrational, for he commanded that he should be believed, he proposed the highest rewards for faith, eternal punishments for disbelief—we can only command voluntary actions, belief is not an act of volition, the mind is even passive, from this it is evident that we have not sufficient testimony, or rather that testimony is insufficient to prove the being of a God, we have before shown that it cannot be deduced from reason,—they who have been convinced by the evidence of the senses, they only can believe it.

From this it is evident that having no proof from any of the three sources of conviction: the mind *cannot* believe the existence of a God, it is also evident that as belief is a passion of the mind, no degree of criminal-

ity can be attached to disbelief, they only are reprehensible who willingly neglect to remove the false medium thro' which their mind views the subject.

It is almost unnecessary to observe, that the general knowledge of the deficiency of such proof, cannot be prejudicial to society: Truth has always been found to promote the best interests of mankind.—Every reflecting mind must allow that there is no proof of the existence of a Deity.

Q.E.D.

## TOPICS FOR DISCUSSION

1    In what way does Shelley's whole argument rest on his assumption that "the senses are the sources of all knowledge to the mind"? Do you agree with this assumption?

2    What are the other steps in his argument? Do they all follow reasonably from the first major assumption? Turn Shelley's argument into a syllogism.

3    What are the degrees of excitement?

4    Would the printing in a college magazine today of an essay like Shelley's cause a public stir? Who would probably be most vilified by any public reaction—the college officials or the student writers?

5    Would you so commit yourself to a principle that you would be dismissed from college, as Shelley and his coauthor were, rather than recant? Is there any issue that moves you to contemplate such happenings? Was Riesman ("Where Is the College Generation Headed?") right about most college students' commitment to principle?

## ... AND COMPOSITION

6    Base an argument on a single assumption and work it out step by step.

7    Have you ever been involuntarily turned from a belief you would have liked to have preserved?

8    Formulate a strong statement of belief on any subject.

THOMAS BABINGTON MACAULAY (1800–1859)  one of the great
spokesmen for English liberalism in his century, turned his talents readily
to success in several careers—as historian, essayist, orator, and public
official both at home and abroad. His celebrated writing style enabled him
to impress a large public. Note the definite movements from topic to
topic, the determined assertions, the agile comparisons used to illustrate the
argument. Critics have pointed out that Macaulay's clarity and force
make it hard for the reader to retain that kind of balance an intellectual
should retain in the presence of rhetoric. The following—a decisive
turn in Macaulay's review of Bacon's works—is typical in its
style, and the content reveals his characteristic allegiances.

# Bacon and Plato

The difference between the philosophy of Bacon and that of his
predecessors cannot, we think, be better illustrated than by comparing his
views on some important subjects with those of Plato. We select Plato,
because we conceive that he did more than any other person towards giving
to the minds of speculative men that bent which they retained till they
received from Bacon a new impulse in a diametrically opposite direction.

It is curious to observe how differently these great men estimated
the value of every kind of knowledge. Take Arithmetic for example. Plato,
after speaking slightly of the convenience of being able to reckon and
compute in the ordinary transactions of life, passes to what he considers
as a far more important advantage. The study of the properties of numbers,
he tells us, habituates the mind to the contemplation of pure truth, and
raises it above the material universe. He would have his disciples apply
themselves to this study,—not that they may be able to buy or sell,—not
that they may qualify themselves to be shopkeepers or travelling merchants,
—but that they may learn to withdraw their minds from the ever-shifting
spectacle of this visible and tangible world, and to fix them on the immutable essence of things.

Bacon on the other hand, valued this branch of knowledge only on
account of its uses with reference to that visible and tangible world which
Plato so much despised. He speaks with scorn of the mystical arithmetic
of the later Platonists; and laments the propensity of mankind to employ,
on mere matters of curiosity, powers, the whole exertion of which is required for purposes of solid advantage. He advises arithmeticians to leave
these trifles, and to employ themselves in framing convenient expressions,
which may be of use in physical researches.

The same reasons which led Plato to recommend the study of arithmetic, led him to recommend also the study of mathematics. The vulgar

362

crowd of geometricians, he says, will not understand him. They have practice always in view. They do not know that the real use of the science is to lead man to the knowledge of abstract, essential, eternal truth. Indeed, if we are to believe Plutarch, Plato carried this feeling so far, that he considered geometry as degraded by being applied to any purpose of vulgar utility. Archytas, it seems, had framed machines of extraordinary power, on mathematical principles. Plato remonstrated with his friend; and declared that this was to degrade a noble intellectual exercise into a low craft, fit only for carpenters and wheelwrights. The office of geometry, he said, was to discipline the mind, not to minister to the base wants of the body. His interference was successful; and from that time, according to Plutarch, the science of mechanics was considered as unworthy of the attention of a philosopher.

Archimedes in a later age imitated and surpassed Archytas. But even Archimedes was not free from the prevailing notion that geometry was degraded by being employed to produce any thing useful. It was with difficulty that he was induced to stoop from speculation to practice. He was half ashamed of those inventions which were the wonder of hostile nations; and always spoke of them slightingly as mere amusements—as trifles in which a mathematician might be suffered to relax his mind after intense application to the higher parts of his science.

The opinion of Bacon on this subject was diametrically opposed to that of the ancient philosophers. He valued geometry chiefly, if not solely, on account of those uses which to Plato appeared so base. And it is remarkable that the longer he lived the stronger this feeling became. When, in 1605, he wrote the two books on the "Advancement of Learning," he dwelt on the advantages which mankind derived from mixed mathematics; but he at the same time admitted, that the beneficial effect produced by mathematical study on the intellect, though a collateral advantage, was "no less worthy than that which was principal and intended." But it is evident that his views underwent a change. When, nearly twenty years later, he published the *De Augmentis,* which is the treatise on the "Advancement of Learning," greatly expanded and carefully corrected, he made important alterations in the part which related to mathematics. He condemned with severity the high pretensions of the mathematicians,— "delicias et fastum mathematicorum." Assuming the well-being of the human race to be the end of knowledge, he pronounced that mathematical science could claim no higher rank than that of an appendage, or an auxiliary to other sciences. Mathematical science, he says, is the handmaid of natural philosophy—she ought to demean herself as such—and he declares that he cannot conceive by what ill chance it has happened that she presumes to claim precedence over her mistress. He predicts,—a prediction which would have made Plato shudder,—that as more and more discoveries are made in physics, there will be more and more branches of

mixed mathematics. Of that collateral advantage, the value of which, twenty years before, he rated so highly, he says not one word. This omission cannot have been the effect of mere inadvertence. His own treatise was before him. From that treatise he deliberately expunged whatever was favorable to the study of pure mathematics, and inserted several keen reflections on the ardent votaries of that study. This fact in our opinion, admits of only one explanation. Bacon's love of those pursuits which directly tend to improve the condition of mankind, and his jealousy of all pursuits merely curious, had grown upon him, and had, it may be, become immoderate. He was afraid of using any expression which might have the effect of inducing any man of talents to employ in speculations, useful only to the mind of the speculator, a single hour which might be employed in extending the empire of man over matter. If Bacon erred here, we must acknowledge that we greatly prefer his error to the opposite error of Plato. —We have no patience with a philosophy which, like those Roman matrons who swallowed abortives in order to preserve their shapes, takes pains to be barren for fear of being homely.

Let us pass to astronomy. This was one of the sciences which Plato exhorted his disciples to learn, but for reasons far removed from common habits of thinking. "Shall we set down astronomy," says Socrates, "among the subjects of study?" "I think so," answers his young friend Glaucon: "to know something about the seasons, about the months and the years is of use for military purposes, as well as for agriculture and navigation." "It amuses me," says Socrates, "to see how afraid you are lest the common herd of people should accuse you of recommending useless studies." He then proceeds in that pure and magnificent diction, which, as Cicero said Jupiter would use if Jupiter spoke Greek, to explain, that the use of astronomy is not to add to the vulgar comforts of life, but to assist in raising the mind to the contemplation of things which are to be perceived by the pure intellect alone. The knowledge of the actual motions of the heavenly bodies he considers as of little value. The appearances which make the sky beautiful at night are, he tells us, like the figures which a geometrican draws on the sand, mere examples, mere helps to feeble minds. We must get beyond them; we must neglect them; we must attain to an astronomy which is as independent of the actual stars as geometrical truth is independent of the lines of an ill-drawn diagram. This is, we imagine, very nearly, if not exactly, the astronomy which Bacon compared to the ox of Prometheus—a sleek, well shaped hide, stuffed with rubbish, goodly to look at, but containing nothing to eat. He complained that astronomy had, to its great injury, been separated from natural philosophy, of which it was one of the noblest provinces, and annexed to the domain of mathematics. The world stood in need, he said, of a very different astronomy— of a *living astronomy,* of an astronomy which should set forth the nature, the motion, and the influences of the heavenly bodies, as they really are.

On the greatest and most useful of all inventions,—the invention of alphabetical writing,—Plato did not look with much complacency. He seems to have thought that the use of letters had operated on the human mind as the use of the go-cart in learning to walk, or of corks in learning to swim, is said to operate on the human body. It was a support which soon became indispensable to those who used it,—which made vigorous exertion first unnecessary, and then impossible. The powers of the intellect would, he conceived, have been more fully developed without this delusive aid. Men would have been compelled to exercise the understanding and the memory; and, by deep and assiduous meditation, to make truth thoroughly their own. Now, on the contrary, much knowledge is traced on paper, but little is engraved in the soul. A man is certain that he can find information at a moment's notice when he wants it. He therefore suffers it to fade from his mind. Such a man cannot in strictness be said to know any thing. He has the show without the reality of wisdom. These opinions Plato has put into the mouth of an ancient King of Egypt. But it is evident from the context that they were his own; and so they were understood to be by Quintilian. Indeed they are in perfect accordance with the whole Platonic system.

Bacon's views, as may easily be supposed, were widely different. The powers of the memory, he observes, without the help of writing, can do little towards the advancement of any useful science. He acknowledges that the memory may be disciplined to such a point as to be able to perform very extraordinary feats. But on such feats he sets little value. The habits of his mind, he tells us, are such that he is not disposed to rate highly any accomplishment, however rare, which is of no practical use to mankind. As to these prodigious achievements of the memory, he ranks them with the exhibitions of rope-dancers and tumblers. "The two performances," he says, "are of much the same sort. The one is an abuse of the powers of the body; the other is an abuse of the powers of the mind. Both may perhaps excite our wonder; but neither is entitled to our respect."

To Plato, the science of medicine appeared one of very disputable advantage. He did not indeed object to quick cures for acute disorders, or for injuries produced by accidents. But the art which resists the slow sap of a chronic disease—which repairs frames enervated by lust, swollen by gluttony, or inflamed by wine—which encourages sensuality, by mitigating the natural punishment of the sensualist, and prolongs existence when the intellect has ceased to retain its entire energy—had no share of his esteem. A life protracted by medical skill he pronounced to be a long death. The exercise of the art of medicine ought, he said, to be tolerated so far as that art may serve to cure the occasional distempers of men whose constitutions are good. As to those who have bad constitutions, let them die;—and the sooner the better. Such men are unfit for war, for magistracy, for the management of their domestic affairs. That however is comparatively of

little consequence. But they are incapable of study and speculation. If they engage in any severe mental exercise, they are troubled with giddiness and fulness of the head; all which they lay to the account of philosophy. The best thing that can happen to such wretches is to have done with life at once. He quotes mythical authority in support of this doctrine; and reminds his disciples that the practice of the sons of Æsculapius, as described by Homer, extended only to the cure of external injuries.

Far different was the philosophy of Bacon. Of all the sciences, that which he seems to have regarded with the greatest interest was the science which, in Plato's opinion, would not be tolerated in a well regulated community. To make men perfect was no part of Bacon's plan. His humble aim was to make imperfect men comfortable. The beneficence of his philosophy resembled the beneficence of the common Father, whose sun rises on the evil and the good—whose rain descends for the just and the unjust. In Plato's opinion man was made for philosophy; in Bacon's opinion philosophy was made for man; it was a means to an end;—and that end was to increase the pleasures, and to mitigate the pains of millions who are not and cannot be philosophers. That a valetudinarian who took great pleasure in being wheeled along his terrace, who relished his boiled chicken and his weak wine and water, and who enjoyed a hearty laugh over the Queen of Navarre's tales, should be treated as a *caput lupinum* because he could not read the Timæus without a headache, was a notion which the humane spirit of the English school of wisdom altogether rejected. Bacon would not have thought it beneath the dignity of a philosopher to contrive an improved garden chair for such a valetudinarian,—to devise some way of rendering his medicines more palatable,—to invent repasts which he might enjoy, and pillows on which he might sleep soundly; and this though there might not be the smallest hope that the mind of the poor invalid would ever rise to the contemplation of the ideal beautiful and the ideal good. As Plato had cited the religious legends of Greece to justify his contempt for the more recondite parts of the art of healing, Bacon vindicated the dignity of that art by appealing to the example of Christ; and reminded his readers that the great physician of the soul did not disdain to be also the physician of the body.

## TOPICS FOR DISCUSSION

1   Throughout his survey of mathematics, astronomy, and so on, what essential difference does Macaulay see between Bacon and Plato? How often do you find Macaulay directly stating the difference? In what ways does he let you know his own preference between the two?

2   What elements of assurance are there in Macaulay's writing? That

is, do you find reasons for believing in the powers of your guide through the material? How is your confidence sustained? Do the subjects considered make any difference? Does their order make any difference? Does the manner of their introduction make any difference?

3  Do you connect content or style with your idea of what is "Victorian"?

4  Similes and analogies enable a writer to make a point, but they can be misleading. Is Macaulay fair in his use of similes and analogies? Consider his reference to Roman matrons at the end of paragraph 1, page 364.

5  Examine the transitions in this text. How does Macaulay assure the reader of both continuity and progress?

6  You would expect balance in an essay using the technique of comparison. Note the repetitions, the parallels in this text. Sometimes parallels exist on a conceptual level, not just in wording. Examine Macaulay's management of his developing argument.

## ... AND COMPOSITION

7  Write a short essay justifying the study of subjects which have no practical applicability. See Bacon's own words on this subject ("Of Studies").

8  Be completely fair in comparing or contrasting two things or persons, one of which you greatly prefer. Use some of Macaulay's methods to progress through the various parts of your comparison.

9  Write an essay considering utilitarian views, as typified in this sentence from page 364: "He was afraid of using any expression which might have the effect of inducing any man of talents to employ in speculations, useful only to the mind of the speculator, a single hour which might be employed in extending the empire of man over matter."

**C. S. LEWIS (1898–1963)** in the following essay is at his best, and most typical: he always welcomed opportunities to score against disbelievers. As evidenced in his selection on language in Part I, C. S. Lewis has a range of interests and accomplishments; in writing about language or literature or fantasy or religion, he plunges. He flourishes his arguments. No matter the topic, it becomes vital, because to his mind it links to first and last things. The issue he grapples with in the following article enlivens the narrative of his life, *Surprised by Joy*—recommended reading.

# What Christians Believe

I have been asked to tell you what Christians believe, and I am going to begin by telling you one thing that Christians don't need to believe. If you are a Christian you don't have to believe that all the other religions are simply wrong all through. If you are an atheist you do have to believe that the main point in all the religions of the whole world is simply one huge mistake. If you are a Christian, you are free to think that all these religions, even the queerest ones, contain at least some hint of the truth. When I was an atheist I had to try to persuade myself that the whole human race were pretty good fools until about one hundred years ago; when I became a Christian I was able to take a more liberal view. But, of course, being a Christian does mean thinking that where Christianity differs from other religions, Christianity is right and they are wrong. Like in arithmetic— there's only one right answer to a sum, and all other answers are wrong; but some of the wrong answers are much nearer being right than others.

The first big division of humanity is into the majority, who believe in some kind of God or gods, and the minority who don't. On this point, Christianity lines up with the majority—lines up with ancient Greeks and Romans, modern savages, Stoics, Platonists, Hindus, Mohammedans, etc., against the modern Western European materialist. There are all sorts of different reasons for believing in God, and here I'll mention only one. It is this. Suppose there was no intelligence behind the universe, no creative mind. In that case nobody designed my brain for the purpose of thinking. It is merely that when the atoms inside my skull happen for physical or chemi- cal reasons to arrange themselves in a certain way, this gives me, as a by-product, the sensation I call thought. But if so, how can I trust my own thinking to be true? It's like upsetting a milk-jug and hoping that the way the splash arranges itself will give you a map of London. But if I can't trust my own thinking, of course I can't trust the arguments leading to atheism, and therefore have no reason to be an atheist, or anything else. Unless I believe in God, I can't believe in thought: so I can never use thought to disbelieve in God.

Now I go on to the next big division. People who all believe in God can be divided according to the sort of God they believe in. There are two very different ideas on this subject. One of them is the idea that He is beyond good and evil. *We* call one thing good and another thing bad. But according to some people that's merely our human point of view. These people would say that the wiser you become the less you'd want to call anything good or bad, and the more clearly you'd see that everything is good in one way and bad in another, and that nothing could have been different. Consequently, these people think that long before you got anywhere near the divine point of view the distinction would have disappeared altogether. We call a cancer bad, they'd say, because it kills a man; but you might just as well call a successful surgeon bad because he kills a cancer. It all depends on the point of view. The other and opposite idea is that God is quite definitely "good" or "righteous," a God who takes sides, who loves love and hates hatred, who wants us to behave in one way and not in another. The first of these views—the one that thinks God beyond good and evil—is called Pantheism. It was held by the great Prussian philosopher Hegel and, as far as I can understand them, by the Hindus. The other view is held by Jews, Mohammedans, and Christians.

And with this big difference between Pantheism and the Christian idea of God, there usually goes another. Pantheists usually believe that God, so to speak, animates the universe as you animate your body: that the universe almost *is* God, so that if it didn't exist He wouldn't exist either, and anything you find in the universe is a part of God. The Christian idea is quite different. They think God *made* the universe—like a man making a picture or composing a tune. A painter isn't a picture, and he doesn't die if his picture is destroyed. You may say, "He's put a lot of himself into it," but that only means that all its beauty and interest have come out of his head. His skill isn't in the picture in the same way that it's in his head, or even in his hands. I expect you see how this difference between Pantheists and Christians hangs together with the other one. If you don't take the distinction between good and bad very seriously, then it's easy to say that anything you find in this world is a part of God. But, of course, if you think some things really bad, and God really good, then you can't talk like that. You must believe that God is separate from the world and that some of the things we see in it are contrary to his Will. Confronted with a cancer or a slum the Pantheist can say, "If you could only see it from the divine point of view, you would realize that this also is God." The Christian replies, "Don't talk damned nonsense."[1] For Christianity is a fighting religion. It thinks God made the world—that space and time, heat and cold, and all the colors and tastes, and all the animals and vegetables, are things that

---

[1] One listener complained of the word *damned* as frivolous swearing. But I mean exactly what I say—nonsense that is *damned* is under God's curse, and will (apart from God's grace) lead those who believe it to eternal death.

God "made up out of His head" as a man makes up a story. But it also thinks that a great many things have gone wrong with the world that God made and that God insists, and insists very loudly, on our putting them right again.

And, of course, that raises a very big question. If a good God made the world why has it gone wrong? And for many years I simply wouldn't listen to the Christian answers to this question, because I kept on feeling "Whatever you say, and however clever your arguments are, isn't it much simpler and easier to say that the world was *not* made by any intelligent power? Aren't all your arguments simply a complicated attempt to avoid the obvious?" But then that threw me back into those difficulties about atheism which I spoke of a moment ago. And soon I saw another difficulty.

My argument against God was that the universe seemed so cruel and unjust. But how had I got this idea of *just* and *unjust?* A man doesn't call a line crooked unless he has some idea of a straight line. What was I comparing this universe with when I called it unjust? If the whole show was bad and senseless from A to Z, so to speak, why did I, who was supposed to be part of the show, find myself in such violent reaction against it? A man feels wet when he falls into water, because man isn't a water animal: a fish wouldn't feel wet. Of course I could have given up my idea of justice by saying it was nothing but a private idea of my own. But if I did that then my argument against God collapsed too—for the argument depended on saying that the world was really unjust, not that it just didn't happen to please my private fancies. Thus in the very act of trying to prove that God didn't exist—in other words, that the whole of reality was senseless—I found I was forced to assume that one part of reality—namely my idea of justice—was full of sense. Consequently atheism turns out to be too simple. If the whole universe has no meaning, we should never have found out that it has no meaning; just as if there were no light in the universe and therefore no creatures with eyes we should never know it was dark. *Dark* would be a word without meaning.

## II

Very well then, atheism is too simple. And I'll tell you another view that is also too simple. It's the view I call Christianity-and-water, the view that just says there's a good God in Heaven and everything is all right—leaving out all the difficult and terrible doctrines about sin and hell and the devil, and the redemption. Both these are boys' philosophies.

It is no good asking for a simple religion. After all, real things *aren't* simple. They *look* simple, but they're not. The table I'm sitting at looks simple: but ask a scientist to tell you what it's really made of—all about the atoms and how the light waves rebound from them and hit my eye and what they do to the optic nerve and what it does to my brain—and, of course, you find that what we call "seeing a table" lands you in mysteries

and complications which you can hardly get to the end of. A child, saying a child's prayer, looks simple. And if you're content to stop there, well and good. But if you're not—and the modern world usually isn't—if you want to go on and ask what's really happening—then you must be prepared for something difficult. If we ask for something more than simplicity, it's silly then to complain that the something more isn't simple. Another thing I've noticed about reality is that, besides being difficult, it's odd: it isn't neat, it isn't what you expect. I mean, when you've grasped that the earth and the other planets all go round the sun, you'd naturally expect that all the planets are made to match—all at equal distances from each other, say, or distances that regularly increased, or all the same size, or else getting bigger or smaller as you go further from the sun. In fact, you find no rhyme or reason (that we can see) about either the sizes or the distances; and some of them have one moon, one has four, one has two, some have none, and one has a ring.

Reality, in fact, is always something you couldn't have guessed. That's *one* of the reasons I believe Christianity. It's a religion you couldn't have guessed. If it offered us just the kind of universe we'd always expected, I'd feel we were making it up. But, in fact, it's not the sort of thing anyone would have made up. It has just that queer twist about it that real things have. So let's leave behind all these boys' philosophies—these over-simple answers. The problem isn't simple and the answer isn't going to be simple either.

What is the problem? A universe that contains much that is obviously bad and apparently meaningless, but containing creatures like ourselves who know that it is bad and meaningless. There are only two views that face all the facts. One is the Christian view that this is a good world that has gone wrong, but still retains the memory of what it ought to have been. The other is the view called Dualism. Dualism means the belief that there are two equal independent powers at the back of everything, one of them good and the other bad, and that this universe is the battlefield in which they fight out an endless war. I personally think that next to Christianity Dualism is the manliest and most sensible creed on the market. But it has a catch in it.

The two powers, or spirits, or gods—the good one and the bad one—are supposed to be quite independent. They both existed from all eternity. Neither of them made the other, neither of them has any more right than the other to call itself God. Each presumably thinks it is good and thinks the other bad. One of them likes hatred and cruelty, the other likes love and mercy, and each backs its own view. Now what do we mean when we call one of them the Good Power and the other the Bad Power? Either we're merely saying that we happen to prefer the one to the other—like preferring beer to cider—or else we're saying that, whatever *they* say about it, and whichever *we* happen to like, one of them is actually wrong, actually

mistaken, in regarding itself as good. Now if we mean merely that we happen to prefer the first, then we must give up talking about good and evil at all. For good means what you ought to prefer quite regardless of what you happen to like at any given moment. If "being good" meant simply joining the side you happened to fancy, for no real reason, then good wouldn't *be* good. So we must mean that one of the two powers is actually wrong and the other actually right.

But the moment you say that, you are putting into the universe a third thing in addition to the two Powers: some law or standard or rule of good which one of the powers conforms to and the other fails to conform to. But since the two powers are judged by this standard, then this standard, or the being who made this standard, is farther back and higher up than either of them, and He will be the real God. In fact, what we meant by calling them good and bad turns out to be that one of them is in a right relation to the real ultimate God and the other in a wrong relation to Him.

The same point can be made in a different way. If Dualism is true, then the Bad Power must be a being who likes badness for its own sake. But in reality we have no experience of anyone liking badness just because it is bad. The nearest we can go to it is in cruelty. But in real life people are cruel for one of two reasons—either because they are sadists, that is, because they have a sexual perversion which makes cruelty a cause of sensual pleasure to them, or else for the sake of something they are going to get out of it—money, or power, or safety. But pleasure, money, power, and safety are all, as far as they go, good things. The badness consists in pursuing them by the wrong method, or in the wrong way, or too much. I don't mean, of course, that the people who do this aren't desperately wicked. I do mean that wickedness, when you examine it, turns out to be pursuit of some good in the wrong way. You can be good for the mere sake of goodness: you can't be bad for the mere sake of badness. You can do a kind action when you're not feeling kind and when it gives you no pleasure, simply because kindness is right; but no one ever did a cruel action simply because cruelty is wrong—only because cruelty was pleasant or useful to him. In other words, badness can't succeed even in being bad *in the same way* in which goodness is good. Goodness is, so to speak, itself: badness is only spoiled goodness. And there must be something good first before it can be spoiled. We called Sadism a sexual perversion; but you must first have the idea of a normal sexuality before you can talk of it being perverted; and you can see which is the perversion, because you can explain the perverted from the normal, and can't explain the normal from the perverted. It follows that the Bad Power, who is supposed to be on an equal footing with the Good Power, and to love badness in the same way as the good one loves goodness, is a mere bogey. In order to be bad he must have good things to want and then to pursue in the wrong way: he must have impulses which were originally good in order to be able to pervert

them. But if he is bad he can't supply himself either with good things to desire or with good impulses to pervert. He must be getting both from the Good Power. And if so, then he is not independent. He is part of the Good Power's world: he was made either by the Good Power or by some power above them both.

Put it more simply still. To be bad, he must exist and have intelligence and will. But existence, intelligence, and will are in themselves good. Therefore he must be getting them from the Good Power: even to be bad he must borrow or steal from his opponent. And do you now begin to see why Christianity has always said that the devil is a fallen angel? That isn't a mere story for the children. It's a real recognition of the fact that evil is a parasite, not an original thing. The powers which enable evil to carry on are powers given it by goodness. All the things which enable a bad man to be effectively bad are in themselves good things—resolution, cleverness, good looks, existence itself. That's why Dualism, in a strict sense, won't work.

But I want to say that real Christianity (as distinct from Christianity-and-water) goes much nearer to Dualism than people think. One of the things that surprised me when I first read the New Testament seriously was that it was always talking about a Dark Power in the universe—a mighty evil spirit who was held to be the Power behind death, and disease, and sin. The difference is that Christianity thinks this Dark Power was created by God, and was good when he was created, and went wrong. Christianity agrees with Dualism that this universe is at war. But it doesn't think this is a war between independent powers. It thinks it's a civil war, a rebellion, and that we are living in a part of the universe occupied by the rebel.

Enemy-occupied territory—that's what this world is. Christianity is the story of how the rightful king has landed, you might say landed in disguise, and is calling us all to take part in a great campaign of sabotage. When you go to church you're really listening in to the secret wireless from our friends: that's why the enemy is so anxious to prevent us going. He does it by playing on our conceit and laziness and intellectual snobbery. I know someone will ask me, "Do you really mean, at this time of day, to reintroduce our old friend the devil—hoofs and horns and all?" Well, what the time of day has to do with it I don't know. And I'm not particular about the hoofs and horns. But in other respects my answer is, "Yes, I do." I don't claim to know anything about his personal appearance. If anybody really wants to know him better I'd say to that person. "Don't worry. If you really want to, you will. Whether you'll like it when you do is another question."

III

Christians, then, believe that an evil power has made himself for the present the Prince of this World. And, of course, that raises problems. Is this state of affairs in accordance with God's will or not? If it is, He's a

strange God, you'll say: and if it isn't how *can* anything happen contrary to the will of a being with absolute power?

But anyone who has been in authority knows how a thing can be in accordance with your will in one way and not in another. It may be quite sensible for a mother to say to the children, "I'm not going to go and make you tidy the schoolroom every night. You've got to learn to keep it tidy on your own." Then she goes up one night and finds the Teddy bear and the ink and the French Grammar all lying in the grate. That's against her will. She would prefer the children to be tidy. But on the other hand, it is her will which has left the children free to be untidy. The same thing arises in any regiment, or trades union, or school. You make a thing voluntary and then half the people don't do it. That isn't what you willed, but your will has made it possible.

It's probably the same in the universe. God created things which had free will. That means creatures which can go wrong *or* right. Some people think they can imagine a creature which was free but had no possibility of going wrong, but I can't. If a thing is free to be good it's also free to be bad. And free will is what has made evil possible. Why, then, did God give them free will? Because free will, though it makes evil possible, is also the only thing that makes possible any love or goodness or joy worth having. A world of automata—of creatures that worked like machines—would hardly be worth creating. The happiness which God designs for His higher creatures is the happiness of being freely, voluntarily united to Him and to each other in an ecstasy of love and delight compared with which the most rapturous love between a man and a woman on this earth is *mere milk and water*. And for that they've got to be free.

Of course God knew what would happen if they used their freedom the wrong way: apparently He thought it worth the risk. Perhaps we feel inclined to disagree with Him. But there's a difficulty about disagreeing with God. He is the source from which all your reasoning power comes: you couldn't be right and He wrong any more than a stream can rise higher than its own source. When you are arguing against Him you're arguing against the very power that makes you able to argue at all: it's like cutting off the branch you're sitting on. If God thinks this state of war in the universe a price worth paying for free will—that is, for making a *real* world in which creatures can do real good or harm and something of real importance can happen, instead of a toy world which only moves when He pulls the strings —then we make take it it *is* worth paying.

When we've understood about free will, we shall see how silly it is to ask, as somebody once asked me: "Why did God make a creature of such rotten stuff that it went wrong?" The better stuff a creature is made of—the cleverer and stronger and freer it is—then the better it will be if it goes right, but also the worse it will be if it goes wrong. A cow can't be very good or very bad; a dog can be both better and worse; a child better and

worse still; an ordinary man, still more so; a man of genius, still more so; a superhuman spirit best—or worst—of all.

How did the Dark Power go wrong? Well, the moment you have a self at all, there is a possibility of putting yourself first—wanting to be the centre —wanting to *be* God, in fact. That was the sin of Satan: and that was the sin he taught the human race. Some people think the fall of man had something to do with sex, but that's a mistake. What Satan put into the heads of our remote ancestors was the idea that they could "be like gods"—could set up on their own as if they had created themselves—be their own masters —invent some sort of happiness for themselves outside God, apart from God. And out of that hopeless attempt has come nearly all that we call human history—money, poverty, ambition, war, prostitution, classes, empires, slavery—the long terrible story of man trying to find something other than God which will make him happy.

The reason why it can never succeed is this. God made us, invented us as a man invents an engine. A car is made to run on petrol, and it won't run properly on anything else. Now God designed the human machine to run on Himself. He Himself is the fuel our spirits were designed to burn, or the food our spirits were designed to feed on. There isn't any other. That's why it's just no good asking God to make us happy in our own way without bothering about religion. God can't give us a happiness and peace apart from Himself, because it isn't there. There's no such thing.

That is the key to history. Terrific energy is expended—civilizations are built up—excellent institutions devised; but each time something goes wrong. Some fatal flaw always brings the selfish and cruel people to the top and it all slides back into misery and ruin. In fact, the machine konks. It seems to start up all right and runs a few yards, and then it breaks down. They're trying to run it on the wrong juice. That's what Satan has done to us humans.

And what did God do? First of all He left us conscience, the sense of right and wrong: and all through history there have been people trying (some of them very hard) to obey it. None of them ever quite succeeded. Secondly, He sent the human race what I call good dreams: I mean those queer stories scattered all through the heathen religions about a god who dies and comes to life again and, by his death, has somehow given new life to men. Thirdly, He selected one particular people and spent several centuries hammering into their heads the sort of God He was—that there was only one of Him and that He cared about right conduct. Those people were the Jews, and the Old Testament gives an account of the hammering process.

Then comes the real shock. Among these Jews there suddenly turns up a man who goes about talking as if He was God. He claims to forgive sins. He says He has always existed. He says He is coming to judge the world at the end of time. Now let us get this clear. Among Pantheists, like the

Indians, anyone might say that he was a part of God, or one with God: there'd be nothing very odd about it. But this man, since He was a Jew, couldn't mean that kind of God. God, in their language, meant the Being outside the world Who had made it and was infinitely different from anything else. And when you've grasped that, you will see that what this man said was, quite simply, the most shocking thing that has ever been uttered by human lips.

I'm trying here to prevent anyone from saying the really silly thing that people often say about Him: "I'm ready to accept Jesus as a great moral teacher, but I don't accept His claim to be God." That's the one thing we mustn't say. A man who was merely a man and said the sort of things Jesus said wouldn't be a great moral teacher. He'd either be a lunatic—on a level with the man who says he's a poached egg—or else he'd be the Devil of Hell. You must make your choice. Either this man was, and is, the Son of God: or else a madman or something worse. You can shut Him up for a fool; you can spit at Him and kill Him as a demon; or you can fall at His feet and call Him Lord and God. But don't let us come with any patronizing nonsense about His being a great human teacher. He hasn't left that open to us. He didn't intend to.

## TOPICS FOR DISCUSSION

1   Could an atheist as well as a Christian be free to think that all ". . . religions, even the queerest ones, contain at least some hint of truth"? Is there any justification for the greater freedom Lewis claims for the Christian?

2   Examine the argument concluding the second paragraph. How does this argument used by Lewis relate to Descartes's "I think, therefore I am"; to the argument that because one can conceive the idea of God, God must exist?

3   Does Lewis establish an essential distinction, or does he create a false dilemma, when he contrasts Christianity and dualism in paragraph 3, page 371.

4   What are the main steps in Lewis's argument, as signified by the three divisions of the article?

5   What qualities in the writing indicate that the language is adapted to a broadcast talk (consider sentence and paragraph length and structure, transitions, tone)?

## . . . AND COMPOSITION

6   Write a paragraph on some aspect of a big question such as good

and evil, immortality, etc. First design your paragraph as a purely literary presentation; then recast the paragraph for oral presentation to a general audience; to children.

7   Write your own essay on religious belief.

8   Write on some change in your own beliefs, examining critically the "before" and "after" phases. Note how Lewis contrasts his later beliefs to his earlier views.

**D. H. LAWRENCE (1885–1930)** wandered the earth, witnessing,
committing himself to people, places, beliefs. "Knowledge is an experience,
not a formula," he says. What he encountered became vivid, and he told
about it. The following is from *Etruscan Places,* a trancelike book,
an evocation of life from Etruscan tombs. Life and belief are close, in
Lawrence. You may remember his essay on Melville, under
"Methods and Demonstrations" in Part I. Lawrence's essential
significance gets some reference in the headnote to that essay.

# Painted Tombs of Tarquinia

To the Etruscan all was alive; the whole universe lived; and the business of man was himself to live amid it all. He had to draw life into himself, out of the wandering huge vitalities of the world. The cosmos was alive, like a vast creature. The whole thing breathed and stirred. Evaporation went up like breath from the nostrils of a whale, steaming up. The sky received it in its blue bosom, breathed it in and pondered on it and transmuted it, before breathing it out again. Inside the earth were fires like the heat in the hot red liver of a beast. Out of the fissures of the earth came breaths of other breathing, vapours direct from the living physical underearth, exhalations carrying inspiration. The whole thing was alive, and had a great soul, or *anima*: and in spite of one great soul, there were myriad roving, lesser souls; every man, every creature and tree and lake and mountain and stream, was animate, had its own peculiar consciousness. And has it to-day.

The cosmos was one, and its *anima* was one; but it was made up of creatures. And the greatest creature was earth, with its soul of inner fire. The sun was only a reflection, or off-throw, or brilliant handful, of the great inner fire. But in juxtaposition to earth lay the sea, the waters that moved and pondered and held a deep soul of their own. Earth and waters lay side by side, together, and utterly different.

So it was. The universe, which was a single aliveness with a single soul, instantly changed, the moment you thought of it, and became a dual creature with two souls, fiery and watery, for ever mingling and rushing apart, and held by the great aliveness of the universe in an ultimate equilibrium. But they rushed together and they rushed apart, and immediately they became myriad; volcanoes and seas, then streams and mountains, trees, creatures, men. And everything was dual, or contained its own duality, for ever mingling and rushing apart.

The old idea of the vitality of the universe was evolved long before history begins, and elaborated into a vast religion before we get a glimpse of it. When history does begin, in China or India, Egypt, Babylonia, even

in the Pacific and in aboriginal America, we see evidence of one under-lying religious idea: the conception of the vitality of the cosmos, the myriad vitalities in wild confusion, which still is held in some sort of array: and man, amid all the growing welter, adventuring, struggling, striving for one thing, life, vitality, more vitality: to get into himself more and more of the gleaming vitality of the cosmos. That is the treasure. The active re-ligious idea was that man, by vivid attention and subtlety and exerting all his strength, could draw more life into himself, more life, more and more glistening vitality, till he became shining like the morning, blazing like a god. When he was all himself he painted himself vermilion like the throat of dawn, and was god's body, visibly, red and utterly vivid. So he was a prince, a king, a god, an Etruscan Lucumo; Pharaoh, or Belshazzar, or Ashurbanipal, or Tarquin; in a feebler *decrescendo,* Alexander, or Caesar, or Napoleon.

This was the idea at the back of all the great old civilizations. It was even, half-transmuted, at the back of David's mind, and voiced in the Psalms. But with David the living cosmos became merely a personal god. With the Egyptians and Babylonians and Etruscans, strictly there were no personal gods. There were only idols or symbols. It was the living cosmos itself, dazzlingly and graspingly complex, which was divine, and which could be contemplated only by the strongest soul, and only at moments. And only the peerless soul could draw into itself some last flame from the quick. Then you had a king-god indeed.

There you have the ancient idea of kings, kings who are gods by vividness, because they have gathered into themselves core after core of vital potency from the universe, till they are clothed in scarlet, they are bodily a piece of the deepest fire. Pharaohs and kings of Nineveh, kings of the East, and Etruscan Lucumones, they are the living clue to the pure fire, to the cosmic vitality. They are the vivid key to life, the vermilion clue to the mystery and the delight of death and life. They, in their own body, unlock the vast treasure-house of the cosmos for their people, and bring out life, and show the way into the dark of death, which is the blue burning of the one fire. They, in their own bodies, are the life-bringers and the death-guides, leading ahead in the dark, and coming out in the day with more than sunlight in their bodies. Can one wonder that such dead are wrapped in gold; or were?

The life-bringers, and the death-guides. But they set guards at the gates both of life and death. They keep the secrets, and safeguard the way. Only a few are initiated into the mystery of the bath of life, and the bath of death: the pool within pool within pool, wherein, when a man is dipped, he becomes darker than blood, with death, and brighter than fire, with life; till at last he is scarlet royal as a piece of living life, pure vermilion.

The people are not initiated into the cosmic ideas, nor into the awakened throb of more vivid consciousness. Try as you may, you can

never make the mass of men throb with full awakenedness. They *cannot* be more than a little aware. So you must give them symbols, ritual and gesture, which will fill their bodies with life up to their own full measure. Any more is fatal. And so the actual knowledge must be guarded from them, lest knowing the formulae, without undergoing at all the experience that corresponds, they may become insolent and impious, thinking they have the all, when they have only an empty monkey-chatter. The esoteric knowledge will always be esoteric, since knowledge is an experience, not a formula. But it is foolish to hand out the formulae. A little knowledge is indeed a dangerous thing. No age proves it more than ours. Monkey-chatter is at last the most disastrous of all things.

The clue to the Etruscan life was the Lucumo, the religious prince. Beyond him were the priests and warriors. Then came the people and the slaves. People and warriors and slaves did not think about religion. There would soon have been no religion left. They felt the symbols and danced the sacred dances. For they were always kept *in touch,* physically, with the mysteries. The "touch" went from the Lucumo down to the merest slave. The blood-stream was unbroken. But "knowing" belonged to the high-born, the pure-bred.

So, in the tombs we find only the simple, uninitiated vision of the people. There is none of the priest-work of Egypt. The symbols are to the artist just wonder-forms, pregnant with emotion and good for decoration. It is so all the way through Etruscan art. The artists evidently were of the people, artisans. Presumably they were of the old Italic stock, and understood nothing of the religion in its intricate form, as it had come in from the East: though doubtless the crude principles of the official religion were the same as those of the primitive religion of the aborigines. The same crude principles ran through the religions of all the barbaric world of that time, Druid or Teutonic or Celtic. But the newcomers in Etruria held secret the science and philosophy of their religion, and gave the people the symbols and the ritual, leaving the artists free to use the symbols as they would; which shows that there was no priest-rule.

Later, when scepticism came over all the civilized world, as it did after Socrates, the Etruscan religion began to die, Greeks and Greek rationalism flooded in, and Greek stories more or less took the place of the old Etruscan symbolic thought. Then again the Etruscan artists, uneducated, used the Greek stories as they had used the Etruscan symbols, quite freely, making them over again just to please themselves.

But one radical thing the Etruscan people never forgot, because it was in their blood as well as in the blood of their masters: and that was the mystery of the journey out of life, and into death; the death-journey, and the sojourn in the after-life. The wonder of their soul continued to play round the mystery of this journey and this sojourn.

## TOPICS FOR DISCUSSION

1  Compare Lawrence's presentation of Etruscan pantheism with C. S. Lewis's discussion of pantheism in "What Christians Believe," paragraph 2, page 369.

2  Discuss the use of similes in this selection.

3  Expatiate on what you think Lawrence may mean by "esoteric knowledge" and "monkey chatter" in paragraph 1, page 380.

4  What is the relationship between emotion and belief in this selection (see paragraph 2, page 380)? In your own thinking?

5  What is Lawrence opposing when he contrasts Greek rationalism and Etruscan symbolic thought in paragraphs 4 and 5, page 380.

## ... AND COMPOSITION

6  Write an essay suggested by your interpretation of the symbolic thought of religious art or artifacts.

7  Write a narrative suggested by paragraph 2, page 380.

8  Research the meanings of the phrase "archetypal image" and write an essay reconsidering Lawrence's selection in the light of your studies. See the works of M. Bodkin, C. G. Jung, and Northrop Frye.

PART *3*

# *Forms and Occasions*

As evidenced in Part 2, the writer often mobilizes his resources for persuasion, but other modes of composition abound. Innumerable occasions call for strategies too numerous and complex for adequate display in any anthology, but certain occasions are prevalent enough or notable enough to permit useful classification. This section offers some standard forms of writing arranged as helpfully as possible in relation to times and places—occasions—for their use.

Perhaps the most public, decorous, and serious form of writing is that of speeches designed to announce large, accepted group purposes. The two inaugural addresses presented in this section exemplify this kind of composition. Appeals, in which an individual finds himself communicating across a gulf to his society, constitute another group. For direct person-to-person communication, there are letters. Analysis is yet another form. Still another is the delivery of information, either directly or indirectly, through the vehicles of irony and satire. Last is characterization, represented by three essays exhibiting a range of possibility in this form.

ABRAHAM LINCOLN (1809–1865)  in the text below confronts a particular
situation with a typical statement put into a pattern standard for such
an occasion. The pattern involves a sober assessment, a recognition of opposing
forces or opinions, a reminder of background assumptions shared by all, and
a reading of the future as it may emerge from the elements recognized
as potential in the present. Any summary of the pattern does less than justice
to the poise and control manifest in Lincoln's phrasing, his parallelisms
and his patterns of sequence such as are found in paragraph 1 ("at this
second appearing," "then," "now," "the future") and in
paragraph 3 ("neither," "each," "both," "any," "other"). And the
diction carries weight, with a biblical, governmental, social tone.

# Second Inaugural Address

Fellow-countrymen: At this second appearing to take the oath of the
presidential office, there is less occasion for an extended address than there
was at the first. Then a statement, somewhat in detail, of a course to be
pursued, seemed fitting and proper. Now, at the expiration of four years,
during which public declarations have been constantly called forth on every
point and phase of the great contest which still absorbs the attention, and
engrosses the energies of the nation, little that is new could be presented.
The progress of our arms, upon which all else chiefly depends, is as well
known to the public as to myself; and it is, I trust, reasonably satisfactory
and encouraging to all. With high hope for the future, no prediction in
regard to it is ventured.

On the occasion corresponding to this four years ago, all thoughts
were anxiously directed to an impending civil-war. All dreaded it—all
sought to avert it. While the inaugural address was being delivered from this

place, devoted altogether to *saving* the Union without war, insurgent agents were in the city seeking to *destroy* it without war—seeking to dissolve the Union, and divide effects, by negotiation. Both parties deprecated war; but one of them would *make* war rather than let the nation survive; and the other would *accept* war rather than let it perish. And the war came.

One eighth of the whole population were colored slaves, not distributed generally over the Union, but localized in the Southern part of it. These slaves constituted a peculiar and powerful interest. All knew that this interest was, somehow, the cause of the war. To strengthen, perpetuate, and extend this interest was the object for which the insurgents would rend the Union, even by war; while the government claimed no right to do more than to restrict the territorial enlargement of it. Neither party expected for the war, the magnitude, or the duration, which it has already attained. Neither anticipated that the *cause* of the conflict might cease with, or even before, the conflict itself should cease. Each looked for an easier triumph, and a result less fundamental and astounding. Both read the same Bible, and pray to the same God; and each invokes His aid against the other. It may seem strange that any men should dare to ask a just God's assistance in wringing their bread from the sweat of other men's faces; but let us judge not that we be not judged. The prayers of both could not be answered; that of neither has been answered fully. The Almighty has His own purposes. "Woe unto the world because of offences! for it must needs be that offences come; but woe to that man by whom the offence cometh!" If we shall suppose that American Slavery is one of those offences which, in the providence of God, must needs come, but which, having continued through His appointed time, He now wills to remove, and that He gives to both North and South, this terrible war, as the woe due to those by whom the offence came, shall we discern therein any departure from those divine attributes which the believers in a Living God always ascribe to Him? Fondly do we hope—fervently do we pray—that this mighty scourge of war may speedily pass away. Yet, if God wills that it continue, until all the wealth piled by the bondman's two hundred and fifty years of unrequited toil shall be sunk, and until every drop of blood drawn with the lash, shall be paid by another drawn with the sword, as was said three thousand years ago, so still it must be said, "The judgments of the Lord, are true and righteous altogether."

With malice toward none; with charity for all; with firmness in the right, as God gives us to see the right, let us strive on to finish the work we are in; to bind up the nation's wounds; to care for him who shall have borne the battle, and for his widow, and his orphan—to do all which may achieve and cherish a just, and a lasting peace among ourselves, and with all nations.

## TOPICS FOR DISCUSSION

1   What is Lincoln's purpose in this address? To what instincts does he direct his appeal? Is he persuasive?

2   Find examples of persuasive language. How important is the connotation of words in an address of this type?

3   Does Lincoln find one side more responsible for the war than the other? How tactfully is this matter handled?

4   Is the diction generally concrete or vague? Elaborate and full of rhetorical maneuver or simple and direct? Cite specific examples to support your conclusions.

## ...AND COMPOSITION

5   Imagine an attitude some particular contemporary of Lincoln's might have taken toward this speech; from that point of view write a commentary.

6   Analyze in detail the diction of the address; remember that it was, in part, a political address.

7   Most of the sentences of the address are short and relatively simple in structure. The last sentence is different, being a paragraph in length and quite complex in structure. Analyze the sentence and imitate its basic pattern.

**JOHN F. KENNEDY (1917–1963)** confronts, as Lincoln did, the identifying, the inaugural situation; and the pattern for such compositions is there: present situation, opposing forces, reliance on a tide larger than man's own powers, and a facing of the future. On this occasion more specifics are needed—it is a first inaugural, and a number of topics need passing mention. Also, it is apparent that much more exhorting is present; phrases of urgency abound. As for rhetorical inducement—parallelisms, appeals to emotion—they are more evident. President Kennedy was speaking for a team and appealing for the allegiance of an electorate which had been almost evenly divided in the campaign just preceding. The speech reveals the influence of the team and the pressure of the need to appeal.

# Inaugural Address

We observe today not a victory of party, but a celebration of freedom —symbolizing an end, as well as a beginning—signifying renewal, as well as change. For I have sworn before you and Almighty God the same solemn oath our forebears prescribed nearly a century and three quarters ago.

The world is very different now. For man holds in his mortal hands the power to abolish all forms of human poverty and all forms of human life. And yet the same revolutionary beliefs for which our forebears fought are still at issue around the globe—the belief that the rights of man come not from the generosity of the state, but from the hand of God.

We dare not forget today that we are the heirs of that first revolution. Let the word go forth from this time and place, to friend and foe alike, that the torch has been passed to a new generation of Americans—born in this century, tempered by war, disciplined by a hard and bitter peace, proud of our ancient heritage—and unwilling to witness or permit the slow undoing of those human rights to which this Nation has always been committed, and to which we are committed today at home and around the world.

Let every nation know, whether it wishes us well or ill, that we shall pay any price, bear any burden, meet any hardship, support any friend, oppose any foe, in order to assure the survival and the success of liberty.

This much we pledge—and more.

To those old allies whose cultural and spiritual origins we share, we pledge the loyalty of faithful friends. United, there is little we cannot do in a host of cooperative ventures. Divided, there is little we can do—for we dare not meet a powerful challenge at odds and split asunder.

To those new States whom we welcome to the ranks of the free, we pledge our words that one form of colonial control shall not have passed

away merely to be replaced by a far greater iron tyranny. We shall not always expect to find them supporting our view. But we shall always hope to find them strongly supporting their own freedom—and to remember that, in the past, those who foolishly sought power by riding the back of the tiger ended up inside.

To those peoples in the huts and villages across the globe struggling to break the bonds of mass misery, we pledge our best efforts to help them help themselves, for whatever period is required—not because the Communists may be doing it, not because we seek their votes, but because it is right. If a free society cannot help the many who are poor, it cannot save the few who are rich.

To our sister republics south of our border, we offer a special pledge—to convert our good words into good deeds, in a new alliance for progress, to assist free men and free governments in casting off the chains of poverty. But this peaceful revolution of hope cannot become the prey of hostile powers. Let all our neighbors know that we shall join with them to oppose aggression or subversion anywhere in the Americas. And let every other power know that this hemisphere intends to remain the master of its own house.

To that world assembly of sovereign states, the United Nations, our last best hope in an age where the instruments of war have far outpaced the instruments of peace, we renew our pledge of support—to prevent it from becoming merely a forum for invective—to strengthen its shield of the new and the weak—and to enlarge the area in which its writ may run.

Finally, to those nations who would make themselves our adversary, we offer not a pledge but a request: that both sides begin anew the quest for peace, before the dark powers of destruction unleashed by science engulf all humanity in planned or accidental self-destruction.

We dare not tempt them with weakness. For only when our arms are sufficient beyond doubt can we be certain beyond doubt that they will never be employed.

But neither can two great and powerful groups of nations take comfort from our present course—both sides overburdened by the cost of modern weapons, both rightly alarmed by the steady spread of the deadly atom, yet both racing to alter that uncertain balance of terror that stays the hand of mankind's final war.

So let us begin anew—remembering on both sides that civility is not a sign of weakness, and sincerity is always subject to proof. Let us never negotiate out of fear. But let us never fear to negotiate.

Let both sides explore what problems unite us instead of laboring those problems which divide us.

Let both sides, for the first time, formulate serious and precise proposals for the inspection and control of arms—and bring the absolute

power to destroy other nations under the absolute control of all nations.

Let both sides seek to invoke the wonders of science instead of its terrors. Together let us explore the stars, conquer the deserts, eradicate disease, tap the ocean depths, and encourage the arts and commerce.

Let both sides unite to heed in all corners of the earth the command of Isaiah—to "undo the heavy burdens and to let the oppressed go free."

And if a beachhead of cooperation may push back the jungle of suspicion, let both sides join in creating a new endeavor, not a new balance of power, but a new world of law, where the strong are just and the weak secure and the peace preserved.

All this will not be finished in the first 100 days. Nor will it be finished in the first 1,000 days, nor in the life of this administration, nor even perhaps in our lifetime on this planet. But let us begin.

In your hands, my fellow citizens, more than in mine, will rest the final success or failure of our course. Since this country was founded, each generation of Americans has been summoned to give testimony to its national loyalty. The graves of young Americans who answered the call to service are found around the globe.

Now the trumpet summons us again—not as a call to bear arms, though arms we need; not as a call to battle, though embattled we are; but a call to bear the burden of a long twilight struggle, year in, and year out, "rejoicing in hope, patient in tribulation"—a struggle against the common enemies of man: tyranny, poverty, disease, and war itself.

Can we forge against these enemies a grand and global alliance, North and South, East and West, that can assure a more fruitful life for all mankind? Will you join in that historic effort?

In the long history of the world, only a few generations have been granted the role of defending freedom in its hour of maximum danger. I do not shrink from this responsibility—I welcome it. I do not believe that any of us would exchange places with any other people or any other generation. The energy, the faith, the devotion which we bring to this endeavor will light our country and all who serve it—and the glow from that fire can truly light the world.

*And so, my fellow Americans, ask not what your country can do for you: Ask what you can do for your country.*

*My fellow citizens of the world: Ask not what America will do for you, but what together we can do for the freedom of man.*

Finally, whether you are citizens of America or citizens of the world, ask of us the same high standards of strength and sacrifice which we ask of you. With a good conscience our only sure reward, with history the final judge of our deeds, let us go forth to lead the land we love, asking His blessing and His help, but knowing that here on earth God's work must truly be our own.

## TOPICS FOR DISCUSSION

1   Parallelism and balance of words, phrases, and sentences were the distinguishing marks of Kennedy's public style. Find examples of parallelism of words, of phrases, and of sentences in this address and analyze each for naturalness, beauty, and logic. Are the balances ever forced? Are any elements made parallel which are not equal? Why is this style effective for public speeches?

2   Why does Kennedy appeal to the revolutionary past of the American people? Has this revolutionary background been altered by its modern context? Has "revolutionary" become a pejorative word?

3   How is the foe described? How conciliatory is Kennedy to this foe?

4   Is the diction specific or general?

5   How much of your reaction to this address is conditioned by the assassination of President Kennedy?

## ...AND COMPOSITION

6   Imitate the following: "Let us never negotiate out of fear. But let us never fear to negotiate."

7   Compare the addresses of Lincoln and Kennedy, touching on the persuasiveness, the rhetoric, and the diction of each.

8   Describe the tone of the address, the way figurative language contributes to this tone, and the kind of reaction the tone would be likely to evoke.

**BARTOLOMEO VANZETTI (1887–1927)**  with his slightly younger friend
Nicola Sacco was convicted of murder and executed in Massachusetts.
The two men were philosophical anarchists, and circumstances of the trial were
such that public opinion was roused all over the world, many holding—as
Vanzetti does in the speech below—that their trial and conviction
came about through prejudice against their beliefs rather than evidence
of guilt. In this statement the defendant, confronted with a situation
requiring of him a very positive stand, rallies a number of arguments which
range through several considerations. The language difficulty, you
will note, does not prevent the marshaling of effective
statements, and the lack of polish in the speaker even sharpens
our awareness of his successive moves in the progress of his defense.

# Last Speech to the Court

What I say is that I am innocent, not only of the Braintree crime,
but also of the Bridgewater crime. That I am not only innocent of these
two crimes, but in all my life I have never stole and I have never killed
and I have never spilled blood. That is what I want to say. And it is not
all. Not only am I innocent of these two crimes, not only in all my life
I have never stole, never killed, never spilled blood, but I have struggled
all my life, since I began to reason, to eliminate crime from the earth.

Everybody that knows these two arms knows very well that I did
not need to go in between the street and kill a man to take the money.
I can live with my two arms and live well. But besides that, I can live
even without work with my arm for other people. I have had plenty of
chance to live independently and to live what the world conceives to be
a higher life than not to gain our bread with the sweat of our brow. . . .

Well, I want to reach a little point farther, and it is this,—that not

only have I not been trying to steal in Bridgewater, not only have I not been in Braintree to steal and kill and have never steal or kill or spilt blood in all my life, not only have I struggled hard against crimes, but I have refused myself the commodity or glory of life, the pride of life of a good position, because in my consideration it is not right to exploit man. I have refused to go in business because I understand that business is a speculation on profit upon certain people that must depend upon the business man, and I do not consider that that is right and therefore I refuse to do that.

Now, I should say that I am not only innocent of all these things, not only have I never committed a real crime in my life—though some sins but not crimes—not only have I struggled all my life to eliminate crimes, the crimes that the official law and the official moral condemns, but also the crime that the official moral and the official law sanctions and sanctifies,—the exploitation and the oppression of the man by the man, and if there is a reason why I am here as a guilty man, if there is a reason why you in a few minutes can doom me, it is this reason and none else.

There is the more good man I ever cast my eyes upon since I lived, a man that will last and will grow always more near and more dear to the people, as far as into the heart of the people, so long as admiration for goodness and for sacrifice will last. I mean Eugene Debs. I will say that even a dog that killed the chickens would not have found an American jury to convict it with the proof that the Commonwealth produced against us. That man was not with me in Plymouth or with Sacco where he was on the day of the crime. You can say that it is arbitrary, what we are saying, that he is good and he applied to the other his own goodness, that he is incapable of crime, and he believed that everybody is incapable of crime.

Well, it may be like that but it is not, it could be like that but it is not, and that man has a real experience of court, of prison and of jury. Just because he want the world a little better he was persecuted and slandered from his boyhood to his old age, and indeed he was murdered by the prison. He know, and not only he but every man of understanding in the world, not only in this country but also in the other countries, men that we have provided a certain amount of a record of the times, they all still stick with us, the flower of mankind of Europe, the better writers, the greatest thinkers of Europe, have pleaded in our favor. The scientists, the greatest scientists, the greatest statesmen of Europe, have pleaded in our favor. The people of foreign nations have pleaded in our favor.

Is it possible that only a few on the jury, only two or three men, who would condemn their mother for worldly honor and for earthly fortune; is it possible that they are right against what the world, the whole world has say it is wrong and that I know that it is wrong? If there is one that I should know it, if it is right or if it is wrong, it is I and this man.

You see it is seven years that we are in jail. What we have suffered during these seven years no human tongue can say, and yet you see me before you, not trembling, you see me looking you in your eyes straight, not blushing, not changing color, not ashamed or in fear.

Eugene Debs say that not even a dog—something like that—not even a dog that kill the chickens would have been found guilty by American jury with the evidence that the Commonwealth have produced against us. I say that not even a leprous dog would have his appeal refused two times by the Supreme Court of Massachusetts—not even a leprous dog. . . .

Before you see us you already know that we were radicals, that we were underdogs, that we were the enemy of the institution that you can believe in good faith in their goodness—I don't want to condemn that— and that it was easy on the time of the first trial to get a verdict of guiltiness.

We know that you have spoke yourself and have spoke your hostility against us, and your despisement against us with friends of yours on the train, at the University Club of Boston, on the Golf Club of Worcester, Massachusetts. I am sure that if the people who know all what you say against us would have the civil courage to take the stand, maybe your Honor—I am sorry to say this because you are an old man, and I have an old father—but maybe you would be beside us in good justice at this time.

When you sentenced me at the Plymouth trial you say, to the best of my memory, of my good faith, that crimes were in accordance with my principle,—something of that sort,—and you take off one charge, if I remember it exactly, from the jury. The jury was so violent against me that they found me guilty of both charges, because there were only two. But they would have found me guilty of a dozen of charges against your Honor's instructions. Of course I remember that you told them that there was no reason to believe that if I were the bandit I have intention to kill somebody, so that they will take off the indictment of attempt to murder. Well, they found me guilty of what? And if I am right, you take out that and sentence me only for attempt to rob with arms,—something like that. But, Judge Thayer, you give more to me for that attempt of robbery than all the 448 men that were in Charlestown, all of those that attempted to rob, all those that have robbed, they have not such a sentence as you gave me for an attempt at robbery. . . .

We were tried during a time that has now passed into history. I mean by that, a time when there was a hysteria of resentment and hate against the people of our principles, against the foreigner, against slackers, and it seems to me—rather, I am positive of it, that both you and Mr. Katzmann has done all what it were in your power in order to work out, in order to agitate still more the passion of the juror, the prejudice of the juror, against us.

The jury were hating us because we were against the war, and the jury don't know that it makes any difference between a man that is against the war because he believes that the war is unjust, because he hate no country, because he is a cosmopolitan, and a man that is against the war because he is in favor of the other country that fights against the country in which he is, and therefore a spy, and he commits any crime in the country in which he is in behalf of the other country in order to serve the other country. We are not men of that kind. Katzmann know very well that. Katzmann know that we were against the war because we did not believe in the purpose for which they say that the war was done. We believe it that the war is wrong, and we believe this more now after ten years that we understood it day by day,—the consequences and the result of the after war. We believe more now than ever that the war was wrong, and we are against war more now than ever, and I am glad to be on the doomed scaffold if I can say to mankind, "Look out; you are in a catacomb of the flower of mankind. For what? All that they say to you, all that they have promised to you—it was a lie, it was an illusion, it was a cheat, it was a fraud, it was a crime. They promised you liberty. Where is liberty? They promised you prosperity. Where is prosperity? They have promised you elevation. Where is the elevation? . . ."

If I understand well, there have been agreement of counsel during the trial in which the counsel of defense shall not produce any evidence of my good conduct in Plymouth and the counsel of the prosecution would not have let the jury know that I was tried and convicted another time before in Plymouth. Well, I call that a one-sided agreement. In fact, even the telephone poles knew at the time of this trial at Dedham that I was tried and convicted in Plymouth; the jurymen knew that even when they slept. On the other side the jury have never seen I or Sacco and I think they have the right to incline to believe that the jury have never approached before the trial anyone that was sufficiently intimate with me and Sacco to be able to give them a description of our personal conduct. The jury don't know nothing about us. They have never seen us. The only thing that they know is the bad things that the newspaper have say when we were arrested and the bad story that the newspaper have say on the Plymouth trial. . . .

It was also said that the defense has put every obstacle to the handling of this case in order to delay the case. That sound weak for us, and I think it is injurious because it is not true. If we consider that the prosecution, the State, has employed one entire year to prosecute us, that is, one of the five years that the case has last was taken by the prosecution to begin our trial, our first trial. Then the defense make an appeal to you and you waited, or I think that you were resolute, that you had the resolute in your heart when the trial finished that you will refuse every appeal that we will put up to you. You waited a month or a month and a half and just lay down your decision on the eve of Christmas—just on the evening of Christ-

mas. We do not believe in the fable of the evening of Christmas, neither in the historical way nor in the church way. You know some of our folks still believe in that, and because we do not believe in that, it don't mean that we are not human. We are human, and Christmas is sweet to the heart of every man. I think that you have done that, to hand down your decision on the evening of Christmas, to poison the heart of our family and of our beloved. I am sorry to be compelled to say this, but everything that was said on your side has confirmed my suspicion until that suspicion has changed to certitude. So that you see that one year it has taken before trying us. . . .

What I want to say is this: Everybody ought to understand that the first of the defense has been terrible. My first lawyer did not stick to defend us. He has made no work to collect witnesses and evidence in our favor. The record in the Plymouth Court is a pity. I am told that they are almost one-half lost. So the defense had a tremendous work to do in order to collect some evidence, to collect some testimony to offset and to learn what the testimony of the State has done. And in this consideration it must be said that even if the defense take double time of the State without delay, double time that they delay the case it would have been reasonable, whereas it took less than the State.

Well, I have already say that I not only am not guilty of these two crimes, but I never commit a crime in my life,—I have never steal and I have never kill and I have never spilt blood, and I have fought against the crime, and I have fought and I have sacrified myself even to eliminate the crimes that the law and the church legitimate and sanctify.

This is what I say: I would not wish to a dog or to a snake, to the most low and misfortunate creature of the earth—I would not wish to any of them what I have had to suffer for things that I am not guilty of. But my conviction is that I have suffered for things that I am guilty of. I am suffering because I am a radical and indeed I am a radical; I have suffered because I was an Italian, and indeed I am an Italian; I have suffered more for my family and for my beloved than for myself; but I am so convinced to be right that if you could execute me two times, and if I could be reborn two other times, I would live again to do what I have done already.

I have finished. Thank you.

## TOPICS FOR DISCUSSION

1  What details in the statement illustrate the political and economic philosophy of Vanzetti?

2  What prejudices does Vanzetti feel worked against him in his trial? If there were such prejudices, would they interfere with the execution of justice in a courtroom today?

3   Controversy still lingers regarding the innocence or guilt of Sacco and Vanzetti, although the most considered opinion is that they were not guilty or at least not proved guilty. Had you an opinion before you read Vanzetti's statement? Did he convince you of his innocence or introduce you to any new doubts? If so, point directly to those passages that may have altered your opinion.

4   Who was Eugene Debs? What connection did he have with Sacco and Vanzetti? What is the general estimate of Debs today?

5   Why are the occasionally broken English and the almost childlike imagery so effective in communicating Vanzetti's feelings?

## ...AND COMPOSITION

6   Read a standard reference work and a standard United States history on this famous case and write a defense or prosecution statement for the trial.

7   Define a radical, comparing, if you choose, Vanzetti's simple and open statement of his radical allegiances with the complexities of modern radicalism, which is both leftist and rightist in its persuasions.

8   Most capital executions involve persons of low or no income and persons from racial minorities. Find some concrete statistics supporting this statement and write an essay considering whether the statistics are attributable to the kind of unequal justice of which Vanzetti speaks or to a preponderance of capital crime among these groups or to both.

GEORGE ORWELL [ERIC BLAIR] (1903–1950)   more fully identified in
Part I, here delivers a vivid example of one kind of writing: the careful
report of an event with its accompanying particulars. Our judgments
about events derive from the actual experiences connected with them. A
clear-eyed delivery of what the experience consists of is often surprisingly
effective; it seems that not till we retell exactly what happened do we
fully realize what has gone on. Note that the occasion provides Orwell with
a number of apparently irrelevant but actually quite pertinent incidents—the
dog, the puddle, the accents and appearances of the men. To see, to
tell—these are often enough to effect an utterly admirable composition:
the event supplies the details, and the writer contrives to let the
reader have the fullest human realization of what happens.

# A Hanging

It was in Burma, a sodden morning of the rains. A sickly light, like
yellow tinfoil, was slanting over the high walls into the jail yard. We were
waiting outside the condemned cells, a row of sheds fronted with double
bars, like small animal cages. Each cell measured about ten feet by ten
and was quite bare within except for a plank bed and a pot for drinking
water. In some of them brown silent men were squatting at the inner bars,
with their blankets draped round them. These were the condemned men,
due to be hanged within the next week or two.

One prisoner had been brought out of his cell. He was a Hindu, a puny
wisp of a man, with a shaven head and vague liquid eyes. He had a thick,
sprouting moustache, absurdly too big for his body, rather like the
moustache of a comic man on the films. Six tall Indian warders were guarding him and getting him ready for the gallows. Two of them stood by with
rifles and fixed bayonets, while the others handcuffed him, passed a chain
through his handcuffs and fixed it to their belts, and lashed his arms tight
to his sides. They crowded very close about him, with their hands always
on him in a careful, caressing grip, as though all the while feeling him to
make sure he was there. It was like men handling a fish which is still alive
and may jump back into the water. But he stood quite unresisting, yielding
his arms limply to the ropes, as though he hardly noticed what was happening.

Eight o'clock struck and a bugle call, desolately thin in the wet air,
floated from the distant barracks. The superintendent of the jail, who was
standing apart from the rest of us, moodily prodding the gravel with his
stick, raised his head at the sound. He was an army doctor, with a gray
toothbrush moustache and a gruff voice. "For God's sake hurry up,
Francis," he said irritably. "The man ought to have been dead by this
time. Aren't you ready yet?"

Francis, the head jailer, a fat Dravidian in a white drill suit and gold spectacles, waved his black hand. "Yes sir, yes sir," he bubbled. "All iss satisfactorily prepared. The hangman iss waiting. We shall proceed."

"Well, quick march, then. The prisoners can't get their breakfast till this job's over."

We set out for the gallows. Two warders marched on either side of the prisoner, with their rifles at the slope; two others marched close against him, gripping him by arm and shoulder, as though at once pushing and supporting him. The rest of us, magistrates and the like, followed behind. Suddenly, when we had gone ten yards, the procession stopped short without any order or warning. A dreadful thing had happened—a dog, come goodness knows whence, had appeared in the yard. It came bounding among us with a loud volley of barks, and leapt round us wagging its whole body, wild with glee at finding so many human beings together. It was a large woolly dog, half Airedale, half pariah. For a moment it pranced round us, and then, before anyone could stop it, it had made a dash for the prisoner and, jumping up, tried to lick his face. Everyone stood aghast, too taken aback even to grab at the dog.

"Who let that bloody brute in here?" said the superintendent angrily. "Catch it, someone!"

A warder, detached from the escort, charged clumsily after the dog, but it danced and gamboled just out of his reach, taking everything as part of the game. A young Eurasian jailer picked up a handful of gravel and tried to stone the dog away, but it dodged the stones and came after us again. Its yaps echoed from the jail walls. The prisoner, in the grasp of the two warders, looked on incuriously, as though this was another formality of the hanging. It was several minutes before someone managed to catch the dog. Then we put my handkerchief through its collar and moved off once more, with the dog still straining and whimpering.

It was about forty yards to the gallows. I watched the bare brown back of the prisoner marching in front of me. He walked clumsily with his bound arms, but quite steadily, with that bobbing gait of the Indian who never straightens his knees. At each step his muscles slid neatly into place, the lock of hair on his scalp danced up and down, his feet printed themselves on the wet gravel. And once, in spite of the men who gripped him by each shoulder, he stepped slightly aside to avoid a puddle on the path.

It is curious, but till that moment I had never realized what it means to destroy a healthy, conscious man. When I saw the prisoner step aside to avoid the puddle I saw the mystery, the unspeakable wrongness, of cutting a life short when it is in full tide. This man was not dying, he was alive just as we are alive. All the organs of his body were working—bowels digesting food, skin renewing itself, nails growing, tissues forming—all toiling away in solemn foolery. His nails would still be growing when he stood on the drop, when he was falling through the air with a tenth of a

second to live. His eyes saw the yellow gravel and the gray walls, and his brain still remembered, foresaw, reasoned—reasoned even about puddles. He and we were a party of men walking together, seeing, hearing, feeling, understanding the same world; and in two minutes, with a sudden snap, one of us would be gone—one mind less, one world less.

The gallows stood in a small yard, separate from the main grounds of the prison, and overgrown with tall prickly weeds. It was a brick erection like three sides of a shed, with planking on top, and above that two beams and a crossbar with the rope dangling. The hangman, a gray-haired convict in the white uniform of the prison, was waiting beside his machine. He greeted us with a servile crouch as we entered. At a word from Francis the two warders, gripping the prisoner more closely than ever, half led half pushed him to the gallows and helped him clumsily up the ladder. Then the hangman climbed up and fixed the rope round the prisoner's neck.

We stood waiting, five yards away. The warders had formed in a rough circle round the gallows. And then, when the noose was fixed, the prisoner began crying out to his god. It was a high, reiterated cry of "Ram! Ram! Ram! Ram!" not urgent and fearful like a prayer or cry for help, but steady, rhythmical, almost like the tolling of a bell. The dog answered the sound with a whine. The hangman, still standing on the gallows, produced a small cotton bag like a flour bag and drew it down over the prisoner's face. But the sound, muffled by the cloth, still persisted, over and over again: "Ram! Ram! Ram! Ram! Ram!"

The hangman climbed down and stood ready, holding the lever. Minutes seemed to pass. The steady, muffled crying from the prisoner went on and on, "Ram! Ram! Ram!" never faltering for an instant. The super-intendent, his head on his chest, was slowly poking the ground with his stick; perhaps he was counting the cries, allowing the prisoner a fixed number—fifty, perhaps, or a hundred. Everyone had changed color. The Indians had gone gray like bad coffee, and one or two of the bayonets were wavering. We looked at the lashed, hooded man on the drop, and listened to his cries—each cry another second of life; the same thought was in all our minds: oh, kill him quickly, get it over, stop that abominable noise!

Suddenly the superintendent made up his mind. Throwing up his head he made a swift motion with his stick. "Chalo!" he shouted almost fiercely.

There was a clanking noise, and then dead silence. The prisoner had vanished, and the rope was twisting on itself. I let go of the dog, and it galloped immediately to the back of the gallows; but when it got there it stopped short, barked, and then retreated into a corner of the yard, where it stood among the weeds, looking timorously out at us. We went round the gallows to inspect the prisoner's body. He was dangling with his toes pointing straight downward, very slowly revolving, as dead as a stone.

The superintendent reached out with his stick and poked the bare brown body; it oscillated slightly. *"He's* all right," said the superintendent.

He backed out from under the gallows, and blew out a deep breath. The moody look had gone out of his face quite suddenly. He glanced at his wrist watch. "Eight minutes past eight. Well, that's all for this morning, thank God."

The warders unfixed bayonets and marched away. The dog, sobered and conscious of having misbehaved itself, slipped after them. We walked out of the gallows yard, past the condemned cells with their waiting prisoners, into the big central yard of the prison. The convicts, under the command of warders armed with lathis, were already receiving their breakfast. They squatted in long rows, each man holding a tin pannikin, while two warders with buckets marched round ladling out rice; it seemed quite a homely, jolly scene, after the hanging. An enormous relief had come upon us now that the job was done. One felt an impulse to sing, to break into a run, to snigger. All at once everyone began chattering gaily.

Several people laughed—at what, nobody seemed certain.

Francis was walking by the superintendent, talking garrulously: "Well, sir, all hass passed off with the utmost satisfactoriness. It was all finished—flick! like that. It is not always so—oah, no! I have known cases where the doctor wass obliged to go beneath the gallows and pull the prissoner's legs to ensure decease. Most disagreeable!"

"Wriggling about, eh? That's bad," said the superintendent.

"Ach, sir, it iss worse when they become refractory! One man, I recall, clung to the bars of hiss cage when we went to take him out. You will scarcely credit, sir, that it took six warders to dislodge him, three pulling at each leg. We reasoned with him. 'My dear fellow,' we said, 'think of all the pain and trouble you are causing to us!' But no, he would not listen! Ach, he wass very troublesome!"

I found that I was laughing quite loudly. Everyone was laughing. Even the superintendent grinned in a tolerant way. "You'd better all come out and have a drink," he said quite genially. "I've got a bottle of whisky in the car. We could do with it."

We went through the big double gates of the prison into the road. "Pulling at his legs!" exclaimed a Burmese magistrate suddenly, and burst into a loud chuckling. We all began laughing again. At that moment Francis' anecdote seemed extraordinarily funny. We all had a drink together, native and European alike, quite amicably. The dead man was a hundred yards away.

## TOPICS FOR DISCUSSION

1   As you remember from "Politics and the English Language," Orwell was deeply concerned with the exactness and effect of words. Make a list of the words used to mark the uncomfortable

atmosphere surrounding the execution. In any case would the connotations have remained the same had synonyms been substituted, or is each word obviously an effective word in the context?

2   Notice the exact, concrete details describing the Hindu prisoner. How do these details affect your reaction to him? How does this description relate to Orwell's central thesis?

3   What does the dog recognize in the prisoner that the guards and officials apparently fail to recognize? How does the puddle episode improve the vision of at least the author? Although the dog may be a creature of fact, his use as a product of the imagination only is particularly vivid. Why?

4   The preponderance of almost trivial detail in the shackling of the prisoner is more than a recounting of a true event. What does it tell you of the author's immediate and lasting reactions? What does it tell you of the ritual of execution? Does it have any effect on you?

5   Any event of this sort cannot help but impress a man, any man. Reactions are as various as the men present, and the stimuli to reactions as various as the multitude of detail crowding the few minutes of the narrative. Why is the shouting of "Ram" so disturbing? Why does Francis's choice of words describing the event annoy a reader but apparently soothe Francis? Why do the men laugh after the execution?

## ...AND COMPOSITION

6   Write a defense or repudiation of capital punishment, basing your remarks most heavily on one specific case which helped you formulate your opinion.

7   Write a short narrative of an impressive experience, paying particular attention to the details which give color to that experience.

8   Executions in most states cost more money than the maintenance of prisoners on life sentences, thus removing one possibly valid reason for capital punishment, the saving of state funds. Why do you think the ritual element has become so important, resulting in such elaborate executions?

**SAMUEL JOHNSON (1709–1784)** critic, conversationalist, dictionary maker, dominates our idea of the literary scene of his time. His wit and unique personal qualities make him one of the most interesting of all the great literary figures, and through James Boswell, his biographer, we have gained one of the most detailed accounts in all the world's history. Johnson's celebrated letter to Lord Chesterfield demonstrates how a letter may move steadily to make a point, with clear divisions: occasion for writing, a detailing of the circumstances, a developing of the writer's feelings which portend a conclusion, and then the conclusion. Something of Johnson's justification for such a letter may emerge from the character you glimpse in our next selection, a letter Lord Chesterfield writes, in a worldly fashion, to his son. But Johnson was later somewhat ashamed of his asperity toward Chesterfield, and it is true that the letter here reveals the touchiness of the great man, as well as his ability in deft attack.

# To the Right Honorable the Earl of Chesterfield

*February 7, 1755.*

MY LORD:

I have lately been informed by the proprietor of *The World,* that two papers, in which my *Dictionary* is recommended to the public, were written by your Lordship. To be so distinguished is an honor which, being very little accustomed to favors from the great, I know not well how to receive, or in what terms to acknowledge.

When, upon some slight encouragement, I first visited your Lordship, I was overpowered, like the rest of mankind, by the enchantment of your address; and I could not forbear to wish that I might boast myself "Le

vainqueur du vainqueur de la terre"; that I might obtain that regard for which I saw the world contending; but I found my attendance so little encouraged, that neither pride nor modesty would suffer me to continue it. When I had once addressed your Lordship in public, I had exhausted all the art of pleasing which a retired and uncourtly scholar can possess. I had done all that I could; and no man is well pleased to have his all neglected, be it ever so little.

Seven years, my Lord, have now passed, since I waited in your outward rooms, or was repulsed from your door; during which time I have been pushing on my work through difficulties, of which it is useless to complain, and have brought it at last to the verge of publication, without one act of assistance, one word of encouragement, or one smile of favor. Such treatment I did not expect, for I never had a Patron before.

The shepherd in Virgil grew at last acquainted with Love, and found him a native of the rocks.

Is not a Patron, my Lord, one who looks with unconcern on a man struggling for life in the water, and, when he has reached ground, encumbers him with help? The notice which you have been pleased to take of my labors, had it been early, had been kind; but it has been delayed till I am indifferent, and cannot enjoy it; till I am solitary, and cannot impart it; till I am known, and do not want it. I hope it is no very cynical asperity not to confess obligations where no benefit has been received, or to be unwilling that the Public should consider me as owing that to a Patron, which Providence has enabled me to do for myself.

Having carried on my work thus far with so little obligation to any favorer of learning, I shall not be disappointed though I should conclude it, if less be possible, with less; for I have been long wakened from that dream of hope, in which I once boasted myself with so much exultation,

    *My Lord,*
    *Your Lordship's most humble,*
    *Most obedient servant,*

                                    SAM. JOHNSON.

## TOPICS FOR DISCUSSION

1  What is the tone of the letter?
2  How much of the tone is the result of the diction? Why?
3  Does Johnson seem excessively proud, or is this a pose assumed for a special purpose?
4  Aside from the specific date and the obviously outmoded practice

of personal patronage, what marks this letter as the work of a writer from an earlier time?

5 "The shepherd in Virgil grew at last acquainted with Love, and found him a native of the rocks." What does this mean in context?

## ...AND COMPOSITION

6 Write a satiric letter.

7 Find Johnson's *Dictionary* in your school library and look through it for other evidences of his wit.

8 Personal patronage is a thing of the past. Should the Federal government (or state governments) participate in the arts by giving financial assistance? If you think so, how could it be done so that the government would not restrict intellectual freedom? If you think not, why not?

**PHILIP DORMER STANHOPE, EARL OF CHESTERFIELD (1694–1773)** in the eighteenth-century world of wit was a man of taste, a patron of the arts, and in general a success in the terms he mentions in his first paragraph below—a man of fortune and figure in the fashionable part of the world of London. Playfully as you may take his letter, it demonstrates solidly this type of communication—made for display, elaborately exploring one subject, becoming something very close to a personal essay. Chesterfield's assumptions about human motivation are extreme enough in themselves to gain him Johnson's enmity: the man of fashion is made one who conducts himself always in terms of gaining something from others, a mode of conduct strikingly different from that of a located, individual, masterful man like Johnson.

# A Letter to His Son

*London, September 5, 1748.*

DEAR BOY:

. . . As women are a considerable or at least a pretty numerous, part of company, and as their suffrages go a great way towards establishing a man's character in the fashionable part of the world (which is of great importance to the fortune and figure he proposes to make in it), it is necessary to please them. I will, therefore, upon this subject let you into certain *arcana,* that will be very useful for you to know, but which you must, with the utmost care, conceal; and never seem to know. Women, then, are only children of a larger growth; they have an entertaining tattle, and sometimes wit, but for solid reasoning, good sense, I never knew in my life one that had it, or who reasoned or acted consequentially for four and twenty hours together. Some little passion or humor always breaks in upon their best resolutions. Their beauty neglected or controverted, their age increased or their supposed understandings depreciated, instantly kindles their little passions, and over-turns any system of consequential conduct, that in their most reasonable moments they might have been capable of forming. A man of sense only trifles with them, plays with them, humors and flatters them, as he does with a sprightly, forward child; but he neither consults them about, nor trusts them with, serious matters; though he often makes them believe that he does both, which is the thing in the world that they are proud of; for they love mightily to be dabbling in business (which, by the way, they always spoil), and, being justly distrustful, that men in general look upon them in a trifling light, they almost adore that man who talks more seriously to them, and who seems to consult and trust them; I say, who seems,—for weak men really do, but wise ones only seem to do it. No flattery is either

too high or too low for them. They will greedily swallow the highest, and gratefully accept of the lowest; and you may safely flatter any woman, from her understanding down to the exquisite taste of her fan. Women who are either indisputably beautiful or indisputably ugly are best flattered upon the score of their understandings; but those who are in a state of mediocrity are best flattered upon their beauty, or at least their graces; for every woman who is not absolutely ugly, thinks herself handsome, but, not hearing often that she is so, is the more grateful, and the more obliged to the few who tell her so; whereas a decided and conscious beauty looks upon every tribute paid to her beauty only as her due, but wants to shine, and to be considered on the side of her understanding; and a woman who is ugly enough to know that she is so, knows that she has nothing left for it but her understanding, which is consequently (and probably in more senses than one) her weak side. But these are secrets which you must keep inviolably, if you would not, like Orpheus, be torn to pieces by the whole sex; on the contrary, a man who thinks of living in the great world must be gallant, polite, and attentive to please the women. They have, from the weakness of men, more or less influence in all courts; they absolutely stamp every man's character in the *beau monde,* and make it either current, or cry it down, and stop it in payments. It is, therefore, absolutely necessary to manage, please, and flatter them, and never to discover the least mark of contempt, which is what they never forgive; but in this they are not singular, for it is the same with men; who will much sooner forgive an injustice than an insult. Every man is not ambitious, or covetous, or passionate; but every man has pride enough in his composition to feel and resent the least slight and contempt. Remember, therefore, most carefully to conceal your contempt, however just, wherever you would not make an implacable enemy. Men are much more unwilling to have their weaknesses and imperfections known, than their crimes; and if you hint to a man that you think him silly, ignorant, or even ill bred or awkward, he will hate you more and longer than if you tell him plainly that you think him a rogue. Never yield to that temptation, which to most young men is very strong, of exposing other people's weaknesses and infirmities, for the sake either of diverting the company, or showing your own superiority. You may get the laugh on your side by it for the present; but you will make enemies by it forever; and even those who laugh with you then, will, upon reflection, fear, and consequently hate you: besides that, it is ill natured, and a good heart desires rather to conceal than expose other people's weaknesses or misfortunes. If you have wit, use it to please, and not to hurt: you may shine, like the sun in the temperate zones, without scorching. Here it is wished for; under the Line it is dreaded.

These are some of the hints which my long experience in the great world enables me to give you, and which, if you attend to them, may prove

useful to you, in your journey through it. I wish it may be a prosperous one; at least, I am sure that it must be your own fault if it is not.

Make my compliments to Mr. Harte, who, I am very sorry to hear, is not well. I hope by this time he is recovered. Adieu!

## TOPICS FOR DISCUSSION

1  What is Chesterfield's conception of women?

2  Chesterfield wrote in the eighteenth century, but are his attitudes necessarily old-fashioned? Are there areas of American life in which these notions are still the prevalent ones? Do you agree with Chesterfield?

3  What is Chesterfield's conception of men? Do you agree?

4  In your opinion do Chesterfield's sharp distinctions between the characters of men and women demonstrate perceptivity on his part? Stupidity? An outmoded habit of thought? Are there modern counterparts of Chesterfield? Without simplifying too much, can you suggest which professions might provoke self-conscious mannerisms, or do all professions have aspects likely to elicit such behavior?

5  Does the letter writer seem well intentioned or merely interested in illustrating his own knowledge of the world?

## ... AND COMPOSITION

6  Write a letter of advice on how to deal socially with men like Chesterfield.

7  Write an essay identifying formal social courtesies as either hypocrisy or tact.

8  Compose a likely answer from Chesterfield to Samuel Johnson's letter.

**JOHN KEATS (1795–1821)**   is what most people mean when they say "poet."
His prose, too, reveals the true ore; his letters are marked throughout
by the quality of genius. Students should read them. On Sunday, February 14,
1819, Keats began a long letter to his brother and his sister-in-law,
George and Georgiana Keats; in that letter, continued at intervals over several
months, Keats communicated his quick, real, unrehearsed thoughts. This
letter is at an opposite pole from the careful public statement of
Lord Chesterfield; here, there cannot be cynicism (though there is some
distrust), and there cannot be mannerism (though the writer is aware of himself)—
there is simply a headlong immediacy. A letter can be a wholehearted pursuit
of what consciousness offers as one human being tries to carry to another
his finest perceptions. And this is the kind of letter John Keats writes.

# A Letter to George and Georgiana Keats

I have this moment received a note from Haslam, in which he expects
the death of his Father, who has been for some time in a state of insensibility—his mother bears up, he says, very well—I shall go to town to-morrow
to see him. This is the world—thus we cannot expect to give away many
hours to pleasure. Circumstances are like Clouds continually gathering and
bursting. While we are laughing, the seed of some trouble is put into the
wide arable land of events—while we are laughing it sprouts, it grows,
and suddenly bears a poison fruit which we must pluck. Even so we have
leisure to reason on the misfortunes of our friends; our own touch us
too nearly for words. Very few men have ever arrived at a complete disinterestedness of Mind: very few have been influenced by a pure desire
of the benefit of others—in the greater part of the Benefactors to Humanity
some meretricious motive has sullied their greatness—some melodramatic
scenery has fascinated them. From the manner in which I feel Haslam's
misfortune I perceive how far I am from any humble standard of disinterestedness. Yet this feeling ought to be carried to its highest pitch, as
there is no fear of its ever injuring Society—which it would do, I fear,
pushed to an extremity. For in wild nature the Hawk would lose his
Breakfast of Robins and the Robin his of Worms—the Lion must starve
as well as the Swallow. The greater part of Men make their way with the
same instinctiveness, the same unwandering eye from their purposes, the
same animal eagerness as the Hawk. The Hawk wants a Mate, so does the
Man—look at them both, they set about it and procure one in the same
manner. They want both a nest and they both set about one in the same
manner—they get their food in the same manner. The noble animal Man
for his amusement smokes his pipe—the Hawk balances about the Clouds
—that is the only difference of their leisures. This it is that makes the
Amusement of Life—to a speculative Mind—I go among the Fields and

catch a glimpse of a Stoat or a fieldmouse peeping out of the withered grass—the creature hath a purpose and its eyes are bright with it. I go amongst the buildings of a city and I see a Man hurrying along—to what? the Creature has a purpose and his eyes are bright with it. But then, as Wordsworth says, "we have all one human heart"—there is an electric fire in human nature tending to purify—so that among these human creatures there is continually some birth of new heroism. The pity is, that we must wonder at it as we should at finding a pearl in rubbish. I have no doubt that thousands of people never heard of have had hearts completely disinterested: I can remember but two—Socrates and Jesus—their Histories evince it. What I heard a little time ago, Taylor observe with respect to Socrates, may be said of Jesus—That he was so great a man that though he transmitted no writing of his own to posterity, we have his Mind and his sayings and his greatness handed to us by others. It is to be lamented that the history of the latter was written and revised by Men interested in the pious frauds of Religion. Yet through all this I see his splendour. Even here, though I myself am pursuing the same instinctive course as the veriest human animal you can think of, I am, however, young, writing at random, straining at particles of light in the midst of a great darkness, without knowing the bearing of any one assertion, of any one opinion. Yet may I not in this be free from sin? May there not be superior beings, amused with any graceful though instinctive, attitude my mind may fall into as I am entertained with the alertness of a Stoat or the anxiety of a Deer? Though a quarrel in the Streets is a thing to be hated, the energies displayed in it are fine; the commonest Man shows a grace in his quarrel. By a superior Being our reasonings may take the same tone—though erroneous they may be fine. This is the very thing in which consists Poetry, and if so it is not so fine a thing as philosophy—For the same reason that an eagle is not so fine a thing as a truth. Give me this credit—Do you not think I strive—to know myself? Give me this credit, and you will not think that on my own account I repeat Milton's lines—

> How charming is divine Philosophy
> Not harsh and crabbed, as dull fools suppose
> But musical as is Apollo's lute—

No—not for myself—feeling grateful as I do to have got into a state of mind to relish them properly. Nothing ever becomes real till it is experienced—even a Proverb is no proverb to you, till your Life has illustrated it. I am ever afraid that your anxiety for me will lead you to fear for the violence of my temperament continually smothered down: for that reason I did not intend to have sent you the following sonnet—but look over the two last pages and ask yourselves whether I have not that in me which will bear the buffets of the world. It will be the best comment on my sonnet; it will show you that it was written with no Agony but that of ignorance;

with no thirst of anything but Knowledge when pushed to the point, though the first steps to it were through my human passions—they went away, and I wrote with my Mind—and perhaps I must confess a little bit of my heart—

> Why did I laugh to-night? No voice will tell:
>     No God, no Demon of severe response,
> Deigns to reply from heaven or from Hell.
>     Then to my human heart I turn at once.
> Heart! Thou and I are here sad and alone;
>     Say, wherefore did I laugh? O mortal pain!
> O Darkness! Darkness! ever must I moan,
>     To question Heaven and Hell and Heart in vain.
> Why did I laugh? I know this Being's lease,
>     My fancy to its utmost blisses spreads;
> Yet would I on this very midnight cease,
>     And the world's gaudy ensigns see in shreds;
> Verse, Fame, and Beauty are intense indeed,
> But Death intenser—Death is Life's high meed.

I went to bed and enjoyed an uninterrupted Sleep. Sane I went to bed and sane I arose.

## TOPICS FOR DISCUSSION

1   How can you tell from the letter itself that it is actually a part of Keats's correspondence and not an "open" or public letter?

2   What is "disinterestedness"?

3   Both of the following sentences appear in this letter: "Very few men have ever arrived at a complete disinterestedness of Mind . . . and "I have no doubt that thousands of people never heard of have had hearts completely disinterested." Is this a contradiction or a complexity of thought produced by exploring a subject?

4   What are the correspondences of the hawk analogy? How is this analogy related to the theme of disinterestedness?

5   How was the disinterestedness of Jesus converted into something else by the interests of men? Does this comment by Keats help to illustrate the term that is the theme of the letter?

## . . . AND COMPOSITION

6   Comment on the several animal analogies in this letter, touching on their aptness, clarity, and effect.

7   "Nothing ever becomes real till it is experienced—even a Proverb is no proverb to you, till your Life has illustrated it." Discuss.

8   Read any one of Keats's great odes ("Ode to Psyche," "Ode on Indolence," "Ode to a Nightingale," "Ode on a Grecian Urn," "Ode on Melancholy," or "To Autumn") and examine it in light of the subjects touched upon in this letter.

**JAMES BALDWIN (1924–     )** in novels, plays, stories, and articles and through speeches and on the air, participates in the fast social changes typical of our time. Here, in the form of a letter to his nephew, he actually addresses other readers—readers who gain assurance that as Negroes they have a special value, and readers who are reminded that as whites they have let injustice happen and have missed knowing a certain quality of experience. The letter is polemical; charges are leveled against evils and against evil or misled men, but the explicit intent is the achievement of social change through enlarged awareness. That kind of achievement is a natural goal for a writer; composition offers that kind of enlightenment.

# *My Dungeon Shook*

DEAR JAMES:

I have begun this letter five times and torn it up five times. I keep seeing your face, which is also the face of your father and my brother. Like him, you are tough, dark, vulnerable, moody—with a very definite tendency to sound truculent because you want no one to think you are soft. You may be like your grandfather in this, I don't know, but certainly both you and your father resemble him very much physically. Well, he is dead, he never saw you, and he had a terrible life; he was defeated long before he died because, at the bottom of his heart, he really believed what white people said about him. This is one of the reasons that he became so holy. I am sure that your father has told you something about all that. Neither you nor your father exhibit any tendency towards holiness: you really *are* of another era, part of what happened when the Negro left the land and came into what the late E. Franklin Frazier called "the cities of destruction." You can only be destroyed by believing that you really are what the white world calls a *nigger*. I tell you this because I love you, and please don't you ever forget it.

I have known both of you all your lives, have carried your Daddy in my arms and on my shoulders, kissed and spanked him and watched him learn to walk. I don't know if you've known anybody from that far back; if you've loved anybody that long, first as an infant, then as a child, then as a man, you gain a strange perspective on time and human pain and effort. Other people cannot see what I see whenever I look into your father's face, for behind your father's face as it is today are all those other faces which were his. Let him laugh and I see a cellar your father does not remember and a house he does not remember and I hear in his present laughter his laughter as a child. Let him curse and I remember him falling down the cellar steps, and howling, and I remember, with pain, his tears, which my hand or your grandmother's so easily wiped away. But no one's

hand can wipe away those tears he sheds invisibly today, which one hears in his laughter and in his speech and in his songs. I know what the world has done to my brother and how narrowly he has survived it. And I know, which is much worse, and this is the crime of which I accuse my country and my countrymen, and for which neither I nor time nor history will ever forgive them, that they have destroyed and are destroying hundreds of thousands of lives and do not know it and do not want to know it. One can be, indeed one must strive to become, tough and philosophical concerning destruction and death, for this is what most of mankind has been best at since we have heard of man. (But remember: *most* of mankind is not *all* of mankind.) But it is not permissible that the authors of devastation should also be innocent. It is the innocence which constitutes the crime.

Now, my dear namesake, these innocent and well-meaning people, your countrymen, have caused you to be born under conditions not very far removed from those described for us by Charles Dickens in the London of more than a hundred years ago. (I hear the chorus of the innocents screaming, "No! This is not true! How *bitter* you are!"—but I am writing this letter to *you,* to try to tell you something about how to handle *them,* for most of them do not yet really know that you exist. I *know* the conditions under which you were born, for I was there. Your countrymen were *not* there, and haven't made it yet. Your grandmother was also there, and no one has ever accused her of being bitter. I suggest that the innocents check with her. She isn't hard to find. Your countrymen don't know that *she* exists, either, though she has been working for them all their lives.)

Well, you were born, here you came, something like fifteen years ago; and though your father and mother and grandmother, looking about the streets through which they were carrying you, staring at the walls into which they brought you, had every reason to be heavyhearted, yet they were not. For here you were, Big James, named for me—you were a big baby, I was not—here you were: to be loved. To be loved, baby, hard, at once, and forever, to strengthen you against the loveless world. Remember that: I know how black it looks today, for you. It looked bad that day, too, yes, we were trembling. We have not stopped trembling yet, but if we had not loved each other none of us would have survived. And now you must survive because we love you, and for the sake of your children and your children's children.

This innocent country set you down in a ghetto in which, in fact, it intended that you should perish. Let me spell out precisely what I mean by that, for the heart of the matter is here, and the root of my dispute with my country. You were born where you were born and faced the future that you faced because you were black and *for no other reason.* The limits of your ambition were, thus, expected to be set forever. You were born into a society which spelled out with brutal clarity, and in as many ways as possible, that you were a worthless human being. You were

not expected to aspire to excellence: you were expected to make peace with mediocrity. Wherever you have turned, James, in your short time on this earth, you have been told where you could go and what you could do (and *how* you could do it) and where you could live and whom you could marry. I know your countrymen do not agree with me about this, and I hear them saying, "You exaggerate." They do not know Harlem, and I do. So do you. Take no one's word for anything, including mine— but trust your experience. Know whence you came. If you know whence you came, there is really no limit to where you can go. The details and symbols of your life have been deliberately constructed to make you believe what white people say about you. Please try to remember that what they believe, as well as what they do and cause you to endure, does not testify to your inferiority but to their inhumanity and fear. Please try to be clear, dear James, through the storm which rages about your youthful head today, about the reality which lies behind the words *acceptance* and *integration*. There is no reason for you to try to become like white people and there is no basis whatever for their impertinent assumption that *they* must accept *you*. The really terrible thing, old buddy, is that *you* must accept *them*. And I mean that very seriously. You must accept them and accept them with love. For these innocent people have no other hope. They are, in effect, still trapped in a history which they do not understand; and until they understand it, they cannot be released from it. They have had to believe for many years, and for innumerable reasons, that black men are inferior to white men. Many of them, indeed, know better, but, as you will discover, people find it very difficult to act on what they know. To act is to be committed, and to be committed is to be in danger. In this case, the danger, in the minds of most white Americans, is the loss of their identity. Try to imagine how you would feel if you woke up one morning to find the sun shining and all the stars aflame. You would be frightened because it is out of the order of nature. Any upheaval in the universe is terrifying because it so profoundly attacks one's sense of one's own reality. Well, the black man has functioned in the white man's world as a fixed star, as an immovable pillar: and as he moves out of his place, heaven and earth are shaken to their foundations. You, don't be afraid. I said that it was intended that you should perish in the ghetto, perish by never being allowed to go behind the white man's definitions, by never being allowed to spell your proper name. You have, and many of us have, defeated this intention; and, by a terrible law, a terrible paradox, those innocents who believed that your imprisonment made them safe are losing their grasp of reality. But these men are your brothers—your lost, younger brothers. And if the word *integration* means anything, this is what it means: that we, with love, shall force our brothers to see themselves as they are, to cease fleeing from reality and begin to change it. For this is your home, my friend, do not be driven from it; great men have done great things here, and will again,

and we can make America what America must become. It will be hard, James, but you come from sturdy, peasant stock, men who picked cotton and dammed rivers and built railroads, and, in the teeth of the most terrifying odds, achieved an unassailable and monumental dignity. You come from a long line of great poets, some of the greatest poets since Homer One of them said, *The very time I thought I was lost, My dungeon shook and my chains fell off.*

You know, and I know, that the country is celebrating one hundred years of freedom one hundred years too soon. We cannot be free until they are free. God bless you, James, and Godspeed.

*Your uncle,*

JAMES

## TOPICS FOR DISCUSSION

1   Is this a real letter, or does it have the characteristics of an essay in letter form, an essay intended, as a letter is not, for public scrutiny?

2   What are the paradoxes involved in Baldwin's use of "innocence"?

3   What does "acceptance" mean?

4   What must the white man do to lose his innocence? Does this letter offer a reasonable explanation of the racial issue facing American society?

## ... AND COMPOSITION

5   Compare the letters of Baldwin and Keats as real letters written to real people and as attempts to define complex subjects.

6   Baldwin quotes the following: "The very time I thought I was lost, My dungeon shook and my chains fell off." Analyze the meaning and aptness of these lines in this letter.

7   Baldwin's answer to racial dissension is not a legal answer. Do you think any of his objectives can be furthered by new laws or by better enforcement of existing ones?

**CHARLES LAMB (1775–1834)** ranks as the most notable English essayist, and in the personal essay below we have him at his best—advancing with playful perspicacity an odd idea from which he manages to extract many reflections. Lamb wrote drama, fiction, criticism; he turned his ability to many things, but in sociability and in essays he was most at home. In this kind of writing the writer relies on himself for his content; he is ready to follow his impulses. At its best—as in Lamb—this procedure may enlarge the realms of consciousness to include a whole range of joy, whimsy, wonderful recollection, and—oddly enough—wisdom.

# The Two Races of Men

The human species, according to the best theory I can form of it, is composed of two distinct races, *the men who borrow, and the men who lend.* To these two original diversities may be reduced all those impertinent classifications of Gothic and Celtic tribes, white men, black men, red men. All the dwellers upon earth, "Parthians, and Medes, and Elamites," flock hither, and do naturally fall in with one or other of these primary distinctions. The infinite superiority of the former, which I choose to designate as the *great race,* is discernible in their figure, port, and a certain instinctive sovereignty. The latter are born degraded. "He shall serve his brethren." There is something in the air of one of this cast, lean and suspicious; contrasting with the open, trusting, generous manners of the other.

Observe who have been the greatest borrowers of all ages—Alcibiades —Falstaff—Sir Richard Steele—our late incomparable Brinsley—what a family likeness in all four!

What a careless, even deportment hath your borrower! what rosy gills! what a beautiful reliance on Providence doth he manifest,—taking no more thought than lilies! What contempt for money,—accounting it (yours

and mine especially) no better than dross! What a liberal confounding of those pedantic distinctions of *meum* and *tuum!* or rather, what a noble simplification of language (beyond Tooke), resolving these supposed opposites into one clear, intelligible pronoun adjective!—What near approaches doth he make to the primitive *community,*—to the extent of one half of the principle at least.

He is the true taxer who "calleth all the world up to be taxed"; and the distance is as vast between him and *one of us,* as subsisted between the Augustan Majesty and the poorest obolary Jew that paid it tribute-pittance at Jerusalem!—His exactions, too, have such a cheerful, voluntary air! So far removed from your sour parochial or state-gathers,—those ink-horn varlets, who carry their want of welcome in their faces! He cometh to you with a smile, and troubleth you with no receipt; confining himself to no set season. Every day is his Candlemas, or his Feast of Holy Michael. He applieth the *lene tormentum*[1] of a pleasant look to your purse,—which to that gentle warmth expands her silken leaves, as naturally as the cloak of the traveller, for which sun and wind contended! He is the true Propontic which never ebbeth! The sea which taketh handsomely at each man's hand. In vain the victim, whom he delighteth to honour, struggles with destiny; he is in the net. Lend therefore cheerfully, O man ordained to lend—that thou lose not in the end, with thy worldly penny, the reversion promised. Combine not preposterously in thine own person the penalties of Lazarus and of Dives!—but, when thou seest the proper authority coming, meet it smilingly, as it were half-way. Come, a handsome sacrifice! See how light *he* makes of it! Strain not courtesies with a noble enemy.

Reflections like the foregoing were forced upon my mind by the death of my old friend, Ralph Bigod, Esq., who parted this life, on Wednesday evening; dying, as he had lived, without much trouble. He boasted himself a descendant from mighty ancestors of that name, who heretofore held ducal dignities in this realm. In his actions and sentiments he belied not the stock to which he pretended. Early in life he found himself invested with ample revenues; which, with that noble disinterestedness which I have noticed as inherent in men of the *great race,* he took almost immediate measures entirely to dissipate and bring to nothing: for there is something revolting in the idea of a king holding a private purse; and the thoughts of Bigod were all regal. Thus furnished by the very act of disfurnishment; getting rid of the cumbersome luggage of riches, more apt (as one sings)

> To slacken virtue, and abate her edge,
> Than prompt her to do aught may merit praise,—

he set forth, like some Alexander, upon his great enterprise, "borrowing and to borrow!"

---

[1] "Gentle torture."

In his periegesis, or triumphant progress throughout this island, it has been calculated that he laid a tythe part of the inhabitants under contribution. I reject this estimate as greatly exaggerated:—but having had the honour of accompanying my friend divers times, in his perambulations about this vast city, I own I was greatly struck at first with the prodigious number of faces we met who claimed a sort of respectful acquaintance with us. He was one day so obliging as to explain the phenomenon. It seems, these were his tributaries; feeders of his exchequer; gentlemen, his good friends (as he was pleased to express himself), to whom he had occasionally been beholden for a loan. Their multitudes did no way disconcert him. He rather took a pride in numbering them; and, with Comus, seemed pleased to be "stocked with so fair a herd."

With such sources, it was a wonder how he contrived to keep his treasury always empty. He did it by force of an aphorism, which he had often in his mouth, that "money kept longer than three days stinks." So he made use of it while it was fresh. A good part he drank away (for he was an excellent toss-pot); some he gave away, the rest he threw away, literally tossing and hurling it violently from him—as boys do burrs, or as if it had been infectious,—into ponds, or ditches, or deep holes, inscrutable cavities of the earth;—or he would bury it (where he would never seek it again) by a river's side under some bank, which (he would facetiously observe) paid no interest—but out away from him it must go peremptorily, as Hagar's offspring into the wilderness, while it was sweet. He never missed it. The streams were perennial which fed his fisc. When new supplies became necessary, the first person that had the felicity to fall in with him, friend or stranger, was sure to contribute to the deficiency. For Bigod had an *undeniable* way with him. He had a cheerful, open exterior, a quick jovial eye, a bald forehead, just touched with grey (*cana fides*). He anticipated no excuse, and found none. And, waiving for a while my theory as to the *great race,* I would put it to the most untheorising reader, who may at times have disposable coin in his pockets, whether it is not more repugnant to the kindliness of his nature to refuse such a one as I am describing, than to say *no* to a poor petitionary rogue (your bastard borrower), who, by his mumping visnomy, tells you, that he expects nothing better; and, therefore, whose preconceived notions and expectations you do in reality so much less shock in the refusal.

When I think of this man; his fiery glow of heart; his swell of feeling; how magnificent, how *ideal* he was; how great at the midnight hour; and when I compare with him the companions with whom I have associated since, I grudge the saving of a few idle ducats, and think that I am fallen into the society of *lenders,* and *little* men.

To one like Elia, whose treasures are rather cased in leather covers than closed in iron coffers, there is a class of alienators more formidable

than that which I have touched upon; I mean your *borrowers of books*—
those mutilators of collections, spoilers of the symmetry of shelves, and
creators of odd volumes. There is Comberbatch, matchless in his depreda-
tions!

That foul gap in the bottom shelf facing you, like a great eye-tooth
knocked out—(you are now with me in my little back study in Blooms-
bury, reader!)——with the huge Switzer-like tomes on each side (like the
Guildhall giants, in their reformed posture, guardant of nothing), once held
the tallest of my folios, *Opera Bonaventuræ*, choice and massy divinity,
to which its two supporters (school divinity also, but of a lesser calibre,—
Bellarmine, and Holy Thomas), showed but as dwarfs,—itself an Ascapart!
—*that* Comberbatch abstracted upon the faith of a theory he holds, which
is more easy, I confess, for me to suffer by than to refute, namely, that
"the title to property in a book (my Bonaventure, for instance), is in exact
ratio to the claimant's powers of understanding and appreciating the same."
Should he go on acting upon this theory, which of our shelves is safe?

The slight vacuum in the left-hand case—two shelves from the ceiling
—scarcely distinguishable but by the quick eye of a loser—was whilom
the commodious resting-place of Browne on Urn Burial. C. will hardly
allege that he knows more about that treatise than I do, who introduced it
to him, and was indeed the first (of the moderns) to discover its beauties—
but so have I known a foolish lover to praise his mistress in the presence
of a rival more qualified to carry her off than himself. Just below, Dodsley's
dramas want their fourth volume, where Vittoria Corombona is! The
remainder nine are as distasteful as Priam's refuse sons when the Fates
*borrowed* Hector. Here stood the Anatomy of Melancholy, in sober state.
There loitered the Compleat Angler; quiet as in life, by some stream side.
In yonder nook, John Buncle, a widower-volume, with "eyes closed,"
mourns his ravished mate.

One justice I must do my friend, that if he sometimes, like the sea,
sweeps away a treasure, at another time, sea-like, he throws up as rich
an equivalent to match it. I have a small under-collection of this nature
(my friend's gatherings in his various calls), picked up, he has forgotten
at what odd places, and deposited with as little memory at mine. I take in
these orphans, the twice-deserted. These proselytes of the gate are welcome
as the true Hebrews. There they stand in conjunction; natives, and natural-
ized. The latter seem as little disposed to inquire out their true lineage as
I am.—I charge no warehouse-room for these deodands, nor shall ever
put myself to the ungentlemanly trouble of advertising a sale of them to
pay expenses.

To lose a volume to C. carries some sense and meaning in it. You
are sure that he will make one hearty meal on your viands, if he can give
no account of the platter after it. But what moved thee, wayward, spiteful

K., to be so importunate to carry off with thee, in spite of tears and adjurations to thee to forbear, the Letters of that princely woman, the thrice noble Margaret Newcastle?—knowing at the time, and knowing that I knew also, thou most assuredly wouldst never turn over one leaf of the illustrious folio:—what but the mere spirit of contradiction, and childish love of getting the better of thy friend?—Then, worst cut of all! to transport it with thee to the Gallican land—

> Unworthy land to harbour such a sweetness,
> A virtue in which all ennobling thoughts dwelt,
> Pure thoughts, kind thoughts, high thoughts, her
>     sex's wonder!

——hadst thou not thy play-books, and books of jests and fancies, about thee, to keep thee merry, even as thou keepest all companies with thy quips and mirthful tales? Child of the Green-room, it was unkindly done of thee. Thy wife, too, that part-French, better-part Englishwoman!—that *she* could fix upon no other treatise to bear away, in kindly token of remembering us, than the works of Fulke Greville, Lord Brook—of which no Frenchman, nor woman of France, Italy, or England, was ever by nature constituted to comprehend a tittle!—*Was there not Zimmerman on Solitude?*

Reader, if haply thou art blest with a moderate collection, be shy of showing it; or if thy heart overfloweth to lend them, lend thy books; but let it be to such a one as S. T. C.—he will return them (generally anticipating the time appointed) with usury; enriched with annotations tripling their value. I have had experience. Many are these precious MSS. of his—(in *matter* oftentimes, and almost in *quantity* not unfrequently, vying with the originals) in no very clerky hand—legible in my Daniel; in old Burton; in Sir Thomas Browne; and those abstruser cogitations of the Greville, now, alas! wandering in Pagan lands. I counsel thee, shut not thy heart, nor thy library, against S. T. C.


## TOPICS FOR DISCUSSION

1   What is Lamb satirizing? Why is the pseudo-anthropological approach a good organizational method?

2   What satirical devices do you find in this essay?

3   Why is paragraph 3 effective?

4   Throughout the essay, what part does punctuation play in creating the satiric effect? Diction? Parenthetical expressions? Italic type?

5   How does Lamb really feel about S. T. C. (Samuel Taylor Coleridge)? How can you tell?

## ...AND COMPOSITION

6   Write a satire by praising that which you intend to mock.

7   Analyze the diction of this essay for general level, appropriateness, clarity, and effect.

8   Paraphrase this classification of men directly without using satire or humor.

# The Concept of Race

What is true of stature applies with far greater force to psychological
characters—of intelligence, special aptitude, temperament, and character.
In the first place, such characters are far more susceptible to changes in
environment (here of course predominantly social environment) than are
physical characters. Second, the social environment shows a greater range
of difference than the physical environment. High innate mathematical
ability would be unable to express itself in paleolithic society or among
present-day savages. The most consummate artistic gifts would find little
scope on a desert island. The temperament which gives its possessor the
capacity for going into a trance or seeing visions is in our modern western
world likely to land its possessor in an asylum, whereas in various
Australian and Asiatic tribes it will further his attainment of power and
practicing as a medicine man or Shaman. A warlike temperament which
would have expressed itself adequately in the early days of Jewish history
would have been at a discount during the Captivity. The same capacities,
of inventiveness and initiative, which would be expressed to the full in a
pioneer country tend to remain latent in conditions of unskilled factory
labour. Certain economic and social conditions favour the expression of
the tendencies to individualism and self-assertion, other conditions favour
the reverse; we can think of early industrialism on the one hand, the
Authoritarian State on the other.

In general, the expression of temperamental tendencies seems to be
determined mostly in the very early years of life, so that changes affecting
the atmosphere of the home and the theories and practice of children's
upbringing will have large effects.

Similarly, the sweeping assertion often made as regards the differences
of women's aptitudes and character from men's undoubtedly refers in the
main to differences brought about by differences in the upbringing of boys

and girls and by the different social and economic status of the sexes. An amusing example is the exclamation of the third-century Greek gossip-writer Athenaeus, "Who ever heard of a woman cook?"

While it is clear that individuals endowed with exceptional combinations of genes will often rise superior to all obstacles, it is equally clear that the quantity of innate talent which a person possesses depends for its realization and expression upon adequate facilities for its cultivation; and that these again depend upon environmental factors such as financial resources, social outlook, and existing educational systems. The chief reason why children from the upper social classes obtain proportionately more scholarships than those from the lower classes is because they have better educational opportunities, not because they are better endowed by heredity.

The bearing of such facts upon problems of race and nationality is obvious. With the best will in the world it is, in the present state of knowledge, impossible to disentangle the genetic from the environmental factors in matters of "racial traits," "national character," and the like. Such phrases are glibly used. In fact they are all but meaningless, since they are not properly definable. Further, in so far as they are capable of definition, the common presupposition that they are entirely or mainly of a permanent or genetic nature is unwarranted.

Do not let me be misunderstood. It is clear that there must exist innate genetic differences between human groups in regard to intelligence, temperament, and other psychological traits. There do exist genetic differences in physical characters; there is every reason to believe that similar differences in psychical characters also exist. However, in the first place this need not mean that the mental differences are highly correlated with the physical—that a dark skin, for instance, automatically connotes a tendency toward low intelligence or irresponsible temperament. Second, the mental differences must be expected to be like the physical, mere matters of general averages and proportions of types—in every social class or ethnic group there will be a great quantitative range and a great qualitative diversity of mental characters, and different groups will very largely overlap one another. Finally, and perhaps most important of all, there exist as yet no means for assigning the shares of genetic constitution and of environment in producing the observed difference of type.

All the evidence we possess goes to show that the expression of such mental characters is to a very high degree dependent on the social environment. Let us first take so-called "national character." There was a time when England was called "merry"; during the nineteenth century that epithet was not applicable. In Elizabethan times the English were among the most musical of the European nations; the reverse is generally held to have been true in late Victorian times. Again, as Hume shrewdly notes in his *Essay of National Characters,* the Spaniards were in earlier times restless

and warlike; whereas in his day and the period immediately preceding it the reverse was the case.

Were these changes due to alteration in the genes or to such influences as the difference between the social atmosphere of the Renaissance and that of early industrialism? The social answer is here far the more likely. In other cases it is manifestly the correct one. For instance, in Carlyle's time, the German "national character" was supposed to be peaceable, philosophic, musical, and individualist. After the Franco-Prussian War it became arrogant and militarist. Now we are witnessing the blossoming of tendencies to state-worship, mass-enthusiasm, and the like which we are once more assured are inherent in it. But it would be inconceivable on any biological theory whatsoever, let alone on that of modern genetics, to believe that the inherent constitution of the German people could change so rapidly. We are, therefore, driven to believe that the change, where it has not been merely an apparent one, due to the bias of the recorder, has been brought about by changes in social atmosphere and institutions.

Let us now examine the problem from a different angle, "racial" rather than "national." It is often asserted that the Nordic "race" is gifted above all others with initiative, originality, and that all the great advances in civilization have been due to the Nordic genius.

What are the facts? The fundamental discoveries on which civilization is built are the art of writing, agriculture, the wheel, and building in stone. All these appear to have originated in the Near East, among people who by no stretch of imagination could be called Nordic or presumed to have but the faintest admixture of genes from Nordic or even Proto-Nordic germ-plasm.

In the classical period, Aristotle (*Politics VII*) gave what appeared even to that great thinker cogent reasons for believing the Nordic barbarians as well as the Asiatic peoples inherently incapable of rising to the level of Greek achievements. The inhabitants of northern climates, he says, though endowed with plenty of spirit, are wanting in intelligence and skill, while the reverse is true of the Asiatics. The Greeks, on the other hand, are endowed with both sets of qualities. The attitude of the Roman invaders of this island toward the ancient Britons must have been very similar to that of the British and Dutch invaders of South and Central Africa toward the Bantu. We have as yet no means of learning whether this latter attitude will be any more justified than that of the dominant peoples of classical times to the barbarian tribes which they subdued.

When we come to matters of detail, facts are equally hostile to the myth of Nordic superiority. For instance, exploration certainly demands initiative. But far from Nordic types being pre-eminent in that domain, Havelock Ellis, in his *Study of British Genius,* has shown that hardly any of the great British explorers were fair-haired or in other ways of Nordic type.

The Nordic myth has many upholders in the United States; but, as Hrdlička has shown in his book *The Old Americans,* the early colonists were mostly round-headed and dark or medium in complexion.

Again, the orthodox Nazi view is that Germany owes her chief achievements to the "Aryan" or Nordic elements in her population. As we shall see later, the Nordic type, besides being fair and tall, is long-headed. But as Weidenreich has shown, the greatest Germans, including Beethoven, Kant, Schiller, Leibnitz, and Goethe, were all moderately or extremely round-headed (cephalic indices 84 to 92)! Already the difficulties in the way of a simple Nordic explanation are apparent to the Nazi "intelligentsia" and they are now introducing such terms as *Nordic-Dinaric* and *Baltic-Nordic* to denote certain very numerous Germans of obviously mixed type,—a procedure which at once robs the "pure race" concept of its meaning. The influential German anthropologist Kossina, in his *Ursprung der Germanen,* says that "Nordic souls may often be combined with un-Nordic bodies, and a decidedly un-Nordic soul may lurk in a perfectly good Nordic body." This may be a convenient method of disposing of certain awkward facts, but it assuredly has no point of contact with biological science: the implication that the genes responsible for "the soul" segregate *en bloc* from those responsible for "the body" is more medieval than Mendelian.

One final example, and I have done. In so far as the Jews constitute a "racial type," they should be long-headed, since this is a distinctive Semite character. But Einstein is, like a large proportion of Jews, extremely broad-headed. The Jewish problem indeed is, from the standpoint of biology, a particularly illuminating one. The ancient Jews were formed as the result of crossing between several groups of markedly distinct types. Later there has always been a certain amount of crossing between the Jews and the non-Jewish inhabitants of the countries where they settled, the most striking examples being the black Jews of Northern Africa and the famous historical case of the Chazars of South Russia. The result is that the Jews of different areas are not genetically equivalent, and that in each country the Jewish group overlaps with the non-Jewish in every conceivable character. The word *Jew* is valid more as a socio-religious or pseudo-national description than as an ethnic term in any genetic sense. Many "Jewish" characteristics are without doubt much more the product of Jewish tradition and upbringing, and especially of reaction against extreme pressure and persecution, than of heredity.

## TOPICS FOR DISCUSSION

1   Since some mental characteristics are genetic in orgin, why does Huxley stress so strongly the social influences on such characteristics?

426  Forms and Occasions

2  What is a "national" characteristic? What is a "racial" characteristic? What does the word "Jew" mean to Huxley?

3  How would you describe the vocabulary of this essay? Is it appropriate to the theme?

4  What do the following mean: "consummate"; "genetic"; "psychical"; "qualitative"; "quantitative"? What would Orwell say about Huxley's diction in this essay generally, in using these words specifically?

5  Are the examples provided by Huxley sufficiently wide in range to support his generalizations regarding alterations of mental character? Can you supply additional examples to support his case?

## ...AND COMPOSITION

6  Define "Aryan" in a short essay after consulting several standard dictionaries and encyclopedias.

7  If Huxley's thesis is true, what special problems are posed for teachers and administrators in slum schools? Do you think these problems have been adequately met thus far?

8  Given the role most women play during their adult lives, do you believe our society undereducates women?

**ERIC HOFFER (1902–    )** a longshoreman in San Francisco, always firmly asserts his background and his working-class allegiances. Reflected throughout his writing are an inquiring mind and a continuing loyalty to the "common man." His books *The True Believer* and *The Ordeal of Change* constitute a pertinacious kind of brooding about contemporary problems from the point of view of an outsider, an original thinker, a philosopher determined to remain an amateur.

## *The Role of the Undesirables*

In the winter of 1934, I spent several weeks in a federal transient camp in California. These camps were originally established by Governor Rolph in the early days of the Depression to care for the single homeless unemployed of the state. In 1934 the federal government took charge of the camps for a time, and it was then that I first heard of them.

How I happened to get into one of the camps is soon told. Like thousands of migrant agricultural workers in California I then followed the crops from one part of the state to the other. Early in 1934 I arrived in the town of El Centro, in the Imperial Valley. I had been given a free ride on a truck from San Diego, and it was midnight when the truck driver dropped me on the outskirts of El Centro. I spread my bedroll by the side of the road and went to sleep. I had hardly dozed off when the rattle of a motorcycle drilled itself into my head and a policeman was bending over me saying, "Roll up, Mister." It looked as though I was in for something; it happened now and then that the police got overzealous and rounded up the freight trains. But this time the cop had no such thought. He said, "Better go over to the federal shelter and get yourself a bed and maybe some breakfast." He directed me to the place.

I found a large hall, obviously a former garage, dimly lit, and packed

with cots. A concert of heavy breathing shook the thick air. In a small office near the door, I was registered by a middle-aged clerk. He informed me that this was the "receiving shelter" where I would get one night's lodging and breakfast. The meal was served in the camp nearby. Those who wished to stay on, he said, had to enroll in the camp. He then gave me three blankets and excused himself for not having a vacant cot. I spread the blankets on the cement floor and went to sleep.

I awoke with dawn amid a chorus of coughing, throat-clearing, the sound of running water, and the intermittent flushing of toilets in the back of the hall. There were about fifty of us, of all colors and ages, all of us more or less ragged and soiled. The clerk handed out tickets for breakfast, and we filed out to the camp located several blocks away, near the railroad tracks.

From the outside the camp looked like a cross between a factory and a prison. A high fence of wire enclosed it, and inside were three large sheds and a huge boiler topped by a pillar of black smoke. Men in blue shirts and dungarees were strolling across the sandy yard. A ship's bell in front of one of the buildings announced breakfast. The regular camp members—there was a long line of them—ate first. Then we filed in through the gate, handing our tickets to the guard.

It was a good, plentiful meal. After breakfast our crowd dispersed. I heard some say that the camps in the northern part of the state were better, that they were going to catch a northbound freight. I decided to try this camp in El Centro.

My motives in enrolling were not crystal clear. I wanted to clean up. There were shower baths in the camp and wash tubs and plenty of soap. Of course I could have bathed and washed my clothes in one of the irrigation ditches, but here in the camp I had a chance to rest, get the wrinkles out of my belly, and clean up at leisure. In short, it was the easiest way out.

A brief interview at the camp office and a physical examination were all the formalities for enrollment.

There were some two hundred men in the camp. They were the kind I had worked and traveled with for years. I even saw familiar faces—men I had worked with in orchards and fields. Yet my predominant feeling was one of strangeness. It was my first experience of life in intimate contact with a crowd. For it is one thing to work and travel with a gang, and quite another thing to eat, sleep, and spend the greater part of the day cheek by jowl with two hundred men.

I found myself speculating on a variety of subjects: the reasons for their chronic bellyaching and beefing—it was more a ritual than the expression of a grievance; the amazing orderliness of the men; the comic seriousness with which they took their games of cards, checkers, and dominoes; the weird manner of reasoning one overheard now and then. Why, I kept wondering, were these men within the enclosure of a federal

transient camp? Were they people temporarily hard up? Would jobs solve all their difficulties? Were we indeed like the people outside?

Up to then I was not aware of being one of a specific species of humanity. I had considered myself simply a human being—not particularly good or bad, and on the whole harmless. The people I worked and traveled with I knew as Americans and Mexicans, whites and Negroes, Northerners and Southerners, etc. It did not occur to me that we were a group possessed of peculiar traits, and that there was something—innate or acquired—in our make-up which made us adopt a particular mode of existence.

It was a slight thing that started me on a new track.

I got to talking to a mild-looking, elderly fellow. I liked his soft speech and pleasant manner. We swapped trivial experiences. Then he suggested a game of checkers. As we started to arrange the pieces on the board, I was startled by the sight of his crippled right hand. I had not noticed it before. Half of it was chopped off lengthwise, so that the horny stump with its three fingers looked like a hen's leg. I was mortified that I had not noticed the hand until he dangled it, so to speak, before my eyes. It was, perhaps, to bolster my shaken confidence in my powers of observation that I now began paying close attention to the hands of the people around me. The result was astounding. It seemed that every other man had had his hand mangled. There was a man with one arm. Some men limped. One young, good-looking fellow had a wooden leg. It was as though the majority of the men had escaped the snapping teeth of a machine and left part of themselves behind.

It was, I knew, an exaggerated impression. But I began counting the cripples as the men lined up in the yard at mealtime. I found thirty (out of two hundred) crippled either in arms or legs. I immediately sensed where the counting would land me. The simile preceded the statistical deduction: we in the camp were a human junk pile.

I began evaluating my fellow tramps as human material, and for the first time in my life I became face-conscious. There were some good faces, particularly among the young. Several of the middle-aged and the old looked healthy and well preserved. But the damaged and decayed faces were in the majority. I saw faces that were wrinkled, or bloated, or raw as the surface of a peeled plum. Some of the noses were purple and swollen, some broken, some pitted with enlarged pores. There were many toothless mouths (I counted seventy-eight). I noticed eyes that were blurred, faded, opaque, or bloodshot. I was struck by the fact that the old men, even the very old, showed their age mainly in the face. Their bodies were still slender and erect. One little man over sixty years of age looked a mere boy when seen from behind. The shriveled face joined to a boyish body made a startling sight.

My diffidence had now vanished. I was getting to know everybody in the camp. They were a friendly and talkative lot. Before many weeks I knew some essential fact about practically everyone.

And I was continually counting. Of the two hundred men in the camp there were approximately as follows:

| | |
|---|---|
| Cripples | 30 |
| Confirmed drunkards | 60 |
| Old men (55 and over) | 50 |
| Youths under twenty | 10 |
| Men with chronic diseases, heart, asthma, TB | 12 |
| Mildly insane | 4 |
| Constitutionally lazy | 6 |
| Fugitives from justice | 4 |
| Apparently normal | 70 |

(The numbers do not tally up to two hundred since some of the men were counted twice or even thrice—as cripples and old, or as old and confirmed drunks, etc.)

In other words: less than half the camp inmates (seventy normal, plus ten youths) were unemployed workers whose difficulties would be at an end once jobs were available. The rest (60 per cent) had handicaps in addition to unemployment.

I also counted fifty war veterans, and eighty skilled workers representing sixteen trades. All the men (including those with chronic diseases) were able to work. The one-armed man was a wizard with the shovel.

I did not attempt any definite measurement of character and intelligence. But it seemed to me that the intelligence of the men in the camp was certainly not below the average. And as to character, I found much forbearance and genuine good humor. I never came across one instance of real viciousness. Yet, on the whole, one would hardly say that these men were possessed of strong characters. Resistance, whether to one's appetites or to the ways of the world, is a chief factor in the shaping of character; and the average tramp is, more or less, a slave of his few appetites. He generally takes the easiest way out.

The connection between our make-up and our mode of existence as migrant workers presented itself now with some clarity.

The majority of us were incapable of holding onto a steady job. We lacked self-discipline and the ability to endure monotonous, leaden hours. We were probably misfits from the very beginning. Our contact with a steady job was not unlike a collision. Some of us were maimed, some got frightened and ran away, and some took to drink. We inevitably drifted in the direction of least resistance—the open road. The life of a migrant worker is varied and demands only a minimum of self-discipline. We were now in one of the drainage ditches of ordered society. We could not keep a footing in the ranks of respectability and were washed into the slough of our present existence.

Yet, I mused, there must be in this world a task with an appeal so

strong that were we to have a taste of it we would hold on and be rid for good of our restlessness.

My stay in the camp lasted about four weeks. Then I found a haying job not far from town, and finally, in April, when the hot winds began blowing, I shouldered my bedroll and took the highway to San Bernardino.

It was the next morning, after I had got a lift to Indio by truck, that a new idea began to take hold of me. The highway out of Indio leads through waving date groves, fragrant grapefruit orchards, and lush alfalfa fields; then, abruptly, passes into a desert of white sand. The sharp line between garden and desert is very striking. The turning of white sand into garden seemed to me an act of magic. This, I thought, was a job one would jump at—even the men in the transient camps. They had the skill and ability of the average American. But their energies, I felt, could be quickened only by a task that was spectacular, that had in it something of the miraculous. The pioneer task of making the desert flower would certainly fill the bill.

Tramps as pioneers? It seemed absurd. Every man and child in California knows that the pioneers had been giants, men of boundless courage and indomitable spirit. However, as I strode on across the white sand, I kept mulling the idea over.

Who were the pioneers? Who were the men who left their homes and went into the wilderness? A man rarely leaves a soft spot and goes deliberately in search of hardship and privation. People become attached to the places they live in; they drive roots. A change of habitat is a painful act of uprooting. A man who has made good and has a standing in his community stays put. The successful business men, farmers, and workers usually stayed where they were. Who then left for the wilderness and the unknown? Obviously those who had not made good: men who went broke or never amounted to much; men who though possessed of abilities were too impulsive to stand the daily grind; men who were slaves of their appetites—drunkards, gamblers, and woman-chasers; outcasts—fugitives from justice and ex-jailbirds. There were no doubt some who went in search of health—men suffering with TB, asthma, heart trouble. Finally there was a sprinkling of young and middle-aged in search of adventure.

All these people craved change, some probably actuated by the naïve belief that a change in place brings with it a change in luck. Many wanted to go to a place where they were not known and there make a new beginning. Certainly they did not go out deliberately in search of hard work and suffering. If in the end they shouldered enormous tasks, endured unspeakable hardships, and accomplished the impossible, it was because they had to. They became men of action on the run. They acquired strength and skill in the inescapable struggle for existence. It was a question of do or die. And once they tasted the joy of achievement, they craved for more.

Clearly the same types of people which now swelled the ranks of migratory workers and tramps had probably in former times made up the bulk of the pioneers. As a group the pioneers were probably as unlike the present-day "native sons"—their descendants—as one could well imagine. Indeed, were there to be today a new influx of typical pioneers, twin brothers of the forty-niners only in a modern garb, the citizens of California would consider it a menace to health, wealth, and morals.

With few exceptions, this seems to be the case in the settlement of all new countries. Ex-convicts were the vanguard in the settling of Australia. Exiles and convicts settled Siberia. In this country, a large portion of our earlier and later settlers were failures, fugitives, and felons. The exceptions seemed to be those who were motivated by religious fervor, such as the Pilgrim Fathers and the Mormons.

Although quite logical, this train of thought seemed to me then a wonderful joke. In my exhilaration I was eating up the road in long strides, and I reached the oasis of Elim in what seemed almost no time. A passing empty truck picked me up just then and we thundered through Banning and Beaumont, all the way to Riverside. From there I walked the seven miles to San Bernardino.

Somehow, this discovery of a family likeness between tramps and pioneers took a firm hold on my mind. For years afterward it kept intertwining itself with a mass of observations which on the face of them had no relation to either tramps or pioneers. And it moved me to speculate on subjects in which, up to then, I had no real interest, and of which I knew very little.

I talked with several old-timers—one of them over eighty and a native son—in Sacramento, Placerville, Auburn, and Fresno. It was not easy, at first, to obtain the information I was after. I could not make my questions specific enough. "What kind of people were the early settlers and miners?" I asked. They were a hard-working, tough lot, I was told. They drank, fought, gambled, and wenched. They were big-hearted, grasping, profane, and God-fearing. They wallowed in luxury, or lived on next to nothing with equal ease. They were the salt of the earth.

Still it was not clear what manner of people they were.

If I asked what they looked like, I was told of whiskers, broad-brimmed hats, high boots, shirts of many colors, sun-tanned faces, horny hands. Finally I asked: "What group of people in present-day California most closely resemble the pioneers?" The answer, usually after some hesitation, was invariably the same: "The Okies and the fruit tramps."

I tried also to evaluate the tramps as potential pioneers by watching them in action. I saw them fell timber, clear firebreaks, build rock walls, put up barracks, build dams and roads, handle steam shovels, bulldozers, tractors, and concrete mixers. I saw them put in a hard day's work after a night of steady drinking. They sweated and growled, but they did the work. I saw tramps elevated to positions of authority as foremen and superintendents.

Then I could notice a remarkable physical transformation: a seamed face gradually smoothed out and the skin showed a healthy hue; an indifferent mouth became firm and expressive; dull eyes cleared and brightened; voices actually changed; there was even an apparent increase in stature. In almost no time these promoted tramps looked as if they had been on top all their lives. Yet sooner or later I would meet up with them again in a railroad yard, on some skid row, or in the fields—tramps again. It was usually the same story: they got drunk or lost their temper and were fired, or they got fed up with the steady job and quit. Usually, when a tramp becomes a foreman, he is careful in his treatment of the tramps under him; he knows the day of reckoning is never far off.

In short, it was not difficult to visualize the tramps as pioneers. I reflected that if they were to find themselves in a singlehanded life-and-death struggle with nature, they would undoubtedly display persistence. For the pressure of responsibility and the heat of battle steel a character. The inadaptable would perish, and those who survived would be the equal of the successful pioneers.

I also considered the few instances of pioneering engineered from above —that is to say, by settlers possessed of lavish means, who were classed with the best where they came from. In these instances, it seemed to me, the resulting social structure was inevitably precarious. For pioneering deluxe usually results in a plantation society, made up of large landowners and peon labor, either native or imported. Very often there is a racial cleavage between the two. The colonizing activities of the Teutonic barons in the Baltic, the Hungarian nobles in Transylvania, the English in Ireland, the planters in our South, and the present-day plantation societies in Kenya and other British and Dutch colonies are cases in point. Whatever their merits, they are characterized by poor adaptability. They are likely eventually to be broken up either by a peon revolution or by an influx of typical pioneers—who are usually of the same race or nation as the landowners. The adjustment is not necessarily implemented by war. Even our old South, had it not been for the complication of secession, might eventually have attained stability without war: namely, by the activity of its own poor whites or by an influx of the indigent from other states.

There is in us a tendency to judge a race, a nation, or an organization by its least worthy members. The tendency is manifestly perverse and unfair; yet it has some justification. For the quality and destiny of a nation is determined to a considerable extent by the nature and potentialities of its inferior elements. The inert mass of a nation is in its middle section. The industrious, decent, well-to-do, and satisfied middle classes—whether in cities or on the land—are worked upon and shaped by minorities at both extremes: the best and the worst.

The superior individual, whether in politics, business, industry, science, literature, or religion, undoubtedly plays a major role in the shaping

of a nation. But so do the individuals at the other extreme: the poor, the outcasts, the misfits, and those who are in the grip of some overpowering passion. The importance of these inferior elements as formative factors lies in the readiness with which they are swayed in any direction. This peculiarity is due to their inclination to take risks ("not giving a damn") and their propensity for united action. They crave to merge their drab, wasted lives into something grand and complete. Thus they are the first and most fervent adherents of new religions, political upheavals, patriotic hysteria, gangs, and mass rushes to new lands.

And the quality of a nation—its innermost worth—is made manifest by its dregs as they rise to the top: by how brave they are, how humane, how orderly, how skilled, how generous, how independent or servile; by the bounds they will not transgress in their dealings with man's soul, with truth, and with honor.

The average American of today bristles with indignation when he is told that this country was built, largely, by hordes of undesirables from Europe. Yet, far from being derogatory, this statement, if true, should be a cause for rejoicing, should fortify our pride in the stock from which we have sprung.

This vast continent with its towns, farms, factories, dams, aqueducts, docks, railroads, highways, powerhouses, schools, and parks is the handiwork of common folk from the Old World, where for centuries men of their kind had been as beasts of burden, the property of their masters—kings, nobles, and priests—and with no will and no aspirations of their own. When on rare occasions one of the lowly had reached the top in Europe he had kept the pattern intact and, if anything, tightened the screws. The stuffy little corporal from Corsica harnessed the lusty forces released by the French Revolution to a gilded state coach, and could think of nothing grander than mixing his blood with that of the Hapsburg masters and establishing a new dynasty. In our day a bricklayer in Italy, a house painter in Germany, and a shoemaker's son in Russia have made themselves masters of their nations; and what they did was to re-establish and reinforce the old pattern.

Only here, in America, were the common folk of the Old World given a chance to show what they could do on their own, without a master to push and order them about. History contrived an earth-shaking joke when it lifted by the nape of the neck lowly peasants, shopkeepers, laborers, paupers, jailbirds, and drunks from the midst of Europe, dumped them on a vast, virgin continent and said: "Go to it; it is yours!"

And the lowly were not awed by the magnitude of the task. A hunger for action, pent up for centuries, found an outlet. They went to it with ax, pick, shovel, plow, and rifle; on foot, on horse, in wagons, and on flatboats. They went to it praying, howling, singing, brawling, drinking, and fighting. Make way for the people! This is how I read the statement that this country was built by hordes of undesirables from the Old World.

Small wonder that we in this country have a deeply ingrained faith in human regeneration. We believe that, given a chance, even the degraded and the apparently worthless are capable of constructive work and great deeds. It is a faith founded on experience, not on some idealistic theory. And no matter what some anthropologists, sociologists, and geneticists may tell us, we shall go on believing that man, unlike other forms of life, is not a captive of his past—of his heredity and habits—but is possessed of infinite plasticity, and his potentialities for good and for evil are never wholly exhausted.

## TOPICS FOR DISCUSSION

1    What does it take to be an "undesirable"? Does Hoffer ever sentimentalize these characteristics?

2    Hoffer frames his analysis of the undesirables with a narrative at the beginning and an evaluation at the conclusion. The pronoun usage which normally helps to create a point of view is not always consistent, nor is Hoffer's position with regard to his subject; sometimes he is one of the tramps, using "us," and sometimes he is the social critic talking of "them." Does this violate any sense of coherence, or does it fit a larger purpose?

3    Does Hoffer blame society for the presence of tramps, or does he find a cause in the individual tramp?

4    Should all migratory workers be included in one group as in Hoffer's essay? Should all pioneers be grouped together? Is the author careless in his larger classifications?

5    Do the pioneers or the tramps have the most to gain from the comparison Hoffer makes of their characteristics?

6    Hoffer generalizes about the lowly from the Old World who "reached the top." Do his examples adequately validate his generalization?

## ...AND COMPOSITION

7    Formulate a national program that might make use of the restless energies of the undesirables.

8    Hoffer's undesirables and Gibbon's early Christians are not remarkably dissimilar, save for the quality and direction of their zeal. Compare these two groups as they are represented in these selections, touching on their similarities and dissimilarities.

9    Hoffer's essay traces the maturation of an idea. Write an essay in which you explain the development of a belief or opinion, including the nature of the idea as well as the major stages of its development.

**EDWARD GIBBON (1737–1794)** wrote his *Decline and Fall of the Roman Empire,* from which the present selection is taken, at a time when it was not politic to challenge accounts of miracles in traditional Christianity. Against this inhibition there mounted the pressure of his accumulation of knowledge about Roman civilization, his balanced critical insight, and his cynicism about mankind. The result, in his writing, was a rich blend of all these impulses into a keen irony—he recounted his information, allowed his judgments to haunt the material, juxtaposed conflicting testimonies, and played cat and mouse with the sensibilities of his readers. He managed to pretend to be tame while leaving great claw marks: ". . . it is much to be lamented that such a cause was not defended by abler advocates." In this kind of writing poise is essential; the material is relentlessly managed, while the writer insists on acting out a cool perspective.

# *Saints, Beggars, and Fakers*

A perpetual stream of strangers and provincials flowed into the capacious bosom of Rome. Whatever was strange or odious, whoever was guilty or suspected, might hope, in the obscurity of that immense capital, to elude the vigilance of the law. In such a various conflux of nations, every teacher, either of truth or of falsehood, every founder, whether of a virtuous or a criminal association, might easily multiply his disciples or accomplices. The Christians of Rome, at the time of the accidental persecution of Nero, are represented by Tacitus as already amounting to a very great multitude, and the language of that great historian is almost similar to the style employed by Livy when he relates the introduction and the suppression of the rites of Bacchus. After the Bacchanals had awakened the severity of the senate, it was likewise apprehended that a very great multitude, as it were *another people,* had been initiated into those abhorred mysteries. A more careful inquiry soon demonstrated that the offenders did not exceed seven thousand; a number, indeed, sufficiently alarming, when considered as the object of public justice. It is with the same candid allowance that we should interpret the vague expressions of Tacitus, and in a former instance of Pliny, when they exaggerate the crowds of deluded fanatics who had forsaken the established worship of the gods. The church of Rome was undoubtedly the first and most populous of the empire; and we are possessed of an authentic record which attests the state of religion in that city, about the middle of the third century, and after a peace of thirty-eight years. The clergy, at that time, consisted of a bishop, forty-six presbyters, seven deacons, as many sub-deacons, forty-two acolytes, and fifty readers, exorcists, and porters. The number of widows, of the infirm, and of the poor, who were maintained by the oblations of the faithful, amounted to fifteen hundred. From reason, as well as from the analogy of Antioch,

we may venture to estimate the Christians of Rome at about fifty thousand. The populousness of that great capital cannot, perhaps, be exactly ascertained; but the most modest calculation will not surely reduce it lower than a million of inhabitants, of whom the Christians might constitute at the most a twentieth part.

The western provincials appeared to have derived the knowledge of Christianity from the same source which had diffused among them the language, the sentiments, and the manners of Rome. In this more important circumstance, Africa, as well as Gaul, was gradually fashioned to the imitation of the capital. Yet, notwithstanding the many favourable occasions which might invite the Roman missionaries to visit their Latin provinces, it was late before they passed either the sea or the Alps; nor can we discover in those great countries any assured traces either of faith or of persecution that ascend higher than the reign of the Antonines. The slow progress of the gospel in the cold climate of Gaul was extremely different from the eagerness with which it seems to have been received on the burning sands of Africa. The African Christians soon formed one of the principal members of the primitive church. The practice introduced into that province of appointing bishops to the most inconsiderable towns, and very frequently to the most obscure villages, contributed to multiply the splendour and importance of their religious societies, which during the course of the third century were animated by the zeal of Tertullian, directed by the abilities of Cyprian, and adorned by the eloquence of Lactantius. But if, on the contrary, we turn our eyes towards Gaul, we must content ourselves with discovering, in the time of Marcus Antoninus, the feeble and united congregations of Lyons and Vienna; and even as late as the reign of Decius we are assured that in a few cities only, Arles, Narbonne, Toulouse, Limoges, Clermont, Tours, and Paris, some scattered churches were supported by the devotion of a small number of Christians. Silence is indeed very consistent with devotion, but, as it is seldom compatible with zeal, we may perceive and lament the languid state of Christianity in those provinces which had exchanged the Celtic for the Latin tongue; since they did not, during the three first centuries, give birth to a single ecclesiastical writer. From Gaul, which claimed a just pre-eminence of learning and authority over all the countries on this side of the Alps, the light of the gospel was more faintly reflected on the remote provinces of Spain and Britain; and, if we may credit the vehement assertions of Tertullian, they had already received the first rays of the faith when he addressed his apology to the magistrates of the emperor Severus. But the obscure and imperfect origin of the western churches of Europe has been so negligently recorded that, if we would relate the time and manner of their foundation, we must supply the silence of antiquity by those legends which avarice or superstition long afterwards dictated to the monks in the lazy gloom of their convents. Of these holy romances, that of the apostle St. James can

alone, by its single extravagance, deserve to be mentioned. From a peaceful fisherman of the lake of Gennesareth, he was transformed into a valorous knight, who charged at the head of the Spanish chivalry in their battles against the Moors. The gravest historians have celebrated his exploits; the miraculous shrine of Compostella displayed his power; and the sword of a military order, assisted by the terrors of the Inquisition, was sufficient to remove every objection of profane criticism.

The progress of Christianity was not confined to the Roman empire; and, according to the primitive fathers, who interpret facts by prophecy, the new religion within a century after the death of its divine author had already visited every part of the globe. "There exists not," says Justin Martyr, "a people, whether Greek or barbarian, or any other race of men, by whatsoever appellation or manners they may be distinguished, however ignorant of arts or agriculture, whether they dwell under tents, or wander about in covered waggons, among whom prayers are not offered up in the name of a crucified Jesus to the Father and Creator of all things." But this splendid exaggeration, which even at present it would be extremely difficult to reconcile with the real state of mankind, can be considered only as the rash sally of a devout but careless writer, the measure of whose belief was regulated by that of his wishes. But neither the belief nor the wishes of the fathers can alter the truth of history. It will still remain an undoubted fact that the barbarians of Scythia and Germany who afterwards subverted the Roman monarchy were involved in the darkness of paganism; and that even the conversion of Iberia, of Armenia, or of Æthiopia, was not attempted with any degree of success till the sceptre was in the hands of an orthodox emperor. Before that time the various accidents of war and commerce might indeed diffuse an imperfect knowledge of the gospel among the tribes of Caledonia, and among the borderers of the Rhine, the Danube, and the Euphrates. Beyond the last-mentioned river, Edessa was distinguished by a firm and early adherence to the faith. From Edessa the principles of Christianity were easily introduced into the Greek and Syrian cities which obeyed the successors of Artaxerxes; but they do not appear to have made any deep impression on the minds of the Persians, whose religious system, by the labours of a well-disciplined order of priests, had been constructed with much more art and solidity than the uncertain mythology of Greece and Rome.

From this impartial, though imperfect, survey of the progress of Christianity, it may perhaps seem probable that the number of its proselytes has been excessively magnified by fear on the one side and by devotion on the other. According to the irreproachable testimony of Origen, the proportion of the faithful was very inconsiderable when compared with the multitude of an unbelieving world; but, as we are left without any distinct information, it is impossible to determine, and it is difficult even to conjecture, the real numbers of the primitive Christians. The most

favourable calculation, however, that can be deduced from the examples of Antioch and of Rome will not permit us to imagine that more than a twentieth part of the subjects of the empire had enlisted themselves under the banner of the cross before the important conversion of Constantine. But their habits of faith, of zeal, and of union seemed to multiply their numbers; and the same causes which contributed to their future increase served to render their actual strength more apparent and more formidable.

Such is the constitution of civil society that, whilst a few persons are distinguished by riches, by honours, and by knowledge, the body of the people is condemned to obscurity, ignorance, and poverty. The Christian religion, which addressed itself to the whole human race, must consequently collect a far greater number of proselytes from the lower than from the superior ranks of life. This innocent and natural circumstance has been improved into a very odious imputation, which seems to be less strenuously denied by the apologists than it is urged by the adversaries of the faith; that the new sect of Christians was almost entirely composed of the dregs of the populace, of peasants and mechanics, of boys and women, of beggars and slaves, the last of whom might sometimes introduce the missionaries into the rich and noble families to which they belonged. These obscure teachers (such was the charge of malice and infidelity) are as mute in public as they are loquacious and dogmatical in private. Whilst they cautiously avoid the dangerous encounter of philosophers, they mingle with the rude and illiterate crowd, and insinuate themselves into those minds whom their age, their sex, or their education has the best disposed to receive the impression of superstitious terrors.

This unfavourable picture, though not devoid of a faint resemblance, betrays, by its dark colouring and distorted features, the pencil of an enemy. As the humble faith of Christ diffused itself through the world, it was embraced by several persons who derived some consequence from the advantages of nature or fortune. Aristides, who presented an eloquent apology to the emperor Hadrian, was an Athenian philosopher. Justin Martyr had sought divine knowledge in the schools of Zeno, of Aristotle, of Pythagoras, and of Plato, before he fortunately was accosted by the old man, or rather the angel, who turned his attention to the study of the Jewish prophets. Clemens of Alexandria had acquired much various reading in the Greek, and Tertullian in the Latin language. Julius Africanus and Origen possessed a very considerable share of the learning of their times; and, although the style of Cyprian is very different from that of Lactantius, we might almost discover that both those writers had been public teachers of rhetoric. Even the study of philosophy was at length introduced among the Christians, but it was not always productive of the most salutary effects; knowledge was as often the parent of heresy as of devotion, and the description which was designed for the followers of Artemon may with equal propriety be applied to the various sects that

resisted the successors of the apostles. "They presume to alter the holy scriptures, to abandon the ancient rule of faith, and to form their opinions according to the subtile precepts of logic. The science of the church is neglected for the study of geometry, and they lose sight of Heaven while they are employed in measuring the earth. Euclid is perpetually in their hands. Aristotle and Theophrastus are the objects of their admiration; and they express an uncommon reverence for the works of Galen. Their errors are derived from the abuse of the arts and sciences of the infidels, and they corrupt the simplicity of the Gospel by the refinements of human reason."

Nor can it be affirmed with truth that the advantages of birth and fortune were always separated from the profession of Christianity. Several Roman citizens were brought before the tribunal of Pliny, and he soon discovered that a great number of persons of *every order* of men in Bithynia had deserted the religion of their ancestors. His unsuspected testimony may, in this instance, obtain more credit than the bold challenge of Tertullian, when he addresses himself to the fears as well as to the humanity of the proconsul of Africa, by assuring him that, if he persists in his cruel intentions, he must decimate Carthage, and that he will find among the guilty many persons of his own rank, senators and matrons of noblest extraction, and the friends or relations of his most intimate friends. It appears, however, that about forty years afterwards the emperor Valerian was persuaded of the truth of this assertion, since in one of his rescripts he evidently supposes that senators, Roman knights, and ladies of quality were engaged in the Christian sect. The church still continued to increase its outward splendour as it lost its internal purity; and in the reign of Diocletian the palace, the courts of justice, and even the army concealed a multitude of Christians who endeavoured to reconcile the interests of the present with those of a future life.

And yet these exceptions are either too few in number, or too recent in time, entirely to remove the imputation of ignorance and obscurity which has been so arrogantly cast on the first proselytes of Christianity. Instead of employing in our defence the fictions of later ages, it will be more prudent to convert the occasion of scandal into a subject of edification. Our serious thoughts will suggest to us that the apostles themselves were chosen by providence among the fishermen of Galilee, and that, the lower we depress the temporal condition of the first Christians, the more reason we shall find to admire their merit and success. It is incumbent on us diligently to remember that the kingdom of heaven was promised to the poor in spirit, and that minds afflicted by calamity and the contempt of mankind cheerfully listen to the divine promise of future happiness; while, on the contrary, the fortunate are satisfied with the possession of this world; and the wise abuse in doubt and dispute their vain superiority of reason and knowledge.

We stand in need of such reflections to comfort us for the loss of some illustrious characters, which in our eyes might have seemed the most worthy of the heavenly present. The names of Seneca, of the elder and the younger Pliny, of Tacitus, of Plutarch, of Galen, of the slave Epictetus, and of the emperor Marcus Antoninus, adorn the age in which they flourished, and exalt the dignity of human nature. They filled with glory their respective stations, either in active or contemplative life; their excellent understandings were improved by study; Philosophy had purified their minds from the prejudices of the popular superstition; and their days were spent in the pursuit of truth and the practice of virtue. Yet all these sages (it is no less an object of surprise than of concern) overlooked or rejected the perfection of the Christian system. Their language or their silence equally discover their contempt for the growing sect, which in their time had diffused itself over the Roman empire. Those among them who condescend to mention the Christians consider them only as obstinate and perverse enthusiasts, who exacted an implicit submission to their mysterious doctrines, without being able to produce a single argument that could engage the attention of men of sense and learning.

It is at least doubtful whether any of these philosophers perused the apologies which the primitive Christians repeatedly published in behalf of themselves and of their religion; but it is much to be lamented that such a cause was not defended by abler advocates. They expose with superfluous wit and eloquence the extravagance of Polytheism. They interest our compassion by displaying the innocence and sufferings of their injured brethren. But, when they would demonstrate the divine origin of Christianity, they insist much more strongly on the predictions which announced, than on the miracles which accompanied, the appearance of the Messiah. Their favourite argument might serve to edify a Christian or to convert a Jew, since both the one and the other acknowledge the authority of those prophecies, and both are obliged, with devout reverence, to search for their sense and their accomplishment. But this mode of persuasion loses much of its weight and influence when it is addressed to those who neither understand nor respect the Mosaic dispensation and the prophetic style. In the unskillful hands of Justin and of the succeeding apologists, the sublime meaning of the Hebrew oracles evaporates in distant types, affected conceits, and cold allegories; and even their authenticity was rendered suspicious to an unenlightened Gentile by the mixture of pious forgeries, which, under the names of Orpheus, Hermes, and the Sibyls, were obtruded on him as of equal value with the genuine inspirations of Heaven. The adoption of fraud and sophistry in the defence of revelation too often reminds us of the injudicious conduct of those poets who load their *invulnerable* heroes with a useless weight of cumbersome and brittle armour.

But how shall we excuse the supine inattention of the Pagan and

philosophic world to those evidences which were presented by the hand of Omnipotence, not to their reason, but to their senses? During the age of Christ, of his apostles, and of their first disciples, the doctrine which they preached was confirmed by innumerable prodigies. The lame walked, the blind saw, the sick were healed, the dead were raised, dæmons were expelled, and the laws of Nature were frequently suspended for the benefit of the church. But the sages of Greece and Rome turned aside from the awful spectacle, and, pursuing the ordinary occupations of life and study, appeared unconscious of any alterations in the moral or physical government of the world. Under the reign of Tiberius, the whole earth, or at least a celebrated province of the Roman empire, was involved in a præternatural darkness of three hours. Even this miraculous event, which ought to have excited the wonder, the curiosity, and the devotion of mankind, passed without notice in an age of science and history. It happened during the lifetime of Seneca and the elder Pliny, who must have experienced the immediate effects, or received the earliest intelligence, of the prodigy. Each of these philosophers, in a laborious work, has recorded all the great phenomena of Nature, earthquakes, meteors, comets, and eclipses, which his indefatigable curiosity could collect. Both the one and the other have omitted to mention the greatest phenomenon to which the mortal eye has been witness since the creation of the globe. A distinct chapter of Pliny is designed for eclipses of an extraordinary nature and unusual duration; but he contents himself with describing the singular defect of light which followed the murder of Cæsar, when, during the greatest part of the year, the orb of the sun appeared pale and without splendour. This season of obscurity, which cannot surely be compared with the præternatural darkness of the Passion, had been already celebrated by most of the poets and historians of that memorable age.

## TOPICS FOR DISCUSSION

1   How does Gibbon characterize the early Christians? What reason does he give for this? Do you find yourself agreeing or disagreeing with him? Is your agreement or disagreement based upon his reasoning and historical knowledge or upon your own religious sentiments?

2   What qualities does Gibbon find in the best of the pagan Romans to account for their resistance to Christianity? Do these seem in the main honorable characteristics? Are these the same characteristics found in Shelley ("The Necessity of Atheism") or Russell ("A Free Man's Worship")?

3   Recount the progress of Christianity covered in this selection. Why

does Gibbon stress those matters which seem to lessen the numbers and the influence of the early Christians?

4   Why does Gibbon retell the story of the metamorphosis of St. James when he obviously does not believe it?

5   This eighteenth-century work is a classic of historical writing as well as a masterpiece of English prose style. What is it about the sentence structure of this work that marks it as clearly not the work of a modern writer, yet clearly the work of a conscientious craftsman? What do the references to other writers tell you of the education of the author?

## ...AND COMPOSITION

6   Imitate the rhythm of the following sentence: "This unfavourable picture, though not devoid of a faint resemblance, betrays, by its dark colouring and distorted features, the pencil of an enemy."

7   What is your judgment of Gibbon's characterization of the early Christians? Would you expect such characteristics in most "believers" in societies of today?

8   Write a paper from the point of view of a contemporary pagan Roman describing the Christians in Rome.

**H. R. TREVOR-ROPER (1914–     )** the eminent Oxford
historian, is a specialist in the Elizabethan period. What really goes on in history
is so complicated, and the possible sequences in the telling are so numerous,
that for most of us any historical account is either baffling or misleadingly
understandable: we must rely on our informant. In the following
account by Trevor-Roper, Raleigh comes before us as already
understood; we inherit the perspective the writer has achieved. The life
of Raleigh is seen as a clear progression of possibilities, each one
linked to those events of his time which provide his story with its maximum
meaning. In a selection about Raleigh following this one, you will see how a poet
considers him, and you will note the difference in the poet's treatment.

# The Last Elizabethan: Sir Walter Raleigh

In 1603 the greatest English royal dynasty came to an end. With
suprising smoothness King James succeeded to Queen Elizabeth. Directly,
that transition made the fortune of a great private dynasty, the Cecils of
Hatfield; incidentally it ruined one of the greatest living Englishmen, Sir
Walter Raleigh.

In November 1603 Sir Walter Raleigh was accused of treason—of
seeking, with Spanish and popish aid, to overthrow the new king and substitute on his throne a puppet-queen. The evidence for this charge was
simple: first, a group of desperate popish gentry in the Midlands, having
hatched an absurd plot in the obscurity of Sherwood Forest, admitted that
they had pleased themselves with the fancy of Raleigh's support; secondly,
a single thrice-perjured witness alternately alleged and denied and re-alleged
that it was so. At his trial at Winchester Raleigh contemptuously dismissed
such evidence and demanded to face his accuser. Was it likely, he asked,
that he would consent to be "a Robin Hood, a Wat Tyler, a Jack Cade,

a John Kett"? And did not the law anyway demand two witnesses? It was in vain. Over against him was the King's Attorney, Sir Edward Coke. No lack of evidence could disconcert that great Panjandrum of the Common Law. "Damnable atheist," he cried, "thou hast a Spanish heart and art thyself a spider of Hell." "Many horse-stealers would escape," declared another sententious lawyer, "if they could not be hanged but by the mouth of two witnesses." These arguments convinced the special judges of that tribunal—Sir Robert Cecil, the King's secretary, Raleigh's former friend, who would himself silently pocket, among other bribes, a pension from Spain; Lord Henry Howard, Raleigh's inveterate enemy, himself a secret papist; their friends, allies and kinsmen. By one of the most famous injustices in our history Raleigh was condemned to death and led out to execution. Then, having submitted to all the formalities of approaching death, he was suddenly, at the last moment, reprieved; the British Solomon admired, in this solemn farce, the evidence of his own magnanimity; and Raleigh disappeared, for fifteen years, into the Tower.

Raleigh's condemnation in 1603 was a climacteric in his personal life and evoked from him his finest poems—his *Passionate Man's Pilgrimage,* his *Petition to the Queen.* He had always been a poet, of all the Elizabethan court-poets "most lofty, insolent and passionate"; but beneath the polished surface of his occasional verse there lay, half-hidden, qualities which separate him from his rivals in that field: an insatiable intellectual ambition, a deep and proud melancholy. He was the patron not only of Spenser but of the disquieting "School of Night": of the atheist Marlowe, "still climbing after knowledge infinite," and, indirectly, of that self-torturing laborious introvert, George Chapman, forerunners of the mystical poets of the new century. So now, on the eve of execution, Raleigh struck a new vein and expressed in poetry his latent metaphysical melancholy:

Give me my scallop-shell of quiet,
My staff of faith to walk upon,
My scrip of Joy, immortal diet,
My bottle of Salvation,
My gown of Glory, hope's true gage,
And thus I'll take my pilgrimage.

Blood must be my body's balmer,
No other balm will there be given,
Whilst my soul, like a white palmer,
Travels to the land of Heaven. . . .

Then, turning like all the poets of that litigious age to the processes of law for his images, he pronounced, indirectly, his sentence on the corrupt and unjust tribunal that had condemned him, and particularly on the King's Attorney, Sir Edward Coke:

From thence to Heaven's bribeless hall,

Where no corrupted voices brawl,
No conscience molten into gold,
Nor forg'd accusers bought and sold,
No cause deferred nor vain-spent journey,
For there Christ is the King's Attorney. . . .

Raleigh's trial, which recreated his poetry and gave him the leisure
to write his most ambitious work, the *History of the World*, was also the
cause of his remarkable posthumous reputation; but legally it was an
outrage, which has to be explained. Of course it was a political trial; and
the politics of the last years of Elizabeth bring us back always to the meteor
of her declining court, Robert Devereux, Earl of Essex.

Raleigh and Essex, famous as rival courtiers, sustaining on the spoils
of church-lands, court offices and war their ambitions, their retinues, their
dependent poets, their elaborate gestures, were nevertheless not court
figures only. Behind the court was the country, divided—like the court—by
brisk party struggles between those who enjoyed and those who coveted
the sweets and opportunities of office: between the Cecils and their ever-
growing system of patronage on the one hand, and, on the other, Essex at
the head of the excluded peers at court, the excluded gentry in the country.
Against the day when the old Queen should die, the parties manœuvred
and counter-manœuvred; then, in 1601, Essex was out-manœuvred and
destroyed; the peers who had rashly followed him made their submission;
and the court at least was united round Sir Robert Cecil, who could now
negotiate from strength with the King of Scots and ensure, under a new
king, the continuation of the old system, the vast monopoly of office which
he had so nearly closed.

But if the court was united, what of the country? If the peers had
forsaken them, the gentry would look to other champions. If Essex was
dead, they would look to his old rival, himself by birth "a bare gentleman."
Raleigh, by his individualism, his isolation, his survival, became the hope
of all whom the Cecil system excluded; and Cecil and his allies the
Howards were convinced that, to complete their monopoly, Raleigh must
be destroyed. In secret letters to the King of Scots they denounced, with
sanctimonious spite, the "atheist" and his friends; and when the King's
mind had been sufficiently poisoned, they struck. A few desperate plotters
mumbled the name of Raleigh. It was enough. The all-powerful secretary,
with unctuous magnanimity, presided over the trial, and could rely on his
own kinsman, Attorney-General Coke, to demand the death-sentence.
Raleigh was ruined; and the empire of Cecil was safe for ever.

Thereafter the excluded gentry, leaderless and resentful, looked from
afar upon the gay, corrupt, extravagant court of James I, and the words
which Raleigh, in his temporary eclipse by Essex, had once applied to the
old court,

Say to the court it glows
And shines like rotten wood

now seemed to them doubly applicable to the new. The great Cecil racket was succeeded by the great Buckingham racket; court and country drifted ever further apart; and the distant protests of the gentry, as they beat inaudibly upon the frivolous world of privilege and pleasure, assumed by opposition a puritan earnestness. Naturally their minds turned to their most distinguished fellow-victim, whose name recalled the happier days of "Queen Elizabeth of glorious memory": the solitary prisoner who now, still insatiable in his boundless intellectual quest, was practising chemistry in a shed under the Tower Wall, or writing for Prince Henry the *History of the World*. "Only my father," exclaimed the indignant prince, "would keep such a bird in a cage." Then, in 1618, the bird was let out, and the second visit to Guiana was followed by the second and final ruin. Fifteen years after his freedom had been sacrificed to Cecil, Raleigh's life was sacrificed to the Spanish ambassador, Count Gondomar. So once again, still on the old charge, he was condemned to death; once again he penned—or rather, as we now know, remade—a valedictory poem, those famous lines inscribed in his Bible:

> Even such is time which takes in trust
> Our youth, our joys and all we have,
> And pays us but with age and dust;

once again he was led out to the block. Only this time there were differences. In 1603, thanks to his "damnable pride," Raleigh had been the most hated man in England—at his trial at Winchester he had barely been brought alive through the crowd; in 1618 he was everywhere hailed as a martyr. In 1603, to the disappointment of the observers, the axe had not fallen; in 1618, to their dismay, it fell.

Thence also sprang the strange history of his later fame. Raleigh, the outrageous intellectual, the arrogant courtier, rich, elegant, flamboyant, with his satin clothes and huge pearl ear-drops, the cosmopolitan, the machiavellian, the atheist, whose casual table-talk had sent a Dorset parson mumping to the Privy Council, was gradually transformed, by their common misfortunes, into the idol of earnest, conventional, parsimonious, provincial, puritan inland squires. In their country houses they transcribed his casual poems, or they had them carved upon their tombs;[1] they expressed their views in pamphlets with such titles as *Sir Walter Raleigh's Ghost*; they read, in half a century, twenty editions of his *History of the World*; and when, in the Great Rebellion, they rose at last and swept away the whole court, the court of Charles I, the last Renaissance court in Europe, they did it in the name of the greatest of all courtiers and virtuosi, Sir Walter Raleigh, whose minor works were first collected and published under the English Republic; whose dreams of a Caribbean Empire became the policy

---

[1] Raleigh's lines "Even such is time . . ." are inscribed on seventeenth century tombstones in Herefordshire, Cumberland and Surrey (see letters in *The Times Literary Supplement*, 12 and 26 October 1951).

of the Puritan Protectorate; whose *Prerogative of Parliaments* was copied out by Sir John Eliot; whose apocryphal works were edited by John Milton;[2] whose *History of the World* was, after the Bible, the favourite reading of Oliver Cromwell. Truly, until Disraeli, no man inspired, or was followed by a more incongruous party than he.

## TOPICS FOR DISCUSSION

1　How is Raleigh the individual characterized? How is Raleigh the last Elizabethan characterized?

2　"Elizabethan" is often imprecise and highly connotative. Is this so in Trevor-Roper's essay?

3　Does the author remain aloof from his subject, or does he commit himself to Raleigh's cause both openly and subtly?

4　Does the essay read like textbook history? If so, what qualities account for this? If not, what qualities make it different from such writing?

5　Is the excerpt from "Passionate Man's Pilgrimage" well used as a document supporting historical assertions? Is this use of poetry (or any work of art) a violation of poetry as you understood it from earlier readings in this text (e.g., Poe, "The Philosophy of Composition"; Cary, "Idea and Form"; Langer, "Living Form")? Can poetry ever be offered as proof of an author's feelings?

6　Why is it paradoxical that after his death Raleigh's supporters came from the groups they did?

## ...AND COMPOSITION

7　Compare the historical facts presented in this essay with those of a standard history book covering the same details. Include in your comparison the facts themselves (were they the same? were any omitted by one writer included by another? was it an important omission?), how they were arranged, and how the authors varied in objectivity.

8　Retell an historical event with which you are familiar, working for the same kind of liveliness you find in Trevor-Roper.

9　Read all of "Passionate Man's Pilgrimage" and comment on the accuracy of Trevor-Roper's reading of it.

[2] Mr. Ernest A. Strathmann has shown (in *The Times Literary Supplement,* 13 April 1956) that *The Cabinet-Council,* which Milton edited and ascribed to Raleigh in 1658, is not in fact by Raleigh but by one "T. B.", possibly Thomas Bedingfield, the translator of Machiavelli's *Florentine History.*

**WILLIAM CARLOS WILLIAMS (1883–1963)**   became by the end of his long
life a special kind of literary figure, a rallying point, an encourager of the
young. A physician in Rutherford, New Jersey, he made that locality a
part of the literature of our time, in novels, poems, and essays. As a
poet Mr. Williams championed American speech and made its flat, abrupt,
common style a part of our literary consciousness. In the selection here
he turns toward American history and evokes the myth of our past,
using references from explorers' accounts. He displays something of the mystery
a person feels when he finds himself caught in the present which has grown
from the tangled past historians cannot ever deliver fully. In this
essay Williams has abandoned conventional order and sequence in favor
of another sort of unity: what Raleigh means in the consciousness of an
informed American observer of our day is built up through allusion, through echoes
of epic forms, and through figures of speech which haunt the whole passage.

# Sir Walter Raleigh

Of the pursuit of beauty and the husk that remains, perversions and
mistakes, while the true form escapes in the wind, sing O Muse; of Raleigh,
beloved by majesty, plunging his lust into the body of the new world—
and the deaths, misfortunes, counter coups, which swelled back to certify
that ardor with defeat. Sing! and let the rumor of these things make the
timid more timid and the brave desperate, careless of monuments which
celebrate the subtle conversions of sense and let truth go unrecognized.
Sing! and make known Raleigh, who would found colonies; his England
become a mouthful of smoke sucked from the embers of a burnt weed.
And if the nations, well founded on a million hindrances, taxes, laws and
laws to annul laws must have a monument, let it be here implied: this
undersong, this worm armed to gnaw away lies and to release—Raleigh:
if it so please the immortal gods.

Sing of his wisdom, O Muse: The truth is that all nations, how remote
soever, being all reasonable creatures, and enjoying one and the same imagination and fantasy, have devised, according to their means and materials,
the same things.

They all have lighted on the invention of bows and arrows; all have targets
and wooden swords, all have instruments to encourage them to fight, all
that have corn beat it in mortars and make cakes, baking them upon slate
stones; all devised laws without any grounds had from the scriptures or
from Aristotle's Politick, whereby they are governed; all that dwell near
their enemies impale their villages, to save themselves from surprise. Yea,
besides the same inventions, all have the same natural impulsions; they
follow nature in the choice of many wives; and there are among them

which, out of a kind of wolfish ferocity, eat man's flesh; yea, most of them believe in a second life, and they are all of them idolators in one kind or another.—

These things, still chewing, he chewed out. And as an atheist, with Marlow, they would have burned him. It was his style! To the sea, then! mixed with soundest sense—on selling cannon to one's enemies.

But through all else, O Muse, say that he penetrated to the Queen!

Sing! O Muse and say, he was too mad in love, too clear, too desperate for her to trust upon great councils. He was not England, as she was. She held him, but she was too shrewd a woman not to know she held him as a woman, she, the Queen; which left an element. Say that he was made and cracked by majesty, knew that devotion, tasted that wisdom and became too wise—and she all eyes and wit looking through until her man, her Raleigh became thin, light, a spirit. He was the whetter, the life giver through the Queen—but wounded cruelly. In this desperate condition, will-less, inspired, the tool of a woman, flaming, falling, being lifted up, robbed of himself to feed her, caught, dispatched, starting, held again, giving yet seeking round the circle for an outlet: this was, herself; but what, O Muse, of Raleigh, that proud man?

Say, first, he was the breath of the Queen—for a few years; say, too, that he had traveled much before he knew her, that he had seen the tropics and explored the Orinoco River for a hundred miles. Then say, O Muse, that now he saw himself afar, that he became—America! that he conceived a voyage from perfection to find—an England new again; to found a colony; the outward thrust, to seek. But it turned out to be a voyage on the body of his Queen: England, Elizabeth—Virginia!

He sent out colonists, she would not let him go himself; nothing succeeded. It was a venture in the crook of a lady's finger, pointing, then curving in. Virginia? It was the nail upon that finger. O Raleigh! nowhere, everywhere —and nothing. Declare, O Muse, impartially, how he had gone with the English fleet to strike at Spain and how she called him back—Sire, do you not know, you!? These women are my person. What have you dared to do? How have you dared, without my order, to possess yourself of what is mine? Marry this woman!

Sing, O Muse, with an easy voice, how she, Elizabeth, she England, she the Queen—deserted him; Raleigh for Leicester, Essex now for Raleigh; she Spenser whom he friended, she "The Faery Queen," she Guiana, she Virginia, she atheist, she "my dear friend Marlow," she rents, rewards, honors, influence, reputation, she "the fundamental laws of human knowl-edge," she prison, she tobacco, the introduction of potatoes to the Irish

soil: It is the body of the Queen stirred by that plough—now all with-drawn.

O Muse, in that still pasture where you dwell amid the hardly noticed sounds of water falling and the little cries of crickets and small birds, sing of Virginia floating off: the broken chips of Raleigh: the Queen is dead.

O Virginia! who will gather you again as Raleigh had you gathered? science, wisdom, love, despair. O America, the deathplace of his son! It is Raleigh, anti-tropical. It is the cold north, flaring up in ice again.

What might he have known, what seen, O Muse?—Shoal water where we smelt so sweet and so strong a smell, as if we had been in the midst of some delicate garden; and keeping good watch and keeping but slack sail—we arrived upon the coast; a land so full of grapes as the very beating and surge of the sea overflow them, such plenty, as well there as in all places else, on the sand and on the green soil on the hills, as well as every little shrub, as also climbing towards the tops of high cedars, that in all the world I think a like abundance is not to be found. And from below the hill such a flock of cranes, mostly white, arose with such a cry as if an army of men had shouted all together.—He might have seen the brother of the king, Granganimo, with copper cap, whose wife, comely and bashful, might have come aboard the ship, her brows bound with white coral; or running out to meet them very cheerfully, at Roanoake, plucked off his socks and washed his feet in warm water. A people gentle, loving, faithful, void of all guile and treason. Earthen pots, large, white and sweet and wooden platters of sweet timber.

Sing, O Muse and say, there is a spirit that is seeking through America for Raleigh: in the earth, the air, the waters, up and down, for Raleigh, that lost man: seer who failed, planter who never planted, poet whose works are questioned, leader without command, favorite deposed—but one who yet gave title for his Queen, his England, to a coast he never saw but grazed alone with genius.

Question him in hell, O Muse, where he has gone, and when there is an answer, sing and make clear the reasons that he gave for that last blow. Why did he send his son into that tropic jungle and not go himself, upon so dangerous an errand? And when the boy had died why not die too? Why England again and force the new King to keep his promise and behead him?


## TOPICS FOR DISCUSSION

1   To William Carlos Williams, Sir Walter Raleigh is too lively and too meaningful to be merely a musty historical fact. Yet Wil-

liams's Raleigh is not just an idea either; rather, he is an attitude, a specific man caught in an endlessly meaningful pose, a gesture with a name. In short Williams is a poet, and Raleigh is that distinctive union of general and specific which poets build, an image. One understands such images best simply by describing them. What facts does Williams include in his portrait of Raleigh? How does he order them? What ideas emerge from this selection and arrangement?

2   The larger elements of this image filter down to the smallest details in Williams's style. His Raleigh is a lover. In how many ways is this fact introduced in the first paragraph?

3   What is the Elizabeth Raleigh loves?

4   What does Raleigh find to love in Virginia?

5   What does Williams find to love in Virginia and in Raleigh?

6   Epic poets from Homer on have asked the Muses to help them tell of heroes; Williams's repeated "Sing, O Muse" reminds us that Raleigh is a hero by reminding us of Homer and Virgil and their heroic poems. What else do these invocations accomplish in the passage? Why does Williams feel that he must have the Muses' help to sing specifically of Raleigh?

7   Beginning writers are often told never to introduce new materials in the conclusion; yet this selection ends with a question, and it is a real question, not a rhetorical flourish. Why is it an appropriate close?

## ...AND COMPOSITION

8   As simply as possible state what Raleigh means to Williams.

9   "Let us try to enlighten ourselves together; let us try to disinter one precious monument from the ruins of centuries." Such, says Voltaire, are the ends to be gained by studying the past. In your opinion, who best achieves these ends with Raleigh, the poet Williams or the historian Trevor-Roper ("The Last Elizabethan: Sir Walter Raleigh")?

10  Try to write a paragraph of your own which generalizes extensively without using generalities.

**WILLIAM FAULKNER (1897–1962)** in successive novels, created from a mixture of history and myth an imaginary county in his native Mississippi. One of his most experimental novels, *The Sound and the Fury,* for which the following passage serves as an introduction, presents its story from bewilderingly limited points of view, so that the reader experiences the whole in terms of separate glimpses. Faulkner's method forms a sequence with the two selections preceding: from history made coherent by the teller (Trevor-Roper), through history as a trance in the teller's sensibilities (Williams), to fiction imposed on the reader as history (Faulkner).

# *Compson: 1699 — 1945*

### IKKEMOTUBBE

A dispossessed American king Called "l'Homme" (and sometimes "de l'homme") by his fosterbrother, a Chevalier of France, who had he not been born too late could have been among the brightest in that glittering galaxy of knightly blackguards who were Napoleon's marshals, who thus translated the Chickasaw title meaning "The Man"; which translation Ikkemotubbe, himself a man of wit and imagination as well as a shrewd judge of character, including his own, carried one step further and anglicised it to "Doom." Who granted out of his vast lost domain a solid square mile of virgin North Mississippi dirt as truly angled as the four corners of a cardtable top (forested then because these were the old days before 1833 when the stars fell and Jefferson Mississippi was one long rambling onestorey mudchinked log building housing the Chickasaw Agent and his tradingpost store) to the grandson of a Scottish refugee who had lost his own birthright by casting his lot with a king who himself had been dispossessed. This in partial return for the right to proceed in peace, by whatever means he and his people saw fit, afoot or ahorse provided they were Chickasaw horses, to the wild western land presently to be called Oklahoma: not knowing then about the oil.

### JACKSON

A Great White Father with a sword. (An old duellist, a brawling lean fierce mangy durable imperishable old lion who set the wellbeing of the nation above the White House and the health of his new political party above either and above them all set not his wife's honor but the principle that honor must be defended whether it was or not because defended it was whether or not.) Who patented sealed and countersigned the grant with his own hand in his gold tepee in Wassi Town, not knowing about the oil either: so that one day the homeless descendants of the dispossessed would

ride supine with drink and splendidly comatose above the dusty allotted harborage of their bones in speciallybuilt scarletpainted hearses and fire-engines.

These were Compsons:

### QUENTIN MACLACHAN

Son of a Glasgow printer, orphaned and raised by his mother's people in the Perth highlands. Fled to Carolina from Culloden Moor with a claymore and the tartan he wore by day and slept under by night, and little else. At eighty, having fought once against an English king and lost, he would not make that mistake twice and so fled again one night in 1779, with his infant grandson and the tartan (the claymore had vanished, along with his son, the grandson's father, from one of Tarleton's regiments on a Georgia battlefield about a year ago) into Kentucky, where a neighbor named Boon or Boone had already established a settlement.

### CHARLES STUART

Attainted and proscribed by name and grade in his British regiment. Left for dead in a Georgia swamp by his own retreating army and then by the advancing American one, both of which were wrong. He still had the claymore even when on his homemade wooden leg he finally overtook his father and son four years later at Harrodsburg, Kentucky, just in time to bury the father and enter upon a long period of being a split personality while still trying to be the schoolteacher which he believed he wanted to be, until he gave up at last and became the gambler he actually was and which no Compson seemed to realize they all were provided the gambit was desperate and the odds long enough. Succeeded at last in risking not only his neck but the security of his family and the very integrity of the name he would leave behind him, by joining the confederation headed by an acquaintance named Wilkinson (a man of considerable talent and influence and intellect and power) in a plot to secede the whole Mississippi Valley from the United States and join it to Spain. Fled in his turn when the bubble burst (as anyone except a Compson schoolteacher should have known it would), himself unique in being the only one of the plotters who had to flee the country: this not from the vengeance and retribution of the government which he had attempted to dismember, but from the furious revulsion of his late confederates now frantic for their own safety. He was not expelled from the United States, he talked himself countryless, his expulsion due not to the treason but to his having been so vocal and vociferant in the conduct of it, burning each bridge vocally behind him before he had even reached the place to build the next one: so that it was no provost marshal nor even a civic agency but his late coplotters them-

selves who put afoot the movement to evict him from Kentucky and the
United States and, if they had caught him, probably from the world too.
Fled by night, running true to family tradition, with his son and the old
claymore and the tartan.

## JASON LYCURGUS

Who, driven perhaps by the compulsion of the flamboyant name given
him by the sardonic embittered woodenlegged indomitable father who
perhaps still believed with his heart that what he wanted to be was a
classicist schoolteacher, rode up the Natchez Trace one day in 1811 with
a pair of fine pistols and one meagre saddlebag on a small lightwaisted but
stronghocked mare which could do the first two furlongs in definitely
under the halfminute and the next two in not appreciably more, though
that was all. But it was enough: who reached the Chickasaw Agency at
Okatoba (which in 1860 was still called Old Jefferson) and went no
further. Who within six months was the Agent's clerk and within twelve
his partner, officially still the clerk though actually halfowner of what was
now a considerable store stocked with the mare's winnings in races against
the horses of Ikkemotubbe's young men which he, Compson, was always
careful to limit to a quarter or at most three furlongs; and in the next year
it was Ikkemotubbe who owned the little mare and Compson owned the
solid square mile of land which someday would be almost in the center
of the town of Jefferson, forested then and still forested twenty years later
though rather a park than a forest by that time, with its slavequarters and
stables and kitchengardens and the formal lawns and promenades and
pavilions laid out by the same architect who built the columned porticoed
house furnished by steamboat from France and New Orleans, and still
the square intact mile in 1840 (with not only the little white village called
Jefferson beginning to enclose it but an entire white county about to
surround it because in a few years now Ikkemotubbe's descendants and
people would be gone, those remaining living not as warriors and hunters
but as white men—as shiftless farmers or, here and there, the masters of
what they too called plantations and the owners of shiftless slaves, a little
dirtier than the white man, a little lazier, a little crueller—until at last
even the wild blood itself would have vanished, to be seen only occasionally
in the noseshape of a Negro on a cottonwagon or a white sawmill hand
or trapper or locomotive fireman), known as the Compson Domain then,
since now it was fit to breed princes, statesmen and generals and bishops,
to avenge the dispossessed Compsons from Culloden and Carolina and
Kentucky, then known as the Governor's house because sure enough in
time it did produce or at least spawn a governor—Quentin MacLachan
again, after the Culloden grandfather—and still known as the Old Governor's even after it had spawned (1861) a general—(called so by pre-

determined accord and agreement by the whole town and county, as though they knew even then and beforehand that the old governor was the last Compson who would not fail at everything he touched save longevity or suicide)—the Brigadier Jason Lycurgus II who failed at Shiloh in '62 and failed again though not so badly at Resaca in '64, who put the first mortgage on the still intact square mile to a New England carpetbagger in '66, after the old town had been burned by the Federal General Smith and the new little town, in time to be populated mainly by the descendants not of Compsons but of Snopeses, had begun to encroach and then nibble at and into it as the failed brigadier spent the next forty years selling fragments of it off to keep up the mortage on the remainder: until one day in 1900 he died quietly on an army cot in the hunting and fishing camp in the Tallahatchie River bottom where he passed most of the end of his days.

And even the old governor was forgotten now; what was left of the old square mile was now known merely as the Compson place—the weedchoked traces of the old ruined lawns and promenades, the house which had needed painting too long already, the scaling columns of the portico where Jason III (bred for a lawyer and indeed he kept an office upstairs above the Square, where entombed in dusty filingcases some of the oldest names in the county—Holston and Sutpen, Grenier and Beauchamp and Coldfield—faded year by year among the bottomless labyrinths of chancery: and who knows what dream in the perennial heart of his father, now completing the third of his three avatars—the one as son of a brilliant and gallant statesman, the second as battleleader of brave and gallant men, the third as a sort of privileged pseudo-Daniel Boone-Robinson Crusoe, who had not returned to juvenility because actually he had never left it— that that lawyer's office might again be the anteroom to the governor's mansion and the old splendor) sat all day long with a decanter of whiskey and a litter of dogeared Horaces and Livys and Catulluses, composing (it was said) caustic and satiric eulogies on both his dead and his living fellowtownsmen, who sold the last of the property, except that fragment containing the house and the kitchengarden and the collapsing stables and one servant's cabin in which Dilsey's family lived, to a golfclub for the ready money with which his daughter Candace could have her fine wedding in April and his son Quentin could finish one year at Harvard and commit suicide in the following June of 1910; already known as the Old Compson place even while Compsons were still living in it on that spring dusk in 1928 when the old governor's doomed lost nameless seventeen-year-old greatgreatgranddaughter robbed her last remaining sane male relative (her uncle Jason IV) of his secret hoard of money and climbed down a rainpipe and ran off with a pitchman in a travelling streetshow, and still known as the Old Compson place long after all traces of Compsons were gone from it: after the widowed mother died and Jason IV, no longer needing to fear

Dilsey now, committed his idiot brother, Benjamin, to the State Asylum in Jackson and sold the house to a countryman who operated it as a boarding house for juries and horse- and muletraders, and still known as the Old Compson place even after the boardinghouse (and presently the golfcourse too) had vanished and the old square mile was even intact again in row after row of small crowded jerrybuilt individuallyowned demiurban bungalows.

And these:

QUENTIN III

Who loved not his sister's body but some concept of Compson honor precariously and (he knew well) only temporarily supported by the minute fragile membrane of her maidenhead as a miniature replica of all the whole vast globy earth may be poised on the nose of a trained seal. Who loved not the idea of the incest which he would not commit, but some presbyterian concept of its eternal punishment: he, not God, could by that means cast himself and his sister both into hell, where he could guard her forever and keep her forevermore intact amid the eternal fires. But who loved death above all, who loved only death, loved and lived in a deliberate and almost perverted anticipation of death as a lover loves and deliberately refrains from the waiting willing friendly tender incredible body of his beloved, until he can· no longer bear not the refraining but the restraint and so flings, hurls himself, relinquishing, drowning. Committed suicide in Cambridge Massachusetts, June 1910, two months after his sister's wedding, waiting first to complete the current academic year and so get the full value of his paid-in-advance tuition, not because he had his old Culloden and Carolina and Kentucky grandfathers in him but because the remaining piece of the old Compson mile which had been sold to pay for his sister's wedding and his year at Harvard had been the one thing, excepting that same sister and the sight of an open fire, which his youngest brother, born an idiot, had loved.

CANDACE (CADDY)

Doomed and knew it, accepted the doom without either seeking or fleeing it. Loved her brother despite him, loved not only him but loved in him that bitter prophet and inflexible corruptless judge of what he considered the family's honor and its doom, as he thought he loved but really hated in her what he considered the frail doomed vessel of its pride and the foul instrument of its disgrace; not only this, she loved him not only in spite of but because of the fact that he himself was incapable of love, accepting the fact that he must value above all not her but the virginity of which she was custodian and on which she placed no value whatever: the

frail physical stricture which to her was no more than a hangnail would have been. Knew the brother loved death best of all and was not jealous, would (and perhaps in the calculation and deliberation of her marriage did) have handed him the hypothetical hemlock. Was two months pregnant with another man's child which regardless of what its sex would be she had already named Quentin after the brother whom they both (she and the brother) knew was already the same as dead, when she married (1910) an extremely eligible young Indianian she and her mother had met while vacationing at French Lick the summer before. Divorced by him 1911. Married 1920 to a minor movingpicture magnate, Hollywood California. Divorced by mutual agreement, Mexico 1925. Vanished in Paris with the German occupation, 1940, still beautiful and probably still wealthy too since she did not look within fifteen years of her actual fortyeight, and was not heard of again. Except there was a woman in Jefferson, the county librarian, a mousesized and -colored woman who had never married, who had passed through the city schools in the same class with Candace Compson and then spent the rest of her life trying to keep *Forever Amber* in its orderly overlapping avatars and *Jurgen* and *Tom Jones* out of the hands of the highschool juniors and seniors who could reach them down without even having to tiptoe from the back shelves where she herself would have to stand on a box to hide them. One day in 1943, after a week of a distraction bordering on disintegration almost, during which those entering the library would find her always in the act of hurriedly closing her desk drawer and turning the key in it (so that the matrons, wives of the bankers and doctors and lawyers, some of whom had also been in that old highschool class, who came and went in the afternoons with the copies of the *Forever Ambers* and the volumes of Thorne Smith carefully wrapped from view in sheets of Memphis and Jackson newspapers, believed she was on the verge of illness or perhaps even loss of mind) she closed and locked the library in the middle of the afternoon and with her handbag clasped tightly under her arm and two feverish spots of determination in her ordinarily colorless cheeks, she entered the farmers' supply store where Jason IV had started as a clerk and where he now owned his own business as a buyer of and dealer in cotton, striding on through that gloomy cavern which only men ever entered—a cavern cluttered and walled and stalagmitehung with plows and discs and loops of tracechain and singletrees and mulecollars and sidemeat and cheap shoes and horselinament and flour and molasses, gloomy because the goods it contained were not shown but hidden rather since those who supplied Mississippi farmers or at least Negro Mississippi farmers for a share of the crop did not wish, until that crop was made and its value approximately computable, to show them what they could learn to want but only to supply them on specific demand with what they could not help but need—and strode on back to Jason's particular domain in the rear: a railed enclosure cluttered with shelves and pigeonholes bearing

spiked dust-and-lintgathering gin receipts and ledgers and cottonsamples and rank with the blended smell of cheese and kerosene and harnessoil and the tremendous iron stove against which chewed tobacco had been spat for almost a hundred years, and up to the long high sloping counter behind which Jason stood and, not looking again at the overalled men who had quietly stopped talking and even chewing when she entered, with a kind of fainting desperation she opened the handbag and fumbled something out of it and laid it open on the counter and stood trembling and breathing rapidly while Jason looked down at it—a picture, a photograph in color clipped obviously from a slick magazine—a picture filled with luxury and money and sunlight—a Cannebière backdrop of mountains and palms and cypresses and the sea, an open powerful expensive chromiumtrimmed sports car, the woman's face hatless between a rich scarf and a seal coat, ageless and beautiful, cold serene and damned; beside her a handsome lean man of middleage in the ribbons and tabs of a German staffgeneral—and the mousesized mousecolored spinster trembling and aghast at her own temerity, staring across it at the childless bachelor in whom ended that long line of men who had had something in them of decency and pride even after they had begun to fail at the integrity and the pride had become mostly vanity and selfpity: from the expatriate who had to flee his native land with little else except his life yet who still refused to accept defeat, through the man who gambled his life and his good name twice and lost twice and declined to accept that either, and the one who with only a clever small quarterhorse for tool avenged his dispossessed father and grandfather and gained a principality, and the brilliant and gallant governor and the general who though he failed at leading in battle brave and gallant men at least risked his own life too in the failing, to the cultured dipsomaniac who sold the last of his patrimony not to buy drink but to give one of his descendants at least the best chance in life he could think of.

"It's Caddy!" the librarian whispered. "We must save her!"

"It's Cad, all right," Jason said. Then he began to laugh. He stood there laughing above the picture, above the cold beautiful face now creased and dogeared from its week's sojourn in the desk drawer and the handbag. And the librarian knew why he was laughing, who had not called him anything but Mr Compson for thirty-two years now, ever since the day in 1911 when Candace, cast off by her husband, had brought her infant daughter home and left the child and departed by the next train, to return no more, and not only the Negro cook, Dilsey, but the librarian too divined by simple instinct that Jason was somehow using the child's life and its illegitimacy both to blackmail the mother not only into staying away from Jefferson for the rest of her life but into appointing him sole unchallengeable trustee of the money she would send for the child's maintenance, and had refused to speak to him at all since that day in 1928 when the daughter climbed down the rainpipe and ran away with the pitchman.

"Jason!" she cried. "We must save her! Jason! Jason!"—and still crying it even when he took up the picture between thumb and finger and threw it back across the counter toward her.

"That Candace?" he said. "Dont make me laugh. This bitch aint thirty yet. The other one's fifty now."

And the library was still locked all the next day too when at three oclock in the afternoon, footsore and spent yet still unflagging and still clasping the handbag tightly under her arm, she turned into a neat small yard in the Negro residence section of Memphis and mounted the steps of the neat small house and rang the bell and the door opened and a black woman of about her own age looked quietly out at her. "It's Frony, isn't it?" the librarian said. "Dont you remember me—Melissa Meek, from Jefferson—"

"Yes," the Negress said. "Come in. You want to see Mama." And she entered the room, the neat yet cluttered bedroom of an old Negro, rank with the smell of old people, old women, old Negroes, where the old woman herself sat in a rocker beside the hearth where even though it was June a fire smoldered—a big woman once, in faded clean calico and an immaculate turban wound round her head above the bleared and now apparently almost sightless eyes—and put the dogeared clipping into the black hands which, like the women of her race, were still as supple and delicately shaped as they had been when she was thirty or twenty or even seventeen.

"It's Caddy!" the librarian said. "It is! Dilsey! Dilsey!"

"What did he say?" the old Negress said. And the librarian knew whom she meant by "he," nor did the librarian marvel, not only that the old Negress would know that she (the librarian) would know whom she meant by the "he," but that the old Negress would know at once that she had already shown the picture to Jason.

"Dont you know what he said?" she cried. "When he realised she was in danger, he said it was her, even if I hadn't even had a picture to show him. But as soon as he realised that somebody, anybody, even just me, wanted to save her, would try to save her, he said it wasn't. But it is! Look at it!"

"Look at my eyes," the old Negress said. "How can I see that picture?"

"Call Frony!" the librarian cried. "She will know her!" But already the old Negress was folding the clipping carefully back into its old creases, handing it back.

"My eyes aint any good anymore," she said. "I cant see it."

And that was all. At six oclock she fought her way through the crowded bus terminal, the bag clutched under one arm and the return half of her roundtrip ticket in the other hand, and was swept out onto the roaring platform on the diurnal tide of a few middleaged civilians but mostly

soldiers and sailors enroute either to leave or to death and the homeless young women, their companions, who for two years now had lived from day to day in pullmans and hotels when they were lucky and in day-coaches and busses and stations and lobbies and public restrooms when not, pausing only long enough to drop their foals in charity wards or police-stations and then move on again, and fought her way into the bus, smaller than any other there so that her feet touched the floor only occasionally until a shape (a man in khaki; she couldn't see him at all because she was already crying) rose and picked her up bodily and set her into a seat next the window, where still crying quietly she could look out upon the fleeing city as it streaked past and then was behind and presently now she would be home again, safe in Jefferson where life lived too with all its incomprehensible passion and turmoil and grief and fury and despair, but here at six oclock you could close the covers on it and even the weightless hand of a child could put it back among its unfeatured kindred on the quiet eternal shelves and turn the key upon it for the whole and dreamless night. *Yes* she thought, crying quietly *that was it she didn't want to see it know whether it was Caddy or not because she knows Caddy doesn't want to be saved hasn't anything anymore worth being saved for nothing worth being lost that she can lose*

### JASON IV

The first sane Compson since before Culloden and (a childless bachelor) hence the last. Logical rational contained and even a philosopher in the old stoic tradition: thinking nothing whatever of God one way or the other and simply considering the police and so fearing and respecting only the Negro woman, his sworn enemy since his birth and his mortal one since that day in 1911 when she too divined by simple clairvoyance that he was somehow using his infant niece's illegitimacy to blackmail its mother, who cooked the food he ate. Who not only fended off and held his own with Compsons but competed and held his own with the Snopeses who took over the little town following the turn of the century as the Compsons and Sartorises and their ilk faded from it (no Snopes, but Jason Compson himself who as soon as his mother died—the niece had already climbed down the rainpipe and vanished so Dilsey no longer had either of these clubs to hold over him—committed his idiot younger brother to the state and vacated the old house, first chopping up the vast oncesplendid rooms into what he called apartments and selling the whole thing to a countryman who opened a boardinghouse in it), though this was not difficult since to him all the rest of the town and the world and the human race too except himself were Compsons, inexplicable yet quite predictable in that they were in no sense whatever to be trusted. Who, all the money from the sale of the pasture having gone for his sister's wedding and his brother's

course at Harvard, used his own niggard savings out of his meagre wages as a storeclerk to send himself to a Memphis school where he learned to class and grade cotton, and so established his own business with which, following his dipsomaniac father's death, he assumed the entire burden of the rotting family in the rotting house, supporting his idiot brother because of their mother, sacrificing what pleasures might have been the right and just due and even the necessity of a thirty-year-old bachelor, so that his mother's life might continue as nearly as possible to what it had been; this not because he loved her but (a sane man always) simply because he was afraid of the Negro cook whom he could not even force to leave, even when he tried to stop paying her weekly wages; and who despite all this, still managed to save almost three thousand dollars ($2840.50 as he reported it on the night his niece stole it; in niggard and agonised dimes and quarters and halfdollars, which hoard he kept in no bank because to him a banker too was just one more Compson, but hid in a locked bureau drawer in his bedroom whose bed he made and changed himself since he kept the bedroom door locked all the time save when he was passing through it. Who, following a fumbling abortive attempt by his idiot brother on a passing female child, had himself appointed the idiot's guardian without letting their mother know and so was able to have the creature castrated before the mother even knew it was out of the house, and who following the mother's death in 1933 was able to free himself forever not only from the idiot brother and the house but from the Negro woman too, moving into a pair of offices up a flight of stairs above the supplystore containing his cotton ledgers and samples, which he had converted into a bedroom-kitchen-bath in and out of which on weekends there would be seen a big plain friendly brazenhaired pleasantfaced woman no longer very young, in round picture hats and (in its season) an imitation fur coat, the two of them, the middleaged cottonbuyer and the woman whom the town called, simply, his friend from Memphis, seen at the local picture show on Saturday night and on Sunday morning mounting the apartment stairs with paper bags from the grocer's containing loaves and eggs and oranges and cans of soup, domestic, uxorious, connubial, until the late afternoon bus carried her back to Memphis. He was emancipated now. He was free. "In 1865," he would say, "Abe Lincoln freed the niggers from the Compsons. In 1933, Jason Compson freed the Compsons from the niggers."

### BENJAMIN

Born Maury, after his mother's only brother: a handsome flashing swaggering workless bachelor who borrowed money from almost anyone, even Dilsey although she was a Negro, explaining to her as he withdrew his hand from his pocket that she was not only in his eyes the same as a member of his sister's family, she would be considered a born lady any-

where in any eyes. Who, when at last even his mother realised what he was and insisted weeping that his name must be changed, was rechristened Benjamin by his brother Quentin (Benjamin, our lastborn, sold into Egypt). Who loved three things: the pasture which was sold to pay for Candace's wedding and to send Quentin to Harvard, his sister Candace, firelight. Who lost none of them because he could not remember his sister but only the loss of her, and firelight was the same bright shape as going to sleep, and the pasture was even better sold than before because now he and TP could not only follow timeless along the fence the motions which it did not even matter to him were humanbeings swinging golfsticks, TP could lead them to clumps of grass or weeds where there would appear suddenly in TP's hand small white spherules which competed with and even conquered what he did not even know was gravity and all the immutable laws when released from the hand toward plank floor or smokehouse wall or concrete sidewalk. Gelded 1913. Committed to the State Asylum, Jackson 1933. Lost nothing then either because, as with his sister, he remembered not the pasture but only its loss, and firelight was still the same bright shape of sleep.

QUENTIN

The last. Candace's daughter. Fatherless nine months before her birth, nameless at birth and already doomed to be unwed from the instant the dividing egg determined its sex. Who at seventeen, on the one thousand eight hundred ninetyfifth anniversary of the day before the resurrection of Our Lord, swung herself by a rainpipe from the window of the room in which her uncle had locked her at noon, to the locked window of his own locked and empty bedroom and broke a pane and entered the window and with the uncle's firepoker burst open the locked bureau drawer and took the money (it was not $2840.50 either, it was almost seven thousand dollars and this was Jason's rage, the red unbearable fury which on that night and at intervals recurring with little or no diminishment for the next five years, made him seriously believe would at some unwarned instant destroy him, kill him as instantaneously dead as a bullet or a lightningbolt: that although he had been robbed not of a mere petty three thousand dollars but of almost seven thousand he couldn't even tell anybody; because he had been robbed of seven thousand dollars instead of just three he could not only never receive justification—he did not want sympathy—from other men unlucky enough to have one bitch for a sister and another for a niece, he couldn't even go to the police; because he had lost four thousand dollars which did not belong to him he couldn't even recover the three thousand which did since those first four thousand dollars were not only the legal property of his niece as a part of the money supplied for her support and maintenance by her mother over the last sixteen years, they did not exist

at all, having been officially recorded as expended and consumed in the annual reports he submitted to the district Chancellor, as required of him as guardian and trustee by his bondsmen: so that he had been robbed not only of his thievings but his savings too, and by his own victim; he had been robbed not only of the four thousand dollars which he had risked jail to acquire but of the three thousand which he had hoarded at the price of sacrifice and denial, almost a nickel and a dime at a time, over a period of almost twenty years: and this not only by his own victim but by a child who did it at one blow, without premeditation or plan, not even knowing or even caring how much she would find when she broke the drawer open; and now he couldn't even go to the police for help: he who had considered the police always, never given them any trouble, had paid the taxes for years which supported them in parasitic and sadistic idleness; not only that, he didn't dare pursue the girl himself because he might catch her and she would talk, so that his only recourse was a vain dream which kept him tossing and sweating on nights two and three and even four years after the event, when he should have forgotten about it: of catching her without warning, springing on her out of the dark, before she had spent all the money, and murder her before she had time to open her mouth) and climbed down the same rainpipe in the dusk and ran away with the pitchman who was already under sentence for bigamy. And so vanished; whatever occupation overtook her would have arrived in no chromium Mercedes; whatever snapshot would have contained no general of staff.

And that was all. These others were not Compsons. They were black:

### TP

Who wore on Memphis's Beale Street the fine bright cheap intransigent clothes manufactured specifically for him by the owners of Chicago and New York sweatshops.

### FRONY

Who married a pullman porter and went to St Louis to live and later moved back to Memphis to make a home for her mother since Dilsey refused to go further than that.

### LUSTER

A man, aged 14. Who was not only capable of the complete care and security of an idiot twice his age and three times his size, but could keep him entertained.

### DILSEY

They endured.

## TOPICS FOR DISCUSSION

1  The late history of the Compson family is compacted into sketches of significant members of this family. Who are the members sketched? What could you anticipate as the contribution of each in this history?

2  What effects are gained from the extraordinarily long sentences that appear so frequently in this selection?

3  The author provides few transitions in chronology between the crucial episodes he recounts, but the reader has a sense of the steady and purposeful progress of time. How is the author able to create this sense of continuity?

4  What is meant by the slight sentence following Dilsey's name? Are there other details of Dilsey found in other portraits?

5  Why would an author begin his novel with a basic outline of his plot? Does this introduction prompt you to continue to read the novel?

## ... AND COMPOSITION

6  Write a Faulkner-like sentence that rambles into paragraph length. Try to give it the same kind of purposefulness which marks Faulkner's style and which creates his effects.

7  Compose a portrait of an imaginary person that focuses on a single but telling event in that person's life. Try to make the past live in the present.

8  Analyze the use of parenthetical elements in this selection. Comment on their frequency, their function, and their effect on readers.

PART *4*

# Selections for Further Analysis

Liberated from preconceptions and stealthy guidance, the student may find the following selections helpful in testing his own judgments and discriminations. The pieces reflect the scope of the entire book, but are left without exercises so that instructors and students may more freely adapt them to individual needs.

These readings are good and can be helpful, but they are samples only—after them come libraries, and the world.

**THOMAS DE QUINCEY (1785–1859)** is best known for his sensational
writings, some of them based on his own experience, as in his most
famous, *Confessions of an English Opium Eater.* Other titles indicate something
of his typical bent: *On Murder Considered as One of the Fine Arts, On
the Knocking at the Gate in Macbeth, Suspiria de Profundis.* He wrote direct
and perceptive biographical sketches of his acquaintances among the
Romantics; most characteristic, however, are the pieces in which he expressed
depths of guilt and anxiety. The following selection on the death of
Joan of Arc demonstrates both his directness, at the beginning,
and his vivid fantasy about guilt and anxiety, when he turns to an
imagined death scene for the judge who sentenced the martyr.

# Joan of Arc

On the Wednesday after Trinity Sunday in 1431, being then about
nineteen years of age, the Maid of Arc underwent her martyrdom. She
was conducted before mid-day, guarded by eight hundred spearmen, to
a platform of prodigious height, constructed of wooden billets supported by
occasional walls of lath and plaster, and traversed by hollow spaces in
every direction for the creation of air-currents. "The pile struck terror,"
says M. Michelet, "by its height"; and, as usual, the English purpose in
this is viewed as one of pure malignity. But there are two ways of explaining all that. It is probable that the purpose was merciful. On the circumstances of the execution I shall not linger. Yet, to mark the almost fatal
felicity of M. Michelet in finding out whatever may injure the English name,
at a moment when every reader will be interested in Joanna's personal
appearance, it is really edifying to notice the ingenuity by which he draws
into light from a dark corner a very unjust account of it, and neglects,
though lying upon the high road, a very pleasing one. Both are from English
pens. Grafton, a chronicler but little read, being a stiff-necked John Bull,
thought fit to say, that no wonder Joanna should be a virgin, since her
"foule face" was a satisfactory solution of that particular merit. Holinshead,
on the other hand, a chronicler somewhat later, every way more important,
and at one time universally read, has given a very pleasing testimony to
the interesting character of Joanna's person and engaging manners. Neither
of these men lived till the following century, so that personally this evidence
is none at all. Grafton sullenly and carelessly believed as he wished to believe; Holinshead took pains to inquire, and reports undoubtedly the general impression of France. But I cite the case as illustrating M. Michelet's
candor.

The circumstantial incidents of the execution, unless with more space
than I can now command, I should be unwilling to relate. I should fear to

injure, by imperfect report, a martyrdom which to myself appears so unspeakably grand. Yet for a purpose, pointing not at Joanna, but at M. Michelet—viz., to convince him that an Englishman is capable of thinking more highly of *La Pucelle* than even her admiring countryman, I shall, in parting, allude to one or two traits in Joanna's demeanor on the scaffold, and to one or two in that of the bystanders, which authorize me in questioning an opinion of his upon this martyr's firmness. The reader ought to be reminded that Joanna D'Arc was subjected to an unusually unfair trial of opinion. Any of the elder Christian martyrs had not much to fear of *personal* rancor. The martyr was chiefly regarded as the enemy of Cæsar; at times, also, where any knowledge of the Christian faith and morals existed, with the enmity that arises spontaneously in the worldly against the spiritual. But the martyr, though disloyal, was not supposed to be, therefore, anti-national; and still less was *individually* hateful. What was hated (if anything) belonged to his class, not to himself separately. Now, Joanna, if hated at all, was hated personally, and in Rouen on national grounds. Hence there would be a certainty of calumny arising against *her,* such as would not affect martyrs in general. That being the case, it would follow of necessity that some people would impute to her a willingness to recant. No innocence could escape *that.* Now, had she really testified this willingness on the scaffold, it would have argued nothing at all but the weakness of a genial nature shrinking from the instant approach of torment. And those will often pity that weakness most, who, in their own persons, would yield to it least. Meantime, there never was a calumny uttered that drew less support from the recorded circumstances. It rests upon no *positive* testimony, and it has a weight of contradicting testimony to stem. And yet, strange to say, M. Michelet, who at times seems to admire the Maid of Arc as much as I do, is the one sole writer amongst her *friends* who lends some countenance to this odious slander. His words are, that, if she did not utter this word *recant* with her lips, she uttered it in her heart. "Whether she *said* the word is uncertain; but I affirm that she *thought* it."

Now, I affirm that she did not; not in any sense of the word *"thought"* applicable to the case. Here is France calumniating *La Pucelle:* here is England defending her. M. Michelet can only mean that, on *à priori* principles, every woman must be liable to such a weakness: that Joanna was a woman; *ergo,* that she was liable to such a weakness. That is, he only supposes her to have uttered the word by an argument which presumes it impossible for anybody to have done otherwise. I, on the contrary, throw the *onus* of the argument not on presumable tendencies of nature, but on the known facts of that morning's execution, as recorded by multitudes. What else, I demand, than mere weight of metal, absolute nobility of deportment, broke the vast line of battle then arrayed against her? What else but her meek, saintly demeanor won from the enemies, that till now

had believed her a witch, tears of rapturous admiration? "Ten thousand men," says M. Michelet himself, "ten thousand men wept"; and of these ten thousand the majority were political enemies knitted together by cords of superstition. What else was it but her constancy, united with her angelic gentleness, that drove the fanatic English soldier—who had sworn to throw a faggot on her scaffold, as *his* tribute of abhorrence, that *did* so, that fulfilled his vow—suddenly to turn away a penitent for life, saying everywhere that he had seen a dove rising upon wings to heaven from the ashes where she had stood? What else drove the executioner to kneel at every shrine for pardon to *his* share in the tragedy! And if all this were insufficient, then I cite the closing act of her life, as valid on her behalf, were all other testimonies against her. The executioner had been directed to apply his torch from below. He did so. The fiery smoke rose upwards in billowing volumes. A Dominican monk was then standing almost at her side. Wrapped up in his sublime office, he saw not the danger, but still persisted in his prayers. Even then, when the last enemy was racing up the fiery stairs to seize her, even at that moment did this noblest of girls think only for *him,* the one friend that would not forsake her, and not for herself; bidding him with her last breath to care for his own preservation, but to leave *her* to God. That girl, whose latest breath ascended in this sublime expression of self-oblivion, did not utter the word *recant* either with her lips or in her heart. No; she did not, though one should rise from the dead to swear it. . . .

Bishop of Beauvais! thy victim died in fire upon a scaffold—thou upon a down bed. But for the departing minutes of life, both are oftentimes alike. At the farewell crisis, when the gates of death are opening, and flesh is resting from its struggles, oftentimes the tortured and torturer have the same truce from carnal torment; both sink together into sleep; together both, sometimes, kindle into dreams. When the mortal mists were gathering fast upon you two, bishop and shepherd girl—when the pavilions of life were closing up their shadowy curtains about you—let us try, through the gigantic glooms, to decipher the flying features of your separate visions.

The shepherd girl that had delivered France—she, from her dungeon, she, from her baiting at the stake, she, from her duel with fire, as she entered her last dream—saw Domrémy, saw the fountain of Domrémy, saw the pomp of forests in which her childhood had wandered. That Easter festival, which man had denied to her languishing heart—that resurrection of spring-time, which the darkness of dungeons had intercepted from *her,* hungering after the glorious liberty of forests—were by God given back into her hands, as jewels that had been stolen from her by robbers. With those, perhaps (for the minutes of dreams can stretch into ages), was given back to her by God the bliss of childhood. By special privilege, for *her* might be created, in this farewell dream, a second childhood, innocent

as the first; but not, like *that,* sad with the gloom of a fearful mission in the rear. The mission had now been fulfilled. The storm was weathered, the skirts even of that mighty storm were drawing off. The blood that she was to reckon for had been exacted; the tears that she was to shed in secret had been paid to the last. The hatred to herself in all eyes had been faced steadily, had been suffered, had been survived. And in her last fight upon the scaffold she had triumphed gloriously; victoriously she had tasted the stings of death. For all, except this comfort from her farewell dream, she had died—died, amidst the tears of ten thousand enemies—died, amidst the drums and trumpets of armies—died, amidst peals redoubling upon peals, volleys upon volleys, from the saluting clarions of martyrs.

Bishop of Beauvais! because the guilt-burdened man is in dreams haunted and waylaid by the most frightful of his crimes, and because upon that fluctuating mirror—rising (like the mocking mirrors of *mirage* in Arabian deserts) from the fens of death—most of all are reflected the sweet countenances which the man has laid in ruins; therefore I know, bishop, that you also, entering your final dream, saw Domrémy. That fountain, of which the witnesses spoke so much, showed itself to your eyes in pure morning dews: but neither dews, nor the holy dawn, could cleanse away the bright spots of innocent blood upon its surface. By the fountain, bishop, you saw a woman seated, that hid her face. But as *you* draw near, the woman raises her wasted features. Would Domrémy know them again for the features of her child? Ah, but *you* know them, bishop, well! Oh, mercy! what a groan was *that* which the servants, waiting outside the bishop's dream at his bedside, heard from his laboring heart, as at this moment he turned away from the fountain and the woman, seeking rest in the forests afar off. Yet not *so* to escape the woman, whom once again he must behold before he dies. In the forests to which he prays for pity, will he find a respite? What a tumult, what a gathering of feet is there! In glades, where only wild deer should run, armies and nations are assembling; towering in the fluctuating crowd are phantoms that belong to departed hours. There is the great English Prince, Regent of France. There is my Lord of Winchester, the princely cardinal, that died and made no sign. There is the Bishop of Beauvais, clinging to the shelter of thickets. What building is that which hands so rapid are raising? Is it a martyr's scaffold? Will they burn the child of Domrémy a second time? No: it is a tribunal that rises to the clouds; and two nations stand around it, waiting for a trial. Shall my Lord of Beauvais sit again upon the judgment-seat, and again number the hours for the innocent? Ah! no: he is the prisoner at the bar. Already all is waiting: the mighty audience is gathered, the Court is hurrying to their seats, the witnesses are arrayed, the trumpets are sounding, the judge is taking his place. Oh! but this is sudden. My lord, have you no counsel? "Counsel I have none: in heaven above, or on earth beneath,

counsellor there is none now that would take a brief from *me:* all are silent."
Is it, indeed, come to this? Alas the time is short, the tumult is wondrous,
the crowd stretches away into infinity, but yet I will search in it for somebody to take your brief: I know of somebody that will be your counsel.
Who is this that cometh from Domrémy? Who is she in bloody coronation
robes from Rheims? Who is she that cometh with blackened flesh from
walking the furnaces of Rouen? This is she, the shepherd girl, counsellor
that had none for herself, whom I choose, bishop, for yours. She it is, I
engage, that shall take my lord's brief. She it is, bishop, that would plead
for you: yes, bishop, SHE—when heaven and earth are silent.

JOHN STUART MILL (1806–1873)   was led by his almost equally famous
father, James Mill, to become one of the earliest accelerated scholars.
As a child he read Latin and Greek and was adept in conversations
about economics, mathematics, philosophy, and politics. The quick clarity of
his thinking appears in the order and neatness of his prose, of which
the following extract from his *Autobiography* is a good example. In this
passage he examines and lucidly explains his discovery that knowing enough
would not necessarily bring happiness: ". . . to know that a feeling
would make me happy if I had it, did not give me the feeling." Mill's
account locates a crucial issue of our time—how to combine training with
education, vocational effectiveness with full human development.

# A Crisis in My Mental History. One Stage Onward

For some years after this I wrote very little, and nothing regularly, for
publication: and great were the advantages which I derived from the
intermission. It was of no common importance to me, at this period, to be
able to digest and mature my thoughts for my own mind only, without any
immediate call for giving them out in print. Had I gone on writing, it would
have much disturbed the important transformation in my opinions and
character, which took place during those years. The origin of this
transformation, or at least the process by which I was prepared for it,
can only be explained by turning some distance back.

From the winter of 1821, when I first read Bentham, and especially
from the commencement of the Westminster Review, I had what might
truly be called an object in life; to be a reformer of the world. My conception of my own happiness was entirely identified with this object. The
personal sympathies I wished for were those of fellow labourers in this
enterprise. I endeavoured to pick up as many flowers as I could by the
way; but as a serious and permanent personal satisfaction to rest upon,
my whole reliance was placed on this; and I was accustomed to felicitate
myself on the certainty of a happy life which I enjoyed, through placing
my happiness in something durable and distant, in which some progress
might be always making, while it could never be exhausted by complete
attainment. This did very well for several years, during which the general
improvement going on in the world and the idea of myself as engaged with
others in struggling to promote it, seemed enough to fill up an interesting
and animated existence. But the time came when I awakened from this
as from a dream. It was in the autumn of 1826. I was in a dull state of
nerves, such as everybody is occasionally liable to; unsusceptible to enjoy-

ment or pleasurable excitement; one of those moods when what is pleasure at other times, becomes insipid or indifferent; the state, I should think, in which converts to Methodism usually are, when smitten by their first "conviction of sin." In this frame of mind it occurred to me to put the question directly to myself: "Suppose that all your objects in life were realized; that all the changes in institutions and opinions which you are looking forward to, could be completely effected at this very instant: would this be a great joy and happiness to you?" And an irrepressible self-consciousness distinctly answered, "No!" At this my heart sank within me: the whole foundation on which my life was constructed fell down. All my happiness was to have been found in the continual pursuit of this end. The end had ceased to charm, and how could there ever again be any interest in the means? I seemed to have nothing left to live for.

At first I hoped that the cloud would pass away of itself; but it did not. A night's sleep, the sovereign remedy for the smaller vexations of life, had no effect on it. I awoke to a renewed consciousness of the woeful fact. I carried it with me into all companies, into all occupations. Hardly anything had power to cause me even a few minutes oblivion of it. For some months the cloud seemed to grow thicker and thicker. The lines in Coleridge's "Dejection"—I was not then acquainted with them—exactly describe my case:

A grief without a pang, void, dark and drear,
A drowsy, stifled, unimpassioned grief,
Which finds no natural outlet or relief
In word, or sigh, or tear.

In vain I sought relief from my favourite books; those memorials of past nobleness and greatness from which I had always hitherto drawn strength and animation. I read them now without feeling, or with the accustomed feeling *minus* all its charm; and I became persuaded, that my love of mankind, and of excellence for its own sake, had worn itself out. I sought no comfort by speaking to others of what I felt. If I had loved any one sufficiently to make confiding my griefs a necessity, I should not have been in the condition I was. I felt, too, that mine was not an interesting, or in any way respectable distress. There was nothing in it to attract sympathy. Advice, if I had known where to seek it, would have been most precious. The words of Macbeth to the physician often occurred to my thoughts. But there was no one on whom I could build the faintest hope of such assistance. My father, to whom it would have been natural to me to have recourse in any practical difficulties, was the last person to whom, in such a case as this, I looked for help. Everything convinced me that he had no knowledge of any such mental state as I was suffering from, and that even if he could be made to understand it, he was not the physician who could heal it. My education, which was wholly his work, had been

conducted without any regard to the possibility of its ending in this result; and I saw no use in giving him the pain of thinking that his plans had failed, when the failure was probably irremediable, and at all events, beyond the power of *his* remedies. Of other friends, I had at that time none to whom I had any hope of making my condition intelligible. It was however abundantly intelligible to myself; and the more I dwelt upon it, the more hopeless it appeared.

My course of study had led me to believe, that all mental and moral feelings and qualities, whether of a good or of a bad kind, were the results of association; that we love one thing, and hate another, take pleasure in one sort of action or contemplation, and pain in another sort, through the clinging of pleasurable or painful ideas to those things, from the effect of education or of experience. As a corollary from this, I had always heard it maintained by my father, and was myself convinced, that the object of education should be to form the strongest possible associations of the salutary class; associations of pleasure with all things beneficial to the great whole, and of pain with all things hurtful to it. This doctrine appeared inexpugnable; but it now seemed to me, on retrospect, that my teachers had occupied themselves but superficially with the means of forming and keeping up these salutary associations. They seemed to have trusted altogether to the old familiar instruments, praise and blame, reward and punishment. Now, I did not doubt that by these means, began early, and applied unremittingly, intense associations of pain and pleasure, especially of pain, might be created, and might produce desires and aversions capable of lasting undiminished to the end of life. But there must always be something artificial and casual in associations thus produced. The pains and pleasures thus forcibly associated with things, are not connected with them by any natural tie; and it is therefore, I thought, essential to the durability of these associations, that they should have become so intense and inveterate as to be practically indissoluble, before the habitual exercise of the power of analysis had commenced. For I now saw, or thought I saw, what I had always before received with incredulity—that the habit of analysis has a tendency to wear away the feelings: as indeed it has, when no other mental habit is cultivated, and the analysing spirit remains without its natural complements and correctives. The very excellence of analysis (I argued) is that it tends to weaken and undermine whatever is the result of prejudice; that it enables us mentally to separate ideas which have only casually clung together: and no associations whatever could ultimately resist this dissolving force, were it not that we owe to analysis our clearest knowledge of the permanent sequences in nature; the real connexions between Things, not dependent on our will and feelings; natural laws, by virtue of which, in many cases, one thing is inseparable from another in fact; which laws, in proportion as they are clearly perceived and imaginatively realized, cause our ideas of things which are always joined together

in Nature, to cohere more and more closely in our thoughts. Analytic habits may thus even strengthen the associations between causes and effects, means and ends, but tend altogether to weaken those which are, to speak familiarly, a *mere* matter of feeling. They are therefore (I thought) favourable to prudence and clear-sightedness, but a perpetual worm at the root both of the passions and of the virtues; and, above all, fearfully undermine all desires, and all pleasures, which are the effects of association, that is, according to the theory I held, all except the purely physical and organic; of the entire insufficiency of which to make life desirable, no one had a stronger conviction than I had. These were the laws of human nature, by which, as it seemed to me, I had been brought to my present state. All those to whom I looked up, were of opinion that the pleasure of sympathy with human beings, and the feelings which made the good of others, and especially of mankind on a large scale, the object of existence, were the greatest and surest sources of happiness. Of the truth of this I was convinced, but to know that a feeling would make me happy if I had it, did not give me the feeling. My education, I thought, had failed to create these feelings in sufficient strength to resist the dissolving influence of analysis, while the whole course of my intellectual cultivation had made precocious and premature analysis the inveterate habit of my mind. I was thus, as I said to myself, left stranded at the commencement of my voyage, with a well-equipped ship and a rudder, but no sail; without any real desire for the ends which I had been so carefully fitted out to work for: no delight in virtue, or the general good, but also just as little in anything else. The fountains of vanity and ambition seemed to have dried up within me, as completely as those of benevolence. I had had (as I reflected) some gratification of vanity at too early an age: I had obtained some distinction, and felt myself of some importance, before the desire of distinction and of importance had grow into a passion: and little as it was which I had attained, yet having been attained too early, like all pleasures enjoyed too soon, it had made me *blasé* and indifferent to the pursuit. Thus neither selfish nor unselfish pleasures were pleasures to me. And there seemed no power in nature sufficient to begin the formation of my character anew, and create in a mind now irretrievably analytic, fresh associations of pleasure with any of the objects of human desire.

These were the thoughts which mingled with the dry heavy dejection of the melancholy winter of 1826–7. During this time I was not incapable of my usual occupations. I went on with them mechanically, by the mere force of habit. I had been so drilled in a certain sort of mental exercise, that I could still carry it on when all the spirit had gone out of it. I even composed and spoke several speeches at the debating society, how, or with what degree of success, I know not. Of four years continual speaking at that society, this is the only year of which I remember next to nothing. Two lines of Coleridge, in whom alone of all writers I have found a true

description of what I felt, were often in my thoughts, not at this time (for I had never read them), but in a later period of the same mental malady:

> Work without hope draws nectar in a sieve,
> And hope without an object cannot live.

In all probability my case was by no means so peculiar as I fancied it, and I doubt not that many others have passed through a similar state; but the idiosyncrasies of my education had given to the general phenomenon a special character, which made it seem the natural effect of causes that it was hardly possible for time to remove. I frequently asked myself, if I could, or if I was bound to go on living, when life must be passed in this manner. I generally answered to myself, that I did not think I could possibly bear it beyond a year. When, however, not more than half that duration of time had elapsed, a small ray of light broke in upon my gloom. I was reading, accidentally, Marmontel's "Mémoires," and came to the passage which relates his father's death, the distressed position of the family, and the sudden inspiration by which he, then a mere boy, felt and made them feel that he would be everything to them—would supply the place of all that they had lost. A vivid conception of the scene and its feelings came over me, and I was moved to tears. From this moment my burthen grew lighter. The oppression of the thought that all feeling was dead within me, was gone. I was no longer hopeless: I was not a stock or a stone. I had still, it seemed, some of the material out of which all worth of character, and all capacity for happiness, are made. Relieved from my ever present sense of irremediable wretchedness, I gradually found that the ordinary incidents of life could again give me some pleasure; that I could again find enjoyment, not intense, but sufficient for cheerfulness, in sunshine and sky, in books, in conversation, in public affairs; and that there was, once more, excitement, though of a moderate kind, in exerting myself for my opinions, and for the public good. Thus the cloud gradually drew off, and I again enjoyed life: and though I had several relapses, some of which lasted many months, I never again was as miserable as I had been.

**WILLIAM BUTLER YEATS (1865–1939)** would be ranked by many as the greatest poet of our time. His poetry, his plays, and his prose deliver a rich interplay of sounds, concepts, and visions; throughout, they are two things at once: documents on current affairs (for Yeats participated in the political and international tides of his time) and marvelously sustained products of art (for Yeats scorned mere immersion in immediate issues and limited endeavors). The following, from his very distinctive autobiography, sketches one of his associates and represents well something of Yeats's distinction—his delivery of particulars, along with a poised judgment which enriches what he says and how he says it.

# The Trembling of the Veil

I shared a lodging full of old books and magazines, covered with dirt and dust, with the head of the Fenian Brotherhood, John O'Leary. "In this country," he had said to me, "a man must have upon his side the Church or the Fenians, and you will never have the Church." He had been converted to nationality by the poems of Davis, and he wished for some analogous movement to that of Davis, but he had known men of letters, had been the friend of Whistler, and knew the faults of the old literature. We had made him the President of our Society, and without him I could do nothing, for his long imprisonment and longer exile, his magnificent appearance, and, above all, the fact that he alone had personality, a point of view not made for the crowd's sake, but for self-expression, made him magnetic to my generation. He and I had long been friends, he had stayed with us at Bedford Park, and my father had painted his portrait, but if I had not shared his lodging he would have opposed me. He was an old man, and my point of view was not that of his youth, and it often took me half the day to make him understand—so suspicious he was of all innovation— some simple thing that he would presently support with ardour. He had grown up in a European movement when the revolutionist thought that he, above all men, must appeal to the highest motive, be guided by some ideal principle, be a little like Cato or like Brutus, and he had lived to see the change Dostoievsky examined in *The Possessed*. Men who had been of his party—and oftener their sons—preached assassination and the bomb; and, worst of all, the majority of his countrymen followed after constitutional politicians who practised opportunism, and had, as he believed, such low morals that they would lie, or publish private correspondence, if it might advance their cause. He would split every practical project into its constituent elements, like a clerical casuist, to find if it might not lead into some moral error; but, were the project revolutionary, he would sometimes temper condemnation with pity. Though he would cast off his oldest

acquaintance did he suspect him of rubbing shoulders with some carrier of bombs, I have heard him say of a man who blew himself up in an attempt to blow up Westminster Bridge, "He was not a bad man, but he had too great a moral nature for his intellect, not that he lacked intellect." He did not explain, but he meant, I suppose, that the spectacle of injustice might madden a good man more quickly than some common man. Such men were of his own sort, though gone astray, but the constitutional politicians he had been fighting all his life, and all they did displeased him. It was not that he thought their aim wrong, or that they could not achieve it; he had accepted Gladstone's Home Rule Bill; but that in his eyes they degraded manhood. "If England has been brought to do us justice by such men," he would say, "that is not because of our strength, but because of her weakness." He had a particular hatred for the rush of emotion that followed the announcement of Gladstone's conversion, for what was called "The Union of Hearts," and derided its sentimentality. "Nations may respect one another," he would say, "they cannot love." His ancestors had probably kept little shops, or managed little farms in County Tipperary, yet he hated democracy, though he never used the word either for praise or blame, with more than feudal hatred. "No gentleman can be a socialist," he said, and then, with a thoughtful look, "he might be an anarchist." He had no philosophy, but things distressed his palate, and two of those things were International propaganda and the Organised State, and Socialism aimed at both, nor could he speak such words as "philanthropy," "humanitarianism," without showing by his tone of voice that they offended him. The Church pleased him little better; there was an old Fenian quarrel there, and he would say, "My religion is the old Persian, to pull the bow and tell the truth." He had no self-consciousness, no visible pride, and would have hated anything that could have been called a gesture, was indeed scarce artist enough to invent a gesture; yet he would never speak of the hardship of his prison life—though abundantly enough of its humours—and once, when I pressed him, replied, "I was in the hands of my enemy, why should I complain?" A few years ago I heard that the Governor of the prison had asked why he did not report some unnecessary discomfort, and O'Leary had said, "I did not come here to complain." Now that he is dead, I wish that I could question him, and perhaps discover whether in early youth he had come across some teacher who had expounded Roman virtue, but I doubt if I would have learnt anything, for I think the wax had long forgotten the seal—if seal there were. The seal was doubtless made before the eloquent humanitarian 'forties and 'fifties, and was one kind with whatever moulded the youthful mind of Savage Landor. Stephens, the founder of Fenianism, had discovered him searching the second-hand bookstalls for rare editions, and enrolled him in his organisation. "You have no chance of success," O'Leary had said, "but it will be good for the *morale* of the country" (*morale* was his great word),

"and I will join on the condition that I am never asked to enrol anybody."
He still searched the second-hand bookstalls, and had great numbers of
books, especially of Irish history and literature, and when I, exhausted over
our morning's casuistry, would sit down to my day's work (I was writing
*The Secret Rose*) he would make his tranquil way to the Dublin Quays.
In the evening, over his coffee, he would write passages for his memoirs
upon postcards and odd scraps of paper, taking immense trouble with
every word and comma, for the great work must be a masterpiece of
style. When it was finished, it was unreadable, being dry, abstract, and confused; no picture had ever passed before his mind's eye. He was a victim,
I think, of a movement where opinions stick men together, or keep them
apart, like a kind of bird-lime, and without any relation to their natural
likes and tastes, and where men of rich nature must give themselves up to
an irritation which they no longer recognise because it is always present.
I often wonder why he gave me his friendship, why it was he who found
almost all the subscribers for my *Wanderings of Usheen,* and why he now
supported me in all I did, for how could he like verses that were all picture,
all emotion, all association, all mythology? He could not have approved
my criticism either, for I exalted Mask and Image above the eighteenth-
century logic which he loved, and set experience before observation,
emotion before fact. Yet he would say, "I have only three followers, Taylor,
Yeats, and Rolleston," and presently he cast out Rolleston—"Davitt wants
to convert thousands, but I want two or three." I think that perhaps it was
because he no more wished to strengthen Irish Nationalism by second-rate
literature than by second-rate morality, and was content that we agreed in
that. "There are things a man must not do to save a Nation," he had once
told me, and when I asked what things, had said, "To cry in public," and
I think it probable that he would have added, if pressed, "To write oratorical
or insincere verse."

**BEN SHAHN (1898–    )** born in Russia, came to the United States in 1906 to become, in time, one of the best-known painters of our country. In this passage from *The Shape of Content,* he touches everything with an expert's confidence. You will note that when he refers to what others say, he can supply his own immediate knowledge on the topic; he is a witness from close, local experience. The writer who can command his subject like this has a great advantage. He is like a person who happens to be where exact and particular things can be seen; he tells others— blocked from such knowing—what is there, as if he is down in a bathysphere telephoning back his reports, or in orbit letting earthbound people know what is visible from the sky.

# Artists in Colleges

On the basis of fairly extensive observation I have concluded that there are about three major blocks to the development of a mature art, and to the artist's continuing to produce serious work within the university situation. And perhaps these major blocks may reach beyond the field of art.

The first of them is dilettantism. Dilettantism, as we all know, is the nonserious dabbling within a presumably serious field by persons who are ill-equipped—and actually do not even want—to meet even the minimum standards of that field, or study, or practice. Dilettantism in the university is best observed in the so-called "smattering" courses themselves, but it is by no means confined to such academic routine; it is a fairly pervasive attitude.

I understand fully the need to educate broadly. And I understand and applaud that breadth of interest that impels the bright human being to dip into or to investigate all sorts of divergent fields. Obviously there is a contradiction here. For to have a broad acquaintance with a number of different studies means that at least some of these studies cannot be met on a professional level.

I think that the university has met the contradiction fairly successfully in some fields, but has certainly not done so in the field of art. For in this field, dilettantism governs the whole departmental attitude, whereas in other fields of study the department itself is regarded seriously, however little may be absorbed by the student whose main interest is elsewhere.

I believe that it is an objective of any one of the major departments within the greater universities to constitute in itself a center for its field, so that individuals and institutions in the practical world customarily look to the university for the most advanced work or opinion obtainable. Ideas and leadership then flow out of the university and into general currency.

And need I cite the leadership of the universities in such fields as that of physics, of all the branches of sociology and psychology, of archaeology and numerous other fields!

In this connection, the Visual Arts Committee Report comments:

> All the timidity that now surrounds the thought of bringing artist and studio into the university, on a par with other fields of scholarship, lately surrounded the same venture with regard to scientists. Just as the scientist has found his place within the university, just as his laboratory has become academically respectable, so the artist and studio, given time and opportunity, should find their places. [And the report also says] Though research laboratories in industry and government contribute increasingly to the advancement of fundamental science, the university is still the primary source of the most important scientific progress.

Students then—even those who do not expect to follow a particular field itself—may still derive some sense of its stature and its real meaning. And the individuals who teach and who work under the university aegis are actually working in the center of their field and not on its fringe. Thus the university may be assured of gaining the foremost talent in such studies, while the teacher himself, the physicist-teacher or the sociologist-teacher, let us say, need not be disillusioned nor bored by the level at which his profession exists.

Quite the opposite is true in the field of art, that is, of creative art. In the first place the university directorship is quite likely to look somewhat askance at its art departments and its art courses as somewhat frivolous. (It is not inconceivable that the great public blind spot toward art extends even to such high places.) The student of art in a college is almost required to guard himself against becoming involved or too serious about his art. He will dabble a bit once or twice during a week, but must not and literally can not make of art a field of major interest.

He may be an art-history student, or an architecture, or an aesthetics student, in which case he will do a little painting "just," as the saying goes, "to get his hand in." Or a student may display a passionate interest in painting; but even in that event he is still required only to play about lightly. He cannot devote either long hours or concentration to his work. The artist-teacher is thus not able to require or to expect serious work from his students—not even from the talented ones. And thus the level of the work that is produced is likely to arouse in him something akin to physical illness, particularly if he is himself an artist of great capability. And then he must perforce ask himself what he is doing there and why he is not off painting his own pictures.

I cannot understand why there should exist such mistrust of creative work. Is it to guard the student against an incautious degree of self-committal? Or is it indecision as to whether art is really a wholly decorous profession? Or is there some conflict in value as between the art that has

already safely taken place, and that which—alarmingly enough—may take place?

Some such conflict appears within the Visual Arts Report itself:

[On page 10, for instance, we read] The Committee believes that the visual arts are an integral part of the humanities and as such must assume a role of prominence in the context of higher education. [Yet, on page 66, we find] It is still doubtful if a student at Harvard can find space or time to apply himself seriously to creative work in the visual arts. [On page 9, the enlightened comment] At no moment in history since the invention of printing has man's communication with his fellow man been so largely taken over by visual media as today. [But, on page 65, we read the following] We do not propose to inject the art school into the academic life, but rather to give the experience of art its rightful place in liberal education.

I wonder whether the university would also suggest offering the *experience* of calculus, of solid state physics; the experience of French or German; the experience of economics, of medieval history, of Greek.

I was one of those asked to give an opinion concerning the desirability of the university for the education of an artist. I expressed preference for the university as against the professional art school. But my rejection of the art school was certainly not on the grounds of its professionalism; indeed that is the one thing that recommends it. My preference for the university is based upon a belief that the very content of the liberal education is a natural content of art, that art will profit by and greatly needs the content of liberal education. Further, that the humanities and the humanistic view have been the companions of art during the great periods of both.

But if dilettantism is to pervade the whole atmosphere of art, and even the very department in which it is taught, then, far from being the best influence for the young artist, the university may prove to be the worst, and may further prove equally unfavorable to the artist-teacher.

The second major block to the development of a mature art and to the artist's thriving within the university community is the fear of creativity itself. The university stresses rather the critical aspects of knowledge—the surveying, the categorizing, the analyzing, and the memorizing. The reconversion of such knowledge into living art, into original work, seems to have diminished. In a few universities—particularly in the East—discouragement of original work has achieved the status of policy. I was told by a department head in one university that in that institution the creative arts are discouraged because "it is felt that they may interfere with the liberal arts." I have never been able to understand actually what he meant, but the result of the policy is brilliantly clear, and that result is that the student misses the vital opportunity to integrate what he knows with what he thinks—that he fails to form the expressive, the creative habit.

In another university I once had occasion to pay a number of visits to its very large ceramics department. I noticed that there was a great leafing about among books whenever a piece of pottery was to be decorated, and that not even the shapes of pieces were original. It seemed to me that the students were missing whatever pleasure there may be in the work. In talking to them, I made the odd discovery that they did not consider themselves capable of originating a decoration; it was not for them. In fact one student explained to me that that was not the course they were taking.

A very trivial incident indeed, but still a disturbing one. Could it be that the students were too impressed by the past of ceramics, by the Greek, the Chinese, the Etruscan, to be able to surmount that and create something of their own? It is not impossible that within the university the pre-eminence of scholarship itself may become an impassable block to creativity, and may over-impress and stifle both the artist-teacher and the student.

The artist who is only a painter may well become intimidated by his degree-bearing brethren. Under the charmed light of their MA's, their PhD's, their accumulated honors and designations, the scholars speak of art in terms of class and category, and under headings of which the artist may never have heard. While he himself may have read extensively about art—and I think that most artists do read a great deal about art, and know a great deal about it—while he may have looked at scores of paintings, have dwelt upon them and absorbed them, his interest has been a different one; he has absorbed visually, not verbally. The idea of classifying such work would never have occurred to him, because to him the work is unique; it exists in itself alone. It is its distinction from other art, not its commonality with other art, that interests him. If the work has no such distinction, if it does not stand alone, he has no reason for remembering it. And yet, surrounded by abstract and learned discussion, his own vision may waver and its reality grow dim.

At the same time I feel that both art history and art theory are of immense value to the creative artist. All such material lends depth and subtlety to art, and it is definitely stimulating to most artists. Only when, in the verbalizing or the teaching process, the original creative necessity is obliterated does art theory or art history tend to suffocate the artist.

I have a young friend who, through most of his high-school years, was given to writing poetry. He is now entering his junior year in the university. The other evening I asked him what sort of verse he had been writing, and whether I might read some of it. He replied, "Oh, I've stopped writing poetry." Then he explained, "There's so much that you have to know before you can write poetry. There are so many forms that you have to master first. Actually," he said, "I just wrote because I liked to put things down. It didn't amount to much; it was only free verse."

Perhaps my young friend would never under any circumstances have become a good poet. Perhaps he should have had the drive and persistence

to master those forms which have defeated him—I myself think he should. But I wonder whether it was made clear to him that all poetic forms have derived from practice; that in the very act of writing poetry he was, however crudely, beginning to create form. I wonder whether it was pointed out to him that form is an instrument, not a tyrant; that whatever measures, rhythms, rhymes, or groupings of sounds best suited his own expressive purpose could be turned to form—possibly just his own personal form, but form; and that it too might in time take its place in the awesome hierarchy of poetic devices.

Scholarship is perhaps man's most rewarding occupation, but that scholarship which dries up its own creative sources is a *reductio ad absurdum,* a contradiction of itself.

And there is the loneliness and isolation of the artist upon the college grounds. Of course we know that many artists have painted alone with great success. But of these we may say that they chose loneliness: loneliness was their theme and their way of painting. Theirs has been a different loneliness from that of the artist who, safely cushioned within the pleasantest and most agreeable environment known to man, must at some point arise from the good conversational table, move off, don his paint-spattered pants, squeeze out his tubes and become involved in the nervous, unsure, tense, and unsatisfactory business of making a picture which will have cohesion, impact, maturity, and an unconscionable lot of sheer work; which will, most uncomfortably, display an indiscreet and unveiled feeling about something; and which will then proceed to violate every canon of good art behavior just delineated by his recent companions.

These latter have no need to create something new. It is enough that they discover the old and bring it home to the common consciousness in all its radiance.

The third major block to the successful functioning of the artist within the university is a somewhat romantic misconception as to what sort of man he is. The more venerable academic element, still under the sway of Trilby, looks upon an artist as a mad genius. This group believes, and I think the public joins it, that an artist has no idea of why he paints; he simply has to. Among the younger and more advanced collegians, the New Criticism has taken over, but the artist himself fares no better. For according to this very avant-garde view, it makes little difference what an artist paints or what he himself happens to think; it is the viewer who really accounts for the meaning of the work, and even he would flounder about hopelessly were it not for the theorist, or critic. In his hands rest all the clues to art; he is the high priest of the art process.

I have one critical fencing companion who assures me that the meaning of one order of art—the nonobjective—is a supra-human, that is, a cosmic one. The artist, as he describes him, is a medium through which all sorts

of ineffable forces flow. Any willing, however, on the part of the artist, any intending, would be an interference, would only destroy the time-space continuum, would render impure the art produced.

And, by implication, that art which is the product of willing and intending must be impure.

As criticism itself flourishes particularly within the universities, so does this particular critical view find its warmest advocates there. In several universities, the critical circle has formed itself into a small cultural nucleus which exerts a powerful influence, one not free of snobbery, upon the arts—a Gorgon-like power that turns the creative artist into stone.

This curious academic mutation is corroborated within the Visual Arts Report in a most understanding passage.

> It is a curious paradox that, highly as the university esteems the work of art, it tends to take a dim view of the artist as an intellectual . . . one encounters the curious view that the artist does not know what he is doing. It is widely believed and sometimes explicitly stated that the artist, however great his art, does not genuinely understand it, neither how he produced it, nor its place in the culture and in history.

At this point I cannot resist a few somewhat crisper lines in this direction from Francis Bacon: "Some there have been," says the philosopher, "who have made a passage for themselves and their own opinions by pulling down and demolishing former ones; and yet all their stir has but little advanced the matter, since their aim has been not to extend philosophy and the arts in substance and value, but only to . . . transfer the kingdom of opinion to themselves."

Before the artist can be successfully oriented within the university environment there will be needed a calmer view toward both the qualities of the man and the qualities of the work. No artist will be at ease with an opinion that holds him to be a mere handyman of art—the fellow who puts the paint on. Nor will any artist rest well with the notion that he is a mad genius—something other than human, either more than human or less than human or tangential to human. The whole notion of genius needs to be reassessed, needs perhaps to be deglamorized somewhat. For genius is certainly much more a matter of degree than of kind. The genius so-called is only that one who discerns the pattern of things within the confusion of details a little sooner than the average man. Thus the genius (again, I insist upon saying so-called) is likely to be impatient with those individuals who fail to discern such patterns, such larger meanings, within common affairs.

If the artist, or poet, or musician, or dramatist, or philosopher seems somewhat unorthodox in his manner and attitudes, it is because he knows—only a little earlier than the average man—that orthodoxy has destroyed a great deal of human good, whether of charity, or of good sense, or of art.

It seems to me that, far from setting the "genius" apart, the university should constitute itself the natural place toward which the young person of such exceptional talent may turn for an education suitable to his talent. Otherwise we announce, in effect, that the broadness of view, the intellectual disciplines, the knowledge content which the university affords are reserved for the unproductive man—the uncreative, the nonbrilliant. Such an assumption would be an absurdity, and yet how often do I hear voiced the sentiment that the university is not for the young person of genius.

Withal the foregoing, I do not attribute to the university an intentional undervaluing of art, nor do I believe that creativeness in other fields is discouraged by intention other than in a few conspicuous instances. In the abstract, I believe that creative art is eminent in the university hierarchy of values. But teaching itself is so largely a verbal, a classifying, process that the merely intuitive kinds of knowing, the sensing of things which escape classification, the self-identification with great moods and movements in life and art and letters may be lost or obliterated by academic routine. They are not to be taught but rather absorbed through a way of life in which intensively developed arts play an easy and familiar part. For it is just such inexact knowing that is implicit in the arts. And actually I believe that it is toward this kind of knowing that the classifications of the classroom reach, if sometimes unsuccessfully.

It is this kind of knowing also—the perceptive and the intuitive—that is the very essence of an advanced culture. The dactyl and the spondee, the heroic couplet, the strophe and the antistrophe may be valuable and useful forms to the poet; but the meaning of the poem and its intention greatly transcend any such mechanics.

**SAMUEL TAYLOR COLERIDGE (1772–1834)**   impressed his contemporaries
and later writers as one of the greatest minds of their acquaintance;
Wordsworth, Hazlitt, Lamb, and John Stuart Mill are among
those who have made such a judgment. He wrote poetry, literary criticism,
and a number of productions hard to classify, except perhaps as
recorded conversation. One of his most illuminating speculations had to do
with how the mind works—he saw it as creative, as something more than
the location where sense impressions are associated. The following
is his account of the source of a great, original, fragmentary poem, "Kubla
Khan," which begins this way: "In Xanadu did Kubla Khan/ A stately
pleasure dome decree:/ Where Alph, the sacred river, ran/ Through caverns
measureless to man/ Down to a sunless sea." Such inspirations are rare;
accounts of their circumstances are to be treasured. And the
report by Coleridge, no matter how fragmentary, is worth pondering.

# A Person from Porlock

In the summer of 1797, the Author, then in ill health, had retired to a lonely farm-house between Porlock and Linton, on the Exmoor confines of Somerset and Devonshire. In consequence of a slight indisposition, an anodyne had been prescribed, from the effects of which he fell asleep in his chair at the moment that he was reading the following sentence, or words of the same substance, in "Purchas's Pilgrimage": "Here the Khan Kubla commanded a palace to be built, and a stately garden thereunto. And thus ten miles of fertile ground were inclosed with a wall." The author continued for about three hours in a profound sleep, at least of the external senses, during which time he has the most vivid confidence, that he could not have composed less than from two to three hundred lines; if that indeed can be called composition in which all the images rose up before him as *things,* with a parallel production of the correspondent expressions, without any sensation or consciousness of effort. On awaking he appeared to himself to have a distinct recollection of the whole, and taking his pen, ink, and paper, instantly and eagerly wrote down the lines that are here preserved. At this moment he was unfortunately called out by a person on business from Porlock, and detained by him above an hour, and on his return to his room, found, to his no small surprise and mortification, that though he still retained some vague and dim recollection of the general purport of the vision, yet, with the exception of some eight or ten scattered lines and images, all the rest had passed away like the images on the surface of a stream into which a stone has been cast, but, alas! without the after restoration of the latter!

**ALBERT EINSTEIN (1879–1955)** is more fully identified in Part 2 of this book. Here he addresses himself to the apparently troublesome question: If science avoids the influence of feelings, how can the methods of science relate to the field of ethics, where feelings do count? In his quick treatment he demonstrates a certain kind of writing—the brief, reasoned statement.

# Science and Ethics

Science searches for relations which are thought to exist independently of the searching individual. This includes the case where man himself is the subject; or the subject of scientific statements may be concepts created by ourselves, as in mathematics. Such concepts are not necessarily supposed to correspond to any objects in the outside world. However, all scientific statements and laws have one characteristic in common: they are "true" or "false" (adequate or inadequate). Roughly speaking, our reaction to them is "yes" or "no."

The scientific way of thinking has a further characteristic. The concepts which it uses to build up its coherent systems do not express emotions. For the scientist, there is only "being," but no wishing, no valuing, no good, no evil—in short, no goal. As long as we remain within the realm of science proper, we can never encounter a sentence of the type: "Thou shalt not lie." There is something like a Puritan's restraint in the scientist who seeks truth: he keeps away from everything voluntaristic or emotional. Incidentally, this trait is the result of a slow development, peculiar to modern Western thought.

From this it might seem as if logical thinking were irrelevant for ethics. Scientific statements of facts and relations, indeed, cannot produce ethical directives. However, ethical directives can be made rational and coherent by logical thinking and empirical knowledge. If we can agree on some fundamental ethical propositions, then other ethical propositions can be derived from them, provided that the original premises are stated with sufficient precision. Such ethical premises play a similar role in ethics to that played by axioms in mathematics.

This is why we do not feel at all that it is meaningless to ask such questions as: "Why should we not lie?" We feel that such questions are meaningful because in all discussions of this kind some ethical premises are tacitly taken for granted. We then feel satisfied when we succeed in tracing back the ethical directive in question to these basic premises. In the case of lying, this might perhaps be done in some way such as this: Lying destroys confidence in the statements of other people. Without such confidence, social co-operation is made impossible or at least difficult. Such co-operation, however, is essential in order to make human life possible

and tolerable. This means that the rule "Thou shalt not lie" has been traced back to the demands: "Human life shall be preserved" and "Pain and sorrow shall be lessened as much as possible."

But what is the origin of such ethical axioms? Are they arbitrary? Are they based on mere authority? Do they stem from experiences of men and are they conditioned indirectly by such experiences?

For pure logic all axioms are arbitrary, including the axioms of ethics. But they are by no means arbitrary from a psychological and genetic point of view. They are derived from our inborn tendencies to avoid pain and annihilation, and from the accumulated emotional reaction of individuals to the behavior of their neighbors.

It is the privilege of man's moral genius, expressed by inspired individuals, to advance ethical axioms which are so comprehensive and so well founded that men will accept them as grounded in the vast mass of their individual emotional experiences. Ethical axioms are found and tested not very differently from the axioms of science. *Die Wahrheit liegt in der Bewährung.* Truth is what stands the test of experience.

JACQUES BARZUN (1907–    )    has the knowledge and the confidence it
takes to provide something very much sought in our day—perspective.
From his position at Columbia University, where he has taught
history and headed the graduate school, he can bring together the culture
of his native France and the developing culture of the United States;
and he can bring to his discussions of the twentieth century the
perspectives of an historian with a strong grounding in the history of the
nineteenth century. In the following selection, he applies to the teaching of science
a critical analysis. He is unwilling for science in the schools to isolate itself
from its own sources and from its essential involvement with the thought of its time.

## The Ivory Lab

> I degrade Physics into an implement of culture, and this is my deliberate
> design.
>
> JOHN TYNDALL
> *Fragments of Science*

Most of the excitement about "higher education" in the last three years
has been about the teaching of history, languages, and "great books." But
the most serious and pressing need in colleges today seems to me to be
the teaching of science. It may appear paradoxical that I speak of a "need"
which everyone believes to be adequately met, but paradox disappears
when the point of view changes. From one point of view, science is taught
in every American college; from another point of view, it is taught in none,
or very few. Looked at in a certain light, science teaching today is the most
efficient, up to date, and worldly-wise. In another light, it is backward,
wasteful and "escapist." Let me explain these contrasts.

Fifty or sixty years ago, science was a new academic subject. People
mistrusted its power to educate, and many of its proponents seemed as if
they could never be educated themselves. The tradition of liberal studies
had always included mathematics, because mathematics was supposed to
train the mind; but the new physical sciences were first seen as manual
arts, messy and expensive, and with no more "discipline" to them than a
pair of elastic-sided boots. At the time of the fight for adding science to
the curriculum, the defensive position was held by Greek and Latin, which
unfortunately adopted a "scorched earth" policy. I mean that they allowed
themselves to be invaded by the "scientific spirit" and in trying to compete
with it reduced their field to a wasteland of verbal criticism, grammar, and
philology. Literature was relegated to a second place and studying the
classics came to mean research into the uses of *utor, fruor,* and *fungor.*

Naturally the classics were exterminated, for science could beat them
at their own game. A young man trained in science could on graduation

get any of a hundred desirable jobs in industry. A young "scientific" classicist could only hope to teach his own subject to a dwindling number of students. That is what invariably comes of trying to put belles-lettres into utilitarian envelopes. As Dean Briggs of Harvard said when the Bachelor of Science degree was established: "It does not guarantee that the holder knows any science, but it does guarantee that he does *not* know any Latin." When the study of classical literature in translation was reintroduced for freshmen at Columbia College a few years ago, the undergraduate department of classics was surprised to find its enrollment in beginning Greek increased 150 per cent: they now had ten students.

But the bitter joke is not on the Classics alone. Having stepped into Greek's vacated place, Science now occupies its position, not with respect to size of enrollment, but with respect to educational attitude. It is now in power and it acts disdainful, holier-than-thou, and prudish. Someone once asked, "What is it that our men of science are guarding like a threatened virginity?" "Oh," was the answer, "they have a Vestal interest in their subject." Considered—somewhat unfairly—in the mass, science teachers may be said to contribute the greatest proportion of backward-looking, anti-intellectual, mechanic-minded members to the faculty. Characteristically, single departments of physical science have in certain institutions tried to set up separate schools, where only their one science would be taught for four years and rewarded with some kind of Bachelor's degree. The intention was to monopolize the student's time, cram him full of "practical" knowledge, and sell him to the highest bidder the moment he had clutched his diploma and redeemed his ten-dollar deposit for apparatus.

Doubtless there is a demand for such prefabricated industrial robots and I see no reason why such schools should not function in a manner useful to the commonwealth—off the campus. But departments that once clamored for admission to university status and have had it for fifty years are unwilling to give up all the *douceurs* of the association. They would still like to profit from the university connection, to color their degree with a faint tincture of liberal teaching—perhaps they would require a year of English and a year of history and economics—and to boast that their own subject, be it chemistry or geology, is also one of the "humanities." They want to eat their cake as many times over as a cow does her cud.

A crowd of evils springs from this ambiguous mood in the present college curriculum. There is an undignified scramble for the student's time, with broad hints on the part of the scientist that the rest of the program is folderol. Repressed antagonisms divide teachers of the humanities (vague, pointless, unpractical subjects—except economics) from teachers of the real stuff represented by science. Moreover, departments of physics and chemistry require mathematical preparation in strict amount and order of time, with the result that all scheduling revolves around their claims. Since

most young Americans discover their vocational bent while undergraduates, the wish to qualify for a profession is a powerful lever to make everyone study science for one or two years under these barbaric conditions. The doctor, the engineer, the research man in any science must gobble up as many courses as he can; and the man uninterested in science must "fulfill the requirement." Both are often judged on their science record, in the belief that it unmistakably reveals "real brains" or the lack of them.

The worst of all this is that neither group of students learns much about science but goes to swell the ranks of the two great classes of modern men—the single-track expert and the scientific ignoramus. Could anything more plainly demonstrate the failure of science to become a subject fit for college teaching? What makes a subject fit for the higher curriculum is surely no novelty: it is that it shall enlighten all the corners of the mind and teach its own uses. The humble three R's begin in strict utility and end up in poetry, science, and the search for the Infinite. They can and should therefore be taught indefinitely. Men have known for three thousand years that other matters of knowledge naturally divide themselves into special and general, that both are needful, but that whereas the special *add* to one's powers, the general *enhance the quality* of all of them.

At a recent educational conference, the Dean of a Midwestern university complained humorously that he was always being asked to give credits for impossible subjects—subjects that, he said, deserve to be called *in-credible*. A transfer student, for example, wanted "points" for seven hours of saw filing. Undeniably saw filing is a necessary art, but its merits as a general enhancer of power and personality stop accruing so soon after study is begun that it is not properly a branch of academic learning. The same is true of still more complex matters like shorthand, typewriting, and dress designing. Farther on in the series, it becomes harder to draw the line: stamp collecting is sub-educational but numismatics is a province of history.

Fortunately there is no doubt whatever about the place of the sciences: they *are* humanities and they belong in the college curriculum. Accordingly, they should be introduced into it *as humanities,* at the earliest possible moment. How? I have some tentative suggestions to make, but first I want to stress the danger of further delay and of the continuance of our present malpractice.

The worst danger is the creation of a large, powerful, and complacent class of college-trained uneducated men at the very heart of our industrial and political system. We may be too near to judge, but it strikes me that one of the conditions that made possible the present folly in Germany was the split among three groups: the technicians, the citizens, and the irresponsible rabble. This becomes persuasively plain if you consider the professional army caste as a group of unthinking technicians. The rabble together with the technicians can cow the citizenry; the technicians—

wedded solely to their workbench—will work for any group that hires; and the rabble, worshiping "science" to the exclusion of less tangible necessaries, are perfectly willing to sacrifice the citizen. They probably think that, if necessary, "science" could manufacture German citizens—out of wolfram.

Such principles will hardly give long life and happiness to a democracy. The only hope for a democratic state is to have more citizens than anything else. Hence technicians must not be allowed to hibernate between experiments, but must become conscious, responsible, politically and morally active men. Otherwise they will find not only that representative government has slipped out of their fingers, but that they have also lost their commanding position. They will be paid slaves in the service of some rabble, high or low. Meanwhile our present stock of citizens must not simply gape at the wonders of science, but must understand enough of its principles to criticize and value the results. As for the rabble, it must be transmuted as fast as it forms, by science and morals both.

All this clearly depends on teaching our easygoing, rather credulous college boys and girls what science is. If they leave college thinking, as they usually do, that science offers a full, accurate, and literal description of man and Nature; if they think scientific research by itself yields final answers to social problems; if they think scientists are the only honest, patient, and careful workers in the world; if they think that Copernicus, Galileo, Newton, Lavoisier, and Faraday were unimaginative plodders like their own instructors; if they think theories spring from facts and that scientific authority at any time is infallible; if they think that the ability to write down symbols and read manometers is fair grounds for superiority and pride, and if they think that science steadily and automatically makes for a better world—then they have wasted their time in the science lecture room; they live in an Ivory Laboratory more isolated than the poet's tower[1] and they are a plain menace to the society they belong to. They are a menace whether they believe all this by virtue of being engaged in scientific work themselves or of being disqualified from it by felt or fancied incapacity.

I return to what might perhaps be done preventively and constructively. To begin with, a change of direction must be imparted to the teaching of science. The fact must be recognized that most students still do not make science their profession.[2] Consequently, for future lay citizens the compulsory science requirement in force nearly everywhere must be justified

[1] To judge by results, it would seem that the poet climbs to the top of his tower to look out on the world and write about it. Why cavil at the building material—at once durable and attractive and requiring no upkeep?

[2] Statistics for the Middle West, based on large freshman enrollments, show that 50 per cent of those taking Chemistry I, 60 per cent of those taking Geology I, 73 per cent of those taking Physics I, 75 per cent of those taking Biology I, and 82 per cent of those taking Botany I, never go further into the science.

by a course explicitly designed for them. Such a course must not play at making physicists or biologists, but must explain the principles of the physical sciences in a coherent manner. A "survey" of all the sciences is out of the question. It would be at once superficial and bewildering. But an intelligent introduction to principles can be given. The assumptions that connect and that differentiate the sciences of matter, of living beings, and of logical relation can be taught; the meaning and the grounds of great unifying theories can be explained, and significant demonstrations and experiments can be shown to and made by the students.

Out of such a course there would surely come a changed attitude on the part of teachers and indeed a change in teaching personnel. At present, side by side with wise men and ripe teachers in the sciences, one finds many highly trained and absolutely uneducated practitioners. One also finds fanatics of the order that Dickens described in Professor Dingo, who, being caught defacing houses with his geological hammer, replied that "he knew of no building save the Temple of Science." Many university scientists openly scorn teaching and use their appointment to boil the pot of individual research. Now a life of research is a worthy one, but no amount of worthy motive justifies false pretenses and fraudulent impersonation—in this case the pretense of imparting knowledge and the impersonation of a teacher.

In the classroom, such men usually are neither civil, nor literate, nor even scientific, for their knowledge of science is purely from inside—a limitation equally bad but more misleading than the limitation of knowing it purely from outside. "What do they know of science who only science know?" They teach it as a set of rules, and speak of the profession as a "game." Drill in manual dexterity they entrust to laboratory assistants, who are only younger editions of themselves, and for whom a good notebook or speed in performing repetitious experiments is the passport to approval. There is seldom any consideration of the students as thinking minds, of the proper allocation of effort among the many interests legitimate at their time of life, nor of the philosophical implications which the words, the history, and the processes of the particular science disclose.

To offset this lamentable state of things, it must be said that two of the professions most concerned with scientific training—engineering and medicine—have lately amended their outlook and made overtures to the humanities. The medical schools have declared that cramming the student with science in college was a poor thing. He had better study other, less "practical," more formative subjects and postpone advanced chemistry and biology until medical school, where they will be taught him again in a fashion better tailored to his needs. This new policy is excellent, but it is not yet sufficiently enforced. The lesser medical schools—and some others—do not trust their own belief in the principle; they still appeal to "practical" views and judge applicants by A's in science.

Similarly, the Society for the Promotion of Engineering Education has passed splendid resolutions approving what they call the "social-humanistic stem"—by which they mean a few branches of non-engineering study; more accurately then, the "social-humanistic faggots." But here again, engineering thought is ahead of the engineer's emotions. When it comes to the test, the student or the program is pushed around to suit engineering subject matter.

If you add to this the important fact that many young Americans choose "engineering" in the belief that this means a career of research in pure science, you may form some notion of the present anarchical mess. The would-be engineer of seventeen finds that what he really wants to work at is pure research in electricity, that is, to be a physicist. He must therefore back water, change his course, and take some new prerequisites. Meanwhile his upbringing as a man and citizen goes by the board. He is caught between two grindstones, each indifferent to the effect of its motion, just as if the boy being put through this mill were not a human being, a student of the university, and a future citizen of the nation. Who is being "practical" now?

Some would probably still maintain that the professional schools in contact with "the world" know best what is the practical view, and that the college is as ever utopian. But there is one curious fact to be added. It is that the scientific professional schools have a way of relaxing their jaws into a smile whenever the market demand for their product decreases: it is a reflex action. They fall in love with the humanities all over again and raise the amount they require for admission, until outside pressure once again lowers the floodgates and the frown succeeds the smile. This self-regulating action is a feat of engineering in itself—or shall I say of doctoring the supply for public consumption?

The question is not whether this is the easy way to go about marketing young men, but whether it is a responsible grown-up way of replenishing the professional class of society. Granted that practice is the test of all schemes and ideals, is this the most practical scheme that American ingenuity can devise? I concede that in the present state of mind of the American public, desire for vocational training takes the lead over anything else. But are the directing members of the university world to follow other people's untutored impulses or to guide and redirect them? We may well ask when we reflect that the first victims of the system are the children of the unthinking public and the public itself. For it is the oldest fallacy about schooling to suppose that it can train a man for "practical" life. Inevitably, while the plan of study is being taught, "practical life" has moved on. "They did it this way three months ago, now they do it this way." No employer who knows anything about men will value a beginner because he knows the ropes of a particular changeable routine. It would be as sensible to

require that newcomers know the floor plan of the factory ahead of time.[3]

The corporations employing the largest numbers of engineers and scientific research men are on this matter way ahead of the colleges. One such firm conducted a survey last year to find out where and how its first-rate executives had been prepared. They came from the most unexpected places—including small liberal arts colleges, the teaching profession, the stage, and the Baptist ministry. It was found that the engineering schools—particularly those sensible ones that make no pretense at intellectual *cachet*—turned out a good average product, but few leaders. The company's own institutes and night courses raised the chance of foremen and district managers—but only up to a point. The survey concluded that what it wanted as material to shape future executives was graduates of liberal arts colleges, trained in history and economics, in philosophy and in good English, and likewise possessed of *an intelligent interest in science and technology*. Gentlemen, the path lies open.

II

My friend Dean Finch, of the Columbia University School of Engineering, might not agree with all I have just said, but I think he would approve of one element in my suggestions which I casually threw in. I mean the utility of history in the teaching of science. He himself is an historian of technology and offers in Columbia College a most valuable course in the subject for the use of "lay" students. What is surprising is that similar courses, accompanied by others in the history of pure science, are not given—indeed required—on every American campus.

The very idea, it must be said, is shrouded in the smoke of battle. When I mention it, some of my scientific colleagues slap me on the back and say "more power to you." They may express doubts about persuading their fellows, or finding good instructors, but they want to see it tried. Moreover they do not feel robbed when in my own teaching of nineteenth-century history I discuss Dalton and Darwin, Liebig and Faraday, Mayer and Clerk Maxwell. Though scientists, these colleagues of mine can see that to complain of general ignorance about the role of science in modern history, and to prevent historians from mentioning it, is to love monopoly above riches.

Others take the view that science has no history because every new

[3] The S.P.E.E. reports: "From its very nature, engineering education operates under changing conditions which constantly challenge its processes and test its results . . . so as to adapt itself to changing needs." (*Draft of a Report*, etc. November 16, 1939, p. 1.) This is fine and good, but it holds true of every other professional subject and most academic ones. The old belief that only a few schools are in touch with the "real world" is untrue, even if the newer belief should prove true that it is best for the world to have the school conform to every change outside.

achievement supersedes previous ones. The history of science, they feel, is nothing but biographical chitchat about scientists. Or else they admit that it is useful to find out what the Middle Ages thought of natural science, but only in order to point the lesson of freedom from church authority and fight anew the old battle of science against religion.

This angry confusion about the history of science is dense but not impenetrable. Three things may be distinguished. First there is historical research into the beginnings of science—Greek or Arabic or Medieval. This goes on as advanced study and concerns undergraduates only in the form of broad tested conclusions. Then there is the biography of scientists, which is of immense educational importance—whatever laboratory men may say. Biography does not mean recounting Newton's imaginary embroilments with women or Lavoisier's perfectly real ones with public finance. It means finding out from the lives of great scientific creators what they worked at and how their minds functioned. How tiresome it is to hear nothing from our scientific departments but Sunday-school homilies on the gameness of Galileo, the patience of Pasteur, and the carefulness of Madame Curie. And how uninstructive! Any man who accomplishes anything in any field is as patient as he has to be, and even little boys know that glass being breakable, you have to be careful.[4]

What would be far more significant and novel, though true, would be to teach that Copernicus gambled on insufficient evidence; that Kepler was chiefly a horoscope-caster; that Faraday probably believed more wrong theories than any man alive—and turned them to good use in experiment; that Darwin, on his own admission, made awful blunders and admired the art of wriggling out of them; that T. H. Morgan's laboratory was rather messy; that Newton could not see how his own astronomy contradicted the Bible; that scientific men have suppressed and persecuted opponents of their theories, and that the best scientific truth can end in a rigid and mistaken orthodoxy—as happened after Newton and Darwin. The point is that science is made by man, in the light of interests, errors, and hopes, just like poetry, philosophy, and human history itself.

To say this is not to degrade science, as naïve persons might think; it is on the contrary to enhance its achievements by showing that they sprang not from patience on a monument but from genius toiling in the mud. I leave unexplained here all that accrues from studying how we came to use atoms or devise Absolute Zero or to state the Law of Conservation of Energy (including the reasons why energy is a better word than the earlier "force") or what steps led first to the abandonment and then to the later salvaging of Avogadro's hypothesis. A good scientist-historian would exhibit the assumptions and habits which affected scientific opinion

---

[4] The self-righteousness of the man of science is universal enough to sustain advertising appeals: "Like the scientist, NEWSWEEK . . . makes it its business to search out truth by continual research, relentless checking and re-checking of the facts." A grim grind!

at important turning points. He would unite science to other thought by discussing the nature of its evidence at various periods. And he would show the role of the pure imagination in all great scientific work. I know Bacon promised that science would level all the minds of its devotees to average size, and he is right insofar as drilling can make ordinary men into patient, careful laboratory workers. But science has not yet managed to get along without ideas, and these come only from men of special, powerful, and irreducible aptitudes. The chronological study of these men and ideas is the proper subject matter for an undergraduate course in the history of science.[5]

I know the common objection offered to all this—to an historical and a synoptic account of scientific principles in place of the "regular" science courses: it is that the substitutes would be merely talk about science and not science itself. Grant this for argument's sake. The objectors miss the point if they do not see that talk about science has a place in the curriculum and that such talk may be good or bad, quite all right or all quite wrong, exactly like talk about art. If science is one of the humanities it must be capable of being looked at and thought about apart from direct doing—at least until we require every concertgoer to write a symphony before being allowed to take his seat at Carnegie Hall. Besides, the synoptic course I have in view would include laboratory work, and it would rest with the scientists themselves whether the students mastered enough of the operative side of true science to keep them from irresponsible talk about it. If science teachers think that a year's drudgery in physics as now given prevents silly notions in those who take it in college, they are either inobservant or illogical.

Doubtless it is bad logic they suffer from—the usual weakness of scientists . . . and of the rest of mankind, who generally want to have things both ways. Take as an example a comment made on the relation of science and history in the excellent study of Lavoisier by J. A. Cochrane. The author complains that "although Lavoisier was at the time of his death and for at least fifteen years before it one of the most eminent men in France, the general historian does not think it worth while to make any mention of him. . . . Science has undoubtedly changed the face of the world, and yet practically the only credit given to it by the historian is the Industrial Revolution . . . and even then the facts are not always accurate."

This is very sound criticism, but the scientist at once reasserts his monopoly: "No doubt the historian, having no qualifications to discuss the progress of science, feels that he had best leave it severely alone, but he

---

[5] Some very useful works already exist which exemplify the historical and inductive method of teaching science; among others: Ostwald's *Schule der Chemie* (translated by E. C. Ramsay), Ida Freund's *The Study of Chemical Composition* and *The Experimental Basis of Chemistry*, Norman Campbell's *Physics: The Elements*, and H. T. Pledge's *Science Since 1500*.

can scarcely claim to trace the evolution of the modern world if he omits one of the most important factors in that evolution." Which will the author have—treatment with inevitable errors or leaving the sacred objects "severely alone"? So long as we act like watchdogs over our little plots, it is obvious that we cannot have the comprehensive views that all profess to desire. Somebody has to take the first step—and suffer for his pains.

But it would be unfair if I gave the impression that the opposition to teaching the history of science to college students was universal or came only from certain scientists. At one great university near New York there was a thriving enterprise of this sort, popular with students and science departments alike. It was given by a young man, equally gifted in the humanities and in his chosen physical science—a budding *uomo universale*, whom fellow scientists were willing to aid, guide, and correct—if need be— on the remoter details of their science. After a few years this course built up a tradition, exerted an influence, reached a kind of perfection in the fulfillment of its aim.

With the war, changes came in staff and direction; the instructor left and the opposition rallied to abolish the course. It will scarcely be believed when I say that the prime mover in this *Putsch* was a philosopher. What inspired him, the Absolute only knows. The science course did not teach any philosophy contrary to his own; it only taught the historical fact that great men of science have employed varying philosophical assumptions to gain their ends. It taught, besides, that the several sciences do not look at the world all in the same way and that so far as science has a unified point of view, it is not exclusive of others—the ways, namely, of art, philosophy, religion, and common sense. Lastly, the course imparted a fair amount of matters of fact and showed how wrong was the man who said: "You don't have to teach the history of science to make a man understand that water is $H_2O$." It is precisely what you have to teach, unless you are willing to barter understanding for mere voodoo formulas.

What more could any philosophy department want? Their students were lucky enough to be taught to think. Is there any other use to make of the four years of college? The world being full of a number of things, it takes practice to think easily about the chief ones. Does philosophy pretend to monopolize cogitation because Descartes said, "Don't doubt I'm thinking!"

The fact is that philosophy has suffered emotionally, like Greek and Latin, from the triumph of science. Philosophy was a minor partner in the defeat of the classics, and that has left it laboring under the same sense of wrong, the same fancied need to be haughty—and even hoity-toity. In the '80s science said: "We bring you the answers. Philosophy will gradually be pushed out as we extend our certainty." Many philosophers agreed and looked for their retirement at the first outrush of some naked Archimedes shouting "Eureka." Other philosophers, courageously holding their ground,

fought as critics of science's faulty logic or extreme arrogance, just as a few classicists kept saying, "Poison gas marks a great step forward but have you taken in the meaning of Thucydides's 'Peloponnesian War'?"

The time has now come for the three-cornered duel on the campus to cease. The classics, philosophy, and science are at once overlapping and complementary disciplines. No need even to adjust boundary differences. The students are well able to take care of seeming conflicts, and in truth profit from them, since opposition reinforces attention by heightening the drama of human thought. Science must be taught, and historically, too, or the people will perish. Philosophy likewise must have a voice in all courses throwing light on the history of ideas. It will save philosophy as a subject and save the students from caddishness and provincialism. But philosophy has other obvious collegiate duties. It must read its great masterpieces with the new generation, expound ethical and metaphysical theory, help teach logic, and do liaison work with historians, scientists, and theologians. Once in a while an original philosopher will arise, unsought, in the midst of his colleagues, and the world will know him to its own profit.

The classics, too, must enter the dance. They hold the key to the meaning of our long journey from the cave to—precisely—the laboratory.

**E. B. WHITE (1899–    )** for years has helped sustain the
lively pages of *The New Yorker's* "Talk of the Town" section, and his
essays have consistently placed him in the forefront of those who apply
quick wisdom of the humanistic kind to current issues. Even in his children's
books, *Stuart Little* and *Charlotte's Web,* he has managed to exemplify
the kind of wit which understands and illuminates while it entertains.

# The Door

Everything (he kept saying) is something it isn't. And everybody is always somewhere else. Maybe it was the city, being in the city, that made him feel how queer everything was and that it was something else. Maybe (he kept thinking) it was the names of the things. The names were tex and frequently koid. Or they were flex and oid or they were duroid (sani) or flexsan (duro), but everything was glass (but not quite glass) and the thing that you touched (the surface, washable, crease-resistant) was rubber, only it wasn't quite rubber and you didn't quite touch it but almost. The wall, which was glass but thrutex, turned out on being approached not to be a wall, it was something else, it was an opening or doorway—and the doorway (through which he saw himself approaching) turned out to be something else, it was a wall. And what he had eaten not having agreed with him.

He was in a washable house, but he wasn't sure. Now about those rats, he kept saying to himself. He meant the rats that the Professor had driven crazy by forcing them to deal with problems which were beyond the scope of rats, the insoluble problems. He meant the rats that had been trained to jump at the square card with the circle in the middle, and the card (because it was something it wasn't) would give way and let the rat into a place where the food was, but then one day it would be a trick played on the rat, and the card would be changed, and the rat would jump but the card wouldn't give way, and it was an impossible situation (for a rat) and the rat would go insane and into its eyes would come the unspeakably bright imploring look of the frustrated, and after the convulsions were over and the frantic racing around, then the passive stage would set in and the willingness to let anything be done to it, even if it was something else.

He didn't know which door (or wall) or opening in the house to jump at, to get through, because one was an opening that wasn't a door (it was a void, or koid) and the other was a wall that wasn't an opening, it was a sanitary cupboard of the same color. He caught a glimpse of his eyes staring into his eyes, in the thrutex, and in them was the expression he had seen in the picture of the rats—weary after convulsions and the frantic

racing around, when they were willing and did not mind having anything done to them. More and more (he kept saying) I am confronted by a problem which is incapable of solution (for this time even if he chose the right door, there would be no food behind it) and that is what madness is, and things seeming different from what they are. He heard, in the house where he was, in the city to which he had gone (as toward a door which might, or might not, give way), a noise—not a loud noise but more of a low prefabricated humming. It came from a place in the base of the wall (or stat) where the flue carrying the filterable air was, and not far from the Minipiano, which was made of the same material nailbrushes are made of, and which was under the stairs. "This, too, has been tested," she said, pointing, but not at it, "and found viable." It wasn't a loud noise, he kept thinking, sorry that he had seen his eyes, even though it was through his own eyes that he had seen them.

First will come the convulsions (he said), then the exhaustion, then the willingness to let anything be done. "And you better believe it *will* be."

All his life he had been confronted by situations which were incapable of being solved, and there was a deliberateness behind all this, behind this changing of the card (or door), because they would always wait till you had learned to jump at the certain card (or door)—the one with the circle —and then they would change it on you. There have been so many doors changed on me, he said, in the last twenty years, but it is now becoming clear that it is an impossible situation, and the question is whether to jump again, even though they ruffle you in the rump with a blast of air— to make you jump. He wished he wasn't standing by the Minipiano. First they would teach you the prayers and the Psalms, and that would be the right door (the one with the circle) and the long sweet words with the holy sound, and that would be the one to jump at to get where the food was. Then one day you jumped and it didn't give way, so that all you got was the bump on the nose, and the first bewilderment, the first young bewilderment.

I don't know whether to tell her about the door they substituted or not, he said, the one with the equation on it and the picture of the amoeba reproducing itself by division. Or the one with the photostatic copy of the check for thirty-two dollars and fifty cents. But the jumping was so long ago, although the bump is . . . how those old wounds hurt! Being crazy this way wouldn't be so bad if only, if only. If only when you put your foot forward to take a step, the ground wouldn't come up to meet your foot the way it does. And the same way in the street (only I may never get back to the street unless I jump at the right door), the curb coming up to meet your foot, anticipating ever so delicately the weight of the body, which is somewhere else. "We could take your name," she said, "and send it to you." And it wouldn't be so bad if only you could read a sentence all the way through without jumping (your eye) to some-

thing else on the same page; and then (he kept thinking) there was that man out in Jersey, the one who started to chop his trees down, one by one, the man who began talking about how he would take his house to pieces, brick by brick, because he faced a problem incapable of solution, probably, so he began to hack at the trees in the yard, began to pluck with trembling fingers at the bricks in the house. Even if a house is not washable, it is worth taking down. It is not till later that the exhaustion sets in. But it is inevitable that they will keep changing the doors on you, he said, because that is what they are for; and the thing is to get used to it and not let it unsettle the mind. But that would mean not jumping, and you can't. Nobody can not jump. There will be no not-jumping. Among rats, perhaps, but among people never. Everybody has to keep jumping at a door (the one with the circle on it) because that is the way everybody is, specially some people. You wouldn't want me, standing here, to tell you, would you, about my friend the poet (deceased) who said, "My heart has followed all my days something I cannot name"? (It had the circle on it.) And like many poets, although few so beloved, he is gone. It killed him, the jumping. First, of course, there were the preliminary bouts, the convulsions, and the calm and the willingness.

I remember the door with the picture of the girl on it (only it was spring), her arms outstretched in loveliness, her dress (it was the one with the circle on it) uncaught, beginning the slow, clear, blinding cascade— and I guess we would all like to try that door again, for it seemed like the way and for a while it was the way, the door would open and you would go through winged and exalted (like any rat) and the food would be there, the way the Professor had it arranged, everything O.K., and you had chosen the right door for the world was young. The time they changed that door on me, my nose bled for a hundred hours—how do you like that, Madam? Or would you prefer to show me further through this so strange house, or you could take my name and send it to me, for although my heart has followed all my days something I cannot name, I am tired of the jumping and I do not know which way to go, Madam, and I am not even sure that I am not tired beyond the endurance of man (rat, if you will) and have taken leave of sanity. What are you following these days, old friend, after your recovery from the last bump? What is the name, or is it something you cannot name? The rats have a name for it by this time, perhaps, but I don't know what they call it. I call it plexikoid and it comes in sheets, something like insulating board, unattainable and ugli-proof.

And there was the man out in Jersey, because I keep thinking about his terrible necessity and the passion and trouble he had gone to all those years in the indescribable abundance of a householder's detail, building the estate and the planting of the trees and in spring the lawn-dressing and in fall the bulbs for the spring burgeoning, and the watering of the grass

on the long light evenings in summer and the gravel for the drive way (all had to be thought out, planned) and the decorative borders, probably, the perennials and the bug spray, and the building of the house from plans of the architect, first the sills, then the studs, then the full corn in the ear, the floors laid on the floor timbers, smoothed, and then the carpets upon the smooth floors and the curtains and the rods therefor. And then, almost without warning, he would be jumping at the same old door and it wouldn't give: they had changed it on him, making life no longer supportable under the elms in the elm shade, under the maples in the maple shade.

"Here you have the maximum of openness in a small room."

It was impossible to say (maybe it was the city) what made him feel the way he did, and I am not the only one either, he kept thinking—ask any doctor if I am. The doctors, they know how many there are, they even know where the trouble is only they don't like to tell you about the prefrontal lobe because that means making a hole in your skull and removing the work of centuries. It took so long coming, this lobe, so many, many years. (Is it something you read in the paper, perhaps?) And now, the strain being so great, the door having been changed by the Professor once too often . . . but it only means a whiff of ether, a few deft strokes, and the higher animal becomes a little easier in his mind and more like the lower one. From now on, you see, that's the way it will be, the ones with the small prefrontal lobes will win because the other ones are hurt too much by this incessant bumping. They can stand just so much, eh, Doctor? (And what is that, pray, that you have in your hand?) Still, you never can tell, eh, Madam?

He crossed (carefully) the room, the thick carpet under him softly, and went toward the door carefully, which was glass and he could see himself in it, and which, at his approach, opened to allow him to pass through; and beyond he half expected to find one of the old doors that he had known, perhaps the one with the circle, the one with the girl her arms outstretched in loveliness and beauty before him. But he saw instead a moving stairway, and descended in light (he kept thinking) to the street below and to the other people. As he stepped off, the ground came up slightly, to meet his foot.

*Appendix*

# CONTENTS LISTED ACCORDING TO RHETORICAL CATEGORIES

Few writers agree on the proper categories of rhetorical classification. For example, some writers treat definition, classification, comparison, and analysis as specific methods or subdivisions of exposition. Others treat definition, analysis, etc., as independent categories equal in weight to the four forms of discourse (narration, exposition, description, and argument).

We have faced the problem of overlap and the inevitable element of arbitrariness in assigning categories by listing the works below under the heading that seems to us best to label the major means employed in the selections. Some pieces are as aptly described by one heading as by another; these are listed under both headings. There is scarcely a work of any length that does not combine several rhetorical strategies; so be prepared to disagree with some of our classifications.

### ANALYSIS

## CONTENTS LISTED ACCORDING TO FORMS AND FUNCTIONS

The writer's audience and his purpose frequently converge to give form to his writing. The particular occasion for a work can give it, at times, its unique shape. We hope the categories used below to analyze the contents of this book will provide a perspective from which to view the relationship between a work's "function" and its form.

## ADDRESSES

### FORMAL

### LECTURES

### PLEA

## ESSAYS AND ARTICLES

### AUTOBIOGRAPHICAL

### CRITICAL

### FICTION

### LETTERS

### PROSE POEMS

*Index of Authors
and Titles*